YEATS
150

IN MEMORIAM
Seamus Justin Heaney
Nobel Laureate
13 April 1939 – 30 August 2013

William Butler Yeats 1865–1939

YEATS 150

Edited by Declan J. Foley

THE LILLIPUT PRESS
DUBLIN

First published 2016 by
THE LILLIPUT PRESS
62–63 Sitric Road, Arbour Hill,
Dublin 7, Ireland
www.lilliputpress.ie

A CIP record for this title is available
from The British Library.

10 9 8 7 6 5 4 3 2 1

TRADE HARDBACK   978 1 84351 645 3
LIMITED EDITION   978 1 84351 644 6

Set in 10 pt on 14 pt Sabon by Marsha Swan
Printed in Navarre, Spain, by GraphyCems

Contents

Explanations of abbreviated book references in essays

Au   *Autobiographies* W.B. Yeats

AVB   *A Vision* (London: Macmillan, 1962)

AVA   *A Critical Edition of Yeats's* A Vision (1925), eds George Mills Harper and
Walter Kelly Hood (London: Macmillan, 1978)

CLI   *The Collected Letters of W.B. Yeats,* vol. 1: *1865–95,* eds John Kelly and
Eric Domville (Oxford: Clarendon Press, 1986)

E & I   *Essays and Introductions* W.B. Yeats

Ex   *Explorations,* Collier edition (New York: Macmillan 1962). Sel. Mrs W.B.
Yeats (London: Macmillan, 1962; New York: Macmillan, 1963)

GYL   *The Gonne–Yeats Letter 1893–1938: Always Your Friend,* eds Anna
MacBride White and A. Norman Jeffares (London: Hutchinson, 1992)

JS & D   *John Sherman and Doya,* ed. with an introduction, collation of the texts, and
notes, Richard J. Finneran (Detroit: Wayne State University Press, 1969)

L   *The Letters of W.B. Yeats,* ed. Allan Wade (London: Rupert Hart-Davis,
1954; New York: Macmillan, 1955)

Myth   *Mythologies* W.B. Yeats

Mem   *Memoirs*

SB   *The Speckled Bird, with Variant Versions,* ed. William H. O'Donnell
(Toronto: McCleeland and Stewart, 1976)

OBMV   *The Oxford Book of Modern Verse, 1892–1935,* chosen by W.B. Yeats
(Oxford: Clarendon Press, 1936)

UP1   *Uncollected Prose by W.B. Yeats* vol. 1, ed. John P. Frayne (London:
Macmillan; New York: Columbia University Press, 1970)

UP2   *Uncollected Prose by W.B. Yeats* vol. 2, eds John P. Frayne and Colton Johnson
(London: Macmillan, 1975; New York: Columbia University Press, 1976)

VP   *The Variorum Edition of the Poems of W.B. Yeats,* eds Peter Allt and
Russell K. Alspach (New York and London: Macmillan, 1957); seventh
printing (New York: Macmillan, 1977)

VPl   W.B. Yeats, *The Variorum Edition of the Poems of W.B. Yeats,* ed. Russell
K. Alspach (New York: Macmillan, 1966)

VSR   *The Secret Rose, Stories by W.B. Yeats: A Variorum Edition,* eds Warwick
Gould, Phillip L. Marcus and Michael J. Sidnell (London: Macmillan, 1992)

YA 10   Yeats Annual (UK), No. 10

YAACTS   Yeats: An Annual of Critical and Textual Studies

Acknowledgments

Acknowledgments bring to the forefront those whose work is inside a book. In a collection of essays such as this there are many people to thank for their kindness, advice and assistance and, most important of all, encouragement to honour the historic occasion this work marks.

To the essayists, my deepest appreciation of your work, patience and understanding of the project: Elizabeth Ansel, Dresden; Dr Penelope Buckley, Kew, Melbourne, for permission to reproduce the essay of the late Vincent Buckley; Rev. Fr John Carroll, Sligo for his essay and photos; Glen Cavaliero (a man who manages without a computer; so nice to receive a handwritten letter in the twenty-first century). Anne Margaret Daniel, New York; Associate Professor Maneck H. Darawula, Florida, for her very kind assistance. Professor Emeritus Denis Donoghue; the family of the late Jim Eccles, photographer, Sligo. Gerry Foley, and Fiona Gallagher, Sligo. Professor Emeritus Warwick Gould, for a most original and interesting essay; Professor Tomoko Iwatsubo, Hosei University, Tokyo; John Kavanagh (another 'Sligo Poet'); Professor Emeritus Patrick J. Keane; Professor Emeritus Francis King, Melbourne for kind permission to reproduce the essay of the late Alec King. Kristóf Kiss, Budapest. Craig Kirk, Albury, NSW Australia. Professor Peter Kuch, University of Otago. NZ Professor José Lanters, University of Wisconsin-Milwaukee. Dr Earl Livings, poet and scholar, Melbourne, for his ongoing friendship, advice, assistance and encouragement in my Yeatsian studies and events. Professor Emeritus Richard Londraville and his more than capable wife / assistant Janis for their friendship, and ever ready assistance with any query. Sam McCready for his kind assistance in providing photographs of the play rehearsals. Kathy McDevitt (née Plowright), Adelaide; Professor Lucy McDiarmid, Montclair State University. Ita McMorrow-Leyden, Sligo. N.J. Mann. Dr Martin Mansergh, Tipperary. Dr Carolyn Masel, Australian Catholic University, Melbourne. James L. Pethica, Williams College MA., USA. Isle of Skye resident, John Purser, a great friend and conversationalist. Hilary Pyle, Yeats Curator Emeritus, NGI, for her ongoing encouragement in my Yeats family studies. Professor Emeritus Ann Saddlemyer of Massey College, another great and kind encourager. Doug Saum of Reno, NV, for his more than kind assistance, advice and friendship over many years. Colin Smythe, publisher, collector. I express my sincere appreciation of Colin's permission to reproduce Tom Henn's essay. Melinda Szüts, Budapest, Hungary. Deirdre Toomey, Research Editor of the *Yeats Annual*. Professor Emeritus Helen Vendler. A special word of thanks to the New York Yeats Society; the iYeats Poetry Competition, the W.B. Yeats Poetry

Prize for Australia; Poetry Ireland, and Orla McArt, Grange Post Primary School, County Sligo, and to each of the poets who kindly gave permission for their prize-winning entries to be reproduced in the book.

To Maureen E. Mulvihill, Florida for her encouragement and advice down the Years, and the many who encouraged me on this project, sincere appreciation and thanks.

To Antony Farrell and Suzy Freeman at The Lilliput Press, an enormous debt is due for their patience, understanding and kindness in accepting this book without a moment's hesitation. To Bridget Farrell is due an equal debt for her editorial work. My sincere and eternal thanks to those Special Subscribers mentioned at the end. Each of you ensured *Yeats 150* would be published.

To my wife Helen for her support and great patience with my Yeatsian activities for the past twenty years, a special appreciation is due.

Illustrations 10 and 13–22 in 'Byzantine Materiality and Byzantine Vision: "Hammered Gold and Gold Enamelling"' courtesy of Longo Editore, Ravenna. Illustrations 1–3, 4, 5, 6, 8, 24, 26, 27, 28, 29, 30, 31, 33 courtesy of a Private Collection, London. Other illustrations courtesy of *The Yeats Annual*.

Photographs of Swans in Sligo town © representatives Estate of Jim Eccles, Sligo.

Photographs of Noh Play © Sam McCready.

The essay 'The Place of Shells' by T.R. Henn is republished by kind permission of Colin Smythe Ltd. This first appeared in *Yeats, Sligo and Ireland*, ed. A. Norman Jeffares (Colin Smythe Ltd, 1980), in the series 'Irish Literary Studies'.

The essay 'Away 'by Deirdre Toomey first appeared in Yeats Annual No. 10 (1993). It is reproduced here by kind permission of Deirdre Toomey and Warwick Gould (eds), *Yeats: An Annual of Critical and Textual Studies* (London).

The essay 'Every Paddler's Heritage' by Maneck H. Darawula, republished by kind permission of Maneck H. Darawula, first appeared in *Prodigal Father Revisited: Artists and Writers in the World of John Butler Yeats*, ed. Janis Londraville (West Cornwall, CT: Locust Hill Press, 2003).

The essay 'Yeats: The Great Comedian' by Vincent Buckley is republished by kind permission of Penelope Buckley. This first appeared in an unknown literary studies periodical in the USA *c*. 1980. I have been unable to make contact with the publisher / editor.

The essay 'Yeats: The Poet' by Alec King is republished by kind permission of Francis King. This first appeared in *The Unprosaic Imagination: Essays and Lectures on the Study of Literature*, ed. Francis King (Nedlands: University of Western Australia, 1975).

Permissions for the unpublished manuscript material in James Pethica's essay, '"Living in an elastic-sided world": John Butler Yeats and Lady Gregory' are due to the National Library of Ireland; to the Manuscript Division of the New York Public Library; and to the Henry W. and Albert Berg Collection, The New York Public Library, Astor, Lenox and Tilden Foundations.

YEATS
150

Introduction

DECLAN J. FOLEY

Neath Ben Bulben's buttocks lies
Bill Yeats, a poet twoice the soize
Of William Shakespear, as they say
Down Ballykillywuchlin way
Ezra Pound, *Pavannes and Divagations*, p. 228

This book of essays celebrates the one hundred and fiftieth anniversary of the birth of W.B. Yeats. These essays reflect the esteem in which the man and his work are held internationally, not alone in the famed halls of academia, but also by the public at large. That there are a number of successful international Yeats poetry competitions, encouraging the creativity of up to five hundred poets annually, reflects the great impact his work has had, and continues to have, on the arts.

The Sligo International Yeats Summer School, now in its fifty-sixth year, brings honour to all involved in ensuring its success year after year. Not just a success in attendance numbers, but more importantly a success in perpetuating scholarship and learning throughout the world. One hallmark of the Sligo Yeats Summer School is that all are welcome to attend. No academic qualification is required, just a desire and yearning for knowledge of the arts, and the great enduring work of the Yeats family which will live on through them. W.B. Yeats elaborates:

> We who care deeply about the arts find ourselves the priesthood of an almost forgotten faith, and we must, I think, if we would win the people again, take upon ourselves the method and fervour of a priesthood.
> We must be humble and half-proud ... .We must baptize as well as preach.
> *Ireland and the Arts*, 1901

The name Yeats has interesting origins, and has its roots in 'gate'. The Merriam-Webster online dictionary explains the origin of LYCH-GATE: 'Middle English *lycheyate*, from *lich* body, corpse (from Old English *līc*) + *gate*, *yate* gate. First Known Use: 15th century.'

In MacLysaght's *Surnames of Ireland* the name 'Yeats / Yates' is described as follows: 'The famous literary and artistic family of Yeats, which has formerly been of Dublin, settled in Sligo at the end of the seventeenth century ... The name means dweller by the gate.'

Once we enter through that 'gate' of the Yeats family, we are introduced to a great and varied artistic world. Prior to the International Yeats Summer School, the work of W.B. Yeats was limited to universities, colleges, and private appreciation. His poetry was, and is still, included in many school curricula. Between his death in January 1939 and the publication of Richard Ellmann's *The Man and the Masks* in 1948 there was not much general work published on W.B., his life and work. The intervening World War disrupted the lives of innumerable academics. Perhaps this interregnum was a blessing in disguise, because it allowed W.B.'s 'great wife' George Yeats – an intellectual partner throughout their marriage – to put his vast collection of papers in an order which continues to assist every academic researcher on Yeats, since Richard Ellmann's initial research in 1948.

In his lifetime, W.B. Yeats's circle, to name but a small number, included: Æ, W.H. Auden, T.S. Eliot, Lady Gregory, Annie Horniman, Edward Martyn, George Moore, Ezra Pound, Arthur Symons and many others involved in the arts, not alone in Ireland but in Europe, Australia, Japan, India and the USA.

In the year 2015 those who study Yeats meet another set of 'dwellers by the gate': internationally renowned academics named Butler-Cullingford, Crotty, Donoghue, Gould, Harper, Henn, Iwatsubo, Jeffares, Keane, Kiberd, Kuch, Kelly, Londraville, Martin, Mann, Murphy, Pethica, Daniel, Schuchard, Toomey, Vendler and many, many, more, who year after year produce further Yeatsian scholarship.

W.B. Yeats gave his entire life to his work in the arts and to Ireland. The landscape of Sligo was the cradle of his civilization, and the inspiration for his early work. He chose 'perfection of the work over perfection of the life' and that we must appreciate.

The adage 'Behind every great man, there is a great woman', was never so true as in the life of W.B. Yeats. To his mother Susan Pollexfen, his sisters Lily and Lolly, his wife George, Lady Gregory, Annie Horniman and, as his daughter Anne said, 'his artistic love affairs' with intellectual ladies in his latter years, there is a great debt owed by the coming generations.

In his oration at the graveside of W.B. Yeats in 1965, his contemporary, Frank O'Connor, said:

> Two centuries after this, if our civilisation endures, there will be people speaking here, and other people will be listening to them, when you and I are in our graves.
>
> I hope that what they praise Yeats for will not be the things that we praise him for. Because that will simply mean that our generation has left its task uncompleted.
>
> I hope that the tradition we establish here today may be the beginning of a new, and a very different, Ireland.
>
> That we in coming days, 'MAY BE THE INDOMITABLE IRISHRY.'

This was a challenge in 1965, as it is today to all who study the life and work of W.B. Yeats. I know from my association with the Australian Yeats Poetry Prize – I am fortunate to be its Convener – that Frank O'Connor would be content by the different ways Yeats is praised today. Daniel Albright (1945–2015) in his *W.B. Yeats – The Poems* (London 1990) writes:

> Yeats's size is difficult to measure. Pound's mean parody of 'Under Ben Bulben' suggests that Yeats appears to be twice the size of Shakespeare only because Ireland is a quarter the size of England ... . – such modern Irishmen as James Joyce, Samuel Beckett, [George] Bernard Shaw, and Yeats himself, have so powerfully shaped European literature that Ireland looms as large as France or Germany on the cultural map. (*Introduction*, p. xvii)

That W.B. Yeats was a native of Ireland, a land where common life was traditionally interconnected with poetry and the arts, and how this interconnectedness continued through the years with Yeats, is best illustrated by W.H. Auden's explanation in *The Dyer's Hand*, where Auden explains how a better poem was written about a small Irish uprising in 1916 than any about the whole of World War II:

> To write a good poem on Churchill, a poet would have to know Winston Churchill intimately, and his poem would be about the man, not about the Prime Minister. All attempts to write about persons and events, however important, to which the poet is not intimately related in a personal way are now doomed to failure. Yeats could write great poetry about the Troubles in Ireland, because most of the protagonists were known to him personally and the places where the events occurred had been familiar to him since childhood. (p. 81)

If ever there was a need to endorse the impact that Ireland had upon the poems Yeats composed, then this last line does so.

In January 1987, I left Sligo with my wife Helen and our children to live in Melbourne. Three years later in January 1990, I visited Sligo for my father's funeral; on calling in to see John Mullaney in his O'Connell Street shop, John mentioned, 'It would be nice to have a Yeats Society in Melbourne.' If anyone had told me about the 'gate' I was about to enter, and what it would lead me to, no doubt I would have laughed, remarking, 'Me, become a Yeats scholar?' For, I cannot deny, that is what I am today, albeit a minor one, on the cusp of my 65th birthday. I have been fortunate to have known the late William M. Murphy, biographer of John Butler Yeats, an invaluable source for Yeats material, and a man who never had any intention of becoming a Yeatsian. His influence on me along with that of Hilary Pyle, the major artistic Emeritus Curator of the Yeats family, and all those involved in the John Butler Yeats Seminars in Chestertown, have been instrumental in my work on the Yeats family.

The intention of this collection of essays when first mooted three years ago was that it would be populated more by scholars than academics, because many of us assumed there would be a number of fine academic publications to mark the event. From previous experience of working with the Yeats family of Sligo, I have discovered they can set the agenda, and in this collection they surely have. There were a number of academics who wanted to be associated with this collection, but due to time constraints could not provide an essay.

I wish to express my sincere appreciation of the essayists who have put their trust in me to collate this collection of essays. Essays that reflect the influence of Yeats around the globe. Each essay is as enjoyable to read and as educational as the next. That this collection will bring more people to study the Yeats family of Sligo is my personal hope. Their Bedford Park neighbour G.K. Chesterton in his *Autobiography* (New York 1936), described the Yeats children in a beautiful little phrase, to honour their presence in his life: 'Willy and Lily and Lollie and Jack.' (p. 140)

At 12 West 44th Street, New York, on 16 March 2003, Janis Londraville's *Prodigal Father Revisited: Artists and Writers in the World of John Butler Yeats* was launched by then Mayor of Sligo, Councillor T. Cummins. As the event was about to begin, the street door opened wide and remained so for a few seconds, though no one was there. I said, 'Here is J.B.Y. coming in!' Who knows what shades will turn up for the launch of *Yeats 150* in the grounds of Merville?

Perhaps W.B. might whisper in the wind among the reeds, 'my glory was I had such friends.'

Seamus Heaney

1939–2013

Poet

Seamus Justin Heaney

13 April 1939 – 30 August 2013

HELEN VENDLER

Seamus Heaney, the most famous English-language poet of his era, and (as was often said) the greatest Irish poet since W.B. Yeats, was in 1995 awarded the Nobel Prize 'for works of lyrical beauty and ethical depth, which exalt everyday miracles and the living past'. His public readings attracted large appreciative audiences not only in Ireland and Great Britain and the United States but also throughout Europe. Heaney, although best known for his work as a poet, was also a prose writer of vigour and eloquence. He also ventured into the adaptation of Sophoclean tragedy when, in conjunction with the Field Day Theatre, he produced English 'versions' (as he preferred to characterize them) of *Philoctetes* (under the title *The Cure at Troy*) and *Antigone* (under the title *The Burial at Thebes*). Heaney was also a notable translator not only of the Anglo-Saxon epic *Beowulf* but also (in 'version' form) of the anonymous Middle-Irish narrative *Buile Suibhne* (rendered as *Sweeney Astray*) and of the Middle-Scots *The Testament of Cresseid* & *Seven Fables* of Robert Henryson. Scattered in various volumes are translations of excerpts from Virgil, Ovid and other poets, and at the time of Heaney's death a limited edition of his translation of Book VI of *The Aeneid* was in preparation. A book-length interview by Dennis O'Driscoll, published in 2008 as *Stepping Stones*, is the fullest rendering of Heaney's own view of his life and work.

Heaney, born in Castledawson, County Derry, Northern Ireland, grew

up as the first child of nine born to Patrick Heaney, a cattle dealer, and his
wife Margaret. Patrick's sister Mary shared the house, and Heaney's first
memory (revealed in 'Mossbawn') was of his aunt Mary making and baking
scones: 'And here is love / like a tinsmith's scoop / sunk past its gleam / in
the meal-bin.' After elementary school in Anahorish, Heaney won a scholar-
ship enabling him to become a boarder at the Catholic St Columb's School in
Derry, a period vividly recalled in the sequence 'Alphabets', in which Heaney
traces his schooling in English, Latin and Irish, a process by which the world
is widened beyond his rural upbringing. During Heaney's time at St Columb's,
his four-year-old brother Christopher was killed in a road accident: the tragedy
is described in one of Heaney's most famous poems, 'Mid-Term Break'.

It was at Queen's University, Belfast, that Heaney began to write poems
under the pen-name 'Incertus': 'I went disguised in it, ... tagging it under my
efforts like a damp fuse. Uncertain.' Heaney left Queen's in 1964 with a First
in English and, after a year at St Joseph's teacher-training college, was for a
year an intermediate-school teacher before being appointed to the staff at St
Joseph's. At this time, he met the English critic and poet Philip Hobsbaum,
who formed in Dublin (as he had in London previously) a group of young
poets who met regularly to read and critique each other's work. Hobsbaum
forwarded Heaney's work to London, where it was seen by Karl Miller, Editor
of the *New Statesman*, who in 1964 published three poems, including the
well-known poem of vocation, 'Digging': 'Between my finger and my thumb /
The squat pen rests. / I'll dig with it.' In 1965, Faber published Heaney's first
volume of poems, *Death of a Naturalist*, which was followed by eleven more
collections. The most substantial collected edition, *Opened Ground: Poems
1966–1996*, was, by the time of Heaney's death in 2013, missing poems from
the volumes published in 2001 (*Electric Light*), 2006 (*District and Circle*) and
2010 (*Human Chain*). In 2009, to celebrate Heaney's seventieth birthday, Faber
brought out a collection of CDs on which Heaney recorded all his published
poems to that point, but no *Complete Poems* was ever issued. A bibliography
of Heaney's work by Rand Brandes was published in 2008.

In 1965, Heaney married Marie Devlin, a teacher and writer; three chil-
dren, Michael, Christopher, and Catherine were born of the marriage. In
1966, Heaney became a lecturer at Queen's University, Belfast, and in 1970,
he accepted an offer to be a visiting lecturer at the University of California,
Berkeley, returning to Queen's in 1971. The California venture introduced
Heaney to the United States and its contemporary poets, both native and
foreign; Czeslaw Milosz, the great Polish poet, was teaching at Berkeley and
became, for Heaney, an example of the life of poetry lived at the highest level

(Heaney was later to write a poem about Milosz entitled 'The Master'). In California, Heaney wrote the remarkable poems in *Wintering Out* (1972), in which his social canvas began to extend itself in several directions. Whereas in his first two books he had been chiefly occupied with his country childhood and its 'calendar customs', he now began to write about social injustice, choosing (in a decision unusual in a man of his generation) to expose the cruelty of Irish society toward women who had borne children out of wedlock. In 'Limbo', a frightened young mother drowns her baby rather than risk discovery; in 'Bye-Child', an 'illegitimate' child, kept hidden alone in a dark hen-house and fed surreptitiously by his mother, is at last freed; he lacks the capacity of speech. The social canvas extends to a candid picture of marital smouldering in 'Summer Home', and, further afield, the poet reaches out to the first of the 'bog bodies' described by P.V. Glob in *The Bog People*. 'The Tollund Man', found strangled, his body preserved by the tannin in the bog, seems to the poet analogous to the murdered contemporary bodies of Northern Ireland. Revolted by the killing in his own country, the poet imagines visiting the Jutland of the bog bodies: 'Out there in Jutland / In the old man-killing parishes / I will feel lost, / Unhappy and at home.'

After Heaney's return to Queen's in 1972, the political 'Troubles' in Northern Ireland, which had increased in intensity and danger since the sixties, determined the move of the poet and his family to the Republic of Ireland, where they lived south of Dublin in Glanmore, County Wicklow, in a cottage that had served as the gatekeeper's lodge of the Synge estate. Heaney had given up his Lectureship at Queen's, and the family lived frugally for four years on his freelance work and Marie's income as an elementary-school teacher. It was at Glanmore that Heaney wrote his most famous volume, *North* (1975), which became (and remains) a site of controversy. In it, Heaney reflected the violence erupting in the North as the political and economic tensions between the dominant Protestant Unionists and the Catholic minority (suffering discrimination in employment and education) came to a head. Placing the 'Troubles' in a larger geographical and historical context, Heaney imagined the long history of killing, of 'neighbourly murder', in the northern regions of Europe; he recalled as well the Viking invasions and the savage execution of enemies: such cruelty was symbolized by the torture of an adulterous medieval woman whose body was found in an Irish bog. In such famous poems as 'Bog Queen' and 'Punishment', Heaney indicts both himself and his culture.

After four years in Glanmore, Heaney moved to Dublin and accepted a Lectureship at Carysfort College (a teaching college), where he served as Head of Department, a task leaving him little time for writing. He was invited to

Harvard for a visiting appointment, arriving in 1981, and was then appointed to the tenured Boylston Professorship of Rhetoric and Oratory, committing himself to teaching at Harvard for one semester every year (and honouring the commitment even in the year he won the Nobel). His wife Marie, facing single motherhood of three children for three months a year, did not flinch, but said to me, 'All I want is for Seamus to be able to write his poems.' Backed by her support, Heaney embarked on a happy and successful career at Harvard, where he taught both Creative Writing and Contemporary Irish Poetry (a course which omitted his own work). He concluded his formal teaching at Harvard in 1997, but from 1998 to 2006 visited for a few weeks each year as the Emerson Poet in Residence. In 1989, while at Harvard, he was elected to the five-year non-resident position of Professor of Poetry at Oxford, delivering three lectures yearly, some of which were collected under the title *The Redress of Poetry* (1995). *Finders Keepers: Selected Prose 1971–2001* gives a broad overview of his prose works – autobiographical, biographical and literary. His critical opinions were forthright, but courteously offered. He wrote widely on Irish, English, Welsh and Scottish authors, but the years in the United States had also introduced him to the work of the post-war American poets, among whom he found Elizabeth Bishop especially sympathetic. He had of course known the work of Eliot and Pound and Frost from his youth, and once, in conversation with me, surprisingly named Frost as his favourite poet. Heaney's prose brought new energy to contemporary critical writing about poetry: brilliantly accurate, it was voiced in a tone of colloquial engagement with his audience. It assumed that poetry was an indispensable part of any culture, serving to bring current concerns to the fore but also to recreate, in free play, the fabric of language.

In *North*, Heaney had continued to use the 'thin' stanza he had explored in his second and third volumes, deriving it from slender forms of poetry in the Irish language, and contrasting it, in later remarks, with the broad pentameters of Wordsworth and Keats and Hopkins, poets that had first inspired him. With increasing frequency, Heaney prolongs his subject matter by composing sequences, gathering a series of short poems under a single title. These, beginning with the seven-member 'A Lough Neagh Sequence' in Heaney's second volume, *Door into the Dark*, take on more and more weight over time until, in 1984, the poet publishes the twelve-member autobiographical sequence 'Station Island' (the title poem for his sixth volume of verse). In another autobiographical sequence, 'Sweeney Redivivus', Heaney exposes himself, under the guise of Sweeney (the bird-hero of *Sweeney Astray*), to ironic questioning of his own history. He has now exhausted, as a primary subject, the earlier narratives of his childhood life and its religious observance; he has left behind the North and its Troubles; he has taken a period of seclusion in Glanmore (recorded in his 1979 seventh volume, *Field Work*), and he now finds himself, in 'On the Road' – the closing poem of 'Sweeney Redivivus' – seeking a new source of poetry. Leaving Christianity behind, he migrates (still in the bird-persona of Sweeney) down to the 'deepest chamber' of a prehistoric cave, finding there, incised in the rock, 'a drinking deer' with its 'nostril flared // at a dried up source.' He resolves to wait there 'until the long dumbfounded / spirit broke cover / to raise a dust / in the font of exhaustion.'

The new energy that seemed unattainable in 'On the Road' arose from an unlikely source: a Polish poet, Czeslaw Milosz, and his contemporaries. These poets, writing under censorship, often turned to allegory as a vehicle of moral meditation, and *The Haw Lantern* (1987), Heaney's eighth volume, betrays their influence in such allegorical poems as 'From the Republic of Conscience', 'From the Frontier of Writing', 'From the Canton of Expectation' and 'The Mud Vision'.

The Haw Lantern's sequence 'Clearances', an elegy for the poet's mother, represents a new venture in Heaney's poetry, as his next volume *Seeing Things* (1991) takes as its subject invisible things. The invisibles include the dead, who remain only as absences; the interior (but invisible) sensings and mountings of which Wordsworth spoke, the abstract geometrical forms living in the architectural space of the mind; the measures of mathematics, perceived even when merely imagined. In 'Song', a poem from the earlier Glanmore period, Heaney had described himself as a poet of the everyday: 'There are the mud-flowers of dialect / And the immortelles of perfect pitch / And that moment when the bird sings very close / To the music of what happens.' Now, in *Seeing Things*, Heaney resolves to leave poetry that is 'Sluggish in the doldrums of what happens' and to turn to those intellectual and emotional invisibles that contend against a material concept of the real.

Heaney's father had died in 1986, completing the erasure of the poet's childhood experience (elegized in 'Clearances' as 'a space / utterly empty, utterly a source'). Patrick Heaney's death lies under Heaney's longest sequence, 'Squarings', included in *Seeing Things*. This is a series of forty-eight twelve-line poems, each consisting of four broad-lined tercets, making a square shape on the page. The sequence itself is subdivided into four groups of twelve poems, each representing a perfect square: 12 (lines per poem) x 12 (poems). In the tenth poem, as the poet contemplates a flooded quarry, he isolates his theme: the irreconcilable confrontation of the invisible and the material. 'Ultimate // Fathomableness, ultimate / Stony up-againstness: could you reconcile / What

was diaphanous there with what was massive?' Heaney confronts the insuffi-
ciencies of both art and nature to human existence: 'How habitable is perfected
form? / And how inhabited the windy light?'

The Spirit Level (1996) praises stoic endurance in the person of the poet's
brother Hugh, who, living among the armed outbreaks in the North, kept
the family farm ('Keeping Going'). But against that patience Heaney sets the
corruption of both kingship and marriage in Aeschylus' Agamemnon. It was
only after the subsidence of the quarter-century of conflict in Northern Ireland
that Heaney could allow his language a violence corresponding to the political
violence he had seen and felt. In the bitter poems comprising 'Mycenae Lookout',
Heaney takes on the persona of the Watchman, who observes, at the return of
Agamemnon and his sexual captive Cassandra from Troy, the obscene fantasies
of the crowd, followed by the murder of both Agamemnon and Cassandra by
Clytemnestra and her lover Aegisthus. The sequence concludes with a fatalistic
view of the perpetual persistence of aggression, of 'besieger and besieged', but
its most memorable lines are those reporting terror and slaughter. And although
The Spirit Level closes with the Northern Irish ceasefire and a 'postscript' of
light, water and swans in County Clare, the inhumanity of the Troubles is not
entirely routed. As the poet realizes the metamorphoses of self over time, he
describes his identity, so solid in childhood, as a phenomenon in perpetual flux:
'You are neither here nor there, / A hurry through which known and strange
things pass.'

Heaney's next two volumes, Electric Light (2001) and District and Circle
(2006), continued in an elegiac atmosphere, with moving vignettes of past and
present; District and Circle contained 'Anything Can Happen', Heaney's poem
on the 2001 destruction of the Twin Towers (adapted from an Horatian ode in
which human destiny is governed not by a benign Providence but by a malign
Fate). A new note was struck in Human Chain (2010), where poems written in
the wake of Heaney's 2006 stroke celebrated, with marked tenderness, family
and friends, 'the ones who have known him all along'. The volume culminates
in a long autobiographical sequence called 'Route 110' in which Heaney draws
parallels between episodes in his own life and events in The Aeneid, especially
Aeneas's sojourn in the underworld and his meeting there with the ghosts of
his father and of Dido.

In 2013, Heaney was hospitalized in Dublin for treatment of an aneu-
rysm. After his departure for the operating room, Marie Heaney, to her sudden
surprise, received on her cell phone a text sent by Seamus as he awaited the
operation. The text included the Latin Noli timere, 'Do not be afraid': Heaney
was quoting from his own poem 'The Master', in which the neophyte seeking

knowledge finds, after an arduous climb to the tower of the Master, 'just the old rules / we all had inscribed on our slates ... . // *Tell the truth. Do not be afraid.*' Heaney died just before the operation was to begin, instantly and with his faculties intact.

Heaney's work was awarded numerous prizes in Ireland, England, the United States and Europe, from his first book (which won both the Gregory Award and the Geoffrey Faber Prize) to his last (which won the Forward Poetry Prize for Best Collection), with the 1995 Nobel (and many others) coming in between. His poetry attracted a large readership, beginning with those in Ireland who remembered rural childhoods and customs resembling his own, and widening over time to the world audiences that heard his unaffected and moving readings or that knew the poems in English or in translation. The poetry was reassuring in its compassion and understanding of human sadness, hostility and loss; it was nostalgic in its reconstruction of a vanished pre-industrial Ireland; it was honest in refusing political ideology and political propaganda; it was humane in its candid depictions of married dissension and married love; and (after a long period of holding back) it allowed itself an outburst of rage at human cruelty and the indifference of fate. Like its author, the work was at home in allusion and etymology, but both were so deftly touched on that they could glide easily into mind or recollection. Heaney's wonderfully modulated rhythms could be angular or lulling, martial or dance-like, melodic or staccato; and his alert revisions of kinds of the Western lyric – the epithalamion, the christening-poem, the pastoral, the elegy, the erotic poem, the *hommage*, the journey poem, the eclogue and the poem of praise – have yet to be described fully. His work gave courage to other poets who, remaining within the tradition, could dare, as he did, to alter it by their individual talent.

In person, Heaney was welcoming, generous and witty; his household in Dublin was the site of warm welcome to visitors from all over the world. His humour arrived in a quip or in repartee rather than in any bravura display. His natural posture was a modest one, from his young days onward, and he remained firmly grounded in the body that never forgot the muscular life of spades and pitchforks. He had a sense of duty that he took only too seriously; he could not dismiss any genuine inquiry or any obligation to family and friends, to whom he was sturdily loyal. He was not sentimental, although he was brimming with sentiment; he gave the appalling its due. His elegy for his sister Ann, who died of cancer, included the full hospital ghastliness of the fright in her face, just as his poem about washing his dying father included his own revulsion from the slack skin of the aged flesh. His high intelligence compelled, throughout his work, second thoughts that queried his first ones;

as he said himself in 'Terminus', 'Is it any wonder when I thought / I would have second thoughts?' Like Chekhov writing about the prison on Sakhalin, he strove – in an atmosphere riddled with dogma, declaration and threat – 'To try for the right tone – not tract, not thesis.'

This is an obituary written for the Bulletin of the American Philosophical Association, Philadelphia, PA.

Academic Essays

The Fairies

William Allingham (1824–89)

Up the airy mountain,
    Down the rushy glen,
We daren't go a-hunting
    For fear of little men;
Wee folk, good folk,
    Trooping all together
Green jacket, red cap,
    And white owl's feather!
Down along the rocky shore
    Some make their home,
They live on crispy pancakes
    Of yellow tide-foam;
Some in the reeds
    Of the black mountain lake,
With frogs for their watch-dogs,
    All night awake.

High on the hill-top
    The old King sits;
He is now so old and gray
    He's nigh lost his wits.
With a bridge of white mist
    Columbkill he crosses,
On his stately journeys
    From Slieveleague to Rosses;
Or going up with music
    On cold starry nights
To sup with the Queen
    Of the gay Northern Lights.

They stole little Bridget
    For seven years long;
When she came down again
    Her friends were all gone.
They took her lightly back,
    Between the night and morrow,
They thought that she was fast asleep,
    But she was dead with sorrow.
They have kept her ever since
    Deep within the lake,
On a bed of flag-leaves,
    Watching till she wake.

By the craggy hill-side,
    Through the mosses bare,
They have planted thorn-trees
    For pleasure here and there.
If any man so daring
    As dig them up in spite,
He shall find their sharpest thorns
    In his bed at night.

Up the airy mountain,
    Down the rushy glen,
We daren't go a-hunting
    For fear of little men;
Wee folk, good folk,
    Trooping all together;
Green jacket, red cap,
    And white owl's feather!

'Every Paddler's Heritage': W.B. Yeats, Hans Christian Andersen, Susan Pollexfen Yeats, S.T. Coleridge and Children's Stories

(For N.H.)

MANECK H. DARUWALA

I

'I am not really dead.' (Hans C. Andersen)

'Think what you would have been now, if instead of being fed with tales and old wives' fables in childhood, you had been crammed with geography and natural history!' (*Charles Lamb to S.T. Coleridge, who had been crammed with everything, 23 October 1802*)

Once upon a time, well over a hundred years ago, a young Irishwoman read her children a story about how once upon a time there was an ugly duckling who turned out to be a swan.

I have forgotten *Grimm's Fairy-Tales* that I read at Sligo, and all of Hans Andersen except 'The Ugly Duckling' which my mother had read to me and to my sisters. I remember vaguely that I liked Hans Andersen better than Grimm because he was less homely, but even he never gave me the knights and dragons and beautiful ladies that I longed for. I have remembered nothing that I read but only those things that I heard or saw. (*Au*, p. 47)

William Butler Yeats, although nicknamed 'William Tell' by his wife, tells us relatively little about his mother and the story of her sad life, and the complicated relationship between mother and son has been told by William M. Murphy and worked out by Deirdre Toomey in her richly suggestive essay, 'Away' (*Yeats Annual, No. 10*). Much has been written – justifiably – of J.B. Yeats's influence on his son. W.B. Yeats, writing *Reveries* in 1914, regards as his mother's gifts both his motherland and his mother tongue: his almost savage love of Sligo, his love of Ireland and of folklore. As a later poem puts it, merging mother and country, 'I carry from my mother's womb / A fanatic heart' (*VP* 506, *ll*. 14–15).

> She would spend hours listening to or telling stories of the pilots and fishing-people of Rosses Point, or of her own Sligo girlhood, and it was always assumed between her and us that Sligo was more beautiful than other places … My memory of what she was like in those days has grown very dim, but I think her sense of personality, her desire of any life of her own, had disappeared in her care for us and in much anxiety about money. (*Au*, p. 31)

Susan Pollexfen Yeats (who died on 3 January 1900) seems to have been deeply unhappy in her marriage. W.B. Yeats knew the profound debt he owed his father, but the poetic debt he owed his mother – who unlike his father had no social status as an artist and did not seem to care for books – seems to have been an emotion-laden and retrospective discovery. When Yeats was a sixty-year-old smiling public man, he explained in one of his most beautiful poems, 'Among School Children', why no one really deserves or can justify a mother's love.

Yeats's contrary parental heritage has been invoked to explain his poetics. Born in the year *Alice in Wonderland* was published, Yeats spent his childhood in the midst of a great efflorescence of children's literature in English as well as a rich Celtic tradition. ' "No one will ever see Sligo as we saw it", Willie told Lily in later years' (*Family Secrets*, p. 9). As the boy grew up he heard and read many more stories – Danish, German, Arabian, Indian and Irish – not always distinguishable in their origins. 'What you love well is your true heritage.' Some of the stories Yeats probably first encountered in Andersen and Grimm were edited by him later in *Fairy and Folk Tales of the Irish Peasantry* (1888) and *Irish Fairy Tales* (1892).[1]

The stories of Andersen – like the poems of Yeats – are crowded with water birds; with ducks and swans and geese and storks, with ravens and nightingales and golden birds and cocks (both the farmyard and the weathervane variety), beautifully illustrated in the versions to which the Yeats children might have had access. In ' "Sailing to Byzantium," Keats, and Andersen',[2] Ernest Schanzer calls Dr H.W. Dulcken's 1864 translation of Andersen's tales, with a frontispiece showing a natural nightingale, Chinese lords and ladies, and a reclining

Emperor, 'the most popular translation of Andersen's tales available during
Yeats's childhood' (p. 376). There were various Dulcken translations, including
what was apparently the most complete English translation available at the
time: Hans Christian Andersen's 1866 *Stories for the Household*, translated
by Dulcken, 'With Two Hundred and Twenty illustrations by A.W. Bayes;
engraved by Dalziel Brothers'; (reprinted in 1870 by George Routledge & Sons,
it is the version used for this essay).[3] The Pre-Raphaelite connections of the
Dalziel Brothers also make this a likely choice for the Yeats household.[4]

Both Celtic folklore and Andersen's fairy tales present a fine fluidity between
species, between natural and supernatural worlds. Sometimes the ducks are
ducks, sometimes they are swans, sometimes the swans are enchanted brothers
and sometimes the frogs are princes and the footmen mice. (And this without
getting into the occasionally painful matter of changelings.) Or, as Yeats put
it in 'The Celtic Element in Literature' (1897), 'Men ... lived in a world where
anything might flow and change, and become any other thing' (*E & I*, p. 178).
The texts of these tales, like their subjects, were prone to metamorphosis, and
Andersen combines a long folk tradition with whimsical authorship. Yeats's
references to Andersen, although scattered over his work, are not entirely
random. As the poet becomes a young man he puts away childish things. When
he gets older, about his late forties, he returns to them. As Yeats grew up he
turned to Celtic lore – to the stories of lovers, dragons and beautiful ladies he
had longed for but never had enough of as a child – and to the discovery of his
Celtic 'roots'; he was often – as caricatures of the time testify – to be seen in the
company of Irish fairies.

Storytelling has long been regarded in the West as a female tradition, not
always positively; Plato in the *Gorgias* refers to old wives' tales (Tatar, xi)[5],
although even children's tales are not always disparaged by poets. Philip Sidney
makes the criterion of poetic value and pleasure the deceptively simple claim
that poetry keeps children from play and old men from the chimney corner – or
as Yeats rephrases it, entertains 'A young girl in the indolence of her youth, / Or
an old man upon a winter's night' (*VP* 359, *ll*. 5–6); this is not so different from
keeping drowsy emperors awake. In any case, as Virginia Woolf asserts in a
different context, 'Anonymous', who gave us these stories, was often a woman.
Yeats associates childhood tales with his mother; and of Mary Battle, who
worked for his uncle, George Pollexfen, he says, 'Much of my *Celtic Twilight* is
but her daily speech' (*Au*, p. 71), casting himself in the role of male folklorists
like the Grimms who – whether they acknowledged it or not – also collected
and reported female wisdom. Fairyland is traditionally a world of women, and
it might have been that the same inclinations that led Yeats to prefer Andersen

to the Grimms also led him to prefer Celtic to continental fairy tales; certainly
your garden-variety fairy tale can be devoid of Celtic glamour, and often even of
fairies. It takes a Niamh or a Maeve to carry off the heart of a sensitive young
poet, and it is not surprising that for a variety of reasons – personal, sexual,
aesthetic, political – Yeats should have preferred Irish folklore, and his passion
for it is certainly well documented in his own work. Most of the critical mate-
rial on Yeats and fairy and folklore naturally concerns Celtic lore, although
there are some richly suggestive essays on individual tales like 'Yeats's Swans
and Andersen's Ugly Duckling' by Rupin W. Desai in *Colby Library Quarterly*
(1971) and ' "Sailing to Byzantium," Keats, and Andersen' by Ernest Schanzer in
English Studies, 41 (1960), which points out a now generally accepted source for
Yeats's poem in Andersen's 'The Emperor's Nightingale' (or 'The Nightingale')
and suggests that 'Every paddler's heritage' in stanza three of 'Among School
Children' is an allusion to 'The Ugly Duckling'. (Warwick Gould's remarkable
essay, ' "A Lesson for the Circumspect:" W.B. Yeats's Two Versions of *A Vision*
and *The Arabian Nights*',[6] also demonstrates the sophistication and complexity
of the connection, placing it in a more adult tradition.) Non-Celtic fairy tales
seem to reappear more directly later in Yeats's poetry, about the time that he is
writing about his mother in his autobiography in his late forties.

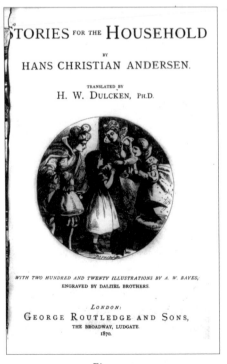

Figure 1

> She read no books, but she and the fisherman's wife would tell each other
> stories that Homer might have told, pleased with any moment of sudden
> intensity and laughing together over any point of satire. There is an essay
> called 'Village Ghosts' in my *Celtic Twilight*, which is but a record of one
> such afternoon, and many a fine tale has been lost because it had not occurred
> to me soon enough to keep notes. My father was always praising her to my
> sisters and to me, because she pretended to nothing she did not feel. She
> would write him letters, telling of her delight in the tumbling clouds ... She
> had always, my father would say, intensity, and that was his chief word of
> praise ... (*Au*, pp. 61–62)

Storytelling, laughter, intensity, nonchalance: these are the Yeatsian
virtues. In fact, the Yeatsian virtues are also the fairy virtues – gaiety, gener-
osity, courtesy, truth-telling, promise-keeping. Deirdre Toomey points out that
'During the 1890s Yeats became increasingly interested in folklore, particu-
larly Irish folklore', but that 'he had been taking notes between 1882 and 1883
of some of his mother's stories: "I wrote nothing but ghost or fairy stories,
picked up from my mother or some pilot at Rosses point"' (Toomey, *YA 10*,
Au, p. 61). Yeats tells us in 'The Message of the Folklorist' that

> Folklore is at once the Bible, the Thirty-nine Articles, and the Book of
> Common Prayer, and well-nigh all the great poets have lived by its light ...
> the Slavonian peasants tell their children now, as they did a thousand years
> before Shakespeare was born, of the spirit prisoned in the cloven pine ...
> Shakespeare and Keats had the folk-lore of their own day, while Shelley had
> but mythology. (*Yeats's Poetry, Drama, and Prose*, p. 263)

Apuleius' second-century story of 'Cupid and Psyche', which had so much
influence on Keats and Yeats and Pater, is such an old wives' tale (told by a
drunken and half-demented old woman). The conception of 'childhood' may
have changed in recent centuries. 'The notion that "adult" and "juvenile" texts
should be kept apart did not become prevalent until the end of the nineteenth
century' according to U.C. Knoepflmacher (p. xiii).[7] Today the Booker committee
might pass over a children's book for fear of not appearing quite grown up. But
every poet was a child once, and it is the intent of this essay to contaminate the
gaiety of Yeats's poetry with the seriousness of children's stories.

II

Despite cultural suppression – including the suppression of the pagan world
and sexist selection – Alison Lurie can still see in the Grimms's tales 'a kind
of pagan bible' and feminist politics (pp. 26 and 16).[8] More recent selection

has doted on the sleeping princess and forgotten the sleeping prince. 'From the point of view of European (and world) folklore, such stories are highly unrepresentative' (p. 19). As Julia Briggs and Dennis Butts point out in 'The Emergence of Form, 1850–90' (*Children's Literature An Illustrated History*, ed. Peter Hunt et al, pp. 130–65), 'the versions of fairy tales that reached Victorian children were already more mediated than their defenders supposed, pre-selected – often strategically cut and bowdlerised ... ' (p. 138). Andersen explicitly Christianized his stories, but even he did not escape bowdlerization – in addition to the distorting mediation of translation. There were three translations from Andersen in England in 1846, and by 1870 (the year of his death) at least twenty-one different collections of Andersen's tales had been published. Not that these translations apparently do Andersen justice. Andersen, it seems, is notoriously hard to translate. At their most beautiful and memorable, as in 'The Snow Queen' (which originates in a folk-tale), they remain a well-loved children's heritage, one of the permanent pleasures of childhood and deeply influential in contemporary literature, whether in adult poetry or in books like Philip Pullman's *His Dark Materials* trilogy. They engaged Yeats, as they engaged Wilde, whose own stories show Andersen's influence. And influence may be even more unpredictable and labyrinthine in a child's mind. Fairy tales are rarely as simple as they seem: 'This is a doubtful tale from faery land, / Hard for the non-elect to understand' (Keats, *Lamia*, Part II, lines 5–6).

Yeats attributes to his mother's influence his love of both natural and supernatural worlds. Perhaps these stories also offered enchantment and escape to an unhappy child. 'In the first twelve years of Yeats's life he was never more than two years in one place.' (*Away*, YA 10). Yeats dwells on the pain of childhood in the opening pages of his autobiography, although Sligo – loved passionately by his mother – becomes an enchanted and 'sacred place': 'Years afterwards, when I was ten or twelve years old in London, I would remember Sligo with tears, and when I began to write, it was there I hoped to find my audience' (*Au*, p. 18). It is not surprising that 'The Ugly Duckling' should have been the favourite of a poet who could write, 'Indeed I remember little of childhood but its pain' (*Au*, p. 11) or speak of 'The ignominy of boyhood' (*VP* 478, l. 45). (Yeats adds, 'I have grown happier with every year of life as though gradually conquering something in myself, for certainly my miseries were not made by others but were a part of my own mind.' [*Au*, p. 11]) The duckling had successors by other names and in more adult plumage: 'Mine inheritance is as the speckled bird, all the birds of heaven are against it.'[9] (Or, in the King James version, 'Mine heritage is unto me as a speckled bird, the birds round about are against her', Jeremiah 12:9). And in Yeats's story, 'The Wisdom of the King' ('Wisdom' in 1895), which begins like a variant of a sleeping beauty or sleeping prince story, the young king is set apart by his wisdom and his imperfect humanity, 'For the feathers of the grey hawk had begun to grow in the child's hair' (*The Secret Rose*, p. 27).

Of Yeats's claim that he had forgotten 'all of Hans Andersen except "The Ugly Duckling" which my mother had read to me',[10] Desai says: 'Two questions that arise are, first, why did "The Ugly Duckling" alone remain so deeply embedded in the poet's memory that nearly forty years later he could thus single it out? And, second, why did his thoughts revert to this favorite story of his boyhood around the time that he wrote his poem "The Wild Swans at Coole"?' (p. 331) Desai answers both questions convincingly, locating the boy's lonely and unhappy identification with the story, and associating the recalled memory with Yeats's unhappy circumstances at the time he wrote 'The Wild Swans at Coole'. But whatever Yeats claims to have forgotten of Hans Andersen, 'The Ugly Duckling' was not the only story that became a part of his consciousness – there were other Andersen stories that seem to have haunted him as well. 'The Wild Swans' and 'The Snow Queen' are powerful magic, and these, along with 'The Ugly Duckling' and 'The Nightingale' (or 'The Emperor's Nightingale' or 'The Emperor and the Nightingale') seem to have been irresistible to generations of children, including William Yeats.

Andersen's stories are frankly the creations of a single author even though they draw on folklore, and his characters are more individualized, even to the point of eccentricity, than the figures of many folktales. Of course Andersen can be 'homely' too – but that does not come across in full force in the selected works that most children encounter; and the Grimm stories, which can also be magical, are often 'homely' even in their supposedly magical moments. One could hardly expect a child who wants princesses and dragons and knights to thrill to the romance of a pre-arranged masculine bargain between the groom and the bride's father, as say, presented by the Grimms's 'Twelve Dancing Princesses' or 'King Thrushbeard' – stories told from the point of view of a Conchubar rather than a Deirdre or a Naoise. Andersen's 'The Shepherdess and the Chimney Sweep' of course gives us the lovers' version. And Andersen, even when he borrows a story from the grimmer tradition, presents romance as necessarily mutual, not a disposing of or acquisition of chattel. As someone frankly making up his stories, he also has more room for whimsy, although the humour of the sensitivity and high breeding which culminate in an infallible pea-detector is probably lost on a serious child. Yeats picks up the humour; on the other hand, Andersen's religiosity (which may have influenced some of Wilde's fairy tales), seems alien to his temperament. And the masochistic piety of tales such as 'The Little Sea Maid' is in fact completely subverted. Andersen's mermaid saves the drowning prince [figure 2]; she 'rejoiced that she had saved his life when he was driven about, half dead, on the wild billows; she thought how quietly his head had reclined on her bosom, and how heartily she had kissed him; but he knew nothing of it, and could not even dream of her.' (*Stories for the Household*, p. 550)

Yeats's mermaid drowns her lover quite by accident. But if she seems to revert to another nineteenth-century type in painting and literature, the *femme fatale*, she is one casually and unthinkingly:

> A mermaid found a living lad,
> Picked him for her own,
> Pressed her body to his body,
> Laughed; and plunging down
> Forgot in cruel happiness
> That even lovers drown.
> ('The Little Mermaid', 1927, *VP* 452–3, *ll.* 1–6)

Figure 2

Like the works of Yeats and Wilde, stories like 'The Tin Soldier', 'The Ugly Duckling' and 'The Little Mermaid' have been seen as a form of auto-biography.[11] Reginald Spink sees The Little Mermaid as a blend of Norse or Danish folklore and Andersen's own projection of himself as the little maid. In its depiction of an undersea world it is far more alluring than any moral tale that Brocklehurst tries to inflict on the astute Jane Eyre. But that is also the problem. Whatever the story loses in translation (and readers claim it lacks Andersen's usual humour), as handed down in the version available to Victorian children who were William Yeats's contemporaries, the mermaid loses both her worlds, progressing from a gifted and lively young mermaid who loves a prince to a self-mutilated martyr translated into someone else's heaven. (Other fairy tales have ogres and witches and giants and wicked step-mothers – but they are not usually about permanently and deliberately self-mutilated heroines.) The mermaid's story reads like a post-colonial or feminist allegory. It combines the horrors of east and west – mutilation and amputa-tion, the story of a crippled victim of Chinese footbinding and a tongueless Philomel – in a moral tale about the rewards of self-abjection and renunciation for the benefit of little girls. Perhaps its popularity in Victorian England speaks for itself – unlike The Little Mermaid. The Little Mermaid, despite her posi-tion of apparent privilege, ends up as a member of that sorry sisterhood of tiny Victorian heroines whose societies – or authors – are so harsh with them that death seems their only hope of upward mobility. In what may only be another imperialist allegory, and without underrating the woe that is in Disney, one may argue it took more than beatification to make The Little Mermaid inter-nationally popular. It took Disneyfication.

A surface reading of 'The Little Mermaid' sometimes gives us a world where (to misapply Susan Sontag) it is spiritually fashionable to be in pain, where body is constantly bruised to pleasure soul. Even in its predecessor – the earlier Danish tale whose sympathies Arnold beautifully reverses in 'The Forsaken Merman' – the poor maid has two choices: the mere world or the churchgoing earthly world. Andersen's story presents a grimmer, more convo-luted problem, and perhaps, a metaphysical bait-and-switch. But this may be too literalist a reading of the story – which can perhaps be read in a more subversive fashion. One can only hope that Victorian children approached it with the sophistication of a Jane Eyre (who, after all, came to know a 'real' Helen Burns). It is not surprising that some of them went on to paint pictures like Edward Burne-Jones's 'The Depths of the Sea' (1887) or write poems like Yeats's 'The Mermaid' – whether or not they were reacting against childhood pieties or reverting to an ancient tradition or to male fears and fantasies of female power. (Yeats knew his Burne-Jones, who, born in 1833, may have been just in time for Andersen.)

The capacity of Andersen's stories to disturb, and our adult memories of that, also testify to their power. Andersen belongs to children everywhere (from Ireland to India), and it is difficult even for grown-up children to be cool and indifferent about him, even about a story never encountered as a child. Perhaps he should be read more subtly. A poem like Yeats's 'The Cap and Bells', which Yeats (bitterly?) called the way to win a lady, may be read in this light. Yeats tells us it is a dream poem, but that does not preclude a child-hood influence. The jester is a male version of the Little Sea Maid (as H.W. Dulcken's translation calls her) who is herself, Spink suggests, a female version of Andersen; he sends his young queen his 'wise-tongued soul' (VP 159, l. 7) and a heart 'grown sweet-tongued by dreaming' (VP 160, l. 17), and finally his cap and bells; although she accepts these in the end, it is not clear that he survives the sacrifice of his art, his identity and of everything else that the cap and bells signify.

Yeats's Countess Cathleen reverses the Little Sea Maid in a different fashion; Christ-like, she sacrifices her human soul to save her people. Andersen's mermaid desperately wants a soul; the Countess loses or 'sells' hers. Yet, like the mermaid, Cathleen is 'saved' despite her bargain (and even, perhaps, because of it).

Yeats's first great poem gives us pagan Celtic glamour which is a more direct challenge to Andersen's Christianized northern world – Oisin would rather go to hell than acquire a Christian soul. The sea maid asks her wise grandmother:

> 'If people are not drowned,' asked the little sea maid, 'can they live for ever? Do they not die as we die down here in the sea?'
>
> 'Yes,' replied the old lady. 'They too must die, and their life is even shorter than ours. We can live to be three hundred years old, but when we cease to exist here, we are turned to foam on the surface of the water, and we have not even a grave here among those we love. We have not an immortal soul; we never receive another life; we are like the green seaweed, which when once cut through can never bloom again. Men on the contrary, have a soul ... '
>
> ... 'Why did I not receive an immortal soul?' asked the little sea maid, sorrowfully. 'I would gladly give all the hundreds of years I have to live as a human being only for one day, and to have a hope of partaking in the heavenly kingdom.'
>
> 'You must not think of that,' replied the old lady. 'We feel ourselves far more happy and far better than mankind yonder.'
>
> 'Then I am to die and be cast as foam upon the sea, not hearing the music of the waves, nor seeing the pretty flowers and the red sun. Can I not do anything to win an immortal soul?'

'No!' answered the grandmother. 'Only if a man were to love you so that you should be more to him than father and mother; if he should cling to you with his every thought and with all his love, and let the priest lay his right hand in yours with a promise of faithfulness here and in all eternity, then his soul would be imparted to your body, and you would receive a share of the happiness of mankind. He would give a soul to you and yet retain his own. But that can never come to pass. What is considered beautiful here in the sea – the fish-tail – they would consider ugly on the earth ... '

The little sea maid sighed, and looked mournfully upon her fish-tail.

'Let us be glad!' said the old lady. 'Let us dance and leap in the three hundred years we have to live. That is certainly long enough; after that we can rest ourselves all the better.'

(*Stories for the Household*, pp. 550–1)

The speaker of Yeats's 'The White Birds' (*VP 121* (30), *l1*) does not think the undersea world so regrettable: 'I would that we were, my beloved, white birds on the foam of the sea!' (*VP 121*). And the world of the sea has much in common with the world of Niamh in Yeats's first great poem (even down to the three hundred years, like its Celtic predecessor); the old lady is the champion of her pagan world as Oisin is of his, or St Patrick of his Christian one. Oisin's is clearly not a world where they marry in churches, and true love needs the sanction of a priest. Niamh, who rides out of the foam to carry off the delighted Oisin, is no silent mermaid either; as she tells Finn: 'now I choose, for these four feet / Ran through the foam and ran to this / That I might have your son to kiss' (*VP 6*, *ll.* 58–59). Obviously Norse and Celtic lore shared many things in common, including the importance of the sea (also developed by Arnold in his 'Forsaken Merman') and a cold hell. Oisin's longing is to undo the Christian transformation so devoutly wished by the mermaid. On the other hand, like Oisin, the sea maid, who is also a singer, leaves behind the world of her father for a lover from another world. Niamh is led to Oisin by the magic of words, and words play a role in how she wins him and how he won her:

> 'I loved no man, though kings besought,
> Until the Danaan poets brought
> Rhyme that rhymed upon Oisin's name,
> And now I am dizzy with the thought
> Of all that wisdom and the fame
> Of battles broken by his hands,
> Of stories builded by his words
> That are like coloured Asian birds
> At evening in their rainless lands.'

> O Patrick, by your brazen bell,
> There was no limb of mine but fell
> Into a desperate gulph of love!
>
> (*VP* 7, *ll.* 62–73)

But in Andersen's tale of female sacrifice the sea maid gives up her voice – her tongue – among other things, to win the prince. Yet her own undersea world is very like the one Niamh carries Oisin into, a world of luminous colour, of sea purples and pearls and silver and gold. 'Through the midst of the hall flowed a broad stream, and on this the sea men and women danced to their own charming songs. Such beautiful voices the people of the earth have not.' (*Stories for the Household*, p. 552)

> O Patrick, by your brazen bell,
> There was no limb of mine but fell
> Into a desperate gulph of love!
> 'You only will I wed,' I cried,
> 'And I will make a thousand songs,
> And set your name all names above,
> And captives bound with leathern thongs
> Shall kneel and praise you, one by one,
> At evening in my western dun.'
>
> ('The Wanderings of Oisin', *VP* 7–8, *ll.* 71–79)

Captives, whether as audience or singers, are not to everyone's taste, but they are also what the Andersen story describes:

> In the castle she was the most beautiful creature to be seen; but she was dumb, and could neither sing nor speak. [The witch, having warned her that it is a 'stupid' exchange, has cut off the Sea Maid's tongue.] Lovely slaves, dressed in silk and gold, stepped forward, and sang before the Prince and his royal parents ... (*Stories for the Household*, p. 554)

Andersen, who is part of the Romantic tradition, deals, in his own fashion (sometimes considered sentimental), with themes that are to become Yeatsian signatures: metamorphosis, spiritual development, a glorification of poetry and the poet, the opposition between nature and art, the forced choice between two worlds. Other themes or images that recur constantly in Andersen, like the rose, are of course everywhere in fairy tales and mythology. Andersen, like an early Romantic, comes down consistently on the side of nature; Yeats, like any alert child (or late Romantic), ignores the message and prefers the golden bird. The princess in Andersen's 'The Swineherd' almost begins to cry when she realizes that what seems like a wonderfully made flower is 'not artificial, it's a *natural* rose!' (p. 247). Nor does she appreciate the honest value of the real nightingale, although her father the Emperor weeps at it. Like Yeats she may well have preferred being the artificial bird of 'The Nightingale' to 'any natural thing', and part of the moral of Andersen's story is her ethical and aesthetic re-education. Yeats was a poet happy to take the story and let the moral go, and his endings are rarely as moral as, say, Oscar Wilde's. Of course, a pious tag at the end of every tale may turn any child into an aesthete.

A story of Andersen's that may have made a lasting impression on both Yeats and Wilde is 'The Swineherd'. But whether or not Wilde was influenced by Andersen here, Yeats's 'A Full Moon in March' is the offspring of an alliance between Wilde and Andersen – between Wilde's *Salomé* and Andersen's 'The Swineherd'. There are, of course, other versions of *Salomé* (hundreds, at least; *Salomé* was, we are told, a French national industry at the turn of the century), as well as other versions of Andersen's tale, such as the Grimm story 'King Thrushbeard'. The heroes of these tales tend to be deliberately irritating or arrogant, although Wilde's Jokanaan is in a class by himself. Unlike the heroes of 'The Swineherd' or 'A Full Moon in March', Jokanaan is decorative (his anatomization by Salomé is a defiant role reversal) but not artistic. Wilde could have presented him much more sympathetically; instead Jokanaan's mind is a sewer rather than a temple of the Holy Ghost.

Some of Andersen's stories end sadly, but his swineherd is naturally a prince (in disguise), although his kingdom is small and the princess is the emperor's daughter. The analogies between the story and Yeats's play are numerous. For example, Andersen's prince disguises or masks himself with black and brown dye and 'A Full Moon in March' opens: *'The swineherd wears a half-savage mask covering the upper part of his face. He is bearded.'* (Eliminating the role of the king – who is of course paternalistic – heightens the drama and the tension between Queen and Swineherd.) The Queen offers her hand and her kingdom to him 'that best sings his passion' with the proviso: 'None I abhor can sing' (VPl, p. 981). Naturally, she is also the judge, and makes the Victoria-like pronouncement: 'No song has moved us yet' (p. 981). Like Andersen's Prince who 'was not to be frightened', Yeats's Swineherd is confident 'Because I look upon you without fear' (p. 982). Both wooers are makers and poets. Andersen's disguised prince is an artist, although he sets nature higher – in the form of the natural rose and the nightingale; he makes a pot with bells that plays an old tune and a musical rattle; Yeats's disguised Swineherd (who is really a swineherd – as far as anyone is really just anybody in these symbolic plays) offers a song. Neither story has a happy ending, although Andersen's

Prince manages to keep his head while those about him are losing theirs. It is characteristic of Yeats's later plays however, that the women he designates princesses keep turning into goosegirls.

GERDA PREPARING TO START.

hand, and slept so that one could hear her; but Gerda could not close her eyes at all—she did not know whether she was to live or die.

The robbers sat round the fire, sang and drank, and the old robber woman tumbled about. It was quite terrible for a little girl to behold.

Then the Wood Pigeons said, "Coo! coo! we have seen little Kay. A white owl was carrying his sledge: he sat in the Snow Queen's carriage, which drove close by the forest as we lay in our nests. She blew upon us young pigeons, and all died except us two. Coo! coo!"

"What are you saying there?" asked Gerda. "Whither was the Snow Queen travelling? Do you know anything about it?"

"She was probably journeying to Lapland, for there they have always ice and snow. Ask the Reindeer that is tied to the cord."

"There is ice and snow yonder, and it is glorious and fine," said the Reindeer. "There one may run about free in great glittering plains. There the Snow Queen has her summer tent; but her strong castle is up towards the North Pole, on the island that's called Spitzbergen."

"Oh, Kay, little Kay!" cried Gerda.

Figure 3

Even Yeatsian works that have deeply rooted Celtic sources, like *Deirdre*,[12] often have fairy tale associations – like the 'Three Little Pigs' or 'The Shepherdess and the Chimney-Sweeper'. What is intriguing for our purposes is Yeats's positioning of the drama in the context of woman's lore. Yeats introduces the three female musicians who are Greek chorus, mythic figures like the fates, female representatives of the oral tradition and of poets everywhere. The story of Deirdre, like any number of fairy tales, begins with the prophecy of a birth (by a Druid), and it ends with Druid incantations by the sea. Yeats replaces this tradition of male wisdom and magic that is power with an explicitly female chorus, and he goes out of his way to gender and develop the opposition between female wisdom and the male arrogance that dismisses it. Fergus and Naoise's belittling of the prophetic foresight of the musicians and of Deirdre not only parallels the usual Cassandra myths, but also the world of fairy and folklore traditionally dismissed by masculine scholarship, or Irish lore dismissed by the scholars even at Trinity College, Dublin. In Yeats's play it proves a fatal mistake. Another way of looking at it might be to say that Fergus and Naoise are superficial readers or unravellers of stories. They take words at face value, dismiss the world of woman's lore or old wives' tales and believe that the world of their heroic code is the real world, while the women are more sophisticated interpreters and critics of the complicated relationship between the real and the ideal world, language and reality, art and history.

Moving on to the poems, the human figures in the early fairy tales who seemed to influence Yeats's poetry were not Snow Whites or Sleeping Beauties or Cinderellas. Andersen gives us some droopy heroines, of course, but he also gives us Eliza (or Elsa) who defies stake, graveyard and public opinion to save her swan brothers; little girls like Gerda who roam the world to save little boys like Kay (the engraving of 'Gerda Preparing to Start' [figure 3] is not unlike the tradition of pictures depicting the arming of a knight, with the substitution of a girl and a reindeer);[13] the overwhelming, powerful, and glamorous Snow Queen who sweeps Kay off to her ice world in her ice sled; the learned princess in the same story who 'wanted to marry, but ... wished for a husband who could answer when he was spoken to, not one who only stood and looked handsome, for that was wearisome' (*Stories for the Household*, p. 327); and of course the robber-girl with her striking red cap, long dagger, pair of pistols (she is well-armed even if one excludes her ability to bite) and splendid stolen horse – and an astonishingly unorthodox relation to her mother: a daughter who calls her mother 'old nanny goat' and takes her by the beard defies all our stereotypes of Victorian girlhood. ' "Good morning, my own old nanny-goat." And the mother filliped her nose till it was red and blue; and it was all done for pure love' (p. 334). A noble savage if there ever was one (despite her shortcomings she is the goddess from the machine in the story), she never does see the error of her ways, nor is she ever reduced to domesticity. The last we hear of her is that she 'was tired of staying at home [her perception of her bandit life], and wished to go first to the north, and if that did not suit her, to some other region' (p. 340). Surely these independent heroines seem a foreshadowing of Yeats's fascination with Niamh and Maeve and Helen, with women warriors who are Helen and Achilles rolled into one. As he put it in 'The Old Age of Queen Maeve',

> in her young age
> She had been beautiful in that old way
> That's all but gone; for the proud heart is gone,
> And the fool heart of the counting-house fears all
> But soft beauty and indolent desire. (*VP* 180–1, *ll.* 18–22)

Of course, a child who grew up next door to Maeve's megalithic cairn and Ben Bulben could hardly escape such a heritage.

Yeats's education seems to follow this tradition of female independence, as did some of the poets and artists he chose to admire. 'I was in all things pre-Raphaelite' says Yeats the autobiographer. This included the cult of the Amazon, especially as practised by D.C. Rossetti and William Morris. Fiona MacCarthy says of the 1996 Morris exhibit at the Victoria and Albert Museum:

> One of the great games at the V&A is spotting the warrior women. Women with bows and arrows, with spears and daggers. The most magnificent are the brawny red-haired heroines taken from Chaucer's *Legend of Good Wimmen* [sic]. Morris designed them [c.] 1860 as embroideries for the walls of the dining room at Red House. (Essay on William Morris, *Times Literary Supplement* No. 4861, 31 May 1996.)

These include 'Helen, who holds a flaming baton ... inscribed "Flamme Troiae."' But then perhaps Yeats's was an education in the etymological sense of a drawing out.

Yeats creates his biography in his books of poetry, and he draws in the process on a variety of genres, including the fairy tale. (The 'real' Maud Gonne is not the issue here, as she seems to have realized herself; or as Yeats put it much later: 'who can tell / Which of her forms has shown her substance right?' 'A Bronze Head', VP 618, *ll.* 10–11.) He was to live, or at least write, his own version of 'The Snow Queen' in volumes of poems like *The Wind Among the Reeds* and *The Green Helmet*. The poet plays the part of Kay in his devotion to an enthralling Snow Queen whose ice crystals affect everything he sees and feels; Olivia Shakespear, like Gerda, is too salutary a love for him, too close to his own soul.

> Pale brows, still hands and dim hair,
> I had a beautiful friend
> And dreamed that the old despair
> Would end in love in the end:
> She looked in my heart one day
> And saw your image was there;
> She has gone weeping away.
> ('The Lover mourns for the Loss of Love', VP 153, *ll.* 1–7)

Gerda does not go weeping away, but she almost does; and the robber girl tells Kay, 'I wonder whether you deserve that anyone should run to the ends of the world for your sake.' The spell is finally broken when Gerda rescues Kay, the ice crystals spell the magic word – 'Eternity' (a sort of predecessor to the rituals

of the Golden Dawn?) – and Kay and Gerda are reunited; but Yeats's story was
not in the end a fairy tale; or, in his telling, not until much later and another
'glad kindness'. Then it ends, perhaps with a question, but with fame, honour,
love: 'All his happier dreams came true – / A small old house, wife, daughter,
son ...' ('What Then?', *VP* 577, *ll.* 11–12).

There are, however, homelier stories for which Yeats seems to be drawing
on Andersen. A very early example (the first version was published on 15 Novem-
ber 1890 [*VP* 131]) is the much-revised 'The Lamentation of the Old Pensioner'.

> There's not a woman turns her face
> Upon a broken tree,
> And yet the beauties that I loved
> Are in my memory;
> I spit into the face of Time
> That has transfigured me.
> (*VP* 132–3, *ll.* 13–18)

Figure 4

Andersen's lamentation, 'By The Almshouse Window', is reversed by Yeats's marvellous last stanza. The accompanying engraving – 'The Old Pensioner' (illustrated by A.W. Bayes and engraved by the Dalziel Brothers [figure 4]) – gives us a sadly dejected old woman sitting by a window looking out at a potted plant; the text tells us she is as lonely as Yeats's speaker, but unlike him, full of regret for lost sexual opportunity. And like him her contemplations are of Time and trees.

> Scarcely have the violets come forth, but there on the rampart, just opposite the beautiful castle of Rosenberg, there is a tree bright with the first green buds. Every year this tree sends forth fresh green shoots. Alas! It is not so with the human heart! Dark mists, more in number than those that cover the northern skies, cloud the human heart. Poor child – thy friend's bridal chamber is a black coffin, and thou becomest an old maid ...
>
> ('By the Almshouse Window', *Stories for the Household*, p. 213)

The problem with Yeats's pensioner is that, unlike the rest of him, his heart has not grown old. Perhaps Andersen's story struck a chord in the young Yeats whose first long poem concerns the fear of Time and of growing old.

There are, of course, aspects of Andersen that we love to forget. Unlike the apparently more authentic Grimm brothers he sometimes seems pious, sentimental and even cute in translation. It is a popular belief that children (like critics of tragic drama) like poetic justice – which is often neither; they also, naturally, wish to convince themselves that nothing ever happens to the good. Yet although the tales of Andersen (like some of the Grimm stories) often have moralistic endings, they are also sometimes unexpectedly disturbing. 'The Storks' (in which the mother stork tries to teach her young to appear not to care – like Yeats's water bird) is a story that seems intolerable even for rough children, let alone sensitive adults. But when Yeats borrows a tale with a moralistic ending, the original moral is almost never Yeats's. The most famous such reversal is of course that at the end of 'Sailing to Byzantium'; Andersen's story is about the superiority of the natural bird over cold artifice. Yeats's bird combines immortal artifice and organic variety of song and subject. (The later bird of 'Byzantium' seems all artifice.)

Another reversal of perception seems to become the basis of an entire poem, 'A Coat'. *Responsibilities* (1914), published the same year as Yeats's reminiscences of his mother in his autobiography, closes with the famous modernist statement:

> I made my song a coat
> Covered with embroideries
> Out of old mythologies

From heel to throat;
But the fools caught it,
Wore it in the world's eye
As though they'd wrought it.
Song, let them take it,
For there's more enterprise
In walking naked.

(*VP* 320, *ll.* 1–10)

It is Yeats's farewell to old mythologies – but not to old fairy tales. The emper-
or's new clothes were equally sumptuous and insubstantial. The tailors in
Andersen's story (based, we are told by F.J. Harvey Darton, in *Children's Books
in England*, 1982, on a Spanish source) are of course frauds and deceivers
who prey on vanity and on people's fears of what other people think, fears of
being shown up, or of seeming foolish, incompetent, stupid or just different.
Or maybe they are minimalist artists, reader-response critics, or poets and liars
who take their colours – their lights and half-lights – from the imaginations
they awaken, and their airy looms are laden with the cloths of heaven.

In any case, Andersen's story ends with the enforced dignity of the
emperor (by now the emperor, as the child points out and everyone knows, has
nothing on, and he knows they know it). For the poet, walking naked becomes
a heroic act. Yeats himself said 'The self-conquest of a writer who is not a man
of action is style',[14] (*Yeats: The Man and the Masks*, p. 138). In the end, the
emperor's clothes and the poet's nakedness – stylistic or otherwise – may be
equally deceptive.

'In dreams begins responsibility' says the headnote to Yeats's volume. The
sleeper in 'The Hour Before Dawn' in this collection goes perversely back to
sleep – but not to dream; there are other poems in *Responsibilities* which suggest
generalized fairy-tale sources which are not necessarily Celtic. The titles, 'The
Three Hermits', 'The Three Beggars', 'The Witch', are of course the stuff of
folklore. 'The Dolls' is somewhat different, reminiscent of various nineteenth-
century stories, including Andersen's (and his empathy for animated toys seems
to survive elsewhere in Yeats). Another possible fairy-tale association in this
volume may be found in 'A Memory of Youth'; the moment of enlightenment
when 'Love upon the cry / Of a most ridiculous little bird / Tore from the cloud
his marvellous moon' is not unlike that in the Grimm story, 'The Goose-Girl
at the Well'.

The next volume of poems Yeats publishes is *The Wild Swans at Coole*.
(The poem which gives its title to the volume may be associated with one of

Andersen's most haunting and influential tales: 'The Wild Swans'.) Desai, in 'Yeats's Swans and Andersen's Ugly Duckling' points out and elaborates the many similarities between this poem and 'The Ugly Duckling' – including the autumnal setting and the fact that both the situation of the poet and the poem are similar to those of the story. The poet, like the ugly duckling, is outside the enchanted and beautiful realm that the swans inhabit: he is a spectator whose 'heart is sore' (p. 334).

He is imperfect, mortal, full 'of unfulfilled longing, of incomplete knowledge' (p. 334). Desai points out that:

> just two years before he wrote the poem, Yeats mentioned Andersen twice, both times with great appreciation, the second time referring specifically to 'The Ugly Duckling'. In 1914, in 'Art and Ideas', Yeats describes how on a visit to the Tate gallery, he was stirred by the sight of paintings he had long been familiar with as a child. One painting in particular, Potter's *Field Mouse* that he remembered 'had hung in our house for years', profoundly affected him: 'I murmured to myself, "The only painting in modern England that could give pleasure to a child, the only painting that would seem as moving as *The Pilgrim's Progress* or Hans Andersen"'. (pp. 330–1)

The second reference was in the opening pages of his autobiography. The extravagance of Yeats's praise is typical, and the juxtaposition with Bunyan may at first seem peculiar. Desai locates the power of 'The Ugly Duckling' over Yeats in his own sad biography. ('The Ugly Duckling' may also be read as a kind of Stupid Hans or runt-of-the-litter story – but it is more. Charles Kingsley's *Water Babies* with its metamorphosis of a chimney sweep into a water baby is a submarine version of such a transformation tale, although it has greater affinities with 'The Little Mermaid'). Unathletic, artistic, dreamy and seemingly hard to teach in Ireland – like the hero or heroine of a fairy tale ('Because I had found it hard to attend to anything less interesting than my thoughts, I was difficult to teach', *Au*, p. 23) – Irish in England ('I was called names for being Irish', p. 33), it was only later that Yeats, set apart by his dark 'Indian' appearance even as a child, came to realize that he had pretty plumage. Most ducklings grow up to be ducks – happily enough, one hopes. The swan's crisis of identity, its 'ugliness', is just a consequence of applying duck standards to someone not a duck. Or, as Blake might have put it, 'One law for the duck and the swan is oppression.'

Perhaps the duckling story can be read as a spiritual and aesthetic pilgrimage, an avian version of the Psyche story which Keats had used for his 'Ode to Psyche' (see my essay 'Keats and the "Ode to Pysche" ', *Victorians Institute Journal* No. 19, 141–88), and which Yeats was later to admire in

Pater and (reinforced by his knowledge of Indian philosophy) develop in his own *Vision* and his theories of the phases of the soul. Aherne says, at least of a certain phase, that 'All dreams of the soul / End in a beautiful man's or woman's body' ('The Phases of the Moon', *VP* 374). What is Yeats's *Vision* but a grown-up version of a duckling becoming a swan, of the soul wheeling its way from phase to phase and incarnation to incarnation? 'Some moralist or mythological poet / Compares the solitary soul to a swan' ('Nineteen Hundred and Nineteen', *VP* 430, *ll.* 59–60). Scholars tell us this is Shelley, but of course it is also Andersen. His story is about loneliness and meta-morphosis; it can be read as a story about physical beauty or the perception of it, but it is as much about spiritual beauty, or the value of individuality, or about human prejudice or the alienation of the outcast or the artist or anyone a little different from the rest of the flock (the Duckling is bitten and hunted and scoffed at, and [figure 5] 'The Duckling Teased by the Goose' is itself an aesthetic or intellectual parable); or it is about artistic longing for a beauty that seems beyond one's reach ('Desiring this man's art and that man's scope'), or just as a hunger for love.

> Now came the autumn. The leaves in the forest turned yellow and brown; the wind caught them so that they danced about, and up in the air it was very cold ... One evening – the sun was just setting in his beauty – there came a great flock of great handsome birds out of the bushes; they were dazzlingly white, with long, flexible necks; they were swans. They uttered a very pecu-liar cry, spread forth their glorious great wings, and flew away from that cold region to warmer lands, to fair open lakes. They mounted so high, so high! And the little ugly Duckling felt quite strangely as it watched them. It turned round and round in the water like a wheel, stretched out its neck towards them, and uttered such a strange loud cry as frightened itself. Oh! It could not forget those beautiful, happy birds. And so soon as it could see them no longer, it dived down to the very bottom, and when it came up again, it was quite beside itself. It knew not the name of those birds, and knew not whither they were flying; but it loved them as it had never loved any one. It was not at all envious of them. How could it think of wishing to possess such loveliness as they had? (*Stories for the Household*, pp. 160–2)

After that autumn when the swans mount high and fly away to warmer lands, the duckling is at last frozen fast one night in the ice despite all his efforts, and is saved and finally resurrected (to a new phase of the soul?) by a peasant in the morning. Although his ostensible mother is protective, the duckling suffers many trials and cruelties and much loneliness through the phases of his young life and the cycle of the seasons; he certainly labours to be beautiful – or to discover that he has always been a swan.

THE DUCKLING TEASED BY THE GOOSE.

And so they came into the poultry-yard. There was a terrible riot going on in there, for two families were quarrelling about an eel's head, and the cat got it after all.

"See, that's how it goes in the world!" said the Mother-Duck; and she whetted her beak, for she, too, wanted the eel's head. "Only use your legs," she said. "See that you can bustle about, and bow your heads before the old duck yonder. She's the grandest of all here; she's of Spanish blood—that's why she's so fat; and do you see, she has a red rag round her leg; that's something particularly fine, and the greatest distinction a duck can enjoy: it signifies that one does not want to lose her, and that she's to be recognized by man and beast. Shake yourselves—don't turn in your toes; a well brought-up duck turns its toes quite out, just like father and mother, so! Now bend your necks and say 'Rap!'"

And they did so; but the other ducks round about looked at them, and said quite boldly,

"Look there! now we're to have these hanging on as if there were

ELIZA AND HER BROTHERS, THE SWANS.

"In what way can I release you?" asked the sister; and they conversed nearly the whole night, only slumbering for a few hours.

She was awakened by the rustling of the swans' wings above her head. Her brothers were again enchanted, and they flew in wide circles and at last far away; but one of them, the youngest, remained behind, and the swan laid his head in her lap, and she stroked his wings; and the whole day they remained together. Towards evening the others came back, and when the sun had gone down they stood there in their own shapes.

"To-morrow we fly far away from here, and cannot come back until a

Figures 5 and 6

Yeats, when he wrote his 'Wild Swans at Coole', did not know how his story would end; the wheeling of Andersen's duckling – who is of course a swan – is borrowed by Yeats's gyring birds, 'wheeling in great broken rings', among many other things. And the speaker's sadness is perhaps not only for the setting nineteen years ago, and his lost love of Maud Gonne, but also for his lost childhood. ('And yet the white & loving creatures Delighted me when young' (*The Wild Swans at Coole: Manuscript Materials by W.B. Yeats*, ed. Stephen Parrish (Ithaca & London 1994), pp. 22–3). These lines could refer to his own childhood as well as that of the swans or the ugly duckling). Manuscripts of the poem vary the years and the count (*The Wild Swans at Coole*, ed. Parrish). He mentions going out counting the swans 'Gaily when I was young' and 'Always when I was young' (pp. 12–13). (See figure 6, 'The Four Swans'.) The first time Yeats walked that shore or heard the bell-beat of swans' wings was perhaps when he heard those stories from his mother. And his feeling for birds – especially water birds – may owe something to those stories as well as his Sligo background. Swans are endemic in Andersen, not only in 'The Ugly Duckling' but in other tales – like the one from which 'The Wild Swans at Coole' borrows its title. Eliza in Andersen's 'The Wild Swans' – one of his most powerful and moving tales – also eventually recognizes the eleven swans who come toward her by the setting sun: 'The swans alighted near her and flapped their great white wings' (p. 564), and she watches as they are transformed into humanity and her brothers. Later,

> She was awakened by the rustling of the swans' wings above her head. Her brothers were again enchanted, and they flew in wide circles and at last far away; but one of them, the youngest, remained behind, and the swan laid his head in her lap, and she stroked his wings; and the whole day they remained together. (*Stories for the Household*, p. 565)

The quiet water, 'the great wood', the familiar birds of Andersen's story all find their counterparts in Yeats's poem, as do the wide circles of the swans:

> I saw, before I had well finished,
> All suddenly mount
> And scatter wheeling in great broken rings
> Upon their clamorous wings.
>   (*VP* 322, *ll.* 9–12)

And perhaps they have counterparts not only in that poem but in earlier and later ones; in 'The White Birds': 'I would that we were, my beloved, white birds on the foam of the sea' (*VP* 121, *l.* 1) or in the much later 'Lullaby'. Here the context is very different, but the enduring tenderness between bird and human is similar, as is the girl's 'protecting care' (*VP* 522, *l.* 18). Andersen's Eliza finally wins the swans back into humanity, but the poet at Coole seems to want to reverse the transformation – *their* hearts have not grown old. The poet in his autobiography insists that he remembered only what he heard and saw; and long before Yeats saw Leonardo's gentle depiction of Leda and the Swan, which is supposed to have inspired 'Lullaby', he probably saw what, in his own life at least, would have been its predecessor and prefigurement: Bayes's illustration, engraved by the Dalziels, of 'Eliza and her Brothers, the Swans' [figure 6], which shows Eliza tenderly kissing one brother while her right hand rests at the base of the arched neck of another; she is, in fact, surrounded by swans.

III

A casual survey suggests that the tales Yeats apparently responds to are those that have long been children's favourites and have been selected and printed over and over again – contemporary English translations still seem to depend heavily on their nineteenth-century predecessors; the translation of *Andersen's Fairy Tales* by Valdemar Paulsen published by Barnes and Noble in 1995 (but originally copyrighted 1916) which I picked up at the local book store in Miami is still remarkably close to H.W. Dulcken's 1870 (1866) *Stories for the Household*, which may have been used by the Yeats family.

THE FOUR SWANS.

brown; the wind caught them so that they danced about, and up in the air it was very cold. The clouds hung low, heavy with hail and snow-flakes, and on the fence stood the raven, crying, " Croak! croak!" for mere cold; yes, it was enough to make one feel cold to think of this. The poor little Duckling certainly had not a good time. One evening—the sun was just setting in his beauty—there came a whole flock of great handsome birds out of the bushes; they were dazzlingly white, with long flexible necks; they were swans. They uttered a very peculiar cry, spread forth their glorious great wings, and flew away from that cold region to warmer lands, to fair open lakes. They mounted so high, so high! and the ugly little Duckling felt quite strangely as it watched them. It turned round and round in the water like a wheel, stretched out its neck towards them, and uttered such a strange loud cry as frightened itself. Oh! it could not forget those beautiful, happy birds; and so soon as it could see them no longer, it dived down to the very bottom, and when it came up again, it was

M

Figure 7

Not all the uses of these tales by Yeats are extensive; there are touches here and there in poems that suggest possible associations, and some of them are poems about children. Perhaps Yeats had, later on, as a father, been reading or meditating or re-telling children's stories. The peculiar phrasing of the lines in 'A Prayer for My Daughter' ('It's certain that fine women eat / A crazy salad with their meat') may take us back (if it doesn't invoke a Waldorf, a Caesar, or a hallucinogenic mushroom salad illustrative of dangers of vegetarianism), not to Andersen this time but to Grimm. In the Grimm story 'The Salad' (not to be confused with 'The Turnip' or 'Rapunzel'), a huntsman accidentally discovers a 'bad salad' which changes him into an ass. In the process of this complicated story (having regained his shape with 'another kind of salad' [*Sixty Fairy Tales*, p. 296]), he feeds the bad salad to a witch, her maid, and the beautiful maiden who is the witch's daughter. 'She ate some, and, like the others, was immediately changed into an ass, and ran out to them in the yard' (p. 298). Of course she regains her human form at the end, after Grimm justice is done, but the story may be as convincing a source for Yeats's turn of phrase as any other. Another possible source for this poem is the Grimms's more obscure 'The Sparrow and His Young Ones', where a sparrow brings up four young ones in a swallow's nest; it is destroyed (either by boys or a high wind), the children escape, and the older bird is saddened that the children are driven into the world before he could properly advise and warn them. However, a happy reunion, tales of experience and some advice follow. 'A Prayer for My Daughter' with its wind and bird and tree images may be like the advice an old bird might have given; although perhaps less practical, the emphasis is on hidden serenity and safety: 'That all her thoughts may like the linnet be ...'; 'If there's no hatred in the mind / Assault and battery of the wind / can never tear the linnet from the leaf.'

On the other hand, the references to swans and paddlers in 'Among School Children' are much more richly evocative and clear, and it seems appropriate that the poet's sudden vision of childhood in stanza III be associated with children's tales. (Also see Ernest Schanzer, p. 376.)

Two other poems, 'In Memory of Eva Gore-Booth and Con Markiewicz' and 'Ego Dominus Tuus', may be illuminated by the introduction of Andersen's 'The Little Match Girl' (also known as 'The Little Match Seller'). There are other tales that may apply to the first poem: Andersen's 'The Tinder-Box' and its probable source, the Grimms's 'The Blue Light', especially since the perpetrators there are convicted of guilt, and escape only by striking their lights. But the first story may well be the best match. Andersen's story is a powerful indictment of a world where children freeze and die within view of dazzling luxury; the little match girl can see the plenty beyond the 'veil' that separates the two worlds as she starves; the wall becomes a window. And the same page that describes the luxury and food (perhaps the little girl is delirious by now) gives us a picture of the frozen child: 'The People Find the Little Match Girl' [figure 8].

> A second [match] was rubbed against the wall. It burned up, and when the
> light fell upon the wall, it became transparent like a thin veil, and she could
> see through it into the room. On the table a snow-white cloth was spread;
> upon it stood a shining dinner service; the roast goose smoked gloriously,
> stuffed with apples and dried plums. And what was still more splendid to

behold, the goose hopped down from the dish, and waddled along the floor, with a knife and fork in its breast to the little girl. Then the match went out, and only the thick, damp, cold wall was before her. She lighted another match. Then she was sitting down under a beautiful Christmas tree; it was greater and more ornamented than the one she had seen through the glass at the rich merchant's. Thousands of candles burned upon the green branches, and coloured pictures like those in the print shops looked down upon them. The little girl stretched forth her hand towards them; then the match went out. The Christmas lights mounted higher. She saw them now as stars in the sky: one of them fell down, forming a long line of fire.

'Now someone is dying', thought the little girl ... (pp. 358–9)

THE PEOPLE FIND THE LITTLE MATCH GIRL.

R-r-atch! how it sputtered and burned! It was a warm bright flame, like a little candle, when she held her hands over it; it was a wonderful little light! It really seemed to the little girl as if she sat before a great polished stove, with bright brass feet and a brass cover. How the fire burned! how comfortable it was! but the little flame went out, the stove vanished, and she had only the remains of the burned match in her hand.

A second was rubbed against the wall. It burned up, and when the light fell upon the wall it became transparent like a thin veil, and she could see through it into the room. On the table a snow-white cloth was spread; upon it stood a shining dinner service; the roast goose smoked gloriously, stuffed with apples and dried plums. And what was still more splendid to behold, the goose hopped down from the dish, and waddled along the floor, with a knife and fork in its breast, to the little girl. Then the match went out, and only the thick, damp, cold wall was before her. She lighted another match. Then she was sitting under a beautiful Christmas tree; it was greater and more ornamented than the

Figure 8

Phillip L. Marcus draws my attention in this context to the use of the goose image in 'A Very Pretty Little Story' ('Related Documents', *The Secret Rose*), a 'three page typescript (carbon) ... found among Lady Augusta Gregory's papers. This is a "folk" version of "The Binding of the Hair" ... The precise extent (if any) of Yeats's involvement in its writing is unknown, but it opens in a whimsical semi-Andersen style:

> In the time long ago, when herons made their nests in old men's beards and turkeys chewed tobacco, and the little pigs ran about with knives and forks stuck in them crying out 'Who'll eat me! Who'll eat me! Who'll eat me!' there lived a queen in a golden palace, having [?] the roof thatched with birds wings.' (*The Secret Rose, Stories by W.B. Yeats: A Variorum Edition*, Phillip L. Marcus et al. (eds) [Ithaca & London 1991] p. 258)[15]

The spread table in Andersen's story may also have its counterpart in 'In Memory of Eva Gore-Booth and Con Markiewicz'. The manuscripts of the early version of the poem have 'The light of evening, Lizadell' preceded by 'A table spread / A table & window to the south' (*The Winding Stair* [1929], pp. 2–3). There are more explicit uses of the window image. In 'Ego Dominus Tuus', Yeats uses the same images, the same juxtaposition of window-gazing, luxury, poverty, food, hunger and death for Keats and his deliberate happiness, although Keats's hunger – directed to 'sweets' – is presented as more childish, and the starving match girl can smell the food she cannot eat.

> I see a schoolboy when I think of him,
> With face and nose pressed to a sweet shop window,
> For certainly he sank into his grave
> His senses and his heart unsatisfied ...
>
> (*VP* 370, *ll.* 55–8)

Keats makes 'luxuriant song' out of his deficient life before he dies; the girl's matches do not keep her warm but light her way to a visionary world and ultimately death.

'In Memory of Eva Gore-Booth and Con Markiewicz' is one of Yeats's loveliest, most haunting poems. 'The light of evening, Lissadell' – the liquid lines drop subtly off the tongue. 'The innocent and the beautiful / Have no enemy but time' Yeats tells us, and the words are so beautiful that we are almost convinced they are true. (Perhaps the realization of other enemies is the loss of innocence.) In this case however, the poem may be more of a fairy tale, a cry of the heart against necessity, than the story. That Yeats seems to be drawing on 'The Little Match Girl' is perhaps clearer in the manuscript versions of the poem, but the published work itself – with its great windows, 'That table', shadows (a manuscript version reads 'dear shadows in the grave') and striking matches, and conflagrations – has much in common with the story. The story tells us 'It was terribly cold; it snowed and was already almost dark, and evening came on the last evening of the year ... Shivering with cold and hunger she crept along a picture of misery ... In all the windows lights were shining, and there was a glorious smell of roast goose, for it was New Year's-eve' (p. 357). Windows in this poem (unlike those in 'The Cap and Bells' or 'Ego Dominus Tuus') look outward; in 'Blood and the Moon', 'dusty, glittering windows' (IV) separate two worlds: blood and the moon, life and death; but these are magic casements, the great windows behind which the privileged live. Some thirty-three years before he wrote the poem Yeats stayed with the Gore-Booths at Lissadell. Like Keats, or even the little match girl, he himself was not grand enough in 1894, he suggests later (in a passage very much like his poem), to quite belong behind those great windows: 'this house would never accept so penniless a suitor' (Mem, p. 78). (Yeats felt an affinity then with Eva Gore-Booth, 'whose delicate, gazelle-like beauty reflected a mind far more subtle and distinguished. Eva was for a couple of happy weeks my close friend' [Mem. p. 78].) According to R.F. Foster, 'This was a level of county society to which the Pollexfens did not aspire; WBY had breached it through the power of art, and the Gore-Booth enthusiasm for the avant-garde.' (W.B. Yeats: A Life, Vol. I, p. 144) Yeats does not describe his younger self directly in this poem, although he was, perhaps, shyer than his gazelle. In this poem, memory, desire and 'pictures of the mind' mix in a dazzling defiance of chronology – and Chronos.

The poem began in politics; the first line was 'But Ireland is a hag' – but politics, or ultimately time, is seen as having invaded a world of summer evenings located between the two 'gazelle's, the second a beautifully delayed and repeated rhyme. The manuscript spells the word various ways: 'gazell', 'gazale', 'gasel'. Gazelles are African or Asian animals, the word itself apparently being of Arabic origin, and in this context evocative of eastern poetry. But 'ghazal' or 'gazal', Persian (and Arabic) in origin, is also a common word for a song or lyric, particularly a lyric with a repeated rhyme (although a 'real' ghazal has intricate rules and repetitions; the OED, which gives its first English citation in 1800, seems to have as many variants as Yeats: gazel, ghazel, ghasel, ghazul. Ghazals tend to be love songs, although an OED citation mentions several written for a city). 'But a raving autumn shears / Blossoms from the summer's wreath'; 'wreath', although the manuscripts suggest it was discovered for its rhyme, has an appropriate circularity, aesthetic, chronological and, as will become apparent, Coleridgean. For this poem may be the offspring of 'the unwritten' (for Yeats) and 'written' traditions of Romanticism, of Andersen and S.T. Coleridge, of Susan Pollexfen Yeats

and J.B. Yeats. Yeats's late romanticism makes a pleasure place out of the revo-
lutionary Romanticism of the first Romantics and the 'pre-literary' Romanticism
of the Andersen his mother read him.

What is lost is not just the way of a class, but of youth and summer
sunshine, of boyhood ('Con Gore-Booth all through my later boyhood had
been romantic to me' [*Mem*, p. 73]) and even childhood. For the pictures of the
mind that Yeats would mix may go well beyond thirty-three years and those
visits to Lissadell, go further back perhaps to childhood memories, pictures,
fairy tales and word associations.

'The Little Match Girl' may not be the only Andersen fairy tale associ-
ated with the poem. Yeats may have been meditating on Japanese silk in 'A
Dialogue of Self and Soul' drafted in the same notebook during the same year
(Clark, Introduction, *The Winding Stair* [1929], p. xxiii), and the first citation
for *kimono* (from the Japanese) in the OED is for 1894 – the year of Yeats's
stay at Lissadell. But although the English rage for Japonisme and kimonos
(which were also Chinese exports) may have been fin de siècle, the pictures of
the mind may have included the silk-gowned members of the Chinese court by
A.W. Bayes engraved by the Dalziel Brothers in their illustrations of Andersen's
'The Nightingale' [figure 9]. The poem is haunting because it unites the ideal-
ized images of 1894 with an even longer lost fairy-tale world, re-'orienting' the
imagination with a world of kimonos, gazebos and gazelles (whether one sees
this as Saidean 'Orientalism' or Rushdian 'orientation'; in Said the West or the
colonizer co-opts the Other; in Rushdie the East or the post-colonial world
writes back. Yeats, western, Irish, post-colonial and honorary Indian fits into
several of these categories).

The gazebo is naturally (and unnaturally) at the centre of this re-orien-
tation. Gazebos are both etymologically and architecturally associated with
things Chinese (not just Chinoiserie). The OED suggests that it may be the
corruption of 'some oriental word' and gives as its earliest, 1752, citation: 'The
Elevation of a Chinese Tower or Gazebo.' Not only did gazebos remain eleva-
tions or towers (often lighted at night) at the time that Yeats was writing the
poem, they remained associated with eastern, specifically Chinese, design;
but Yeats's most influential source here is probably the great pleasure dome
of Coleridge's Xanadu – now Shangdu to the Chinese – his transformation
perhaps of Marco Polo's description of a great yurt (*The Times*, 23 May 1998).

'Kubla Khan' is the incarnation and model of all Romantic theory. Its
pleasure dome reconciles oppositions, fuses complexities of past and future,
earth and air, East and West, Abyssinia and China, 'feminine' and 'masculine',
poetry and history, dream and waking, human and non-human, architecture

and anatomy. It is the archetypal Romantic poem – and that is how Yeats seems
to have regarded it in the scattered references of his essays. 'Kubla Khan' was,
for decades, not only Yeats's lyric ideal as his edition by Arthur Symons[16] (the
one cited in this essay) suggests, but was also associated by Yeats with eastern
wisdom: 'Then I think … of the magic of Christabel or Kubla Khan, … and
wisdom, magic, sensation seem Asiatic. We have borrowed directly from the
East and selected for admiration or repetition everything in our own past that
is least European, as though groping backward toward our common mother'
(Yeats, *E & I*, 'An Indian Monk', 1932, p. 432).

THE COURTIERS FIND THE NIGHTINGALE.

And then the Nightingale began to sing.
"That is it!" exclaimed the little girl. "Listen, listen! and yonder
it sits."
And she pointed to a little grey bird up in the boughs.
"Is it possible?" cried the cavalier. "I should never have thought
it looked like that! How simple it looks! It must certainly have lost
its colour at seeing such grand people around."
"Little Nightingale!" called the little kitchenmaid, quite loudly,
"our gracious Emperor wishes you to sing before him."
"With the greatest pleasure!" replied the Nightingale, and began to
sing most delightfully.
"It sounds just like glass bells!" said the cavalier. "And look at its
little throat, how it's working! It's wonderful that we should never
have heard it before. That bird will be a great success at court."
"Shall I sing once more before the Emperor?" asked the Nightingale,
for it thought the Emperor was present.

Figure 9

   The great gazebo may be a political or an aesthetic utopia, an ironic spec-
tacle that may invite a mocking 'gaze' (another etymology for *gazebo*, perhaps
associated with the notion of making a gazebo of oneself) or an ideal world
that blends a lighted Yeatsian tower, the Irish Renaissance or Pater's 'house
beautiful' (as Phil Marcus suggests), the Shelleyan dawn predicted in the

Dedication to *Laon and Cythna*, fairy tales and Romantic poetry. It is like Tennyson's fairy built city from 'Gareth and Lynette', ever in progress: 'They are building still, seeing the city is built / To music, therefore never built at all, / And therefore built for ever.' It embodies the urge of the Romantic artist or the fallen angel to remake paradise – or this world. In *Women in Love* (p. 236) Birkin talks of Gudrun and Winifred:

[Birkin] And every true artist is the salvation of every other.
[Gerald] I thought they got on so badly as a rule.
[Birkin] Perhaps, but only artists produce for each other the world that is fit to live in.

Perhaps, in the end, no adult creates for another a world that is fit to live in. But art (with its suspension of belief and disbelief, of fanaticism) may not only come closest, it sweetens and expands the human imagination by allowing it to conceive the possibility of such a world. We have questions about Kubla Khan's labour practices, and we know Lissadell is full of stuffed animal trophies. Yeats does not really describe or praise the interior of Lissadell. Like Coleridge, Yeats rebuilds Lissadell (and Xanadu) – perhaps as it never used to be – not in brick or stone but in the air and the mind; Yeats gives us not one Abyssinian maid with a dulcimer (Eva Gore-Booth was a poet) but two girls in silk kimonos. The speaker of 'Kubla Khan' longs to revive the girl's song in his mind, Yeats to mix pictures of the mind with the girls. Both sunny and girdled paradises are threatened by time and politics; ancestral voices prophesying war were, sadly enough, always heard in Ireland. The remains of each survive: the recently discovered site of Xanadu in Mongolia testifies to the architectural accuracy of Coleridge's 'vision' (and of his sources); the old Mongolian lady who told the man from *The Times* 'that she had not realised that there was another country outside China' also has a certain Andersenian appeal; and Yeats's great gazebo is the legacy of modern Ireland and the world. The gazebo, like its predecessors – Lissadell, Xanadu – is, Yeats suggests by juxtaposition, a specific place, not a vague Utopia but an earthly paradise. 'Paradise' is, by its Avestan etymology, a park, an enclosure, a pleasure place according to Xenophon (OED), and by definition a foreign space (in Hindi, pardesh). All paradises are lost paradises we are told, and Yeats's tribute was to remake Lissadell in air and with a mouthful of air, like Coleridge's Xanadu. The speaker of 'Kubla Khan' is ostracized in the end as taboo; the speaker of Yeats's poem convicted of creative 'guilt'. The same guilt, perhaps, which Coleridge found so unbearable that he abandoned the authorship of his poem to a dream. Because as Yeats spelt out and Coleridge knew in his so-called fragments and in endless revisions of 'The Ancient Mariner' – re-making the work or paradise is not possible without re-making the self. (The Old Persian origin of 'paradise' is pairidaeza, from pairi (around) + diz (to mould, form) [OED]). Coleridge believed that the perfect form for a poem was the Greek *ouroboros*, the serpent biting its own tail, and 'Kubla Khan' ends where it begins, with the creation of the pleasure dome – this time in eternity and in air; and in our imagination. Yeats's poem has its own circularities, its images of eternity; the entire poem is woven in the enclosed rhyme scheme of the more ecstatic portions of 'Kubla Khan' (it also picks up some of Coleridge's rhymes) and it ends on the same quickening beat and encircling rhyme scheme (abba) as its great predecessor. Like 'Kubla Khan' (although this is most obvious in the Crewe manuscript in Coleridge's own handwriting, which was not 'discovered' until 1934)[17] it is separated into two parts. Each poem opposes 'we' or 'I' to 'they' or 'all' – the artist and the audience separated, shut in or out, by the taboo of a magic circle; and literally enchanted – as in spellbound by words. The second part of Coleridge's poem – the building of the dome in air – mirrors the first (some have seen them as examples of his Primary and Secondary Imagination), just as 'The shadow of the dome of pleasure' … 'Floated midway on the waves' (wherever 'midway' might be). Yeats's poem also deals with images and 'pictures of the mind' and memory. The first twenty-line movement of Yeats's poem is circular in itself; the last line rhymes with the first and the fourth, the last two lines reflect the opening; the repetition of words, the rhyme scheme, and the liquid consonants continue throughout:

> The light of evening, Lissadell,
> Great windows open to the south,
> Two girls in silk kimonos, both
> Beautiful, one a gazelle …
>   mix
> Pictures of the mind, recall
> That table and that talk of youth,
> Two girls in silk kimonos both
> Beautiful, one a gazelle.

>   II
> Dear shadows, now you know it all …

The second part, set in a different time and a different world, also comes round. 'Kubla Khan' – following Coleridge's devotion to the contraries that make a great poem – is constructed of light and shadow, fire and ice, art and war, the river of life and the ocean of death, a wailing woman and a damsel with a dulcimer, and so on. Yeats's manuscript also gives us 'sunlight', 'shadow', 'hill' and 'forest'. ~~A Georgean~~ house under a hill / The glittering sunlight of my our / A glittering summer evening of youth / A dinner in the sunlight' and lines like 'Sunlight~~ garden~~' and '~~Memories of sea & hill~~'. The published version begins with 'The light of evening' and moves on to 'Dear shadows'. (The manuscript also has '~~Dear ghosts~~'.) 'A raving autumn shears blossom from the summer's wreath' and pictures of the mind become an old and 'skeleton-gaunt' image of politics. Like Kubla Khan who hears ancestral voices, the speaker, the shadows, or all of us, are '~~Instructed now beyond the grave~~' (*The Winding Stair* [1929], pp. 4–7).

'In Memory of Eva Gore-Booth and Con Markiewicz' opens, like 'Kubla Khan', on an ideal picture; and Yeats re-wrote the poem until the syntax of the final version insists that the first agent of change, the villain, is time:

> The light of evening, Lissadell,
> Great windows open to the south,
> Two girls in silk kimonos, both
> Beautiful, one a gazelle.
> But a raving autumn shears
> Blossoms from the summer's wreath;
> The older is condemned to death ...

Even politically, the sisters seem to react or be acted upon. Both poems have gentle feminine ideals and poet figures associated with eastern paradises: girls in silk kimonos (one a poet, we know) and an Abyssinian damsel with a dulcimer as well as wild women; Coleridge's perhaps imaginary woman wails by the moon for her demon-lover (we are never quite sure whether he or she is the demon, or whether the term qualifies the ardour of his love-making). But there is also another contrast, between the 'girls' – only one is a gazelle; the other, Yeats tells us in his *Memoirs* (p. 78), was wild, a tomboy on horseback (like a figure out of Andersen) – and his boyish vision of romance; in 'On a Political Prisoner' she was wild 'like any rock-bred, sea-borne bird' (*VP* 397, l. 11). Yeats transfers the raving to his autumn, but even his gazelle is transformed by politics. (And Time has rendered them 'Dear shadows' – an echo perhaps or an unconscious pun on 'gazelle'.) And the end of Yeats's poem seems richly ambiguous in syntax and vocabulary: who should run, the speaker or the 'Dear shadows'? What exactly should the sages know? Are 'they' who convicted 'us' of guilt the sages? Or enemies? Or an audience – as in 'Kubla Khan'? Are the sages like 'The Seven Sages' (also part of *The Winding Stair*), 'old men ... massed against the world' (*VP* 486, *l.* 14), beggarly but wise like the match seller's grandmother? Or are they to be associated with Coleridge himself in his role as a sage? (See *Yeats, Coleridge and the Romantic Sage* by Matthew Gibson.) Is the guilt that of aspiring to gazebos – aesthetic, spiritual, or political – or simply incarnation, the crime of death and birth? Or the guilt of having to choose between 'Perfection of the life, or of the work' as in 'The Choice', thereby losing two paradises (earthly and heavenly) instead of one?

THE NIGHTINGALE SINGING BEFORE THE EMPEROR.

brilliantly ornamented with diamonds, rubies, and sapphires. So soon as the artificial bird was wound up, he could sing one of the pieces that he really sang, and then his tail moved up and down, and shone with

Figure 10

Eva Gore-Booth died at fifty-six of bowel cancer, and, despite the harsh description in the poem, she was actually five years younger than Yeats. Politically different in their strategies, they were often on the same side (as in the Roger Casement fight). Perhaps Coleridge might have been startled (as Shelley might not) had the damsel with the dulcimer led a protest march. That is a risk of taking a living woman for a muse. But perhaps what Yeats mourns is the laying aside of the dulcimer. Perhaps, as Phillip L. Marcus (who revealingly analyses Yeats's own aesthetic choices in a cultural and political context in *Yeats and Artistic Power* [YAP]) suggests, this is what Yeats meant; he might have been mourning the loss of the poet. Jon Stallworthy quotes Yeats's letters to Eva Gore-Booth from Esther Roper's *Poems of Eva Gore-Booth*, 1929, in *Between the Lines*: 'Writing to Eva in 1916, Yeats says: "Your sister and yourself, two beautiful figures among the great trees of Lissadell, are among the dear memories of my youth" ... In 1898, when she decided to publish her first book of poems, he wrote to her: "I think it is full of poetic feeling and has great promise"' (p. 166). In 'The Quiet Revolutionary', Declan J. Foley and Janis Londraville tell us of the conflict in Gore-Booth's own life:

> Perhaps Eva Gore-Booth would never have been a great poet, even if she had kept her poems 'longer on the anvil'; but some of the limitations of her work resulted from her dedication to her social causes. She may have deprived us of greater poetry by her support of union movements, her fight for the rights of women to earn a fair wage, and her quest to force parliaments to give due and proper democratic recognition to the rights of the underprivileged (p. 163).

Gore-Booth's poems show an authentic gift, but had she made the choice of the perfection of the work above that of the life it is not clear that the work would have been better – and the world might have been worse. Perhaps it was the sheer impossibility of the choice, Yeats's inability to settle finally for one or the other that kept him a great and interesting poet.

> Dear shadows, now you know it all,
> All the folly of a fight
> With a common wrong or right.
> The innocent and the beautiful
> Have no enemy but time;
> Arise and bid me strike a match
> And strike another till time catch;
> Should the conflagration climb,
> Run till all the sages know.
> We the great gazebo built,
> They convicted us of guilt;
> Bid me strike a match and blow.
> (*VP* 476, *ll.* 21–32)

'Common' is an ambiguous word in context – does it signify that the fight is universal, shared with the speaker, class-associated or just undistinguished? And 'folly' has its own ambiguities. 'All the folly of a fight' seems critical. Perhaps it can also be associated with 'All that delirium of the brave', or the excess of love that 'bewildered' the revolutionaries of Easter 1916. But a gazebo is also a folly. (Jon Stallworthy also suggests this submerged echo.) 'Gazebo' occurs first in the manuscript and they are part of the same architectural and natural – or anti-natural – metaphor. The poem opens with the 'chaste' Greek revival architecture of Lissadell – great windows open to the south – and ends with the extravagance of gazebos and follies. 'Folly', French in its etymology, suggests foolishness, but also *folie*, pleasure, and a folly is also a pleasure garden (even sometimes a clump of trees; what Yeats seemed to remember most fondly of Lissadell was the women and the trees). As The Folly Fellowship points out, 'true follies are unconscious creations', and they cite Gwyn Headley and Wim Meulenkamp from *Follies: Grottoes and Garden Buildings*: a folly is in the eye of the beholder. Follies were fashionable in Ireland and England, the commonest form being a tower, and, of course, gazebos are a kind of folly. In Yeats's poem the dead women's folly may also be the living man's. The speaker's 'guilt' is that he is implicated in the folly as the others are in the gazebo; Yeats, after all, changes the agency of gazebo-building from 'I' to 'we' in the manuscript (whether this includes the sisters or Maud Gonne or friends like Lady Gregory and John Synge). The solitary poet speaker, the 'I' of Coleridge, becomes 'we', reminding us that the Irish version was also a great political accomplishment – a making of national identity. (And even Coleridge's 'dome in air' is built today with the collaboration of his reader.)

A folly was an extravagant construction, in this case – 'All the folly of a fight' – let's say, Ireland's exotic answer to the imperialist politics of the Crystal Palace, which itself caught fire several times in the early 1920s before it finally burned down in 1936. But the metaphor goes beyond politics. The poem opens on the light of evening and a summer day, but a raving autumn follows. Gazebos and follies also arrest the seasons, try to manipulate and defy time, creating an eternal summer; great gazebos sound humorous, and ironic, but they are also great works constructed there in nature's spite. Shangdu was Kubla Khan's summer palace, and his ancestral voices are prophetic in the poem: it was torched by the first Ming emperor. Yeats uses Coleridge's pleasure dome and Andersen's emperor again for 'Byzantium' – which is the great anti-natural, urban, and nocturnal anti-type of Coleridge's Xanadu. But the geography of his Lissadell seems not unlike that of Coleridge's Xanadu: 'Lissadell is a place of haunting beauty lying near the point of Sligo Bay, between the heather-covered mountains and "the great waves of the Atlantic" ... not far from Knocknarea and Maeve's cairn' (p. 165), says Jon Stallworthy, in *Between the Lines: Yeats's Poetry in the Making*, Oxford 1963, quoting Esther Roper's introduction to *Poems of Eva Gore-Booth*, 1929 (p. 5). The landscape of Lissadell may haunt still, but it is the power of the poem that makes the house unforgettable to us. And Coleridge's 'Kubla Khan' is quoted today in Mongolia.

In the end, inspiration, hope – in 'Kubla Khan', in 'The Little Match Girl' and in 'In Memory' – is otherworldly. Abyssinia and Lissadell were once the locations of paradise or the geography of Eden, and the little match girl's grandmother is in paradise. Shangdu was destroyed, like so much in Ireland, by war and politics. But Romantic fire is creative and destructive, and Yeats suggests setting the match to time. Could the speaker of 'Kubla Khan' revive within him the Abyssinian maid's symphony and song, could the 'Dear shadows' 'Arise' and bid the poet strike a match, the world might still catch fire, still appreciate the pleasure dome of Xanadu or the great gazebo built by Yeats and his friends.

We don't really know how beautiful or just Kubla Khan's historical palace was. Coleridge himself may have needed the intervention of dreams or the myth of an opium reverie. The experience may not endure. But whatever the artist's personal or political realities, poems like 'Kubla Khan' are made by poets who write as if already free.

Both Coleridge and Yeats believed that their minds were stretched by a childhood immersed in fairy and folklore.[18] And underlying 'In Memory of Eva Gore-Booth and Con Markiewicz', it seems, are Coleridge's 'Kubla Khan' and two very different tales by Andersen: one of supposedly Chinese luxury and magic and art and fireworks on an Emperor's birthday, and another of childhood misery and poverty in a European city on New Year's Eve and a match that does the impossible. The match that lights up a visionary world provides little warmth against the night or the cold despite the visions of a burning stove and candles. The match girl's last match takes her out of time into death. The early 21 September 1927 manuscript of the poem suggests a clear connection in some cancelled phrases: 'Dear ghosts return& strike a match'(6–7), 'till years be gone', and a 'pyre' and 'final embers'; its end – 'I the great gazebo built / They brought home to me the guilt / Bid me strike a match and blow' – merges the two worlds divided by the match girl's crystal window pane (or veil) as art can. But not only art: Constance Markiewicz, born on the privileged side of the great windows, spent her last years among the Dublin poor who loved her. Part of the 'folly' of the sisters was action, the pursuit of social justice (also a family tradition) rather than of a small, furry, mammal – the unspeakable in pursuit of the uneatable, as Wilde called it. But that introduces fauna from another poem ('On a Political Prisoner'); 'In Memory' gives us no harriers or foxes, only gazelles. In any case the Gore-Booth sisters' political strategies were not Yeats's, and this is not an analysis of their relative merits. Yeats criticized in Shelley his own passion for reforming the world, and 'vague Utopias' may not be fair – but it is not indifferent. Yeats's bitterness was directed against his perception of those qualities, especially in Constance Markiewicz, which he seemed to recognize and fear in himself (not just in Maud Gonne), and he uses similar terminology – the ditch of 'On a Political Prisoner' recurs in 'A Dialogue of Self and Soul' – to describe himself; so it is the Red Countess and not her sister who evokes the most passionate response and becomes a touchstone, the subject of some of his loveliest – if most controversial – poems, including 'On a Political Prisoner'. Perhaps they take their greatness from their bitterness. For all the complaints and poems that begin 'Why should I blame her ... ' and proceed to count the ways, the figures who command Yeats's poetry – and his praise, however bitter – are women of action and courage and intellect, artists, writers, warriors and revolutionaries. '[S]oft beauty and indolent desire' ('The Old Age of Queen Maeve', *VP* 181, *ll.* 22) are neither aesthetic nor dramatic, neither Yeatsian nor fairy-tale virtues. In the second part of 'In Memory' the apparent bitterness of the first (and the didacticism of the manuscript) melts away into tenderness: 'Dear shadows ... ', although Yeats still sees the fight – any fight, right or wrong – as folly.

In the opening temptation, creation, and fall scene of *Dorian Gray*, the protagonist – innocent and beautiful – discovers Time. When Lord Henry reveals Dorian to himself he tells him not to squander his beauty and his youth in good deeds, that youth is the one thing worth having. Time in this poem is the one thing worth having; if we are all, as Pater quotes Victor Hugo at the end of *The Renaissance*, '*condamnés*', the wisest, according to Pater, 'among "the children of this world" ', spend it 'in art and song' (p. 190). And yet Yeats's poem wants more than this. It wants to save the world as well as the self. The 'I' becomes 'we' at the end, which seems to include all of them: 'We the great gazebo built'. They are at last together on the same side, thanks to time – builders of follies and gazebos, positioned against 'they' – like the speaker of 'Kubla Khan'. The bitterness is not against the fighter but against time and the world. The poem moves beyond the partisan and the political, suggesting that these are the consequences not of being on the wrong side but on any side – alive – part of the complexities of mire and blood which saturate this book of poems. It is a rather unelegiac ending, reminiscent of the Dedication of *Laon and Cythna*. Action like this is an extravagance, a folly, building gazebos, but it's what we have. *The Tower* ends with an elegy, and *The Winding Stair* begins and ends with elegies – for the living and the dead. At the time Yeats wrote 'In Memory ... ', both Eva Gore-Booth and Constance Markiewicz were shadows and therefore ('now you know it all') in possession of the wisdom that is the property of the dead; and, it seems here, of the artist. The manuscript talks of life and art, of natural and aesthetic creation: 'All those cradles left to fill, / And works of intellectual fire' (*The Winding Stair*, p. 7). Yeats saves that last phrase for 'Blood and the Moon' (as Phillip Marcus points out). In 'In Memory' Yeats sets up the gazebo (an open, perhaps lighted, tower), mocked but also mocking, in 'Blood and the Moon' the 'powerful emblem' of the tower 'In mockery'. 'In Memory' anticipates the progression of *The Winding Stair*. In 'Blood and the Moon', as in 'A Dialogue of Self and Soul', Yeats recognizes the value of folly:

> Saeva indignatio and the labourer's hire,
> Everything that gives our blood and State magnanimity of its
>   own desire:
> Everything that is not God consumed in intellectual fire.

God consuming the heavens with a kiss is an image Yeats uses in his early poetry, and the notion of the world ending in fire is common to many mythologies. Yeats, who knew Kabir, may have known one of his most famous *doha*s about a fire in the sky. (O'Shea lists a 1914 translation of Kabir, *One Hundred Poems of Kabir*, among Yeats's books, p. 144.) And he certainly knew Pater's *Renaissance* and its obsession with the imagery of fire (see my essay on Pater in *The Victorians Institute Journal*, 16, pp. 85–128). 'In Memory' ends with fire because there is always the hope that art – the Romantic city of the imagination, Blake's condition of fire, Shelley's revolutionary 'sparks, my words among mankind' … 'from an unextinguished hearth', Yeatsian creative fire from the 'Song of Wandering Aengus' through the Byzantium poems and 'Lapis Lazuli', perhaps even Pater's gemlike flame – can light the match that annihilates time.

Near the end of Andersen's story the little match seller rubs another match against the wall and her grandmother – also wise in her afterlife – appears.

> 'Grandmother!' cried the child, 'Oh! Take me with you! I know you will go when the match is burned out. You will vanish like the warm fire, the warm food, and the great glorious Christmas tree!'
>
> And she hastily rubbed the whole bundle of matches, for she wished to hold her grandmother fast. And the matches burned with such a glow that it became brighter than in the middle of the day; grandmother had never been so large or so beautiful. She took the little girl in her arms, and both flew in brightness and joy above the earth, very, very high, and up there was neither cold, nor hunger, nor care – they were with God!
>
> But in the corner, leaning against the wall, sat the poor girl with red cheeks and smiling mouth. The New Year's sun rose upon a little corpse! The child sat there, stiff and cold, with the matches of which one bundle was burned. 'She wanted to warm herself', the people said. No one imagined what a beautiful thing she had seen, and in what glory she had gone in with her grandmother to the New Year's-day. (*Stories for the Household, p.* 359)

The matches that conjure up visions for the little girl are themselves luxuries, and lighting a whole bundle of them is an extravagance. In the Paulsen version, she even fears lighting the first match. 'If only she could light a match! But what would her father say at such a waste!' In a poor or utilitarian world, writing poetry or building gazebos or lighting visionary matches is a wasteful virtue. And the flame in this story is not hard or gemlike but a magical conflagration. It doesn't save her life, but it enables her first to see visions and then to escape time. By the time they discovered her frozen body, the little match seller was far away with God and her grandmother: 'up there was neither cold, nor hunger, nor care' (p. 359). The final, marvellous ending of Yeats's poem gives us the prospect of what we saw in Andersen's story: the girl strikes one match after another to the end of time.

> Arise and bid me strike a match
> And strike another till time catch; ...
> Bid me strike a match and blow.

Or, as Yeats puts it in another poem:

> The herald's cry, the soldier's tread
> Exhaust his glory and his might:
> Whatever flames upon the night
> Man's own resinous heart has fed.
>   (VP 438, ll. 13–16)

This is the reverse of Andersen's Tin Soldier who is consumed by fire – leaving only a little tin heart (apparently not resinous).

It is possible to read Andersen's tale as encouraging pious escape from the world rather than social change; but that reading might ignore its bitter portrait of the harsh indifference of the privileged and the savage lives of the poor. Good and evil are common themes in children's stories, but this story presents them in terms of class and capital. 'Pity would be no more, / If we did not make somebody Poor.' A world which presents a child's only escape as death can be no consolation to an adult. The story itself may provide another submerged connection to the origins of an elegy which begins somewhat critically but ends as a tribute to Eva Gore-Booth and to Con Markiewicz – who fought for the children of Dublin and died not much better off than the poor she fought for – who pursued not just vague Utopias (the poem refers to the younger sister here) but also a world where children would never go hungry or die of exposure again. In the end they are all on the same side.

Perhaps children's stories provide an alternate world of enchantment (or, to use Yeats's words, of an enchanter calling), a world where, despite the perils, promises are kept and devotion and wit and honesty and kindness and courage are rewarded. Protagonists in children's stories, like their counterparts in Romantic poems, often exercise what may seem wasteful virtues to their more single-minded and goal-oriented siblings (or to a cost-effective society): they are courteous and kind to the apparently irrelevant and humble, and to birds and beasts and insects and trees. Sometimes in fairy tales, unlike real life, hearts are not had as gifts but hearts are earned – at least by one side. Lovers climb glass mountains, outwit wizards and witches, and learn the language of birds and bees for the love of a sleeping princess or an amnesiac prince. Fairy tales some-times give us a hopeful world where everything can be survived, even death.

Yeats's poems, building gazebos, dreaming of a life beyond death, aspire to these things. And the appeal of these stories is not merely escapist – although escapism, like boredom, is an unjustifiably maligned and underrated source of creativity in art and science. Paradoxically, the influence of these tales seems to grow as Yeats becomes less a poet of the Celtic Twilight and more of a modernist. The emblematic titles of Yeats's great books of poems – *The Wild Swans at Coole, The Tower, The Winding Stair* – are also fairy-tale titles. 'Goldsmith and the Dean, Berkeley and Burke have travelled' his winding stair – but so have Rapunzel and the twelve dancing princesses. Berkeley knows about this pragmatical, preposterous pig of a world – but so does the swineherd of Andersen's tale and of 'A Full Moon in March'. Yeats helped create his own heritage, but what he loved well may have included the brothers of Elsa as well as the children of Lir.

'I have forgotten *Grimm's Fairy-Tales* that I read at Sligo, and all of Hans Andersen except "The Ugly Duckling" which my mother had read to me and to my sisters … ' says Yeats. To some extent, criticism depends on memory, poetry on forgetting. What Yeats forgot of Andersen became a part of his consciousness. Yeats's use of Andersen is very different from his use of Celtic sources. (Celtic folklore was also his mother's gift, although not hers alone, but the unhomely stories of poet-lovers and kings and fairy queens which gave him some wonderful poems and plays are of a different variety – although both kinds share the fairy tales' archetypal appeal.) There are no invocations of magical names or assumptions of rich associative knowledge on the reader's part. 'The domain of culture begins when one HAS forgotten what-book' (Ezra Pound, 'Rappel à l'Ordre', *Guide to Kulchur*, 1938, p. 191. From *Ezra Pound, A Critical Anthology*, ed. J.P. Sullivan, Harmondsworth 1970). Yeats not only 'forgot' Andersen, he associated him with the realm of a literate mother who supposedly 'read no books' (*Au*, p. 40). Never having heard of post-literacy, he wrote of the middle class that they are ' ... people who have unlearned the unwritten tradition which binds the unlettered, so long as they are masters of themselves, to the beginning of time and to the foundation of the world, and who have not learned the written tradition which has been established upon the unwritten.' ('What Is "Popular Poetry"?' 1901, *E & I*, p. 6)

Andersen, son of a shoemaker and a washerwoman, was himself a child of the Romantic Movement, and Andersen's stories in their varied metamorphoses still give enduring pleasure. When Andersen travelled abroad he displayed a card in his hotel room saying: 'I am not really dead.' Although we are told that this concerned his distrust of foreign doctors and fear of live burial (Richard Boston, *TLS*, 1 June 2001), it has a wider application.

Whatever Andersen may have thought of himself (and he wanted to be more than the most influential of all kinds of writers – one of children's books), he seems associated by Yeats with a time from which he claims to 'have remembered nothing that I read but only those things that I heard or saw.' In addition to the spoken word so valued by Romantic poets, nineteenth-century editions of Andersen offered numerous images of ugly ducklings, nightingales singing to Chinese emperors, long-legged cranes, emperors with and without their clothes, swineherds wooing princesses, wild robber girls, boys being swept to faraway worlds on ice sleds by gorgeous queens, girls wandering through worlds of ice and snow to rescue them, and of course breathtaking pictures of wild swans.

In the end, perhaps it is their simplicity that renders some Yeatsian passages incomprehensible to us – we look for sources, justifiably enough, in Plato and Plotinus but not at a parent's knee where so many rhymes and stories begin.

NOTES

1. Patrick Kennedy's 'The Twelve Wild Geese' has many similarities with Andersen's 'The Wild Swans' (here geese are swans and swans are geese), and his 'The Haughty Princess' is a version of the Grimm tale 'King Thrushbeard' – which may also have provided material for Andersen's 'The Swineherd'. 'The Little Weaver of Duleek Gate' by Samuel Lover is a very vivid Irish variation of the Grimm story 'The Valiant Tailor'.
2. Ernest Schanzer, ' "Sailing to Byzantium", Keats, and Andersen' in *English Studies* 41 (December 1960, dated 1956), pp. 376–80.
3. I would like to thank George L. Valcarce, Photographer, Instructional Photography and Graphics, Florida International University, for his remarkable work in making all but one of the figures used in this essay from a microfilm version of the 1870 text lent to me by courtesy of the Houghton Library, Harvard University. For Figure 8, unexpectedly retrieved from a paper copy of the microfilm, and much else, I am very grateful to Janis Londraville, editor of *Prodigal Father Revisited*,

where the earlier version of this essay appeared. My thanks to Marsha Swan for the figures in this version, and to Bridget Farrell. Finally, I am deeply grateful to our editor, Declan Foley.

4. The Dalziel Brothers and Dulcken were also responsible for the famous *Arabian Nights Entertainments* with various illustrators published by Ward, Locke and Tyler between 1864 and 1865.

5. Maria Tatar, *The Classic Fairy Tales*, A Norton Critical Edition (New York 1999).

6. Peter L. Caraccioloa (ed.), *The Arabian Nights in English Literature* (New York 1988), pp. 244–80.

7. U.C. Knoepflmacher, *Ventures into Childland: Victorians, Fairy Tales, and Femininity* (Chicago and London 1999).

8. Alison Lurie, *Don't Tell the Grown-ups: Subversive Children's Literature* (Boston 1990), pp. 16 and 26.

9. Rupin W. Desai also quotes this from Ellmann's *Yeats: The Man and the Masks* (1948); Desai cites a later edition of the story from *Fairy Tales*, ed. Svend Larsen, trans. R.P. Keigwin (Odense 1950).

10. Rupin W. Desai, 'Yeats's Swans and Andersen's Ugly Duckling' in *Colby Library Quarterly*, Series IX, no. 6 (June 1971) pp. 330–5.

11. In *Hans Christian Andersen and His World* Reginald Spink speaks of the literary qualities and sources of the tales (e.g. E.T.A. Hoffmann for 'Little Ida's Flowers' or *A Thousand and One Nights* for 'The Tinder Box', their ironies, allegories, sophisticated humour and prose poetry. He writes, 'The Nightingale' is a tribute to Jenny Lind, 'The Swedish Nightingale' (setting natural song over the fashionable Italian opera of the day); it is also an allegory that sets up true poetry, the real nightingale, 'which has never been heard of at court', against academic literature, the mechanical nightingale, 'which always sang the same tune'. This is of course very different from Yeats's version of the story in 'Sailing to Byzantium'.

12. See my essay, 'Yeats and the Mask of Deirdre: "That love is all we need."' *Colby Library Quarterly*, 37, No. 3, pp. 247–66. To Phillip L. Marcus, from whom I have learned so much, these essays, like much of my other work, owe more than I can express.

13. Compare the later 'Arming and Departure of the Knights' (1895–6), designed by Edward Burne-Jones and woven by Morris & Co. located in the Birmingham Museum and Art Gallery. Women on horseback, real or mythic or Sidhe, Constance Gore-Booth or Niamh, are important to Yeats's poetry.

14. Richard Ellman, *Yeats: The Man and The Masks* (New York 1979), p. 138.

15. My sincere thanks for this and other valuable suggestions, and for generously sharing his vast knowledge of Yeats to Phillip L. Marcus; to David G. Riede for his insightful suggestions about the manuscript, enduring encouragement, and excellent advice; my thanks to Donald G. Watson, former Chair of the English Department at Florida International University, for our discussions of children's stories and to him and our current chair, James M. Sutton, for their consistent support of my research and writing.

16. Edward O'Shea's catalogue lists this as one of the editions of Coleridge owned by Yeats (#403, p. 61). See Matthew Gibson, who also refers to the influence of

Symons's introduction on Yeats.

17. 'I have worked on *Kubla Khan* for thirty years and I do not know if it is a poem about poetry or politics, or is in three sections or five, or is satirical or celebratory. Whether it makes different sense if you are a lesbian or a royalist. I could speculate about whether it is a complete poem or a fragment, but answers to the questions I described would be negotiable' (J.C.C. Mays, quoted on the epigraph page of *Reading The Eve of St Agnes*, 1999, by Jack Stillinger). One could add to the list of parts alone. In Arthur Symons's edition, *Poems of Coleridge*, which Yeats owned, 'Kubla Khan' is in four parts – the six lines beginning with 'The shadow of the dome of pleasure' float freely, reflecting the earlier passage to which they are usually anchored. W.M. Rossetti's 'Kubla Khan' (in Coleridge's *Poetical Works*), on the other hand, is one undivided and ecstatic poem (although there is a page break). But whatever the poem on the page may be, the poem in the mind may be said to resolve itself into two parts, like Yeats's.

18. Here is Coleridge at twenty-five looking back at his eight-year-old self: 'I read every book that came in my way without distinction – and my father was very fond of me, & used to take me on his knee, and hold long conversations with me. I remember, that at eight years old I walked with him one winter evening from a farmer's house, a mile from Ottery – & he told me the names of the stars – and how Jupiter was a thousand times larger than our world – and that the other twinkling stars were Suns that had worlds rolling round them – & when I came home, he shewed me how they rolled round – /. I heard him with a profound delight & admiration; but without the least mixture of wonder or incredulity. For from my early reading of Faery Tales, & Genii &c &c – my mind had been habituated *to the Vast.*' (Letter to Thomas Poole, Collected Letters, I, #210, 354).

Sligo children escorting the swans from Cole's Lough to Sligo Quay. c. 1960

Swans making their way from Cole's Lough to Sligo Quay
via Wolfe Tone Street. Note the interest of the horse

Away

DEIRDRE TOOMEY

'my mother died years ago'

On 4 January 1900 Yeats wrote to Lady Gregory, telling her of the death of his mother. Yeats's response to the event, as delivered to closest friend and confidante, is oblique and flat:

> It has of course been inevitable for a long time; & it is long since my mother has been able to recognize any of us ... I think that my sister Lilly & myself feel it most through our father... It will be a big blow to Jack & there was no softening of the news, for it came suddenly; and he was devoted to his mother. [1]

The failure of affect is displayed without check; Susan Yeats is *Jack's* mother, in the only sentence which admits of a sense of loss. Yeats had been present when his mother died, yet displays so little feeling that she might well have been dead several weeks, rather than a day. He wrote to Maud Gonne – the letter does not survive – and she responded kindly, if vaguely.[2] In a letter of condolence written on 20 May 1900 to Olivia Shakespear on the death of her mother, Yeats reinforces the impression of insensibility. Early in the process of *rapprochement* after the end of their affair,[3] he seeks to console Olivia Shakespear with folk beliefs concerning the continuing presence of dead mothers: but he concludes by saying, 'when a mother is near ones heart at all her loss must be the greatest of all losses'.

This seems to state the position; apparently Yeats excludes himself from the category. Yet the letter does indicate some personal feelings displaced onto folk-beliefs: 'The Irish poor hardly think of a mothers death as dividing her very far from her children & I have heard them say that when a mother dies all things go better with her children for she has gone where she can serve them better ...'[4]

Yeats also kept the order of service for Susan Yeats's funeral in his library,[5] and, in November 1900, he had an odd conversation with John Masefield (whom he had only just met) on the subject of dead mothers in Irish folk belief:

> I heard him tell of an old Irish woman with whom he had been talking ... .
> He asked her about the life of a spirit after bodily death, & the woman had
> given him various particulars then added: 'But of course, Mothers always
> stay by their children, as long as any one of them can need her help' ... then
> she paused. 'And after that ... they go on.'[6]

Susan Yeats's death had had a supernatural accompaniment: her sister Elizabeth had heard the banshee crying on the night of her death.[7] According to her death certificate, Susan Yeats died of 'General Paralysis' of a duration of six years. The term refers to General Paralysis of the Insane, that is, a neuro-syphilis, but Susan Yeats's decline had been the result of a series of strokes. The death certificate therefore misdiagnosed her condition, but in a manner which indicated how her decline and death were viewed by the family doctor, W.B. Gordon-Hogg. General Paralysis of the Insane was only identified as a neurosyphilis in the early twentieth century and up to that point it had a much less specific identity. Thomas Austin, in the most influential nineteenth-century account of the illness,[8] emphasizes that the condition is quite distinct from ordi-nary paralysis, and this distinction must have been generally accepted. Austin gives a full account of the disease, stressing the mental collapse, delusions, mutism, final paralysis and imbecility that characterized it. A key element in Austin's history of the disease is his emphasis on the trauma which he believed consistently precipitated it – 'moral anguish' at a series of traumatic events, such as bankruptcy, the death of children or close relatives, or the failure of a marriage. He argued that a sensitive person – one with 'moral hyperaesthesia' – might react to such events by developing a cerebral disease.[9] In all likelihood, the certifying doctor, in misdiagnosing Susan Yeats's illness, was reacting to what he knew of her married life.[10]

II
'What youthful mother ... '

The Susan Yeats presented in *Autobiographies* is a fragmented figure, who does not appear until a Sligo full of Pollexfens and Middletons has been dramatized. Indeed neither parent enters the narrative for fifteen pages, in which a host of Pollexfen and Middleton relatives surround the child. John Butler Yeats is described before Susan Yeats, an exceptional reversal of the usual ordering of memory – that is unless the anonymous figure who holds the child up to 'an Irish window' is she. Remarkably, for a man with many relatives living, including his father, Yeats opens with a descent into the pain and misery of childhood:

> My first memories are fragmentary and isolated and contemporaneous, as though one remembered some first moments of the Seven Days. It seems as if time had not yet been created, for all thoughts are connected with emotion and place without sequence.
>
> I remember sitting upon somebody's knee, looking out of an Irish window at a wall covered with cracked and falling plaster ... . After that come memories of Sligo, where I live with my grandparents ... I know that I am very unhappy and have often said to myself, 'When you grow up, never talk as grown-up people do of the happiness of childhood'. I may have already had the night of misery when, having prayed for several days that I might die, I began to be afraid that I was dying and prayed that I might live. There was no reason for my unhappiness ... . Some of my misery was loneliness and some of it fear of old William Pollexfen, my grandfather. (*Au*, pp. 5–6)

There was, however, a reason. He and his sisters, bereft of their parents, had been dumped in Sligo in the midst of a complex, bewildering and threatening family of grandparents, aunts and uncles. He concludes this first stretch of memory: 'Indeed I remember little of childhood but its pain', although again – his father being still alive[11] – he qualifies 'my miseries were not made by others but were part of my own mind' (*Au*, p. 11).

This first memory seems datable to 1869 when J.B. Yeats, financially pressed, left his three eldest children at Sligo, taking his wife, pregnant with Robert, to London. The family was not reunited until the winter. The fact of the existence of a mother is acknowledged once and very obliquely in the first twenty or so pages of *Autobiographies*. She only enters the picture fully with the death of Robert: 'I heard feet running past and heard somebody say in the passage my younger brother, Robert, had 'died ... . I heard people telling how my mother and the servant had heard the banshee crying the night before he died.' (*Au*, p. 27) [12]

Susan Yeats thus enters the narrative with death, again a most unusual presentation in autobiographical writing.

Yeats represents himself as being, in the main, alone as a small child in Sligo, with the rest of the family in London. This is an adult distortion of memory which, however, contributes to a strong impression of the misery of abandonment. Dating his preface to *Reveries over Childhood and Youth*, Christmas Day 1914, Yeats insisted on the authority of memory, no matter how imperfect: 'I have changed nothing to my knowledge; and yet it must be that I have changed many things without my knowledge; for I am writing after many years and have consulted neither friend, nor letter, nor old newspaper, and describe what comes oftenest into my memory.' (*Au*, p. 3)

The wretched saga of the period 1869 to 1877 can be summarized as follows. In 1869 the three children, Willie aged four, Lily aged three and Lolly aged one, spent the period from summer to December in Sligo, without their parents, in order to save money. From 1872 to 1874, Susan Yeats and the four children stayed at Sligo for the same reason – Robert, the fourth child, died there in 1873. The family was reunited in London in October 1874. Jane, the last child, died in June 1876 in London; the family went back to Sligo that summer, with John Butler Yeats returning later to London. In the autumn the twelve-year-old Yeats was sent from Sligo to join his father, the rest of the family (except Jack) returning to London in January 1877. These trips from London to Sligo and back were epic affairs. In order to travel free on the Pollexfen ships, the Yeatses would have had to go by train from London to Liverpool and then take the thirty-hour route around Northern Ireland to Sligo. In the first twelve years of Yeats's life he was never more than two years in the one place.

That this unsettled, fragmented and chaotic early life traumatized the young Yeats is made abundantly clear in *Reveries over Childhood and Youth*. Chaos and insecurity also nullified his mother. Susan Pollexfen, the 'most beautiful girl in Sligo', became Susan Yeats, a plainly dressed silent woman, perpetually knitting and mending clothes in order to save money, and, eventually, a mute madwoman isolated in an upper room in Bedford Park. This story has been told from a position of overwhelming partisanship by William M. Murphy in his two studies of the Yeats family, and he relentlessly condemns Susan Yeats for failing to understand her husband's determination to adopt the life of an unsuccessful bohemian painter. In his first study, Murphy engages in an orgy of victim-blaming, arguing that Susan Yeats was culpably deficient in those qualities which might have made her a successful wife for John Butler Yeats: 'she could not escape the false gods of her family'. Finally, at a loss for a stronger argument, Murphy blames Susan Yeats's inability to relish a life of financial insecurity, alienation and separation from the country which she loved, on the 'imperfect protoplasm' of the Pollexfens.[13] That such a concept could be invoked in a monograph published in 1971 demonstrates the uncritical character of Murphy's advocacy of John Butler Yeats.

Yet what actually happened? J.B. Yeats was not, when he met Susan Pollexfen, ignorant of her family's characteristics, value or standards. He had been her brother's friend for some years. He must also have been aware of her passionate love for Sligo. Thus, in marrying a provincial young woman, reserved – like all her family – with strong, silent feelings and no intellectual interests, deeply tied to her place of birth and with conventional notions of family life he consciously made a choice of someone very dissimilar to himself When describing marriage from his own viewpoint to his son, in a letter of 1916, J.B. Yeats characterized the thing he called 'a wife' in excruciatingly negative and contemptuous terms, clearly derived from this assessment of Susan Yeats:

> People seem to have quite forgotten *what* a wife is. A man may admire one woman and be in love with another, and all sorts of wanton fancies in his restless heart may play continually about a third, There is one woman whom *he accepts* and she is his wife – all her limitations, her want of intellect, even her want of heart All her infirmities and all her waywardness he accepts and would not have them altered. If there be such a woman she is his wife. The feeling grows slowly. It is not affection as it is not passion. It is just *husband's feeling*, and she has doubtless a corresponding *wife's feeling*.[14]

Yet the destructive career which J.B. Yeats pursued, from barrister to unsuccessful professional artist; from landed gentleman, to near bankrupt, dependent for financial aid first upon his parents and parents-in-law and then, even more bizarrely, upon his children, seems almost designated to cause the maximum suffering to the wife he had freely chosen.[15] During the first decade of his marriage he was able to distance himself from the disasters of his family life by periodically depositing wife and children in Sligo and re-entering a bachelor world, a world which was to be his refuge for the duration of the marriage. In such masculine circles, J.B. Yeats was unquestionably a delightful companion and entertaining conversationalist. Yet his marriage produced six children in ten years; so, while choosing to inhabit a male environment of artists and writers he continued to burden his wife with a child every eighteen months or so until the death of Jane, the youngest, from pneumonia.

Susan Yeats suffered financial instability – fields and houses vanishing into a bottomless pit – her husband's marital alienation, the death of two children. In addition she was condemned to spend the greater part of her time in London, which she hated, rather than Sligo. She conveyed to her children her dislike of London and England, and an extraordinary worship of Sligo as a sacred place.

According to the account in *Autobiographies,* Susan Yeats seems to have been revitalized when the family moved back to Ireland in the 1880s. Howth, where they settled for two years, operated as a substitute for Sligo, and Yeats presents his only positive memories of his mother from this period:

> I have no doubt that we lived at the harbour for my mother's sake ... she loved the activities of a fishing village. When I think of her, I almost always see her talking over a cup of tea in the kitchen with our servant, the fisherman's wife, on the only themes outside our house that seemed of interest – the fishing-people of Howth, or the pilots and fishing-people of Rosses Point. She read no books, but she and the fisherman's wife would tell each other stories that Homer might have told, pleased with any moment of sudden intensity and laughing together over any point of satire. There is an essay called *Village Ghosts* in my *Celtic Twilight* which is but a record of one such afternoon, and many a fine tale has been lost because it had not occurred to me soon enough to keep notes. (*Au,* p. 61)[16]

When the family moved back to London again, the estrangement was obviously too much for her: 'her sense of personality, her desire of any life of her own, had disappeared' (*Au,* p. 31). In 1887, the year of their return, she suffered two strokes. A cerebral haemorrhage affecting the left hemisphere could have caused aphasia, paralysis and mental confusion: but there were clearly also non-organic factors in her illness. By about 1898 J.B. Yeats was ready to admit to Lily that he had been a 'bad husband and a bad father'.[17]

Yeats's reaction to his mother's illness in his letters is inhibited. In February 1888, writing to Katharine Tynan, he erupts on the subject of his own general lack of feeling; 'I have woven around me a web of thoughts I wish to brake through it, to see the world again', providing a focus for his anxiety in his inability to respond to the distress of his cousin, Alexander Middleton

> Yesterday I went to see – in a city hotel – an acquaintence who has had sudden and great misfortunes, come in these last few days to a crisis ... . We talked of all manner of things ... meanwhile I saw his hands and eyes moving restlessly and that his face was more shrunken than when I saw him some months before. Of course all this pained me at the time but I know, now that he is out of my sight, that if I heard that he was dead I should not think twice about it. So thick has the web got. An accident to one of my MSS or a poem turning out badly would seem of more importance ... it is all the web. (*CLI,* p. 48; see also *Au,* p. 42)

The sense of a personal crisis relating to failure of feeling seems directed at more than the financial problems of a second cousin. The account of Susan Yeats's last years of life, in *Autobiographies,* is brief and almost ashamed in tone:

> I remember all this very clearly and little after it until her mind had gone in a
> stroke of paralysis and she had found, liberated at last from financial worry,
> perfect happiness feeding the birds at a London window. (*Au*, p. 62)

Is it possible, as Murphy implies, that Susan Yeats inspired little affection in her
children and that the fractured account of her in *Autobiographies* is a product
of a genuine lack or etiolation of feeling, or that her exclusion from *Memoirs*,
in which she is only mentioned once, in passing, indicates her unimportance for
Yeats? The account Yeats gives, in a letter of 1908, of her decline might rein-
force this interpretation: 'My mother was so long ill, so long fading out of life,
that the last fading of all made no noticeable change in our lives'.[18] Lily Yeats
does not demonstrate much affection in her manuscript memoir; the comment.
'Mama was very silent and undemonstrative', some notes on Susan Yeats's
unusual eyes (one blue, one brown) and a basic account of her illnesses do not
add up to a record of strong feeling. Yet Lily was so much her father's daughter
that one might not expect more; her tie to John Butler Yeats was over close.[19]

Jack Yeats, despite being brought up separately in Sligo with his grand-
parents after his seventh year, provides singular evidence of attachment to his
mother. After he married and moved to Devon in 1894, he continued to write
regularly to her. Although, by this time, Susan Yeats was not mentally compe-
tent, the letters[20] are long, affectionate and addressed as if to a perfectly sane,
active woman. He includes in one letter an account of cider pressing, in another
a childhood memory of 'Willy', illustrated with little pen-and-ink sketches.
Jack seems also to have sent his mother a cheque with each letter: no doubt
these were swiftly cashed by J.B. Yeats. When, in his letter to Lady Gregory of
January 1900, Yeats referred to Jack's love for his mother, he did not overstate
the case.

III
'Never to leave that valley ...'

In early 1888, shortly after Susan Yeats's second stroke, Yeats began to draft
John Sherman (*CLI*, p. 57). In many ways the novel seems an attempt at
reparation for the dreadful tragedy of his mother's life. It is a bizarre, almost
Russian tale, and seems, at least in the first section, to show more the influence
of Turgenev (of whom Yeats thought highly[21] at this time) than any English
or Irish models. The somnambulistic, dream-like narrative and the strong
Oedipal motif combine to disturbing effect, especially when one considers
that Yeats insisted that 'there is more of myself in it than in any thing I have
done' (*CLI*, p. 245–6). The crucial relationship of the novel is that between

the aimless, drifting hero (an only child) and his widowed mother. This close, dependent relationship does not trouble John Sherman, who sees no urgent reason to marry, save for money. Indeed Sherman is presented (unusually in the fiction of a late-Romantic poet) as largely devoid of romantic feeling: 'I am not, you see, the kind of person who falls in love inconveniently' (*JS&D*, p. 47). Sherman's closest human tie is with his mother: the dead father is not even mentioned. Mrs Sherman is patently modelled upon Susan Yeats; she is silent and isolated, 'solitary because silent', conventional and provincial; like Susan Yeats she is constantly knitting: 'A spare, delicate-featured woman, with somewhat thin lips tightly closed as with silent people, and eyes at once gentle and distrustful, tempering the hardness of the lips' (*JS&D*, p. 49). Margaret Leland, to whom the hero briefly becomes engaged, is plainly modelled on Laura Armstrong, Yeats's 'first love'. Although he re-touched the novel after meeting Maud Gonne (*CLI*, p. 230), he did not attempt to alter either Margaret Leland or Mary Carton[22] in order to accommodate this new image. The structure of the work was so essentially 'right' in psychic terms that even the power of his feelings for Maud Gonne could not destabilize it.

The complete lack of passion in John Sherman's attitude to Margaret is something which she vehemently attacks:

> 'You have no feeling; you have no temperament ... Don't you see,' she replied with a broken voice, 'I flirted all day with that young clerk? You should have nearly killed me with jealousy.' (*JS&D*, p. 71–2)

Although her reaction and assumptions are utterly conventional, they are also shrewd. Sherman has drifted dreamily into this engagement, but has little emotional investment in it. His realization that he loves Mary Carton – an idealized mother-figure and, like his own mother, a Ballah / Sligo woman, conventional and rule bound – is bound up with a magnificently expressed nostalgia for Ballah / Sligo itself:

> All this while the mind of Sherman was clucking over its brood of thoughts. Ballah was being constantly suggested to him ... . A certain street-corner made him remember an angle of the Ballah fish-market. At night a lantern, marking where the road was fenced off for mending, made him think of a tinker's cart, with its swing-can of burning coals ... . Delayed by a crush in the Strand, he heard a faint trickling of water near by; it came from a shop window where a little water-jet balanced a wooden ball upon its point. The sound suggested a cataract with a long Gaelic name, that leaped crying into the Gate of the Winds at Ballah. Wandering among these memories a footstep went to and fro continually, and the figure of Mary Carton moved among them like a phantom. (*JS&D*, pp. 91–2)[23]

This passage, in which Ballah is recreated from fragments of London, is a paradigm of the recreation of a perfect internal world from something broken or destroyed. Yeats, when seeking to express the quality of the novel to Katharine Tynan, begins by accenting the novel's obsession with *place* (Ballah / Baile) and moves with an inevitable progression to his own childish feeling for Sligo and to his mother's enduring loyalty to her place of birth:

> I studied my characters in Ireland & described a typical Irish feeling in Sherman's devotion to Ballah ... . I remember when we were children how intense our devotion was to all things in Sligo & still see in my mother the old feeling. (*CLI*, p. 275)

That John Sherman's final love object is a mother figure is confirmed in the conclusion of the novel with rare, arid, almost sinister, explicitness:

> Something in her voice told of the emotion that divides the love of woman from the love of man. She looked upon him whom she loved as full of a helplessness that needed protection, a reverberation of the feeling of the mother for the child at the breast. (*JS&D*, p. 111)

John Sherman is a remarkable example of the art work as reparation.[24] Yeats creates an idealized mother–son relationship and allows it to extend itself into a love-relationship in which the beloved is a replication of the mother. Although superficial aspects of Sherman's persona, the husk of the character, derive from Yeats's cousin, Henry Middleton, the protagonist is close to a self-portrait, as Yeats acknowledged in his last reluctant printing of the story:

> I ... can see ... a young man – was I twenty-three? And we Irish ripen slowly – born when the Water-Carrier was on the horizon, at pains to overcome Saturn in Saturn's hour, just as I can see in much that follows his struggle with the still all-too-unconquered Moon, and at last, as I think, the summons of the prouder Sun. Sligo, where I had lived as a child ... is Ballah ... and he who gave me all of Sherman that was not born at the rising of the Water-Carrier has still the bronze upon his face, and is at this moment, it may be, in his walled garden, wondering, as he did twenty years ago, whether he will ever mend the broken glass of the conservatory, where I am not too young to recollect the vine-trees and grapes that did not ripen. (*JS&D*, p. 40)[25]

This is one of Yeats's most emotion-laden prefaces; and it is a purely personal emotion.

IV
'Was I twenty-three? ... I was twenty-three.'

By January 1889, Susan Yeats was gradually retreating from life and beginning a long descent into mutism. On 31 January, Yeats wrote to Katharine Tynan, ' ... you ask about my Mother, She is as usual, that is to say feable and unable to go out of doors, or move about much' (*CLI*, p. 136). On the previous day Yeats's life had been transformed by his first meeting with Maud Gonne:

> I was twenty-three when the troubling of my life began ... she drove up to our house in Bedford Park with an introduction from John O'Leary to my father. I had never thought to see in a living woman so great beauty. It belonged to famous pictures, to poetry, to some legendary past. A complexion like the blossom of apples, and yet face and body had the beauty of lineaments which Blake calls the highest beauty because it changes least from youth to age, and a state so great that she seemed of divine race. (*Mem*, p. 40)

What connects Yeats's romantic obsession with a tall, beautiful, independent, wealthy, cosmopolitan revolutionary and feminist with the fate of his mother, a slight, dependent, conventional, provincial woman? Explanations (as well as non-explanations) of the dynamics of Yeats's love for Maud Gonne abound. Many writers take Yeats's love as a *fait accompli*. It is as it were, not worth analysis. He met her, she was very beautiful, they shared nationalist ideals, and that was that for the next twenty-five years. The most sophisticated analysis to date (that of John Harwood) argues that Yeats had created, over several years, an *imago* of a beautiful quasi-supernatural woman, and that Maud Gonne walked into a fully prepared role: yet as he points out, it is not just that Maud Gonne steps 'into Niamh's shoes', but that the ' "faery bride" subsequently assimilates the mortal woman'.[26] From this point on, Harwood argues, Yeats worked with great intensity assimilating an *imago* of Maud Gonne into his imaginative world: 'Maud Gonne did not overpower his imagination; his imagination overpowered "Maud Gonne" and then he began, in life, to enter a relationship with "the image he had made"' (*YA 9*, p. 18). The word was made flesh – and then the flesh was made word again. The only thing missing from this astute analysis is the question 'Why Maud Gonne, in January 1889?' She was probably the most beautiful woman whom Yeats had met, but it does seem remarkable that, after his adolescent infatuation with Laura Armstrong,[27] he had remained completely free of romantic or sexual attachments for nearly five years. Even given that his closest female friend of this period was Katharine Tynan, 'a simple bright looking Biddy',[28] to whom even under strong moral pressure he was unable to feel attracted, the hiatus is arresting.

It has been argued that overwhelming romantic love is often a reaction to an 'object loss', to a traumatic or distressing event in the lover's life,[29] a death, an illness, a separation, even a major disappointment. The distress is erased by 'being in love' and by the consequent over-valuation of the beloved. Yeats had suffered bouts of anxiety arid depression in 1887 and 1888, which are referred to in his letters to Katharine Tynan: 'In bad spirits ... I had one of my dreadful despondent moods on ... like a burnt out taper ... one of my "collapses"' (*CLI*, pp. 75, 77, 92, 118). In January 1888 Yeats underwent a terrifying experience at a Dublin séance:

> ... my whole body moved like a suddenly unrolled watch-spring, and I was thrown backward on the wall ... I was now struggling vainly with this force which compelled me to movements I had not willed, and my movements became so violent that the table was broken. I tried to pray ... For years afterwards I would not go to a séance ... and would often ask myself what was that violent impulse that had run through my nerves. Was it a part of myself – something always to be a danger perhaps: or had it come from without, as it seemed? (*Au*, pp. 103–5)

These depressions and crises do not seem completely unconnected with his mother's illness and decline and an inevitable, if only half conscious, meditation by Yeats on the innumerable negative aspects of his parents' marriage. In the first period of his love for Maud Gonne, his feelings for her were symbiotic: '[s]he seemed to understand every subtlety of my own art and especially all my spiritual philosophy' (*Mem*. p. 61). This sense of spiritual and emotional fusion, recalled in 'Among School Children'

> ... it seemed that our two natures bent
> Into a sphere from youthful sympathy, (*VP* 443)

presented an absolute antithesis to his parents' polarized uncommunicative marriage.

A reflection of the link between the major love of his life and a 'dead' mother is found in the first two drafts of *The Speckled Bird*, written between 1896 and 1898. In these early versions Michael's dead mother is identified by his father with the Virgin and remembered as a 'star of beauty'; 'his father had begun to talk a good deal about his dead wife and call her by the names of the Mother of God' (*SB*, p. 124). When Michael and his father hear that Margaret, daughter of the dead woman's sister, is a replica of the dead wife / mother, both are deeply moved, although they have not seen the child: ' "She is like my wife. She is like my wife" ... "Oh, father, do ask my cousin to come and stay with us. I never see anyone here and she is like my mother too." ' (*SB*, pp. 126–7)

So it is made clear that the hero is destined to fall in love with a young girl who exactly resembles his dead (and unknown) mother. This is a second fictional attempt to transform and idealize biographical material, with a father-son unit replacing the mother-son unit of *John Sherman*.[30]

His meeting with Maud Gonne, and his obsession with her, coincided, as he recalls in *Autobiographies*, with the end of his uncritical admiration for his father: 'When I was in my 'teens I admired my father above all men ... but when I was twenty-three or twenty-four I read Ruskin's *Unto This Last* ... and we began to quarrel' (*Ex,* p. 417). The physical fight between Yeats and his father with which *Memoirs* opens is datable to before 1892 (when Jack went to Manchester) but, as Yeats indicates, after 1889:

> I began to read Ruskin's *Unto This Last*, and this, when added to my interest in psychical research and mysticism, enraged my father ... . One night a quarrel over Ruskin came to such a height that in putting me out of the room he broke the glass in a picture with the back of my head. Another night when we had been in an argument over Ruskin or mysticism ... he followed me upstairs to the room I shared with my brother. He squared up to me, and wanted to box, and when I said I could not fight my own father replied, 'I don't see why you should not'. My brother ... started up in a violent passion ... . My father fled without speaking. (*Mem,* p. 19)

Jack's fury at his father is telling, as is J.B. Yeats's extravagant rage at being challenged by his sons. Yeats's love for Maud Gonne, despite, or perhaps because of its unrequited nature, gave him the strength to emancipate himself from his father and his family – although he continued to live in Bedford Park until 1895. The period from 1889 to 1896 marks a significant opening out in Yeats's life: he met Florence Farr and Olivia Shakespear, joined the Rhymers' Club, entered a bohemian literary world and became close friends with Arthur Symons and Lionel Johnson; he joined the Golden Dawn, had his first play produced and had his first consummated love affair. Despite his dwelling on the unhappiness caused by his love for Maud Gonne, the obsession coincided with a positive transformation of his life.

Finally, in 1896, he was befriended by Lady Gregory, a widow some thirteen years his senior, an obvious mother substitute and an influence in his life very much opposed to Maud Gonne. In fact, as he later insisted, Lady Gregory came to operate as an entire family-system for him: '[s]he has been to me mother, friend, sister and brother' (*Mem,* pp. 160–1). When he received the news of her illness in February 1909 he lapsed into a state of mental confusion and dream-like condensation, ' ... my mind wandered ... I thought my mother was ill and that my sister was asking me to come at once: then I remembered that my mother died years ago' (*Mem,* p. 160).

V
'Away'

During the 1890s Yeats became increasingly interested in folklore, particularly
Irish folklore, although a concern with folk tales goes back to his teens and to his
hearing his mother tell 'stories Homer might have told'. His first recorded collec-
tion took place in August 1887 in Sligo (*CLI*, p. 33), but he had been taking notes
between 1882 and 1884 of some of his mother's stories: 'I wrote nothing but
ghost or faery stories, picked up from my mother (or some pilot at Rosses Point)'
(*Au*, p. 129). This interest also represented one of a range of reactions against
the rationalism and materialism of his father. His early anthologies and his first
original collection, *The Celtic Twilight* (1893), incline very much towards the
lighter and more playful aspects of Irish folklore – and he at this time subscribed
to the thesis that there was almost no 'dark side' to Irish folk tradition:

> In Ireland we hear but little of the darker powers, and come across any who
> have seen them even more rarely, for the imagination of the people dwells
> rather on the fantastic and capricious, and fantasy and caprice would lose
> their freedom which is their breath of lift, were they to unite them with either
> evil or with good.[31]

The first topic of common interest which Yeats and Lady Gregory discussed
in August 1896 was folklore and she noted in her diary that after his depar-
ture from Tulira, she began collecting folklore for him. That this represented
some link between them is supported by the fact that she began to type up the
material for him when she arrived in London in February 1897, and that the
first book of his which she read was *The Celtic Twilight*. By the summer of
1897 this was clearly a firm bond, the frame of their expanding friendship: 'We
searched for folk-lore – I gave him over all I had collected & took him about
looking for more – And whoever came to the door, fishwoman or beggar or
farmer. I would get on the subject.'[32] Thus began nearly five years of collecting.
In *Dramatis Personae* Yeats identifies the therapeutic nature of this activity. In
summer 1897, the affair with Olivia Shakespear over, and no further advanced
in his relations with Maud Gonne, he was depressed and frustrated: 'Lady
Gregory brought him from cottage to cottage collecting folk-lore' (*Au*, p. 399).
In a manuscript draft of the same passage he is franker, 'a love affair had gone
wrong. I was worn out, incapable of work & as I found out afterwards to
keep me in the open air Lady Gregory began that great collection of folk lore,
published many years later.'[33]

Yeats had been collecting folklore himself, mainly in Sligo, for a decade
or so and his early practice as a collector was more 'scientific' than that of

the 'scientific' folklorists whom he deplored; 'There are innumerable little turns of expression and quaint phrases that in the mouth of a peasant give half the meaning … the gesture and voice of the peasant tale-teller' (*UP1*, p. 174).[34] Thus Yeats had reached, by the early 1890s, the position of realizing that context (situation, gesture, idiom, audience reaction) was semantically as important as tale or *histoire* – a point taken by anthropologists and folklorists in the 1930s. The context of his collecting with Lady Gregory is itself significant. What did country people on the Coole estate and elsewhere in Galway make of the appearance in their cottages and fields of a female land owner and a young male companion, both black-clad, both Protestant, asking for 'faery' beliefs? Did this affect the histories which were produced? Oral cultures totalize, and the country people's responses would be governed by their reading of the questioners as well as the questions; they would have responded to the whole context, not just to an inquiry. The introductory material to 'Irish Witch Doctors' makes clear the fear that rural people had of the priests – 'for he is afraid of the priests' (*UP2*, p. 219).

Yeats and Lady Gregory, as Protestants, would not condemn or betray their pagan belief-system to the parish priests, and thus 'the country people spoke so freely, indeed, that they were afraid for themselves afterwards' (*UP2*, p. 219). Yeats recalled that he was given folklore in Sligo only because of his family connections and that '[a] few miles northward I am wholly a stranger, and can find nothing. When I ask for stories of the faeries, my answer is … "They always mind their own affairs and I always mind mine" ' (*Myth*, p. 94, see also *Au*, pp. 400–1). The people of south Galway talked to Yeats because 'Lady Gregory was my friend' (*Au*, p. 401) and the passage's manuscript draft records that 'The secular leaders had thought her [AG] a Home Ruler, the priests had been contented so long as the people came to confession & to Mass, beliefs older than Christianity remained.'[35] The wife of Fagan the Witch Doctor was clearly troubled by the look of Yeats and Lady Gregory and asked the latter 'Are you *right*?'[36] By this she meant human, real, non-supernatural. Their only first-hand account of being 'away' was given (after much pressure) by Mrs Sheridan, who worked for Lady Gregory. Others who had been 'away' … believe that they must be silent' (*UP2*, p. 230). Content analysis of the six folklore essays indicates that Lady Gregory's and Yeats's borderline status (Protestant but nationalist) allowed the country people to tell dark, uneuphemized tales. Typically they did not present their material as fables, traditional or wonder tales, but directly, as actual experience: 'There was little attempt to reconcile old & new, a word spoken, an association touched, & the picture on the screen was changed.'[37]

The six essays are dominated by the theme of 'away', that is of those who are stolen by the faeries, usually because they are young and strong, children, young men and women, and young mothers being the most popular victims.[38] However, older people were also taken. Sometimes those abducted seem to die (i.e. they are 'taken'), in other cases they appear to become paralysed or demented, affected by the 'fairy stroke' [poc sidhe]. A young, healthy woman or girl would be magically replaced by 'an old woman with long teeth, that you'd be frightened, and the face wrinkled and the hands' (UP2, p. 103). The country people asserted that death, disease and substitution were part of the supernatural illusion, the real person being elsewhere. This motif predominates in 'Prisoners of the Gods', 'The Broken Gates of Death', 'Ireland Bewitched', 'Irish Witch Doctors' and, of course, 'Away', the climax of the series. It is the ruling motif of the essays and, unlike the consciously playful and fantastic anecdotes illustrating this belief collected in The Celtic Twilight (1893), the material is sombre, focusing on disease, madness and premature death, and is ridden with what Yeats identified as 'the pathos of many doubts' (UP2, p. 95).

Although the last essay was not published until 1902, much of it was drafted by 1898, as internal references indicate. The material is highly repetitive. Yeats was in the grip of an obsession with the material – '[t]hat experience is my obsession' (Au, p. 401). His comprehension of the distinct nature of oral narrative led him to retain repetitions and formulate phraseology tied to traditional ideas and beliefs that are fundamental characteristics of oral texts.

In the last essay his theoretical attitude to the phenomenon is clearest and the oral accounts are most striking, not least in their insistence on ugly detail – far removed from the picturesque and naive accounts collected in The Celtic Twilight (1893). The use of the informants' own words is insistent:

> My own mother was away for twenty-one years, and at the end of every seven years she thought it would be off her, but she never could leave the bed. She could but sit up and make a little shirt or the like for us … … There was Kitty Flannery at Kilchreest … For seven years she had everything she could want … . But she ate no food all that time … at the end of the seven years all left her, and she was glad at the last to get Indian meal … . Sure there was a fairy in the house at Eserkelly fourteen years … She never kept the bed, but she'd sit in the corner of the kitchen on a mat, and from a good stout lump of a girl that she was, she wasted to nothing, and her teeth grew as long as your finger, and then they dropped out. And she'd eat nothing at all only crabs and sour things. And she'd never leave the house in the daytime, but in the night she'd go out and pick things out of the fields she could eat … She died as quiet as another, but you wouldn't like to be looking at her after the teeth fell out … . There was a girl at Kilkerran of the same name as my own, was lying on a mat

for eight years … . She never got off the mat for anyone to see, but one night … a working man … saw the outer door open, and three or four boys and girls come in, and with them a piper or a fiddler … and they danced, and the girl got up off the mat and joined them. And in the morning … he … said 'You were the best dancer among them last night.' (*UP2*, pp. 268, 274, 276, 279)[39]

A mass of complementary tales is presented, all of which insist that the apparently paralysed, deranged, or dead person is really elsewhere; working or playing, or nursing the children of the *sidhe* or even bearing their children. In this essay Yeats also delineates the theology of the belief:

This substitution of the dead for the living is indeed a pagan mystery, and not more hard to understand than the substitution of the body and blood of Christ for the wafer and the wine in the mass; and I have not yet lost the belief that some day, in some village lost among the hills or in some island among the western seas … I will come to understand how this pagan mystery hides and reveals some half-forgotten memory of an ancient knowledge or of an ancient wisdom. (*UP2*, p. 275)

Yeats's sacramentalizing of the folk-belief argues for some considerable personal investment. When Yeats drafted 'Away' in 1898, Susan Yeats had been 'away' for a decade. From 1897 onwards Yeats heard countless tales of the afflictions of Irish country people that exactly matched his mother's story, except that in the 'West of Ireland a pre-Christian belief-system gave status and some degree of protection to the sufferers. The paralyzed figure in the corner of the kitchen was regarded with awe, rather than with embarrassment.' Yeats emphasizes strongly, in 'Away', the importance of not injuring the 'substitute':

I was always convinced that tradition, which avoids needless inhumanity, had some stronger way of protecting the bodies of those, to whom the other world was perhaps unveiling its mysteries, than any mere command not to ill-treat some old dead person, who had maybe been put in the room of one's living wife or daughter or son. I heard of this stronger way last winter from an old Kildare woman, that I met in London. She said that in her own village, 'there was a girl used to be away with them, you'd never know when it was she herself that was in it or not till she'd come back, and then she'd tell she had been away. She didn't like to go, but she had to go when they called to her, and she told her mother always to treat kindly whoever was put in her place … for, she'd say "If you are unkind to whoever is there, they'll be unkind to me".' (*UP2*, p. 278)[40]

Yeats gathered this tale with Lady Gregory in Chiswick on Sunday 19 December 1897; after interviewing the old woman, they went to Blenheim Road for tea with Lily and Lolly. Lady Gregory, in her diary account, gives no indication of any knowledge of the existence of Susan Yeats, hidden away in an upstairs room, perhaps experiencing (in Yeats's belief-system) the mysteries of the 'other world'. The radical contrast between Susan Yeats's position and that of Irish country people suffering from paralysis or depressive withdrawal would have been thrown into relief by this conjunction of events.

Yeats's obsession with 'the dead' and life after death, the major occult concerns of his life, were, during the 1890s, fed solely by folklore and tales of 'away'.[41] So powerful was the material that he gathered and so overwhelming was the impact of 'that mysterious life' that by late 1898 he gained the courage to return to spiritualism, abandoned after the traumatic séance of January 1888. He sought thus to supplement the beliefs and experiences of Irish peasants with direct encounters with spirits and ghosts. In late 1898 he contracted a well-known medium, Charles Will who gave public séances at 61 Lamb's Conduit Street, Holborn. Yeats probably attended his first séance there in early 1899, and later came to believe that he had been placed in contact with Leo Africanus by Williams.[42] Séance attendance became increasingly important to him. 'I found much that was moving, when I had climbed to the top storey of some house in Soho or Holloway and, having paid my shilling, awaited, among servant girls, the wisdom of some fat old medium' (*Ex*, p. 30). By 1914 he was a regular sitter: 'I lived in excitement, amused to make Holloway interpret Aran' (*Ex*, p. 32). 'I began a study of "Spiritualism" not only in its scientific form but as it is found among the London poor, and discovered that there was little difference except that, the experience of the cottagers was the richer' (*Au*, p. 400). This fusion of folklore and spiritualism was realized in 'Swedenborg, Mediums and the Desolate Places', completed in October 1914. On 6 June 1914, when Yeats was sitting with Felicia Scatcherd, a spirit had come 'who called herself my mother. She was impressing my father that he might believe in the other world'– J.B. Yeats was an agnostic. Yeats made some notes giving information about his mother when he wrote up the séance the next day.[43] As Yeats was notorious for his ability to influence the spirits at séances, we might assume that the separation between his parents – and indeed its significance for him – had been on his mind.

In 1938 a ghostly mother destroyed by marriage returns to trouble *Purgatory*, presented, in the ordering of *Last Poems and Two Plays*, from beyond the grave. The play is extraordinary in its absolute rejection of catharsis, in its violence and apparent nihilism, and in its realization of the primal scene on stage via the mechanism of a supernatural vision of an endlessly re-enacted past.[44] The central situation is that of *The Speckled Bird*, but the family romance is complicated by two generations of sons, and is brutally de-idealized.

The Old Man's desire is to end his mother's torment, her purgatorial re-enactment of her wedding night, which will endlessly result in the birth of a parricide:

> ... ... O my God
> she does not understand – her agony, her agonised joy,
> or her remorse begin all over again ...
> ... ...
> She did not [know] the worst because
> She died in giving birth to me
> But now [being] a soul in purgatory
> She knows it all ... [45]

In the ruined house the ghostly mother must, like the ghosts in 'Swedenborg, Mediums and the Desolate Places', relive her agony forever, unless her son's murder of *his* son will undo the cause by undoing the end. The Old Man sacrifices father and son to free his mother's soul:

> Study that tree.
> It stands there like a purified soul.
> All cold, sweet, glistening light.
> Dear mother, the window is dark again,
> But you are in the light because
> I finished all that consequence. (VPl, p. 1049)

Yeats not only outdoes *Oedipus Rex* by representing parricide and infanticide by the same actor, but – and in Ireland – by presenting the primal scene on stage. 'The Old Man' watches as the ghosts re-enact his conception;

> ... They mount the stairs.
> She brings him into her own chamber.
> And that is the marriage-chamber now.
> The window is dimly lit again
>
> Do not let him touch you! ...
> ... she must live
> Through everything in exact detail,
> Driven to it by remorse, and yet
> Can she renew the sexual act
> And find no pleasure in it, and if not,
> If pleasure and remorse must both be there
> Which is the greater? (VPl, p. 1046)

There is such a slaughtering of social taboo in *Purgatory* that it is incon-
ceivable to construe these horrifying exhibitions as solely expressive of Yeats's
fear of a degenerated Ireland.[46] The lullaby which the Old Man sings after
killing his son is, in its fusion of dead child and infant self in a recreation of the
family romance, too disturbing and psychically primary to be a by-product of
eugenic anxieties.

> 'Hush-a-bye baby, thy father's a knight,
> Thy mother a lady, lovely and bright.'
> No, that is something I read in a book
> And if I sing it must be to my mother
> And I lack rhyme. (VPl, p. 1048)

The *dénouement* rejects catharsis for an eternal repetition:

> .... Dear God
> ....
> Her mind cannot hold up that dream.
> Twice a murderer and all for nothing.
> And she must animate that dead night
> Not once but many times!
> O God!
> Release my mother's soul from its dream!
> Mankind can do no more. Appease
> The misery of the living and the remorse of the dead. (VPl, p. 1049)

VI
' ... a man of genius takes the most after his mother'

William M. Murphy has stated plainly that Susan Yeats contributed 'almost
nothing' to her son's character or genius.[47] Yet she made two overwhelmingly
powerful contributions to Yeats's values and writing. She gave him 'love of
the Unseen Life and love of country' (E & I, p. 204); she imprinted in all her
children a belief that Ireland, and especially Sligo, was a sacred place; she gave
their country of origin paramount value: '[t]his love was instinctive and left
the soul free' (Au, p. 472). By contrast, J.B. Yeats was a rootless cosmopolitan
rationalist, as happy in New York as in London or Dublin as long as he had a
congenial circle and a supply of money from some source or other:

> I and my sister had spoken together of our longing for Sligo and our hatred of
> London. I know we were both very close to tears and remember with wonder

… that I longed for a sod of earth from some field I knew, something of Sligo to hold in my hand. It was some old race instinct like that of a savage … . Yet it was our mother, who would have thought its display a vulgarity, who kept alive that love … and it was always assumed between her and us that Sligo was more beautiful than other places. I can see now that she had great depth of feeling, that she was her father's daughter. (*Au,* p. 31)

Inasmuch as Yeats is an *Irish* poet and a poet of *Irish* place, landscape and legend, of 'the cairn-heaped grassy hill / Where passionate Maeve is stony-still' (*VP* 3), we can thank Susan Pollexfen. When Yeats quotes his father's remark that it was 'by marriage with a Pollexfen' that the Yeatses had 'given a tongue to the sea cliffs', he calls it 'the only eulogy that turns my head' (*Au,* p. 23), acknowledging the centrality in his writings of identification with the very land of Ireland:

The very feel of the familiar Sligo earth puts me in good spirits. I should like to live here always not out of liking for the people so much as for the earth and the sky here, though I like the people too. (*CLI,* p. 33)

I wanted to be united, not to a people only but to a soil & not … as it was to day or yesterday but as it was thousands of years [ago] to get down under the codes, abstractions … to say 'Mother Ireland'.[48]

Yeats recalls Susan Yeats almost as part of Nature: 'my Sligo-born mother whose actions were unreasoning and habitual like the seasons' (*Au,* p. 167). She gave value to folklore, legend, country wisdom, the irrational, traditional 'unthinking' 'lunar' side of life, all that J.B. Yeats rejected. Her telling 'stories Homer might have told' imprinted on the adolescent Yeats not merely a superficial attraction to folk material, but a sense of such discourses as repositories and expressions of truth and value. One could also see Yeats's strong attraction to orality and communal production of art – 'friend by friend, lover by lover' (*Ex,* p. 221) and his subtle sense of the unique character of oral narrative as deriving from his mother's storytelling.[49] 'She would spend hours listening to stories or telling stories of the pilots and fishing-people of Rosses Point, or of her own Sligo girlhood' (*Au,* p. 31). He stresses, with pride rather than apology, 'she read no books' (*Au,* p. 61).

When Yeats articulates Mrs Sherman's attitude to Ballah, he patently represents his mother's feeling for Sligo: 'Her old home had long seemed to her a kind of lost Eden, wherewith she was accustomed to contrast the present. When, in time, this present had grown into the past it became an Eden in turn. She was always ready for a change, if the change came to her in the form of a return to something old' (*JS&D,* p. 99).

Yeats's conceptions of folklore involved a belief in a holistic primal universe, a record of which remained in folk literature: 'the unwritten tradition which binds the unlettered ... to the beginning of time and the foundation of the world' (E & I, p. 6). A declaration of such a position was made in 'The Celtic Element in Literature', given first as a lecture in December 1897:

> Once every people in the world believed that trees were divine and could take a human or a grotesque shape and dance among the shadows; and that deer, and ravens and foxes, and wolves and bears, and clouds and pools, almost all things under the sun and moon, and the sun and moon, were not less divine and changeable ... . Men ... lived in a world where anything might flow and change, and become any other thing: and among great gods whose passions were in the flaming sunset, and in the thunder ... worshipped nature and the abundance of nature ... (E & I, pp. 174, 178)

The belief is reiterated in 'Gods and Fighting Men':

> Children play at being great and wonderful people, at the ambitions they will put away for one reason or another before they grow into ordinary men and women. Mankind as a whole had a like dream once: everybody and nobody built up the dream bit by bit, and the ancient story-tellers are there to make us remember what mankind would have been like ... . The Fianna ... are set in a world so fluctuating and dream-like, that nothing can hold them from being all that the heart desires. (Ex, p. 20)

In an extraordinary passage in 'By The Roadside', Yeats recalls an experience of 1901, when he felt, while listening to country people singing in Irish, a sensation of being reunited with the primal holistic world:

> The voices melted into the twilight, and were mixed into the trees, and when I thought of the words they too melted away ... . I was carried so far that it was as though I came to one of the four rivers, and followed it under the wall of Paradise to the roots of the Trees of Knowledge and of Life. There is no song or story handed down among the cottages that has not words and thoughts to carry one as far ... . (Myth, pp. 138–9)

Folk material placed Yeats in symbiotic contact with an original, preverbal, atemporal, unseparated world, 'in illo tempore'. Mircea Eliade has sought to demonstrate that a belief in this primal, perfect place is universal and that there has been a powerful attraction in all human societies to a cyclical conception of history, that allows a return to the original golden period, an abolition of time and a periodic restarting of history.[50]

And for Yeats this belief in a perfect primal world was constructed from his mother's Paradisial, hierophanic conception of Sligo:

I ... am certain that a man should find his Holy Land where he first crept upon the floor, and that familiar woods and rivers should fade into symbol with so gradual a change that he may never discover, no, not even in ecstasy itself that he is beyond space, and that time alone keeps him from Primum Mobile, Supernal Eden, Yellow Rose over all. (*E & I*, p. 297)

NOTES

1. Autograph letter signed (hereafter ALS), Berg Collection, New York Public Library. Susan Yeats was a non-person to Lady Gregory.
2. 'It is always terrible to see one one loves go through the door of death & mystery before one yet life is such a short thing in eternity that we shall soon meet them again, & perhaps under happier conditions' *Gonne-Yeats Letters*, p. 119.
3. Their affair had ended *c*. March 1897, but Yeats recorded a dream or vision of Olivia Shakespear of *c*. 10 March 1900. They had, therefore, been in contact again as early as then. 'Visions Diary', 10 April 1900 (unpub., present where-abouts unknown).
4. ALS, Lilly Library, Bloomington, Indiana.
5. Yeats kept a copy of the standard Anglican burial service (*YL*, 2313). Susan Yeats was buried at Acton Cemetery on 6 January 1900. Jack Yeats arranged and paid for a plaque to be erected in St John's church, Sligo. See William M. Murphy, *Prodigal Father: The Life of John Butler Yeats (1839–1922)* (Ithaca and London 1978), p. 216, n. 105. Hereafter cited as *Prodigal Father*.
6. John Masefield, *Letters to Reyna*, edited by William Buchan (London 1983), p. 297. Masefield also recalls Yeats's having shown him a photograph of the family including his mother: 'I saw from this photograph that she was very like Yeats's sister, Lolly: a beautiful woman from Sligo, with dark-brown hair, and I should say an imagination of wonder & delight' (p. 492).
7. *Prodigal Father*, p. 217.
8. Thomas Austin, *A Practical Account of General Paralysis* (London 1859).
9. *Ibid.* pp. 77–82.
10. Dr Gordon-Hogg; had been in practice at Priory Avenue, Bedford Park, since 1889. He was a friend of J.B. Yeats as well as being the family doctor. See William M. Murphy (ed.), *Letters From Bedford Park: A Selection from the Correspondence (1890–1901) of John Butler Yeats* (Dublin 1972), pp. 21, 28.
11. Yeats 'fear[ed]' that some surviving friend' might be 'offended with my book' (*Au*, p. 3), and his memories aroused resentment in his immediate family, particularly in J.B. Yeats. William M. Murphy assumes that the plain speaking of the first tranche of autobiography (by a man nearly fifty years old) can be ascribed to the 'Pollexfen in him' (*Prodigal Father*), p. 448.
12. The episode was, by 1914, probably linked by Yeats with Maud Gonne's identical experience before the death of her first child (*Mem*, p. 47).
13. *The Yeats Family and the Pollexfens of Sligo* (Dublin 1971), p. 54. See, however, John Harwood, *Olivia Shakespear and W B. Yeats: After Long Silence* (London

1989), pp. 34–6, for a 'critique of Murphy's attitude and a discussion of the impli-
cations for Yeats of his parents' unhappy marriage'. Helen Vendler, in a rigorous
review of *Prodigal Father*, presented the case against J.B. Yeats ('J.B.Y.' [*The New
Yorker*, 29 January 1979, pp. 66–77]). Murphy responded by devoting a lecture at
the 21st Yeats International Summer School to a defence of his position. In doing
so, he made his bias (and indeed his antifeminist stance) all too clear. In the course
of this *apologia*, he dismissed Susan Yeats as 'a dull and commonplace housewife'
and concluded, complacently, that the misery of her life was worthwhile: '[a]ll in
all, with due sympathy for the unlucky Susan, I rather like the way things turned
out.' See his 'Home Life among the Yeatses' in A. Norman Jeffares (ed.), *Yeats,
Sligo and Ireland* (Gerrards Cross 1980), pp. 170–88.

14. 6 January 1916, quoted from *Prodigal Father*, p. 216. In J.B. Yeats's *Early Memories*
(Dublin 1922) Susan Yeats is almost completely erased. She is mentioned twice,
casually and obliquely: 'whose sister I afterwards married', 'my wife's relations',
Yeats's recording of his father's praise of his mother, 'she pretended to nothing she
did not feel' (*Au*, p. 61), must be qualified by documents such as this letter and
Early Memories.

15. When George Pollexfen died in 1910, J.B. Yeats was astonished and enraged to
find that he had been excluded from the will. The estate was about £50,000, He
wrote many angry letters to [W.B.] Yeats on this subject. He interpreted this
action as evidence that his brother-in-law had no humanity, despite the fact that
Susan Yeats's portion of her brother's estate had been divided among her chil-
dren. Yet there were two obvious reasons for Pollexfen's action. First, he prob-
ably saw no reason to throw good money after bad, given J.B. Yeats's record.
Second, he might well have harboured over decades strong, if unexpressed, feel-
ings concerning the unhappiness of his favourite sister's married life and J.B.
Yeats's responsibility for this.

16. It seems likely that other unattributed folk tales and anecdotes in *The Celtic
Twilight* (such as those in 'Kidnappers' and 'Drumcliffe and Rosses') might derive
from Susan Yeats.

17. Undated letter from J.B.Y. to Lily Yeats, Coll. Michael Butler Yeats. Yeats
concludes '*Louis Lambert*' with a recollection of the 'wisdom deeper than intel-
lect' of a passage of Balzac's *La Recherche de l'absolu*. The novel would have
had formidable significance for a child of J.B. Yeats. The eccentric protagonist
Balthazar Claes, marries a conventional religious woman of no intellect and loses
her fortune and his in a lunatic quest for the universal element. Tortured by his
indifference and by the prospects of bankruptcy, she becomes paralysed and, after
a long illness, dies. Claes then battens on his children and finally characterizes
himself as a 'prodigal father' (The *Quest of the Absolute*. trans. Ellen Marriage
(York and London 1901), p. 214, *YL*, p. 103. The sentence which so moved Yeats
and is quoted by him (*E & I*, p. 446) is Balzac's description of Mme Claes: 'Blessed
are the imperfect, for theirs is the Kingdom of Love' (p. 32).

18. To Mabel Dickinson, 11 May (MS Bancroft Library, University of California at
Berkeley) the letter concerns the inevitability of Synge's death. Yeats insists that
he has never experienced the 'reality' of death before (although he qualifies this by

admitting that it is the death of Synge's imagination which most distresses him). He forgets, for the while, the deaths of Beardsley, Wilde, Dowson and Johnson – but not the death of his mother. I am grateful to Ronald Schuchard for a transcript of this letter.

19. In 1917 she wrote, to John Quinn ' ... not only do I love him as my father but as my greatest friend. When I think of his age and the distance he is off I cannot keep away my tears' (*Prodigal Father*, p. 474). As early as the 1890s Lily had become something of a proxy wife for her father.

20. Coll. Michael Butler Yeats. The last surviving letter is of December 1899.

21. Sec *CLI*, p.108. The novel might well be compared to Turgenev's novella, *The Two Friends*.

22. William M. Murphy, in an otherwise solid biographical analysis of the novel, has sought to make a case for Mary Carton's being modelled on Katharine Tynan. The grounds presented for this argument are that Katharine Tynan was his closest female friend at the time of the composition of the novel and that he had once – under strong moral pressure from friends – proposed to her and been rejected. However Mary Carton is represented as being a beauty, whose classic looks are unrecognized in provincial society: she is also conventional, unintellectual and governed by notions of duty. Katharine Tynan was a plain young woman, but clever, a talented writer and adventurous enough to set up a kind of salon at her father's farm. Further, she was a political radical, a Parnellite at a time when this alignment resulted in her receiving hate-mail. There seems but the slightest ground for Murphy's conjecture. Mary Carton – unlike the other characters in *John Sherman* – is a creature from the deeps of Yeats's psyche. See Murphy's 'William Butler Yeats's *John Sherman*: an Irish Poet's Declaration of Independence', *Irish University Review* (Spring 1979), pp. 92–111, at pp. 100–1.

23. Richard J. Finneran ingeniously suggests that the name 'Ballah' derives from Blake's 'Beulah', and there might have been such an association. However, as it is simply a phonetic anglicization of *Baile* [a place / town], the most common and basic of all Irish place names, it must have seemed to Yeats, in London, quintessentially Irish. See *JS&D*, pp. 21–2. The passage also describes the genesis of 'The Lake Isle of Innisfree'.

24. For a full discussion of this concept, see Hanna Segal, *Dreams, Phantasy and Art* (London and New York 1991) esp. ch. 7. 'Art and the Depressive Position'. It could be argued in terms of Segal's thesis, in which Art / Imagination is distinguished from fantasy / daydreaming by art's accommodation of painful reality that *John Sherman* is a somewhat marginal work. Certainly the plot of the novel avoids those painful aspects of reality which Yeats was experiencing daily at Blenheim Road. However, the work is saved from being mere fantasy-compensation, by its markedly depressed monochrome tint, its sadness of tone, the modifying factor on an optimistic narrative line. And one painful aspect of Yeats's life which is fully incorporated is his hatred of London and longing for Sligo. I am grateful to Riccardo Steiner for drawing my attention to Hanna Segal's work.

25. Yeats had been persuaded to include his 'two early stories' in *The Collected Works in Verse and Prose* (Stratford-upon-Avon 1908) vol. vii, by his publisher A.H.

Bullen, and in particular by Bullen's assistant, Miss Edith Lister.

26. See 'Secret Communion: Yeats's Sexual Destiny' (*YA* 9, pp. 3–30). At p. 16 Martin Bergmann reports a similar strategy in the life of a patient: 'When I fell in love I wrote the whole scenario myself and only later looked around for a list of characters.' See 'On the Intrapsychic Function of Falling in Love', *Psychoanalytic Quarterly* 49 (1980) 56–76. at p. 67. However, this patient's 'scenario' was not 'The Wanderings of Oisin'.

27. Datable to *c*. 1883–4. See *CLI*, p. 155. The sheer *normality* of Yeats's infatuation with Laura Armstrong forms a contrast to his later obsession with Maud Gonne.

28. So described by Gerard Manley Hopkins, who met her in 1886. See Claude Colleer Abbott (ed.), *Further Letters of Gerard Manley Hopkins including his Correspondence with Coventry Patmore*, 2nd edn (London 1956), p. 373.

29. See Robert Bak, 'Being in love and Object Loss', *International Journal of Psychoanalysis*, 54 (1973) 1–7.

30. The abandonment of the dead mother-beloved identification in the last two versions of the novel is probably linked to Maud Gonne's revelations to Yeats of December 1898. See my 'Labyrinths: Yeats and Maud Gonne' (*YA* 9, 95–131) at p.107, where I argue that Yeats's aversion to marriage and his shock when he discovered that Maud Gonne had had two children was linked to the depressing circumstances of his parents' marriage. André Green has discussed the problem of a symbolically dead mother in *On Private Madness* (London 1986). In Chapter 7, 'The Dead Mother', Green discusses the problem not of an actual dead mother, but of a mother whose depression 'brutally transforms a living object, which was a source of vitality … into a distant figure, toneless, practically inanimate' (p. 142) – a fair description of Susan Yeats for the last decade of her married life.

31. He appended a retraction in 1902: 'I know better now.' (*Myth*, p. 37, n. 1).

32. 13 November 1897. See *Lady Gregory's Diaries, 1892–1902*, edited by James Pethica (Gerrards Cross 1996).

33. *MS NLI 30, 754.*

34. For a fuller discussion of Yeats's folklore interests and their significance, see Warwick Gould, 'Frazer, Yeats and the Reconsecration of Folklore' in Robert Fraser (ed.), *Sir James Frazer and the Literary Imagination* (London 1990), pp. 121–53.

35. *MS NLI 30, 754.*

36. Lady Gregory, *Visions and Beliefs in the West of Ireland* (Gerrards Cross 1970), p. 70. For a similar usage see *Cathleen ni Houlihan*: 'Is she right, do you think? Or is she a woman from beyond the world?' (*VPl*, p. 225). 'Not right' means either being possessed of supernatural powers, or being supernatural.

37. *MS NLI 30, 754.* Irish culture does not lack wonder tales, *märchen* or fables, rather the reverse. When Douglas Hyde was collecting folklore in Irish in the late 1880s, he found abundance of such tales; the massive 'The King of Ireland's Son' (which he published in cut form) is a classic wonder tale. However, Hyde makes clear in his introduction to *Beside the Fire* (London 1890) his lack of interest in 'conversational anecdotes rather than set stories' (p. xxxv). Just as Hyde directed his storytellers away from this material, Yeats and Lady Gregory directed them towards it and away from wonder tales.

38. Yeats had of course treated this motif, albeit in a lighter, more fantastic vein, in *The Land of Heart's Desire*. In the draft of *Au*, pp. 400–1, he terms his knowledge of 'away' at this period as 'slight' and 'casual' (*MS NLI* 30, 754). Part of the dynamic of *Cathleen ni Houlihan* also derives from this folk motif. The supernatural being who takes Michael Gillane away from domestic life is a politicized version of the Others who summon the young and healthy to work for them: 'It is a hard service that they take that help me ...' (*VPl*, p. 229). Indeed the fact that Gillane is about to be married stems from the motif; ' ... [when] a young, handsome and strong man ... dies about his marriage day he is believed to die, I think, because a woman of "the others" wants him for herself'. (*UP2*, p. 80).

39. Yeats does not modify the narratives which Lady Gregory took down, although he changes names and places. See *Visions and Beliefs in the West of Ireland* (Gerrards Cross 1970), pp. 139, 132, 137, 110.

40. Yeats had been troubled for some years by violence shown to those believed to be changelings. He had discussed the Clonmel Witch Burning case with Mary Battle in 1895. See Genevieve 'Yeats, Clodd, *Scatologic Rites*, and the Clonmel Witch Burning' (*YA* 4, pp. 207–15).

41. Although the Theosophical Society had given Yeats a theory of Karma and reincarnation, which he had been happy to pass on to Maud Gonne, the Golden Dawn offered no teaching on life after death. Yeats's early reading of Swedenborg, whose works offer a detailed and pedantic account of life after death, was largely governed by his interest in Blake. Recently Jahan Ramazani has questioned the seriousness of Yeats's belief in life after death and reincarnation in an elegant study of Yeats's poetry of death. This questioning has a certain strangeness, for it is as if one were, in a study of Marx, to question the seriousness of his belief in the labour theory of value, or the class struggle. Ramazani argues that Yeats's belief in reincarnation was part of a defence against a fear of death, that it was a reaction formation. Freud used this concept in the area of sexuality and of feeling, but it could be applied to ideology or belief-system. Yet to identify the psychic roots of a belief-system central to a person is not to invalidate sincerity. Reaction formation could be said to be at the root of many strongly and sincerely held beliefs. Ramazani produces no very convincing evidence for his case and one might conclude that his own distaste for such beliefs is paramount. Indeed, the attitude of the critic might suggest some reaction formation. See *Yeats and the Poetry of Death* (New Haven 1990).

42. In *Leo Africanus*, Yeats recalls the séance with Williams as having taken place shortly after an episode in Dublin in which he put Bessy Sigerson in a trance: this is dateable by the *Visions Notebook* to 12 December 1898. He had probably discussed Williams's career before November 1898. Williams had been the medium involved in the famous 1871 transit of Mrs Guppy, which Yeats mentions in an unpublished letter to Edmund Clodd of 6 November 1898. Williams's exposure as a cheat in 1878 must have been well known: he had regularly manifested the popular spirit, John King the Pirate, but was caught with King's beard in his pocket: see also *Ex*, p. 55.

43. See Steve I. Adams and George Mills Harper, 'The Manuscript of "Leo Africanus"'

(*YA 1*, pp. 3–47, at pp. 11–13). Yeats records a conversation which he had with Miss Stead, who told him of her own dead brother's manifesting at a séance, and of the ghost's speaking of differences with Miss Stead's father on the issue of Home Rule. Yeats noted the way in which the spirits' idiom is distorted by that of the medium, so that, when Susan Yeats spoke of trying to contact J.B. Yeats, she used the expression 'gone East' (to New York) as if she were American, like Mrs Wreidt, the medium (*MS MBY*: diary begun June 1908). See also *YVP* 3, p. 107.

44. In *Purgatory* Yeats dramatizes the eternity of Karmic punishment, drawing on a work very important to him in his youth, Ráma Prasád's *The Science of Breath and the Philosophy of the Tatwas … with Fifteen Introductory & Explanatory Essays on Nature's Finer Forces* (London 1890). Prasád insists that evil or destructive acts done in one lifetime are re-enacted in reverse in the next; the murderer endlessly suffers the terror of his victim in his next existence, 'that picture of the ebbing life of the victim is now part and parcel of his constitution, the pain, the terror and the feeling of despair … His life is miserable; slowly but surely it wanes away. Let the curtain fall on this scene. The incarnated thief now comes on the stage … He is doomed to a lonely house. The picture of somebody coming into the house … perhaps strangling him, makes its appearance with the fullest strength' (pp. 134–5). Prasad's central image of a cosmic gallery or Akashic record of images of all human acts of all times, being constantly projected back into human consciousness, is patently absorbed in the magic lantern realization of the past in *Purgatory*; and Prasad's powerful representation of the murderer and the lonely house in the setting and *dramatis personae* of the play.

45. *Purgatory Manuscript Materials including the Author's Final Text*, edited by Sandra F. Siegel, first and second drafts (Ithaca and London 1986), pp. 53, 79.

46. Yeats's 'explanation' of his play in response to Father Terence Connolly's queries is deteriorationist and eugenic in its thrust: 'In my play, a spirit suffers because of its share, when alive, in the destruction of an honoured house; that destruction is taking place all over Ireland today. Sometimes it is the result of poverty, but more often because a new individualistic generation has lost interest in the ancient sanctities… I have founded my play on [mesalliance] partly because of my interest in certain problems of eugenics … ' *(Irish Independent, The Irish Times, 13 August 1938)*. Of course a eugenic / deteriorationist argument is a part of the play's 'meaning'; it was conceived in tandem with *On the Boiler*. Yeats's curtain speech had been, 'I wish to say that I have put into this play not many thoughts that are picturesque, but my own belief about this world and the next' *(Irish Independent, 11 August 1938)*. Yeats was wisely guarded in his 'explanations': despite a good reception from puzzled but impressed audiences ('even to hardened playgoers the effect was uncanny', *Irish Independent*, 13 August 1938) a predictable controversy arose as to the legitimacy of Yeats's use of Catholic dogma given his non-Christian belief system (*The Irish Times*, August 14, 16, 17, 18, 19, 20, 1938).

47. *The Yeats Family and the Pollexfens of Sligo*, p. 8. John Kelly, in a somewhat Bowlbyan reading of the relationship, concludes that Susan Yeats's influence on her son was non-existent if not negative, save in the matter of her love for Sligo. His analysis of 'maternal deprivation' is tied to his exploration of Yeats's dependence

upon Lady Gregory. See ' "Friendship is the only house I have": Lady Gregory and W.B. Yeats', in Ann Saddlemyer and Colin Smythe (eds), *Lady Gregory Fifty Years After* (Gerrards Cross 1987) pp. 196–8.

48. *MS NLI* 30, 754.

49. In fact it could be argued that his comparison of his mother's folk tales to Homer shows an instinctive grasp of Homer's orality (first fully argued by Milman Parry and Albert Lord). This is supported by a remarkable statement in 'The Philosophy of Shelley's Poetry': 'all the machineries of poetry are part of the convictions of antiquity' (*E & I*, p. 74), which is close in arguments to Parry's thesis that oral poetry is identifiable by its use of formulae, 'groups of words ... regularly employed under the same metrical conditions to express a given, essential idea'. See Adam Parry (ed), *The Making of Homeric Verse; the Collected Papers of Milman Parry* (Oxford 1971) p. 272.

50. See Mircea Eliade, *Le Mythe de l'éternel retour. Archétypes et répétition* (Paris 1949) *passim*. Yeats's early and continued concern with magical other worlds, such as *Tír na nÓg*, is part of the same obsession, For a full discussion of Yeats's interest in both cyclical and linear theories of history, see Marjorie Reeves and Warwick Gould, *Joachim of Fiore and the Myth of the Eternal Evangel in the Nineteenth Century* (Oxford 1987) pp. 202–71.

Byzantine Materiality and Byzantine Vision: 'Hammered Gold and Gold Enamelling'

WARWICK GOULD

(Institute of English Studies, UK)

I think if I could be given a month of Antiquity and leave to spend it where I chose, I would spend it in Byzantium a little before Justinian opened St. Sophia and closed the Academy of Plato. I think I could find in some little wine shop some philosophical worker in mosaic who could answer all my questions, the supernatural descending nearer to him than to Plotinus even ... I think that in early Byzantium, and maybe never before or since in recorded history, religious, aesthetic and practical life were one, and that architect and artificers – though not, it may be, poets, for language had been the instrument of controversy and must have grown abstract – spoke to the multitude and the few alike. The painter and the mosaic worker, the worker in gold and silver, the illuminator of Sacred Books were almost impersonal, almost perhaps without the consciousness of individual design, absorbed in their subject matter and that the vision of a whole people.[1]

'Sailing to Byzantium', one of W.B. Yeats's greatest and best-known poems, was written in 1926. 'In a sense', said Richard Ellmann, Yeats 'had been writing it all his life.'[2] It opens what is also his greatest book of poems, *The Tower* (1928), his first substantial collection of new work after the award of the Nobel Prize in 1923. It gave rise to a secondary creation, 'Byzantium', following correspondence with Thomas Sturge Moore, Yeats's fellow poet and the designer of the dust jackets for a number of his later books. 'Byzantium', one of the great masterpieces of *The Winding Stair* (1933), even supplied that book's working title – *Byzantium* – as well as the theme for preliminary and indeed final art-work for Sturge Moore's cover design.

Both poems take their point of departure from the ageing poet's preoccu-pation with death and the afterlife seen as a process of alchemical transforma-tion of the 'weary heart into a weariless spirit'. That phrase belongs, as we shall see, to a story written in 1896.[3] If for no other reason than to prove the truth of Ellmann's brilliant throwaway remark, I will proceed chronologically from the nineties until near his death – looking before and after.

My subject, then, is less the poems themselves than their hinterland of thought, much of which is to be found, as my headnote indicates, in *A Vision*, first published on 15 January 1926 despite having a title-page date of 1925. Instead of merely celebrating afresh Yeats's long enthusiasm for Byzantine iconography, I focus on his interest in the materiality of the Byzantine vision, and what, for Yeats, that materiality might open up for Irish artists and designers – workers in mosaic, designers of Celtic crosses, those working with metals, or in the book arts. My case study of what he brought back from Byzantium and how it might inflect Irish design, focuses on the work of a young book illus-trator and stage designer, whom Yeats tutored, Norah McGuinness (1904–80).

'Sailing to Byzantium' charts a one-way passage towards death and trans-figuration, setting sail from Ireland, and opening with a rejectionary gesture sternwards, 'That is no country for old men' – a line with which Yeats was strangely dissatisfied, later even preferring 'Old men should quit a country where the young' in preparation for a radio broadcast.[4] The poem fares forward to what only seems a new destination in his imaginary – Byzantium. A frequent traveller in North America, an incessant traveller in Ireland, England, France and, less frequently, Italy, Yeats never actually went any further eastwards than Venice, Ravenna and Ferrara, in 1907, and, in 1925, Sicily. What since only 1930 has been officially known as Istanbul remained for Yeats Byzantium, founded in 660 BC by the Greek, Byzas. After Constantine the Great made it the new eastern capital of the Roman Empire in AD 330 it became Constantinopolis, but, as Byzantium, was destined to remain a country of Yeats's mind.

The interplay of what he saw as Byzantine and Latin influences upon Celtic art in Ireland was a very early interest of Yeats's, and it informed an enduring set of his aesthetic preferences. After the award of the Nobel Prize in 1923, these suffused an entirely new phase in his creative career, as Byzantine materi-ality and its iconography dominated his attempts to build a personal system of thought, an occult mythology of both personality and history, which embraced the universal history of art and artifice in *A Vision*, first published privately in 1926 and later revised in 1937. 'Sailing to Byzantium' was the poem which flowered from that obsessive interest, written 'to recover my spirits', as he told Olivia Shakespear, and first published in his *October Blast*.[5]

For its second printed incarnation, on 11 November 1927 (the year after its composition), 'Sailing to Byzantium' appeared in a 'total' context designed by – and for – Norah McGuinness (plates 1–3).[6]

Plate 1. Stories of Red Hanrahan and The Secret Rose *(Macmillan, 1927): Top Board and Spine*

Plate 2. Stories of Red Hanrahan and The Secret Rose *(1927), illustrated by Norah McGuinness in Byzantine style, as suggested by Yeats. Variant Binding*

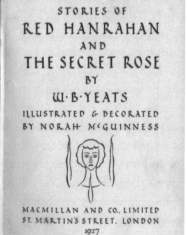

Plate 3. Stories of Red Hanrahan *etc. (1927) title page*

While his Cuala Press volumes were used by him to try his poems on a coterie audience of admirers and collectors, this second version was an artist's book. All its stories dated from before 1897, but many had been later rewritten at various times, with especially radical revision and augmentation of the Hanrahan stories by Lady Gregory in 1904. Reissuing such old work in a new edition of just 1885 copies was strange enough. Not only had they been published many times, but they were still very much in print from the same publisher, in a serviceable trade text and arrangement, *Early Poems and Stories*, revised as recently as 1925. Now entitled *Stories of Red Hanrahan and the Secret Rose*, and with the words 'Illustrated and Decorated by Norah McGuinness' on the title page in a typeface which she seems to have designed, and with that newly added dedication to the poem now positioned as a proem to the Hanrahan stories, this book was very much a vehicle for Norah McGuinness's illustration (plate 4).

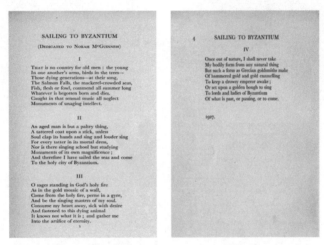

Plate 4. Stories of Red Hanrahan *etc. (1927) Dedicatory Poem*

I YEATS'S EARLY BYZANTINE INTERESTS

To explain how the poem came to be inserted into this particular context and what light this might shed upon it and the poet, we now go back to the 1890s. In 1899 Yeats wrote up a Dublin lecture on 'The High Crosses of Ireland' by the scholar Margaret Stokes, author of *Early Christian Art in Ireland* (1887) and an authority on its forty-five carved stone High Crosses. She can be seen in an 1897 photograph in Co. Kildare, sketching and photographing the High Cross of Moone, seemingly putting her old academic gown and cap to good use in the rain (plate 5).

Stokes's interest was in the iconography of such crosses, and, as registered in Yeats's summary, she had listed the Christian legendary subjects 'repeated over and over again on different crosses such ... as Noah entering the Ark, Daniel in the Lion's Den, the Fall of Man, David playing upon his harp, Jacob wrestling with the Angel mixed with 'chariots and hunting scene[s]', *topoi* which had been used 'to describe Heaven to [a Celtic] people who still remembered 'the great plain', 'the land of the ever living', 'the land of the living heart' where the dead heroes lived in 'the delight of war and of the chase'.[7] Stokes demonstrated the iconography 'of these Christian subjects from the Byzantine Guide for Painters, compiled at Mount Athos, from the works of Panselinos, an eleventh century painter. In using this medieval text-book to interpret *Early Christian Art in Ireland*, she discerned the confluence of two currents, one Byzantine, the other Latin.'[8]

Plate 5. Miss Margaret Stokes sketching the High Cross of Moone, Co. Kildare, 1897

Yeats signed his review of the lecture 'Rosicrux', concealing his identity whilst displaying his private modern occultism. In disputing her reading of antique Irish 'Paradises' in these High Crosses in favour of a more modern 'mystical' approach, he offered his explanation 'doubtfully' because, having 'met young Catholics of deep piety, and some that have heard voices and seen visions' he was now 'certain that some day one among them, having become scholour [*sic*] as well as visionary, and having mastered the mysticism of the Middle Ages, will tell us how much of it is reflected in the crosses and illuminated missals of this country'.[9]

This intense national focus implied a syncretic desire to link the *unum necessarium* of his day, a new national culture, to his own preoccupations with the mystical life. He readily admitted his inherent anachronism: ' ... the mystics I have read, wrote either much earlier or much later than the time to which Miss Stokes refers this diagram, and I have read their mysticism for its own sake, and not with any thought of its historical changes.'[10]

He had published *The Secret Rose* in 1897, and with a synthesized Rosicrucian design with some Celtic imagery and typography, on its gilded stamped blue boards as executed by Althea Gyles (plate 6), to illustrate a passage in *The Tables of the Law*. In plate 7, she is to be seen seated on the right in a Chelsea Studio, with Constance Gore-Booth, 1898, two bold Irish art students of the Slade School in London.

Plate 6. Wraparound design of
The Secret Rose *(1897) by Althea Gyles*

Plate 7: Constance Gore-Booth and Althea Gyles in a Chelsea Studio, 1898

Gyles used a Celtic knotwork style and worked to what must have been Yeats's programme, given that Gyles was not a member of his Rosicrucian Order, the Hermetic Students of the Golden Dawn. The ultimate source is an early eleventh-century French sacramentary by Nivardus (plate 8), though Gyles as an art student might well have worked from a facsimile by Lord John Thynne (plate 9). One of these – there may also have been further copies by Thynne in private collections – had been in the South Kensington Museum (now the V&A), since the 1860s.[11]

Plate 8 Nivardus: The Sacramentary Fleury, 11th C.,
f. 9, Getty Museum and Gyles's Book Cover, 1897

Plate 9. Nivardus: The Sacramentary Fleury, 11th C., *f. 9,*
Getty Museum and V&A facsimile by Lord John Thynne, c. 1862

So, why does Yeats also insert Byzantium – as he does – into supercharged descriptions of a Connemara occult temple and, later, into the domestic interior of an old Dublin house, and these at the culmination of his Irish stories, with their admixture of Christian and Rosicrucian symbolism? I refer to the final triptych, in which an unnamed narrator fails in his attempt to apply the doctrine of spiritual alchemy in his own life:

> I looked out into the darkness, and it seemed to my troubled fancy that all
> those little points of light filling the sky were the furnaces of innumerable

divine alchemists, who labour continually, turning lead into gold, weariness into ecstasy, bodies into souls, the darkness into God; and at their perfect labour my mortality grew heavy, and I cried out, as so many dreamers and men of letters in our age have cried, for the birth of that elaborate spiritual beauty which could alone uplift souls weighted with so many dreams.[12]

Just as material alchemy turns materials of a lesser value into gold, so spiritual alchemy burns bodies into souls, and both processes – analogues of each other – are figured in mosaic, whereby firing fuses raw materials – some of considerable value, such as lapis lazuli – into imperishable beauty, permanent art, the 'artifice of eternity'. Well might Yeats, then, in 'Byzantium' ponder whether 'golden handiwork' is, or is not, 'miracle'.[13] But by 1896 Yeats had travelled no farther than Paris, where from February 1894, he was wont to stay with MacGregor Mathers, his Golden Dawn magus, in Auteuil. With touching penury and vaunting ambition, Mathers had decorated the hall and stairway in a Byzantine style, if with Egyptian subject matter. Ella Young remembered all along the hallway and on the wall which climbed the stairs were 'frescoes in mosaic' of 'images of Egyptian deities', made of 'thin paper of various colours: paper cut in tiny longitudinal pieces and fitted together with the utmost exactitude', which Mathers claimed to have executed by himself in the course of one night.[14]

Something of this 'tawdry cheapness' of materials goes to the essence of the gap between the aspiration and the material reality of most Golden Dawn art and regalia, as Maud Gonne famously noted. But in his mind Yeats had clearly been much farther afield. In a late part of the story the narrator, clearly in a state of heightened aesthetic excitement, brought on by the 'mysterious glamour' of Michael Robartes and clearly under the influence of 'fumes of … incense' is inducted into a temple of The Order of the Alchemical Rose on the Connemara coast of the west of Ireland, where he finds himself 'in a marvellous passage, along whose sides were many divinities wrought in a mosaic not less beautiful than the mosaic in the Baptistery at Ravenna, but of a less severe beauty; the predominant colour of each, which was surely symbolic, being repeated in the lamps that hung from the ceiling, a curiously-scented lamp before each divinity.'[15]

The octagonal Battistero degli Ortodossi or Neone Baptistery near the cathedral was built at the beginning of the fifth century, and the mosaics in the dome were added by Bishop Neone shortly after 450. The baptism of Christ is depicted in the centre against a gold background, while the twelve apostles with gold and white drapery are depicted radially against a deep blue, lapis lazuli background. Twelve swags give a petal-like effect to the central design (plate 10).

There can be no doubt that Yeats's figure comes from the Battistero Neoniano for, as the scene in the Connemara Temple of the Alchemical Rose continues, we become gradually aware that the scene describes a drug-induced delusory perception of a ritual, during which the petals of a mosaic rose in a domed ceiling come alive, descend and dance orgiastically with the human participants:

> Upon the ceiling was an immense rose wrought in mosaic; and about the walls, also in mosaic, was a battle of gods and angels, the gods glimmering like rubies and sapphires ... Pillars supported the roof and made a kind of circular cloister, each pillar being a column of confused shapes, divinities, it seemed, of the wind, who in a whirling dance of more than human vehemence, rose playing upon pipes and cymbals; and from among these shapes were thrust out hands, and in these hands were censers ... as I turned from the pillars towards the dancers, I saw that the floor was of a green stone, and that a pale Christ on a pale cross was wrought in the midst. I asked Robartes the meaning of this, and was told that they desired 'to trouble His unity with their multitudinous feet'.

Plate 10. Battistero degli Ortodossi (Battistero Neoniano), cupola and pillars, early 5th C.

There is a preview, as it were, of those 'marbles of the dancing floor' which 'break bitter furies of complexity' of 'blood-begotten spirits', purging the 'fury and the mire of human veins' in the second Byzantium poem, with its 'agonies of trance' (*VP* 497–8). This is a fairly well-worn floor: the point is made by that most brilliant of early Yeats symbologists, Giorgio Melchiori.[16] But Yeats's self-referentiality is such that his early symbolic preoccupations grow, eventually exfoliating, as new knowledge of material forms of beauty come to interest him. Here I'm concerned with what happens to that mosaic rose in the agonies of trance and dance.

The dance wound in and out, tracing upon the floor the shapes of petals that copied the petals in the rose overhead, until gradually I sank into a half-dream, from which I was awakened by seeing the petals of the great rose, which had no longer the look of mosaic, falling slowly through the incense-heavy air, and, as they fell, shaping into the likeness of living beings of an extraordinary beauty. Still faint and cloud-like, they began to dance, and as they danced took a more and more definite shape, so that I was able to distinguish beautiful Grecian faces and august Egyptian faces, and now and again to name a divinity by the staff in his hand or by a bird fluttering over his head; and soon every mortal foot danced by the white foot of an immortal; and in the troubled eyes that looked into untroubled shadowy eyes ... Sometimes, but only for a moment, I saw a faint solitary figure with a veiled face, and carrying a faint torch, flit among the dancers, but like a dream within a dream, like a shadow of a shadow ... it was Eros himself ... a voice cried to me from the crimson figures, 'Into the dance! there is none that can be spared out of the dance; into the dance! into the dance! that the gods may make them bodies out of the substance of our hearts' until the narrator understands 'with a great horror that I danced with one who was more or less than human, and who was drinking up my soul as an ox drinks up a wayside pool; and I fell, and darkness passed over me.

Going into the temple, the narrator had 'marvel[led] exceedingly how these enthusiasts could have created all this beauty in so remote a place, and half persuaded to believe in a material alchemy, by the sight of so much hidden wealth; the censer filling the air, as I passed, with smoke of ever-changing colour.'

It is, of course, a drug-induced delusion. The narrator 'awoke suddenly ... and saw that I was lying on a roughly painted floor, and that on the ceiling, which was at no great distance, was a roughly painted rose, and about me on the walls half-finished paintings.' (*Variorum Secret Rose*, pp. 145–8).

Yeats's earliest diagram of the Golden Dawn rose is in his 1893 white vellum manuscript book, in the National Library of Ireland. It would seem that a twenty-two petalled rose (one for each of the paths of the Tree of Life, or the Tarot Trumps), on the ceiling of the seven-sided Vault of the Adepts in Clipstone St, London, was revealed to new Adepts at the conclusion of the Adeptus Minor Ritual 5° = 6° that Yeats underwent on 20–21 January 1893.[17] Plate 11 compares its design with that of the Neone Baptistery Cupola.

Golden Dawn art is irredeemably tawdry, as we have seen; each initiate making his / her own implements out of base materials – cardboard or what-ever. But if one compares that Ravenna Baptistery with its twelve apostles and twelve petal-like swags to the Golden Dawn Lamen, or cross (Yeats of course had to make his own), the twelve outer petals of the central twenty-two petalled rose make something of a similar pattern (plate 12).[18] I will leave the byways of the Order of the Golden Dawn and its fictional analogue, the Order of the

Alchemical Rose, at the portal of the Second Order (Ordo Rubidae Rosae et Aurea Crucis) for the moment, noting only that the symbolism of the rose as a living spiritual force is developed in the Mariolatrous 1897–8 version of *The Speckled Bird*. There the flames of a crimson stained-glass – no doubt, a rose-window in a chapel depicting some sort of martyrdom of Our Lady become 'petals of a great rose' in some sort of visionary experience.[19]

Yeats's early actual visual sources for Ravenna mosaics are, as I say, not known, and coloured reproductions of them must have been very scarce in 1896.[20] If his initial interest may have been stimulated by the writings of Margaret Stokes,[21] it is possible – but I stress this is research in progress – that the Victoria and Albert Museum in South Kensington would have been the place to go, to see examples of mosaic work, as well as being of course the temple of the Arts and Crafts movement for which Ruskin, Morris and Sir William Lethaby had written so much about Venice and other places such as Ravenna, famous for Byzantine mosaics.[22]

Plate 11. Battistero Neoniano, cupola and pillars, Golden Dawn Lamen with tracing by Donald Pearce of WBY's GD Rose from 1893 notebook, NLI 30,548

Plate 12. Battistero Neoniano, cupola and pillars, and Golden Dawn Lamen

II RAVENNA

By the time Yeats actually went to Ravenna in May 1907, his mind would have been further fired by the conversation and wonderfully atmospheric essays on cities of his former co-tenant in Fountain Court, Arthur Symons. Symons, an inveterate traveller, had been to Constantinople in 1902 and published two essays on that city in 1903.[23] He was to collect essays on Ravenna, Venice, Siena, Florence and others in *Cities of Italy* in October of 1907.[24] His Ravenna essay, though not published until 1904, could have been read by Yeats before he went there in 1907.[25] Given that for Yeats, much of what he knew came from Symons the talker, one imagines that not only during the period of their dwelling in the Inner Temple, 1895–6, but thereafter, 'holy cities' such as Venice and Ravenna would have been a subject of their conversations. Here is Symons on the dome mosaic of the Baptistery:

> I remember ... the lapis lazuli which makes a sky in the dome of the Baptistery, against which the twelve Apostles walk in gold and white robes with jewelled crowns in their hands, and the green grass, on which a shadow turns and darkens with their feet, as the circle goes around with the sun.[26]

It is frequently the case, when one looks comparatively at the writings of Symons and Yeats, to find that Symons 'got there first' but that Yeats did much more with identical subject matter, frequently filtered through Symons. I've often wondered why Yeats wrote so little about Italy, as well as choosing to write about places Symons had not visited, but then reflect on the lines 'Caught in that sensual music all neglect / Monuments of unageing intellect' (VP 407). 'Unageing' is a word used by Yeats only that once in a poem, and never in his prose or letters. He uses 'ageing' only once in a poem ('The Tower', VP 427). Symons finds Ravenna 'as if worn out, languid with fever; it has not aged gracefully. Its miraculous mosaics, so nearly unaging [*sic*], are housed inside rough walls, through which the damp creeps, staining the marble columns with strange, lovely colours of decay' – apt reading for Yeats, I would suggest, in preparing for, or reflecting on his own experiences.[27]

Yeats had gone straight to Florence by 10 April, and then on to Urbino, Ferrara, Rimini, Ravenna, and thence by sea to Venice. In Ravenna he would have seen the Basilica di S. Apollinare in Classe with its wondrous apse, upon which Symons's depressingly descriptive, if powerfully impressionistic poem 'S. Apollinare in Classe: Ravenna' is focused (plates 13–14).[28]

Other images that evidently stayed with Yeats for a lifetime include the 'starlit dome' of the fifth-century century mosaics in Mausoleo di Galla Placidia (plate 15), the Processions of Female Saints (left) and of Martyrs (right) in the nave of the Basilica di S. Apollinare Nuovo which always recall for me the 'sages standing in God's holy fire' of the poem (plates 16–18).

Plate 13. S. Apollinare in Classe: the Apse, 6th C. AD

Plate 14. S. Apollinare in Classe: the Apse, detail

Plate 15. Interior of the 'starlit dome' of the Mausoleo de Galla Placida, Ravenna, early 5th C. AD

Plate 16. Nave of S. Apollinare Nuovo, early 6th C. AD

Plate 17. S. Apollinare Nuovo, Procession of Martyrs 'in God's holy fire', r.h. nave, detail

Plate 18. S. Apollinare Nuovo, Procession of female saints, l.h. nave, detail

Then there are in the same Basilica the mosaics of the Emperor Justinian and the Empress Theodora (plates 19, 20), and numerous examples of bird imagery (plates 21, 22) as well, of course, as the two baptisteries. I should stress that, in making what seem to me to be obvious connections between these visual images and the language and symbols in the two Byzantium poems, I am not insisting that these are Yeats's exclusive or unique visual sources: 'there is always a phantasmagoria',[29] says Yeats, and everything about his passion for things Byzantine is phantasmagoric: the bird upon the golden bough of the second poem has a tenth-century source (Luitprand had been first sent there in 949, in the reign of Constantinus VII Porphyrogenitus), while his Byzantine passion in *A Vision* is for the age of Justinian (b. *c.* 482, reigned from 527, d. 565) and Theodora. We shall see later that the same is not true of his illustrator, Norah McGuinness, but then she worked in visual media.

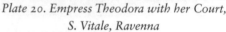

Plate 19. The Emperor Justinian,   Plate 20. Empress Theodora with her Court,
Basilica di S. Vitale, Ravenna   S. Vitale, Ravenna

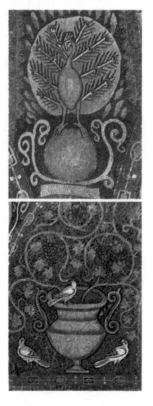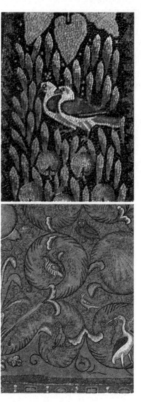

Plates 21 and 22, Bird imagery, S. Vitale, Ravenna

Symons, of course, had been to Venice many times, and his essay on the subject, first published in 1894 and thereafter augmented, sees the city itself as a 'superb, barbaric patchwork in which the East and the West have an equal share', St Mark's as 'one vast mosaic ... an immense jewel, a piece of goldsmith's work in which the exquisite and the fantastic are carried to so rare a beauty, in their elaborate intermingling', its 'majestical roof fretted with golden fire' – words from Shakespeare which Symons does not hesitate to patch into his own patchwork. He is mildly obsessed with the imagery of marble floors and mosaics: thus, when he visits the neighbouring island of Torcello, it is the mosaics and marbles of its cathedral that preoccupy him.[30] Frustratingly, very little survives by way of record of this tour, except by implication in his writings, where its profound effect on his imagination may be seen in a number of poems (principally drawing on Castiglione's *Book of the Courtier* and his memories of Urbino), and in allusions to other art works in Ferrara, Siena, and Florence to be found in revisions to his fiction and in new essays for *Discoveries* and other pieces. Thus, in 'Poetry and Tradition' (August 1907, immediately on his return from the Italian trip) he recalled: 'When I was at Siena, I noticed that the Byzantine style persisted in faces of Madonnas for several generations after it had given way to a more natural style in the less loved faces of saints and martyrs. Passion had grown accustomed to those narrow eyes, which are almost Japanese, and to those gaunt cheeks, and would have thought it sacrilege to change.'[31]

Plate 23. Duccio: Madonna and Child
(detail, c. 1300-10), Siena.

Clearly thinking of the influence of Duccio di Buoninsegna (active 1278–1318, see plate 23), Yeats concludes that '... a writer must not ... ignore the examples of the great Masters in the fancied or real service of a cause'.[32] As always with Yeats, an aesthetic implied an ethic, the one developing as the other was articulated, in moral behaviour, or in style.[33] In 'The Tragic Theatre' (August 1910) he writes, 'If we are painters, we shall ... leave out some element of reality as in Byzantine painting, where there is no mass, nothing in relief; and so it is that in the supreme moment of tragic art there comes upon one that strange sensation as though the hair of one's head stood up.'[34]

On his return, he set about revising those early stories, so that the 1908 text of *The Tables of the Law* incorporates a revised iconography incorporating new enthusiasms for the Byzantine style.

> The ... Sienese School ... alone of all the schools of the world pictured not the world but what is revealed to saints in their dreams and visions. The Sienese alone among Italians ... could not or would not represent the pride of life, the pleasure in swift movement or sustaining strength, or voluptuous flesh. They were so little interested in these things that there often seemed to be no human body or head at all under the robe of the saint, but they could represent by a bowed head, or uplifted face, man's reverence before Eternity as no others could, and they were at their happiest when mankind had dwindled to a little group, silhouetted upon a golden abyss, as if they saw the world habitually from far off.[35]

III MACLAGAN AND LUITPRAND

'I have read somewhere that in the emperor's palace at Byzantium was a tree made of gold and silver, and artificial birds that sang', Yeats writes in a note to the first publication of 'Sailing to Byzantium'.[36] In fact, he'd known since 25 April 1910,[37] though his source was oral: we'll catch up with his later reading on the subject. Eric Maclagan told him that in late Byzantium there had been artificial birds which could be made to sing – by a hydraulic process – in artificial trees. Maclagan, by then working at the V&A, was an expert in ecclesiastical embroidery, and an habitué of Yeats's Monday evenings at home in Woburn Buildings. Yeats had stayed in Maclagan's rooms in Christ Church when he lectured on 'The Theatre' in Oxford, from 17–19 May 1902, and had housed Maclagan in Woburn Buildings upon occasion. I've often wondered whether Yeats had used his name when seeking to disguise the identity of Samuel Liddell MacGregor Mathers, the mage of the Golden Dawn, under the name of Samuel Maclagan, in the 1902 version of his novel, *The Speckled Bird*. Maclagan had helped his sisters in 1902–3 with the design for altar cloths, and again for ecclesiastical banners in Loughrea cathedral, and in 1904 he had published with Yeats's publisher an edition of Blake's *Jerusalem*.[38]

Maclagan had been reading Liutprand, or Liudprand (*c.* 922–72), Bishop of Cremona, and a confidential secretary to the ruler of Italy, Berengar II of Ivrea. Liutprand had been despatched as ambassador in 949 to the court of Constantine II, a miserable time covered in Liutprand's *Antapodosis* ('Retribution'), and again in 968, this time to the court of Nicephorus Phokas. Liutprand's written accounts of Constantinople and the Byzantine court are wonderfully fresh, but they were not translated until 1930. Maclagan told A. Norman Jeffares that he'd been the oral source.[39] Maclagan was a brilliant and learned linguist, but tenth-century Latin would not have been easy for Yeats. (Lionel Johnson had had to supply the Latin passages in *The Tables of the Law*.[40])

IV ADEPTUS EXEMPTUS

Yeats actually tried to rewrite a poem for a Golden Dawn initiation into the utterly exalted Adeptus Exemptus Grade of 7=4, for which there was no set ritual in England, but which was back in play amid increasing rivalry between claimant bodies in the fissiparous Golden Dawn, with consequent grade inflation at all levels.[41] Mathers conferred the 7=4 grade upon himself as a kind of honorary degree. Yeats's holograph of the poem (plate 24) is to be found in his PIAL notebook, dated Nov 4 [1915].[42]

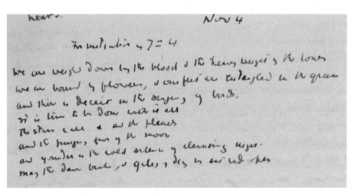

Plate 24. *For Initiation of 7=4, 4 Nov., [1915], NLI MS 36,276*

For Initiation of 7=4

We are weighed down by the blood and the heavy weight of the bones
We are bound by flowers, & our feet are tangled in the green
And there is deceit in the singing of birds
It is time to be done with it all

The stars call & all the planets
And the purging fire of the moon
And yonder is the cold silence of cleansing night
May the dawn break, & gates of day be open

This reworks R.W. Felkin's Whare Ra temple mantra, which was to be repeated every day for four weeks in preparation for taking the rite.

1. Earthborn and bound our bodies close us in,
Clogged with red clay and shuttered by our sin – We must arise.

Flowers bind us round and grasses catch our feet,
Bird songs allure and blossom scent is sweet – We must arise.

Mountains may beckon and the seas recall,
Cloud-forms delude, and rushing streams enthrall – We must arise.

Planets encircle with their spiral light,
Stars call us upward to our: faltering flight – Thus we arise.

Sunrays will lead us higher yet and higher,
Moonbooms our Souls scorch with their purging fire – Thus we arise.

Into the darkness plunge, fearless of pain,
Coldness and silence cleanse us again – Still we arise.

Open ye gates of Light – Doors open wide!
Gaze we within at the glories ye hide – We have arisen![43]

Yeats had certainly seen Felkin's effort, hackneyed as it is by its inability to escape from cliché, some of it biblical, and from the prison-house of trite rhyme. Yeats has tried to lift it above the 'brown rice' level (it comes in the midst of complex advice on self-purification during a preparatory month prior to initiation). The images of the natural world implicit in

Flowers bind us round and grasses catch our feet,
Bird songs allure and blossom scent is sweet ...

Mountains may beckon and the seas recall,
Cloud-forms delude, and rushing streams enthrall

lie somewhere very much behind the first stanza of 'Sailing to Byzantium'. He has yet to cash these vague banalities of bird songs, blossom scent, seas and rushing streams into the specifically Irish world of 'those dying generations' of 'birds in the trees', 'salmon-falls', 'mackerel-crowded seas' and whatever is 'begotten, born, and dies' so 'Byzantium' as a destination has yet to suggest itself to Yeats's mind, and its high purpose to an 'aged man', the study of 'Monuments of unageing intellect', 'Monuments of its own magnificence' the study of images found in a 'holy city'. Musing on the origins of poems in Yeats's 'habitual thought', Ellmann remarks that Yeats 'had to secure a dramatic structure and the more dense and powerful Byzantine symbolism before the idea took on full poetic significance'.[44] But he does have that one line which is unique to him: 'It is time to have done with it all', a line which prefigures 'That is no country for old men'.

V STOCKHOLM, 1923

With these gestures to what was now becoming the 'tradition' of Yeats's mind, I jump forward to December 1923, when Yeats was presented with his Nobel Prize in Stockholm, and saw the the brand new Stadthus, or Town Hall, with its mosaic-lined Gyllene salen, or 'Golden Hall', designed by Einar Goseth and based on Swedish mythological figures such as that of the Queen of Malaren (plate 25). He remarked shortly after in 'The Bounty of Sweden' (written in 1924, first published 1925) that the Stockholm Town Hall, decorated by many artists, working in harmony with one another and with the design of the building as a whole, and 'yet all in seeming perfect freedom', carried 'the mind backward to Byzantium'.[45] There can be little doubt, I think, that so recent a venture into mosaic and national myth would subsequently have been pressed by Yeats upon Norah McGuinness.

Plate 25. Gyllene salen, Stockholms Stadhus (1923). Mosaics by Einar Goseth

VI PREPARING FOR THE VOYAGE: YEATS'S BYZANTINE READING

The world of Byzantium in Yeats's mind was gradually revived from his massive immersion in universal history in preparing to write *A Vision*, privately printed for subscribers in 1925 and issued early in 1926. Yeats was an eclectic and even idiosyncratic scholar, but his intake of reading about the reign, especially, of Justinian and Theodora was prodigious.[46] My headnote offers its central focus, the reign of Justinian (*c.* AD 527– 65). Sixth-century Byzantium for Yeats had been 'that great age of building in which one may conclude Byzantine art was perfected ... the moment when Byzantium became Byzantine and substituted for formal Roman magnificence, with its glorification of physical power, an architecture that suggests the Sacred City in the Apocalypse of St. John.' The passage bears repetition:

> I think if I could be given a month of Antiquity and leave to spend it where I chose, I would spend it in Byzantium a little before Justinian opened St. Sophia [AD 537] and closed the Academy of Plato [AD 529]. I think I could find in some little wine shop some philosophical worker in mosaic who could answer all my questions, the supernatural descending nearer to him than to Plotinus even ... I think that in early Byzantium, and maybe never before or since in recorded history, religious, aesthetic and practical life were one, and that architect and artificers – though not, it may be, poets, for language had been the instrument of controversy and must have grown abstract – spoke to the multitude and the few alike. The painter and the mosaic worker, the worker in gold and silver, the illuminator of Sacred Books were almost impersonal, almost perhaps without the consciousness of individual design, absorbed in their subject matter and that the vision of a whole people ... (*AVB* 279–81, cf. *AVA*, *CW*13 158–9).

In Josef Strygowski's *Origin of Christian Church Art* Yeats (and later, Norah McGuinness) would have found a whole chapter on 'Hiberno-Saxon Art in the Time of Bede', one which, while stressing its Byzantine connections, also insists that Celtic ecclesiastical art is 'no mere pale reflection of Roman or Byzantine art, but an art which, in comparison with these, shows no less individuality than do the remains of buildings, sculptures and paintings of Hither Asia'.[47]

Other books available for consultation in Yeats's collection of Byzantine and Celtic Art studies offered more by way of Byzantine history as illustrated by Byzantine art, even in its courtly amusements, which lie behind the image of the golden bird on the golden bough. Yeats's easy familiarity with his sources characteristically disdains bibliographical exactitude: the remark 'I have read somewhere that in the emperor's palace at Byzantium was a tree made of gold and silver, and artificial birds that sang' in a note to the poem's first publication[48] gestures to the fact that by this time he had read something of Liutprand of Cremona at last, surely in Gibbon's *Decline and Fall of the Roman Empire.*

While Richard Finneran picks out:

> [The Emperor's] fanciful magnificence employed the skill and patience of such artists as the times could afford; but the taste of Athens would have despised their frivolous and costly labours: a golden tree, with its leaves and branches, which sheltered a multitude of birds, warbling their artificial notes, and two lions of massy gold, and of natural size, who looked and roared like their brethren of the forest.[49]

surely the following from pp. 87–8 is even more apposite:

> When [Liutprand] approached the throne, the birds of the golden tree began to warble with their notes, which were accompanied by the roarings of the two lions of gold. With his two companions, Liutprand was compelled to bow and to fall prostrate; and thrice he touched the ground with his fore-head. He arose; but, in the short interval, the throne had been hoisted by an engine from the floor to the ceiling, the Imperial figure appeared in new and more gorgeous apparel, and the interview was concluded in haughty and majestic silence. In this honest and curious narrative, the bishop of Cremona represents the ceremonies of the Byzantine court, which are still practised in the Sublime Porte, and which were preserved in the last age by the dukes of Moscovy or Russia ... [50]

With his attention drawn to such mechanical marvels, there is little wonder that he later sought to educate in Byzantine culture the young stage-designer, Norah McGuinness.

7. SICILY AND ROME, 1925

Then in January 1925, short of breath and with high blood pressure, Yeats went to Sicily with his wife and Ezra Pound, and saw, and in historical order, the late Byzantine mosaics in Cefalù, Palermo and Monreale. Mosaics dominated the various cultural sites, a matter of their permanence as an art form, the 'artifice of eternity', but a whole essay might be devoted to what Yeats saw in the rest of the Palazzo Reale. The manager of the Hotel des Palmes proudly showed him Richard Wagner's suite and signature, and told him that the Cappella Palatina had provided the composer with his model for the Chapel of the Grail in *Parsifal.*

Russell Elliott Murphy has covered the Yeatses' excursions in an article valuable for its lists and descriptions of Yeats's collection of postcards, photo-graphs and prints relating to Byzantine mosaics and other souvenirs of his trip to Capri, Sicily and Rome in 1925. The article's title compresses its chief preoccupations: '"Old Rocky Face, look forth": W.B. Yeats, the Christ Pantokrator, and the Soul's History (The Photographic Record)'.[51]

In Christian iconography, the Christ Pantokrator depicts Christ as the omnipotent, or 'Ruler of All'. Predominantly of the Eastern Church, the surviving examples of such an icon are all comparatively late, and the earliest surviving example of the icon of Christ as a stern, all-powerful judge of humanity dates from the sixth or seventh century in St Catherine's Monastery, Mt Sinai. In mosaics, the Pantokrator frequently dominates the late Byzantine apse or dome church decorations – as it does in the apses or domes, of cathedrals, chapels and churches in Cefalù, Palermo and Monreale – almost as a Christian embodiment of Zeus, with stern countenance, right hand raised in blessing, and a New Testament for Judgement in His left, against a gold background, sometimes with Greek letters inlaid. Christ's fingers often represent the Greek letters of the Christogram, ICXC ('Jesus Christ').[52] Murphy's catalogue focuses upon his own great interest in – which amounts to an obsession with – this particular icon, but whether it was, as he repeatedly asserts, the focus of Yeats's interest remains our question.[53] Though his listings are highly important for the serious scholar, this thesis doggedly downplays Yeats's earliest formative experiences of Byzantine mosaics and does so, moreover, without displaying a single image.[54]

Murphy takes his point of departure from a passage in A Vision (1925), which he offers as a headnote to his essay.

> ... can even a visionary of today wandering among the mosaics of Rome and Sicily, fail to recognise some one image seen under his closed eyelids? To me it seems that He, who among the first Christian communities was little but a ghostly exorcist, had in His assent to a full Divinity made possible this sinking-in upon a supernatural splendour, these walls with their little glimmering cubes of blue and green and gold.' (AVB 280–1, CW13 159)

The baffling question is why, beyond his headnote and one or two other stray references in A Vision, Murphy should think this particular icon of Christ to be of overpowering significance to Yeats. As corrected in 1937, the headnote passage reads almost identically, but with a crucial textual change, here highlighted in bold: '... can even a visionary of today wandering among the mosaics at Ravenn[e]a or in Sicily ... (AVB 280–1, emphasis added). This exchange of 'Rome' for 'Ravenne' (corrected after the 1937 edition to 'Ravenna') is rather bashfully conceded by Murphy, but he quite dismisses its significance.[55] For him, the Sicilian and Roman mosaics as seen by Yeats in 1925 are 'the Real Thing, Byzantium in the flesh' (ibid.). This rather suggests that what Yeats had seen in Ravenna and Venice in 1907 was not the 'Real Thing'. For Murphy, the Sicilian trip was 'a study tour in connection with A Vision', and he implies that if Ravenna and its mosaics had really been important to Yeats, he should have revisited them in 1925, an assumption wholly unreasonable given the realities of travel in 1925 for a sixty-year old man in such poor health.[56]

Yeats's periods are of course arbitrarily fixed, and the Sicilian cathedrals, churches and chapels that he saw date from *c.* 1131 through the rest of the twelfth century. Yeats's general point is they were created just when Sicilian Byzantine art, expressing the apogee of Norman power and capital, also presages some gradually approaching humanism.[57] Yeats's Byzantine references are carefully historicized, and while the great focus of his interest remains in fifth- and sixth-century Byzantine art and design, i.e. the Ravenna period, the gradually evolving nature of Byzantine iconography and the lateness of its Sicilian manifestations also have their period interest and importance for him at the end of the fourth section, AD 1 – 1050 of the 'Dove or Swan' part of *A Vision*. Thus Yeats's chosen period ends with 'that stern majesty, borrowed it may be from the Phidean Zeus – if we can trust Cefalù and Monreale', even as the Virgin 'put[s] off her harsh Byzantine image' (*CW13* 163, *AVB* 285).

The impact of Ravenna on Yeats nearly twenty years before the Yeatses' trip to Sicily is simply not weighed by Murphy, who therefore did not appreciate that, for Yeats in *A Vision*, what really matters is the state of Byzantine material culture 'in Byzantium, a little before Justinian opened St. Sophia and closed the Academy of Plato'. In 'early Byzantium ... the painter, the mosaic worker, the worker in gold and silver, the illuminator of sacred books, were almost impersonal, almost perhaps without the consciousness of individual design, absorbed in their subject-matter and that the vision of a whole people' (*AVB* 279–80).

This culture predates that of Norman Sicily by some six centuries, but the ensuing series of circular arguments in an over-elaborate thesis, press home relentlessly and with ritual scolding of all previous commentators. It is simply not the 'indisputable' case, as Murphy insists, that '([t]he matter of Yeats's deeper purposes for viewing these aside for the moment', Yeats 'travelled through Sicily and Italy for the express purpose of visiting the Christ Pantokrators in the Byzantine mosaics to be found in the apses of cathedrals and chapels in Palermo, Monreale, Cefalù and Rome'.[58]

Whilst researches into that icon may have been the inner research agenda of Murphy's own visit in 1992 because it dominates the residual collection of postcards and images, the simple fact is that Christ Pantokrator dominates the twelfth-century churches that Yeats saw, and so the images available for him to buy.[59] Yeats travelled to see Byzantine mosaics in all their materiality, with their changing and growing dynamism and fluidity, to complement the extensive studies he had already made of the subject. Only once does Murphy allow for the converse of his thesis, when he concedes, 'the reader may honestly conclude that in view of the apparent variety of photographic images [which] Yeats acquired at the Palazzo Reale, [that] it was mosaics in general and not any particular interest of his in the Christ Pantokrator to be found in the apse there, as well as other depictions of Christ, that drew him to the chapel [the Cappella Palatina]'.[60]

Perhaps it is Murphy's over-enthusiasm for this icon that leads to his strangest assertion, viz., that Yeats had postcards depicting 'Christ in the aspect of the Pantokrator' from Ravenna.[61] Were it true, such would mark a major discovery, viz. of the world's earliest such usages of the icon.[62] It is apparent, too, that he misreads the rhetoric of Yeats's 'some one image' ('some one' being a catchphrase of growing importance in Yeats's expository prose[63]).

But the truth is that in Sicily Yeats was completing his Byzantine education for 'Dove or Swan'. The cathedrals, chapels and churches that he saw are remarkable for their accommodation of Islamic motifs and arabesque abstract designs, especially in the lower reaches of their walls and their stupendously patterned marble floors, inlaid with differently coloured marbles and semi-precious stone (plate 26), which leave the reader of 'Byzantium' to wonder if it is these which come to supplant the rose-petal patterned floor of the dance in 'Rosa Alchemica' as quoted above with those designed to 'break' the 'mire-and blood bitter furies of 'complexity' as in the poem (*VP* 497–8). The 'little glimmering cubes of blue and green and gold' (*CW13* 159) also certainly caught the 'pitiless intellect' of the Pantokrator in all his 'stern majesty' (*CW10* 212; *AVB* 285; *CW13* 159) especially for a Yeats alarmed at the growing movement to theocratize the Irish Free State.

Plate 26. Arabesque floor design, Cefalù Cathedral

From his seat in the Irish Seanad, Yeats opposed the movement towards state censorship, and, far from surrendering to any attempt to apply the strictures of late Byzantine vision to modern life, though without renouncing the appeal of Byzantine style, the 'artifice of Eternity', for modern Celtic art, Yeats declared:

> For centuries the Platonizing theology of Byzantium had dominated the thought of Europe. Amidst the abstract splendour of its basilicas stood saints with thought-tortured faces and bodies that were but a framework to sustain the patterns and colours of their clothes. The mosaics of the Apse displayed a Christ with face of pitiless intellect [plates 27–29], or a pinched, flat-breasted virgin holding a child like a wooden doll [plate 30]. Nobody can stray into that little Byzantium chapel at Palermo, which suggested the chapel of the Grail to Wagner, without for an instant renouncing the body and all its works and sending all thought up into that heaven the pseudo Dionysius, the Areopagite, fashioned out of the Platonic ideas.[64]

Within fifty years of the death of St Thomas [1225–74] the art of a vision had faded, and an art of the body, an especial glory of the Catholic Church, had inspired Giotto. The next three centuries changed the likeness of the Virgin from that of a sour ascetic to that of a woman so natural nobody complained when Andrea del Sarto chose for his model his wife, or Raphael his mistress, and represented her with all the patience of his 'sexual passion'.[65]

Nevertheless, the materiality and mystery of 'little glimmering cubes of blue and green and gold' remained. During the Sicily trip Yeats was still correcting proofs of *Early Poems and Stories* (published in September 1925) and this may well have been the moment at which he revised his alchemical romance *Rosa Alchemica* (written and first published in 1896, and revised on a number of subsequent occasions) so that references to Byzantine mosaics become a more pervasive part of its iconography, as illustrated by the following example. From 1896 to 1925 a passage in which the unnamed narrator described the furnishings of his private library in Dublin, decorated to conform with every aspect of his extravagant tastes, the following passage had stood:

> ... [T]apestry, full of the blue and bronze of peacocks, fell over the doors, and shut out all history and activity untouched with beauty and peace ... I looked in triumph at the birds of **Hera, glowing in the firelight as though they were wrought of jewels; and** to my mind, for which symbolism was a necessity, they seemed the doorkeepers of my world, shutting out all that was not of as affluent a beauty as their own ... (*Variorum Secret Rose*, 128, emphasis added)

The words highlighted are revised to '... Hera, glittering in the light of the fire as though of Byzantine [later Byzantine] mosaic, and ...'[66]

Plate 27. Choir and apse of Cefalù Cathedral with   Plate 28. Christ Pantokrator in the
Christ Pantokrator, c. 1135 AD.   apse of Monreale Cathedral, 12th C.

Plate 29. Nave, Monreale Cathedral

There is something of an extraordinary sensory challenge in comparing a tapestry to a mosaic throwing back light. Robartes' eyes similarly 'glitter in the firelight, through the incense cloud' (*VSR*, p. 132) but in that instance, his drugged incense is clearly beginning to induce synaesthesia in the narrator, until it leaves 'the peacocks to glimmer and glow as though each separate colour were a living spirit', the narrator being 'drowned in a tide of green and blue and bronze feathers' (*ibid*. pp. 133, 135). So remarkable is this hashish-induced premonition of what mosaic would 'alchemically' come to represent for Yeats, that it brings to mind Yeats's famous definition – *obiter dicta* as it were, to Cecil Salkeld – of Eternity as 'the glitter on the beetle's wing ... it is something infinitely short' (*NC*, p. 249).

VII STORIES OF RED HANRAHAN AND THE SECRET ROSE

I return to that 1927 *Stories of Red Hanrahan and the Secret Rose*, and to its new, Byzantine context and iconography. *October Blast*, privately printed in just 350 copies at the Yeats sisters' Cuala Press in Dublin, had been finished in the first week of June 1927, but not published until October. Before then, its contents had evidently also been submitted to Macmillan in London for inclusion in *The Tower*, which was not published until February 1928.

In 1975 I wrote to Norah McGuinness, who kindly sent me copies of Yeats's letters to her. She died in 1980. The letters were published in an appendix to a new edition of the Variorum Edition of *The Secret Rose* (first published in 1981) in 1992.[67] I draw the following account from my publication of them. McGuinness had graduated from the Metropolitan School of Art in Dublin in 1923 and was at that time connected with the Abbey Theatre, where she designed costumes and masks for *The Only Jealousy of Emer*, directed by Lennox Robinson under Yeats's supervision and presented by the Dublin Drama League at the Abbey on 9 and 10 May 1926. In that production McGuinness danced the part of the Woman of the Sidhe.[68]

Yeats had thereafter sought work for Norah McGuinness with Macmillan from early 1925,[69] parrying, for the moment, the firm's inevitable suggestion that she might illustrate his books. After seeing her illustrations to Laurence Sterne, he relented, writing to his editor, Sir Frederick Macmillan, that while he had always feared having his stories emptied into 'some very British nursery', he had been encouraging her to consider the Byzantine influence on Irish art.

> I suggested to Miss McGuinness the other night that she might, if you cared for the idea, illustrate some stories of mine in the style of Byzantine wall-pictures – we spent the evening looking through photographs of Sicilian mosaics and the like and she went away full of the idea. The reason why I want Byzantium is that there was great Byzantine influence upon Ireland.[70]

Yeats then cited wooden crucifixes in the Byzantine style in Irish private collections, and went on to suggest to Sir Frederick a North Connaught tradition of such art down to 'about 80 years ago' before suggesting that 'a little book containing RED HANRAHAN and THE SECRET ROSE stories' might 'suit admirably for a first experiment ... the two sections could be put together if you wanted a larger book'.[71] When the book had been published, Yeats wrote to Lady Gregory:

> I am also sending you the new edition of "Red Hanrahan" with the archaic illustrations. I lent the artist a lot of Byzantine mosaic photographs & photographs of old Irish crusafixes & asked her to re-create such an art as might have been familiar to the first makers of the tales. The result is I think amusing & vivid.[72]

Sir Frederick Macmillan had so liked 'Sailing to Byzantium' that he then asked to put the poem into the book, saying that it had been McGuinness's idea but also seeking a 'prelude' to this Byzantine experiment in integrated book design. While it certainly could have been the publisher's idea, it could also have been Yeats's, or a joint idea of McGuinness and Yeats routed through McGuinness's agency.[73] Yeats had 'thought first of doing a preface to explain why I put it there' but then thought that 'the dedication to the maker of the pictures' was 'a better explanation'.[74] Preferring to keep himself in the background, he did not directly communicate with Sir Frederick about the volume until that letter of 23 August 1927, when he finally sent a manuscript of 'Sailing to Byzantium' with his approval and precise instructions about the placing of the dedication.[75] The book was published on 11 November 1927, with the printed dedication to McGuinness.

Karen E. Brown, an art historian working very much outside the tradition of Yeats scholarship, has thought about Irish images in the Byzantine style. She reproduces and discusses Yeats's photograph of 'Natività di Gesù' from the Church of the Martorana, Palermo, of which Yeats also retained three postcards.[76] The sequence of images in plates 30–32 show clearly the very similar iconography of the two Nativities, that of the side chapel in the Cappella Palatina, and that in the arched roof of the nave of La Martorana, Palermo. Despite his strictures about flat-chested Virgins in 'The Censorship and St. Thomas Aquinas' quoted above, this remains the dominant icon that Yeats brought back to Ireland from Sicily.

Plate 30. Cappella Palatina, Palermo. The
Nativity, above arch in the apse, with dual
images of (i) journeying and (ii) adoring Magi

Plate 31. 'Natività di Gesù' (The Nativity) from Chiesa di
S. Maria dell'Ammiraglio (church known as La Martorana),
Palermo, and Yeats's image of it

Plate 32. The Nativity, La Martorana, 12th C.

Plate 33. Yeats's photograph of The Nativity from La Martorana,
and Norah McGuinness's frontispiece to Stories of Red Hanrahan
and The Secret Rose

VIII CURVILINEAR LINES: CAVES, MOUNDS, DOMES, WOMBS AND TOMBS[77]

Yeats, it seems, was taken even before he went to Sicily with curvilinear forms, and the starlit cave, unicorn and fountain of Charles Ricketts's design for the endpapers of the various volumes of the 1920s *Collected Works* (plate 34) seems to echo those starlit domes of the Ravenna mosaics (see above, plates 4–5). He wrote to Charles Ricketts, on 5 November [1922]:

> My dear Ricketts: yesterday my wife brought the books up to my study, & not being able to restrain her excitement I heard her cry out before she nocked the door 'You have perfect books at last.' Perfect they are – servisable & perfect. The little design of the unicorn is a masterpiece in that difficult kind. You have given my work a decoration of which one will never tire & all I have done will gradually be put into this form. It is a pleasure to me to think that many young men here & elsewhere will never know my work except in this form.[78]

Such abstract symbols of divinity were everywhere in Byzantine ecclesiastical architecture, and many of the photographs of Byzantine mosaic decorations in O[rmonde] M[addock] Dalton's massive *Byzantine Art and Archaeology* include architectural details such as the arch, usually of the apse or narthex of ecclesiastical buildings.[79] Dalton, with his 467 illustrations, devotes entire chapters to carvings in ivory, murals, mosaics, illuminated manuscripts, textiles, pottery and glass; metal-work, goldsmith's work and jewellery; coins and engraved gems and other forms of ornament; as well as to iconography, and Yeats (or Nora McGuinness) left certain paper strips in Yeats's copy, which were available at the time of O'Shea's initial cataloguing, i.e. between 1971 and eventual publication in 1985, but which were no longer in the volume when I inspected it at the National Library of Ireland in April 2013. Thus O'Shea records such a marker in the opening where a plate of the Nativity somewhat lurking in the roof of the nave of La Martorana, is dimly visible. No doubt as supplemented by Yeats's Alinari print as shown in plates 31 and 33, Norah McGuinness's inspiration for the cave of her frontispiece is revealed.

The cave is itself an arch or dome, as we have seen in the nativity scenes above (plates 30–33) while the Church of the Martorana, Palermo, is intricately caverned with wondrous domes and arches. Many of McGuinness's other illustrations, for example, that for 'The Crucifixion of the Outcast', or the black and white drawing for 'The Death of Red Hanrahan' (plates 35, 36) offer similar curvilinear structures or patterns but none is so striking as that of the frontispiece (plate 33) where the mound or hill conceals the Celtic deity with her sacred symbols of Cauldron, Whetstone, Sword and Spear.

Yeats was, as we have seen, obsessed with the objectification of text possible if an author had control of book cover design. In that same excited reply on seeing the Charles Ricketts end-papers, he wrote,

My own memory proves to me that at 17 there is an identity between an authors imagination & paper & book-cover one does not find in later life. I still do not quite separate Shelley from the green covers, or Blake from the blue covers & brown reproductions of pictures, of the books in which I first read them. I do not separate Rossetti at all from his covers. (CL InteLex, no. 4200)

Plate 34. Charles Ricketts's
endpaper to various volumes
of the 1920s Collected
Works of W.B. Yeats

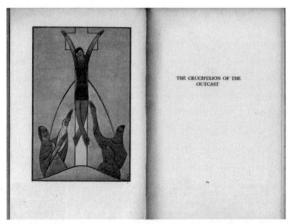

Plate 35. Stories of Red Hanrahan and The Secret
Rose (1927), illustrated by Norah McGuinness in
Byzantine style, as suggested by Yeats

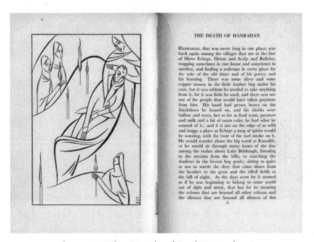

Plate 36. 'The Death of Red Hanrahan',
by Norah McGuinness

Plate 37. Carved ivory book cover, Museo
Nazionale, Ravenna, 6th C., as in Dalton,
Byzantine Art and Archaeology *(1911), p. 210*

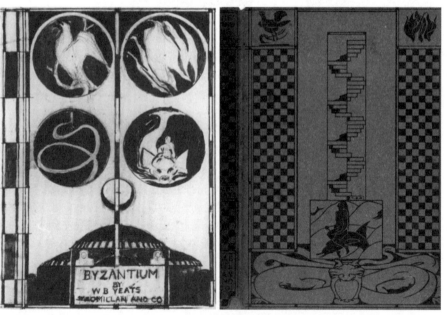

Plates 38 and 39. Sketch of proposed cover design for Byzantium, *later* The Winding
Stair and Other Poems, *1933, by Thomas Sturge Moore (Senate House Library,*
London), and Thomas Sturge Moore's dustjacket replicating top board (blind)
and spine (gilt) of The Winding Stair *(1933)*

Dalton has a whole illustrated section on carved-ivory book covers, including a reproduction of a sixth-century ivory book cover in the museum at Ravenna (pp. 209–10; see plate 37) in the very section marked (at pp. 212–13) by yet another paper slip. Remarkably, the one illustrated feature bas-relief figurines under a central dome.

'Those images that yet / Fresh images beget' said Yeats in 'Byzantium', and suffice it to say that Byzantium nearly became the title of his next book, *The Winding Stair*. A drawing by Thomas Sturge Moore in the Senate House Library of the University of London includes symmetrically placed pairs of plaquettes of birds in a tree and in flames, a winding gyre and a boy on a dolphin (with what appear to be very large ears). Each of these is grouped under two symmetrically domed arches, but underneath the arches is the double dome of Hagia Sophia (plate 38). Yeats told Thomas Sturge Moore:

> Yes I have decided to call the book 'Byzantium'. I enclose the poem from which the name is taken, hoping that it may suggest symbolism for the cover. The poem originates from a criticism of yours. You objected to the last verse of 'Sailing to Byzantium' because a bird made by a goldsmith was just as natural as anything else. That showed me that the idea needed exposition. Gongs were used in the Byzantine churches ... I wrote this poem last spring. The first thing I wrote after my illness.[80]

However, by the time that Sturge Moore had finalized his cover for *The Winding Stair* (1933) (plate 39), economic reality had banished the use of gold stamping as seen on Sturge Moore's previous covers for Yeats. The bird, flames, boy on dolphin, winding stair, mosaic lozenge background, sit above a strange serpent, but again, bilateral symmetries prevail, with the blind-stamped chequer-board lozenges reinforcing the mosaic effect, best seen in the printed dustjacket rather than the identical blind stamping (plate 38). The replacement of the dome of Hagia Sophia with the Winding Stair motif may even be read as indicating Yeats's near exhaustion with Byzantium, his return to Galway, though further poems with Byzantine allusions followed – such as 'The Mother of God' (*VP* 825) – while new references to Byzantine topography and art were infused back into older texts. Even a poem of 1903, 'The Old Age of Queen Maeve', is somewhat effortfully rewritten with a Byzantine frame tale (*VP* 180 *et seq.*).

On closer inspection, and guided by a new and stunning discovery by Robert Nelson, Distinguished Professor of Art History and the History of Culture at Chicago, it is possible to be even more certain of what it was Yeats showed to McGuinness in his library, what dominant Byzantine images she carried away with her, and what it was in the Byzantine style that drew Yeats into his preoccupation with the era of Justinian and Theodora.

Plate 40. 10th C. Icon of St Michael,
Treasury of S. Marco, Venice

Plates 41 and 42. Stories of Red Hanrahan and The Secret Rose *(1927), illustrated by*
Norah McGuinness in Byzantine style, as suggested by Yeats, and from O. M. Dalton,
Byzantine Art and Archaeology, *1911 Plate of 'Enamelled Book Cover', St Michael, Venice*

I refer to a gold enamelled, cloisonné icon in the Treasury of the Basilica di
S. Marco, Venice (plate 40). Nelson focuses on cloisonné enamel in re-examining
Yeats's reading in O.M. Dalton's vast book,[81] what the poem refers to as
'Hammered gold and gold enamelling'. The icon in question is now thought

to be a twelfth-century silver gilt icon of St Michael, on wood and with gold cloisonné enamel and precious stones.[82] In any event, the icon was an apt model for McGuinness's cover, and Nelson is obviously right that Dalton's black and white illustration in Yeats's copy is McGuinness's source (see plates 41–42), whether or not Yeats had seen the original in Venice in 1907.[83]

How curious is the early life of 'Sailing to Byzantium'! It gains a dedicatee after it is published, it propagates in twentieth-century Irish Art the Byzantine vision of her mentor, it offers a new livery for an old book, and helps Yeats, instead of vanishing just then into some imagined transfiguration, to repatriate Byzantium and Byzantine materiality back into Ireland. As Yeats wrote a short time later for a comment on his own work for a radio broadcast of his poems on BBC Belfast, 8 September 1931:

> Now I am trying to write about the state of my soul, for it is right for an old man to make his soul, and some of my thoughts upon that subject I have put into a poem called 'Sailing to Byzantium'. When Irishmen were illuminating the Books of Kells [in the eighth century] and making the jewelled croziers in the National Museum, Byzantium was the centre of European civilisation and the source of its spiritual philosophy, so I symbolise the search for the spiritual life by a journey to that city.[84]

Plates 43 and 44 show a couple of Celtic shrines, or book boxes, Yeats would have seen in the National Museum, and in Trinity College, Dublin. With these images in mind, 'Sailing to Byzantium' and 'Byzantium' may even be seen, perhaps, as a new variant on a very old Irish form: the wonder voyage to the Islands of the Blessed, to Tír na nÓg. More certainly, they offer some atonement for Yeats's having 'doubted' Margaret Stokes's insistence that late antique / medieval Irish renditions of Paradise were Byzantine in inspiration and iconography. The 'scholar' who now would revise his interpretation was Yeats himself, putting Byzantine inspiration into the service of his own *Vision*, his own philosophy, rather than into that of the Rosicrucian mysticism he had studied so ardently as a young man.

It is apt, then, that 'Sailing to Byzantium' replaces the three Rosicrucian stories in *The Secret Rose* which he had divorced from that book as long ago as 1908. In doing so Byzantine iconography returns to Ireland as defiantly as the poem voyages out of it.

This paper is, it may be, merely a piece of patchwork, a review of the work of others, for the scholar is a *sartor resartus*, a patcher repatched. He or she works – like MacGregor Mathers – in patches glued together from the papers of others, artisanship perhaps without permanence. In 'Two Kinds of Asceticism', one of Yeats's great *pensées* on permanence and impermanence, and written when he had just returned from Italy in 1907, Yeats argues that 'no mind is more valuable than the images it contains'.[85] In 'The Municipal Gallery Revisited' he found his 'permanent or impermanent images' (VP 602), yet another apt comment from a man who strove always to create a 'permanent self' in his work, knowing that words themselves made this an intrinsically destabilizing dream, when compared to the permanence of material in that most concrete of arts, Byzantine mosaic.

Plates 43 and 44. An Cathach Shrine, 11th C. National Museum, Dublin, and Shrine of Book of Dimma, 11th C., TCD, Dublin

NOTES

1. W.B. Yeats, *A Vision* (London 1962), pp. 279–80; hereafter *AVB*. The passage is unchanged except in the punctuation of the contraction from its first appearance in *A Vision: An Explanation of Life founded upon the Writings of Giraldus and upon certain Doctrines attributed to Kusta ben Luka* (London: privately printed for subscribers only by T. Werner Laurie Ltd., 1925), hereafter *AVA*.

2. Richard Ellmann, *Yeats, The Man and the Masks* (New York 1948, rev. edn, Penguin, 1979), p. 258.

3. *The Secret Rose, Stories by W.B. Yeats: A Variorum Edition*, eds Warwick Gould, Phillip L. Marcus and Michael Sidnell (Basingstoke 1992), p. 128. Hereafter *Variorum Secret Rose*.

4. See W.B. Yeats, *Later Articles and Reviews: Uncollected Articles, Reviews, and Radio Broadcasts written after 1900*, ed. Colton Johnson (New York 2000), pp. 322, 409.

5. Yeats's letters are best found in an electronic edition, *The Collected Letters after 1907 of W.B. Yeats*, ed. John Kelly, published by InteLex in 2003. Hereafter *CL InteLex*, 4290, 5 September 1926; *October Blast* (Dublin 1927), pp. 1–2.

6. W.B. Yeats, *Stories of Red Hanrahan and The Secret Rose*, Illustrated & Decorated by Norah McGuinness (London 1927).

7. W.B. Yeats, *Early Articles and Reviews: Uncollected Articles and Reviews Written between 1886 and 1900*, eds John P. Frayne and Madeleine Marchaterre (New York 2004), pp. 430–2.

8. See Margaret Stokes, *Early Christian Art in Ireland* (London 1887), pp. 125–8.

9. W.B. Yeats's spellings are always given without emendation.

10. See *Early Articles and Reviews*, p. 432.

11. I am profoundly grateful to Miss Pamela Robinson of the Institute of English Studies for alerting me to this image (the original is now in the Getty Museum) and to Dr Rowan Watson for an image of the Thynne facsimile (plate 9) in the Victoria and Albert Museum.

12. See *Variorum Secret Rose*, pp. 128–9.

13. *The Variorum Edition of the Poems of W.B. Yeats*, eds Peter Allt and Russell K. Alspach (New York 1956, rev. 1966), p. 497. Hereafter *VP*.

14. See Ella Young, *Flowering Dusk* (Toronto 1945), pp. 105–6, quoted in *CL Intelex* (to Lady Gregory, 25 April, [1898]: see also *Collected Letters, II* (1895–1900), p. 214 and n. 1.

15. *Ibid.* 145v., v(vv) meaning variant(s).

16. Giorgio Melchiori, *The Whole Mystery of Art: Pattern into Poetry in the Work of W.B. Yeats* (London 1960), pp. 220 *et seq.* Melchiori believes that Yeats was probably 'struck at first, in the nineties, by a reproduction of the mosaic in the dome of the Ravenna Baptistery' (p. 225). There is a possibility of a circular supposition here, in that Yeats retained among his collection of Byzantine images, photographs and postcards, several from Ravenna, including two Alinari prints of mosaics in the dome of this Baptistery: see Russell Elliott Murphy, '"Old Rocky Face, look forth": W.B. Yeats, the Christ Pantokrator, and the Soul's History (The Photographic Record)' in Richard J. Finneran (ed.), *Yeats: An Annual of Critical and Textual Studies,* xiv, 1996 (Michigan 1998), pp. 69–117 at pp. 80–1, n. 14. Hereafter 'Murphy'. It is possible that Melchiori drew upon images included in the exhibitions which formed the basis of D.J. Gordon (ed.), *Images of a Poet* (Manchester 1961), pp. 81 and ff. Items 182–3. See also below n. 20 and Murphy, pp. 80–1, n. 14.

17. See R. A. Gilbert, *The Golden Dawn Companion: A Guide to the History, Structure and Workings of the Hermetic Order of the Golden Dawn* (Wellingborough 1986), pp. 98–102, 144; Ellic Howe, *The Magicians of the Golden Dawn: the Documentary History of a Magical Order 1887–1923* (London 1972), pp. 84, 97.

18. See Donald R. Pearce, 'The Systematic Rose', *Yeats Annual No. 4* (1986), pp. 195–200, esp. p. 198.

19. See Yeats's *The Speckled Bird: An Autobiographical Novel with Variant Versions*, ed. William H. O'Donnell (Basingstoke 2003), p. 100. Hereafter *Speckled Bird*.

20. See also the Pre-Raphaelite and *fin de siècle* references to Ravenna cited by D.J. Gordon and Ian Fletcher in the 'Byzantium' section of *Images of a Poet* (see above n. 16), pp. 81 and ff. Items 182–3 in Gordon's catalogue of the Yeatses' Alinari prints show views of the dome of this Baptistery: their date is unknown (see p. 90). George Yeats bought Guiseppe Galassi's *Roma o Bisanzio. I Mosaici Di Ravenna E Le Origini Dell'Arte Italiana* (Roma: La Libreria Dello Stato, 1930, *YL*, 725) in Rome in 1934.

21. See Margaret Stokes, *Early Christian Art in Ireland* (London 1887), pp. 125–8, also pp. 177–8 on Ravenna, Classe and evidence of Byzantine influences on Irish architecture, much as she claimed there had been from the ninth to the thirteenth centuries in Ireland.

22. I am grateful for the assistance of Dr Rowan Watson of that Museum, who is advising me on how to take that research forward.

23. 'Constantinople: An Impression', *Harper's Monthly Magazine* 106 (May 1903), 863–70, reprinted in *Cities* (London 1903); 'Constantinople: Three Aspects', *Saturday Review* 95 (13 June, 1903), 741–2.

24. Arthur Symons, *Cities of Italy* (London 1907), not published until October.

25. The Ravenna essay had been published in *Harper's Monthly Magazine* 109 (September, 1904), 618–25.

26. *Ibid.* p. 182.

27. Symons, *Cities of Italy*, p. 175. The book was published in October, 1907.

28. Arthur Symons, *The Fool of the World and Other Poems* (London 1906), p. 58.

29. W.B. Yeats, *Essays and Introductions* (London 1961), p. 509.

30. Arthur Symons, *Cities of Italy* (see above nn. 24–5), pp. 71–118, esp. pp. 78–80, 107–8.

31. W.B. Yeats, *Early Essays,* eds George Bornstein and Richard J. Finneran (New York 2007), p. 187.

32. *Ibid.*

33. See, e.g. *ibid.* p. 185.

34. *Ibid.* pp. 177–8. 'We may not find either mood in its purity, but in mainly tragic art one distinguishes devices to exclude or lessen character, to diminish the power of that daily mood, to cheat or blind its too clear perception. If the real world is not altogether rejected it is but touched here and there, and into the places we have left empty we summon rhythm, balance, pattern, images that remind us of vast passions, the vagueness of past times, all the chimeras that haunt the edge of trance; and if we are painters, we shall express personal emotion through ideal form, a symbolism handled by the generations, a mask from whose eyes the disembodied looks, a style that remembers many masters, that it may escape contemporary suggestion; or we shall leave out some element of reality as in Byzantine painting, where there is no mass, nothing in relief, and so it is that in the supreme moment of tragic art there comes upon one that strange sensation as though the hair of one's head stood up.'

35. *Variorum Secret Rose,* 152v.

36. *VP* 825, first found in *October Blast* (Cuala, 1927, 23).

37. *CL InteLex* 1345, 30 April 1910 to Lady Gregory.

38. See *CL InteLex*, 3 June 1902, 26 July [1903] and *passim* to Eric Maclagan; E.R.D. Maclagan and A.G.B. Russell (eds), *The Prophetic Books of William Blake: Jerusalem* (London 1904). Maclagan's own copy, dated 'Jan. 1904' in a private collection, London, interleaved with corrections, indicates that a further edition was planned. It did not appear. See also *Speckled Bird,* pp. 16 *et. seq.,* and nn.

39. The information is in the first (1968) edition of the *Commentary* (p. 196): see also *A New Commentary on the Poems of W.B. Yeats,* ed. A. Norman Jeffares (London 1984), pp. 215–6, hereafter *NC*. While the source in Liutprand's *Antapodosis* is

cited in A. Norman Jeffares, 'The Byzantine Poems of W.B. Yeats', *Review of English Studies* (January 1946), 44–52 at 48, n. 9, Maclagan is not mentioned there. Maclagan did not die until 1951. His son, Professor Michael Maclagan of Oxford also told Richard J. Finneran, George Mills Harper and William M. Murphy, the editors of *Letters to W.B. Yeats* (London 1977), that his father had actually lent Yeats a copy of Liutprand, 'who is the prime source for the trees and birds of the Byzantine Court', and that he has 'at one moment actually shared lodgings' with Yeats (1, p. 126).

40. See *Variorum Secret Rose*, p. 264.

41. NLI MS 36, 276 (2). I am enormously grateful to Mr Colin McDowell and Dr Neil Mann for assistance with the burgeoning literature of these obscure quarrels among early twentieth-century occultists. Nick Farrell, whose text of Yeats's draft is inaccurate, comments 'The poem is too close to the original Felkin ritual' and 'think[s] Yeats might have suggested it as a replacement' without offering any evidence, remarking further 'It was not used in New Zealand, which was a shame'. See Nick Farrell, *King over the Water: Samuel Mathers and the Golden Dawn* (Dublin n.d.), pp. 139–40.

42. Richard Ellmann, *Yeats: The Man and the Masks*, p. 119.

43. For another, more preliminary, attempt in a manuscript, see Edward O'Shea, *A Descriptive Catalog of W.B. Yeats's Library* (New York & London 1985), item 2013, p. 356. Hereafter *YL*. I am grateful to Colin McDowell and Neil Mann for alerting me to this reference.

44. Richard Ellmann, *Yeats: The Man and the Masks*, p. 119.

45. This first appeared in *The London Mercury* and in *The Dial*, September 1924, and was collected in *The Bounty of Sweden* (Dublin 1925). The present text is quoted from W.B. Yeats, *Autobiographies*, eds William H. O'Donnell and Douglas N. Archibald (New York 1999), hereafter *CW3*, p. 406.

46. The books he owned, consulted and annotated included O.M. Dalton's massive *Byzantine Art and Archaeology* (Oxford 1911); W.G. Holmes's *The Age of Justinian and Theodora: a History of the Sixth Century A.D.* (London 1905), 2 vols.; Margaret Stokes's *Handbook and Guide to Irish Antiquities Collection. Early Christian Art in Ireland. National Museum of Science and Art, Dublin* (Dublin 1911) and Josef Strygowski's *Origin of Christian Church Art* (Oxford 1923), tr. O.M. Dalton and H.J. Braunholtz. See *YL*, items 461, 903, 2009, 2026. The transcriptions of Yeats's marginalia in these entries are far from accurate, but the books themselves, which I have consulted on several occasions, are now in the National Library of Ireland.

47. Strygowski, p. 233, but the whole chapter is also important for the background to Yeats's determination to revive Byzantine styles in modern Celtic art.

48. *VP* 825, first found in *October Blast* [Cuala, 1927], 23. In 'My own Poetry', a BBC reading on 3 July 1937, Yeats explained that the tree and bird were a 'symbol of the intellectual joy of eternity, as contrasted with the instinctive joy of human life'. See W.B. Yeats, *Later Articles and Reviews: Uncollected Articles, Reviews, and Radio Broadcasts written after 1900*, ed. Colton Johnson (New York 2000), p. 286; hereafter *CW10*.

49. *VP* 825. In his edition of Yeats's *Poems*, 2nd edn (New York 1997), p. 615 (London: Macmillan), Richard Finneran claims this was found in volume 6 of J.B. Bury's edition of Gibbon's *The History of the Decline and Fall of the Roman Empire* (London 1909–14), *YL*, 746, where in fact an early *précis* of Luitprand 'describ[es] the decorations of the emperor's square, but at the time of Theophilus' (who ruled 829–42 AD): 'His fanciful magnificence employed the skill and patience of such artists as the times could afford; but the taste of Athens would have despised their frivolous and costly labours: a golden tree, with its leaves and branches, which sheltered a multitude of birds, warbling their artificial notes, and two lions of massy gold, and of the natural size, who looked and roared like their brethren of the forest' (p. 81). However, see next footnote. Jeffares (*NC*, pp. 215–6), thinks it comes from a 'well-known passage' in Liutprand of Cremona, related to him *c.* 1910 by Eric Maclagan. The pages are unmarked in *YL*, 746.

50. *Ibid.* pp. 87–8. In a recent translation of the *Antapodosis* of Luitprand, the passage reads 'In front of the emperor's throne stood a certain tree of gilt bronze, whose branches, similarly gilt bronze, were filled with birds of different sizes, which emitted songs of the different birds corresponding to their species. The throne of the emperor was built with skill in such a way that at one instant it was low, then higher, and quickly it appeared most lofty; and lions of immense size (though it was unclear if they were of wood or of brass, they certainly were coated with gold) seemed to guard him, and, striking the ground with their tails, they emitted a roar with mouths open and tongues flickering. Leaning on the shoulders of two eunuchs, I was led into this space, before the emperor's presence. And when, upon my entry, the lions emitted their roar and the birds called out, each according to its species, I was not filled with special fear or admiration, since I had been told about all these things by one of those who knew them well. Thus, prostrated for a third time in adoration before the emperor, I lifted my head, and the person whom earlier I had seen sitting elevated to a modest degree above the ground, I suddenly spied wearing different clothes and sitting almost level with the ceiling of the mansion. I could not understand how he did this, unless perchance he was lifted up there by a pulley of the kind by which tree trunks are lifted. Then, however, he did not speak at all for himself, since, even if he wished to, the great space between us would render it unseemly, so he asked about the life of Berengar and his safety through a minister. When I had answered him reasonably and when his interpreter gave a sign, I left and was soon received in the hostel assigned to me.' See *The Complete Works of Luidprand of Cremona*, translated with an introduction and notes by Paolo Squatriti (Washington, D.C. 2007), pp. 197–8. On the Byzantine automata, see Gerard Brett, 'The Automata in the Byzantine "Throne of Solomon"', *Speculum* 29 (1954), 477–87.

51. Murphy: for full citation, see above, n. 15.

52. The Greek characters *Iota* (I) and *Sigma* (Σ) being the first and last letters of Jesus (Ιησους), the letters X&C representing *Chi* (X) and *Sigma* (ς), the first and last letters of Christ (Χριστος). The Cefalù Pantokrator (plate 26) has the Latin words 'Factus Homo Factus Hominis Factique Redemptor Iudico Corporeus Corpora Corda Deus', roughly 'Made man, Maker of Man, and Redeemer of what I made, I Judge in Body the Bodies and Hearts as God.'

53. Murphy: see esp. pp. 80–1.

54. See especially pp. 80–1 n. 14; pp. 90–6.

55. See Murphy, p. 71.

56. Murphy does pause over Curtis Bradford's information that Yeats 'did not return to Ravenna, being fearful of its miasmal air'. See Curtis Bradford, 'Yeats's Byzantium Poems: A Study of their Development' in John Unterecker, *Yeats: A Collection of Critical Essays* (Engelwood Cliffs, NJ: Prentice-Hall, 1963), pp. 93–4, and Murphy, p. 77. That Bradford does not cite a source I find less worrying than does Murphy: Bradford was, after all, very closely working at the time on Yeats's MSS with Mrs Yeats, for whom Yeats's health had been of paramount concern. And, as we have noted, Symons had found Ravenna 'languid with fever' (see above n. 27).

57. In so far as distinctions can be discerned between the various twelfth-century Pantokrators in Cefalù, Palermo and Monreale, it could be argued that a milder Pantokrator is to be found in the later depictions. See, e.g. the lavish illustrations in Rodo Santoro, *The Palatine Chapel and Royal Palace* (Palermo 2010), pp. 42–3 and Lisa Sciortino, *The Cathedral of Monreale* (Palermo 2012), p. 43.

58. Murphy, p. 101, emphasis added.

59. Murphy assumes that Yeats's Sicilian journey can be dated from Pound's letters, which in turn assumes that the Yeatses and Pounds travelled together for the entire journey. Ann Saddlemyer is rather more definite: the Yeatses left for Sicily on 5 January, spent 'not much more than a fortnight' with the Pounds, made day trips to Cefalù and Monreale from Palermo, and found the mosaics at Monreale more exciting (seen in 'better weather') than those in the Palazzo Reale. Whilst of course there must have been more than one visit to the Cappella Palatina, Cefalù's Cathedral, with its apse dominated by the earliest and perhaps the harshest of the Sicilian domed icons of Christ Pantokrator (see plate 26), could certainly have been visited in a one-day visit. Without further explanation, Saddlemyer believes that 'Sicily was on the whole a disappointment': see her *Becoming George: The Life of Mrs W.B. Yeats* (Oxford 2002), p. 340.

60. Murphy, p. 95. I endorse this view, having seen all the Sicilian and Ravenna mosaics.

61. Murphy, pp. 80–1, n. 15.

62. *Ibid.*: Murphy confuses the Pantokrator with Christ as Redeemer (i.e., making the blessing sign, but without his New Testament and so not as a Judge) surrounded by Angels from S. Apollinare Nuovo.

63. A special sub-category of Yeats's use of 'some' with an air of studied vagueness, as in 'some stray cactus' for mescal (*Essays and Introductions*, p. 283). Out of dozens of such usages in Yeats's prose, one might compare it to 'I have often had the fancy that there is some one myth for every man, which, if we but knew it, would make us understand all he did and thought', or 'there is for every man some one scene, some one adventure, some one picture that is the image of his secret life' (*Essays and Introductions*, pp. 107, 95), or 'the creative power of the lyric poet depends upon his accepting some one of a few traditional attitudes, lover, sage, hero, scorner of life. They bring us back to the spiritual norm' (*AVB* 234).

64. Yeats soon found that he had to defend the statement about Wagner and the Cappella Palatina against the challenge of Annie Horniman, and did so robustly, writing to the Editor of the *Irish Statesman* on 13 October 1928: 'Miss Horniman is in the right when she says that Wagner got part of the painted scene, that represents the Chapel of the Grail, from the Certosa of Pavia, part from the Alhambra, and she might have added part from that fine Cathedral in Siena which is striped like a zebra. But she is wrong in supposing that I spoke of his deplorable stage scenery. Wagner paid a visit to Palermo towards the end of his life, and, though Ellis' translation of Glasenapp's biography makes no mention of the journey, it is recorded on the wall of the Hotel des Palmes, and should Miss Horniman visit there the manager will show her Wagner's room and I think the pen he wrote with, and some guide will bring her to the Capella Palatina where Wagner went day after day seeking – unless local patriotism deceive itself – an idea powerful enough to call into his hearer's mind the Chapel of the Grail.' (*CL InteLex* 5176). The Yeatses had, it would seem, also stayed at the Hotel des Palmes.

65. See 'The Censorship and St. Thomas Aquinas' in *CW10*, pp. 212 & nn. The piece was first published in the *Irish Statesman* on 22 September 1928.

66. *Variorum Secret Rose*, p. 128 and 128v, cf., 'a supernatural splendour, these walls with their little glimmering cubes of blue and green and gold' (*AVB* 280–1; *CW13* 159).

67. *Variorum Secret Rose*, pp. 271–86.

68. Liam Miller, *The Noble Drama of W.B. Yeats* (Dublin 1977), pp. 246–8, and plate xxiii). Norah McGuinness's own memories of the occasion, on which a droll remark by Yeats about her gold body paint leading to her poor performance, is vividly retold in her 'Young Painter and Elderly Genius', in *W.B. Yeats, 1865–1965: A Centenary Tribute*; Supplement to *The Irish Times*, 10 June 1965, vi.

69. *CL InteLex*. See accession nos. 4693, 4712, and London, British Library, Additional MS 55003, ff. 85–7, to Sir Frederick Macmillan, 4 January and 17 April 1925, hereafter BL, Add. MS.

70. *CL InteLex*, accession 4959, to Sir Frederick Macmillan, 14 Dec., 1926.

71. BL, Add. MS 55003, ff. 95–6. For Yeats's numerous alternative suggestions which show his close practical interest in book-making, see *Variorum Secret Rose*, p. 280, n. 34, which includes the following deduction: 'At no point does Yeats seem to have entertained the idea that the section headed ROSA ALCHEMICA and including 'The Tables of the Law' and 'The Adoration of the Magi' should be included in this "first experiment". The implication is that after so much rearrangement of his text, he had come to see each of these sections as discrete entities, and had stopped seeing the three last-named stories as indivisibly part of an entity called *The Secret Rose*.'

72. *CL InteLex* 5081 [24 February 128].

73. London, BL, Add. MS 55003, f. 99; 55657 f. 466, 25 August 1927. See also *Variorum Secret Rose*, p. 281 and n. 38. It is likely that Yeats initiated the idea, but allowed Norah McGuinness to propose it to Macmillan herself, probably at a meeting with Sir Frederick on 25 May 1927 (BL, Add. MS 55652 f. 500, 17 May 1927). Sir Frederick Macmillan wrote to Norah McGuinness on 14 July 1927, to

acknowledge receipt of the smaller decorations or vignettes, and added 'I have not heard anything from Mr. Yeats about the additional poem, but I am rather expecting a letter from him so perhaps we shall hear soon. Of course, if he adds a poem to the volume it will certainly be a good thing' (BL, Add. MS 55656, f. 533).

74. *CL InteLex* Accession Number: 5018. In this letter, marked 'Private', Yeats wrote to Sir Frederick Macmillan on 23 August [1927]: 'Miss McGuinness tells me that you would like to have my poem 'Sailing to Byzantium' as a prelude to the volume of my stories which she is illustrating. I thought first of doing a preface to explain why I put it there but I think the dedication to the maker of the pictures a better explanation. I enclose the poem which should be followed by "To the secret rose" the old prelude to the book.': see *Variorum Secret Rose*, pp. 281–2.

75. ' "To the secret rose" should be dated 1896, I have dated "Sailing to Byzantium" 1926' *(*BL, Add. 55003, f. 99). In the event, 'Sailing to Byzantium' was included on the first recto (p. 3) after the half-title headed STORIES OF RED HANRAHAN, and the words '(DEDICATED TO NORAH MCGUINNESS)' appeared under its title. The printed date is in fact 1927: no date is given after 'To the Secret Rose', which appears in the corresponding position in the section headed THE SECRET ROSE. The change of date could have been made by Yeats himself: proof of sheet B, including 'Sailing to Byzantium', was sent to him on 7 September and returned by 14 September 1927 (BL, Add. MS55003, f. 100; BL, Add. MS 55658, ff. 103, 299): see *Variorum Secret Rose*, pp. 281–2.

76. Karen E. Brown, *The Yeats Circle, Verbal and Visual Relations in Ireland, 1880–1939* (Farnham 2011). See Ch. 3, 'W.B. Yeats, Norah McGuinness and Irish Modernism', pp. 65–89. See however *Variorum Secret Rose*, Appendix 5, pp. 271–86, and Murphy, p. 94, item 46 (Brogi No. 11373).

77. See also Murphy, pp. 103 & ff.

78. *CL InteLex*, No. 4200. For Yeats on the symbolism of caves and fountains, see *Essays and Introductions*, pp. 80–5.

79. Oxford: Clarendon, 1911, *YL*, 461.

80. ALS Texas. Bridge, 164. 4 October [1930] InteLex Accession Number: 5390.

81. Robert S. Nelson, *Hagia Sophia, 1850–1950: Holy Wisdom Modern Monument* (Chicago 2004), pp. 132–3.

82. See cat. item 58 in *Byzantium 330–1453*, ed. Robin Cormack and Maria Vassilaki (London: Royal Academy of Arts, 2009), cover image and pp. 116–7. The original measures 46.5 x 35 x 2.7 cm.

83. *Byzantine Art and Archaeology*, fig. 306, *YL*, 461.

84. See W.B. Yeats, *Later Articles and Reviews*, ed. Colton Johnson (New York 2000), p. 392. The passage was cut from the broadcast as delivered, and it may also be found in *Yeats's Poems*, ed. A. Norman Jeffares (London: Macmillan, 1989), p. 576, and in *NC*, p. 213.

85. *Essays and Introductions*, p. 286.

A. E. I. O. U.: *George Russell, National Being*

JOSÉ LANTERS

George Russell (1867–1935), who came to be known as 'Æ', was a man of many talents. Poet, painter, theosophist, organizer of agricultural co-operatives, and writer on economics, newspaper editor: he did it all. But Russell was, above all, a man you went to for assistance. In literary circles, Æ is less known for his own poetry than for his unfailing encouragement of other writers, especially those at the beginning of their careers. His friend Simone Téry summed up his talent for supporting others as follows:

> Have you doubts regarding Providence, the origin of the universe and its end? Go see Æ.
>
> Are you seeking information on Gaelic literature, the Celtic soul, Irish history? Go see Æ – Are you interested in painting? Go see Æ – Do you want to know the exports of eggs or how best to cultivate bees? Go see Æ – Do you find society badly run, and want to better it? Run to Æ ... – You doubt yourself? Find life insipid? Æ will give you confidence, will comfort you. – Do you need a friend? Æ is always there.[1]

For Irish writers, Æ was indeed always there. James Joyce was one of these writers.

George Russell appears several times in Joyce's *Ulysses*.[2] Leopold Bloom is overtaken in the street by 'the eminent poet, Mr Geo. Russell' in the 'Lestrygonians' episode: 'His eyes followed the high figure in homespun, beard and bicycle, a listening woman at his side. Coming from the vegetarian.

... Those literary ethereal people they are all. Dreamy, cloudy, symbolistic. Esthetes they are' (*Ulysses*, p. 136). Leopold Bloom, being the unethereal and earthy person he is, is mainly interested in food, it being lunchtime, and in the woman at Russell's side – who may or may not be Lizzie Twigg, one of the women who answered his ad in the paper which asked for a lady 'to aid gentleman in literary work' (*Ulysses*, p. 136). Russell did have an ethereal side, which sometimes got on people's nerves. The Rev. Stopford Brooke, very solid himself and editor of the well-known *A Treasury of Irish Poetry*, told a friend: 'George Russell, the Irish poet, came in to dine. And he talked – opalescently. ... Everything he saw was either opalescent or irridescent, and I wished at times he would opalescence himself into an irridescent vision' (Kain, p. 19). If Russell's head was sometimes in the clouds, however, his feet were planted firmly on the ground. In the same year of his dinner with Stopford Brooke, 1898, Æ wrote to Yeats: 'I have found that around Mt Nephin the atmosphere is so thick with faerys that you draw them in with every breath' – only to continue: 'I may have to go to Arran Isles in a week or so. I have written to the P[arish] P[riest] there offering to organise a bank'.[3] The dreamer was really a very practical man.

In *Ulysses*, Stephen Dedalus encounters Russell in the National Library in the 'Scylla and Charybdis' episode an hour or so after Bloom sees him in the street. Through Stephen's eyes, again we see 'a tall figure in bearded homespun', 'an ollav, holy-eyed' (*Ulysses*, p. 151). Stephen is concerned with his poverty and his future as a poet. Russell is rumoured to be putting together a volume of poems by young writers, but while James Stephens and Padraic Colum are mentioned in connection with the project, Stephen is not. (Russell indeed failed to include Joyce in his collection.) He is, however, in Æ's debt, in that he owes him money; or does he? He muses: 'Five months. Molecules all change. I am other I now. Other I got pound ... .' But, he concludes, 'I, ... am I by memory ... ', and therefore, 'A. E. I. O. U.' (*Ulysses*, p. 156). Actually, Stephen owes Æ more than money, for Russell has been making the young poet the topic of his conversation. In the 'Aeolus' episode, J.J. O'Molloy tells Stephen: 'Æ has been telling some yankee interviewer that you came to him in the small hours of the morning to ask him about planes of consciousness. Magennis thinks you must have been pulling Æ's leg.' (*Ulysses*, p. 115) Stephen is inwardly excited and apprehensive: 'Speaking about me. What did he say? What did he say? What did he say about me? Don't ask.' (*Ulysses*, p. 116)

Stephen does not ask, but we have no such scruples. We already know what James Joyce's *Ulysses* says about George Russell; but what did George Russell say about James Joyce? What did he say about other writers mentioned in 'Scylla and Charybdis' who also owed Æ a debt? And what did they say about him? Let us first look at Joyce and the story Russell told the Yankee interviewer about Stephen.

One summer night in 1902, Joyce decided to call upon Russell, on a whim. It was ten o'clock at night. Æ was not at home, but Joyce walked up and down the street until Russell returned at midnight. Joyce then knocked at the door and asked if it was too late to talk to him. 'It's never too late', Russell generously replied, and let him in. They talked for hours: Joyce complained about Yeats, spoke negatively about other writers and read Russell his poems but told him he was not interested in his opinion. Russell told young Jim what he thought anyway: to be more experimental and to steer away from traditional and classical forms. Joyce also asked Russell about his theosophical beliefs. Initially, Æ thought he had a convert on his hands, but Joyce quickly disabused him of that notion. He was merely collecting material for future reference. After the meeting, Æ wrote to Sarah Purser: 'I expect to see my young genius on Monday and will find out more about him. I wouldn't be his Messiah for a thousand million pounds. He would be always criticising the bad taste of his deity' (Denson, pp. 42–3). Around the same time Æ wrote to Yeats:

> I want you very much to meet a young fellow named Joyce ... . He is an extremely clever boy who belongs to your clan more than to mine and more still to himself ... . Moore who saw an article of this boy's says it is preposterously clever. Anyhow I think you would find this youth of 21 with his assurance and self-confidence rather interesting. He is I think certainly more promising than Magee. (Denson, p. 43)

(The pseudonym of W.K. Magee was, of course, John Eglinton, and he also appears in *Ulysses*.) Yeats and Joyce did meet, in a café. Neither was impressed with the other. Joyce told Yeats: ' "I am not, as you see, treating you with any deference, for after all both you and I will be forgotten".' Yeats later told his friends that he had never seen combined in one person ' "[s]uch a colossal self-conceit with such a Lilliputian literary genius" '.[4]

Joyce was always happy to accept the help of others, and always did so with bad grace. When he went off to France in December 1902, Russell wrote to Maud Gonne and Lady Gregory to find acquaintances in Paris who might be of help to Joyce. Joyce entrusted his manuscripts to George Russell – 'to flatter him for future use' as he told his brother Stanislaus (Ellmann, p. 109). And future use there would be. Two years later, Joyce was again leaving Ireland for the continent, this time with Nora Barnacle. The fare to Zurich for two plus luggage was eight pounds ten shillings, which Joyce borrowed from his literary acquaintances. Lady Gregory gave five pounds; Joyce repaid her by writing an unfavourable review of her *Poets and Dreamers* for the *Daily Express*. In *Ulysses*, Buck Mulligan castigates Stephen for writing badly about 'that old hake Gregory's' book: 'She gets you a job on the paper and then you go and slate her drivel to Jaysus. Couldn't you do the Yeats touch?' (*Ulysses*, pp. 177–8). George Russell gave ten shillings and said he 'pitied the poor girl whom Joyce would certainly abandon'.[5] Joyce repaid him by writing several poems he knew Russell would not like, telling his brother: 'So damn Russell … damn vegetable verse and double damn vegetable philosophy!' (Ellmann, p. 121).

George Russell was not above criticizing his literary colleagues either, but his comments were never self-serving or mean-spirited, and often prompted by fair-mindedness and the perception of injustice done to others. In 1914, for example, he wrote to John Quinn:

> I did not care much for Lady Gregory's book *Our Irish Theatre*. She central-izes herself a great deal too much, and I think she gives too little credit to the Fays [Frank and Willie Fay, who shaped the acting style of the Abbey theatre actors] … . I think historians of movements ought to be generous to those obscure folk who work at the foundations and did all the hard work, unthanked, when nobody looked on or praised them. I knew all about their work before Yeats or Lady Gregory came on the scene at all, and I always felt the Fays never got the credit they were entitled to get. It was at their sugges-tion, not Yeats or Lady Gregory's, that the National Theatre was formed. (Denson, pp. 96–7)

Æ had been great friends with Yeats, but in 1916 he wrote to George Moore: 'He bores me terribly now, and he was once so interesting … . Why can't he be natural? Such a delightful creature he was when young! And at rare moments when he forgets himself he is still interesting as ever almost' (Denson, p. 110).

Russell knew that most writers in his circle did not have his generosity and fair-mindedness. The thought of George Moore working on his assessment of the Literary Revival and its representatives – later published as *Hail and Farewell* – caused Æ a certain amount of anxiety. He wrote to John Quinn in 1909:

> George Moore … has now turned with renewed ferocity to his farewell book. He told me a couple of weeks ago 'Russell, I have just written over 2000 words about you'. I nervously enquired whether I might see them, but he said: 'No, you will see them later on', and I don't know what the fiend has written. Anyhow, we are good friends and I don't think he intends to say anything very hard. I think he is probably keeping most of his satire for the Church and W.B.Y. (Denson, p. 67)

Æ was right about Moore: the satire is very gentle. This is some of what he said about Russell.

The reason I have not included any personal description of Æ is because he exists rather in one's imagination, dreams, sentiments, feelings, than in one's ordinary sight and hearing, and try as I will to catch the fleeting outlines, they escape me; and all I remember are the long, grey, pantheistic eyes that have looked so often into my soul and with such a kindly gaze.

Those are the eyes, I said, that have seen the old Celtic Gods; for certainly Æ saw them when he wandered out of the accountant's office in his old shoes, into Meath, and lay under the trees that wave about the Druid hills ... . Never did a doubt cross my mind that these great folk had appeared to Æ until he put a doubt into my mind himself, for he not only admitted that he did not know Irish (that might not be his fault, and the Gods might have overlooked it, knowing that he was not responsible for his ignorance), but that he did not believe in the usefulness of the Irish language.

But how, then, am I to believe that the Gods have appeared to you? ...

The Gods, he answered, speak not in any mortal language; one becomes aware of their immortal Presences.[6]

By his own account, Moore then becomes annoyed at the conversation and goes off to talk to John Eglinton, who, he says, has never communed with the Gods. When the third part of Moore's *Hail and Farewell, Vale*, appeared in 1914, Æ was not comforted. He wrote: 'Moore's Vale is out, the most scandalous of all his books. I escaped with a halo, but halos fixed on one's brow by the wicked don't add to one's glory. I can't help liking Moore in spite of his bad taste. He is no hypocrite and is never afraid to say what he thinks.' (Denson, p. 96)

Russell was also not afraid to express his thoughts; they just happened to be a good deal more generous than Moore's, and were often combined with positive action. In 1909, Æ encountered James Stephens, then the young author of *Insurrections*. 'He is quite a boy', Æ wrote to Quinn, 'but I think he has great promise.' (Denson, p. 66) When Macmillan rejected a selection of Stephens's poems, Æ commented: 'I asked him to let me see the verses he sent because I doubted whether he had yet acquired any faculty of self-criticism.' He then asked if he could submit a different set of poems, because 'Stephens has I think more talent than any of our younger writers here'. (Denson, p. 71) Ultimately, however, Æ did not think Stephens's talent was in verse: 'he has a great splash of genius, and is poor and I wanted to help him. I think he will be a great story-teller, and he has got a masterpiece or 2 concealed in his skull. Anyhow he is one of the most vivid, vital and delightful persons I know in Ireland, entirely loveable.' (Denson, p. 74) By 1913 he is pleased to see that Stephens 'has suddenly leaped up to the fame which I had prophesied from the first writing' (Denson, p. 78) but regrets that there are no younger men than he appearing on the Irish literary scene.

Russell's earlier protégé, James Joyce, first met James Stephens in 1912, and their initial meeting was not so promising. Stephens wrote about the encounter: 'We were very different-looking people. Joyce was tall, which I wasn't; he was thin, which I wasn't; he wore specs, which I didn't; he looked down at me, which I couldn't; he rubbed his chin at me, which I wouldn't.' (Ellmann, p. 333) Much later in his career, however, Joyce apparently came round to Æ's opinion of Stephens, and designated him as the man to finish *Finnegans Wake* in the event of his own untimely death, noting that they shared a name, James, a birthday, 2 February, and a birthplace, Dublin (Joyce was very superstitious about such coincidences). Stephens was more amused than bemused by the idea, and later wrote:

> Well, I was astonished. I was admired at last. Joyce admired me. I was beloved at last: Joyce loved me. Or did he? Or did he only love his birthday, and was I merely coincident to that? When I spoke about my verse, which was every waking minute of my time, Joyce listened heartily and said 'Ah'. He approved of it as second of February verse, but I'm not certain that he really considered it to be better than the verse of Shakespeare and Racine and Dante. And yet he knew the verse of those three exhaustively! ... So upon our next birthday I sent him a small poem ... . Joyce reported back to me that he was much obliged. He practically said 'Ah' to my poem, and I could almost see him nibbing his chin at it. (Ellmann, p. 593)

Stephens and Joyce were very different in other ways, too. Where Joyce had shamelessly borrowed money from Æ, Stephens had to be coaxed into accepting gifts. In 1915, Russell wrote to him: 'Your letter seems to indicate financial difficulties. Is that so? Can I help according to my means? You know, James darling, I would do what I could if you let me know.' (Denson, pp. 106–7) When Stephens was ill two years later, Æ felt he needed to be sent on a holiday, and conceived a plan: 'if a dozen of his friends contributed two or three pounds apiece we could hand Mrs Stephens the money for the purpose and let her go with James to some good hotel in a mild quarter of Ireland.' (Denson, p. 121) Stephens, of course, was to be kept in the dark as to the source of the money.

George Russell had a hand in starting the writing careers of many important Irish writers, and he is perhaps to be forgiven a little bias in favour of the writers of his own country. In 1925 he wrote to Ernest Boyd:

> I do not find as much pure literature in all the States with one hundred and ten million people as came out of Ireland in the last thirty years. Wilde, Shaw, Moore, Synge, Yeats, Hyde, Lady Gregory, James Stephens, Padraic Colum, Sean O'Casey, Standish O'Grady, Corkery and the rest. Perhaps it is only ignorance of American writers makes me think this or national egomania. (Denson, p. 167)

As for the English poets, he wrote to Frank O'Connor in 1934, after he had moved to England: 'It is this sensation of emptiness which frightens me here. The poets like Eliot and Spender have no light in their minds. They are the dead end, and when Eliot writes a volume of criticism of poetry the effect is to make me never want to read poetry any more in the world, the criticism is so dry and joyless.' (Denson p. 209) Ezra Pound he at first designated 'the keeper of a literary museum', but later he wrote of his *Selected Poems*: 'The book almost convinces me that the man of talent, if he be serious enough about his art, may approach the work of genius.'[7]

In spite of Russell's worries about the scarcity of young writers of promise on the Irish literary scene after James Stephens, there were, of course, a few more, and they received the same encouragement from Russell that he had given their predecessors. In 1926 he recommended Liam O'Flaherty to Seán Ó'Faoláin: 'My feeling about O'Flaherty is that he is a genius when he imagines and creates, and a goose, a delightful goose, when he thinks and reasons ... . O'Flaherty is a clever fellow and in ten years time his intellect will have developed and then if he keeps his genius he may do something really big.' (Denson, p. 172) In 1930 he recommended Frank O'Connor to Macmillan & Co: 'He is a young man of very great talent, an admirable poet and something of a scholar.' (Denson, p. 189) Æ was never far wrong. Meanwhile, he complained, 'Yeats takes himself very seriously as senator. I wish he would write poetry.'

George Russell's final protégé was the poet Patrick Kavanagh. From 1927 onwards, Kavanagh had bicycled the twenty-four mile return journey every week from the black hills of his village of Mucker in County Monaghan to Dundalk to buy a copy of Æ's paper *The Irish Statesman*. The paper had introduced him to contemporary Irish poetry, and in 1929 Æ had accepted three of Kavanagh's poems for publication. One day in 1931 Æ opened his front door, and there was Kavanagh, who had walked all of the sixty miles from County Monaghan to Dublin to see him. The end of 1931 was a bad time for Russell. His friend Kingsley Porter had drowned in a boating accident, and his wife was very ill in hospital. Kavanagh recalls his first impression of the man who opened the door to him: 'I was afraid of that man. He looked like a man who had awakened from a dark trance. His eyes stared at me like two nightmare eyes from which there was no escape.' (Summerfield, p. 263)

Æ invited him in, they talked, and when Kavanagh left again Æ gave him a pile of books to take with him, including Emerson, Dostoyevski, Whitman, Stephens, Plato, Hugo and others. Kavanagh returned to Monaghan by train, which was just as well. In a 1946 interview, Kavanagh recalled his visit to Æ:

He was very good to me, quite friendly. He made tea for me. I admired the fact that he was a good man, and I know that there is a tendency now to make little of him on account of his work, but I think he himself was a great work. I never met Yeats but I would say Æ was a much holier man. I'd say greater in every way, except that Yeats was a very fine writer, but I liked Æ. I think that any man who contributes virtue, goodness and that kind of nobility which really is something, produces a union of hearts far more than any Wolfe Tonery.[8]

Upon Æ's death, Mrs Yeats is supposed to have told her husband: 'Æ was the nearest to a saint you or I will ever meet. You are a better poet but no saint.' (Summerfield, p. 286)

Characteristically, Russell saw his own admirable qualities as reflections of the goodness of others. In 1934, a year before his death, he wrote to the English poet Ruth Fitter:

I only want to say you were an angel to come here. You are one of the best companions. You have the airy element in your nature predominant so that you never get entangled in things like those with the watery nature. You will rise above London and its fogs and its business because of that airy element, which makes you a free creature as far as mortals may be free. All my friends whom I love have that airy nature, all I loved. If you ever come across James Stephens you will find he has it … . I have only enough of it to adore it in others.' (Denson, p. 214)

James Stephens, for one, recognized that George Russell had plenty of airiness when he said of him: 'He inclined to sit on the top of the morning all day.' (Kain, p. 19)

Just hours before he died, Æ told Oliver St John Gogarty (who was portrayed as Buck Mulligan in Ulysses): 'I have realized all my ambitions. I have had an astounding interest in my life. I have great friends. What more can a man want?' (Summerfield, p. 284)

NOTES

1. *George Russell (Æ)*, R.M. Kain and J. H. O'Brien (Lewisburgh, PA 1976), p. 15 [hereafter Kain].
2. *Ulysses*, James Joyce (New York 1986), hereafter *Ulysses*.
3. *Letters from Æ*, ed. Alan Denson (London 1961), pp. 26–7 [hereafter Denson].
4. *James Joyce*, Richard Ellmann, rev. edn (Oxford 1982), p. 101 [hereafter Ellmann].
5. *Nora: A biography of Nora Joyce*, Brenda Maddox (London 1988), p. 65.
6. *Hail and Farewell*, George Moore, ed. Richard Cave (Gerrards Cross, 1985), p. 142.
7. *That Myriad Minded Man: A Biography of G.W. Russell 'Æ', 1867–1935*, Henry Summerfield (Gerrards Cross 1975), p. 235 [hereafter Summerfield].
8. *Patrick Kavanagh: Sacred Keeper*, Peter Kavanagh (The Curragh 1979), pp. 48–9.

Elegy and Affirmation in W.B. Yeats's The Winding Stair

PATRICK J. KEANE

I

The text we know as *The Winding Stair and Other Poems* (1933) combines *The Winding Stair* (New York: Fountain Press, 1929) and *Words for Music Perhaps* (Cuala Press, 1932). The Fountain Press edition, limited to 642 signed copies (one of which I own), is a slender volume consisting of just a half-dozen poems, two ('Death' and 'Oil and Blood') quite short. The others are 'In Memory of Eva Gore-Booth and Con Markiewicz', 'A Dialogue of Self and Soul', 'Blood and the Moon', and the eleven-poem sequence, *A Woman Young and Old*, almost completed before 1928 but, Yeats notes (*Variorum,* p. 831), 'left out' of *The Tower* for 'some reason' he couldn't 'recall', but which seems obvious given the presence of the parallel 'Man' sequence in *The Tower*. Both the 1929 and the 1933 volumes begin with the same five poems. Between them and *A Woman Young and Old*, Yeats added twenty-three poems, several little more than epigrams, but also including such major poems as the two Coole Park elegies and 'Vacillation'. And, to his insertion of the lyrics first printed in *Words for Music Perhaps*, originally opened by 'Byzantium' he added 'Crazy Jane Talks with the Bishop', in which Jane, dramatically embodying the volume's fusion of sexuality and spirituality, punningly but seriously insists that 'Nothing can be sole or whole / That has not been rent.'

My focus on the shape of the 1933 volume, the way in which Yeats hammered these materials into unity, is less editorial than thematic. It is significant that 'A Dialogue of Self and Soul', my principal text in this essay, retains its centrality, and that both the 1929 *Winding Stair* and the 1933 volume begin with the elegy for Con and Eva and end with another elegy, 'From "The Antigone" ' which itself concludes the sequence *A Woman Young and Old*. Those two poems have much in common. Not only is their genesis related (both echo important passages in Sophocles' *Antigone*), they were in fact drafted (the ink has blotted through the original) on reverse sides of the same sheet of paper. In that sense, the volume is rondural, ending where it begun. As befits a collection named for the winding stair in Yeats's Norman tower, its design is circular. This pattern is so thematically significant that the poet, by beginning and ending the 1933 as well as the 1929 collections with elegies for women, made sure it survived the rearrangement necessitated by the fusion of the two volumes and the additional poems. To employ a Joycean pun from another rondural text, *Finnegans Wake*, *The Winding Stair and Other Poems* may be lengthy (actually, Yeats's longest collection) and variegated, but it is most definitely *not* 'whorled without aimed'.

That volume can be read from a variety of perspectives and with differing thematic emphases. Dialectical critics will emphasize the playing out of Yeats's lifelong debate between the claims of soul and body, what he calls the *primary* and the *antithetical*. Feminist or gender critics may focus on Yeats's experimental attempts, primarily but not only in the Crazy Jane and 'Woman Young and Old' sequences, to engage experience from the perspective of a woman. 'The Mother of God', part of the triad beginning with 'Leda and the Swan' and ending with 'The Second Coming', is a dramatic monologue by Mary, a simple village girl who 'bore / The Heavens in my womb'. I have myself been interested in the volume's circuitous design, and in the ring-construction of *A Woman Young and Old*. In the case of that sequence, I believe I have found, rather than imposed, a cyclical pattern in which concentrically-paired poems, I and XI, II and X, III and IX, IV and VIII, V and VII, rotate around the central poem, 'Chosen' (VI). Such approaches to the book are not mutually exclusive. One might say that while each is only a *part* of the truth, it is a part of the *truth*.

Yeats himself has described the 'exultant weeks' in which he wrote many of the poems gathered in *Words for Music Perhaps*. Referring to his convalescence from lung congestion in the spring of 1929, he announced that 'life returned to me as an impression of the uncontrollable energy and daring of the great creators' (*VP* 831). While exultant energy is certainly present in many of these poems, the feeling of the 1933 volume as a whole is bittersweet and elegiac. That is obvious in the case of the opening poem, 'In Memory of Eva Gore-Booth and Con Markiewicz', and in the Coole Park poems, Yeats's celebration of Lady Gregory and of the Anglo-Irish tradition in its twilight, as well as in such mini-lyrics as 'Spilt Milk' and 'The Nineteenth Century and After'. In the former, all that has been thought and done, done and thought, is now thinned out, 'Like milk spilt on a stone'; in the latter, the 'great song' of Romanticism will 'return no more', leaving us, as Matthew Arnold was left at Dover Beach, with the 'rattle of pebbles on the shore / Under the receding wave.'

But in the major poems, mutability – from the autumn of the body to the decline and fall of a tradition – is countered by affirmation. 'After the final No there comes a Yes', says Wallace Stevens. Yeats's Yes is sometimes poignant, sometimes astringent, often weighted down with *blood*. There is a glory in the degradation of haughty Jonathan Swift, the 'heart in his blood-sodden breast' (in 'Blood and the Moon') having 'dragged him down into mankind'. In the mini-poem immediately following, the 'miraculous oil' exuded by entombed bodies of 'holy men and women' is contrasted, rather grotesquely, to the buried bodies of 'vampires full of blood', their shrouds 'bloody', their lips 'wet'. We behold, from the perspective of the Delphic oracle, 'great Plotinus swim' through life's buffeting seas toward paradisal Elysium; 'But the Golden Race looks dim, / Salt blood blocks his eyes.' Mary ponders 'This fallen star my milk sustains, / This love that makes my heart's blood stop.' 'Veronica's Napkin', used to wipe Christ's face, focuses, not on the Pole-Star symbolic of 'the Father and His angelic hierarchy', but on a 'different pole': the crucifix of human, suffering Jesus, and 'where it stood / A pattern on a napkin dipped in blood.'

This blood-drenched pattern is at its most mythological and excessive in 'Her Vision in the Wood', the longest poem in *A Woman Young and Old* (VIII), its violence unrestrained even by Yeats's favorite and most ceremonial stanza, *ottava rima*. At 'wine-dark midnight in the sacred wood', the enraged speaker, 'too old for a man's love', but still 'imagining men', and imagining as well that she 'could / A greater with a lesser pang assuage / Or but to find if withered vein ran blood', tears her 'body that its wine might cover / Whatever could recall the lip of lover', then, raising withered fingers, stares at her 'wine-dark' nails. Her sexual self-mutilation initiates a vision of her 'heart's victim and its torturer': her equally 'blood-bedabbled' lover, that Adonis-like 'thing all blood and mire, that beast-torn wreck'. For all its power, this poem is overly theatrical. But a remarkably carnal spirituality dominates both the Crazy Jane sequence (most notably in her triumphant debate with the Bishop and in the splendid 'Crazy Jane and Jack the Journeyman'), as well as this volume-ending sequence, especially in the bittersweet 'lot of love' heroically if less bloodily embraced by the erotic Neoplatonist of 'Chosen', the still point at the centre of *A Woman Young and Old*.

The gravitational pull is seldom without its epiphanic moment. It is sometimes rhapsodic – as in the 'blest' embrace of life at the climax of Self's peroration in the 'Dialogue' with Soul. Or in that later, unexpected moment in 'Vacillation', IV, when the poet, a 'solitary man' in his fifties in a crowded restaurant – book open on the table, cup empty – is gazing vacantly at shop and street, when his 'body of a sudden blazed; / And twenty minutes more or less / It seemed, so great my happiness, / That I was blesséd and could bless' – a reciprocity privately echoing Self's earlier more expansive and inclusive cry: 'We are blest by everything, / Everything we look upon is blest.' And there is that other moment, at Glendalough, a beautiful and sacred site, when, characteristically uncertain if the source of light is external or internal, received or bestowed, knowing only that 'all my heart seemed gay' – the revivified poet asks:

> What motion of the sun or stream
> Or eyelid shot the gleam
> That pierced my body through?
> What made me live like these that seem
> Self-born, born anew?

Also suspended between the human and the spiritual is the retrospective woman of 'A Last Confession'. In this poem, IX in the Woman Young and Old sequence, an older and wiser woman repudiates her own 'dissembling' and 'coquetry' in the concentrically-related 'A First Confession' (and in the earlier stanzas of 'A Last Confession' itself). She also looks back to the bird which, in poem VII of this sequence, the *aubade* 'Parting', she had insisted (echoing Juliet) was not the lark but the nightingale, 'night's bird and love's', whose 'song reproves / The murderous stealth of day.' Now, having given 'what other women gave / That stepped out of their clothes', she looks ahead: an anticipatory vision of soul-reunion as a spiritual but passionate embrace of true but severed lovers. Experiencing love's 'misery' in life, they will, she believes, come together in eternity, 'when this soul, its body off, / Naked to naked goes', enabling the lovers to 'Close and cling so tight, / There's not a bird of day that dare / Extinguish that delight.' This woman has benefitted from Yeats's reading of Swedenborg's and Milton's accounts of the incandescent sexual intercourse of angels, but her language and her ecstasy wrung from suffering have, finally, a radiance all their own.

There is a question, remarked Denis Donoghue a half-century ago, that 'storms and cries through the entire' volume, *The Winding Stair and Other*

Poems: 'In a world of mutability, what remains, what is possible, where does Value reside?'[1] Mutability resonates throughout *The Winding Stair*, a volume suffused by the atmosphere evoked (in 'At Algeciras', a poem designated 'A Meditation upon Death') as 'Greater glory in the sun, / An evening chill upon the air.' The theme of 'ruin, wreck, and wrack' ('The Results of Thought') begins with 'In Memory of Eva Gore-Booth and Con Markiewicz', the volume's opening poem, where 'a raving autumn shears / Blossom from the summer's wreath'. This Atropos-like levelling wind leaves the two women, once beautiful young girls in silk kimonos, 'withered old', 'skeleton gaunt' and, finally, 'shadows'. Mutability is there in the 'broken, crumbling battlement' Soul implicitly compares to the poet's aging human body in 'A Dialogue of Self and Soul', and in the cruelly rhetorical *ad hominem* question that 'Soul', the spiritual spokesman, directly poses: 'Why should the imagination of a man / Long past his prime remember / Things that are emblematical of love and war?' It is there in the equally cruel, and self-damning, observation flung at an aged but unrepentant Jane by a lesser spiritual spokesman, the Bishop of that sequence: 'Those breasts are flat and fallen now, / Those veins must soon be dry.' The predicament is flatly summarized by the young woman in 'Her Anxiety': 'All true love must die, / Alter at the best / Into some lesser thing.'

Throughout the volume, whether in the form of rejection or consolation, answers to this altering and diminution are sought, and Yeats goes about them in ways that are various, if always characteristically 'Yeatsian'. Anticipating Yeats by a decade or more, Robert Frost had addressed the dilemma by imagining, in one of his finest sonnets, the song of the belated oven bird as a response to the question posed by change, mutability, the alteration into some lesser thing:

> There is a singer everyone has heard,
> Loud, a mid-summer and a mid-wood bird,
> Who makes the solid tree trunks sound again.
> He says that leaves are old and that for flowers
> Mid-summer is to spring as one to ten.
> He says that early petal-fall is past,
> When pear and cherry bloom went down in showers
> On sunny days a moment overcast;
> And comes that other fall we name the fall.
> He says the highway dust is over all.
> The bird would cease and be as other birds
> But that he knows in singing not to sing.

> The question that he frames in all but words
> Is what to make of a diminished thing.

In contrast, Yeats *has* 'words', and he *never* knew how '*not* to sing'. Self insists that 'we must sing'; Jane's very 'body sings on'; as does Yeats's most extraordinary posthumous persona, the wave-whitened bone of the woman in 'Three Things'. Lying on the shore, that discarnate bone, its ineradicable memories lodged in its marrow, continues to sing of human love long after death and decomposition. What to make of a diminished thing is precisely the question framed in many of the poems in *The Winding Stair*, from the issues raised in the autumnal twilight of the volume-opening elegy for those 'dear shades', Eva and Con, to the final Sophoclean elegy for Antigone, echoing, as in Self's 'we must sing', Tennyson's elegiac 'I do but sing because I must' (*In Memoriam*, XXI:23): 'Pray I will and sing I must, / And yet I weep – Oedipus' child / Descends into the loveless dust.' That heart-breaking final phrase may be countered by the irrepressible voice from the bone on the desiccated shore, or by the Woman Old's anticipation of posthumous reunion with her true lover 'when this soul, its body off, / Naked to naked goes.' But in 'From "The Antigone" ', love is made all the more poignantly vivid in its negation, present by its very absence. And so we weep as well as sing.

Even in the triumphant 'Dialogue', Soul, at a disadvantage despite his imperious summons, lands a few blows, especially hurtful to a poet just sixty-two, but in uncertain health. Why, indeed, should the imagination of a man 'long past his prime' remember things emblematical 'of love and war'? Half-listening, half-ignoring his would-be spiritual guide and tormenter, the Yeatsian Self, as we'll see, has an ultimate answer. But the question of mutability is hardly to be dismissed. It must be engaged, poignantly registered, and somehow, if only in the purity of its lyric evocation, transcended – as in the opening poem, the elegy for Con and Eva, in many of the poems in *Words for Music Perhaps,* and in the lines in which Antigone 'Descends into the loveless dust', in the poem that concludes *A Woman Young and Old* and *The Winding Stair* as a whole.

II

The Woman Young and Old sequence is finally getting the attention it deserves. Many of the other lapidary lyrics in the 1933 *Winding Stair* have long been well-known, most notably the Crazy Jane poems and the marvellous 'After Long Silence', with its beautifully cadenced and heartbreaking recognition of the price of wisdom, its concurrence in the Shavian axiom that youth is wasted on the young: 'Bodily decrepitude is wisdom; young, / We loved each other and were ignorant.' Love, human and divine, figures in the charming little dialogue-poem, 'For Anne Gregory', and the lesser-known 'Her Anxiety', already mentioned, is a response to the immediately preceding dialogue poem, 'Young Man's Song'. This Yeatsian debate is internal, between the young man and his 'heart'. The speaker fears that his beloved, like all things mutable, 'will change', that in time she will deteriorate 'into a withered crone'. But 'heart' – a paradoxically passionate Neoplatonist able to penetrate to the metaphysical 'truth' underlying mere appearance – replies in 'noble rage' that 'She would as bravely show / Did all the fabric fade', because her archetypal self exists in eternity: 'No withered crone I saw / Before the world was made.'

As that last line indicates (it echoes the title and refrain of poem II of *A Woman Young and Old*), Heart is not isolated in this volume. For Crazy Jane, that most heterodox of spiritualists, 'All things remain in God', and Jane's male counterpart, Tom the Lunatic, believes that everything 'Stands in God's unchanging eye / In all the vigour of its blood. / In that faith I live or die.' Speaking in *propria persona* in 'Quarrel in Old Age', the one *overt* Maud Gonne poem in *The Winding Stair*, Yeats, desperate to believe, and buttressed by Swedenborg and Plotinus, insists that Maud, though now wrinkled with age, still lives in all her original, heroic early beauty, striding like the goddess of spring, bearing her shield (or 'targe', hence the awkward 'Targeted') like Athena:

> All lives that has lived;
> So much is certain;
> Old sages were not deceived;
> Somewhere beyond the curtain
> Of distorting days
> Lives that lonely thing
> That shone before these eyes
> Targeted, trod like Spring.

In 'Young Man's Song', even as a projection into the future, the speaker's mere thought of his beloved reduced to bodily decrepitude is an offence to the heart, which retains the true – the quintessential and unalterable – image of the beloved in her archetypal and unchanging state (Yeats is eroticizing, here as so often in this volume, the eternity envisioned by Plotinus). 'Abashed' by the report of the heart, which 'cannot lie', the speaker kneels abjectly in the 'dirt' emblematic of his brief but traitorous surrender to the distorted perspective of a fallen world. That he ends with a humble yet hyperbolic rhetorical flourish – calling upon 'all' to 'bend the knee / To my offended heart / Until it pardon me' – emphasizes the winning, chivalrous, but necessarily less-than-fully persuasive argument of the poem, an argument that *almost* but not quite brings us to our knees.

Certainly, the beloved herself is not persuaded, though she longs to be convinced. Going beyond the young man's internal dialogue between 'I' and 'Heart', 'Her Anxiety', a short poem worth dwelling on for a moment, presents the young woman's response, or challenge.

> Earth in beauty dressed
> Awaits returning spring.
> All true love must die,
> Alter at the best
> Into some lesser thing.
> *Prove that I lie.*
>
> Such body lovers have,
> Such exacting breath,
> That they touch or sigh.
> Every touch they give,
> Love is nearer death.
> *Prove that I lie.*

Shelley's climactic question and petition to the West Wind, 'If winter comes, can spring be far behind?' was poignant precisely because it wasn't merely rhetorical: the succession of nature's seasons provides no equivalent guarantee that emotional or political 'winter' will be followed by 'spring' renewal in the *human* world. Yeats's young woman presents an earth 'dressed' in 'beauty' even in winter, a bride garmented in snow awaiting the return of spring. But earth, anticipating her annual re-greening, 'awaits' in confidence. The titular 'anxiety' is not hers, but that of the female speaker, who emphasizes the painful contrast between cyclical nature – ever-changing, yet ever-beautiful and enduring – and human transience, epitomized here less by physical decay than emotional change. The young woman acknowledges her experiential conviction that true love 'must die' or, at best, alter into 'some lesser thing'.

Again, what are we to make of a diminished thing? Is her initial refrain-line, '*Prove that I lie*', addressed to her lover, or to her own heart? In the preceding poem, the young *man's* heart, which we are told '*cannot* lie', refuted his scep-tical, materialist self. Less easily persuaded by metaphysical faith or by what Crazy Jane calls 'heart's-truth', and echoing the Renaissance notion that the *petite mort* of intercourse decreased actual life, the young woman reinforces her pessimistic conclusion with a precise calculus of the exacting cost lovers must pay for sexual ecstasy: 'Every touch they give, / Love is nearer death.'

But there is another inverse ratio at work in the poem. While love – consumed, like the sexual act itself, in its own performance – lessens, the incremental refrain gains in passionate intensity. If in the first stanza, *'Prove that I lie'* was stoic, sceptical, perhaps even a flippant challenge to the young man's heart-dictated faith in permanence, here it seems to hover between a plangent plea and an urgently felt demand to be presented with a deeper metaphysical 'truth' that will 'prove' her *apparent* truth – that Eros must inexorably yield to Thanatos – to be a 'lie'. 'Her Anxiety' beautifully epitomizes the pathos of mutability and, simultaneously, the desperate longing for some imperishable and irrefutable truth. Her plea that someone 'prove' her sad wisdom wrong seems to require no-nonsense cerebral evidence; yet John Keats, who elegized the 'beauty that must die', also spoke, in the 'Vale of Soul-making' letter, of the 'proovings of [the] heart'.[2]

III

It is time to turn to some of the major poems in *The Winding Stair*. In part, the volume is a twilit, autumnal elegy – historical, cultural, political, personal – sung over the Anglo-Irish aristocratic tradition, epitomized by Lady Gregory, embodied and in part bartered away by the Gore-Booth sisters (whose politics, especially Con's revolutionary activism, conservative Yeats deplored), and nostalgically and vestigially visible in the Georgian houses of both Lady Gregory and the Gore-Booth sisters, Coole Park and Lissadell, respectively. The volume's beautiful opening lines, from the complex double-elegy 'In Memory of Eva Gore-Booth and Con Markiewicz' (a poem written in the abba tetrameters of Tennyson's *In Memoriam*), establish the elegiac tone:

> The light of evening, Lissadell,
> Great windows open to the south,
> Two girls in silk kimonos, both
> Beautiful, one a gazelle.
> But a raving autumn shears
> Blossom from the summer's wreath ...

That poem goes on, of course, to severely criticize the dead sisters, for either 'Conspiring among the ignorant' or dreaming of 'Some vague Utopia', and growing 'old and skeleton-gaunt, / An image of such politics'. And yet he had often thought, while they were alive, 'to seek / One or the other out and speak / Of that old Georgian mansion, mix / Pictures of the mind', recalling 'the talk of youth, / Two girls in silk kimonos, both / Beautiful, one a gazelle'. With that rondure, its perfection troubled by the late caesuras before 'mix' and 'both', the poem's opening movement ends. The second and final movement begins tenderly and ends in a stunning apocalyptic reversal, in which the previously judgmental poet allies himself not only with aristocratic Con and Eva ('*We* the great gazebo built'), but in a way with their later politics, submitting himself to *their* incendiary authority:

> Dear shadows, now you know it all,
> All the folly of a fight
> With a common wrong or right.
> The innocent and the beautiful
> Have no enemy but time.
> Arise and bid me strike a match
> And strike another till time catch;
> Should the conflagration climb,
> Run till all the sages know.
> We the great gazebo built,
> They convicted us of guilt;
> Bid me strike a match and blow.

In a more embittered version of the Anglo-Irish motif, the decline of the great tradition associated with Swift, Berkeley, Burke, and (to a lesser degree) Goldsmith recurs in 'Blood and the Moon'. There a sardonic Yeats sets up his own aristocratic edifice, Thoor Ballylee, as a 'powerful emblem', singing it 'rhyme upon rhyme / In mockery of a time / Half dead at the top.' The mockery, the 'savage indignation' (to quote Yeats's translation of *saeva indignatio* in 'Swift's Epitaph'), even the image of dying from the top down, are all Swiftian. At this early point, 'Blood and the Moon' seems a haughtier variation on 'The Seven Sages', one of more tendentious poems in this volume, where 'wisdom', experiential and irrational, comes from 'beggary' rather than from the 'Whiggery' hated by Yeats's Anglo-Irish Foursome. In 'Blood and the Moon', we are told that 'wisdom is the property of the dead'. Among the properties of 'the living' is 'power', as well as everything else that 'has the stain of blood' – that blood with which so much in this volume is sodden and stained. It is only in the poem's final movement – set near the 'top', the upper chamber of the lonely tower itself – that we hear the authentic elegy for now powerless Georgian Ireland: a plangent night-music echoing Burke's great melody, and hinting at, rather than ranting about, the replacement of the gorgeously aristocratic by the less splendidly tinctured democratic:

> Upon the dusty, glittering windows cling,
> And seem to cling upon the moonlit skies,
> Tortoiseshell butterflies, peacock butterflies,
> A couple of night-moths are on the wing ...

Central to this darkling motif are the two Coole Park poems, Yeats's tributes to Augusta Gregory and to the tradition she embodied. In the first, a meditation upon 'an aged woman and her house' set in a characteristically Yeatsian mingling of darkness and light ('A sycamore and a lime tree lost in night / Although that western cloud is luminous'), the poet looks before and after, fusing the thirty or more years in which he spent almost every summer at Coole, constructing, with others, 'great works ... / For scholars and for poets after us.' This projected composite figure – 'traveller, scholar, poet' – in effect evokes those of us who visit Coole. In a move reminiscent of Walt Whitman, we are directly addressed, and, in this case, petitioned to stand amid the ruins of the great house. Recognizing the 'powerful character' of that woman, the 'compass-point' upon which the Irish Renaissance 'seemed to whirl', we are to 'dedicate ... / A moment's memory to that laurelled head'.

The second poem, 'Coole Park and Ballylee, 1931', written two years later, is more emphatic about physical, cultural and imaginative decline. Altering (with the help of Coleridge's river Alph which ran through underground caverns) the actual topography of Coole and Ballylee, Yeats gives us a half-literal, half-symbolic scene: an underground river and a flooded lake bordered by 'a wood / Now all dry sticks under a wintry sun', and suddenly signatured by a 'mounting swan' – 'Another emblem there!' Yeats proudly registers what was achieved by himself and other guests and creative workers gathered at Coole by Lady Gregory, that 'last inheritor', reduced to the disembodied 'sound of a stick upon the floor'. Now, where 'ancestral trees / Or gardens rich in memory glorified' a lost tradition, with 'all that great glory spent', the poem moves toward an inevitable but magnificent sense of an ending. In the final *ottava rima* stanza, Yeats allies himself with the conservative rather than the revolutionary aspect of Romanticism, an alignment justified less by the visionary politics of his true poetic precursors, Blake and Shelley, than by the thinking and poetry of later, conservative, Wordsworth and Coleridge, who made their peace with Burke, and cognitively internalized revolution, relocating it in what Wordsworth called 'the mind of man'. Yeats positions himself in that great lineage:

> We were the last romantics – chose for theme
> Traditional sanctity and loveliness;
> Whatever's written in what poets name

> The book of the people; whatever most can bless
> The mind of man or elevate a rhyme.
> But all is changed, that high horse riderless,
> Though mounted in that saddle Homer rode
> Where the swan drifts upon a darkening flood.

Many Irish Catholic readers resent, with considerable political justification, Yeats's commemoration, and idealization, of the Anglo-Irish Protestant Ascendancy. But Yeats, like Pindar, is an elegist singing his dirge over a dying aristocratic tradition; and, as Hegel reminds us, 'the owl of Minerva flies only at twilight'. I've dwelt on these celebrations of Lady Gregory's Coole Park, not only because they are part of the elegiac pattern of *The Winding Stair*, politically and in terms of the volume's notable emphasis on women, but simply because the lines are so wonderfully resonant. But there are other, even more significant motifs to explore.

IV

To some extent, one must, without being procrustean, read *The Winding Stair* as a dialectical response to *The Tower* (1928), a largely but not exclusively 'feminine' and life-affirming answer to that – again, largely but hardly exclusively – 'masculine' and death-oriented volume. The crucial move, in 'A Dialogue of Self and Soul', is the embrace of cyclical recurrence countering the ostensibly nature-transcending spirituality of 'Sailing to Byzantium', the opening poem of *The Tower*. Another response, of course, is 'Byzantium' itself, a *Winding Stair* poem in which Yeats, pressed by his friend and book-designer Sturge Moore, ostensibly set out to sharpen the cleavage between his transcendent golden bird and the world of 'whatever is begotten, born, and dies'. What the astonishing final stanza of 'Byzantium' *actually does* is to have it both ways, ending by more intensely fusing rather than dividing the two realms. But I will not re-immerse us in the familiar Byzantine complexities of mire and blood, 'That dolphin-torn, that gong-tormented sea' affirming creative generation, sexual and artistic, yet yearning toward its spiritual source. Instead, I want to engage those same antinomies as they play out in 'A Dialogue of Self and Soul', and in Part VII of the sequence entitled 'Vacillation': an alternating six-line debate between 'The Soul' and 'The Heart' which is, in effect, a revisiting of 'A Dialogue of Self and Soul' in stichomythy.

In 1932, having completed 'Vacillation', Yeats wrote to his most intimate correspondent, Olivia Shakespear, to tell her that he had just reread his entire

poetic canon. He connects the old pagan-Christian debate between Oisin and
Patrick (in *The Wanderings of Oisin*, 1889) with the more recent exchange
between Heart and Soul in 'Vacillation', VII. As Yeats's predilection for the
debate-form reveals, his allegiances are provisional and subject to the counter-
truths of polar opposition. Nevertheless, late Yeats locates the vital sources of
creation within the fecund human heart, a heart that may be a corrupt 'rag-
and-bone shop', but which is nevertheless the place 'where all the ladders start'
('The Circus Animals' Desertion'): the 'heart' identified (in the immediately
preceding lines, at the conclusion of Part VI of 'Vacillation') as the 'blood-
sodden' root from which 'are sprung / Those branches of the night and day /
Where the gaudy moon is hung'.

Insisting that Yeats was *not* a religious poet but that Christians should read
him despite his dangerous doctrines because he was above all an 'honest man',
Peter Allt, writing three-quarters of a century ago, brilliantly encapsulated
Yeats's 'mature religious *Anschauung*'. It consisted, he said, of 'religious belief
without any religious faith, notional assent to the reality of the supernatural'
combined with 'an emotional dissent from its actuality'.[3] As if to prove Allt's
point, Yeats cites in the letter to Olivia Shakespear a line from the next and
final section of 'Vacillation' in order to clarify what he now thought of as the
motif dominating all his poetry: 'The swordsman throughout repudiates the
saint, but not without vacillation. Is that perhaps the sole theme – Usheen and
Patrick – "so get you gone, Von Hügel, though with blessings on your head" '
(*Letters*, [Wade] p. 798). He was quoting the final line of 'Vacillation', which
ends with the Poet – having chosen as his exemplary figure, 'Homer ... and his
unchristened heart' – blessing, yet courteously if condescendingly rejecting his
contrary, the Saint, here represented by the Catholic theologian and mystic,
Baron von Hügel. This finale is surprisingly jaunty. Not so the poem's penulti-
mate movement, which, he told Olivia, 'puts clearly an argument that has gone
on in my head for years' (*Letters*, [Wade] p. 789). Written in iambic pentam-
eter couplets, 'Vacillation', VII, is a career-concentrating debate between Saint
('Soul') and Poet ('Heart'). In fact, Part VII was originally subtitled 'Dialogue
of soul & heart':

> *The Soul.* Seek out reality, leave things that seem.
>
> *The Heart.* What, be a singer born and lack a theme?
>
> *The Soul.* Isaiah's coal, what more can man desire?
>
> *The Heart.* Struck dumb in the simplicity of fire?

The Soul. Look on that fire, salvation walks within.

The Heart. What theme had Homer but original sin?

Heart does not dispute this 'notional' distinction between Platonic-Plotinian 'reality' and the mere semblance of phenomena; but the poet, emotionally dissenting, cannot simply 'leave' the things of this world, complexities of mire and blood providing as they do the resinous fuel of his art. 'What', cries Heart, 'be a singer born and lack a theme?' Soul next repairs to the Hebrew Bible and to the great symbolic act in which the lips of the prophet were cleansed, touched by the burning coal brought to him from God's holy fire by the Seraphim (Isaiah 6:5–7). But what happens to the purified lips and tongue if they happen to be those of a born singer? Heart, unwilling to be consumed, is indignant, even appalled, at the prospect of being 'struck dumb in the simplicity of fire'. Forty years earlier, in 'To the Rose upon the Rood of Time' (1892), Yeats had drawn back from total absorption in the spiritual. The attraction and resistance in that early poem initiated Yeats's characteristic pattern, that dialectic of notional assent and emotional dissent registered here in Heart's acknowledgment of the fire's spiritual significance while, simultaneously, drawing back from any such occult or spiritual cleansing.

The crucial distinction – between Christian self-denial and Homeric self-affirmation – was registered by Yeats in annotating Nietzsche in 1902, three decades before he wrote 'Vacillation'. In an antithesis crucial to understanding much if not all of his subsequent thought and work, he grouped under the heading NIGHT: 'Socrates, Christ', and 'one god– denial of self, the soul turned towards spirit, seeking knowledge.' And, under the heading DAY: 'Homer' and 'many gods' – affirmation of self, the soul turned from spirit to be its mask &instrument when it seeks life'.[4] In 'Vacillation', VII (as in 'A Dialogue of Self and Soul', where 'Self' plays the role of 'Heart'), 'Heart' is spokesman of 'Day': the self-affirming, life-seeking, unchristened, Homeric part of Yeats himself, at once acknowledging but resisting the nocturnal self-denying, knowledge-seeking, Socratic-Platonic-Christian 'soul turned towards spirit', and consumed in the 'simplicity of fire'.

Soul's final ploy is a mixture of hellfire threat and redemptive promise. Heart is directed to 'Look on that fire, salvation walks within', a more pious version of the purging Byzantine 'flames begotten of flame'. Elsewhere in *The Winding Stair*, both Crazy Jane and Yeats himself (in 'The Choice') refuse purification or a proffered 'heavenly mansion', choosing instead to 'rage in the dark', or reside in the precarious 'mansion' Love has 'pitched' in 'the place of excrement'. Heart's defiant retort in the form of a rhetorical question – 'What theme had Homer but original sin?' – similarly sets against Socrates, Plato, Plotinus, Isaiah and Christ the great pagan poet of love and war, Helen and Achilles, the 'Homeric' theme culturally wrenched, with the help of Nietzsche, into another context so as to intensify the clash with Christian and Neoplatonic theology. Such 'salvation' and sanctifying grace as Yeats's Homer finds, he finds not in any spiritual purging or transcendent heavenly mansion but *within* all that human turbulence and passion held by orthodox Christians to derive from the primal scene of rebellion in Eden. Yet, paradoxically if predictably, Yeats makes his 'unchristened' Homer a notional 'believer' in lot-blackening original sin. Again, Yeats accepts religious terminology, in order to alter it, triumph over it, or somehow incorporate it as the tragic stimulus in a more expansive, heroic vision which laicizes spirit.[5]

Yeats's pivotal poem in this process, the poem at the centre of *The Winding Stair*, is 'A Dialogue of Self and Soul'. I'll deal with 'Dialogue' at considerable length, not only in its genesis, including its occult and poetic 'sources', but as a poem in which Neoplatonism, Christianity, Milton and the whole Body-Soul *débat*-tradition become recipients of Dionysian news from Yeats at his most Nietzschean, full of a self-redemptive astringent joy. To understand what Yeats is up to here is to see what is going on in *The Winding Stair* as a whole – indeed, I believe, in much of Yeats's canon as a whole.

5

A number of critics have thought *The Winding Stair* a book erroneously or at least misleadingly titled. Presumably because, influenced by the opening line of 'Dialogue', Soul's 'I summon to the winding ancient stair', they have taken the emphasis to be on the transcendent ascent rather than the cyclical winding. But the 'winding stair' of this volume, the spiral staircase within Thoor Ballylee – that 'winding, gyring, spiring treadmill of a stair' which Yeats declares, in the opening movement of 'Blood and the Moon', to be his 'ancestral stair', still bearing the 'Odour of blood' – is not only, or even primarily, a *scala coeli* or Jacob's ladder by which we mount to spiritual vision. Soul would have it so, of course, in 'Dialogue'; but the protagonist, the *antithetical* Self, is not to be bullied into submission. Imperiously commanded to fix his 'wandering' attention 'upon' spiritual ascent and 'ancestral night', Self remains diverted by the greatest of Yeats's fused symbols: the 'ancient blade' (given Yeats as a gift by an admirer, Junzo Sato) scabbarded and bound in complementary 'female' embroidery. That sheathed and fabric-wound sword – 'emblems of the day against the tower / Emblematical of the night', fusing the sacred and the profane, war and love, the phallic and the vaginal – becomes Yeats's symbol of gyring life, set against the vertical ascent, at once spiritual and phallogocentric, urged upon him by the Neoplatonic Soul. But before reengaging this embodied symbolism, let us briefly explore the schematic, astrological-occult dry bones beneath the flesh. We will then return to the poetry.

In a series of congested notes intended to accompany the 1933 volume, Yeats explained his now central symbolism. After discussing towers and winding stairs, he cited a Neoplatonic passage underlying several of the poems of *A Woman Young and Old*. In a note at the back (p. 26) of the 1929 volume (a note written at Rapallo in March 1928) he'd said he had 'symbolised a woman's love as the struggle of the darkness to keep the sun from rising from its earthly bed', a symbol he had 'changed' in the final stanza of 'Chosen', to 'that of the souls of man and woman ascending through the Zodiac'. This early note had ended vaguely and inaccurately: 'in some Neoplatonist or Hermatist – whose name I forget – the whorl changes into a sphere at one of the points where the Milky Way Crosses the Zodiac.' In the 1933 note, having been reminded by that 'learned mystic', Frank Pearce Sturm, who had originally brought the passage to his attention in January 1926, Yeats identified the unknown Neoplatonist, the 'learned astrologer' mentioned in the final stanza of 'Chosen', as the fourth-century Neoplatonist Macrobius. In the relevant passage, from his *Commentary* on Cicero's *Somnium Scipionius* (Scipio's Dream), Macrobius spoke of the 'descending soul by its defluction' being drawn – not, as Yeats mistakenly reversed it, from whorl to sphere – 'out of the spherical, the sole divine form, into the cone', or whorl, or gyre.

I have two reasons for bringing up this esoteric material, 'a little of which', as William York Tindall once said of Yeats's *A Vision*, 'seems too much, his business none of ours.' First, I believe that – in the *poetry* at least – Yeats is having some fun with all this arcana. The female speaker of *A Woman Young and Old* takes her Neoplatonic astrology with some seriousness. At the same time, when, in the poem 'Chosen', she is asked, by 'some new-married bride', about her 'utmost pleasure with a man', one detects a note of sophisticated, tongue-in-cheek humour in her comparison of the moment of post-coital stillness to the drifting of hearts on the miraculous stream, 'Where – wrote a learned astrologer – / The Zodiac is changed into a sphere.' Surely she would not be solemnly pedantic in this immediate context. For one thing, we know something about her temperament from the preceding poem, 'Consolation', in which she had mischievously stood Neoplatonic and Christian doctrine on its head with a *felix-culpa* variation in which she informs the sages that 'the crime of being born' (and note that she does not decriminalize it) can be 'forgot' by returning, in the temporary amnesia of sexual ecstasy, to the scene of the crime!

This is the same woman who, in 'Parting', the poem immediately following 'Chosen', passionately and cunningly 'offer[s] to love's play / My dark declivities.' To have this experienced and playful eroticist answer the youthful bride as she does with *no* saving urbanity would be to parody the role assigned by Dryden to Donne, who 'perplexes the minds of the fair sex with nice speculations of philosophy, when he should engage their hearts and entertain them with the softness of love'. Leaving Dryden's gender-condescension aside, I am assuming that the new-married bride has not come fresh from a perusal of *A Vision*, or of John Donne (the stanza, metre, and imagery of whose 'Nocturnall upon St. Lucies Day' Yeats borrows for 'Chosen'), or of Macrobius, and also that she has not been corresponding with 'that too little known mystic and poet, Dr. Sturm'.

There is another reason to trot out this esoteric annotation to 'Chosen'. In a cancelled portion of the note first published in 1987 (in my *Yeats's Interactions with Tradition*), Yeats went on to describe the opening movement of 'A Dialogue of Self and Soul' as a 'variation on Macrobius'. It was a variation he thought 'may be familiar', for he'd found – in 'those *Intimate Journals of Paul Gauguin* which have attained a popularity so alarming that our Board of Censorship has put them on the index' – the following comment by Gauguin on that strange but haunting novel *Séraphita* by Balzac, one of Yeats's favorite writers: ' "The Colossus" – Balzac – remounts to the pole, the world's pivot; his great mantle shelters and warms the two germs, Seraphitus, Seraphita, fertile souls ceaselessly uniting, who issue from their Boreal Mists to traverse the whole universe, teaching, loving, creating' (Yeats Archives, SUNY Stony Brook, 30.3286). Despite the sublimated yet fertile sexuality Gauguin rightly detected, Balzac's Swedenborgian novel moves toward a climactic journey to ice-capped mountain tops culminating in an arrow-like ascent to, and mystical union with, God, as opposed to what Yeats elsewhere calls the 'winding movement of nature', the *antithetical* 'path of the serpent' (*Mythologies*, p. 340).

As it plays out in 'A Dialogue of Self and Soul', the 'variation' takes the form of a rejection of the vertical ascent. Self chooses the movement downward into life, rather than upward, out of it: not (to quote the Preface to *A Vision*) Christ's ascent into an abstract heaven, but Oedipus' descent 'into an earth riven by love'. As a disciple of such Neoplatonists as Macrobius and of the spiritual mentor (the ghost of Scipio's grandfather) in the Ciceronian text he was glossing, Soul is unaware (in Blake's phrase) that 'Eternity is in love with the productions of time', that man's fall is an alternate form of fulfilment and perfection, albeit profane. Thus Soul deplores the descent into the gyre of 'fallen' human life and austerely commands total concentration on reversing that descent. The obvious 'variation' that Yeats (with the happy collaboration of Gauguin's reading of Balzac) plays on Macrobius is that mutinous Self, rejecting the stern summons to 'the steep ascent', sets up opposing gyre-symbols – the sword and silk-wound sheath, 'emblematical of love and war' – and chooses fertile, ceaseless rebirth rather than escape from the cycle of mutability.

In the opening movement of the poem, the half in which there is still a semblance of actual dialogue, hectoring Soul repeatedly demands that Self 'fix' every thought 'upon' the One, 'upon' the steep ascent, the straight line of saint or sage, 'upon' the occult Pole Star, 'upon' the spiritual quarter where all thought is done. But the recalcitrant Self remains diverted by the Many, by earthly multiplicity, by the sword wound in embroidery replicating the serpentine windings of nature. Similarly, in Cicero's text, despite the rhetorical admonition of Scipio's ghostly ancestor, 'Why not *fix* your attention *upon* the heavens and contemn what is mortal?' young Scipio admits he 'kept turning my eyes back to earth'. According to Macrobius, Scipio 'looked about him everywhere with wonder. Hereupon his grandfather's admonitions recalled him to the upper realms.'[6] Though the agon between the Yeatsian Self and Soul is identical to that between young Scipio and his grandfather's spirit, the Soul in Yeats's poem proves to be – unsurprisingly since he is given less than half a chance – a considerably less successful spiritual guide than that formidable ghost.

Turning a largely deaf ear to Soul's advocacy of the upward path, Self (revealingly called 'Me' in the drafts of the poem) has preferred to focus downward on life, brooding on the consecrated Japanese blade upon his knees with its tattered but still protective wrapping of 'Heart's purple'. That 'flowering, silken, old embroidery, torn / From some court-lady's dress and round / The wooden scabbard bound and wound' makes the double icon 'emblematical' not only of 'love and war', but of the ever-circling gyre: the eternal, and archetypally female, spiral. When Soul's paradoxically physical tongue is turned to stone with the realization that, according to his own austere doctrine, 'only the dead can be forgiven', Self takes over the poem. He goes on, of course, to win his way, despite considerable difficulty, to a *self-redemptive* affirmation of life.

VI

Self begins his peroration defiantly: 'A living man is blind and drinks his drop. / What matter if the ditches are impure?' This 'variation' on Neoplatonism, privileging life's filthy downflow, or 'defluction', over the Plotinian pure fountain of emanation, is followed by an even more defiant rhetorical question: 'What matter if I live it all once more?' 'Was *that* life?' asks Nietzsche's Zarathustra. 'Well then! Once more!' (*Thus Spoke Zarathustra*, 3.2) But Self's grandiose and premature gesture is instantly undercut by the litany of grief that Nietzschean Recurrence, the exact repetition of the events of one's life, would entail – from the 'toil of growing up', through the 'ignominy of boyhood' and the 'distress' of 'changing into a man', to the 'pain' of the 'unfinished man' having to confront 'his own clumsiness', then the 'finished man', old and 'among his enemies'. Despite the Self's bravado, it is in danger of being shaped, deformed, by the judgmental gaze of others. This leads to that crucial question that has bedevilled much post-Hegelian and, more recently, feminist thought: how to overcome passive acceptance of the Gaze, of a discipline imposed by the Other. Soul's tongue may have turned to stone, but other forces, still malignant but now *visual*, have palpable designs upon the assaulted Self:

> How in the name of Heaven can he escape
> That defiling and disfigured shape
> The mirror of malicious eyes
> Casts upon his eyes until at last
> He thinks that shape must be his shape?

To quote a *Tower* poem, 'Ancestral Houses', this would be to lose the Self's ability to 'choose whatever shape it wills', and to 'never stoop to a mechanical / Or servile shape, at others' beck and call'. Yeats brilliantly co-opts the assertion of Robert Browning's arrogant Duke – 'I choose never to stoop' – in support of Nietzschean 'master morality' as opposed to 'slave morality'. If 'Dialogue' is Yeats's 'central' poem – in that, as Lawrence Lerner once put it, it has the 'most repercussions' in his work – that centrality is enhanced by its absorption of so many influences outside the Yeatsian canon as well. Quite aside from the whole Body-Soul debate tradition, and the internalized combat between Plotinus's Neoplatonism and Nietzsche, this Yeatsian *psychomachia* incorporates many poems in the Romantic tradition, including Blake's proto-feminist *Visions of the Daughters of Albion* and another Browning poem, 'Childe Roland to the Dark Tower Came'.

The gleam of the 'malicious eyes' that cast upon Self a distorting lie so powerful that he falls victim to it is borrowed from the opening stanza of Browning's compelling quest-poem, in which the first thought of Childe Roland was that he was being 'lied' to by that hoary and sadistic cripple, 'with *malicious eye* / Askance to watch the working of *his lie* / On mine.' Even closer to Self's temporarily mistaken belief that that 'defiling' shape 'cast upon' him by mirroring eyes 'must be his shape' is the initially deluded, masochistic cry of Blake's Oothoon (2: 36–9) for her *'defiled* bosom' to be rent away so that she 'may *reflect* / The image' of the very man (the moralistic sadist, Theotormon, who, having raped her, now brands her 'harlot') whose 'loved' but unloving 'eyes' have cast upon her precisely this 'defiled' shape – one of Blake's, and now Yeats's, grimmest ironies. But both recover. Self's eventual victory, like Oothoon's, is over severe moralism – what Nietzsche brilliantly psychoanalysed as the divisive but, once overcome, ultimately fruitful 'bad conscience' that would reduce the body to an object of defilement and degradation. In Yeats's case it seems, above all, a triumph over his own Neoplatonism or Gnosticism: an instance of Nietzschean *Selbstüberwindung,* creative 'self-overcoming', for, as Yeats said, 'we make out of the quarrel with others, rhetoric, but of the quarrel with ourselves, poetry' (*Mythologies,* p. 331).

Yet the spiritual tradition is not simply dismissed, here any more than in the Crazy Jane or Woman Young and Old sequences. For Yeats, the world of experience, however dark the declivities into which the generated soul may drop, is never utterly divorced from the world of light and grace. Indeed, the water imagery branching through Self's peroration subsumes pure fountain and impure ditches, since there is a continuum. The Plotinian overflowing fountain cascades down from the divine One through mind or intellect (*nous*) to the lower depths. As long, says Plotinus, as *nous,* or even the generated soul, maintains its gaze on, and contemplation of, God (the First Cause or 'Father'), it retains the likeness of its Creator (*Enneads* 5.2.4). But, writes Macrobius (succinctly glossing Plotinus's Hypostatic fountain), the soul, 'by diverting its attention more and more, though itself incorporeal, degenerates into the fabric of bodies' (*Commentary* 1.14.4).

This clarifies the position of the Yeatsian Self as perceived from Soul's perspective: viewed *sub specie aeternitatis,* Self is an emanation of, and a falling off from, the higher Soul. When the attention, supposed to be fixed on things above, is diverted below – down to the 'blade upon my knees' wound in tattered silk and, still further downward, to life's 'impure' ditches – the lower Soul (or Self) has indeed degenerated into the world of nature and the 'fabric', the tattered embroidery or mortal dress, of bodies. And yet, as usual in later Yeats, that degradation is also a triumph, couched in terms modulating from stoic contentment to fierce embrace:

> I am content to live it all again
> And yet again, if it be life to pitch
> Into the frog-spawn of a blind man's ditch,
> A blind man battering blind men;

> Or into that most fecund ditch of all,
> The folly that man does
> Or must suffer, if he woos
> A proud woman not kindred of his soul.
>
> I am content to follow to its source
> Every event in action or in thought;
> Measure the lot, forgive myself the lot!
> When such as I cast out remorse
> So great a sweetness flows into the breast
> We must laugh and we must sing,
> We are blest by everything,
> Everything we look upon is blest.

Mere contentment suggests awareness of another and higher spiritual 'source', external to the self. But here, following everything to the 'source' within, Self spurns Soul's tongue-numbing doctrine that 'only the dead can be forgiven'. Instead, having pitched with vitalistic relish into life's filthy frog-spawn, Self audaciously (or blasphemously) claims the power to forgive *himself*. In a similar act of self-determination, Self 'cast[s] *out*' remorse, reversing the defiling image earlier 'cast *upon*' him by the 'mirror of malicious eyes'. Self's own passive mirror has turned lamp and Christian redemption has been secularized, with the autonomous Romantic imagination as redeemer. The sweetness that 'flows into' the self-forgiving breast redeems the frog-spawn of the blind man's ditch and even that 'most fecund ditch', the painful but productive folly that is the bitter fruit of unrequited love. (It would violate decorum – and is hardly necessary – for Yeats to name the 'proud woman not kindred of his soul'.) That sweet flow also displaces the infusion (*infundere*: 'to pour in') of Christian grace through divine forgiveness. It is a move at once redemptive and heretical: a confirmation of man's claimed autonomy, a prideful *non serviam*, and a stubborn clinging to sensuous beauty, however bittersweet the attendant pain and folly.

That the battered Self can end in ecstasy is in large part a tribute to Yeats's masterly fusion of his two principal precursors, Blake and Nietzsche. If, as Yeats rightly said (*Essays and Introductions*, p. 112), Blake's central doctrine is a Christ-like 'forgiveness of sins', the sweetness that flows into the suffering but *self-forgiving* 'breast', the breast in which Blake also said '*all* deities reside', allies the Romantic poet with Nietzsche. He had been preceded by the German Inner Light theologians, but it took Nietzsche, the son of a Protestant minister, to most radically transvalue the Augustinian doctrine that man can only be redeemed by divine power and grace, a foretaste of predestinarianism made more uncompromising in the strict Protestant doctrine of the salvation of the elect as an unmerited gift of God. One must find one's *own* 'grace', countered Nietzsche. He who has 'definitively *conquered himself*, henceforth regards it as his own privilege to punish himself, to pardon himself' – in Yeats's phrase, 'forgive myself the lot'. Clemency must replace self-hatred; we must cast out remorse and cease to despise ourselves: 'Then you will no longer have any need of your god, and the whole drama of Fall and Redemption will be played out to the end in you yourselves!'[7]

While Yeats could never bring himself to endorse Nietzschean atheism, the final chant of Self in 'Dialogue' – 'We must laugh and we must sing / We are blest by everything, / Everything we look upon is blest' – is clearly the product of Yeats's brilliant in-gathering of Blake and Nietzsche. To be sure, Self's final lines are riddled with echoes: along with Shakespeare's chastened Lear ('We'll live, / And pray, and sing, and ... laugh') and the Wordsworth of 'Tintern Abbey' (sure 'that all which we behold / Is full of blessings'), there is, minus his orthodox 'kind saint', Coleridge's wa014snake-blessing Mariner, who tells us that, having perceived the previously 'slimy' creatures in all their iridescent vital beauty, 'A spring of love gushed from my heart, / And I blessed them unaware.' But the critical figures remain Blake and Nietzsche. Yeats's citation of Gauguin on *Séraphita* in the unpublished note to 'Dialogue' may confirm Balzac's role as one of Yeats's European conduits to spiritual philosophy; but then Yeats, discussing Balzac's 'romanticization of power', remarked, in 1924, that 'All Nietzsche is in Balzac'. Thus, it is largely under the twin auspices of Blake and Nietzsche, as manipulated by Yeats, that Self in 'Dialogue' can find, rather than everlasting pain, the bliss traditionally reserved for those who follow the ascending path.

Yeats believed that Nietzsche's thought 'flows always, though with an even more violent current, in the bed Blake's thought has worn', and that 'Nietzsche completes Blake and has the same roots', especially Blake in his 'praise of life – "all that lives is holy".' Yeats specifically identifies this Blake with Nietzsche 'at the moment when he imagined the Superman as a child' (*Essays and Introductions*, p. 130; *Letters*, p. 379; *Autobiography*, pp. 474–5). That occurs in Zarathustra's speech on the threefold metamorphosis of the spirit, from burdened camel to defiant lion to the value-creating 'child' and his 'sacred Yes'. In Self's peroration in 'Dialogue', Yeats himself 'completes' a presumably truncated Blake with Nietzsche by fusing childlike 'joy', which Nietzsche's Zarathustra shared with Blake, with the painful but finally ecstatic acceptance of Eternal Recurrence: Nietzsche's 'highest formula of affirmation which is at all attainable', but a Dionysian doctrine anathema to Blake, for whom cyclicism was the final dehumanizing nightmare. That part of the 'completion' is forced, but *not* Yeats's association of Zarathustra's 'sacred Yes' with the final chant (in *Visions of the Daughters of Albion*) of Blake's heroine Oothoon, an affirmation addressed to everything we look upon: 'Sing your infant joy! / Arise and drink your bliss, for everything that lives is holy!'(8:214–5). Self is a living man who, defying Neoplatonism, 'drinks his drop', ending in precisely that state of 'infant joy'.

It is, however, in the American poet Hart Crane's clarifying phrase (in his poem 'Passage'), 'an *improved* infancy', what Blake calls 'organiz'd' or 'higher' Innocence, and Nietzsche, in his preface to *The Gay Science*, 'a *second* dangerous innocence in joy'. For, given the preceding struggle, there is nothing naive or simplistic in Self's hard-earned, all-embracing ecstasy. And it is an embrace *inclusive* in both perception and what is perceived. No matter how unapologetically autonomous Yeats generally is, however far-fetched and idio-syncratic his occult and reincarnational preoccupations, here, like Wordsworth in the final stanza of the Intimations Ode (following four repetitions of 'I' by the pivotal 'Thanks to the human heart by which *we* live'), Yeats insists that it is not just 'I', or even 'such as I', that must laugh and must sing. He claims that '*We* are blest by everything, / Everything *we* look upon is blest.' Yeats's alteration of the spiritual tradition completes Blake with that Nietzsche whose exuberant Zarathustra, jumping 'with both feet' into 'golden-emerald delight', also jumps into a cluster of images and motifs we would call – remembering the dancer of 'Among School Children', the birds of Byzantium, and the transfigu-ration of Cuchulain – Yeatsian:

> In laughter all that is evil comes together, but is pronounced *holy* and *absolved by its own bliss*; and if this is my *alpha* and *omega*, that all that is heavy and grave should become light, all that is body, dancer, all that is spirit, bird – and verily that *is* my alpha and omega: oh, how should I not lust after eternity and the nuptial ring of rings, the ring of recurrence? (*Thus Spoke Zarathustra*, 3:16)

The response of Self, who ends by commandeering the spiritual vocabulary Soul would monopolize, is a fierce, even furious, affirmation of a Nietzschean Eternal Recurrence rather than escape from the labyrinth of human life, with all its tangled antinomies of joy and suffering. To the extent that Yeats permits a fair engagement between Soul and Self, he of course subverts the whole tradition of Body-Soul debates – from Plato, Plotinus, and *Scipio's Dream*, through Milton's *Comus* and Marvell's debate-poems – leaving the spiritual spokesperson with a petrified tongue, and giving Self a final chant which is among the most rhapsodic and resonant in that whole tradition of secularized supernaturalism Yeats inherited from the Romantic poets and from Nietzsche.

It is also the vision of Crazy Jane and the Woman Young and Old: those preeminent female spokespersons for the life-affirming vision that dominates *The Winding Stair*. Forced to choose between 'perfection of the life or of the work', Yeats, Poet rather than Saint, will choose the latter. But, a dialectician to the end, he will prefer a middle term between blood and the moon, between, on the one hand, Soul's 'breathless starlit air' or the Byzantine 'moonlit or a starlit dome', and, on the other, the frog-spawn or the fury and the mire of human veins. Fusing sacred and secular, he celebrates what he calls 'profane perfection' ('Under Ben Bulben'). It is in *that* faith that Yeats lives and dies: a faith best and most inclusively symbolized by Sato's consecrated sword, both spiritual *and* phallic, and protected, adorned, and crucially *completed* by 'That flowering, silken, old embroidery, torn / From some court-lady's dress and round / The wooden scabbard bound and wound.'

Such Romantic symbolism may seem antiquated – until we see their connection to, and distance from, that 'proud woman not kindred of his soul.' Against this scabbarded sword and embroidery, we might cite three earlier Maud Gonne poems. Back in 1899, Yeats had famously wished to spread beneath the feet of his beloved 'The heaven's embroidered cloths'. When, in a poem written a decade later, 'Reconciliation', recording her 1903 marriage, when Maud 'went from' him, he 'could find / Nothing to make a song about but kings, / Helmets and swords, and half-forgotten things / That were like memories of you.' In the title phrase of another poem, written in 1905, he advises us, 'O do not love too long, / Or you will grow out of fashion / Like an old song.' Returning to 'Dialogue', we can finally name the 'proud woman not kindred of his soul', and find in that poem's central icon of sword and silk half-forgotten and out-of-fashion things that were like memories of Maud.

But the lovelorn heart, the place 'where all the ladders start', is not where the ladders *end*. In 1911, in 'Friends', Yeats has asked, 'What of her that *took / All* till my youth was gone?' In old age, in 'The Circus Animals' Desertion', he counters with another hyperbolic half-truth; that it was the playwriting and the poetry that '*took all* my love, / And not those things that they were emblems of.' In 'A Dialogue of Self and Soul', as always in Yeats's mature work, 'a personal emotion has been woven into a general pattern of myth and symbol' (*Autobiographies*, p. 151). Whatever the labyrinthine autobiographical associations of his central symbol, in the overarching design of *The Winding Stair*, the sword's embroidery is another emblem of 'reconciliation', with its entwined and tattered fabric – mutable, female and ultimately life-affirming – palpably re-enacting the spiralling of the winding stair itself.

NOTES

1. Denis Donoghue, 'On 'The Winding Stair', in *An Honoured Guest : New Essays'*, ed. D. Donoghue and J. Mulryne (New York 1966), pp. 107, 123.

2. Keats, 'Ode to Melancholy': *The Letters of John Keats,* 2 vols., ed. Hyder E. Rollins (Cambridge, Massachusetts 1958), vol. 2, pp. 102–4.

3. Peter Allt, 'W.B. Yeats', *Theology* 42 (1941), pp.81–99.

4. Diagram drawn by Yeats on p. 122 of a Nietzsche anthology of 'Choice Selections from His Works' given him by John Quinn: *Nietzsche as Critic, Philosopher, Poet and Prophet,* ed. Thomas Common (London 1901).

5. For a full, luminous reading of 'Vacillation', see Helen Vendler's essay, *Yeats Annual No 18* (2013): pp.151–68.

6. Macrobius, *Commentary on the Dream of Scipio,* trans. W.H. Stahl (New York 1952), pp. 152–3, 155.

7. Nietzsche, *Daybreak* (§437, §79), trans. R.J. Hollingdale (Cambridge 1996), pp. 186–7, 48. Yeats read this book, translated in 1913 by J.M. Kennedy as *Dawn.*

Reading 'The Cold Heaven'

DENIS DONOGHUE

When I started thinking of myself as a student of modern poetry and of Yeats in some particulars, I hardly adverted to 'The Cold Heaven', it was not one of the classic poems. I'm sure I never quoted it. That was a lamentable failure. To be specific: I should have observed that when J.R. Mulryne and I brought together a book of invited essays called *An Honoured Guest: New Essays on W.B. Yeats* (1965), one of the essayists, T.R. Henn, to whom we had assigned *Responsibilities*, wrote a page about 'The Cold Heaven' without claiming that he was in full possession of it. I should have pursued the question to see at least what the problems were. Belatedly, this is one of my aims in the present essay.

But there is a larger consideration. When I was starting out in literary criticism, I took T.S. Eliot as my master. His early essays on Marvell, Donne, and on the Elizabethan dramatists seemed to indicate what literary criticism was, especially when his understanding of literature, notably of poetry and drama, was verified, it seemed to me, in his observations on the verse of *The Revenger's Tragedy* and in several essays by Allen Tate and R.P. Blackmur. Not by John Crowe Ransom. I delighted in Ransom's poems and in his prose when I became preoccupied with style. When I submitted to him, as editor of *The Kenyon Review,* an essay I had written on Yeats's Crazy Jane poems, I received a handwritten reply of acceptance and a promise that he would publish it in an early number of the journal. That filled several of my days with wonder and joy. Kenneth Burke was another story. I entered into correspondence with

him and kept it up for several years, but I think I disappointed him in the
end, even as a devoted pupil. I failed to learn what his notion of 'symbolic
action' meant, unless it was the grammar of a certain language, the fulfilment
of its 'logic' before it takes a psychological or otherwise expressive form. But
I didn't sufficiently realize how different these and other critical masters were,
one from another. Cleanth Brooks was determined to find certain qualities in
language in its supreme moments. William Empson was occupied with ambi-
guity because an ambiguity in language pointed to a corresponding quandary
or knot in a writer's feelings, being pulled in different directions at once. He
thought that the great value of a language was that it accommodated these
quandaries and was not defeated by them. But none of these big critics, apart
from Eliot, showed me what literary criticism was or what it should be. If it
was a game, it apparently had no rules. You could do anything you wanted to
do, subject to the sad consideration that whatever you wanted was merely that:
it had no further authority. However, I gradually started thinking that I might
place beside the chosen poem a goodly number of companionable sentences,
in decent prose, as a context in which a student's reading of the poem might
proceed. An essay placed beside the poem in this way would probably be an
essay in appreciation; else why write it at all?

I now think I should have taken more seriously, that is more strictly, what
Eliot says in 'The Function of Criticism', that criticism should have an end in
view, and that the end 'appears to be the elucidation of works of art and the
correction of taste.'[1] 'Elucidation' may be hard to achieve, you may have to see
how the poem is ordered, the system of energy by which it gets from first word
to last. You may have to put before your assumed readers some facts that they
are not likely to know. 'The correction of taste' may seem to be redundant.
How do I know that an inferior taste is there to be corrected, unless someone
has written an account of the poem which I find repellent? How do I know that
my taste is such as to correct other readers? But Eliot's formula can be modi-
fied. I can write an account of the poem and leave it to hypothetical readers to
decide whether it exhibits good taste or not-so-good taste. I understand Eliot's
concern with taste as an attempt to adumbrate a better way of being alive.

Why not? The elucidation of works of art and the correction of taste offer
a morally charged formula, they presuppose discipline, purity of heart, work
sufficient to the occasion, and other decencies. They also presuppose not neces-
sarily 'close reading' but what Reuben Brower called 'reading in slow motion',
as if you were leading someone arduously though happily through a poem in a
foreign language.

II

'The Cold Heaven' was one of six poems added to make up the 1912 edition of *The Green Helmet and Other Poems* (1910). It was later transferred to *Responsibilities* (1914), where it is now generally read. I give the text as it appeared in the *Collected Poems* (1950) and, with the lines numbered, in the *Variorum Edition of the Poems of W.B. Yeats* (1987):

1: Suddenly I saw the cold and rook-delighting heaven
2: That seemed as though ice burned and was but the more ice,
3: And thereupon imagination and heart were driven
4: So wild that every casual thought of that and this
5: Vanished, and left but memories, that should be out of season
6: With the hot blood of youth, of love crossed long ago;
7: And I took all the blame out of all sense and reason,
8: Until I cried and trembled and rocked to and fro,
9: Riddled with light. Ah! When the ghost begins to quicken,
10: Confusion of the death-bed over, is it sent
11: Out naked on the roads, as the books say, and stricken
12: By the injustice of the skies for punishment?

I start with some details before coming to wider considerations. The only textual variant of any significance is in the first line: every edition from 1912 to 1931 had 'Heaven', but this was becalmed to 'heaven' in 1933, 1950 and thereafter. Of course the capital was retained in the title, but not necessarily in the lines that followed. Yeats took care to retain Heaven, giving it its capital, only when he personified it – 'But masterful Heaven had intervened to save it.' Or when it was accompanied by theologically resonant terms such as 'God' and 'Immortality'. Otherwise he was inconsistent about the capital. The *Concordance* is no help, since it prints every word in capitals. Still with the title and the first line: 'cold' is the standard weather-word, the sky looks cold, there is no ambiguity unless we recall that Yeats promised to write for his iconic fisherman a poem 'maybe as cold / And passionate as the dawn.' Passionate, I suppose, because the dawn looks as if it is determined to become day; the cold of usual dawns is extended to mean independent, resolute, or some such human quality. 'Suddenly I saw ... ' is Yeats's challenge to the apparent objectivity of the natural world; he claims to take apprehensive possession of what he sees.

Deirdre Toomey has explained 'rook-delighting'. Yeats started drafting the poem when he was travelling by train, on 21 February 1911, from Manchester to Norwich by way of London. He was to see an amateur production of *The*

Countess Cathleen, directed by Nugent Monck, the play he had written for
Maud Gonne in 1899. He had wanted her to play the Countess, but she declined
on the consideration, or the excuse, that it would divert her from urgent polit-
ical activities. Yeats started to draft the poem while the train was approaching
Norwich. Toomey notes that South Norwich is 'celebrated for its vast rook-
eries, icy marshes and wetlands'. Norfolk, 'particularly the Yare Valley, has
the largest rook colonies in Western Europe.'[2] The prospect of seeing a new
production of *The Countess Cathleen,* sixteen years after the one in Dublin
written for Maud Gonne, 'must have stirred very powerful emotions of "love
crossed long ago", as well as a painful examination of conscience', writes
Toomey. I don't know why it should provoke an examination of conscience,
but we take Yeats's word for this as for much else.

Line 2: a strong hyperbole for the 'cold' of line 1. There is no reason to
think that fire, one of the four elements, burns merely to destroy. 'Look on that
fire, salvation walks within.' I don't understand the visual image of ice burning
and becoming but the more ice. It is not a morning poem with sunlight. I grant
that ice gleams, but I am carried forward more by the verve of the line than by
anything I grasp with the eye or the eye of the mind.

Line 3: 'And thereupon': a favorite gesture in Yeats's poems, especially
where, as here, a new burst of energy is needed. It has not the same prov-
enance as 'Suddenly'. 'Suddenly' is inaugural, it proclaims a perception upon
no authority but its own. In this case it summons the reader to be present,
to listen, to pay attention. 'And thereupon' invokes a cause: something has
happened or been done, and as a result the poet can proceed without hesitation.
'Imagination and heart.' Yeats thought of imagination as Blake did, and distin-
guished it from mere reason, as in his 'William Blake and the Imagination':

> He had learned from Jacob Boehme and from old alchemist writers that
> imagination was the first emanation of divinity, 'the body of God', 'the
> Divine members', and he drew the deduction, which they did not draw, that
> the imaginative arts were therefore the greatest of Divine revelations, and
> that the sympathy with all living things, sinful and righteous alike, which the
> imaginative arts awaken, is that forgiveness of sins commanded by Christ.[3]

Heart is much the same for Yeats as for anyone else, a faculty of responsive-
ness. Driven wild, it would approach the sublime form of itself. In the seventh
section of 'Vacillation' it disputes with the Soul, bringing the debate to an end
with 'What theme had Homer but original sin?' It speaks up for body and time.
Lines 3–5 anticipate lines 18–21 of 'A Bronze Head':

> ... Propinquity had brought
> Imagination to that pitch where it casts out

> All that is not itself. I had grown wild
> And wandered murmuring everywhere, 'My child, my child!'

Line 4: 'Every casual thought of that and this' is administered by reason. Blake is again the instructor. As Yeats says:

> The reason, and by the reason he meant deductions from the observations of the senses, binds us to mortality because it binds us to the senses, and divides us from each other by showing us our clashing interests; but imagination divides us from mortality by the immortality of beauty, and binds us to each other by opening the secret doors of all hearts.[4]

'Opening the secret doors of all hearts' is not explicit, it depends on a theory of Natural Law that Yeats has not expounded.

Line 5: The sentence that started in line 3 should have ended, I think, with 'memories'. The addition of seventeen words is awkward, especially their beginning with 'that should be out of season / With the hot blood of youth ...' Should be? Ought to be? Not the memories I want to have? A question of taste arises: Yeats is saying more than he feels. 'Out of season': untimely.

Line 6: 'The hot blood of youth, of love crossed long ago.' Of youth and of love together do much of the work of rhyme. It would be perverse to separate them from Maud. If Yeats's love for her was 'crossed' or star-crossed, it is hard to know why, in line 7, he takes all the blame. He didn't, in the poem 'Friends' that precedes this one in *The Green Helmet and Other Poems:*

> And what of her that took
> All till my youth was gone
> With scarce a pitying look?
> How could I praise that one?
> (*VP* 315–16)

'That one', in Irish-English idiom, is a gruff dismissal.

Line 7 is the line I most dislike in Yeats's poems: its only competitor for me in that regard is the line in 'The Tower' about Mrs. French, 'Gifted with so fine an ear.' The repetition of 'all' is loud. I don't think it is a valid intensive. I am not surprised to learn from the *Concordance* that Yeats used 'all' twice as often as any other word in the poems, the next claimant in that category being 'old'. He liked 'all' so much that he insisted on repeating it: 'all, all are in my thoughts to-night being dead.' 'But in the grave all, all, shall be renewed.' I see, by the way, that J. Hillis Miller, in one of his several essays on 'The Cold Heaven', misquoted the poem by omitting the first 'all'.[5] I can't condone the misquotation, even when, as here, it improves the poem. In *The Structure of*

Complex Words William Empson has a chapter on 'All in *Paradise Lost*' in which he maintains that this word in Milton's poem 'is a prominent feature of the style, with a set of tricks of its own – a Wagnerian *motif* – you could hardly parody Milton without bringing it in.' Milton is 'an absolutist, an all-or-none man.' 'All else is unimportant beside one thing, he is constantly deciding; he delights in the harshness of a theme which makes all human history turn on an absolutely trivial action.'[6] Yeats's motifs are different. 'My instructors identify consciousness with conflict', and while his imagination is ready to disinter 'any rich, dark nothing' to set his mind going, he is never content unless he can bring forward an 'all' to challenge it. Toomey argues that 'the misery caused by Maud Gonne's long rejection of him is a punishment for sins in a previous life', and she finds warrant for such punishment in a book that Yeats, she reports, read with great care, Ráma Prasád's *Nature's Finer Forms* (1890). It is a Yeatsian motif, and he probably believed it. In the play *Purgatory* the Old Man says that the souls in Purgatory that 'come back / To habitations and familiar spots' 're-live / Their transgressions, and that not once / But many times.' Eliot found the play shocking because, he said, 'I cannot accept a purgatory in which there is no hint, or at least no emphasis upon Purgation.'[7] Yeats can't have taken all the blame, since he notes that the way he took it was 'out of all sense and reason.' That phrase, as a second thought, questions the first.

Line 8: Generally in Yeats's poems to cry is to cry out, in protest or rage, though I recall that Crazy Jane on the Mountain 'cried tears down'. In 'The Cold Heaven', as the manuscripts show, he had tears to report. To tremble is not always sexual, but Crazy Jane concedes that 'when looks meet / I tremble to the bone.' 'Rocked' is unusual, though it turns up twice in 'The Indian upon God':

> My spirit rocked in evening light, the rushes round my knees,
> My spirit rocked in sleep and sighs; and saw the moorfowl pace ...

Much of the work is done by the repeated 'ands' deploying three intransitive verbs and one subject. For once, the verbs, free of objects, have unlimited resonance. These lines, like some other words in 'The Cold Heaven', have a general air of meaning rather than a commitment to a primary or specific meaning, though 'sighs' intimate desire. Hillis Miller has noted that there are eleven 'ands' in the poem, an unusually high number.[8] Some of them are innocuous, 'to and fro', 'that and this'. But those in the first part of line 8 are not. 'Until I cried and trembled and rocked to and fro.' If the poem were written out as prose, several of the 'ands' would be replaced by commas. The decency of prose would call for 'cold, rook-delighting' and 'cried, trembled, and rocked.' But commas have doubtful acoustic value, the voice hardly knows what to do with them, or with parentheses, as in some of Jorie Graham's poems. Most of the 'ands' in 'The Cold Heaven' are crowded into the middle lines; there is only one in the great sweep of the final question. In line 8 the repeated 'ands' give the experience a note of the frantic, but I'm not sure how it does this. 'And' is often equivocal. Elizabeth Bishop has a poem, 'Over 2,000 Illustrations and a Complete Concordance', in which she looks through a gazetteer before recalling some of her travels and ruefully remarks, 'Everything only connected by "and" and "and" '.[9] 'Only' tips the scale. Evidently she wants a more ample connection among her experiences. But what, other than 'and', could it be? Walter Pater, recommending an impressionist sense of experience, writes severely of language:

> And if we continue to dwell in thought on this world, not of objects in the solidity with which language invests them, but of impressions, unstable, flickering, inconsistent, which burn and are extinguished with our consciousness of them, it contracts still further: the whole scope of observation is dwarfed into the narrow chamber of the individual mind.[10]

If language invests objects with solidity they don't deserve, such that an impressionist sense of life must be left to French painters, Yeats's 'ands' may be hopeless, exorbitant to the experiences they have under their care. But they have particular work to do, as Bishop's, too, have in the final lines of 'The Armadillo':

> O falling fire and piercing cry
> and panic, and a weak mailed fist
> clenched ignorant against the sky![11]

The three 'ands' keep the lines going at the same level of invocation as the initial 'O'.

Line 9: 'Riddled with light.' This is the only use of 'riddled' in Yeats's poems. According to the OED, it can mean either perforated as by bullets or like a sieve. 'Light', rushing into one's mind not as a single blaze or beam but from many sources, as through a sieve. Figurative as it is, and therefore implying intensity of sensation, cognitive by definition, it has not severed connection with the 'saw' of line 1, but it may also be the light that blinds. We receive the force of the phrase without enquiring too narrowly what it means. Everything depends on the glow the word 'light' already has in one's mind. 'Ah!' is a long sigh, but it doesn't give any indication of how it is to be read. To interpret it, one has to look to the words that come after. The interjection is omitted from the *Concordance* though it is used in the poems 88 times. Indeterminate, it anticipates the image it sighs to think of. 'The ghost': the soul, separated from its theological companions, cooled as by the reduction of 'Heaven' to 'heaven'.

'To quicken', to come into its new mode of life. Rare in the poems, 'quicken' in Yeats is usually a noun referring to the mountain-ash or rowan-tree.

Line 10: 'Confusion of the death-bed over': as when Lear, confused indeed and thinking Cordelia alive, says 'This feather stirs; she lives! ... Look on her, look, her lips, / Look there, look there!'

Lines 10–12: Yeats often ended a poem with a question, as in 'Among School Children', 'The Second Coming', and 'Leda and the Swan':

> Did she put on his knowledge with his power
> Before the indifferent beak could let her drop?

Yes or no. But in 'The Cold Heaven' the question is nearly an assertion, coming with the authority of 'the books' – 'old books' in one of the manuscripts.[12] We are not invited to answer yes or no. To arrive at 'the injustice of the skies', you would only have to believe, as Yeats did, in Reincarnation, and then believe that you are punished in your next life for the crimes you have committed in this one. Or even for the bad things you couldn't have helped doing, as in several Greek tragedies. Hence the injustice of the skies. Much of the Vision, in both versions, is an attempt to imagine the form one's life-after-death might take. Yeats was not much of a Christian, so he found it easy to dispense with the idea of a singular God, as in Eliot's poems, who provides for purgation and forgiveness. If you assume many gods, one or more of them will probably be vindictive, like the Furies, given to thunderous interventions. I find no evidence that Yeats, as early as 1911, had worked out the system he was to project in A Vision. I doubt that he had at his fingertips such motifs as the Dreaming Back or the Phantasmagoria. In 1911, I think, he had only the few occult notions he recited in 'Swedenborg, Mediums, Desolate Places', dated 1914, largely gathered from the stories Lady Gregory wrote down from elders in the cottages at Coole or Yeats heard in Aran. The blame of line 7, all or less, needed only a god with a good memory of one's life. 'The skies' is another variant of 'Heaven' or 'heaven', further distanced from theology.

III

The poem began, as the manuscripts indicate, with a few scribbles in a railway-carriage at night. No particular genre was indicated. Yeats sometimes started on a poem by writing out the gist of it in prose and picking a few words that had rhyming possibilities, as in 'The Fascination of What's Difficult'. But not this time. 'As though ice burned and yet was the more ice' was the first line that stayed the course after the scribbles, prefaced by 'It seemed'. Metrically, we have a poem in twelve lines, three quatrains, rhyming or slant rhyming *abab, cdcd, efef.* We almost expect a rhyming couplet, making it a sonnet. Five of the lines have twelve syllables, as if he had alexandrines in his ear, and the other lines run between thirteen and fifteen. Ten lines have six stresses, in my reading, the remaining two have seven and five. The tune is iambic hexameter, despite the dactyl of the first word, 'suddenly'.

But the metre is overruled by the syntax, as it generally is in Yeats's poems. In his essay on Spenser he says that Spenser was 'liberated from the minute felici-ties of phrase and sound that are the temptation and the delight of rhyme',[13] but he himself had no wish to be so liberated. Among the modern poets in English he is one of the most accomplished rhymers, but he still gives first place to the sentence, if only because he thinks of poetry as discourse, something that he or someone else might say. One of the lessons Ezra Pound hoped to learn from Yeats in 1908, according to Hugh Kenner, was how to 'fit the sentence into the stanza', a practice in which Yeats was a master.[14] He must do the best he can with the metre, because it enables the rhythm; the rhythm emerges from the tension between syntax and metre. The submission of the metre, even if we call it submission, is not abject. Syntax has to allow the rhythm to happen. We are reading a poem, not an essay; there must be a tune.

In this poem there are three declarative sentences, followed by a question. The first sentence coincides with the first two lines, and acts with the subjec-tive authority of 'Suddenly I saw ... ' and 'seemed'. These are irrefutable. The second reports the consequence, in lines 3 to 6, with no more authority than 'And thereupon ... ' This sentence doesn't obliterate the metre, but it imposes its own style, such that we hardly notice that 'heaven' gets its rhyme in 'driven' – a rhyme Yeats could have found in Wordsworth, Poe, Byron, Tennyson and other poets when 'heaven's' sentence is already over and 'driven' finds its rapid syntactical completion in 'So wild ... ' The rhyme is hardly noticed. For the same reason, the rhyme of 'ice' and 'this' passes without fuss. In the next quatrain the rhyme of 'season' and 'reason' is predictable, few other rhymes with 'season' being available. The rhyme of 'ago' and 'fro' does not detain a reader. In the third and last quatrain, the verb 'quicken' makes 'stricken' nearly inevitable. In 'The Island of Statues' 'quicken' completes a rhyme with 'sicken', but that was the only other occasion on which Yeats gave it rhyming duty. The rhymings of 'quicken' and 'stricken', and of 'sent' and 'punishment' are the only rhymes likely to register on a reader. But they do.

W.K. Wimsatt's essay, 'One Relation of Rhyme to Reason', argues that the best rhymes relate different parts of speech, as in Pope:

> Bless'd with each talent and each art to please,
> And born to write, converse, and live with ease;
> Should such a man, too fond to rule alone,
> Bear, like the Turk, no brother near the throne;
> View him with scornful, yet with jealous eyes,
> And hate for arts that caus'd himself to rise;

Wimsatt's main argument is 'that the greater the difference in meaning between rhyme words the more marked and the more appropriate will be the binding effect.' He continues: 'But where there is need for binding there must be some difference or separation between the things to be bound. If they are already close together, it is supererogatory to emphasize this by the maneuver of rhyme.'[15] If rhyming links the same part of speech, there should be a difference of function, as again in Pope:

> Dreading ev'n fools; by flatterers besiege
> And so obliging that he ne'er obliged;
> Like Cato, give his little Senate laws,
> And sit attentive to his own applause.[16]

Here, Wimsatt notes, the same part of speech is rhymed, but one verb is active, one passive, one noun is plural, one singular. Small differences, perhaps, but enough to enforce different functions.

I have seen Wimsatt's essay questioned, but it seems to me to withstand the questions.[17] Most studies of rhyme need a distinction between rhymes that draw attention to themselves and those that don't: 'manifest' and 'latent', 'resonant' and 'curt' are among the suggestions I have seen to mark the difference. In Yeats's poem, 'heaven' and 'driven' are different parts of speech; so are 'ice' and 'this'. 'Season' and 'reason' are not, but there is a saving twist of function in the idiom of 'out of season'. 'Ago' and 'fro' are saved by the slight difference between two syllables and one. 'Quicken' and 'stricken' break Wimsatt's rule the more boldly because they make a noticeable rhyme, hard not to hear, but 'quicken' is in the infinitive mood, 'stricken' is a past participle. The final rhyme, 'sent' and 'punishment', fulfils the rule; different parts of speech, and one syllable rhyming with a word of three. Some of these rhymes are hardly more than nominal. Kenner has given us an appropriate idiom to differentiate them: 'The ceremony of Yeatsian rhymed stanzas renders rhymes audible or inconspicuous according as congruences are being ensheaved or simply iterated, and a Japanese poet without rhyming his sounds may rhyme a crow with the night.'[18] This sentence posits a Poundian aesthetic according to which poetry consists of congruences found, retrieved, assembled, with 'rhymes' of culture not necessarily acoustic. It is close to another version, also Poundian, sometimes called 'juxtaposition without copula', which might as well be called 'juxtaposition without rhyme', the congruences being left to speak for themselves. So we have 'ensheaved', gathered up like corn into a sheaf, for a purpose. 'Simply iterated': but the iteration can't be simple, there must be a cause of it. Rhymes that are not audible may as well be called silent: 'inconspicuous' implies visual values. The rhymes in the last quatrain of Yeats's poem are indeed ensheaved, brought together for a reason, and therefore audible, indeed sonorous.

There is also a notable difference of tone between the lines. Lines 1–2 are end-stopped on 'ice', even though the sentence continues after the comma. Lines 3–6 have an end-stop only in 'ago'. Lines 7 and 8 are end-stopped, with the complication of the last phrase, 'Riddled with light.' Line 9 is end-stopped, even though the question continues till the end of the poem. These arrangements have the effect of making the poem gather strength as it proceeds – it gets better all the time – and the strongest line is the last. But it is hard to be more specific about cause and consequence, apart from remarking the Nietzschean tone throughout.

IV

The most notable feature of 'The Cold Heaven' is the audacity with which Yeats drives his chariot from one experience to another, the verve of the transitions. The poem is a play in three acts. The first line starts the whole experience off, simply but irrefutably: he looks out the window of a railway carriage on a winter night and sees a flock of rooks against the sky. 'Rook-delighting' implies that there is a sustaining relation of some kind between birds and sky, but none between Yeats and sky. The second line is a claim of seeming: if it seemed so to Yeats, we are in no position to question it. Poets of an idealist disposition are always ready to say that if something seems to them to be the case, it is the case. Wallace Stevens's 'Description without Place' begins:

> It is possible that to seem – it is to be,
> As the sun is something seeming and it is. The sun is an
> example. What it seems
> It is and in such seeming all things are.[19]

This starts modestly, something is 'possible'. But in next-to-no time Stevens, a good idealist for the moment, talks himself into certainty. Yeats does as much. He saw something, and we take his unambiguous word for it. What he makes of the experience is declared in the second line: 'That seemed as though ice burned and was but the more ice.' That appearance could not seem so to anyone but

Yeats: it has no traction as an experience to which he can appeal for general assent. We concede to it, giving him the benefit of a large doubt. We believe that it means something to Yeats, though we don't know what. And yet on the strength of an experience so meagrely shared, he can say 'And thereupon' and propel us into another experience, wild indeed, which only a reader attuned to the sublime could appreciate. Lines 7 to 9 about blame are also clear. Yeats was inclined to report that, as 'Vacillation' has it, 'Responsibility so weighs me down', and that 'My conscience or my vanity [is] appalled'. We are free to protest that the claims of conscience, and those of vanity, are not equally strong. 'Riddled with light' is a problem because we can't know what 'light' means and we have to guess which tradition of light Yeats is invoking. Even Samuel Johnson couldn't define it; as in Boswell's *Life* on 11 April 1776, he said to Boswell: 'We all *know* what light is, but it is not very easy to *tell* what it is.'[20] It is a 'complex word' in Empson's sense, though it doesn't appear in his book. The speculation in the last quatrain is clear as Yeats's speculations go, but we may well ask what relation obtains among the three sentences and the final question. None, if we count only relations common to whatever tradition we live by. But there is also, in Yeats's poems generally and this one in particular, what R.P. Blackmur called 'a felt unity of disproportions': 'Yeats combines elements any one of which is disproportionate, even incongruous, taken by itself, and his unity – what he is taken all together – is an imaginative, a felt unity of disproportions.'[21] But that sentence moves the question of unity from any particular poem to the 'complete works' – 'what he is taken all together' – as if we could find unity in the composite figure of the poet though not in any of the poems. Blackmur also quotes a passage from one of Yeats's letters to Dorothy Wellesley, dated 10 July 1937:

> I begin to see things double – doubled in history, world history, personal history. At this moment all the specialists are about to run together in our new Alexandria, thought is about to be unified as its own free act, and the shadow in Germany and elsewhere is an attempted unity by force. In my own life I never felt so acutely the presence of a spiritual virtue and that is accompanied by intensified desire. Perhaps there is a theme for poetry in this 'double swan and shadow'. You must feel plunged as I do into the madness of vision, into a sense of the relation between separated things that you cannot explain, and that deeply disturbs emotion.[22]

'Thought about to be unified as its own free act' sounds like the Yeats who has read Gentile's *The Theory of Mind as Pure Act* (1922). 'The madness of vision': this is the 'matter and impertinency mix'd: reason in madness' that Edgar diagnosed in the ruined Lear of the fourth act. 'The relation between separated things that you cannot explain': you cannot explain it because you have no idea what it is and no certainty that there is such a relation, except for the conviction that there must be one. But these speculations carry us beyond 'The Cold Heaven' or aside from it. Four separated things enforced themselves without explanation in that poem. The last one, given in the ostensive form of a question, is the most challenging. Is the poem throughout what it demonstrably becomes, a trembling meditation on death, warding off the ghosts that hover over one's deathbed, or a speculation to make them less punitive by diagnosing their behaviours in advance? Yeats was ill, off and on, from 1927 till his death in 1939, but from the beginning of his adult life he was never short of a reason to think of death – his own or someone else's. Shortly after the assassination of Kevin O'Higgins on July 10 1927 he wrote 'Death':

> Nor dread nor hope attend
> A dying animal;
> A man awaits his end
> Dreading and hoping all;
> Many times he died,
> Many times rose again.
> A great man in his pride
> Confronting murderous men
> Casts derision upon
> Supersession of breath;
> He knows death to the bone –
> Man has created death.
>   (VP 476)

These highly dubious lines may be read along with other questionable lines from 'The Tower':

> I mock Plotinus' thought
> And cry in Plato's teeth,
> Death and life were not
> Till man made up the whole,
> Made lock, stock and barrel
> Out of his bitter soul,
> Aye, sun and moon and star, all,
> And further add to that
> That, being dead, we rise,
> Dream and so create
> Translunar Paradise.
>   (VP 415).

The final lines of 'The Cold Heaven', grand as they are, are bound to seem timid by comparison with the lines just quoted. 'The Cold Heaven' ends with a sense of dread and little hope: 'sent / Out naked on the roads' doesn't hold out much hope of creating 'Translunar Paradise', 'sent' at the end of its line is a strong dismissal. What we feel in the lines from 'The Tower' is mostly dread, despair, that what he is saying can't be true but must be proclaimed as if it were a truth desperately won. 'Man has created death' is true if it means that man has invented the emotions that surround one's death. But not true otherwise. It isn't even true that 'Nor dread nor hope attend / A dying animal', as anyone who has seen an animal dying will testify. The three sentences and a question that make up 'The Cold Heaven' insisted on occupying Yeats's mind with that pressure, and left him to turn the sequence of disproportions into a semblance of achieved order. That is what, in this instance, the madness of vision came to: we have a rigmarole of apprehensions without a relation among them in sight, but we have to take them as somehow related.

What do we expect of such a poem? Usually, one experience, real or imagined, understood, brought to fully apprehended unity. Here, not quite. There are three loosely related experiences with gaps between them, ending with a question that does not call for an answer. The gaps are bold, we have to leap from one experience to the next. Reasons are not given. If we find that the poem makes for unity, it cannot be in a strictly rational form. If we refer, with Blackmur, to a felt unity of disproportions, we ascribe that unity to the complete poetry rather than to any particular poem. We are not forbidden to intuit a certain unity of tone, if we find this to be not just a poem by Yeats but a Yeatsian poem, characteristic of his tunes in the middle years of his style. That is as much unity as we have any hope of finding.

In much the same spirit we say that the poem is a lyric, in the sense that none of the experiences invoked is allowed to escape from an implied consciousness, Yeats himself as we learn from Deirdre Toomey's essay.

What kind of poem, then, are we reading? I think of it as an instance of 'the shorter romantic lyric', comparable in all but length to the longer romantic lyric so fully described by M.H. Abrams in *Natural Supernaturalism* and several essays. I withdraw my suggestion, several pages ago, that Yeats had no strong interest in the question of genre: most of the poems in *Responsibilities* are short romantic lyrics. The poet, a qualified observer, looks at a landscape, takes at least partial subjective possession of it, and is driven to problematic feelings about love, responsibility and death. He does these things on his own authority: he deems himself to be an autonomous person, speaking not especially to you or me but to anyone willing to overhear what he has to say. He does not offer himself as a representative man, speaking for everyone: the question with which the poem ends insures against that misconception. He might nearly be thought to be communing with himself, such that that question is more a wondering than a question, as if to say I wonder what it will be like after I die.

The shorter romantic lyric, then, but that description may not tell us enough. I have been impressed by Helen Vendler's proposal for the understanding of lyric poetry. It is based – or could be – on Yeats's 'A Dialogue of Self and Soul'. We have two principles in conflict. Self speaks up for body, earth, history and tradition, Soul for spirit, darkness, ancestral night, scorning the earth. It is a dialogue until Self brings it to an end and takes over the second part of the poem. Vendler construes the two principles as different choices in the discrimination of lyric from another kind of literature. She is content to relegate Self to the novel, and let it deal with time and space, history, politics, war and character. Soul is 'independent of time and space'. It is the human voice when it is 'alone with itself, when its socially constructed characteristics (race, class, colour, gender, sexuality) are felt to be in abeyance'.[23] Felt, I assume, by the speaker, the lyric poet. Vendler's distinction of Self and Soul is strikingly essentialist, she would have us think that the concerns of the novel are transient while those of Soul are eternal, categorical. I am not sure that the distinction is feasible except as a psychological conceit. But the difference she proposes between the two principles alerts us to one mark of 'The Cold Heaven', that it is indeed a lyric in Vendler's sense, it is Soul, a voice speaking as if alone, nearly independent of everything else that has ever happened it. It is alone with this experience: it speaks from within it and as if there were nothing else in the world but the sky, the birds and a single mind provoked to speak on its own authority.

Nearly every aspect of such a soul-poem has become politically questionable. I've been reading a collection of essays according to which 'I' is permitted only to say 'We', and the autonomous person should in decency slip away as a dishevelled anonymity into any community willing to admit it.[24] Yeats will have none of this: he presents himself, to himself at least, as a mind thinking, a man at large in the world without apology, a presence not to be put by.

As for readers: I see, in the same collection of essays, that we (or they) are not afflicted with the same humiliations that are enforced upon writers: we are permitted to remain autonomous, self-possessed, choosing our company, reading 'The Cold Heaven', for instance, pretty much as we please. I don't understand how we are exempted from the disabilities the poets allegedly suffer from: we have done nothing to deserve such a privilege. We are allowed to be what, conventionally, we have conceded the lyric poem to be, for the time being master of its own space, free to speak without interruption, at least until it is shouted down. The speaker of 'The Cold Heaven' may be shouted down in the end, if someone in the audience notes that the last question in the poem posits one fate for the soul and doesn't allow for any other. A tiresome reader could protest: if not that fate, what's the alternative? Yeats doesn't offer a second choice. 'Will this be my fate?' he asks, without inviting a response. I assume that he was by himself in that railway carriage.

What is 'The Cold Heaven' worth? Why do I find myself recalling it, reading it over, committing it to memory? It can only be because I value the experiences it brings forward and the harmony, formal in the end, it establishes among them. But we may be a little more specific. Geoffrey Hill, in conversation with Rowan Williams in 2008, said:

> I can think of quite a number of twentieth-century poets who add to the stock of available *actuality* – that is to say that their poems, having been written, become part of the pile-up of that plethora of actual things with which our culture is virtually submerged. 'The stock of available reality' means that once this thing has been written, everything else in one's comprehension has to adjust itself slightly around it.[25]

'The stock of available reality' comes from Blackmur. In a review of Norman Macleod's *Horizons of Death*, he wrote: 'The art of poetry is amply distinguished from the manufacture of verse by the animating presence in the poetry of a fresh idiom: language so twisted and posed in a form that it not only expresses the matter in hand but adds to the stock of available reality.'[26] Blackmur's sentence and Hill's use of it make the gist of a philosophic argument about fact and value, value intrinsic and extrinsic; the actual and the real. Both writers are dismayed by the plethora of actual things and the need, short of despair, to live selectively among them. Both writers believe that the imagination, concentrated upon actualities, can redeem some of them, or – as Yeats tended to do – project values aside from them or despite them. On another occasion Blackmur said that 'it is the peculiar business of poetry and the other arts to qualify with form and order so much of experience as can be made intelligible.'[27] Not all of it can be made intelligible, but some of it can be redeemed – Eliot's words – enough such that a value can be glimpsed among its particles. Not all of 'The Cold Heaven' has made the experience – the matter in hand – intelligible: some of it – lines 5 to 8 – falls with the syntax that purports to sustain it. But the strength of the poem is in its culmination, and the best of that is the rhyme of 'sent' and 'punishment', where the rational imagination has found a value among the rhymes.

Can I be a little more specific? Many pages ago I glossed 'the correction of taste' as Eliot's attempt to adumbrate a better way of being alive. Blackmur's sentence about adding to the stock of available reality, and Hill's reading of that, amount to much the same redemption. Yeats's poem – I speak somewhat against Blackmur here – adds a little to the stock of available reality by raising a question – the final question – most of his readers would never have thought of raising, or never in his terms. That is enough.

NOTES

1. T.S. Eliot, *Selected Essays* (London 1963), p. 24.
2. Deirde Toomey: 'The Cold Heaven': *Yeats Annual* No. 18 (2013), p. 193.
3. Yeats, *Essays and Introductions* (London 1961), p. 112.
4. *Ibid*. p. 112.
5. J. Hillis Miller, *Others* (New Jersey 2001), p. 173.
6. William Empson, *The Structure of Complex Words* (London 1985), p. 101.
7. T.S.Eliot, *On Poetry and Poets* (London 1957), p. 258.
8. J. Hillis Miller, *Others,* supra, p. 174.
9. Elizabeth Bishop, *The Complete Poems 1927–1979* (New York 1983), p. 68.
10. Walter Pater, *The Renaissance: Studies in Art and Poetry: The 1893 Text,* edited by Donal L. Hill (Berkeley and Los Angeles 1980), p. 187.
11. Elizabeth Bishop, 'The Armadillo': *The Complete Poems 1927–1979* (New York 1983), p. 104.
12. David Holdeman (ed.), *'In the Seven Woods'* and *'The Green Helmet and Other Poems': Manuscript Materials by W.B. Yeats* (Ithaca and London 2002), p. 241.
13. W.B. Yeats, *Essays and Introductions* (London 1961), p. 357.
14. Hugh Kenner, *Mazes* (San Francisco 1989), p. 36.
15. W.K. Wimsatt, Jr., *The Verbal Icon: Studies in the Meaning of Poetry* (Kentucky 1954), p. 164.
16. *Ibid*. p. 161.
17. John Creaser, 'Rhymes, Rhyme, and Reading' : *Essays in Criticism,* Vol. 62, No. 4, pp. 438–60.
18. Hugh Kenner, *The Pound Era* (Berkeley and Los Angeles 1971), p. 93.
19. Wallace Stevens, *Collected Poems* (London 1955), p. 339.
20. Quoted in W.R. Johnson, *The Idea of Lyric: Lyric Modes in Ancient and Modern Poetry* (Berkeley 1982), p. xi.
21. R.P. Blackmur, *Form and Value in Modern Poetry* (New York 1957), p. 59.
22. W.B. Yeats, *Letters on Poetry from W.B. Yeats to Dorothy Wellesley* (London 1940), pp. 149–150.
23. Helen Vendler, *Soul Says: On Recent Poetry* (Cambridge, Massachusetts 1995), p. 7.
24. Mark Jeffreys (ed.), *New Definitions of Lyric:Theory, Technology, and Culture* (New York and London 1998).
25. Quoted in Matthew Sperling, *Visionary Philology: Geoffrey Hill and the Study of Words* (Oxford 2014), p. 35.

26. R.P. Blackmur, 'Statements and Idyls', *Poetry*, Vol. 46 No. 2, May 1935, p. 108.
27. R.P. Blackmur, *Outsider at the Heart of Things: Essays by R.P. Blackmur*, ed. James T. Jones (Chicago 1989), p. 39.

Suspended Endings – Nothing 'but' Yeats

PETER KUCH

'To understand a sentence means to understand a language. To understand a language means to be a master of technique' – Wittgenstein, *Philosophical Investigations*, §199.

Holidays can bring their own luxuries. At Christmas I was able to make time to re-read Alt and Alspach's edition of *The Collected Poems of W.B. Yeats*, a book I was given as a graduation present many years ago. What I brought away was a rekindled admiration for the intensity and mastery of Yeats's diction, two personal observations and two intellectual debts. The first personal observation, oddly enough, is that the word 'but' occurs 478 times[1] in *The Collected Poems of W.B. Yeats,* and the second is that the *OED* lists some 30 ways in which the word 'but' can be used.

My first intellectual debt is to Helen Vendler's *Our Secret Discipline: Yeats and Lyric Form*, a brilliant 'clearing of the ground of Yeatsian stylistics' (xiv) published by Harvard University Press in 2007. Until then, as Vendler herself rightly points out, there had not been a book in which a reader 'could find descriptions of the inner and outer formal choices Yeats made, the cultural significance his forms bore for him, or the way his forms – in all their astounding variety – became the material body of his thoughts and emotions.' (xv)[2]

My second intellectual debt is to Nicholas Grene's *Yeats's Poetic Codes*, published by Oxford University Press a year later, and nominated by Seamus

Heaney as one of his favourite books for 2008. Seeking to prevent Yeats's poetry from being overwhelmed by the enormous amount of biographical and historical study that had been produced in the previous ten years, as stimulating and insightful as it often proved to be, Grene focuses attention on what he calls the 'codes of practice developed to create the poems and situate them in relation to the poet, the reader, and the implied world.' Such codes, he suggests, include the reference points of dates and places; recurrent images and symbols; and 'Yeats's distinctive rhetorical usage of "this" and "that", and "here" and "there", together with his deployment of grammatical tense and mood.'[3] As Grene shrewdly observes, Yeats is 'a mannered writer with certain favourite words which reappear frequently throughout the canon.'[4] But one 'word' he has overlooked is the word 'but', which, as I say, occurs 478 times.

At this point I should clarify what I mean by 'use' and 'usage'. My guide here is the Prague school Mukarovsky's concept of 'foreground', which denotes 'the appearance in the text of some item or construction with unusual or noticeable frequency.'[5] In what follows, I am not interested in investigating whether or not Yeats uses the word 'but' in a grammatically correct way. In fact, I will be relying on Quirk, Greenbaum, Leech and Svartvik's *A Grammar of Contemporary English* and Huddleson and Pullum's *The Cambridge Grammar of the English Language* to identify and categorize the 478 occurrences; it is the sheer frequency and the variations in frequency that aroused my curiosity.

As I hope to demonstrate, Yeats's use of 'but' is as distinctive as his use of 'this' and 'that' and 'here' and 'there', particularly in managing what he himself referred to as 'the quarrel with ourselves' that he saw as quintessential to the making of poetry while observing that he himself characteristically suspended rather than concluded such quarrels. As Theodor Adorno has remarked: 'a successful work is not one which resolves contradictions in a spurious harmony, but one which expresses the idea of harmony negatively by embodying the contradictions, pure and uncompromised, in its innermost structure.'[6] The grammatical and syntactical flexibility of 'but', as I hope to show, frequently enabled Yeats successfully to achieve such an embodiment. There are three usages that I would like to focus on: the use of **'but now'**; the use of **'but'** to bring the nouns in a noun phrase or clause into creative collision; and the use of **'but'** as a syntactic hinge for the opposites, the antinomies, the doubling, the binary oppositions, the thesis / antithesis that was so characteristic of Yeats's dialogical imagination, and consequently so fundamental to his creativity.

But first, to the *OED* which informs us that 'but' derives from the Old English adverb, preposition and conjunction: *be-ūtan, būtan, būta*, meaning 'on the outside', 'without', 'except',[7] though this derivation is essentially a phonetic one as *butan* as a word does not survive in modern English. Bruce Mitchell, in his definitive *Old English Syntax,* says that it is arguable 'butan' functioned as an adversative conjunction in Old English.[8] The semantic and grammatical functions of the modern word 'but' – at least as an adversative conjunction – were generally fulfilled by the word 'ac'. The Beowulf poet uses butan only 7 times in 3182 lines:

705   Ealle buton anum (*as a preposition with the dative* C. I.1. a)

965/6   þæt he for **mundgripe** minum scolde
         licgean lifbysig, butan his licswice.
         (*as a conjunction with verb in subjunctive of condition*)

Whereas **ac** occurs some 67 times as in:

109   ne gefeah he þære fæhðe, **ac** he hine feor forwræc,

338   Wen ic þæt ge for wlenco, nalles for wræcsiðum,
         ac for higeþrymmum Hroðgar sohton."

595   **Ac** he hafað onfunden þæt he þa fæhðe ne þearf,

In Middle English, the form retaining the long vowel, *bouten, boute, bout,* occurs as an adverb and a preposition, though this was shortened to *būten, būte, but* as a conjunction with uses arising immediately out of the prepositional sense (*OED*). This, and several other developments, can be seen, for example, in the *Prologue* to the *Canterbury Tales,* where Chaucer uses 'but' some 47 times. To take just three examples, examples that also occur with similar frequency in Yeats's poetry: the first with 'but' as an adverbial, governing the noun phrase that follows, where 'but' in the sense of 'only' operates as both a modifier and an intensifier.

> Ther was also a Nonne, a PRIORESSE,
> That of hir smylyng was ful simple and coy;
> Hire gretteste oothe was **but** by Seinte Loy;[9]

The second, where 'but' operates as a preposition, to quote the *OED*, 'appending a statement which is not contrary to, but is not fully consonant with, or is contrasted with, that already made' (analogous to the German=*aber*, meaning 'nevertheless', 'yet', 'however' **24 a**). Used in this way 'but' admits the possibility of irony, which can be suggested as in the description of the Clerke of Oxenford:

> For him was levere have at his beddes heed
> Twenty bookes, clad in blak or reed,
> Of Aristotle, and his philosophie,

> Than robes riche, or fithele, or gay sautrie.
> **But** al be that he was a philosophie,[10]

Or the irony can be more pointed, as when a detailed account of the *Doctour of Phisik's* apparently comprehensive knowledge of medical authorities and his preoccupation with diet is followed by the crisp observation that: 'His studie was **but** litel on the Bible.'[11] Syntactically, as Quirk *et al.* point out, 'but' in such instances 'denotes a contrast', and 'the contrast may be in the unexpectedness of what is said in the second conjoin in view of the content in the first conjoin.'[12]

In modern English 'but' can be used as a preposition, an adverb, a conjunction, a noun, an adjective or a pronoun. Used as a preposition, an adverb and a conjunction, the word 'but' can suspend or postpone the ending of a poem – in the sense of permitting the introduction of more material – by marking a spatial or temporal shift, by facilitating elaboration, by operating as a syntactic hinge that links a 'truth' with its 'counter truth', or by liberating an emotional response to the poem that ripples far beyond its reading. For the moment I want to focus on just one form, the locution '**but now**', though I should mention in passing that some of the attraction might reside in its phonetic versatility because rhetorically as opposed to metrically it can function as an iamb (bŭt nów), a trochee (bút nŏw), or a spondee (bút nów) depending on syntax.

The 'now' in 'but now', as Huddleston and Pullum point out, can mark a deictic shift as in the line from *The Wanderings of Oisin*, '**But now** hearts cry that hearts are slaves',[13] though it is most frequently used, particularly in that poem, to mark temporal shifts. As the *OED* explains, but now 'can pass' from the prepositional 'into the adverbial sense' of 'just now, only at this moment.' In *The Wanderings of Oisin* this usage occurs in lines such as: '**But now** the moon like a white rose shone / In the pale west, … ';[14] and '**But now** a wandering land breeze came / And a far sound of feathery quires.'[15] When Oisin responds to St Patrick about the baleful effects of Christianity, he says:

> **But now** two things devour my life;
> The things that most of all I hate:
> Fasting and prayers.[16]

'But now' does not occur in *Crossways*, and it is only used four times in *The Rose* – once in 'Fergus and the Druid'; twice in 'Cuchulain's Fight with the Sea'; and once in 'A Dream of Death', where it is deployed with a brutal simplicity – and then only in the final revision of the poem.[17]

> She was more beautiful than thy first love,
> **But now** lies under boards.[18]

'But now' is not used again for another eighty poems – though there is an inter-esting variation in '*He mourns for the Change that has come upon him and his Beloved, and longs for the end of the World*' in the line 'And now my calling is but the calling of a hound'[19] – after which there is a gap of a further hundred poems before it is used again. What proves to be the final use in 'Nineteen hundred and Nineteen' from *The Tower* is comparable with the most common usage in *The Wanderings of Oisin*. Here 'but now' simply distinguishes the present from the past:

> O but we dreamed to mend
> Whatever mischief seemed
> To afflict mankind, **but now**
> That winds of winter blow
> Learn that we were crack-pated when we dreamed.[20]

In the two remaining uses however, the distinction between the present and the past is at once more dramatic and more personal; in 'Reconciliation', in *From the 'Green Helmet' and Other Poems*, 'but now' dramatically splits the poem, separating the numbing public heartbreak of rejection from a muted but urgent plea for a renewed intimacy;[21] and in 'The Wild Swans at Coole' where 'but now' anchors the final verse of the poem to return the speaker to the present, a present nevertheless refulgent with memory.

> **But now** they drift on the still water,
> Mysterious, beautiful;
> Among what rushes will they build,
> By what lake's edge or pool
> Delight men's eyes when I awake some day
> To find they have flown away.[22]

Even though the fourteen extant drafts of 'The Wild Swans at Coole' reveal the difficulty Yeats had in managing the tonal and temporal schemes of the poem, he begins to use the locution '**but now**' as early as the fifth draft,[23] and it remains a fixed point in the nine drafts that follow. It is as if his attempts to yoke the emotions he experienced nineteen years before the moment that he stands on the lake's shore come to rest very early in the process of composition on a locution that was a distinctive feature of his early poetry, a poetry he had himself char-acterized as a poetry of 'longing and complaint', the 'cry of the heart against necessity',[24] 'the call of the heart, the heart seeking its own dream', a poetry that needed to be counteracted with a poetry 'of insight and knowledge'.

One of the most common and arguably the most distinctive way Yeats uses 'but' in *The Collected Poems* is defined by the *OED* under 6a as follows: 'By the omission of the negative accompanying the preceding verb, 'but' passes into the adverbial sense of: Nought but, no more than, only or merely.' So, for example, in 'The Fisherman' in *The Wild Swans at Coole*, Yeats defines his idealized figure as

> A man who does not exist,
> A man who is **but** a dream;[25]

– two lines which can be unpacked as 'A man who is (in the sense of an ideal) yet who is not (in the sense of actually existing), / A man who is but a dream' (in the sense of 'nought but, no more than, only, merely' a dream). What is distinctively Yeatsian here is the way the adverbial sense creates an arc, an electrical discharge, between the nouns 'man' and 'dream' by appearing to qualify or perhaps even disparage what has either accrued significance within the poem or, because it is a symbol or a motif, has brought significance to the poem. In this case, 'dream' as a Yeatsian symbol brings significance to the poem while the word 'man' accrues significance because it is repeated eight times, five times in a negative sense and three times in a positive sense, in the 34 lines prior to the coupling of 'A man who does not ... / A man who is ... '. By passing into the adverbial sense of 'nought but, no more than, only or merely' the word 'but' at once accords (the conjunctive is arguably still a trace) even as it seems to undercut the significance of the two nouns.

Other examples where Yeats employs 'but' to perform a similar function include lines such as:

> That life and letters seem
> **But** an heroic dream[26]– from 'A Woman Homer Sung'

> Your beauty can **but** leave among us
> Vague memories, nothing but memories.[27] – from 'Broken Dreams'

> The rhetorician would deceive his neighbours
> The sentimentalist himself; while art
> Is **but** a vision of reality.[28]– from 'Ego Dominus Tuus'

> What had the Caesars **but** their thrones?[29]– from 'Demon and Beast'

And three of my favourites:

> Plato thought nature **but** a spume that plays
> Upon a ghostly paradigm of things;[30]– from 'Among School Children'

and

What's water **but** the generated soul?[31]– from 'Coole Park and Ballylee, 1931'

and

What theme had Homer **but** original sin?[32] – from 'Vacillation'.

What increases the electrical discharge, the arcing between significant nouns in the last two examples, is Yeats's framing them as questions. As Brian Arkins points out questions are themselves a distinctive Yeatsian code. 'Questions are important at the beginning of poems – fifteen poems begin with a question – in the middle of poems where they are consistently found, and especially at the end of poems: an astonishing forty-two poems end with a question.'[33] In the 374 poems that comprise the lyrical section of Yeats's poems, there are 337 questions. The two examples I have quoted above come from the middle rather than the end of poems, and so might not be considered as powerful as ending a poem with a question, though using a question to frame the way 'but' simultaneously enriches and limits the noun clause and connects the reader in a way that increases the electrical discharge. Arguably, to take one of the examples, the full power of 'What theme had Homer **but** original sin' derives as much from the way the assertion confronts the reader as a question as it does from the way the word 'but' juxtaposes the interrogative elliptical noun clause 'What theme had Homer' with the noun phrase 'original sin'.

Finally, I would like to look at Yeats's use of **'but'** as a way of holding in creative tension the opposites, the antinomies, the doubling in ways that elicited similarities even as they released differences, invoked harmonies even as they unleashed dissonances – an attitude towards language and rhythm and a cast of mind that was fundamental to his creativity. 'To me', he once said, 'all things are made of the conflict of two states of consciousness';[34] and elsewhere: 'I see things doubled, doubled in history, world history, personal history.'[35] Such doubling was not simply a matter of dynamic opposition, as various critics who have adopted a range of approaches to elucidate this seminal aspect of Yeats's work point out.

Biographers and historians have speculated about the ways his hyphenated Anglo-Irish identity might have shaped his work, whether in terms of the creative tension that potentially exists between the Celtic and the Irish modes, the rural and the metropolitan, the peasant and the aristocrat, or the values the poet attributed to Georgian Ireland, 'the people of Burke and Grattan', as opposed to the Irelands of William Martin Murphy and de Valera. Post-colonial critics see these binary oppositions writ large in terms of the imperial versus the

colonial, centre versus margin, settler versus native. Others trace the double-
ness through Yeats's desire to write sacred poetry and drama in an increasingly
secular world, whether in terms of the tensions between ancient measures and
modern rhythms, magic and mysticism, the hieratic and the popular, or the
arcane and the demotic. For others, it is the political and linguistic tension
embedded in the poet's literary inheritance, the inescapable fact, as he himself
said, that he owed 'his soul to Shakespeare, to Spenser, to Blake, perhaps to
William Morris, and to the English language', with the result that, as he says,
'my hatred tortures me with love, my love with hate.'[36] Finally, others argue
that post-structuralism holds the key, whether with différance operating as
'difference' and 'deferral' or within self-reflexivity as the 'perpetual unfinished-
ness of the narrated subject.'

Seminal to all of these theories are the grammatical and phonetic func-
tions of the word 'but'. To take three examples: one from the early poetry; one
from the group known as the 'Last Poems'; and finally another from the early
poems – where, in each poem, the word 'but', whether conjunction, preposition
or adverb, holds in creative tension various antimonies, binary oppositions,
truths and counter truths.

In 'The Song of Wandering Aengus', for example, symbolic contraries
coexist throughout the poem as silver is opposed to gold and the moon to
the sun. A sacred hazel supplies material for a fishing rod for which a berry
can be used as bait. The natural self transforms into the supernatural as the
'little silver trout' that has been caught becomes a 'glimmering girl', who then
calls the fisherman by name before fading into 'the brightening air', leaving
him with a remembered vision that compels him to search the world until he
finds her. However, what I wish to remark is the opposition that is engendered
between plural uses of the word 'and' and a single use of the word 'but'.

The first verse of 'The Song of Wandering Aengus', which describes catching
the trout, consists of two co-ordinate clauses of four lines each joined by the
conjunction 'and'. In fact 'and' is used six times in the first verse to mirror the two
halves; three times in the first clause to join three co-ordinate clauses that come
after the main clause; and twice in the second clause to join the two co-ordinate
clauses that precede the second main clause. The first and second verses are also
linked by a conjunction: 'When I had laid it on the floor / I went to blow the fire
aflame'. The transformation of fish to sky-woman occurs immediately after this,
at lines 11 and 12. It is marked by the noun clause 'something rustled on the
floor' introduced by 'but', which it could be argued functions either as a conjunc-
tion or a preposition. What is germane to my argument, however, is the disrup-
tion, the single substitution of 'but' in a sequence of and's.

I went out to the hazel wood,
Because a fire was in my head,
And cut **and** peeled a hazel wand,
And hooked a berry to a thread;
And when white moths were on the wing,
And moth-like stars were flickering out,
I dropped the berry in a stream
And caught a little silver trout.

When I had laid it on the floor
I went to blow the fire aflame,
But something rustled on the floor,
And someone called me by my name:
It had become a glimmering girl
With apple blossom in her hair
Who called me by my name and ran
And faded through the brightening air.[37]

My second example is from the 'Municipal Gallery Revisited' where, in the middle of a passage of reported speech in the second verse, 'but' announces a revisionist history of revolutionary Ireland, a radical challenge to a nationalist discourse that is in danger of becoming hegemonic. Greeting the speaker of the poem as he enters the Municipal Gallery, to which he is returning after thirty years, are realist commemorations of people and events that exemplify fidelity to faith and fatherland. They affect him, until a 'counter-truth' asserts itself in a way that cannot be denied.

'This is not', I say,
'The dead Ireland of my youth, **but** an Ireland
The poets have imagined, terrible and gay.'[38]

It is not religion or politics or warfare that have brought Ireland into being; it is the poets, and specifically those associated most closely with him, John Millington Synge and Lady Augusta Gregory, who he had named and honoured in his acceptance speech for the Nobel Prize fourteen years before his return to the Municipal Gallery that forms the occasion of this poem.

My final example is one of my favourite Yeats poems, a poem I always find difficult to read because of the intensity of its emotion, an emotion that ripples out from the final two lines, via a single sentence pivoted on 'but', as if the word 'but' were some huge rock that was heaved into a still pool of water. This is at once the most eloquent and the most powerful use of the word to suspend the ending of a poem in the sense that what it evokes continues to ripple and echo in the mind. As Seamus Heaney has remarked, though in another context:

> [such a poem] ... satisfies the contradictory needs which consciousness experiences at times of extreme crisis, the need on the one hand for a truth-telling that will be hard and retributive, and on the other hand the need not to harden the mind to a point where it denies its own yearnings for sweetness and trust.[39]

In closing, all I want to do is simply to point out that 'but' is used three times in twelve lines: the first and second uses echoing one another as adverbs qualifying the same verb, but equally in opposition to one another as they position themselves as the horns of the dilemma: 'Time can but make it easier to be wise' as against 'Time can but make her beauty over again.' What Time promises on the one hand, in terms of experience bringing wisdom, it seems to take with the other by remaking her beauty in such a dramatic way that it threatens to unman wisdom. What the heart yearns for, the mind rejects. The poem, of course, is 'The Folly of Being Comforted'; and what the word 'but' releases is the incurable heartache of rejection, the tension between a love that cannot yield but that will never be returned, that constantly desires reassurance knowing full well that such reassurance would be empty, hollow, even if it were offered.

The Folly of Being Comforted

One that is ever kind said yesterday:
'Your well-belovèd's hair has threads of grey,
And little shadows come about her eyes;
Time can **but** make it easier to be wise
Though now it seems impossible, and so
All that you need is patience.'
                                        Heart cries, 'No,
I have not a crumb of comfort, not a grain.
Time can **but** make her beauty over again:
Because of that great nobleness of hers
The fire that stirs about her, when she stirs,
Burns but more clearly. O she had not these ways
When all the wild summer was in her gaze.'

O heart! O heart! if she'd **but** turn her head,
You'd know the folly of being comforted.[40]

NOTES

1. The figure of 478 does not include any of the variants printed in the Alt and Alspach edition.
2. I am sensible of the criticisms of some of Vendler's readings advanced by Nicholas Meihuizen, 'Yeats, Vendler, and Byzantium', *Irish University Review*, 44:2, pp. 234–53 though I feel he tends to overstate his case the more he pursues his analysis.
3. Nicholas Grene, *Yeats's Poetic Codes* (Oxford 2008), p. 3.
4. Grene, p. 3.
5. R. Fowler, *Linguistic Criticism* (Oxford 1986), pp. 71–4; cited in Brian Arkins, *The Thought of W.B. Yeats* (Oxford 2010), p. 156.
6. T.W. Adorno, *Prisms* (Cambridge, Massachusetts 1981), p. 32 quoted in Brian Arkins, *The Thought of W.B. Yeats,* p. 6.
7. The diacritic is a modern addition (albeit used occasionally in Old English). Note also that the OED entry for 'but' remains unrevised since its publication in 1888. The new *Dictionary of Old English* sets out its entries under I Adverb, II Preposition, and III Conjunction. I am indebted for this and for other guidance on Old and Middle English and for grammar in general to Dr Greg Waite.
8. Bruce Mitchell, *Old English Syntax* (Oxford 1985): I, §1773; II, §3626–46.
9. F.N. Robinson (ed.), *The Works of Geoffrey Chaucer*, 2nd edn, 1957; (London 1970), p. 18, *ll.* 118–20.
10. Robinson (ed.), *Works*, p. 20, *ll.* 293–7.
11. Robinson (ed.), *Works*, p. 21, *ll.* 438.
12. Randolph Quirk, Sidney Greenbaum, Geoffrey Leech, Jan Svartvik, *A Grammar of Contemporary English* (London 1973), §9.54, p. 564. See also David Weber, *English Prepositions: A Historical Survey*, Master's Diploma Thesis, Department of English and American Studies, Faculty of Arts, Masaryk University, 2012. Supervisor: Prof. Dr. Václav Blažek, Csc.
13. W.B. Yeats, 'The Wanderings of Oisin', eds Alt and Alspach, *The Variorum Edition of the Poems of W.B. Yeats* (New York 1973), p. 19, *ll.* 280–1.
14. *VP* 12, *ll.* 152–3.
15. *VP* 13, *ll.* 165–6.
16. *VP* 24, *ll.* 378–60.
17. Wayne K. Chapman, *Yeats's Poetry in the Making: Sing Whatever is Well Made* (London 2012), pp. 16–20. Note that 'but' is not introduced into the poem until revision number 3 when it is introduced as: 'But that I carved these words.' Chapman notes that: 'The refurbished self projected in the new poem seems less tolerant than the former one was to indulge in sentiment for the sake of itself.'
18. *VP* 123, *ll.* 11–12.
19. *VP* 153, *ll.* 8.
20. *VP* 431, *ll.* 84–8.
21. *VP* 257.
22. *VP* 323, *ll.* 25–30.
23. *The Wild Swans at Coole: Manuscript Materials by W.B. Yeats*, ed. Stephen Parrish (Ithaca and London 1994), pp. 3–39. NLI 13, 587 (1) I^r: 'But now they

drift on the still water / Mysterious, beautiful'. Note that the word 'but' by itself occurs at this key point in the third draft. NLI 30, 416, 3ʳ.

24. Letter to Katharine Tynan, March 1888.

25. *VP* 348, *ll.* 35–6.

26. *VP* 255 *ll.* 20-1.

27. *VP* 356, *ll.* 14–15.

28. *VP* 369, *ll.* 46–8.

29. *VP* 401, *l.* 50.

30. *VP* 445, *ll.* 1–2.

31. *VP* 490, *l.* 8

32. *VP* 502, *l.* 77.

33. Brian Arkins, *The Thought of W.B. Yeats* (Oxford 2010), p. 167.

34. Yeats to Ethel Manin, 20 October [1938]. *The Letters of W.B. Yeats*, ed. Alan Wade (London 1954), p. 918.

35. Yeats to Dorothy Wellesley, 4 May 1937. *The Letters of W.B. Yeats*, p. 887.

36. Yeats, W.B. 'A General Introduction for my Work' in *Essays and Introductions* (London 1961), p. 519.

37. *VP* 149–50. 'The Song of Wandering Aengus'.

38. *VP* 601–4. 'The Municipal Gallery Revisited'. Note Wayne K. Chapman, *Yeats's Poetry in the Making: Sing Whatever is Well Made* (London 2012), p. 192 where the line 'But Ireland / ~~in the glory of her passion~~ / ~~As~~ / The poets have imagined, terrible & gay occurs in the fifth draft or the third ink draft of 17 drafts of the poem (the first 2 drafts are jottings in pencil).

39. Seamus Heaney, *Opened Ground: Poems 1966-1996* (London 1998), p. 464.

40. *VP* 199–200. 'The Folly of Being Comforted'. Only a late draft of this poem exists. See David Holdeman (ed.), *W.B. Yeats: 'In the Seven Woods' and 'The Green Helmet and Other Poems': Manuscript Materials by W.B. Yeats* (Ithaca and London 2002), p. 45. The relevant lines are:

> Time can but make it easier to be wise
> But heart there is no comfort not a grain
> O heart O heart if she'd but turn her head

Collecting Yeats and Publishing Lady Gregory's Coole Edition

COLIN SMYTHE

The major part of Part 1 of this essay was first published in the Spring 1971 issue of The Private Library, *the Journal of the Private Libraries Association. Book prices are of course way out of date. I have added a postscript, made a few edits, and have added footnotes to update the text where necessary.*

1

My interest in William Butler Yeats started in 1963, the year I graduated from Trinity College, Dublin. I had long been interested in mythology and I was in Hodges Figgis, the Dublin booksellers one day when a friend bought a copy of Yeats's *Mythologies* (1959).[1] It was the first time that I had realized that Yeats wrote about such things and I avidly started to read his prose writings.

I had gone through such squirrel activities as collecting stamps and rocks, but I had no active collecting interest at the time. I was introduced to Michael Walshe who ran the Rare Book Department of Hodges Figgis, which was virtually inaccessible if you didn't know where it was, at the rear of the shop. He had brought out an excellent catalogue of Irish books in 1962 which contained a very comprehensive collection of books by Yeats, Cuala Press, Lady Gregory,

Synge and anybody else you care to mention. Pricewise it was the last catalogue with bargains, but unfortunately most of its contents had been sold by the time I arrived on the scene and I was only able to buy one or two books from it.

The first Yeats first edition that I bought from Michael (for £10/-/-) was a copy of *The Trembling of the Veil* (1922), which I chose for its beauty as much as for its author. At the beginning I was almost too careful in what I bought, turning down many books because I thought the price was too high; for example, refusing to pay £10 for a complete run of *The Yellow Book*, and then rushing back to get it when I had discovered what it was selling for elsewhere. This sort of thing happened all too often when I later realized what the book I'd turned down was worth, so the tempo of my buying speeded up, as I realized that if I did not build up a good collection extremely quickly, I would not have enough money to do so. This was amply justified by future events. For example I bought the *United Irishman* edition of Yeats's *Where There is Nothing* for £15 in 1965: I recently (in the early 1970s) saw a copy in a catalogue for £250; similarly I paid about £25 for *The Wanderings of Oisin* (Wade 2 [Allan Wade's *A Bibliography of the Writings of W.B. Yeats* (London 1951, 1958, 1968)]); the latest copy fetched over £500. I bought from catalogues, at Sotheby's, Christie's and Hodgson's, thereby getting a bad name with many dealers who thought I was cheating at the game and that I should have bought through them. However, the only time I really went for something big, I commissioned the firm of Bernard Quaritch to bid for me, and insisted that I remain anonymous should the press get interested; I had no desire to see headings like 'Dublin student pays £650 for Yeats's first book' across their pages. This sum I paid for a copy of his *Mosada*, plus of course Quaritch's commission: it was a poorish copy in that the cover had torn down the spine and been stuck back together with adhesive tape which had badly yellowed. I spent hours removing the tape and cleaning the cover and I was fortunate in getting rid of most of the staining, and if it wasn't as good as new, it was certainly much improved.[2] Incidentally I was not far out regarding the press. *The Irish Times* article, headed 'Yeats' First Edition', stated that the buyer wished to remain anonymous, but Quaritch had informed them it would be in Dublin the following day.

I remember the first auction I sent in bids for. Having carefully discussed the likely prices with Michael Walshe (whom I expected to turn up nice things for me practically every day), I sent off my list of bids for about fifteen items. I wanted them all very much so I placed bids that were about 50% higher than the last auction price, but to my surprise I only got one item, Yeats's *Poems Written in Discouragement*, privately printed by the Cuala Press in an edition of fifty copies and inscribed by WBY with a note saying it was printed in November 1913. (In fact it was printed the month before, according to Cuala Press records.)

I also wrote to booksellers in the USA and got quite a large number of books offered at surprisingly low prices: I had expected far higher. On the whole I bought all that were offered me, kept the ones I wanted and sold the remainder for about what I paid for the whole lot. I was extremely fortunate in that I had Michael Walshe to advise me, as without him I would have made many mistakes, and his sources of supply also seemed limitless. He seemed to be able to dig up some rare and desirable book, magazine, or something, whenever he rummaged in the long line of cupboards under the bookcases. This back room was Michael's undisputed territory for many years and it was only when Neville Figgis left university and came to work in Hodges Figgis as well, that the department became modernized and moved up front into the glare of the public gaze. Eventually Michael left to open a bookshop dealing almost exclusively in eighteenth-century books and earlier. He and his bookselling partner Noel Jameson had a fascinating bookshop in Molesworth Lane where Michael was in his element.[3]

Soon after I started collecting the poet's books as what might be termed a full-time occupation, Michael suggested that I start collecting the first editions of Lady Gregory, which I did, using as my guide his original catalogue which had three and a half pages of Gregory items. For a long time it was the only guide to her publications other than a few library catalogues. Later I came across the John Quinn sale catalogue of 1923 which gave a great deal of valuable information. I was all too aware of the lack of an adequate bibliography of her publications such as Allan Wade had made for Yeats and I decided that if I could I would produce a similar work for Lady Gregory. I eventually got this accepted as my thesis for an M.Litt. Degree at the University of Dublin (TCD), but it was never completed because publishing took up all my time from 1966 onwards.

In two and a half years I had gathered together a collection that contained about two thirds of all Yeats's publications. Nearly all the items carry some story over their purchase or association, and the stories attached to some of the more interesting ones are given below.

When I bought Yeats's *Deirdre* (Wade 9) I found slipped into it his *Alterations to Deirdre* (Wade 70) which was a four page leaflet handed out at Mrs Patrick Campbell's production of the play on 27 November 1908. If you think how many people can fit into a drawing room, you can appreciate how rare this leaflet was and is. Obviously the bookseller had never noticed or failed to appreciate what it was.

I was also fortunate in getting a copy of *The Golden Helmet* (Wade 74) printed for that great man John Quinn in an edition of fifty copies.[4] When Yeats signed books, he normally put a pen stroke through his name on the title page, but in this case it seems that he cut the entire name out. People have asked me why I think that this was done by Yeats, to which my reply has been that the book has an inscription which goes thus: 'To Mary D. M. Collenson / This play is a first draft of / my play, "The Green Helmet" / which is in verse & I hope a / much better play. Do not / judge me by this. / W B Yeats / August 29 / 1922': who else would have been mad enough to cut up the title page? Maybe he'd made a mess of a signature.

In his later life Yeats became a close friend of the Duchess of Wellington, Dorothy Wellesley, and their correspondence was published in *Letters on Poetry* (Wade 325) in 1940. After Yeats died Wellesley continued to write letters on poetry to him and this very one-sided correspondence was published by her as *Beyond the Grave*. It stated on the title page that it could be purchased from the printer C. Baldwin of Tonbridge Wells, so I wrote off to him in the hope that he might have copies, but he replied that he had never sold any copies; it had been privately printed for the Duchess who had all of them. I wrote off to the Duke of Wellington and was informed that the only copy that he knew of was owned by his daughter: dead end. Imagine my delight when a few weeks later, Neville Figgis offered me a copy of this book which had been inscribed by the author to his father, William Fernsley Figgis (1874–1956), known in the book trade as 'W.F.'

One other book that I prized was a copy of Katherine Tynan's book of poems, *Shamrocks*, inscribed by her 'To dear Willie Yeats, with the belief in him and affectionate friendship of the writer, May 30th 1887.' Certainly she had no doubt as to his genius.

At one time Liam Miller of the Dolmen Press and I were going to do a bibliography of the Cuala Press, but unfortunately this never got completed.[5] Up to then, all that there had been was Maxwell's bibliography of the Press, published in 1932 with the full co-operation of the Yeats sisters, who even provided the special Irish paper used for his edition. Unfortunately, as he only printed thirty copies, this is even more difficult to get hold of than the books themselves. Its format and binding are identical to the press books. I was fortunate in having one of Maxwell's own copies with his bookplate, which Michael Walshe had bought at the Maxwell sale, and I got it out of him by the promise of a bound Xerox copy for his own reference, otherwise he'd have never parted with it.

One of the Press books, *Discoveries*, is inscribed by Yeats: 'Ben Jonson's old title "Discoveries" / W B Yeats / PS. Unicorn was drawn by Robert Gregory'. It also has parts of three finger prints of the poet in the smudged ink.

Synge's *Poems and Translations* was not only published by the Cuala Press, but also in a similar styled edition by John Quinn, for copyright protection purposes in the USA. The Yeats sisters had no end of difficulties over their edition after they started setting on Friday 13th. Unfortunately Synge died before it was published. I was lucky to pick up both for the price of one: at the time Quinn's printings were not at all appreciated and his publications / printings could be picked up for a pound or two, that is, those others not written by Yeats.

Estrangement was one of six proofed bindings I was given by the binders, Brindley & Co. of Eustace Street, Dublin. In the most extreme case, Elizabeth Corbet Yeats had cut the text block away from the casing and made a number of comments about the quality of each gathering, such as 'This stitching shows badly' or 'This stitching looks rough'. She certainly had a high standard, but I wonder whether she expected every copy to be checked at the end of the binding process and discarded if they didn't match her exacting standard.[6]

Of the Cuala Press books, not surprisingly I found that the privately printed items were the most difficult to get hold of and in some ways the most interesting. On the whole these editions had a much smaller print run, often of no more than fifty copies. As with the Maxwell bibliography I had to get photocopies taken of E.R. McClintock Dix's *Printing in Armagh* (1910) and *Printing in Ennis, Co. Clare* (1912) before Michael would sell them to me as a special privilege, after weeks of entreaties. Both of these were published in editions of fifty copies. Among the privately printed items were two publications of poems by Lyle Donaghy, *At Dawn Above Atherlow* (1926) and *Into the Light* (1934). Donaghy acted the Christ in Lady Gregory's Passion play, *The Story Brought by Brigit*, and was specially chosen for the part by her. Eileen Crowe played the part of the Mother. When Lennox Robinson's *History of the Abbey Theatre* was published in 1951, these were virtually the only two parts in any of the plays where the names of the players were omitted. Looking back through the list of Cuala Press books, I thought how the popularity of the Press has increased in the past half-decade, and the prices that the books used to fetch. In 1964 Yeats books would fetch over ten times the price of some of the others. Edward Dowden's *A Woman's Reliquary* could not be sold for a pound then and Hodges Figgis might have four or five in stock at any one time which would not move. A Yeats would fetch £12 or more. Now Yeats is nearer £50 on occasion and Dowden closer to £20, a rather better increase in value on the part of Dowden's title.

I was proud of my Cuala / Dun Emer Press collection, even more so than the Yeats. I had all the published volumes (77 in number); most of the privately printed items including *Poems Written in Discouragement* (inscribed); the complete run of *Broadsides* in 84 parts in their folders, which were published monthly from 1908 to 1915; the series of 12 published in 1935 under the editorship of Yeats and F.R. Higgins, bound and signed by the editors; and the 1937 series, edited by Yeats and Dorothy Wellesley, similarly bound and signed. I had a virtually complete set of the greetings cards, missing not more than five out of one hundred and fifty, and similarly a collection of the hand-coloured prints, again missing only about five out of one hundred and thirty odd. To finish the collection off I had a number of Dun Emer leather and cloth bindings (the latter handpainted) and an eight by nine foot Dun Emer carpet with a William Morris-style design.[7]

No collection would be complete without items to do with the poet, and this includes those that attacked him. I was fortunate in getting a copy of that scurrilous pamphlet *Souls for Gold* written by Frank Hugh O'Donnell, attacking Yeats's *The Countess Cathleen* which quoted on the front cover the words of one of the devils in the play as Yeats's own. O'Donnell had these pamphlets pushed through the letter boxes of many important people in Dublin and as a result there was an outcry against the play and even the Archbishop of Dublin said that, while he had not read the play, if it was as bad as people made out it really should be banned. Surprisingly few of these ephemera survived.

I haven't always been lucky in getting what I want at auctions. This has not only been due to prices going higher than expected, but other outside influences have come into play. On one occasion there was a set of the *Collected Works of W.B. Yeats* (1908) with the Chapman & Hall imprint coming up at Sotheby's and I had a premonition that I would not get there in time. The journey from my flat to Sotheby's usually took half an hour, give or take a few minutes, so on this occasion I gave myself an extra three quarters of an hour for the underground journey, but the train got stuck between two stations for just over fifty minutes, and in spite of running all the way from Green Park station to the auction rooms, I arrived just as the lot I wanted was being knocked down. It really was most frustrating.

I got one book as a result of what I consider a psychic experience. While I was still living in a flat in Pembroke Road, Dublin, I was listening to an opera when I must have dozed off for a moment, because I saw myself walking into Webb's Bookshop on the Dublin quays. The following day, I went round there and told the manager that he had a book for me. He denied this, and I said: 'You must have: go and find something for me.' He went off to his back office and returned with a copy of Lady Gregory's *A Book of Saints and Wonders* which was inscribed by Yeats to Maud Gonne, and it was going for just £5/-/-. Of course I bought it without a moment's hesitation.

1965 was the year of the Centenary of Yeats's birth and I agreed with Hodges Figgis to collaborate over a special exhibition, lending a large number of my major items for it. A special catalogue was prepared, in which both my and the other lenders' assistance was gratefully acknowledged, but when the books were laid out, there was no indication as to whether an item belonged to Hodges Figgis or to a lender. Red markers were used both to indicate books on loan as well as books sold. This gave a very misleading picture as to who owned what, and if I had not been as retiring a person as I was at the time, I would have insisted that due acknowledgment to the lender *by name* should have been made under each of the relevant items. As I said earlier, I had kept quiet about buying *Mosada* and later when I sold my collection, it appeared as 'the collection of a Dublin man'. Later, I became rather more publicity-conscious when selling Colin Smythe Ltd publications.

During my burrowings about for Yeats items, I not unnaturally came across a number of hitherto unrecorded Yeats items and variants mostly sold to me by Michael Walshe, which I assiduously reported to Russell K. Alspach who was preparing a new edition of Wade's *Bibliography*. Some of these he acknowledged and promised to put in his next *Additions to Wade*, such as an inverted blind stamping of the front cover design of the 1913 edition of Yeats' *Poems* (Wade 99), a volume called *The Voice of Ireland* (1923), to which I had given the provisional number of Wade 314A, sending him both the bibliographical descriptions of the first and greatly revised second edition, and also a book called *Irish Tales* to which I gave a provisional Wade number of 215A. On getting my copy of the new edition of Wade, which appeared four years after our correspondence, I found that there was no mention of the inverted front cover design on *Poems*, only a bibliography of the second edition of *The Voice of Ireland*, which did refer to the existence of a first edition that Alspach said he had not seen, in spite of the fact that I gave a far more detailed description of both volumes than his own description of the second edition. Wade 215A was also in, but with an inaccurate (or poorly proof-read) description of the title page.[8]

Through force of circumstances I decided later in 1965 that I wanted to set myself up in publishing and I nagged a friend of mine into letting me publish a book he had written for school leavers called *One for the Road*. Its author Peter Bander joined the company first as joint Managing Director of Colin Smythe Ltd with me before concentrating on a separate publishing company,

Van Duren Publishers. To provide working capital for this venture, I decided to sell my Yeats and Cuala Press collections, if possible as a whole. I held onto my Lady Gregory collection in the hope that I might be able to complete my thesis.[9] I went to Liam Miller of the Dolmen Press,[10] a good friend whose publications I collected,[11] and he put me in touch with the Dublin City Librarian Máirín O'Byrne.[12] She was immediately fired with enthusiasm for the idea and determined to get hold of the collection if she possibly could. The first thing was to agree on a valuation, over which I had the invaluable help of Neville Figgis. I first went through the list of over five hundred items and valued them individually, and then Neville went through it, checking my valuations and changing them where he thought them wrong. Although some things were higher at his valuation than at mine, and *vice versa*, in the end our valuations did not differ by more than £100 or so. The Library also got an independent valuation which, I am glad to say, confirmed ours, and a figure of £6,500 was agreed on as the sale price. Máirín then went about the difficult task of convincing the City Fathers of the wisdom of purchasing 'a lot of old books', as they were called by one. It took some time and I was away from Dublin when they finally came to a decision that it was a worthwhile investment. Events have certainly justified the wisdom of this decision as the collection's value has vastly increased since then. The first I knew of the decision was a letter from her which read: 'We've got it!! I am not really sober this minute with excitement.' On my return to my Dublin flat, I had hardly set foot in my front door before she was round to collect the books, which took up over sixty feet of shelf space.

I am still collecting the works of Lady Gregory, of course, and hoard every edition and reprint and binding variant of her works that I can get hold of, to add to UCG's collection.[13] Through the generosity of Major Richard Gregory I had a complete set of all the rare John Quinn limited editions of her works in perfect condition, and have also gathered together dozens of theatre editions of her plays. The Maunsel editions of Lady Gregory's *Seven Short Plays* are extremely complex and the theatre editions of these plays are even more so: I had to evolve a progression table for the latter, giving all the variations, with which I can speedily place any of the theatre editions. Of course mavericks do turn up on occasion and make it necessary to modify my list. At present, although I cannot be sure, I suspect that there are a minimum of nine issues of each play, and I doubt whether I shall ever get a complete collection of all of them. I have just got twenty in six years, so I am less than a third of the way to my goal. I have found that my experience as a publisher has been of the greatest assistance in my bibliographical work and as a result I would always recommend that all bibliographers should have some publishing experience, especially on the production side, to get into the mind of the people producing the books: variants can so often be accidental rather than deliberate.

I was also extremely fortunate that during the time I was working on this bibliography, a friend of mine, Miss Frances-Jane French was working on the bibliography of the chief publishing house of the Irish Literary Revival, Maunsel & Co. which was launched in 1904 and finally sank in 1924 at the hands of the Official Receiver. Her *Bibliography of the Abbey Theatre Series*, published by the Dolmen Press, was reviewed in *The Private Library* a few issues back.[14]

Before I left Dublin to come to live and work in England, I had met two of the three people who, in 1971, knew more about Lady Gregory than anybody else; Ann Saddlemyer, then at the University of Victoria, British Columbia, and Dan Murphy of the City University, New York. (The third was Elizabeth Coxhead, but I did not meet her until some time after I had moved to Gerrards Cross, when I found that she lived on the other side of the village.) I have been very fortunate in receiving a great deal of help from all three over my Gregory project. In 1966 the Dolmen Press published Ann Saddlemyer's *In Defence of Lady Gregory: Playwright*, and the author wrote in my copy 'With best wishes, and great expectations for "The Definitive Lady G" '. It was only when the Coole Edition of Lady Gregory's works was well under way three years later that the prophetic nature of the dedication occurred to me. At the time I thought it referred to my bibliography, and then had forgotten all about it.

When I lectured on Lady Gregory at the Yeats International Summer School in Sligo in 1968 at T.R. Henn's invitation, some of the American lecturers[15] there suggested that I should republish her works. The idea then began to take shape: I got to know her grandchildren, principally Major Richard Gregory and his sister Mrs R. de Winton (Anne Gregory), whose book of childhood memories of Coole Park[16] we also published. In 1964 Major Gregory sold most of his grandmother's papers to the Berg Collection of the New York Public Library, but fortunately for me he had kept Lady Gregory's own copies of her works, and it was in these that she had made her revisions for future editions, so our company's edition is certainly the Definitive Edition.

The first action that had to be taken was to deal with the copyright situation. Many of the copyrights were still held by Putnams and I had to buy the remainder of their stock of *The Selected Plays of Lady Gregory* before they would release them.[17] We then checked up on the terms of Lady Gregory's will and much to our surprise and consternation we found that the copyrights should have been handed over to the three grandchildren jointly by the executors when Richard had reached the age of twenty-five. This had never been done, it seems, and as one of the executors, Thomas Kiernan, had died in 1967, a deed of conveyance had to be signed by Mrs Gough. Curiously enough, when Daniel Murphy was checking up on the copyright situation for his 1965 US Capricorn paperback edition of *Our Irish Theatre*, Mr Kiernan had told him that they had been transferred, but there was no documentary proof of this. When Major Gregory sold the collection in 1964 he was under the impression that he held the copyright and he sold all rights in the unique unpublished material to the Library. The only difficulty was that they were not his alone to sell. Not unnaturally the Library was in a state of considerable anxiety, and it took a year to tidy up the situation, but I am glad to say it has now been done.

I then set about asking leading figures in the field of Anglo-Irish literature to contribute forewords to the various volumes of the edition, which originally was only going to contain twelve volumes, but has now gone up to eighteen and may go even higher, because I continue to find hitherto unpublished material. I asked Dr T.R. Henn[18] whether he would be prepared to act as joint general editor of the Coole Edition and I am very glad to say that he agreed. It was he who had in 1965 got Dublin University to accept my Gregory bibliography as an M.Litt. thesis subject and we have been good friends ever since. Having gathered my list of foreword writers, I then approached Oxford University Press in New York to see whether they would be prepared to take a proportion of each edition to distribute in the United States, as without this sort of help I would not have had the sort of money required to finance the edition – Dan Murphy was convinced I'd lose my shirt on the project. I hoped their assistance would allow me to bring out the edition at a reasonable speed; otherwise it would have taken years longer. Fortunately Oxford agreed.[19]

I called the series The Coole Edition for two reasons. Coole Park was Lady Gregory's home from 1880, when she married Sir William Gregory, until her death fifty-two years later. The second reason goes back to before World War II. Yeats and Macmillan were preparing a new edition of his 'Collected Works', and this was to have been called 'The Coole Edition'. However, the poet's death and the War put a stop to these plans. The sheets had already been signed for this edition and they were later used for Macmillan's Definitive Edition of the *Poems* (Wade 209–210) published in 1949 in England and for a limited signed edition of the *Variorum Poems* (1957) (Wade 211n) in America.[20]

The Gregory family and I felt that the use of the name Coole was not altogether suitable to an edition of Yeats's works, so I used it to make sure that the idea would not be revived some time in the future. As it was, after Lady Gregory's death, her name had been dropped from the title page of *The Unicorn from the Stars* when it was included in Yeats's *Collected Plays*, by accident or design.[21] Yeats's reputation so overshadowed the other figures of the Irish Literary Revival that I half-seriously feared that one day in the developing myths, Lady Gregory might have been further written out of the story.[22] But I do not see how anybody could have justified the name of Lady Gregory's home for an edition of Yeats's works: the Sligo or Thoor Ballylee Edition would have been much more appropriate. After all, in his poem 'Blood and the Moon', Yeats had written:

> I declare this tower is my symbol; I declare
> This winding gyring, spiring treadmill of a stair is my ancestral stair.

I determined that The Coole Edition would not only be just a new edition of Lady Gregory's works, but also be worthy of a collector, so I have been making it a uniform edition bound in dark blue buckram, blocked in gold, with light blue laid endpapers and top edges gilt, and the critics have been unanimous in praising the production, and the cover designs by Dara O'Lochlainn (whose father Colm founded the Three Candles Press and might also be called 'The Father of Irish Typography').

One day Elizabeth Coxhead asked me whether I wanted any copies of her biography of Lady Gregory. She told me there were just over a thousand available and if she did not take them, they were going to be remaindered in Australia. I said that I would take the lot, and sold them at just over half the original price, and paid Elizabeth a royalty on them.[23]

Having got the edition together, I then set about getting a suitable launching pad and I was fortunate that our Chairman, Sir Robert Mayer (of Youth and Music and Children's Concerts fame)[24] was a great friend of Erskine Childers, then Minister for Health and Tánaiste (Deputy Prime Minister) of the Republic of Ireland,[25] and we asked him whether he would be agreeable to launching the series, and this he was only too delighted to do. Through his help it was arranged that the reception would be held at the Irish Embassy in London on the publication day of the first three volumes, 4 May. The printing schedules therefore had to work round this date, allowing for time for review copies to be sent off. Imagine my near hysteria when I first discovered that just as the copies were to be bound, *Visions and Beliefs in the West of Ireland* had been printed on the wrong paper, which would have resulted in books being half as thick as they should have been. On top of this, after the sheets had been reprinted, I discovered that Tonbridge Printers had hoped to fit the new sheets into the old casings, and had not ordered any more buckram so everything was terribly delayed and I was extremely worried that I would not get copies in time for publication. Fortunately they borrowed some buckram from

Hazell, Watson & Viney and so got a few copies to me in time. For some reason Hazells, who were doing all the other volumes for me at that time, had to farm out *Visions* to one of the other companies in the British Printing Corporation group, and that was the start of my headaches. I wanted to use 11 pt Pilgrim type for the books, but they hadn't got it so we had to make to do with 11 pt Plantin instead. Tonbridge also had to print the jacket again. First they printed it in four colours instead of three: well, I didn't mind that if I only had to pay for three colours. However, I then discovered they had made the spine far too narrow, so I couldn't have used them even if I had tried: it would have looked ridiculous. This book proved to be a great nuisance to Hazells and Tonbridge, both of whom lost heavily on it.[26]

In spite of all these worries and difficulties, *Visions and Beliefs in the West of Ireland*, *Cuchulain of Muirthemne* and *Gods and Fighting Men* all appeared on time and had a very good send-off from Mr Childers who had first read the books in his youth, and the critics have been unanimous in praising the edition, with the only negative comments coming from an Irish reviewer who wished that the book could have been produced in Ireland. But I have had experience of one of the largest Irish printers when I first started in publishing, and that is why they were printed in England.

So we progress: I planned for the four-volume *Collected Plays* to be published at the beginning of 1971,[27] to coincide with new productions of some of Lady Gregory's plays at the Abbey Theatre and then a further three volumes in March, *A Book of Saints and Wonders*, *The Kiltartan Books* and *Poets and Dreamers*, and that is where we are at present.

II

The original 1970 article finished at this point. There were publishing delays to the last three titles mentioned, however: *The Kiltartan Books* only got published in early 1972 (though review copies got sent out, and copies were on sale before Christmas), and *Poets and Dreamers* and *A Book of Saints & Wonders* only appeared on 17 June 1974. The Coole Edition was then somewhat extended, with the number of volumes increasing from the original eighteen to twenty-one.

When Robert Gregory's widow Margaret was placed in a nursing home in 1973 and her home in Budleigh Salterton was cleared, amongst the effects found was the typescript of Lady Gregory's autobiography *Seventy Years*, which we added to the Edition as volume 13, publishing it on 1 July 1974. I also arranged with Oxford University Press and the Berg Collection of the New York Public

Library, the owner of the typescript and MSS, that the complete two-volume edition of Lady Gregory's Journals, then being edited by Daniel J. Murphy, and originally to be published by OUP, should also be included, as volumes 14 and 15. The first volume was only published in 1978 as checking the editor's notes took me some time, and even longer for the second volume, which only appeared in 1988,[28] as the notes provided were incomplete and error-strewn, particularly those for Book 44, to which I added another 150. I also wrote an Afterword to the volume describing the chequered history of Lady Gregory's unpublished works following her death, and Yeats's problems with an over-zealous, over-protective and aggressive Margaret who was ignoring and over-riding all Lady Gregory's spoken and written wishes.

The volumes of *Shorter Writings* are now being edited by James Pethica, Lady Gregory's official biographer, whose edition of *Lady Gregory's Diaries 1892–1902* we published in 1996.[29] The nineteenth volume, *Mr Gregory's Letter-Box*, was published in 1981. I had produced a biographical index for this, but am embarrassed to say that due to errors on my part, I had to issue a sheet of *Errata and Addenda* for it, most of the corrected and new information being provided by Richard Hawkins of the Royal Irish Academy, to whom I am most grateful. I am presently working on a biographical index for Sir William Gregory's *Autobiography* (volume 19) which will use her original text rather than the pared down version used in John Murray's 1894 edition.[30] The Robert Gregory volume has long been abandoned: the General Editors – then Tom Henn and I – over-estimated the amount of material we could use that had not or would not appear elsewhere, as has the volume of lectures, now to form part of the collection of shorter writings, and I plan to replace it with one edited by James Pethica, containing Lady Gregory's first Irish Writings, written between 1883 and 1893, prior to meeting Yeats, including 'An Emigrant's Notebook', *A Phantom's Pilgrimage*, 'A Philanthropist' and 'A Gentleman'.

As to the Yeats Collection in the Dublin City Library, I have since 1965 added a further 600 odd books to it (including about 200 translations), these being more recently published titles as well as books that fill gaps in my orig-inal collection. I continue to add to it when I can, so there are now over 1,100 items catalogued (though a number of the original entries, such as those for the Cuala prints and greetings cards each relate to over a hundred items).

The inaccuracies Russell K. Alspach made in the information I'd given for the third edition of the Wade bibliography he later recognized and made a conciliatory approach in 1979, apologizing for not crediting me for the infor-mation I'd provided and asking me to assist him editing the fourth edition. He must have already been in ill health, however, as I did not hear from him again and the next thing I knew was that he had died, and Oxford University Press, who had taken over the Soho Bibliography Series from its founder / publisher Rupert Hart-Davis, offered me the role of Editor of that edition. Russell Alspach had been a professor at the University of Massachusetts in Amherst and his colleague Professor David R. Clark met me when I was staying in New York the following year and handed over all the research notes Prof. Alspach had already prepared. The third edition took the Yeats publications up to 1965 and I was to update it up to 1980 and deliver it by the end of 1982. That seemed an easy enough job, until I started comparing the text of the earlier editions with what information I had started gathering, and found a lot of inconsistencies, errors and omissions. There were, for example, dozens of books with Yeats contributions that should have been in the first 1951 edition, and had not been picked up in the second and third editions. This did not bode well for the rest of the bibliography. I pointed out the problems to John Bell, my editor at OUP, saying that I needed to double-check every entry from 1885 to the present, and I was effectively given an open-ended contract. To see every single book mentioned by Wade and his editors and add page references to all the contributions to periodicals has taken a long time, and to that end I visited libraries and collections throughout the UK, Ireland, the USA and Canada, finding as I did so many items unrecorded by Wade, Rupert Hart-Davis and Russell Alspach, quite apart from the results of the surge in overseas popularity in Yeats's works in other languages.

I am using 31 December 1989 as my general cut-off date as that was the original termination date of copyright in the UK at the time – fifty years from the end of the year of the author's death. I am 400,000 words into the project, and still have some way to go. Oxford subsequently returned the Soho series to Duff Hart-Davis, Rupert Hart-Davis's son, without being aware that my contract was still valid. This initially put me in a quandary, but then I realized that as I had rewritten and often enlarged every single descriptive entry, I no longer had to worry about earlier copyrights. I severed my contract with Oxford and following discussions with the British Library it looked as if its publications department would take it, but I delayed too long, and the BL's recent budget cuts hit hard, so many projects including mine were cancelled, and I am presently without a publisher. I think it likely I shall do a bit of self-publishing: it's not as if I am without a little experience in the field.

NOTES

1. Bought on 11 June 1963. I still have the copy, and I can say that purchase redirected the course of my life.
2. And it is one of only twenty copies known to still exist of the 100 printed. I have seen ten of these and most are in no better condition than my copy. A review copy inscribed by Yeats at the time of publication and again by him to John Quinn was sold in 2014 for £100,000. A fine copy of *The Wanderings of Oisin* would probably fetch about £5,000 now. Today's likely prices of other books listed here: the *United Irishman* edition of *Where There is Nothing* (Wade 41) £1,500; *Poems Written in Discouragement* (Wade 107) £2,000; *Deirdre* and *Alterations to Deirdre* (Wade 69 and 70) £1,250; *The Golden Helmet* (Wade 74) £2,000; *Beyond the Grave* (Wade 336A) £100; *Discoveries* (Wade 72), inscribed by WBY, £2,000; the Quinn edition of Synge's *Poems and Translations* (Wade 244) £750; the Dix titles, about £500 each); *Souls for Gold*, perhaps £500, while the copy of Lady Gregory's *A Book of Saints and Wonders* inscribed by WBY to Maud Gonne, would go for £5,000, no problem.
3. This was named Falkner Greirson & Co., respelling the names of two famous eighteenth-century Dublin booksellers, George Faulkner (or Falkner) and George Grierson (both of whom had known Swift, with Falkner having been his publisher). Michael died in 1974, but Noel continued through various vicissitudes until his death thirty years later. (See http://www.independent.co.uk/news/obituaries /noel-jameson-6148573.html)
4. As well as being a copyright protector and friend of Yeats, Lady Gregory and Synge, John Quinn (1870–1924) was a great collector of books and manuscripts, owning, among other things, the manuscripts of Joyce's *Ulysses* and Eliot's *The Waste Land* and many Conrad manuscripts. By the time he died, he had become the twentieth century's most important patron of living literature and art, having owned such famous pictures as Matisse's *Blue Nude*, Picasso's *Three Musicians* and Rousseau's *Sleeping Gypsy*, to name but three. He sold his book collection in 1923, but unfortunately he was too much ahead of his time and the sale was unsuccessful, fetching only about 212,000 dollars, for a total of nearly 12,000 lots. Fifty of these (the Conrad items) raised about half the total figure.
5. The bibliography was not to be. Without telling me he was doing so Liam wrote, and in association with the Cuala Press, published *The Dun Emer Press, later the Cuala Press, with a List of the Books, Broadsides and Other Pieces printed at the Press* (1973). It lacked a list of the prints and greetings cards and underestimated their number, as Liam did not check my erstwhile collection of these in the City Library. He mentions 97 prints and 129 greetings cards, while the City Library's collection contains 130 and 145 respectively, and I know both sets are incomplete.
6. Brindley's allowed me to go through their Cuala Press accounts, and from these I saw that a number of the titles published between 1939 and 1943 had more copies printed and bound than their limitations stated (and this must have been standard practice with the other titles):

Title	limitation	number bound
W.B. Yeats *Last Poems and Two Plays*	500	525
Louis MacNeice *The Last Ditch*	450	500
Frank O'Connor (trs.) *A Lament for Art O'Leary*	130	160
W.B. Yeats *If I Were Four-and-Twenty*	450	500
C. Bax (ed.) *Florence Farr, Bernard Shaw & W.B.Yeats*	500	530
Frank O'Connor *Three Tales*	250	280
Patrick Kavanagh *The Great Hunger*	250	280
Elizabeth Bowen *Seven Winters*	450	480
Jack B. Yeats *La La Noo*	250	280
Frank O'Connor *A Picture Book*	450	480
Joseph Hone (ed.) *The Love Story of Thomas Davis*	250	280

I regret to say I made no note as to other titles they bound at this time. Did I not see entries for them, or did binding quantity and limitation match? I don't remember, but suspect the latter. Perhaps Miss Yeats ordered extra copies to be able to throw out those she considered sub-standard.

7. Some years later the City Library had the carpet restored, at which time it was recognized as being a very early Donegal carpet and therefore rather more valuable than had it been a product of Dun Emer Industries.

8. This I did find rather irritating, but as he hadn't acknowledged my assistance the errors could not be laid at my door. I found later that *Irish Tales* was one of a set of three Ariel Booklets published by Putnam's Knickerbocker Press. It had been derived from their 1891 two-volume edition of *Representative Irish Tales* (Wade 215). Wade notes that those were published in two different bindings, but there are more, including a pair in publisher's deluxe full leather, copies of which I came across on eBay about ten years ago. Putnam also decided to reissue the collection under the title *Irish Tales* as part of its Ariel Booklets series, which measure 5½ x 3¾ inches, and are bound in red limp ecrasé leather. They were published in about 1903, as nos. 77–9 in the series, No. 77 containing the Carleton stories, 78 those by Maria Edgeworth and the Banim brothers, and 79 the Lover and Lever tales. Had Putnam been publishing these a decade earlier they would have published a four volume series, each story with Yeats's original 1891 introductory essay, but in 1903, there was a problem. The story 'Father Tom and the Pope' which appeared in the second volume of *Representative Irish Tales*, with Yeats's essay, was in 1891 universally believed to have been written by William Maginn, but in 1895 Samuel Ferguson's widow announced that her late husband was its author, so it was published over Ferguson's name as Ariel Booklet no. 86, without any introduction.

These Ariel Booklets are rare, and I have not yet been able to see a copy of the Lover / Lever volume, which is far, far rarer than the other two. Years ago, I found one copy listed in the *National Union Catalog* as being in the Ohio Wesleyan University Library, but it had gone missing prior to 1977 when the records of their holdings were computerized so, drawing from the layout and contents of the other two volumes I have created an hypothetical bibliographical description for it. I believe it will prove to be accurate when compared with a copy if / when one turns up, but in nearly forty years I have not come across another, and at the time of writing (December 2014) there is no copy to be found in any library linked to WorldCat, the *NUC's* successor. Nor have I heard of any copy in a private collection. Frustrating.

9. I still have not finished the bibliography, but I do intend to include it in the twenty-first volume of The Coole Edition. I sold my collection in 1975 to the Library of University College Galway, now called the James Hardiman Library, NUI Galway. Sadly their cataloguing now is still less detailed than that on the sale catalogue I made up, so it is of little use from the bibliographical point of view.

10. Liam Miller was one of the greatest typographers of the twentieth century and his Dolmen Press, which had started off as a private press before becoming a leading Irish publishing company, produced some of the most beautiful books published at that time. I had invested in the company in 1965, but it was only in 1987 after Liam's death and the bankruptcy of the company that I discovered I had been the third largest shareholder in it after Liam and his wife. Colin Smythe Limited purchased almost all the book stocks – over 150,000 books – and still have a number of them in print nearly thirty years on.

11. This collection is now in the Library of the University of Waterloo, Ontario.

12. Born in 1919 and dying in 2008, Máirín had been appointed Dublin City Librarian in 1961, and Dublin City & County Librarian in 1967, a position she held until her retirement in 1984. A measure of the regard in which she was held amongst her peers was her election as President of the Library Association 1966–7, and she was one of its honorary (life) vice presidents, an honorary fellow of the Library Association of Ireland and a member of An Chomhairle Leabharlanna / the Library Council 1958–82.

13. Though with less energy now than in the past.

14. *The Private Library*, Second Series, vol. 2, no. 3, 1969, pp. 131–2. Frances-Jane French (1929–2002) was connected with this firm because a cousin of hers, Joseph Maunsell Hone (W.B. Yeats's biographer), was one of its founders, and the company took its name from his own middle name with a variant spelling and a different pronunciation. She was also an Irish genealogist, and most of her later life was devoted to the subject. A Dublin 'character', she was, as the *Daily Telegraph* obituary of 16 November 2002 noted, 'instantly recognisable in the city's streets as her black-clad figure progressed in busy little steps with the determination of a battle tank'. She gained her M.Litt. degree in 1969 for her *History of the House of Maunsel and A Bibliography of Certain of its Publications* [those by J. M. Synge] coupled with *A Bibliography of the Tower Press Booklets (First and Second Series 1906–1908)* (1967, 1968) and *The Abbey Theatre Series of Plays, A Bibliography* (1969).

15. The most vociferous was Professor Lester Conner (1920–2005) who taught at Chestnut Hill College, Philadelphia PA from 1962 to 1990, and was a long-time lecturer at the Yeats International Summer School, Sligo. His *A Yeats Dictionary* (which had, so he said, existed for decades as a collection of index cards in a shoebox) was finally published in 1998.

16. Anne Gregory, *Me & Nu, Childhood at Coole*, illustrated by Joyce Dennis (1973).

Her husband, Brigadier Robert de Winton, commanding the British garrison, was assassinated on 10 February 1947 by Maria Pasquinelli over the Trieste agreement as he was about to ceremonially hand Pula (now in Croatia) over to the Yugoslav authorities. Considered a heroine by many in Italy, her death sentence by an Allied military tribunal was commuted to life imprisonment, of which she served seventeen years, and in 1964 she was pardoned by Italian President Antonio Segni, and released. She died in 2013, aged 100 years. Her motive was initially puzzling, until her confession was published in *Corriere della Sera*: 'I rise in rebellion, with the firm intent of killing the man who is unfortunate enough to represent the Four Great Powers that, at the conference in Paris, in violation of justice, against humanity, and against political wisdom, have decided to tear out once again from the maternal womb the lands most sacred to Italy, condemning them either to the experiments of a new Danzig or, with a chilling sensibility and complicity, to the Yugoslav yoke – a synonym to our indomitable Italian people of death in *foibas*, of deportation, of exile.' (*The Daily Telegraph*, 8 July 2013.) Foibas, or foibes, were deep karst sinkholes mainly in Venezia Giulia, Istria and Dalmatia, into which many local Italians were thrown by Yugoslav Partisans from 1943–9. The term came to cover all Yugoslav murders of hundreds if not thousands of Italians.

17. Long before I had even started publishing, I had visited Putnams' trade counter in London, asked what Gregory titles they had in stock, and on 28 April 1965 I bought the stock of all the dozen or so individual plays that were still in print, including ten cloth-bound copies of *Mirandolina* (1924) which were described to me as being a limited edition, but I was doubtful of this. (But I know to the day when they went out of print!) Dublin's Talbot Press had also been very helpful in giving me the years that its Gregory titles went out of print – it often acted as Putnam's Dublin distributor for her works, and in the 1960s still had their sales records.

18. Thomas Rice Henn (1901–74), the doyen of Anglo-Irish literary critics of his time, CBE 1945, Senior Tutor 1945–7 and President 1951–61 of St Catharine's College Cambridge, and among many other works of criticism, author of one of the first studies of Yeats, *The Lonely Tower* (1950), and editor of J.M. Synge's works in 1963. He received hon. Litt. Ds from Dublin University (TCD) and the University of Victoria, BC, Canada. I published his *Last Essays, Mainly on Anglo-Irish Literature* (1976) and *Five Arches, A Sketch for an Autobiography*, with 'Philoctetes', and Other Poems, as a double volume in 1980. Born in Albert House on the outskirts of Sligo, his family home, Paradise, Co. Clare, was destroyed by fire in 1970, some years after it had been sold by his brother. I had met him in January 1965 when he spent a term as a visiting lecturer at TCD.

19. I also agreed to an offer from Captain Tadhg McGlinchey of Irish University Press that it should publish a deluxe edition of 250 copies on special paper, with a special binding. I think he thought of it as a successor series to the Cuala / Dun Emer set. The sheets of each edition were to be printed at the same time as the Smythe / OUP sheets, and the first sets of sheets were sent to IUP, but my progress in the production of the series was too slow for him, and the deal was cancelled some time before IUP went into liquidation in 1974. A very few sets of sheets were bound in IUP bindings for display purposes, I think, and have since appeared

on the rare book market, but the bulk I bought back from the liquidators, and a number of the volumes I then bound up with a slip giving our publication details. Tadhg had also suggested that IUP took over the distribution of all Colin Smythe Ltd's titles, which would be stocked in Ireland, and we had serious discussions. Fortunately they came to nothing, as I would have been in a very difficult position when IUP collapsed.

20. The Coole Edition was to have been published by Charles Scribner's Sons in America rather than by Macmillan. Sheets of an engraved illustration by Edmund Dulac, also prepared for that edition, were mislaid, according to information given me by Charles Scribner III, and so were not transferred to Macmillan with the signed pages.

21. I suspect that this can be traced back to Yeats's annoyance with Margaret Gregory, Robert's widow and sole heir, during the previous year over her failing to keep to the terms of Lady Gregory's invalid 10 November 1931 codicil to her Will – it had only been signed by one witness instead of the legally necessary two – that stated 'I wish the final decision as to arrangement and publication of any of the material left unarranged, to be made by my friend of so many years, W.B. Yeats, whose verdict would be final.' He may well have felt it likely that if he included Lady Gregory's name, Margaret might have somehow caused problems.

22. I need not have worried: a fair number of critical writings and biographies, mostly of high quality, have been published over the intervening years: – Hazard Adams, *Lady Gregory* (1973); Elizabeth Coxhead, *Lady Gregory, A Literary Portrait* (1961, revd 1966); Michèle Dalmasso, *Lady Gregory et la Renaissance Irlandaise* (1982); Anne Dedio, *Das dramatische Werk von Lady Gregory* (1967); Anne Fogarty (ed.) *Irish University Review: A Journal of Irish Studies*, vol. 34, no. 1, Lady Gregory (2004); Anne Gregory, *Me & Nu: Childhood at Coole*, with a foreword by Maurice Collis (1970); Judith Hill, *Lady Gregory, An Irish Life* (2005); Brian Jenkins, *Sir William Gregory of Coole: A Biography* (1986); Mary Lou Kohfeldt, *Lady Gregory, The Woman Behind the Irish Renaissance* (1985); Edward A. Kopper Jr., *Lady Isabella Persse Gregory* (1976); Sam McCready (intro. by James Pethica), *Coole Lady – The Extraordinary Story of Lady Gregory* (2006); E.H. Mikhail, *Lady Gregory: An Annotated Bibliography of Criticism* (1982); E.H. Mikhail (ed.), *Lady Gregory, Interviews and Recollections* (1977); James Pethica (ed.) *Lady Gregory's Diaries 1892–1902* (1996); Ann Saddlemyer, *In Defence of Lady Gregory, Playwright* (1966); Ann Saddlemyer & Colin Smythe (eds) *Lady Gregory, Fifty Years After* (1987); Colin Smythe, *A Guide to Coole Park, Home of Lady Gregory*, with a foreword by Maurice Craig (1973); revd, with a foreword by Anne Gregory (1983, revised 1995, 2003); Colin Smythe (ed.), *Robert Gregory, 1881–1918* (1981); Colm Tóibín, *Lady Gregory's Toothbrush* (2002).

23. Very sadly, Elizabeth killed herself on the railway track at Gerrards Cross, aged seventy years, in 1979 soon after I'd republished her *Daughters of Erin*, and I had the melancholy task of writing an appreciation of her for the local paper.

24. Sir Robert, who had been born in Mannheim, Germany on 5 June 1879, died on 9 January 1985. Founder of the Robert Mayer Children's Concerts in 1923, he was knighted for services to music in 1939.

25. He was later to be elected the fourth President of Ireland, succeeding Eamon de Valera, in 1973. Tragically he died the following year.
26. Their financial loss was increased by the fact that whoever they had got to do the gilding of the top edges of the pages of *Visions and Beliefs* used real gold leaf, instead of a gold-coloured metallic foil, and they could only charge us for the much cheaper product.
27. I planned to publish the *Plays* on 1 March 1971 and had been informed by J.C. Trewin, the Literary Editor of *The Times* (and father of Ion Trewin) that he had written a very favourable review that was to appear in the paper that day. Unfortunately its publication clashed with its printers' one-day-strike, so the review was never printed, though I did get a proof of the text.
28. This was published on 22 February 1988 because of delays over the top-edge gilding, and it was too late to insert a cancel title to change the copyright details which give the publication date as 1987.
29. James Pethica is in fact the third editor to have been appointed. Donald J. Gordon was the first, and on his death, Mary Fitzgerald Finneran. She too died before doing any work on the project.
30. I had Sir William's *Autobiography* typeset in 1981, and at that time attempted the index, which was a failure. I, with James Pethica and others, attempted it again a decade later, and advanced it considerably, but it has only been with the advent of the internet, Wikipedia and other sources that a comprehensive index can be attempted. But one has to face up to the fact that there are a lot of errors 'out there', so one is only half-safe as to accuracy. If there's any doubt, one must double-check elsewhere. In one case, I was searching for details for an entry on Charles Elmé Francatelli (1805–76), a chef Gregory mentions as being at the St James's Club, better known as Crockford's, a gambling 'hell' in St James Street, when he joined it in 1842. There was considerable variance in the entries on the net about the important events in his life, such as the years he worked as chief cook to Queen Victoria, so I set out to search primary sources, principally the newspapers in the online British Newspaper Archive, a search that became a compulsion, and I ended up producing a 20,000 word article on his life and on Crockford's, which was published in *Petits Propos Culinaires* 102 in 2014 and 2015, about nine months after I had started my search. At the time I type this, this index is over 31,000 words in length, but I am hopeful the book will be published in 2016, the bicentenary of Sir William's birth. This will depend on whether I succumb to further sidetracks – I very much hope not.

The Middle Realm

NEIL J. MANN

Yeats is justly celebrated for his evocation of Sligo and the Irish landscape, but it is precisely that – an evocation. The names of Ben Bulben, Rosses Point or Kyle-Na-No evoke presences in the mind, as if Yeats is summoning elemental powers, and there are few details to give them specificity. Those who know the places can readily supply the detail; those who have never seen even a picture will respond to the sounds and sense of place, but will not gain a clear image. Even the descriptions tend to be impressionistic moments or traits. For instance, Innisfree on Lough Gill is described in terms that are evocative not precise: 'midnight's all a glimmer, and noon a purple glow, / And evening full of the linnets wings' (*Variorum Poems,* 117). But Yeats is not describing an experience, he is summoning up the lake isle in his mind while standing 'on the roadway, or on the pavements grey' of the city, and this is an island of desire – 'I will arise' indicates both future and resolve – not of sensuous engagement.

Yeats's poetry is seldom concerned primarily with external perception, concentrating on the visionary world of the mind's eye. Even the most powerful evocations of an external world tend to be inward views, whether the mountain of Knocknarea or the island of Innisfree, the woods of Coole or the stream at Glendalough, the tower at Ballylee or the halls of Tara, the houses of Dublin or the pavements of Byzantium. The landscapes of Sligo are peopled with traditional countryfolk and spirits, and the physical world blurs into the mythic. Scenes of natural place are both real and dreamlike: the immediacy of 'the wandering water gushes / From the hills above Glen-Car' is followed by images of a bathing star and of trout whose dreams are troubled by fairies. A rural domestic scene is evoked in detail but in the negative: 'He'll hear no more the lowing / Of the calves on the warm hillside / Or the kettle on the hob / Sing peace into his breast' (*VP* 88).

In part because Yeats's poetry does not deal with 'normal experience', I.A. Richards in *Science and Poetry* (1926) asserted that he had 'made a violent repudiation, not merely of current civilization but of life itself, in favour of a supernatural world'. This seems to ignore much of the poetry that deals with contemporary Dublin and politics, but it is true that 'September 1913', for instance, moves to a storied Irish past and that the achievement of 'Easter 1916' is the way it places political events in the context of timeless values and myth. The poetry consistently transcends material reality.

Yet, though Yeats was clearly a believer in supernatural reality and spiritually aware, he seems to have little interest in God or religious experience. T.S. Eliot quoted Richards's opinion and went on to dismiss Yeats's supernatural world as 'the wrong supernatural world' because it 'was not a world of spiritual significance, not a world of real Good and Evil, of holiness or sin, but a highly sophisticated lower mythology' (*After Strange Gods*). When Eliot made these comments in a lecture in 1933, he was championing the higher religion with the force of a convert, having been received into the Church of England in 1927, but, within his own terms at least, he was probably right. Yeats's interest is generally situated at the intermediate level rather than either the numinous or the phenomenal; it is neither Eliot's 'world of spiritual significance' nor the world of 'normal experience', what Richards thinks of as 'life itself'.

But Yeats considers that, as a poet, he is concerned with life itself, with what animates the material and the experience from which spiritual experience arises: 'If it be true that God is a circle whose centre is everywhere, the saint goes to the centre, the poet and artist to the ring where everything comes round again' (*Collected Works*, vol. 4, p. 209; 1906). Poet and artist focus on the intermediate world of creation and human emotion: the soul of the world and the soul of humanity. Yeats claimed that his 'philosophy of life' in the 1880s was that 'Nothing was worthy of respect but passion in its moment of splendour and nobility in its hour of pride or of sweetness' (*Yeats and Theatre*, p. 64). Passion means both suffering and desire, which the Buddha saw as tying humanity to the wheel of rebirth, but its intensity reveals 'immortal moods in mortal desires, an undecaying hope in our trivial ambitions, a divine love in sexual passion' (*CW* 4, p. 143; 1895). The link of the fleeting experience to an eternal realm makes them symbols and methods of approach to that Platonic level.

The imaginative writer differs from the saint in that he identifies himself – to the neglect of his own soul, alas! – with the soul of the world, and frees himself from all that is impermanent in that soul, an ascetic not of women and wine, but of the newspapers. Those things that are permanent in the soul of the world, the great passions that trouble all and have but a brief recurring life of a flower and seed in any man, are indeed renounced by the saint, who seeks not an eternal art, but his own eternity. The artist stands between the saint and the world of impermanent things. (*CW* 4, p. 208; 1906)

Some years later, Ezra Pound would summarize similar ideas more pithily: 'Literature is news that stays news' (*ABC of Reading*, 1934). Poets ignore the contingent and accidental realities of events in order to look at the human drama behind them and to look to their inner, essential life. Their concerns are the very bonds of desire, from which potential saints, intent on perfecting their soul, attempt to free themselves:

> The intellect of man is forced to choose
> Perfection of the life, or of the work,
> And if it take the second must refuse
> A heavenly mansion, raging in the dark.
> ('The Choice', *VP* 495; 1932)

The artist chooses perfection of the work – or the attempt at it – and in so doing renounces heaven or release, but also sees how the impermanent world reflects the eternal.

When writing about these spiritual states in the early works, Yeats uses the word 'moods' to underline the evanescence of any individual expression in a human being, but notes that they are 'immortal' and unchanging, 'the gods of ancient days still dwelling on their secret Olympus, the angels of more modern days ascending and descending upon their shining ladder' (*CW* 4, p. 143; 1895). Aphrodite or Niamh moves from lover to lover, inspiring each one and changing in each one but unchanging in herself. This fascination with the permanence of the transient, was supplemented by his interest in Irish folklore, since the Sidhe, the Tuatha Dé Danaan and legendary figures such as Maeve, Deirdre and Cuchullain link the individual to the race and collective memory.

Yeats's ideas about the nature of the Irish fairies, the Sidhe, changed with time, but in 1889, he thought that 'quite beyond any kind of doubt many of them were long ago gods in Ireland' (*CW* 9, p. 81) and that the 'fairies are the lesser spiritual moods of that universal mind, wherein every mood is a soul and every thought a body' (*CW* 9, p. 184; 1890). One of the ways in which they differ from humanity is the purity of their passions, their 'unmixed emotions', 'their untiring joys and sorrows' ('The Untiring Ones' [1893], *Mythologies,*

p. 77). In this they are allied with the tragic figures of Corneille and Racine, or those of Shakespeare when they are 'amid the great moments', where 'all is lyricism, unmixed passion, "the integrity of fire" ' (Preface to *Plays for an Irish Theatre* [1911], *Variorum Plays,* 1297).

The shared folklore of the Sidhe is placed in the same sphere as artistic creations and religious figures by Michael Robartes in '*Rosa Alchemica*': Roland, Hamlet, Faust, Lear and Beatrice as well as the Virgin Mary and Aphrodite. Despite appearances, Robartes affirms that these figures are not the creations of writers or worshippers but are themselves 'always making and unmaking humanity, which is indeed but the trembling of their lips' (*Mythologies,* p. 275). The artists give them expression and they are manifested in humanity but they are independent of any human being.

This realm may be supernatural but only just, and is perhaps better seen as the hidden or the subtle natural. It is the level of the Self when it advocates the value of human life in 'A Dialogue of Self and Soul' even 'if it be life to pitch / Into the frog-spawn of a blind man's ditch' (*VP* 479). 'Masterful images' may grow 'in pure mind' but begin 'where all the ladders start / In the foul rag-and-bone shop of the heart' ('The Circus Animals' Desertion', *VP* 630). The speaker of 'Sailing to Byzantium' may choose to sail from the country of 'sensual music', where the lovers and birds are 'dying generations', and he may call on the 'sages standing in God's holy fire' to be the 'singing masters of my soul', but he chooses to incarnate in an undying bird, a form both natural and arti-ficial, and to sing not of eternity but 'what is past, or passing, or to come' (*VP* 408). When the Soul tells the Heart to 'Seek out reality, leave things that seem', the poetic Heart cannot follow – 'What be a singer born and lack a theme?' – choosing the example of Homer whose theme was 'original sin' ('Vacillation' VII, *VP* 502). This may be 'the wrong supernatural world', but Yeats would probably include Eliot with the religious writer Von Hügel:

> Homer is my example and his unchristened heart.
> The lion and the honeycomb, what has Scripture said?
> So get you gone, Von Hügel, though with blessings on your head.
>
> (*VP* 503)

'Coole and Ballylee, 1931': Yeats's Elegy for the Poetic Demesne[*]

TOMOKO IWATSUBO

W.B. Yeats first described the gestation of 'Coole and Ballylee, 1931' in a letter from Coole to his wife George on 3 February 1932:

> I am tired owing to the fact that I have at last found a rich theme for verse.
> I am turning the introductory verses to Lady Gregorys 'Coole' (Cuala) into
> a poem of some length – various sections with more or less symbolic subject
> matter. Yesterday I wrote an account of the sudden ascent of a swan – a
> symbol of inspiration I think. (#5583)[1]

His use of 'at last' here may carry weight as he had informed George in the previous month that he had been 'writing much poetry' (#5561) and had recently finished twenty-one poems including 'Vacillation' (#5571).[2]

It was 'at last', in a way, for him to return to Coole Lough and the swan(s) in his poetry after setting out on the construction of his own actual as well as textual tower in Ballylee more than a decade earlier around 1917. 'Coole and Ballylee, 1931', where Yeats returns from Thoor Ballylee to Coole Lough, is in part a sequel to 'The Wild Swans at Coole', from where, symbolically, he had set out on his tower-building enterprise, which was intimated with the poem's

* This essay is based on part of my PhD thesis submitted to the University of York. I am
  deeply grateful to my supervisor Professor Hugh Haughton for his invaluable advice
  and generous support.

final question: 'Among what rushes will they build ... ' (p. 323).[3] The phrase 'But all is changed' (p. 492) which appears in the third last line of 'Coole and Ballylee, 1931' links with 'The Wild Swans at Coole', which contains the recollected scene of the swans in 1899 and the poet's reflections 'All's changed' (p. 322), which itself resonates with 'All changed, changed utterly' (p. 392) in 'Easter, 1916', its contemporary in terms of the writing period.[4]

In Yeats's poetic 'demesne', Coole and Ballylee are neighbours with contrasting as well as shared characteristics. The two places share their values of 'custom' and 'ceremony' in antithesis to 'arrogance and hatred' ('A Prayer for My Daughter', p. 406). It was 'For an old neighbour's friendship' that Yeats 'chose the house' in Ballylee ('My Descendants', p. 423). As if winding up – or 'dreaming back' – his construction project in Ballylee, the water in the opening stanza of 'Coole and Ballylee, 1931' leads us, starting right below 'my window-ledge' of Thoor Ballylee – which has now become firmly established in his poetic terrain – back to Coole Lake, a symbolic point of departure. The water on the way 'drop[s]' 'through "dark" Raftery's "cellar",' referring us back to Yeats's first visit to Ballylee and his initiation into the stories in the neighbourhood through Lady Gregory over three decades earlier, which he recorded in his 1899 essay on the local blind Gaelic poet Raftery and his muse ('"Dust hath closed Helen's Eye"')[5]. Four years after departing from Thoor Ballylee as its resident and writing the final poem set in the tower ('A Dialogue of Self and Soul') in late 1927, Yeats opened his monumental *ottava rima* proleptic elegy for his poetic demesne with a metonymic representation of his tower: 'Under my window-ledge the waters race ... ' (p. 490). This highly economical presentation of the tower juxtaposed with the watercourse is also yet another variation of the iconic image – 'The tower set on the stream's edge' (p. 326) – in his 1918 elegy for Robert Gregory, the 'inheritor' of Coole, set in the bare tower Yeats had recently obtained.

The opening stanza highlights the connection between Coole Park and Thoor Ballylee by knitting Cloon River and Coole Lough together – as if 'the best knit to the best' – by the course of water which serves as an emblem of the journey of the soul.[6] The subterranean water under the tower had sometimes half surfaced in Yeats's poetic text, as in the case of the original third stanza of 'My House' in 'Meditations in Time of Civil War'. The stanza was entirely deleted from the text of the poem on its inclusion in *The Tower*: 'The river rises, and it sinks again; / One hears the rumble of it far below / Under its rocky hole ... / Symbols of the soul ... / The subterranean streams, / Tower where a candle gleams, / A suffering passion and a labouring thought ... ' (420n.).[7] Yeats had focused on the upper structure of the tower, as if he had dictated

that the 'subterranean streams' should stay 'below'.[8] The time may have 'at last'
been ripe for him to put those aspects of the tower which he had repeatedly
suppressed in his verse on Thoor Ballylee – 'That hidden stream an emblem of
the soul' (in the words of an early draft of the poem)[9] and the Coole dimension
– into the foreground of his verse. The underground water finally surfaces in
his text in 'Coole and Ballylee, 1931', just as the water finally 'rise[s] in a rocky
place / In Coole demesne' (*VP* 490):

> Under my window-ledge the waters race,
> Otters below and moor-hens on the top,
> Run for a mile undimmed in Heaven's face
> Then darkening through 'dark' Raftery's 'cellar' drop,
> Run underground, rise in a rocky place
> In Coole demesne, and there to finish up
> Spread to a lake and drop into a hole.
> What's water but the generated soul?

Over three pages of laborious drafts of 'an account of the sudden ascent
of a swan' (#5583), preserved in the 'large manuscript book bound in white
vellum' (*WMP*, xvi, pp. 174–81), allow us to see why Yeats wrote to George he
was 'tired' (#5583). 'An Image of inspiration', a phrase similar to 'a symbol of
inspiration' in the letter, is found struck out in one of those early drafts (*WMP*,
pp. 176–7). Five days later Yeats expressed confidence about the poem in prog-
ress: 'My poem on Coole may grow into the finest I have written for some
years' (to George Yeats, 8 February [1932] #5590).

'Coole and Ballylee, 1931' is the second of the paired elegies which stand
out in Yeats's oeuvre. 'Coole Park, 1929', the earlier written, was an occasional
poem Yeats wrote for Lady Gregory – a 'Poem on Coole to go with Lady G s /
Cuala essays', as he wrote above its 'Prose sketch'.[10] As a prologue to Gregory's
Coole (Cuala, 1931), her 'farewell' essays to the demesne,[11] it was titled 'Coole
Park' and inscribed and dated at the end 'W.B. Yeats. September 7th. 1929'.[12]
The year '1929' was added to the title on its inclusion in *Words for Music
Perhaps and Other Poems* (Cuala, 1932), where the second elegy, written after
the publication of *Coole* (July 1931), was first published, titled 'Coole Park
and Ballylee 1932'. The poem was retitled 'Coole and Ballylee, 1931' on its
inclusion in *The Winding Stair and Other Poems* (Macmillan, 1933). A heavily
revised late ink draft of the poem has the title 'Coole 1932' and is dated 'Feb 13
– 1932'.[13] Yeats's note below that date records his idea of bringing two elegies
together into 'a single poem' with several headings, which testifies to the fact
that the two poems were closely related in his mind.[14] 'Coole Park' served as

a prologue to *Coole*; 'Coole and Ballylee, 1931' may serve as an epilogue, not only to *Coole* but also to the whole literary construction rooted in the property of Coole Park – the 'place where', Lady Gregory had once remarked, 'so many children of our minds were born' – and Thoor Ballylee.[15]

'Coole Park, 1929' seems to be more closely related to Yeats's own autobiographical essays than to Lady Gregory's *Coole*. Among the drafts of the autobiography begun in 1915 and completed 'at the end of 1916 or the beginning of 1917' is found Yeats's account of his encounter with Coole.[16] Writing about Lady Gregory's 'house [which] is at the edge of [a] lake', Yeats explained how he 'found at last what [he] had been seeking always, a life of order and of labour, where all outward things were the image of an inward life' (*Mem*, p. 101). The first elegy also seems partly a versification of the last section (VI) of 'The Stirring of the Bones' (written in 1920–2, published in 1922), towards the end of which he writes: 'If [her personal] influence were lacking, Ireland would be greatly impoverished, so much has been planned out in the library or among the woods at Coole'.[17] Earlier in the same autobiographical essay Yeats observes 'the woods at Coole … are so much … knitted to my thought that when I am dead they will have … my longest visit'.[18] 'Dramatis Personae: 1896–1902', which would be written in 1934, two years after Lady Gregory's death, and covers his first years at Coole, may serve as a prose postscript companion to and commentary on 'Coole Park, 1929'.

The second elegy 'Coole and Ballylee, 1931', by contrast, though this has not, as far as I am aware, been argued before, has a strong intertextual connection with *Coole*.[19] It seems likely, based on its intertextual relationship with *Coole*, that reading Lady Gregory's memoir in part inspired Yeats to write the second elegy, with a swan and the lake – absent from the first elegy – finally at its centre leading to further autobiographical meditation. 'Coole Park, 1929', which might have been headed 'A flight of Swallows', had he pursued the idea of making the two elegies 'a single poem', revolves around the metaphor of swallows, as Yeats had planned from the outset in the 'Prose sketch' of the poem.[20] The lake is found in its early drafts, but did not remain in the poem.[21] The first elegy 'Coole Park, 1929' constructs a monument to the golden age of Lady Gregory's Coole and closes with a stanza which might serve as an anticipatory epitaph for Lady Gregory. The second elegy 'Coole and Ballylee, 1931' meditates on departure – in many senses – of Lady Gregory and Coole Park and of Yeats himself.

As we know from her journals, Lady Gregory 'began writing a sort of farewell' to Coole on 24 March 1927 (*J2*, p. 178). A week later (31 March) she was 'writing' and 'sowing and planting' – half preparing for and half withstanding the coming disintegration of her Coole – when Margaret, Robert's widow, was sent 'the Deed of Sale ... to sign' (*J2*, p. 180): 'I don't know if I shall realise then, I cannot now, that Coole has passed altogether away from us. / I go on writing my little "Farewell" to the things around me – to the rooms. And I go on sowing and planting in the garden.' On the next day Lady Gregory put '[her] name as witness to the sale of Coole – all-house-woods-gardens ... ' (*J2*, p. 180). Visiting Dublin to see Yeats 'before they go to the south of Spain for his convalescence' that autumn, she recorded Lennox Robinson's comment on Coole she heard from Yeats ('Balzac would have written 200 pages about the staircase only at Coole') and added: 'So perhaps I am not wasting time in writing of my surroundings' (28 October 1927, *J2*, p. 209).

Lady Gregory read to Yeats from her essays on Coole while she was writing them in 1928.[22] Yeats himself read them. She quotes his letter in her journal entry dated 23 Oct 1930 (*J2*, p. 559): 'Yeats writes about my *Coole* that is to be printed at Cuala. "It is a lovely book – as I read it I felt myself to be on the very spot you wrote about ... ".'[23] The word 'spot' would enter the second elegy: 'A spot whereon the founders lived and died' (p. 491). Her passages about the swans on the lake in the chapter titled 'Woods, Visions, and the Lake' included a quotation from Yeats's poem 'The Wild Swans at Coole' among others, which must have once again brought back to him memories centring on that land-mark poem. The composition of 'The Wild Swans at Coole' had 'immortalised' itself and the swans at Coole Lough, and its composition had nearly coincided with Yeats's venturing on the construction of the tower which he would name 'Thoor Ballylee' in 1922.[24] Reading Gregory's text may well have inspired him to write a second – and the last – poem set by that lake, after about a fifteen-year interval.[25]

Her quotation of the first eight lines and the penultimate stanza from 'The Wild Swans at Coole' occurs in her prose which is woven with memories, folk-lore, topographical details and literary quotations, including Synge's – with Yeats as a *dramatis persona* appearing here and there.[26] Lady Gregory prefaced Yeats's poem with George Moore's autobiographical recollection of the 'thirty-six' swans 'striving to rise from [the] surface' of Coole Lough in 1899 from his passage depicting the early period of their Irish literary movement.[27] Yeats's stanzas were followed – after the meta-narrative foregrounding of her writing process (' ... I had written so far ... ') – by Gregory's account of the 'stately' sailing of a swan family she and Yeats had recently observed at Coole. It is as if it were an implicit postscript to Yeats's question 'Among what rushes will they build ...?' at the close of the poem:

And yesterday evening, August sixteenth, 1928, some days after I had written so far, Yeats having come to stay for a while, we walked down to the river in the evening ... And there ... two swans were sailing along towards the lake, one leading, one to the rear, very white and stately; and between them, in single file three cygnets, grey. And Yeats said 'I have known your lake for thirty years, and that is the first time a swan has built here. That is a good omen' ... [28] They passed on, dignified, not breaking their line until they were out of sight in the wider water, beyond a ridge of rocks. (*Coole*, pp. 37–8)[29]

Yeats's solitary swan in 'Coole and Ballylee, 1931' stands out against the backdrop of all these grouped swans.[30] It evokes the flight of Shelley's in *Alastor* and recalls the comparison of 'the solitary soul' to a swan which 'leap[s] into the desolate heaven' in 'Nineteen Hundred and Nineteen'.[31] It is also in contrast to those Yeats reported from Coole to his daughter Anne around the very time of his composition of the elegy: 'sixty two wild swans on the Lake, this is seven or eight more than I ever saw ... '[32] He told her 'I have been writing a poem which contains a description of a wild swan suddenly flying up from the side of the Lake ... ' (#5584.), referring to the following lines:

At sudden thunder of the mounting swan
I turned about and looked where branches break
The glittering reaches of the flooded lake. (p. 490)

The close relationship between Yeats's 'Coole and Ballylee, 1931' and Gregory's *Coole* is not confined to the swans. It seems likely that her text served as a prose inspiration for the water's journey from Ballylee to Coole in the opening stanza.[33] Several pages before their observing the swans 'sailing' from the river to the lake, 'the wider water, beyond a ridge of rocks', Gregory noted the topographical details of the mysterious course of 'Our own river', accompanied by some quotations from a French writer:

Our own river that we catch a glimpse of now and again through hazel and ash, or outshining the silver beech stems of Kyle Dortha, has ever been an idler. Its transit is as has been said of human life 'from a mystery through a mystery to a mystery'; suddenly appearing, as a French writer has put down in his book ... And dipping presently under great limestone flags that form a natural bridge ... Then, flowing free, it helps to form a lake, whose full-ness, finding no channel above ground is forced 'de chercher sa route par les passages souterains ... '; into which it flows under the very shadow of the Dun of the ancient legendary King Guaire ... (*Coole*, pp. 27–8)

Her comparison of the 'transit' of the river to 'human life' ('"from a mystery through a mystery to a mystery"') as well as a legendary figure ('under the very shadow of the Dun of the ancient legendary King Guaire ... ') could have prompted Yeats to describe the river water running over- and underground, in the process naming a deep pool '"dark" Raftery's "cellar"' by combining words quoted from a poem by Raftery and Yeats's early essay on it.[34] The final destination of the water indicated at the end of the first stanza ('Spread to a lake and drop into a hole')[35] also corresponds to her account: 'Then, flowing free, it helps to form a lake, whose fullness, finding no channel above ground is forced "de chercher sa route par les passages souterains de lac vers la mer" ... ' (*Coole*, p. 28). The watercourse knitting the two places together in the first stanza itself, meta-poetically, embodies the intertextuality between *Coole* and 'Coole and Ballylee, 1931'.

The association of the water with the soul articulated at the end of the first stanza ('What's water but the generated soul?') leads to the sudden appearance – like the water Gregory illustrates ('suddenly appearing') – of the swan / soul in front of the poet in the second and third stanzas. The unnamed 'wood' '[u]pon the border of that [lake]' with 'a copse of beeches' in the second stanza of the present poem was named 'Kyle Dortha', as in Gregory's text, in some of the poem's early drafts.[36] The metaphor vividly capturing the moment's picture which occupied the poet's view at the end of the second stanza ('where branches break / The glittering reaches of the flooded lake') seems likely to have originated from the source of her textual river 'shining through the spreading beech trees of Kyle Dortha ... ' (*Coole*, p. 30).[37]

Yeats's second 'anticipatory elegy' for Coole – and Ballylee this time – was probably '[begotten]' – to use a verb in the first elegy ('those walls begot') – in this way, while he was staying in the place to keep Lady Gregory company in her final days.[38] It was during his last and longest winter at Coole that Yeats composed 'Coole and Ballylee, 1931'. Asked by the family of Lady Gregory, who was terminally ill, Yeats had been staying at Coole more 'continuously' than ever – probably especially since October 1931.[39] The visit to Coole offered him the last opportunity to work there. Lady Gregory's 'never delivered' note – 'her own anticipatory farewell' – to Yeats, in retrospect, synchronized with his writing of the elegy.[40]

Yeats was not only 'turning the introductory verses to Lady Gregorys 'Coole' (Cuala) into a poem of some length' (#5583), but was in part 'turning' her *Coole* into an elegy for the two places, by extending to Ballylee that mysterious water Gregory describes. The poem captures the final stage of Coole Park and Lady Gregory – and also of Yeats himself at Coole – poised on the verge of departure, which is symbolized by the swan's '[drifting] upon a darkening flood', perhaps with a faint echo from the final stanza of 'The Wild Swans at Coole' ('they drift on the still water ... ,' p. 323). It is as if not only 'a last inheritor' but the 'demesne' itself were metamorphosed into the single symbolic swan on the brink of disappearance.[41] The reappearance of the word 'darkening' (' ... darkening through "dark" Raftery's "cellar" drop ... ') as the penultimate word in the poem (' ... the swan drifts upon a darkening flood ... ') indicates the imminent 'drop[ping] into a hole' as formulated in the first stanza, suggesting the continuous, 'winding' water's journey.

'Coole and Ballylee, 1931' underwent two of Yeats's most radical 'architectonic' revisions: one is the transposition of a stanza to the opening of the poem during composition, and the other is the removal of a stanza from the poem after the first publication.[42] In an early draft the present first stanza appears as the fifth stanza, following the image of 'poor Arab tribesman and his tent' at the end of the preceding fourth stanza and beginning a section where the poet meditates on his life and work (WMP, pp. 182–5). The stanza set in Ballylee was originally written in that context, and the stanza on the 'choice' followed it as the sixth stanza, continuing the meditations.

In the later draft dated 'Feb 13 – 1932' the Ballylee stanza is transposed to the beginning, as in the published text (WMP, pp. 190–1). This revision resulted in bringing together two separate passages containing water (the former first and fifth stanzas). The river water now directly leads from Ballylee to the swan and the lake at Coole in the present second stanza ('Upon the border of that lake's a wood ... ', 490]. This revision, which echoes the one executed after the first publication of 'The Wild Swans at Coole' (the transposition of the original third stanza to the end of the poem), also highlights the correspondence between the present first stanza and the final stanza, both invoking Raftery (who inevitably recalls Part II of 'The Tower') and sharing the word 'darkening', as if they were mirroring each other.

The other architectural revision was the removal of the 'choice' stanza from the poem on its inclusion in The Winding Stair and Other Poems after the first publication. The deleted stanza was also collected in the same volume as an independent poem 'The Choice'. The revision, which may reflect Yeats's departure from Coole, removes the whole question of choice from the elegy.

The title of the elegy also underwent a dramatic change with the late entrance of the name Ballylee. A typescript signed 'WB Yeats', which is preserved in the Berg Collection, New York Public Library, carries the title 'COOLE. 1932'.[43] This ribbon copy was 'Removed from inside front cover of Gregory. Journal. y. 46', according to 'a note' in the collection.[44] This suggests it was the copy Yeats gave Lady Gregory and that the title of the poem she knew did not include 'Ballylee'. It is in Yeats's revision of another typescript that we first find the name Ballylee in the title of the poem: 'Coole & Thoor

Ballylee 1931'.[45] While the two place names in the title continued to vacillate between Coole and Coole Park, Ballylee and Thoor Ballylee in drafts, and even after publication concerning Coole / Coole Park, the name Ballylee stayed thereafter.[46] The year 1932 in the title of the elegy in *Words for Music Perhaps and Other Poems*, published in the same year, probably signified not only the actual year of composition but also the year of Lady Gregory's death.[47] On the other hand, the present revised date of 1931, used since *The Winding Stair and Other Poems*, refers to the final full year Yeats and Lady Gregory shared at Coole, the longest time since his first visit in 1896. In early February 1931, according to Lady Gregory's record, they went to see Ballylee together. This was to see the 'new thatch' there (*J2*, p. 592) and the last recorded visit of theirs to Ballylee. Yeats incorporated Thoor Ballylee in the second elegy, which was made 'plainly visible' (#5030) by his last-minute inclusion of the place name in the title of the poem. With the present title 'Coole and Ballylee, 1931', Yeats formally joined the great symbol of Lady Gregory, Coole Park, with his 'permanent symbol' (#5030) and 'powerful emblem' ('Blood and the Moon') which he had established as Thoor Ballylee.

NOTES

1. Quotations of Yeats's letters are from *The Collected Letters of W.B. Yeats*, gen. ed. John Kelly, InteLex Electronic Edition, 2002. Each letter's accession number follows the number symbol. Quotations preserve Yeats's original spellings.

2. 'I have finished my group of poems which I now call "Vacillation"... I have written all my recent verse into the big MSS ... 21 poems in all ... ' ([24 January 1932] #5571).

3. Quotations of Yeats's poems are from *The Variorum Edition of the Poems of W.B. Yeats*, ed. Peter Allt and Russell K. Alspach, corrected 3rd printing (New York: Macmillan, 1966 [1957]) unless otherwise indicated, and page numbers are cited in parentheses.The titles of the poems 'Coole and Ballylee, 1931', as well as 'A Prayer for My Daughter' and 'Easter, 1916' are as they were printed in *The Winding Stair and Other Poems* and *Michael Robartes and the Dancer*, respectively.

4. See *W.B. Yeats: The Poems*, ed. Daniel Albright (London: J. M. Dent, 1994), p. 550. In its first publication the poem was titled 'Coole Park and Ballylee 1932' and the phrase in question was 'But fashion's changed ... ' See *Words for Music Perhaps and Other Poems*, reprinted (Dublin: Cuala 1932; Shannon: Irish UP, 1970) pp. 9–11.

5. *Mythologies* (London and New York: Macmillan, 1959) [hereafter *Myth*], pp. 22–30.

6. 'Upon a House shaken by the Land Agitation': ' ... the sweet laughing eagle thoughts ... / That comes of the best knit to the best ... ', p. 264. See Paul de Man, *The Rhetoric of Romanticism* (New York: Columbia UP, 1984) for what he calls the 'dual role of the emblem image' in Yeats's poetry, pp. 133–43, 194–5.

7. In the drafts of 'The Phases of the Moon' Yeats repeatedly includes the underground water as if it were one of the essential features of the tower, *The Wild Swans at Coole: Manuscript Materials by W.B. Yeats*, ed. Stephen Parrish (Ithaca, NY: Cornell UP,

1994) [hereafter *WSC*] pp. 316–7, pp. 324–5. In a fair copy with revisions is still found ' ... or it may be / He chose it for the river bubbling up / From subterranean caverns, images that / Shelleyan like the first or natural wisdom ...' (*WSC*, pp. 354–5), but the subterranean water has totally disappeared – as if itself mimicking the mysterious water disappearing – in a typescript with revisions (*WSC*,p. 366).

8. 'O how this mother swells up toward my heart! / *Hystericapassio!* Down, thou climbing sorrow, / Thy element's below... ' 2.4.52–4. William Shakespeare, *The Tragedy of King Lear*, ed. Jay L. Halio, updated ed. (Cambridge: Cambridge UP, 2005[1992]) p. 162.

9. *Words for Music Perhaps and Other Poems: Manuscript Materials by W.B. Yeats*, ed. David R. Clark (Ithaca, NY: Cornell UP, 1995) [hereafter *WMP*], pp. 184–5. See also 'hidden water' and 'hidden streams', *WMP*, pp. 190–1.

10. Written on the recto of the thirteenth leaf of 'Rapallo notebook "D" ' (*WMP*, xvii, pp. 104–5).

11. *Lady Gregory's Journals*, ed. Daniel J. Murphy, vol. 2 (Gerrards Cross: Colin Smythe, 1987) [hereafter *J2*], p. 178.

12. Lady Gregory, *Coole,* reprinted (Dublin: Cuala, 1931; Shannon: Irish UP, 1971). See also Lady Gregory,*Coole,* Completed from the Manuscript and Edited by Colin Smythe with a Foreword by Edward Malins (Dublin: Dolmen Press, 1971). The poem, according to Yeats's letter to Lady Gregory on 30 September 1929, had not yet been finished at the end of September: 'however though [the poem] has taken a new leap into life today it is not finished – & now I must not delay longer' (#5289).

13. *WMP*, pp. 194–5. A prose sketch is headed 'Coole Park II' (*WMP*, pp. 170–1).

14. See *WMP*, p. 194, 194n.:'"A flight of Swallows"' (for the first elegy, 'dated'), '"The Wood" or "Swan & Waters"' (for the first three stanzas of the second elegy), '"The House"' (for the fourth and fifth stanzas) and '"The Comment" or "The high horse" or "The last romantics"' (for the sixth and seventh stanzas). The stanzas of the first elegy were numbered with Roman numerals only in the text published in *Coole*among its published texts. As to the second elegy, while stanzas in an ink draft and typescripts carry Roman numerals, no published texts are with numbered stanzas. Yeats had decided not to number stanzas in the paired elegies on their inclusion in *Words for Music Perhaps and Other Poems*.

15. In her 'cautiously' written letter to stop Yeats from publishing 'The New Faces' 'just now', R.F. Foster, *W.B. Yeats: A Life, I: The Apprentice Mage, 1865–1914* (Oxford: Oxford UP, 2000), p. 477.

16. *Memoirs: Autobiography – First Draft: Journal* [hereafter *Mem*], ed. Denis Donoghue (London: Macmillan, 1972), pp. 9, 13.

17. *Autobiographies*, ed. William H. O'Donnell and Douglas N. Archibald (New York: Scribner, 1999), vol. III of *The Collected Works of W.B. Yeats* [hereafter *Au* (CW3)] pp. 7, 285–6.

18. *Au* (CW3),p. 283.

19. It seems the intertextuality between *Coole* and 'Coole and Ballylee, 1931' has never been discussed. A.Norman Jeffares quotes from Gregory's passages on the river and the swans in *Coole* in his commentary on 'The Wild Swans at Coole': A. Norman Jeffares, *A New Commentary on the Poems of W.B. Yeats* (London:

Macmillan, 1984), pp. 131, 132. Daniel Harris remarks that 'Coole Park, 1929' 'emphasizes Coole's cultural importance', 'balancing *Coole*'s modest and private focus on family, literature, local geography ... ': *Yeats: Coole Park and Ballylee* (Baltimore, MD: Johns Hopkins UP, 1974), p. 225. Roy Foster, introducing his account of 'Coole Park, 1929', notes that the 'tone [of *Coole*] is proudly elegiac, and WBY was ready to match it', following his quotation of Gregory's passage on the shelf whose front is filled with Yeats's books from a chapter not included in the book's publication from Cuala in 1931: *W.B. Yeats: A Life, II: The Arch-Poet, 1915–1939* (Oxford: Oxford UP, 2003) [hereafter *Life II*], p. 391. 'Poem ['Coole Park, 1929'] and book [*Coole*] took their place in the historicizing process which enshrined both house and literary revival together ... ', *Life II*, p. 408.

20. *WMP*, p. 194, 194n. ' ... address the swallows ... ', *WMP*, pp. 104-5.

21. In early drafts of the first stanza the lake was incorporated in the landscape, as in ' ...shadowed in foliage, the lake luminous ...' (*WMP*, pp. 106–7, 110–11, 122–3). In a later draft where the water is last found ('A windy water s edge'), the adjective 'luminous' modifies the cloud instead of the lake (*WMP*, pp. 156–7), as in the published text.

22. On 6 May 1928 at 82 Merrion Square she read 'the "Library" to Willie – he had asked if I had any articles that would make a volume for the Cuala Press. He seemed to like it very much, said "it has style" ' (*J2*, p. 255). On 19 August 1928, according to her record, 'I read the Garden one, just finished, and he likes it and wants it with one or two others for a Cuala volume. So I'll finish the "Woods and Lake". I think these should be enough. He doesn't want a big book' (*J2*,p. 308). On 30 August 1928 she read him 'my rough copy of the "Woods and Lake", and he liked it and says the three, it, the "Library", the "Garden", will make a little book for Cuala' (*J2*, p. 311). Lady Gregory notes in her journal entry Yeats's comments on the 'cygnets' as 'a good omen', which would enter her essay as well. See John Kelly, *A W.B. Yeats Chronology*(Basingstoke: Palgrave Macmillan, 2003), pp. 257, 259, 261, 262.

23. Only the 'Stray envelope addressed to Coole, postmark "OCT 23 [1930]",' is preserved in the Berg Collection (#5395).

24. 'The most striking animals of the larger turloughs (including Coole) are the birds which arrive in winter. The most famous of all the birds here of course are the swans, immortalised in Yeats's famous poem ... ' John Feehan and Grace O'Donovan, *The Magic of Coole* (Dublin: Stationery Office, 1993), p. 20.

25. Lady Gregory, for instance, records her experience of hearing Yeats's poems (to be included in *October Blast*) during composition and reading them after publication: 'I had heard him read or repeat the poems little by little, but they are even finer than I thought ... ' (*J2*, p. 203).

26. See, for instance, *Coole*, p. 31: ' ... I think it was these Coole woods and not those of Alban that were in Synge's mind later when he wrote "Who'll pity Deirdre has lost the twilight in the woods with Naisi, when beech trees were silver and copper and ash trees were fine gold." For when staying here he never went out upon the roads, these sylvan walks were his delight.'

27. *Coole*, pp. 36–7. George Moore, *Hail and Farewell: Ave, Salve, Vale*, ed. Richard

Cave, 2nd edn (Gerrards Cross: Colin Smythe, 1985 [1976]), pp. 190–1.

28. This ellipsis is in the original.

29. Yeats wrote about the same swan family to Margaret Gregory on 30 August [1928] (#5153).

30. In an early draft written below his prose 'scenario' headed 'Coole Park II' is found the plural 'wild swans' (WMP, pp. 170–1), which soon becomes the singular 'mounting swan' on the verso of the next leaf in the same notebook (WMP, pp. 172–3).

31. See *Alastor*, ll. pp. 275–80: ' ... the seashore. A swan was there, / Beside a sluggish stream among the reeds. / It rose as he approached, and with strong wings / Scaling the upward sky, bent its bright course ... / His eyes pursued its flight ...'*Shelley: Poetical Works*, ed. Thomas Hutchinson, 2nd edn, corrected by G.M. Matthews (London: Oxford UP, 1970) p. 21.

32. 3 February [1932] #5584. Two months later on 7 April 1932 Yeats wrote to Anne from London: ' ... the only swans are those tame creatures in the parks ... ' (#5632).

33. There is no reference to Ballylee in his prose sketch of the poem (WMP, pp. 170–1). His revision of 'the first stanza' to 'second' in the scenario may have been made when he moved the Ballylee stanza to the opening of the poem.

34. *Myth*, pp. 23–4, 28.

35. It went '... and run into a hole ...' in *Words for Music Perhaps and Other Poems*, p. 9.

36. WMP, pp. 170–1, 172–3.

37. The rhyming words 'break / lake' are written below an early draft (WMP, pp. 170–1).

38. '"Coole Park, 1929" ... was already written as a kind of anticipatory elegy ... ', *Life II*, p. 439.

39. Yeats wrote in 'The Death of Lady Gregory', dated 'June 19, 1932', 'I had been at Coole continuously for a year, with the exception of brief periods when business called me away ... ' (*J2*, p. 638). 'Lady Gregory's family have asked me to stay here ... ' (to T. Sturge Moore, 22 October [1931] #5527).

40. *Life II*, pp. 437, 439.

41. Roy Foster suggests the association between Gregory and the swan (*Life II*, pp. 439–40): ' ... the mysterious swan also leads directly to the journey of the soul, and then to the dying Gregory herself ... He already knew ... how cut adrift he himself would feel when his fellow romantic, her work done, vanished like the swan into darkness.'

42. See Helen Vendler, *Our Secret Discipline: Yeats and Lyric Form* (Oxford: Oxford UP, 2007) pp. 3–4: '[Yeats] was also seeking the "right" architectonic form: his well-known rearrangement of the completed stanzas of "The Wild Swans at Coole" to create an entirely different ending is merely one instance of his keen critical awareness of the import of different structural shapes.'

43. WMP, pp. xxiii-iv, 196–7.

44. WMP, pp. xxiii-iv.

45. WMP, pp. xviii.

46. See WMP, p. 196n. and Richard J. Finneran, *Editing Yeats's Poems* (London: Macmillan, 1983), p. 34 for transformations of the title. 'Park' was posthumously added back to the title in *The Poems of W.B. Yeats* (1949) (Wade 210).

47. See *Life II*, p. 439: ' ... identifying it as an ode on Gregory's death ... '

Yeats and the Oxford Book of Modern Verse*

LUCY MCDIARMID

The 1936 *Oxford Book of Modern Verse*, edited by Yeats, is the most insulted anthology of poetry ever made. Lord Alfred Douglas, Oscar Wilde's boyfriend, furious that he had not been included in the anthology, sent Yeats a telegram that said, 'Your omission of my work from the absurdly-named Oxford Book of Modern Verse is exactly typical of the attitude of the minor to the major poet.'[1] More sensible people also had complaints. W.H. Auden, in his 1939 essay 'The Public v. the Late Mr. William Butler Yeats', called the book 'the most deplorable volume ever issued under the imprint of that highly respected press.'[2] And about a month before the volume was due to be published, in the midst of a frenzy of confused correspondence about permissions, inclusions, exclusions and so forth, the Secretary to the Delegates of Oxford University Press wrote in a private note to the Assistant Secretary, 'I am very sorry that Yeats did not die too soon to finish.'[3]

No one has a good word to say about the *Oxford Book of Modern Verse*. It was disparaged in reviews at the time by (among many) John Hayward in the *Spectator*, H.A. Mason in *Scrutiny* and Stuart Hampshire in the *Oxford*

---

* This essay revises a lecture originally delivered at the Yeats International Summer School in 2011. I am grateful to James Pethica and Anne Margaret Daniel for the invitation to speak. I would also like to thank Robert Alden Rubin for letting me see his excellent dissertation on Yeats's *Oxford Book of Modern Verse* before it was on the web, and Marjorie Howes for help with Yeats's *Collected Letters*.

Magazine.[4] Yeats's most recent biographer, Roy Foster, calls many of its selections 'bizarrely chosen'.[5] But the book is too eccentric to dismiss: I'd like to look at the *OBMV* afresh and from another point of view. The question to ask is not, why did Yeats pick such dreadful poems? No; the question to ask is, what can we learn about Yeats not by judging his selections but by studying this volume as it is? And so this essay will not focus on Yeats's aversion to what would now be considered canonical modernist poetry; it will look instead at what he put in the volume.[6]

Consideration of the contents of the *OBMV* brings into view the importance of the words 'friends' and 'friendship' in Yeats's prose and poetry. Yeats famously wrote of Lady Gregory in *Estrangement*, 'Friendship is all the house I have.'[7] In the most-quoted lines from 'The Municipal Gallery Revisited' – most quoted by politicians – Yeats says, 'Think where man's glory most begins and ends, / And say my glory was I had such friends' (p. 604).[8] When the painter Sir William Rothenstein praised a book Yeats had sent him, Yeats wrote back, 'I thank you for your letter. I wrote for my friends & not the general public & so am entirely content when my friends are pleased.'[9] Both the famous introduction (forty-two pages long) to the *OBMV* and the poems selected for it privilege poetry in the context of intimacy; poems written for friends to read or to read aloud to friends, poems discussed over coffee, wine, dinners; and poets' friendships enjoyed over visits and in houses, 'in some good company', as Yeats put it in the late poem 'Are You Content?' (p. 605). The preponderance of poems are in fact written by Yeats's friends, especially his friends in the mid-1930s when he was working on the anthology, and his encounters at that time, in person, determined many of the selections.

In his early essays, Yeats's paradigm for poetry experienced through 'the living voice' required a cohesive social group of listeners and performers. In this model 'wild-eyed men spoke harmoniously to murmuring wires while audiences in many-coloured robes listened, hushed and excited ... ,' a golden age of oral poetry.[10] But implicit in the *OBMV* and in the letters Yeats wrote at the time is another kind of model. Poetry is still inseparable from the social community, the extra-poetic life off the page, a life of voices, but that life is imagined as a small group of friends, talking, reading one another's poems, revising them, reading them again. What the selection of poems in the *OBMV* reveals about Yeats is that at this point in his career he believed that poetry thrives in a world of private conversations; that it is both inspired by and circulates through intimate friendships.

To understand the nature of the *OBMV* as a volume, consider the many poems in which Yeats lists his friends, poems in which the list, the serial invocation, forms the primary structure of the poem. The earliest of these is 'Friends'

(1912), which begins, 'Now must I these three praise', and then describes, without naming them, Lady Gregory, Olivia Shakespear, and Maud Gonne (p. 315). There are so many other examples that it could be said invoking and thereby 'gathering' a group of friends is one of the most basic structures of Yeats's imagination. To mention just a few: in 'In Memory of Major Robert Gregory', each friend gets a stanza: 'Lionel Johnson comes the first to mind', 'And that enquiring man John Synge comes next', 'And then I think of old George Pollexfen' (pp. 324, 325). 'All Souls' Night' invokes, one person to a stanza, [William Thomas] Horton, Florence Farr Emery and MacGregor Mathers (pp. 471–3). 'Coole Park, 1929' lists the 'friends' in a single stanza: Hyde, Synge, Shawe-Taylor and Hugh Lane (p. 489); and in 'The Municipal Gallery Revisited' the list of friends (Gregory, Synge, Hugh Lane) reflects the paintings Yeats sees on the wall (pp. 601–4).[11]

And so in the *OBMV*, Yeats follows this same paradigm in both the introduction and in the selections of poets: a small circle of friends is summoned and gathered within the volume. To say this is not quite the same as saying, *He puts a lot of his friends' poetry in the volume.* Of course, that's the case: most of the poets in the volume cannot be found in other, major anthologies of modern poetry and are included precisely because they were Yeats's friends or because he had some personal connection with them.[12] It's not simply that he packs them in: it's that, as the introduction to the volume shows, when asked to create an anthology of 'modern verse', Yeats thinks in terms of the chronology of his own life, and the groups of literary friends he has had over the years; and he invokes them as he invoked friends in all of the poems just mentioned: 'Now must I these three praise'. He thought of his father's friends who were also friends of his (Edwin Ellis, York Powell), the Rhymers (Rolleston, Rhys, Symons, Dowson, Johnson), the Irish Revivalists (Lady Gregory, Synge, Æ, Padraic Colum, Gogarty), his Dublin companions (Gogarty, Higgins, MacGreevy), and his London friends of the mid-30s, at the time he was making the anthology (Walter Turner, Vita Sackville-West, Dorothy Wellesley, Margot Ruddock).

To show how the implied scene of the intimate conversation of friends is embodied in the 1936 anthology, I'll look first at the introduction, a piece of prose famous in its own right, which Stuart Hampshire, reviewing the anthology in 1937, thought superior to the poetry. Hampshire wrote, 'It is the prose, not the verse, which makes this book magnificent and exciting.'[13] Mrs Yeats thought it (Yeats said) 'the best bit of prose I have written for years'.[14] Then I'll look at the distinctively Yeatsian parts of the poetic content, three poets of the many who are only included in the *OBMV* and not in other contemporary anthologies.[15] This approach will show what kinds of friends Yeats wants to engage in intimate conversation.

THE INTRODUCTION TO *THE OXFORD BOOK OF MODERN VERSE*

Although no poems by Count Eric Stanislaus Magnus Andreas Harry Stenbock (1860–95) appear in the *OBVM*, its introduction made him famous, providing the series of epithets by which he has been known ever since. He appears in a short passage about the poets of the 1890s. Yeats writes, 'My father gave these young men their right name', and then he says, 'When I had described a supper with Count Stenbock, scholar, connoisseur, drunkard, poet, pervert, most charming of men, he said "they are the Hamlets of our age." '[16]

The lines create two social scenes. In the outer framework, Yeats is in conversation with his father, telling him about a visit and supper; he quotes, admiringly, his father's epithet ('the Hamlets of our age'). Contained within this framework is the supper at which Yeats found Stenbock 'most charming of men'. Count Stenbock, son of an English mother and a Swedish-German father, was heir to an estate in Estonia. He studied at Oxford and published several volumes of poetry between 1881 and 1893. From 1887 onwards he lived primarily in England and got to know Lionel Johnson and others of the '90s poets as well as Yeats. An alcoholic addicted to opium, Stenbock travelled with a doll whom he identified as his son: he called it 'le petit comte' and paid to have it educated. He also travelled with a dog and a monkey. Stenbock is said to have tried out a 'different religion every week' when he was at Oxford; at home in Estonia, he kept snakes, lizards, toads and salamanders in the bedroom, and 'reindeer, a bear, and a fox' in the garden. He died the first day of Wilde's first trial: he was attacking someone (a 'member of his household', it's said) with a poker and fell backwards, striking his head on a grate in the fireplace.[17]

Stenbock is a poet so minor that Yeats didn't include him in the anthology, but this apparent digression is actually central to Yeats's mindset. The vignette typifies the way Yeats privileges aristocracy, table talk ('most charming of men'), transgressive sexuality and transgressive behaviour generally, especially among his friends. 'Pervert', Yeats writes affectionately, obviously revelling in putting that term between 'poet' and 'most charming of men'. The supper and its conversation were presumably described in some detail to John Butler Yeats, who must have enjoyed his son's account of the occasion. He was evidently thinking of the 1890s poets' brooding personalities as well as their self-destructive habits when he came up with 'the Hamlets of their age'.

Like the passage about Stenbock, Yeats's anthology is shamelessly eccentric, charming, backward-looking, elitist and unapologetically personal. The introduction tells, as autobiography, the story of its author's encounters with poets. Its subject is not an introduction to modern poetry but the evolution of

WBY's taste, described in a series of vignettes. Primacy is given less to poetic texts than to conversation and face-to-face interaction. In short, this is auto-biography presented as literary history, because the period covered by the anthology is co-extensive with Yeats's adult life.

In some of these vignettes, the conversations and encounters Yeats remembers have less to do with the kind of poetry these people are writing than with Yeats's evaluation of their bodily – and especially their sexual – vigour. The *Oxford Book of Modern Verse* has an almost eugenic subtext that the introduction makes clear: 'masculinity' is privileged; that is, Yeats's idea of masculinity, which is associated not with conventional heterosexuality but with somatic health and energy.

This, for instance, is from the opening paragraph: 'Gerard Hopkins remained unpublished for thirty years. Fifty-odd years ago I met him in my father's studio on different occasions, but remember almost nothing. A boy of seventeen, Walt Whitman in his pocket, had little interest in a querulous, sensitive scholar.'[18] The scale by which Hopkins is judged appears to be based on perceived masculinity, because – whatever about Whitman's sexual preference – his poetry radiated an earthy, hearty, liberated sexuality, unlike the poetry of a 'querulous, sensitive scholar' (who was also a Jesuit, and therefore celibate). That 'boy of seventeen' appeared to be looking for masculine poetic role models; 'Walt Whitman in his pocket' suggests he wanders around the city, taking out a volume of Whitman, in his free-spirited way, to read whenever the impulse strikes: you wouldn't need to carry a book in your pocket if you were reading at home. And indeed, the passage implies, why would a healthy, energetic 'boy of seventeen' want to read poems by a 'querulous, sensitive scholar'? Later in the introduction Yeats makes this criterion explicit: 'John Synge', he writes, 'brought back masculinity to Irish verse with his harsh disillusionment.'[19]

Consider also the introduction's description of William Ernest Henley, whom Yeats (age 23) remembers this way: 'Henley lay upon the sofa, crippled by his incautious youth, dragged his body, crutch-supported, between two rooms, imagining imperial might.'[20] Again the implicit criterion of masculinity is hinted at: Henley (who had had one leg amputated) has been 'crippled' by his 'incautious youth', though other sources say he had tuberculosis. Henley is not appraised as a writer but critiqued as a role model for the emerging poet: 'For a young man, struggling for expression, despairing of achievement, he remained hidden behind his too obvious effectiveness.'[21] Yeats found this blustery manner a cover for some inner self that was never revealed. But (for what it's worth) another writer found all this bluster inspiringly macho: Robert Louis Stevenson wrote Henley into *Treasure Island*. It was (Stevenson wrote) 'the sight of your maimed strength and masterfulness that begot Long John Silver ... the idea of the maimed man, ruling and dreaded by the sound, was entirely taken from you.'[22]

Lady Gregory is also enlisted to help the general argument: a conversation with her is adduced in oblique support of the superior sexual vigour of Irish poets: 'I showed Lady Gregory a few weeks before her death a book by Day Lewis. "I prefer", she said, "those poems translated by Frank O'Connor because they come out of original sin." '[23] Lady Gregory gives posthumous approval to Yeats's judgment.

The dominant argument – the only explicit argument – in the introduction's history of 'modern verse' is what Yeats calls the 'revolt against Victorianism', by which he means 'a revolt against irrelevant descriptions of nature' and 'scientific and moral discursiveness'.[24] The poets who made that 'revolt' were his friends, the 1890s 'decadent' poets Dowson, Johnson and the rest. Yeats presents this literary development as a conversation around a table: 'Poets said to one another over their black coffee – a recently imported fashion – "We must purify poetry of all that is not poetry" ... Poetry was a tradition like religion and liable to corruption, and it seemed that they could best restore it by writing lyrics technically perfect'.[25]

The coffee-drinking poets were the ones Yeats's father christened 'Hamlets'. Of them Yeats writes,

> Some of these Hamlets went mad, some drank, drinking not as happy men drink but in solitude, all had courage, all had suffered public opprobrium – generally for their virtues or for sins they did not commit – all had good manners ... all had gaiety, some had wit ... Some turned Catholic ... that too was a tradition ... Lionel Johnson was the first to convert ...[26]

Yeats writes movingly of these poets in his poem 'The Grey Rock', which begins 'Poets with whom I learned my trade, / Companions of the Cheshire Cheese ... ' (p. 270). That 'ancient eating house in the Strand', as Yeats calls it in his autobiography, formed the setting of their friendship; they were Yeats's first experience of the group of intimate friends whose conversation kept poetry circulating. Yeats's own relative bodily vigour, acquired perhaps from reading the outdoorsy Whitman and Synge, distinguishes him from the self-destructive decadents; he is a survivor. But he loves those poets, and if they died young, they died so that Yeats might live and write post-Victorian poetry.

Having established, then, an important moment in the history of 'modern verse', the revolt against Victorian descriptiveness, Yeats introduces the next literary period in the most famous sentence of the introduction. 'Then,' writes Yeats, 'in 1900 everybody got down off his stilts; henceforth nobody drank absinthe with his black coffee; nobody went mad; nobody committed suicide; nobody joined the Catholic church; or if they did I have forgotten.'[27] This brilliant contribution to literary history is typical of the *OBMV* not only in its glancing allusions to the social life that takes place around tables but in its flaunting dismissal of mere fact: 'or if they did I have forgotten.'

Like the series of appositives about Count Stenbock ('poet, pervert, most charming of men'), this passage links rhetorically and syntactically aspects of behaviour someone more conventional than Yeats might not connect: drinking absinthe and joining the Catholic Church, for instance. The flourish of the final clause, with its theatrical nonchalance – 'or if they did I have forgotten'– forms the perfect finale to the preceding hyperbole. The phrase's self-confidently gestural quality emphasizes the gestural nature of all the previous clauses. And of course, what Yeats says is more or less true: Stenbock died in 1895, Dowson and Wilde (also in the anthology) in 1900, and Johnson in 1902.

The 1890s poets drink, use absinthe, and commit suicide, and they will never see the new poetic styles their self-destructive ways helped bring into being. From the eugenic point of view, they are tossed aside, like Hopkins and Henley. But the new poetic world that followed is not one that Yeats can easily categorize. From this point on, Yeats's narrative of literary history becomes fragmented: he doesn't have a paradigm for what happened to verse in English after the poets got off their stilts. In a series of roman-numeraled sections, he offers opinions of various types of poetry and individual poets – folk-songs, Irish poets, Ezra Pound, or 'Auden, Day Lewis, and their school.' And in a sentence that has become notorious, Yeats explains why he doesn't like the poets of the Great War: 'passive suffering is not a theme for poetry.'[28] Or, to use Yeats's own gendered discourse, 'passive suffering' doesn't produce a poetry of 'masculinity'; it isn't vigorous and energized.

THE POETIC CONTENT OF THE *OBMV*

And so the most *outré* of the poets Yeats includes – poets not included in other anthologies of modern poetry – are flamboyant and vigorous.[29] In the interest of explaining the eccentricities of the Yeatsian *mentalité* in the anthology, this section will focus on three poets whose inclusion is glaringly inappropriate in a book of 'modern verse'. Only Yeats would anthologize them so excessively.

Wilfrid Blunt (six poems), Oliver Gogarty (seventeen poems – more than any other poet in the anthology) and Dorothy Wellesley (eight poems, very long ones) were all friends of Yeats and all wealthy. They had big houses, houses with names – Newbuildings Place, Renvyle, Penns in the Rocks – where Yeats was a guest. (In fact Gogarty himself said of the *OBMV*, 'Only titled ladies and a few friends admitted.')[30] In their distinct ways they were transgressive and liberated, with an aura of extravagance and sexuality around them that Yeats enjoyed. All of them radiated 'masculinity' (Wellesley was a lesbian, and Yeats used that word of her, approvingly).[31] Their poems use a fairly traditional vocabulary, and Blunt and Gogarty wrote in traditional forms and rhythms. All wrote in complete syntactic units (not fragments), and their subject matters tended to be erotic or heroic and their tones relatively free of irony.

The oldest of these is Blunt (1840–1922), a wealthy Sussex landowner, Catholic, anti-imperialist, anti-Semitic, a philanderer, a minor poet, married to Byron's granddaughter – and 'most charming of men'. Yeats came to know Blunt through Lady Gregory, who had had an affair with him in 1882–3. In 1914 Yeats and Pound (with Lady Gregory's help behind the scenes) organized the famous 'peacock dinner' for Blunt, a testimonial occasion in which six younger poets visited Blunt at Newbuildings and dined on a peacock culled from Blunt's flock.[32] In a formal toast to Blunt on that occasion, twenty-two years before the *OBMV*, Yeats explained why he saw Blunt as the first post-Victorian – and therefore the first 'modern' – poet . 'When you published your first work', Yeats said to Blunt in 1914,

> it was the very height of the Victorian period. One no longer wrote as a human being with an address, living in a London street, having a definite income, and a definite tradition, but one wrote as an abstract personality ... instead of abstract poetry, you wrote verses which were good poetry because they were first of all fine things to have thought and said in some real situation of life. They had behind them the drama of actual life. We are now at the end of Victorian romance – completely at an end ... The whole movement is over, but the work that survives is this work ... [33]

As, in Yeats's view, the first poet to break with Victorian poetic style, Blunt is the first poet in the anthology, inaugurating 'modern verse'.[34]

In the introduction, Yeats says he first knew Blunt 'as a fashionable amateur who had sacrificed a capacity for literature and the visible arts to personal adventure', but later realized that some of his sonnets 'were permanent in our literature'.[35] It is nevertheless the poems of 'personal adventure' that Yeats anthologizes; the poems in the *OBMV* foreground Blunt as romantic lover and as anti-imperialist, both roles he had played 'in some real situation of life'. One such role is notable in the first poem Yeats anthologized, Blunt's 'double-sonnet' to 'Esther' (Esther was in reality, in the words of Elizabeth Longford, 'the most famous courtesan of the late Victorian age'[36]):

> When I hear laughter from a tavern door,
> When I see crowds agape and in the rain
> Watching on tiptoe and with stifled roar
> To see a rocket fired or a bull slain ...
> ************ And when I keep
> Calmly the count of my own life and see
> On what poor stuff my manhood's dreams were fed
> *********************************
>
> – Then I remember that I once was young
> And lived with Esther the world's gods among.[37]

To Yeats this poem sounded refreshingly modern after Tennyson, but to anyone younger than Yeats, Blunt sounds like a man of the nineteenth century, which he was, writing in nineteenth-century diction and syntax (e.g. 'my manhood's dreams').

Yeats also anthologized one of Blunt's prison sonnets from the sequence *In Vinculis*. Blunt had gone to Ireland during the Land War in 1887 and spoken at a banned meeting. He was trying – hoping – to get arrested. The police pulled him off the platform twice, and after the second time, he said, 'Are you all such damned cowards that not one of you dares arrest me?' With that challenge, the police took the hint and arrested him.[38] Blunt was put in Galway Gaol, where he wrote sonnets inside a Bible. Oscar Wilde, reviewing them, said, 'Prison has had an admirable affect on Mr. Blunt as a poet',[39] and thought them better than the love sonnets:

> Honoured I lived e'erwhile with honoured men
> In opulent state. My table nightly spread
> Found guests of worth, peer, priest and citizen,
> And poet crowned and beauty garlanded.
> ***************
>
> To-night, unwelcomed at these gates of woe
> I stand with churls, and there is none to greet
> My weariness with smile or courtly show
> Nor, though I hunger long, to bring me meat.[40]
> *******************

Whatever about 'modern verse', there's very little about Ireland or politics in this poem except its origin. Its main emphasis is on what it feels like for a rich, important man used to giving dinner parties to be hungry in prison alongside 'churls'. But Yeats liked this poem because it didn't manifest 'passive suffering': as he wrote in a review of the volume in 1888, Blunt 'writes like one who is intent on living his life out ... ʼ⁴¹ Blunt's appeal was not simply that he did not sound like Tennyson but that he made grand gestures in love and politics: he got himself arrested, he had many love affairs, he tried out bull-fighting, he travelled by camel through Arabian deserts, he spoke Arabic and he was altogether as colourful a figure as Count Stenbock – but survived a long time to tell his story.

Gogarty (1878–1957) also made grand gestures, and one of them appealed to Yeats so much that he told the story in the introduction to the *OBMV*. Irish writer and physician, famous as Buck Mulligan in *Ulysses*, a close Dublin friend of Yeats's, Gogarty exemplified the kind of high spirits Yeats did not find in the war poets:

> Twelve years ago Oliver Gogarty was captured by his enemies [the anti-Treaty side in the Irish Civil War], imprisoned in a deserted house on the edge of the Liffey with every prospect of death. Pleading a natural necessity he got into the garden, plunged under a shower of revolver bullets and as he swam the ice-cold December stream promised it, should it land him in safety, two swans. I was present when he fulfilled that vow. His poetry fits the incident, a gay, stoical – no, I will not withhold the word – heroic song.⁴²

There certainly is no 'passive suffering' here: healthy, athletic and 'masculine', Gogarty acted also with an intuitive sense of the cinematic and a gesture as stagey as Blunt's demand to be arrested. For this alone, even if his poetry were less good than it is, Gogarty would have deserved a place in Yeats's anthology.

But as Yeats's editor at Oxford, Charles Williams, wrote in a letter to an official at the press, 'Mr Gogarty is better than I feared.'⁴³ What he is, in fact, is an Irish cavalier poet, nonchalant and somewhat smart-ass, as in this typical Gogarty poem ('Palinode'):

> I have been full of mirth
> I have been full of wine;
> And I have trod the earth
> As if it all were mine;
> And laughed to bring to birth
> The lighter lyric line.
>   * * * * *
> A few more years to flow
> From miracle-working Time,
> And surely I shall grow
> Incapable of rhyme,
> Sans Love and Song, and so
> An echo of a mime.⁴⁴

With his lilting 'lighter lyric line', Gogarty's poems not only do not suggest 'passive suffering'; they never invoke suffering at all. They are not just cavalier; they are anti-gravitas. By their rhythm, their pace, their vocabulary and their insistent merriness, they defy sorrow and suffering altogether. Yeats may especially have liked these poems so much because he 'improved' them, as in fact he did many of the poems by lesser known poets in the *OBMV*. Frank O'Connor mentions Gogarty's remark as the two of them went to visit Yeats: Gogarty said, 'He's writing a few little lyrics for me, and I'd like to see how he's getting on.'[45]

Dorothy Wellesley (1889–1956), the third and final of Yeats's eccentric favourites in the anthology, did not make grand gestures or little jokes, but her sexual freedom, her title, her wealth and her house and grounds made her poetry appealing to Yeats. When he knew her, in the mid-1930s, she had left her husband, the Duke of Wellington, and had taken women lovers: first Vita Sackville-West (whose poems Yeats also included in the *OBMV*) and then Hilda Matheson. Yeats was a frequent guest at her Sussex house Penns in the Rocks, which he hoped would function in his life as a second Coole Park, a peaceful rural environment presided over by a titled woman, a place where he could write and where literary conversation could flourish.

Unlike Gerard Hopkins, Wellesley was 'manly'. As Yeats wrote to her in a much quoted letter, 'What makes your work so good is the masculine element allied to so much feminine charm – your lines have the magnificent swing of your boyish body.'[46] Perhaps one source of that 'masculine' element was Yeats himself, who 'improved' some of Wellesley's poems also. The typical Wellesley poem essentializes its subject. Her poems are in retreat from the contemporary: they move chronologically backward to the point at which she views her subject in its remotest cultural context, which is usually classical or biblical. Her poem 'Fire' goes from 'an oblong electric tube … set in the wall' (i.e. a radiator) to Empedocles and Heraclitus. Her poem 'Horses' starts with 'garden-pony' and 'Suffolk Punch' and ends with 'Nordic tales of young gods riding races.'[47]

Wellesley's best poem in the *OBMV* is an excerpt from a longer poem called 'Lenin'. Yeats wrote Wellesley that he wanted to include this poem because 'There are a certain number of revolutionary ignoramuses who will be surprised to find it there.'[48]

> So I came down the steps to Lenin.
> With a herd of peasants before
> And behind me, I saw
> A room stained scarlet, and there
> A small wax man in a small glass case.

Two sentinels at this feet, and one at his head,
Two little hands on his breast:
Pious spinster asleep; and I said
'Many warrants these delicate hands have signed.'
A lamp shone, red,
An aureole over him, on his red hair;
His uniform clothed him still.
Greedy of detail I saw,
In those two minutes allowed,
The man was not wax, as they said,
But a corpse, for a thumb nail was black,
The thing was Lenin.

Then a woman beside me cried
With a strange voice, foreign, loud,
And I, who fear not life nor death, and those who have died
Only a little, was inwardly shaken with fear,
For I stood in the presence of God;
The voice I heard was the voice of all generations
Acclaiming new faiths, horrible, beautiful faiths;
I knew that the woman wailed as women wailed long ago
For Christ in the sepulchre laid.
Christ was a wax man too,
When they carried Him down to the grave.[49]

The poem dehistoricizes but does not altogether depoliticize Lenin. Yeats himself is responsible for the political edge of the beginning; Wellesley originally wrote, 'Much writing these delicate hands have done', but Yeats changed the line to 'Many warrants these delicate hands have signed.'[50] Studying this figure closely, the poem's tourist-speaker soon realizes that the 'small wax man' is not wax: 'The thing was Lenin.' Then the woman beside her cries out, and Wellesley realizes that to her, he's a God; and so Wellesley sees the dead Lenin as if he were the dead Christ. Typically, Wellesley has begun with the contemporary and moved back to the remote past. What might Yeats have liked about this poem? It's about Lenin but it's not 'Communist'; his line about the 'warrants' critiques Communism. And the vision in the final lines reveals the presence of a god in this secular state. Soviet Russia is transformed as it is seen in a mythic context.

But also, I think, Yeats was interested in the intense visual focus on the recumbent dead body in what functioned as a coffin, albeit a see-through one. James Pethica, in his introduction to the Cornell edition of Yeats's *Last Poems*, mentions Yeats's interest in 'death as a starting point for potential new discovery', which is what happens in a somewhat different way in 'Lenin'.[51] Indeed, in his later work Yeats often focuses on bodies in coffins, as in, for instance, the late poem 'In Tara's Halls', where the one-hundred-year-old 'Lay in the coffin, stopped his breath and died' (p. 609), or in 'Vacillation', where Yeats praises 'men who come / Proud, open-eyed, and laughing to the tomb' (p. 501) and mentions Saint Teresa's body lying 'undecayed in tomb' (p. 503).

Wellesley's 'Lenin' and Yeats's coffin poems suggest another context altogether for the *Oxford Book of Modern Verse*, namely, that it forms part of Yeats's 'preparation for death'. It is part of the deliberate packaging of ideas that he made in many different ways in the late 1930s. In a letter to Laura Riding about the *OBMV*, Yeats wrote,

> I am a despotic man, trying to impose my will upon the times (an anthology one instrument) not co-operative. My anthology has however a first domestic object, to get under one cover poems I want to read to myself, to a friend, or to my children. I do not care whether a poem has been in a hundred anthologies. I do not think that a reason for including or excluding it. If I give my anthology to a man, or as is more likely to a woman, I must be able to say this is my table of values.[52]

The phrase 'get under one cover' is reminiscent of what Yeats famously wrote to Lady Elizabeth Pelham weeks before his death: 'When I try to put all into a phrase I say, "Man can embody truth but he cannot know it. I must embody it in the completion of my life." '[53] It is the same impulse to compress and package his thought for posterity. The phrase 'this is my table of values' suggests an association with the original title of 'Under Ben Bulben', which was 'His Convictions'. Yeats was thinking of the *Oxford Book of Modern Verse* as a compact, unitary package of all his poetic 'values'. Judging by the many poems he anthologized but no one else did, these were not anyone else's poetic values, but for Yeats, the book was a legacy.

NOTES

1. Stallworthy, 'Yeats as Anthologist', pp. 188–9.
2. Auden, 'The Public v. the Late Mr. William Butler Yeats', p. 47.
3. As quoted in Alden, *Some Heroic Discipline*, p. 14.
4. As cited in Foster, *W.B. Yeats: A Life. II. The Arch-Poet*, pp. 565, 566.
5. Foster, p. 554.
6. For another interpretation of the *OBMV*, see McDiarmid, *Poets and the Peacock Dinner: the literary history of a meal*, pp. 162–6.

7. Yeats, 'Estrangement', *Autobiography*, p. 323.

8. Page numbers in parentheses refer to the *Variorum Edition of the Poems*.

9. *Collected Letters,* #6433, 4 November 1935.

10. Yeats, 'Samhain: 1906. Literature and the Living Voice', *Explorations*, pp. 205–6.

11. See Vendler, pp. 295–6, for an analysis of the way Yeats writes in 'vignettes'.

12. See Rubin, *Some Heroic Discipline ...* , for a discussion of the contemporaneous *Faber Book of Modern Verse* (1936) edited by Michael Roberts.

13. As quoted in Foster, p. 566.

14. As quoted in Stallworthy, p. 185.

15. That is, poets not included in the *Faber Book of Modern Verse* or the Untermeyer *Modern American and Modern British Poetry*.

16. *OBMV*, x.

17. Information about Stenbock is taken from three sources: http://www.tartaruspress.com/stenbock.htm; http://www.mmhistory.org.uk/cce/Jo/; and http://oasis.lib.harvard.edu/oasis/deliver/~ber00001.

18. *OBMV*, v.

19. *OBMV*, xiv.

20. *OBMV*, vi.

21. *OBMV*, vi.

22. Stevenson, *Letters to His Family and Friends*, Vol. 1, p. 316.

23. *OBMV*, xv.

24. *OBMV*, ix.

25. *OBMV*, ix.

26. *OBMV*, x.

27. *OBMV*, xi–xii.

28. *OBMV*, xxxiv.

29. See, for instance, *The Faber Book of Modern Verse* (1936) and the Untermeyer *Modern British and Modern American Poetry*.

30. As quoted in Foster, p. 564.

31. Wellesley, *Letters on Poetry ...* , p. 113.

32. For more detailed commentary on the dinner, see *Poets and the Peacock Dinner: the literary history of a meal*.

33. F.S. Flint Papers, Harry Ransom Center, University of Texas at Austin. Grateful acknowledgment also to Oliver Flint and Siddhimala (Linda Flint) for permission to quote from the Flint papers.

34. His poems do not, however, begin the anthology. Notoriously (but interestingly), the selection that opened the volume was Pater's description of the *Mona Lisa*, printed as if it were poetry.

35. *OBMV*, vi.

36. Longford, *Pilgrimage of Passion*, p. 34.

37. *OBMV*, p. 2.

38. See Longford, pp. 239–69, for a detailed account of Blunt's arrest and trial.

39. Wilde, 'Poetry and Prison', *Pall Mall Gazette* XLIX:7425 (3 January 1889), p. 3. See Rubin for a discussion of Yeats's review of the same book.

40. *OBMV*, p. 3.

41. Yeats, 'The Prose and Poetry of Wilfred [*sic*] Blunt', in *Uncollected Prose*, Vol. 1, p. 124.
42. *OBMV*, xv.
43. As quoted in Rubin, pp. 54 and 211.
44. *OBMV*, p. 184.
45. O'Connor, *My Father's Son*, p. 104.
46. Wellesley, *Letters on Poetry from W.B. Yeats to Dorothy Wellesley*, p. 113.
47. *OBMV*, pp. 309, 311, 314, 316.
48. *Letters on Poetry ...* , p. 31.
49. *OBMV*, pp. 2–321.
50. *Some Heroic Discipline ...* , p. 341.
51. *Last Poems*, xxiv.
52. *Collected Letters,* #6541, 26 April 1936.
53. *The Letters of W.B. Yeats*, p. 922.

Homecoming: Yeats and Sligo

ANNE MARGARET DANIEL

W.B. Yeats writes about Sligo in his first surviving letter, dating from sometime in autumn of 1876. Willie was eleven, in England with his father, replying to his little sister Lily, who was in Sligo and had sent him a drawing of a mountain he already knew well. John Butler Yeats had left the rest of the family behind, after one of his characteristically fraught visits to his wife at her family's home, and taken Willie off with him to Slough, where JBY was painting landscapes at Burnham Beeches. In his letter, after some boyish preamble – to be expected from a grubby little fellow who kept newts in a jar and who stored his lizards atop his books – Willie leads off with his pet lizards and then thanks Lily, specifically, for her art: 'My lizards walked off one night. Mrs Earl came in to cettle the books on top of the cupboard on which were the lizards but when she found them gone she was afraid to touch the books lest she should put hand on them.' And then he compliments her landscape: 'I recognised Knocknoray'.[1]

It's very Willie to have misspelled the name; he could never spell. Remember him saying that he learned grammar from Shakespeare. But of course Willie recognized Knocknarea, that real mountain that already featured prominently in his imaginative landscape – together with its larger fellow across the waters, Ben Bulben. Knocknarea, the feminine, and Ben Bulben, the masculine, mountains – standing like a protective lion's paws on either side of the beloved town and its river, with strands, waterfalls, lakes, and people and their homes, sheltered in between.

Lily, the artist of Knocknarea, was the only Yeats child born in County Sligo, in the seaside village of Enniscrone, during a family holiday there. But all the children spent their summers, and sometimes more, in Sligo for many years. John Butler Yeats and Susan Mary Pollexfen married in Sligo town on 10 September 1863, a year after they had met through Susan's brother George, a school friend of JBY's on the Isle of Man. The young couple stayed in the west for their honeymoon – they went to Galway, to the railway hotel. Lily, in her classic and acerbic style, told the story of their honeymoon in a letter in 1928, when she was staying at the same hotel: 'It was here Papa and Mama came over 60 years ago on their honeymoon. Mama had never stayed in a hotel, and Papa got ill, and she tried to light a fire and failed, and Papa got cross and said it would take a coach and four to wait on her, and then she went out for help and stood on the landing and looked down the great well to the hall, and heard some children on the top floor saying their prayers, and felt homesick.'[2] That the newlywed Susan Yeats could feel homesick for Sligo while just down the road in Galway is a testament to the effect that the place they, too, regarded as home always had on her soon-to-arrive children.

Susan Yeats had married an up-and-coming Trinity College man, reading law at the time and set to be a successful barrister and, someday, Queen's Counsel – like his contemporary Edward Carson, who would decimate Oscar Wilde in 1895. It is hard to recognize John Butler Yeats from that description today. He remained in the law when Willie and Lily were born, but by the time Susan had her last four children, two of whom died in childhood, JBY had given up the law and begun his study of art, and career as a painter, in London.

It is quite safe to say that, though Susan Yeats found herself homesick in Galway, she was much more so in London, a place she hated. And Willie, though raised also in London, and living in that city for many years of his adult and working life, was homesick in London too. But the same homesickness that paralysed Susan did wonders for WB's imagination. Throughout the late 1860s and 1870s, Susan eagerly, if a bit sadly that such a trip was largely necessitated by her husband's lack of money, often came home to Sligo with her children. In 1868, they were there from early summer through Christmas time, and in 1872 they arrived for what would be almost two years. The handsome, dark-haired little Yeatses were spoiled by Susan's younger brothers and sisters, and had plenty of cousins to play with there. Lily was closest to her big brother; just slightly more than a year separated them in age. Lolly, Robert and Jack were not old enough to roam and play with the oldest two Yeatses; and Lily and Willie shared the most there.

In his early letter to Lily you can feel Willie's link to her, to the place where she was – and where he wished he too could still be. We can trust his early letters better than we can trust his later, sometimes self-serving and much-revised, autobiographies and memoirs and retrospective accounts, for Yeats's true feelings about many things. However, one thing he does not revise in those later works is his love for Sligo. He revisits it, yes, but does not revise – from the first Willie's gratitude for the place, and affection for it, are clear.

What did young Willie love about Sligo? First, having family there. Second, the landscape and freedom to range, both physically, and imaginatively, within that landscape. As one of his Pollexfen aunts said, in damning London (and, as Willie realized at the time, JBY along with it), 'Here you are somebody. There you will be nobody at all.'[3] Though determined to prove the last statement wrong, and succeeding brilliantly in this, Yeats knew the truth of the first all his life.

It was very important for him to situate the Yeatses in Sligo, too – so that his Sligo connections were not exclusively through his mother's people, the Middletons and Pollexfens. That John Yeats, his great-grandfather, had been rector at Drumcliffe from 1811 to 1846 was tremendously important to Willie – after all, he dictated that he should be buried there, and not in Sligo town, in the churchyard of St John's with his mother's family and his own little brother. William Pollexfen came to Sligo in the early 1830s and joined his cousin Elizabeth Middleton's son, also William, in the Middleton milling and shipping business. Pollexfen married Elizabeth's daughter, also Elizabeth, in 1837.[4] Susan was their eldest daughter. Jack lived with his grandparents in Sligo longer than any of the other children did, and his siblings envied him this.

From their grandparents' home on the hill, Merville, the little Yeatses looked down at the town, what they regarded as Grandfather's harbour, and Ben Bulben. Lily, as an old woman, writing to Joseph Hone in 1939, remembered Merville in affectionate detail:

> In our day it was a solid house, big rooms – about 14 bedrooms, stone kitchen offices & a glorious laundry smelling of soap full of white steam & a clean coke fire with rows of irons heating at it. Our grandmother's storeroom like a village shop – a place with windows & a fireplace – shelves & drawers & delicious smell of coffee – the house was of blue grey limestone – the local stone – 60 acres of land round it – a very fine view of Ben Bulben.[5]

The house still stands over Sligo, now the residence of the Sisters of Nazareth who own and operate the adjoining healthcare facility.

JBY addressed two well-known letters to his wife at Merville during their separation in the early 1870s. In one, he soothed her for something about which she needed no soothing:

> You must be a good wife & heroic & not vex yourself about having to stop
> in Sligo till June or May. I know Merville is not a very pleasant house but
> I think it is pleasanter to be there than to be here with no money & not
> enough servants & a husband unsuccessful (you would perhaps put up with
> the husband but the anxiety & the work would simply kill you).[6]

JBY was miserable at Merville, where no one really liked him because of his utter
failure to support his family, and where he did nothing to try to make anyone like
him, either – but he was the only member of the family who didn't like it there.
The others quite loved being in the big house on the hill, looking over the sea and
out the back windows above the stables at the broadside of Ben Bulben.

JBY also worried over Willie in Sligo. He always had his own reasons for
thinking of his first-born son, as we can see here, in 1872:[7]

> I am continually anxious about Willy – he is almost never out of my thoughts.
> I believe him to be intensely affectionate but from shyness, sensitiveness and
> nervousness very difficult to win and yet he is worth winning. ... Bobby is
> robust and hardy and does not mind rebuffs but Willy is sensitive, intel-
> lectual and emotional – very easily rebuffed and continually afraid of being
> rebuffed – so that with him one has to use great sensitiveness – sensitiveness
> which is so rare in Merville. Above all keep him from that termagant Agnes
> ... I think he was greatly disimproved by Merville – he was coming on again
> from being so much with his mother and away from his Grandfather and
> dictatorial young aunts.

Agnes was one of his 'dictatorial' young Pollexfen aunts who Willie liked
most. When in the summer of 1895 she burst into the Yeats home in London
and had to be committed again to a mental institution, he was horribly upset.
Even twenty years after that, writing his memoirs, Willie was so roiled up
about the recollection that Lily and Lolly advised he leave it out.

Poor Bobby, mentioned in this letter too, was actually the child about
whom JBY should have been worried. He died just before his third birthday,
the following year, in Sligo. Willie was in the library when he heard the flurry
of alarm in the hall and the announcement that Bobby was dead. He and Lily
were set at a table and drew pictures of ships with the flags at half-mast, as they
had seen them in town and on the ships that day for their little brother.[8] Robert
Corbet Yeats is buried in the churchyard where his parents were married; you
can see his simple marker there today. Biographers agree that Susan Yeats never
recovered from Bobby's death – and that the death of her last child, Jane Grace,
at less than a year old in 1876 in London, compounded her intensifying depres-
sion and deep unhappiness.

When Willie came many years later to set down his own first memories of
Sligo, he put it, vitally, in the present tense: 'where I live with my grandparents.'[9]

Sligo and its host of childhood memories was, to Yeats, always now. One of his earliest memories involves the harbour, its boats and his grandparents' house:

> I am sitting on the ground looking at a mastless toy boat with the paint rubbed and scratched … I may already have had the night of misery where, having prayed for several days that I might die, I began to be afraid that I was dying and prayed that I might live. There was no reason for my unhappiness. Nobody was unkind, and my grandmother has still after so many years my gratitude and my reverence. The house was so big that there was always a room to hide in, and I had a red pony and a garden where I could wander, and there were two dogs to follow at my heels, one white with some black spots on his head and the other with long black hair all over him.[10]

Yeats kept the red pony for many years – he recurs, in a teenage memory, later.

Like all the Yeats children, Willie was rather afraid of his grandfather, but also admired him tremendously:

> [T]here was a great scar on his hand made by a whaling-hook, and in the dining room was a cabinet with bits of coral in it and a jar of water from the Jordan for the baptizing of his children and Chinese pictures upon rice-paper and an ivory walking stick from India that came to me after his death.[11]

Grandfather Pollexfen was indeed something of a deity:

> I think I confused my grandfather with God, for I remember in one of my attacks of melancholy praying that he might punish me for my sins, and I was shocked and astonished when a daring little girl – a cousin, I think – having waited under a group of trees in the avenue, where she knew he would pass near four o'clock on the way to his dinner, said to him, 'If I were you and you were a little girl, I would give you a doll.'[12]

Yeats remembered vividly the night and following day when his grandfather swam ashore from a wrecked steamer on which he had struggled to save the crew and passengers, getting them all into lifeboats, though some of the boats were then upset and eight men drowned: '[M]y grandfather suffered from that memory at intervals all his life, and if asked to read family prayers never read anything but the shipwreck of St. Paul.'[13] Yeats's grandmother was a gentle woman, who loved her garden and drew delicate pictures of its flowers upon some of that Chinese rice-paper. From her both Yeats and his mother had their love of a good garden, and bright flowers in it.

In the gloomy garden at Bedford Park in London, young Yeats planted sunflowers, and one of his few happy letters from Blenheim Road is to Katharine Tynan about growing things: 'After breakfast I got out on the roof under the balcony and arranged a creeper that climbs over it. Everything seemed so delighted at the going of the east wind – so peaceful and delighted. It all most seemed that if you listened you could hear the sap rising in the branches – bubble bubble.'[14] Yeats always noticed plants and flowers, being very taken by vivid tropical ones in the south of France and California during his travels there, and had a garden he loved at Riversdale.

Young Willie also got into the nautical spirit of what Jack illustrated as Sailor Town, rather politically: 'I had a little flagstaff in front of the house and a red flag with the Union Jack in the corner. Every night I pulled my flag down and folded it up and laid it on a shelf in my bedroom.' The stable boy at Merville, his pal Johnny Healy, furnished Yeats with a songbook that influenced him, both imaginatively and politically:

> He had a book of Orange rhymes, and the days when we read them together in the hayloft gave me the pleasure of rhyme for the first time ... presently, when I began to dream of my future, I thought I would like to die fighting the Fenians. I was to build a very fast and beautiful ship and to have under my command a company of young men who were ... as brave and handsome as the young men in the story-books, and there was to be a big battle on the sea-shore near Rosses and I was to be killed.[15]

Willie loved Rosses Point, where he and his cousin George 'rowed in the river-mouth or were taken sailing in a heavy slow schooner yacht'. And he loved the mysterious family house there, Elsinore – a summer place for Middletons and Pollexfens but best-known as Uncle George's house by the 1890s. Yeats probably liked the name as much as anything, at first – a place where the little dark-haired boy could play Hamlet and look for ghosts: 'There were great cellars under the house, for it had been a smuggler's house a hundred years before ... A pilot had told me that, after dreaming three times of a treasure buried in my uncle's garden, he had climbed the wall in the middle of the night and begun to dig but grew disheartened "because there was so much earth".'[16]

The first time I came to Sligo as a girl I climbed up the old inner stairs, still jutting from the wall, as high as I dared to take pictures of the patterns on what was left of the ceiling. You could, standing in the stairs, now long fallen, see out the windows over the whole of Memory Harbour. The red-gold apple trees in the jungle of grass in what remained of the walled garden still had sweet apples that tasted nothing like apples you've ever bought. The house has, alas, been allowed since, indeed encouraged, to completely go to ruin. Under its ivy, it is still possessed of beauty.

Sligo formality annoyed Yeats: 'sometimes my grandmother would bring me to see some old Sligo gentlewoman ... and I would sit upon my chair, very bored, while my elders ate their seed-cake and drank their sherry.' He preferred the company of the family's servants, who engaged him in town life, told him stories, and prompted his writings: 'My walks with the servants were more interesting; sometimes we would pass a little fat girl, and a servant persuaded me to write her a love-letter.' This was not a successful attempt, by the way – presaging many of Yeats's later love-letters and poems that failed. But the servants' stories fired his imagination. 'All the well-known families had their grotesque or tragic or romantic legends, and I often said to myself how terrible it would be to go away and die where no one would know my story. Years afterward, when I was ... in London, I would remember Sligo with tears, and when I began to write, it was there that I hoped to find my audience.'[17]

Yeats had many first experiences of young manhood in Sligo: for instance, he was first drunk there.

> I had been out yachting ... and it had come on very rough. I had lain on deck between the mast and the bowsprit and a wave had burst over me and I had seen green water over my head. I was very wet and very proud. When we got to Rosses again, I was dressed up in an older boy's clothes so that the trousers came down below my boots, and a pilot gave me a little raw whiskey. I drove home on an outside car and was so pleased with the strange state in which I found myself that for all my uncle could do I cried out to every passerby that I was drunk, and went on crying it through the town and everywhere until I was put to bed by my grandmother and given something to drink that tasted of blackcurrants and so fell asleep.[18]

He also found out about sex in Sligo.

> I asked everybody how calves were born, and because nobody would tell me, made up my mind that nobody knew. They were the gift of God ... and children must come in the same way, in a cloud and a burst of light. That made me content until a boy of twelve or thirteen, who had come on a visit for the day, sat beside me in a hay-loft and explained all the mechanism of sex ... His description [which involved what the boy had been up to with an older lad, whose 'pathic' he was, as Yeats delicately put it, using that old word Byron liked] ... made me miserable for weeks.[19]

Willie was made to go to church regularly, and didn't like it. We see in his memory of church in Sligo Yeats's early inability to carry a tune, and perhaps why this was: 'I took pleasure in the words of the hymn, but never understood why the choir took three times as long as I did in getting to the end.' He liked the sermons, sometimes, and passages from the Apocalypse, but these 'were no compensation for all the repetitions and for the fatigue of so much standing.' Willie was spared church when JBY came for a brief visit; JBY did not go with the family, and instead went his own way to teach his son to read properly. 'He was an angry and impatient teacher, and flung the reading-book at my head, and next Sunday I decided to go to church.'[20]

Willie liked reading with Lily, though, and during their first proper reading lessons, in Sligo at Esther Merrick's home, he had the inspiration of a commemorative sword many decades before Sato's celebrated gift: 'When we had learned our lesson well, we were allowed to look at a sword presented to her father who had led troops in India or China, and to spell out a long inscription on the silver scabbard.'[21]

Children raised on the classic children's stories of the day could not but appreciate the sea. The globe had long been circumnavigated, and as the eighteenth century was one of exploration and imperialism, the nineteenth was one of exploitation and trade. Stories of the sea – of the shipwrecked, of pirates, of new found lands and wonders – had been popular since the days of Hakluyt and Raleigh, Defoe and Swift, and were finding a particular currency in the 1870s and 1880s as children's stories. Yeats loved it when Robert Louis Stevenson, whom he much admired and who wrote the best of these stories, praised 'The Lake Isle of Innisfree'. From Sligo, in October of 1894, he wrote a thank-you note back to Stevenson immediately.[23] The gardens at Merville were decorated with ships' figureheads – though, one assumes, not the half-naked women always most popular for ships. A woman aboard is bad luck; but a nude figurehead, so sailors long believed, calms a rough sea – hence the great number of such figureheads. Here is Lily, once more – note the romance of the sail already giving way to the inglorious utility of steam, as best memorialized in J.M.W. Turner's *Fighting Temeraire* (1838). Sligo is a place of significant nostalgia for Lily, and all her siblings, as adults:[22]

> [Our family] ran a fleet of fast sailing vessels between Sligo – Portugal and Spain. What they traded in I don't know. Salt was, I think, the cargo they brought back from Portugal. In our day these gay little ships' lives were over, and as old black hulls they were used as lighters and clustered round the great corn steamers from America and the Black Sea, yellow corn being poured into them with a delicious rushing sound as the steamers lay out in the deep water anchorage at Rosses Point. Uncle George used to name them for us and tell of his one adventure when as a young man he had gone in the Bacalieu to Portugal. In time the sailing ships were replaced by steamers, and the Ballisodare and Sligo mills were bought, and when we were children the firm was big and rich and proud.

And the Pollexfens and Middletons enjoyed, during the Yeats children's youth, their own resort – rather like ancient Romans with a palazzo and a villa in town. They bought Rosses Point as an investment and summer-holiday spot, very convenient to the whole stretch of harbour. Said the *Sligo Independent*, observing Rosses Point on one afternoon not long after the purchase:

Its light house and whitewashed cottages, with the well tilled lands adjoining, gave it a look of peace and comfort, with which we hope soon to see elegance combined, as we know of no place more favourably situated for the purpose of being made a fashionable sea-side resort. We are confident that its new and enterprising proprietor, William Middleton, Esq., will take advantage of its highly picturesque situation by making it what it ought to be, the Brighton of the West.[23]

Willie would write poems about the Brighton of the West, to be sure, but, just as surely, he never called it that.

As business people, the Pollexfens were little regarded as being part of Sligo county society, yet they were certainly not excluded. The Pollexfens and the Gore-Booths of Lissadell House, for example, were not particularly social friends, but Willie and Jack were invited to things like cricket matches and races at Lissadell. [Dermot Healy had some of these invitations from the Gore-Booth girls to the Yeats boys, which I understand from him were borrowed some time ago, and not returned.] Yeats much admired the Great Houses of County Sligo and wrote more of Lissadell and Hazelwood than he would of Merville or Rathedmond or Elsinore. Imaginatively, he was drawn to the great houses of Sligo that he knew – the ones close by, Markree and Hazelwood and most of all Lissadell. He would stay at two of them, and make one of them, and its evening light, famous in his elegy for the two daughters of the house, Eva and Constance Gore-Booth (later Countess Markiewicz).

When he was exiled to London alone with his father, he found ponds, where he sat 'imagining ships going in and out of the reeds and thinking of Sligo.' He made a friend of an old naval officer who used to sail his cutter yachts in the Round Pond in Kensington Gardens, and who sang Yeats 'a sailor's song about a coffin ship which left Sligo after the great famine, that made me feel very important', for the servants at Sligo had told him the story. Lily was as homesick as he was: in Holland Park, late in life, Yeats had the intense memory of a conversation they had there: ' … of our longing for Sligo and our hatred of London. I know we were both very close to tears and remember with wonder, for I had never known any one that cared for such mementoes, that I longed for a sod of earth from some field I knew, something of Sligo to hold in my hand.' Being bullied at school for being Irish didn't help – for his Sligo accent and his turns of phrase he was mocked as 'Mad Irishman'. 'I had a harassed life and got many a black eye and had many outbursts of grief and rage.' Why, Yeats thought, couldn't he be more like William Pollexfen? 'I was ashamed of my lack of courage, and wanted to be like my grandfather, who thought so little of danger that he had jumped overboard in the Bay of Biscay after an old hat.' One potentially kindred spirit, the school's only Irish master, made matters worse by saying 'it was a scandal I was so idle when all the world knew that any Irish boy was cleverer than a whole class-room full of English boys. A description I had to pay for later', Yeats remembered gloomily.[24]

Going home to Sligo from the docks in Liverpool was for a long time the only thing that made London bearable. Willie liked best the Pollexfen & Middleton ship *The Liverpool*, because it had been a blockade runner during the American Civil War[25]– Yeats's pro-southern sympathies were more romantic than democratic. The family was hostile to JBY on land and by sea, in person and by proxy –'Sometimes my father came too, and the sailors when they saw him coming would say : There is John Yeats and we shall have a storm', for he was considered unlucky.[26]

As he returned to Sligo as a teenager, Yeats spent more and more time out of doors, often with Johnny Healy, climbing the mountains and trout fishing, sometimes riding the red pony still in the Merville stables. His one outing at a hunt on the red pony was not a success, except in Yeatsian terms: 'He balked at the first jump, to my relief, and when a crowd of boys began to beat him, I would not allow it. They all jeered at me for being afraid. I found a gap and when alone tried another ditch, but the pony would not jump that either; so I tied him to a tree and lay down among the ferns and looked up into the sky.'[27] This behaviour, this imaginative part of childhood, Willie never lost.

It is no accident that, after his hideous early-teenage years in London, Willie first began composing poetry when he was once more living beside the sea in Ireland. He was at the Erasmus Smith High School in Dublin, but taking the train in to classes from the new family home in Howth. It wasn't Sligo, but felt enough like home for him – and for his mother, who was happier there than she had been in years – to be at home there. 'I have no doubt that we lived at the harbour for my mother's sake ... When I think of her, I almost always see her talking over a cup of tea in the kitchen with our servant, the fisherman's wife ... [of] the fishing-people of Howth, or the pilots and fishing-people of Rosses Point.'[28]

In the winter of 1881 the children all escaped to Sligo as soon as the school vacations let them: Lough Gill froze over that year, and the Yeatses skated on it, Willie not well but enthusiastically, Lily remembered, wearing red socks that flashed their colour as he skidded over the ice.[29] The Garavogue and lake froze again in 1895, when Yeats was delighted to be back in town and tried skating again, though he was happy to stop when the 'Miss Gore Booths ... made coffey on the shore.'[30]

Yeats began getting deeply interested in mysticisms, including theosophy and the occult, in Dublin in the mid-1880s; The Dublin Hermetic Society and its successor Dublin Theosophical Society were, as Roy Foster has memorably characterized them, 'WBY's university'.[31] If so, his Sligo education was the grade school and prep school for these modes of thinking, believing and feeling. The stories he had in Sligo from local people primed him and made him receptive to freedom in belief, and in imagination. Particularly influential during his Dublin time was a young man from Lurgan who Yeats explained to Katharine Tynan was 'a mystic of medieval type', George Russell.[32] Russell, 'Æ', shared Yeats's belief that this world is less real than it is the shadow of another, better one. This view of our everyday factual-actual world as the shadow, and the dream or faery or visionary world as the real one has been characterized by critics as Yeats's own version of Neoplatonism (though he would not read Plato until Lionel Johnson gave him a volume some years later),[33] or Yeats's version of Blake – but it was begotten, born and lives in Yeats's Sligo world.

When he had to go back to London in early 1887, Yeats was wretched, homesick and depressed by 'this meloncholy London'.[34] The new Yeats house in Bedford Park at least had a study for Willie, and Jack painted a map of Sligo on the walls for him.[35] Yeats assuaged his homesickness, or possibly made it worse, by sitting in that study and working on his collection of folk and fairy tales, most of which he had first heard as a child in Sligo in some form or other, and on *John Sherman*, his autobiographical novel with Sligo fictionalized as 'Ballah'. And he was writing Sligo poems – 'Down by the Salley Gardens' stands out.

When Willie fled London for Sligo in August of that year, Yeats fetched up where he was happiest: at Rosses Point and at Elsinore. He worked hard on *John Sherman* in situ, as it were, and also on *The Wanderings of Oisin*, of which he finished a first draft in town at his grandparents' house – no longer Merville, but Charlemont now, on the harbour. He also wrote some shorter poems set in the nearby landscape – like 'The Protestants' Leap'. Returning to London again for another miserable year, 1888, Willie tried hard not to leave Sligo in his mind, and, one afternoon in mid-December as he stood in The Strand looking into a window-display, he had what James Joyce would have called an epiphany. Feeling an intense emotion that sparked personal memory for him, he rushed home with a new poem in his head. Lily remembers him bursting in the door 'with all the fire of creation & his youth'.[36] The poem is set in a place Yeats had planned to live in a cottage by himself, ever since JBY read a passage from Thoreau's *Walden* to him when he was a boy. Here is an early draft of the start of the poem, as Willie soon after sent it to his friend Katharine Tynan, insisting that to 'live alone on that Island' is 'an old day dream of my own':[37]

I will arise and go now and go to the island of Innisfree
And live in a dwelling of wattles – of woven wattles and wood work made
Nine bean rows will I have there, a yellow hive for the honey bee
And this old care shall fade.
There from the dawn above me peace will come down dropping slow
Dropping from the veils of morning to where the household cricket sings
And noontide there be all a glimmer, midnight be a purple glow
And evening full of the linnets wings.

Yeats is one of the great revisers of his own work, something one can instantly see if you know the poem as published by heart (as many folk do). As Yeats says in one of his celebrated late readings for BBC radio, 'The Lake Isle of Innisfree' was, and likely still is, his best known work. 'When I was a young lad in the town of Sligo, I wanted to live in a hut on an island in Lough Gill called Innisfree.'[38] Yeats admitted the poem was 'my first lyric with anything in its rhythm of my own music'.[39]

1889 marked two things for Yeats: the publication of his first book of poems, which the Sligo Independent reviewed favourably because of his references to local places;[40] and the first time he didn't make the annual trip, with his siblings, to Sligo – because he had met Maud Gonne, and chose to stay in London that summer instead. His imagination, fed for so long by Sligo and all the roots there, had a new focus. When Yeats did return to Ireland, it wasn't until 1891 – and he did not come to Sligo, but hung around Dublin waiting for Gonne to arrive.

Bouncing back and forth from London to Dublin, Willie came to Sligo next in the autumn of 1892, broke and needing a place to live, and mourning the death of his grandmother in October. His grandfather died the following month. During this sad autumn in Sligo town Willie began collecting his thoughts for The Celtic Twilight, finding solace in how he would present his ideas born in Sligo folklore and a now lost childhood. His Uncle George's servant Mary Battle was a help to him – he later admitted much of The Celtic Twilight was in her voice.[41] Yeats also began drafting in the wake of his grandparents' deaths the poems of his intensely elegiac Sligo volume, The Wind Among the Reeds. 'The Fiddler of Dooney', the lyrical ballad concluding with the dancers in heaven, was the poem he wrote between the deaths of his grandparents. And at this time he wrote his play, The Land of Heart's Desire, also set there, and sharing its plot of a young bride stolen by the fairies with 'The Host of the Air'. With William and Elizabeth Pollexfen dead, Willie Yeats literally could not go home again. Yet it is easy to see from what he began thinking of and writing at the time, that he refused to accept this: the power of his poetic imagination could, and would, preserve his Sligo for him – and for others.

When he came back to Sligo in 1894, he stayed as usual with Uncle George – but also with the Gore-Booths at Lissadell. Willie liked Constance and Eva, though he was closer to Eva – the gazelle – and recommended Irish fairy tales for them to read. Con was, at the time, spoken for – an unpublished correspondence exists between her and a young man of another western-county great house from this time, indicating their betrothal, which was never realized. However, Willie thought he might have a chance with Eva, though rather fortunately he was too broke to seriously pursue her. At Uncle George's house in the winter of 1894 he finished revising his drafts for *Poems* 1895. He left Sligo in May of 1895, stopping in Dublin at Lady Wilde's house to offer his support in person for her son, who was about to be tried in London on charges of 'acts of gross indecency'.

When Yeats returned to Sligo again the following summer, he was serving as an authority on Celticism for Arthur Symons, showing his London flatmate around the West. He enjoyed being a houseguest of Edward Martyn at Tulira Castle in Galway, and during that summer, Yeats met the person who would relocate him just a bit to the south, for his poetic, artistic and political inspirations: Lady Augusta Gregory. Though they had crossed paths in London in 1894, it was at Coole that minds met. Arthur Symons, who was present, knew just what had happened, and in seeing Yeats click with Gregory – he referred to her as 'La Strega' – soon mourned the loss of his kindred spirit and literary London collaborator.[42] Symons and Yeats came for a brief visit to Rosses Point together, during which Symons met Yeats's siblings, and JBY reported to Susan Lolly's statement that 'all the natives men & women fell in love with Arthur Simmonds.'[43]

From now on, though, Yeats had a new place to be in the West, new folk and fairy tales to hear from someone who could translate them directly to him from the Irish, and a patroness who would become like family to him – though he was not like family to hers. In the summer of 1897, he went to Rosses Point, but eagerly headed in July with Æ to Coole and its swan-spotted lake, its walled garden and the catalpa tree, the great copper beech 'autograph tree', and its seven woods. Yeats had undergone an imaginative change of venue. Notably, he did not reciprocate for Gregory. Though they travelled over Ireland and Europe and America, to Italy and to London and to Dublin many times, there is no record of Yeats ever bringing her to see Sligo, to visit this landscape that meant so much to him. Perhaps the two simply didn't mix for him – in reality, at least. Yeats felt the conflict keenly. 'Certain woods at Sligo, the woods above Dooney Rock and those above the waterfall at Ben Bulben, though I shall perhaps never walk there again, are so deep in my affections that I dream about them at night;

and yet the woods at Coole, though they do not come into my dream, are so much more knitted to my thought … '[44]

Sligo was, with the advent of Coole and Ballylee, and the publication of *The Wind Among the Reeds* in 1899, set into the frame of reveries of youth – but hardly gone, and never forgotten. Just as Jack's map of Sligo had adorned his brother's study walls at Bedford Park, so his watercolour 'Memory Harbour' hung in Woburn Buildings for very many years. As long as Uncle George lived – until 1910 – Yeats would visit him in Sligo, though with increasing infrequency, and leaving it to Lily to come and nurse him through his final illness. He came up from Coole for the funeral and stayed at the Imperial Hotel, like a visitor, a tourist. Sligo superstitions remained strong, though. He wrote from the hotel to Lady Gregory, 'Lily heard the banshee as well as the nurse. He died the night after at the same hour the Banshee had cried out.'[45]

Yeats would not return to Sligo again until 1929. The visit has gone virtually unnoticed, which is remarkable – for Yeats brought his whole young family with him to show them his home. He came to Markree Castle, the home of Senator Cooper, for a week, and then George and the children joined him at Ewing's Golf Links Hotel at Rosses Point for a week's holiday. Two uncollected letters from this visit survive: 'My dear George,' he wrote from Markree on 29 August 1929, 'we have three rooms at Ewings Hotel Rosses Point, from Thursday, which will give us a couple of days sight-seeing at Sligo. I have done another stanza of the poems for Lady Gregory's book [Coole] and so I am idling today. Mrs. Cooper is driving me into Sligo and round the lake.'[46] Where did they go? Who did they visit? Where did they stop? Did he succeed in remembering which was the Lake Isle of Innisfree this time? Pause at Dromahaire? Veer on up the road on the way back to Markree to walk up Knocknarea, or into the Allt, once more?

From Rosses Point, Yeats wrote to Mrs Cooper, lyrically, in thanks during that family holiday week:

> I am very grateful to you for certain quiet & happy days in a place & amid scenery beautiful in themselves & beautiful because of what they seemed to me in childhood, when they seemed to lie just on the edge of the known world like the Garden of the Hesperides. Somewhere beyond our furthest carriage drive lay both. The children are delighting in the sands of the Rosses.[47]

One can only imagine how Yeats felt, after having been so ill in late 1928 and early 1929 – when he for the first time really thought he would die – as he watched his young children delighting in the sands of that level shore, following in the wet footsteps of Willie and Lily and Lolly and Jack – and of the fairies.

As far as we know, Yeats never returned to Sligo until he was brought there to be buried. He came to Coole, he came to Longford, but not to Sligo.

And he died ten years later, in France, at a hotel where he and George had stayed before. The building that was the Idéal Séjour, so very misnamed, and the little hillside graveyard that tilts perilously and is very, very full today, remain in Roquebrune. Yeats had asked George that he be buried immediately in France upon his death, though not permanently, and without publicity: as George told Tom MacGreevy, 'his actual words were "If I die here bury me up there [in the churchyard above the hotel, on a hill] and then in a years time when the newspapers have forgotten me, dig me up and plant me in Sligo." ' [48]

Upon word of Yeats's death a campaign to have him re-interred in Dublin, headed by Lennox Robinson, began at once. When George permitted 'Under Ben Bulben' to be printed on 3 February in *The Irish Times, The Irish Press* and the *Irish Independent*, this campaign swiftly fell silent. Yeats's memorial today is where he wanted it to be. Louis MacNeice was among the throng at Drumcliffe on 17 September 1948; the photographs of the funeral procession show not only the family members – George, Anne, Jack, Michael – in their cars, the dignitaries like Sean MacBride – but groups of townsfolk on foot, some pushing bicycles that had brought them there; and little boys in boots standing in the fields, watching.[49]

Yacht owned by a first cousin of the Yeats family, 'Fatty' Jackson, at Rosses Point, c. 1930. Jackson managed the Pollexfen business after George Pollexfen's death.

Yeats endures today in memory harbour, sailor town, the land of heart's desire. W.B. told Lily when they were old, in 1936, 'No one will ever see Sligo as we saw it.'[50] No. But thanks to him, one can see the shadows of what he saw in his mind's eye forever, superimposed on the living landscape of a place where change comes to pass, but the topography beneath, the bones under the skin, remain.

Speaking of his brother's famous watercolour, Yeats wrote:

> When I look at my brother's picture *Memory Harbour* – houses and anchored ship and a distant lighthouse all set close together as in some old map – I

recognize the blue-coated man with the mass of white shirt the Pilot I went
fishing with, and am full of disquiet and of excitement, and I am melancholy
because I have not made more and better verses. I have walked on Sindbad's
yellow shore and never shall another's hit my fancy.[51]

There is still a blue-coated man with a white shirt overseeing the channel
at Rosses Point; he is known to the people of Sligo as 'The Metal Man', and to
some, as 'The only Sligoman never to tell a lie'. Maeve's mountain and her cairn
– to which, when you go, you must carry a stone – oversee Sligo to the south. To
the north are Ben Bulben's steep channelled sides, boggy top, and massive head
thrust forward at the sea. Shallow, tidal Lough Gill and the islands scattered
over its surface lie to the east. The fossil prints of seashells in the rocks you pick
up on the level shore at Rosses Point (the shells that give Sligo its name, place
of shells) are to the west. No one will ever see Sligo quite as Yeats saw it, but
what he shared of it through his writings is indelible upon the landscape now,
and will be hereafter.

NOTES

1. W.B. Yeats (WBY) to Susan Mary Yeats (Lily), [autumn 1876], *The Collected
   Letters of W.B. Yeats, Volume 1, 1865–1895*, ed. John Kelly and Eric Domville
   (Oxford 1986), pp. 3–4.

2. Lily Yeats to Ruth Pollexfen Lane-Poole, quoted in R.F. Foster, *W.B. Yeats: A
   Life, Vol. I, The Apprentice Mage, 1865–1914* (Oxford 1998), p. 7. For the chron-
   ological and biographical details of WBY's life throughout, my debt is to Foster
   and his two-volume critical biography of Yeats: R.F. Foster, *W.B. Yeats: A Life,
   Vol. I, The Apprentice Mage, 1865–1914* (Oxford 1998); and R.F. Foster, *W.B.
   Yeats: A Life, Vol. II, The Arch-Poet, 1915–1939* (Oxford 2003).

3. W.B. Yeats, *Autobiographies* (London 1961), p. 27.

4. See Foster I, pp. 9–11.

5. Lily Yeats to Joseph Hone, 19 May 1939, quoted in William M. Murphy, *Family
   Secrets: Yeats and His Relatives* (Syracuse, New York 1995) p. 395, n. 19.

6. JBY to Susan Yeats, February 1873, quoted in Foster I, p. 12.

7. JBY to Susan Yeats, 1 November 1872, quoted in Foster I, p. 16. See also William
   M. Murphy, *Prodigal Father: The Life of John Butler Yeats 1839–1922* (Syracuse,
   New York 2001) p. 82, n. 49, preserving JBY's spelling of 'tarmigant'.

8. *Autobiographies*, p. 27.

9. *Autobiographies*, p. 5.

10. *Autobiographies*, pp. 5–6.

11. *Autobiographies*, pp. 6–7.

12. *Autobiographies*, p. 8.

13. *Autobiographies*, p. 13.

14. WBY to Katharine Tynan, 11 April 1888, *Letters* 1, p. 58.

15. *Autobiographies*, pp. 12; 14.

16. *Autobiographies*, pp. 15; 16.

17. *Autobiographies*, pp. 17; 18.

18. *Autobiographies*, p. 18.

19. *Autobiographies*, p. 26.

20. *Autobiographies*, p. 24.

21. *Autobiographies*, p. 25.

22. Lily Yeats, Scrapbook 6, quoted in Foster I, p. 19.

23. *Sligo Independent*, 4 April 1868, quoted in Foster I, p. 23.

24. *Autobiographies*, pp. 28, 30, 31, 35–6, 37.

25. *Autobiographies*, p. 49.

26. *Autobiographies*, p. 51.

27. *Autobiographies*, p. 53.

28. *Autobiographies*, p. 61.

29. *Family Secrets*, p. 44.

30. *Letters* I, p. 447.

31. Foster I, p. 46.

32. *Letters* I, p. 73.

33. Richard Ellmann, *Yeats: The Man and the Masks* [1948] (Oxford 1979), p. 143.

34. *Letters* I, p. 92.

35. *Family Secrets*, p. 62.

36. Quoted in Foster I, p. 79.

37. *Letters* I, p. 121.

38. W.B. Yeats, recording, BBC Radio, 4 October 1932 (2:02), via http://writing.upenn.edu/pennsound/x/Yeats.php

39. *Autobiographies*, p. 153.

40. Foster I, p. 86.

41. *Autobiographies*, p. 71.

42. John Butler Yeats, *Letters to His Son W.B. Yeats and Others, 1869–1922*, ed. Joseph Hone (London 1944), pp. 151–2.

43. *The Collected Letters of W.B. Yeats, Volume 2, 1896–1900*, ed. Warwick Gould, John Kelly and Deirdre Toomey (Oxford 1997), p. 52, n. 10.

44. *Autobiographies*, p. 377.

45. *Intelex Yeats* 1910, WBY to Lady Gregory from Imperial Hotel, Sligo [28 September 1910].

46. *Intelex Yeats* 1929, WBY to George Yeats from Markree Castle, Collooney [29 August 1929].

47. *Intelex Yeats* 1929, WBY to Lilian Stella Cooper [5 September 1929].

48. R.F. Foster, *The Irish Story: Telling Tales and Making it Up In Ireland* (Oxford 2002), p. 80.

49. See *e.g.* plates 30–1, Foster II, pp. 424–5.

50. Lily to Ruth Pollexfen Lane-Poole, 23 June 1936, quoted in *Family Secrets*, p. 150.

51. *Autobiographies*, p. 52.

Desolation of Reality: W.B. Yeats and the Nihilism of His Age

BRUCE STEWART

> Where does spirit live? Inside or outside
> Things remembered, made things, things unmade?
> What came first, the seabird's cry or the soul
> Imagined in the dawn cold when it cried?
> ...
> (Set questions for the ghost of W.B.)
>
> Seamus Heaney, *Seeing Things* (1996)

If Seamus Heaney sets these questions for W.B. Yeats, it is not alone because Yeats is something of an expert on the location of the spirit but because he is also implicated in forging the bond between spirit and nation which Irish poets made their 'trade' in the revolutionary period and long after. Yeats had many beliefs regarding spirit and nation, typically holding them in that close juncture which is almost the brand-mark of his intellectual system: 'Many times man lives and dies / Between his two eternities, / That of race and that of soul.'[1] The effect of this juncture is to make his readers feel that the term *soul* is metaphorical since we don't commonly believe that nations literally possess souls – though Yeats apparently did. He also, of course, believed that individuals have souls and it is worth pointing out that the word *soul* occurs one hundred and fifteen times in his *Collected Poems*. Now, belief in the

ontological existence of a non-material principle of human identity is not a
common feature of modern thinking – and nor, indeed, is it the hallmark of
Literary Modernism. This is tellingly illustrated by certain remarks in T.S.
Eliot's 'Tradition and the Individual Talent' where he speaks parenthetically of
'the metaphysical theory of the substantial unity of the soul' in such a way as
to suggest that he is filled with dubiety in regard to the locality of the same.[2]
Eliot's thinking is readily traceable to an intellectual background in Brahmin
America which embraced William James's *Varieties of Religious Experience* as
well as Dewey's *Pragmatism*. While Yeats knew Emerson and Thoreau, he had
no such intellectual background and regarded Huxley and John Stuart Mill as
the daemons of the anti-metaphysical tradition. Neither Emerson nor Thoreau
had corrosive things to say about human psychology or the immortal soul.

Yeats possessed firm beliefs on the question of spiritual life even if those
beliefs were not always self-consistent or entirely satisfactory from the philo-
sophical standpoint – nor need they have been in relation to his achievement
as a poet. So far as his ideas had a centre, they revolved around his preoccupa-
tion with the privileged position of the human imagination in its relation to
the *Anima Mundi* – that is, 'the great memory of Nature' – and the practical
relationship between all of this and the art of poetry.

On the autobiographical and biographical planes, it is incontestable that
his espousal of these ideas arose from a virulent reaction against a materialism
that he found suffocating and a metropolitanism which he found insufferable.
In Reveries Over Childhood and Youth Yeats famously wrote:

> I am very religious, and deprived by Huxley and Tyndall, whom I detested,
> of the simple-minded religion of my childhood, I had made a new religion,
> an almost infallible church, of poetic tradition, of a fardel of stories, and of
> personages, and of emotions, inseparable from their first expression, passed
> on from generation to generation by poets and painters with some help from
> philosophers and theologians.[3]

There is reason to question the complete truth of this sentence considered as
a record of an earlier state of mind since it speaks more keenly of a felt need
than a definite belief and does so in pseudo-Catholic terms which – given his
Protestant childhood – immediately cancel the dogmatic weight of the asser-
tion; a form of irony, in fact. (Besides which, psychological *lack* and religious
conviction are not the same thing at all.) Yet, in the main, it does echo in an
almost statutary way the consistent sense of Yeats's many depositions on the
matter. Some of those were odder than others, and none so odd as the one
to be met with in 'General Introduction to My Work', written in 1937 – an
extraordinary apologia in which a great deal is intentionally divulged and an

equal amount unintentionally revealed about his exploration and exploitation of religious ideas:

> I was born into this faith, have lived in it, and shall die in it; my Christ, a legitimate deduction from the Creed of St. Patrick as I think, is that Unity of Being Dante compared to a perfectly proportioned human body, Blake's 'Imagination' what the Upanishads have named 'Self': nor is this unity distant and therefore intellectually understandable, but imminent, differing from man to man and age to age, taking upon itself pain and ugliness, 'eye of newt, and toe of frog'.[4]

This is a highly condensed summary of many points of personal belief concerning the role of human imagination in the cosmic scheme of things to which – for chiefly polemical reasons – he here adds the unlikely supposition that St Patrick might condone the wildly unitarian association of Christ and Dante, William Blake and Gautama Buddha with some further light from William Shakespeare whose witches on a Scottish heath provide the final phrase. But though there are numerous passages in the *Autobiographies*, the *Memoirs*, the *Essays & Introductions* and the *Letters* that amplify the questions touched upon here, it is the poetry itself that provides the essential record of Yeats's spiritual convictions and tests them at the same time.

'Where does the spirit live?' It is pertinent to mention that, in writing that line, Seamus Heaney was reflecting on the death of his own father at a short distance from that sad event. That is to say, the question is eschatological rather than metaphysical in the sense of reflecting an interest in the mind-body dichotomy in living beings: he wants to know where his father is now – if *now* can be used to describe the location of a soul in eternity. Yeats too – increasingly in later poems – was preoccupied with the *au-delà*, though characteristically under the semantically ambivalent form of 'the *artifice* of eternity' [my italics]. Whether this means that *eternity* is a contrivance of poets or that it is effectively created by them is a point that must be addressed in any serious reading of his philosophical ideas, if only to despatch it as aesthetically irrelevant. It certainly does not mean, in Yeats, that eternity exists independently of the human imagination; but, if dependent on imagination, it is not so much actual eternity as an imagined place with all the said attributes except the ontological stamp of 'the thing in itself'. In other words, it does not really exist, or if so, it exists in the sense that Lafayette said of love that it is 'a reality in the realm of the imagination'. The Yeatsian thesis might be, of course, that such imagined things are the most real of all.

One (perhaps banal) aspect of the question is the persistence of human identity, bodily or spiritual, after the supercession of life – something that naïve

religionists of all kinds take more or less on faith. On this matter, Yeats wrote
in 'The Tower':

> Death and life were not
> Till man made up the whole,
> Made lock, stock and barrel
> Out of his bitter soul,
> Aye, sun and moon and star, all,
> And further add to that
> That, being dead, we rise,
> Dream and so create
> Translunar paradise.
>
> (CP, p. 223)

This seems to mean, *inter alia*, that the tandem of life after death is an inven-
tion – what might be called a 'construct', à la mode – inspired by human
passions that required such a notion as the necessary correlate of our fraught
condition. William Wordsworth's 'succedaneum and a prop to our infirmity'
in *The Prelude* (Book II, p. 214) comes to mind. In reaching this position,
Yeats professes to 'mock Plotinus' faith / And cry in Plato's teeth', thus setting
the belief in a separate domain of ideal forms normally associated with these
philosophers at nought.[5] At other times, of course, he preferred to invoke that
very belief as when, in 'Among School Children', he poses the question:

> What youthful mother, a shape upon her lap
> Honey of generation had betrayed,
> And that must sleep, shriek, struggle to escape
> As recollection or the drug decide,
> Would think her Son, did she but see that shape
> With sixty or more winters on its head,
> A compensation for the pang of his birth,
> Or the uncertainty of his setting forth?
>
> (CP, p. 244)

It is easy to miss the point that it is the 'shape upon her lap' – an infant child
– who has been 'betrayed' *into* life by the pleasure of sexual congress on its
mother's part, and that it is the baby who 'struggles to escape' *from* life under
the influence of its latent memories of an anterior condition. Again, the case
is just as Wordsworth described it in 'Ode to Immortality' when he spoke of
the soul as 'trailing clouds of glory' when it first enters the 'prison house' of
mortal life. By contrast, Yeats's idea of immortality is radically inseparable

from his concept of the imagination in which he is utterly unlike Wordsworth, whose pantheistic remake of Christian theology was destined to calcify into Orthodox Anglicanism in later years. By contrast, in 'Sailing to Byzantium', where he makes a poem out of his yearning for lost youth, Yeats coins the deservedly renowned phrase in the context of a prayerful plea to the 'singing masters of his soul':

> Consume my heart away; sick with desire
> And fastened to a dying animal
> It knows not what it is; and gather me
> into the *artifice of eternity*.
>
> (*CP*, p. 18; my italics)

It is worth noting that the climactic phrase in this, the penultimate, stanza was prefigured in Yeats's mystical story of 1897 'The Tables of the Law', in which he wrote: '[T]he world only exists to be a tale in the ears of coming generations; and terror and content, birth and death, love and hatred, and the fruit of the Tree, are but instruments for that supreme art which is to win us from life and gather us into eternity like doves into their dove-cots.'[6] This poses a problem to common-sense: is there a heaven or is there not? Is it merely a state of aesthetic apprehension created by artists through their artefacts? If so, the poet may have wasted his sea-journey – an irony that the poem bitterly comprehends in its adumbration of the ageing process and its mechanical alternative: perpetual existence as a clockwork bird. Yet, if eternity is indeed an 'artifice' in keeping with the 'unshakable belief' that Yeats professed in the thesis 'that whatever of philosophy has been made poetry alone is permanent', then the literary imagination is indeed the gateway to eternity and in effect its onlie begetter.[7] Of the numerous essays in which Yeats struggled to rationalize this idea under the influence of his theosophical initiation, the 1901 essay on 'Magic' is the most predicative as to form and content. In it he enumerated three famous propositions amounting – in paraphrase – to the assertion that our minds and memories continually flow into each other and are part of 'the great memory of Nature herself' (that is, *Anima Mundi*), and that poets can access this memory through the use of symbols.[8] This formula allows the artist to participate in the processes of divine making – and likewise the manufacture of history – through his engagement with the intrinsically spiritual processes of imagination. What it does not assert, and what Yeats would later assert, is that the spiritual is itself a product of imagination or, more precisely, the modality of the imagination when operating in the highest possible way.

In 'Under Ben Bulben', his poetic testament, Yeats offered an emphatic pronouncement on the relationship between individual and universal mind, and did so in the context of man's natural fear of death and annihilation:

> A brief parting from those dear
> Is the worst man has to fear.
> Though grave-diggers' toil is long,
> Sharp their spades, their muscles strong.
> They but thrust their buried men
> Back in the human mind again.
>
> (CP, p. 398)

The immediate effect of these verses is a form of philosophical consolation that argues for the power of memory to overcome the finality of death rather than the more positive assertion (already met with in 'The Tower') that 'life and death were not / Till man made up the whole'. That idea might itself be taken as a poetical redaction of the common notion that men are distinguishable from animals by their capacity to foresee their own extinction and that human consciousness is largely conditioned by that difference. Yet more is meant by it: Yeats seems to suggest that 'the human mind' is the primary embodiment of a higher spiritual agency that employs birth and death as the necessary phases of its own perpetual renewal, alteration and expression. Yet if Yeats's conception of permanence and transience in mortal affairs is cosily related to the idea of a continual process of incarnations by which 'that which is above' penetrates 'that which is below' (the case of 'Leda and the Swan' being a prime instance of this hermetic principle) then a more disturbing idea is also present – that of nation, since:

> Many times man lives and dies
> Between his two eternities,
> That of race and that of soul,
> And ancient Ireland knew it all.
>
> (CP, p. 398)

The position of race in this system of thought is acutely important since it provides a more particular and more passionate context for 'human mind' than the oriental idea of the individual's ultimate absorption in Buddhist Nirvana. Indeed, the claim made here for 'ancient Ireland' is a blasphemous privileging of one national context over another which Buddhism and theosophy by their very nature must deny (and not because of a cultural partiality to the alternative nationhood of India).

At the close of his 'General Introduction', Yeats wrote: 'I am no Nationalist except in Ireland for passing reasons; State and Nation are the work of the intellect, and when you consider what comes before or after them they are, as Victor Hugo said of something or other, not worth the blade of grass God gives for the nest of the linnet.'[9] Here his objection was to the Irish Free State, which proved such a disappointing outcome of his revivalist enthusiasms in an early period. You might say he thought he deserved better than a petty-bourgeois pietistic country in which the mind-forged manacles of man made for the clatter of rosary beads. Yet Yeats was profoundly nationalist in the sense that his conception of spirituality as a force in the world was attached to 'race' as its primary ground at the level of the actual and the ideal. In his introduction to the three-volume edition of *The Works of William Blake* (1893), produced with Edwin Ellis, he wrote: '[S]ystems of philosophy and dogmas of religion are to the mystic of the Blakean school merely symbolic expressions of racial moods or emotions, the essences of truth seeking to express themselves in terms of racial memory and experience.'[10] He went on: 'The German produces transcendental metaphysics, the Englishman positive science, not because either one has discovered the true method of research, but because they express their racial moods or affections.'[11] He might have added – as he did in his explication of the term 'Unity of Being' in 'The Trembling of the Veil' – 'Have not all races had their first unity from mythology that marries them to rock and hill?';[12] or, later in the same decade: 'Is there nation-wide multiform reverie, every mind passing through a stream of suggestion, and all streams acting and reacting upon one another, no matter how distant the minds, how dumb the lips?'[13]

To say, then, that Yeats was a nationalist for 'passing reasons' is to say that he was a nationalist by reason that his conception of the imagination was rooted in the idea of national and racial life. (Tawdry biographical accounts will always link the origins of his nationalism to his infatuation with Maud Gonne.) In a cultural context, the relationship was reciprocal, as he famously said: 'There is no great literature without nationality, and no great nationality without literature.'[14] But in the spiritual context, the matter was darker, and reveals a darker conception of the Irish race than the propagandist in Yeats – whose role he so slightly rates in the 'General Introduction' – suggests or could suggest. Once again, it is the later poems which provide the chief record of this conception and incidentally reveal the animus that turned him against a more genial view of modern Irish nationhood.

II

In 'The Statues' W.B. Yeats celebrates an imaginary Ireland which he regards as providing a bulwark against modernity, introduced to view in the form of the rebarbative phrase 'this filthy modern tide'. In so doing, he presupposes that the Irish peasantry have preserved 'their ancient deposit' of mythology and wisdom in the amber of defeat following the overthrow of the Gaelic lords during the sixteenth- and seventeenth-century religious wars.[15] The poem contains several hieratic phrases, not least an ambiguous reference to 'our proper dark' considered as the medium or agency by which the spirit of the 'Heroic Period' of Celtic pre-history and the more recent revolutionary period of nationalist history united to form a cornerstone for the modern Irish state.

> When Pearse summoned Cuchulain to his side
> What stalked through the Post Office? What intellect,
> What calculation, number, measurement, replied?
> We Irish, born into that ancient sect
> But thrown on this filthy modern tide
> And by its formless spawning fury wrecked,
> Climb to our proper dark that we may trace
> The lineaments of a plummet-measured face.
>
> (CP, p. 376.)

There are several points in this stanza which jar today – as they must have jarred with the majority of Irishmen when they were written. That ringing phrase 'We Irish', gleaned from the writings of the Bishop Berkeley, involves a specific degree of colonial double-vision as numerous critics have remarked.[16] For Yeats, as a descendant of the same class as the bishop and idealist philosopher, the epithet serves to assert that the Anglo-Irish are the best part of the Irish nation both in their own character and through their resemblance to the beaten native aristocracy. By a similar sleight of hand, he co-opted the more patently colonial term 'Irishry' and yoked it with the term 'indomitable' to create one of those ringing phrases that involve a short substantive and a Latinate modifier (such as 'invulnerable tide' or 'unappeasable host' in other instances). In 'Under Ben Bulben', his consciously wrought poetic testament, Yeats asks the reader to cast his mind on 'other days' – meaning the ancient past – 'that we in coming days may be / Still the *indomitable Irishry*' [italics mine].[17] His poem 'The Statues' is part and parcel of the same prescription set forth there and fortified in the more overtly polemic pages of his 'General Introduction for My Work', the discarded (and impractically vatic) preface where he writes: 'If Irish literature goes on as my generation planned it, it may do something to keep the "Irishry" living … . It may be indeed that certain characteristics of the "Irishry" must grow in importance.'[18] Seemingly the Yeatsian plan for Ireland is that it should proceed in the future by returning radically to the past, which is hardly what the new Irish state achieved in kowtowing to the Vatican on the one hand, while building the Ardnacrusha Hydro-Electric dam on the other. How modernism eventually took root in Ireland is a complex question, but in any construction it is widely at variance with Yeats's prescription: imaginative revivification of ancient forms through the work of the poets and playwrights.

Viewed in this light, 'our proper dark', so far from hinting at a doubtful capacity for rational thought, locates the most imaginative element of Irish spiritual life in an irrational – even anti-rational – impulse that found its original expression in the heroic deeds of ancient Irish heroes and was later embodied by the self-sacrifice of the 1916 leaders who gave their lives in the state of mind that he had earlier characterized as 'all the delirium of the brave' in his account of the Protestant patriot-martyrs of 1798 ('September 1913' – CP, p. 120).

For Yeats, from start to finish, Irish life had a psychic and a literary value at variance with the social values and religious beliefs of the ordinary people (the Roman Catholic majority) although it was precisely to them that he turned to fuel his own ideals. As Seán O'Faoláin saw the case:

> It was [Yeats's] immense good fortune to be born into an Ireland where that traditional memory still flourished, and so to see her as an ancient land, old as Judaea and Egypt, with an ancient soul and an ancient aura, to find in her people a great dignity and a great simplicity and a great sense of wonder. Out of it all he created an aesthetic based on the instinctive life of the soul and the passionate life of the body as against such destructive things as cold character and sterile knowledge that generalises all spontaneous life away into obstructions.[19]

Hence the folklore of the peasantry might be seen as the remnant of ancient wisdom and heroic passions that stood in some relation to the oldest traditions of the Aryan peoples. In this he was encouraged by his collaborator Lady Gregory: 'If [she] had not said when we passed an old man in the woods, "That man may know the secret of the ages", I might never have talked with Shri Purohit Swāmi or made him translate his Master's travels in Tibet'.[20] It hardly mattered that maintaining a reservoir of myth and folklore for revivalists to draw on would involve the perpetuation of superstitious terrors in the Irish countryside (about which Joyce was equally touchy and derisive in *A Portrait of the Artist*); and it was with some surprise that Yeats found himself pilloried in the *Cork Examiner* in March 1895 when a peasant woman was found to have been burnt to death by a husband who believed she was a changeling.[21] In his 'General Introduction' – composed at much the same time as 'The Statues' – Yeats quoted Arnold Toynbee's view of the Irish, whom the latter regarded as originating in a race of nomad-warriors quite distinct from the settled peoples who created urban civilization. Yet all has changed: '[m]odern Ireland', he wrote, 'has made up her mind, in our generation, to find her level as a willing inmate in our workaday world'.[22] This was the antipode of the ideal of Irishness that Yeats had tried to foster, and it was in these circumstances that he chose Patrick Pearse as the modern embodiment of the irrational forces that governed Irish society in more heroic days.

In identifying Pearse as a member of the 'ancient sect' of Ireland rather than the herald of a modern country, Yeats was not – as some readings suggest – casting him in the character of an enlightened nation-builder (a role for which he was tolerably well-suited in his actual character as a political thinker and a school-master). Instead, Yeats arranged the forces of his poem in such a way that Pearse is aligned not with the Pythagorean quantities of harmony and reason but with the 'vague Asiatic immensities' of pre-Hellenic despotism. In the emotional scheme of the poem he represents heroic 'passion' of the sort associated with Cuchulain in the first instance. Only secondarily – through his antithetical self – does he bring on the 'calculation, number, measurement' which effect the completion of his partial nature in accordance with Yeats's theory of masks and anti-selves (outlined in *A Vision*), making it possible for an Irish state to come into existence. Yeats's poem 'The Statues' thus speaks centrally of a new order based on irrationality transforming under the pressure of tragic action into rationality and new nationhood: race converting into state-ship but statehood of a kind that ought still to bear the memory of its origins in the anterior condition of the nomad-warrior of ancient Ireland. That was to be the legacy of the Irish literary revival and the reason why Yeats should feel warranted in asking the question of his own play *Cathleen Ni Houlihan* in 'The Man and the Echo': 'did that play of mine send out / Certain men the English shot?' (*CP*, p. 393.) In its refusal of spiritless democracy and its adumbration of atavistic forces in Irish historical memory, *Cathleen Ni Houlihan* – his play of April 1902 on the 1798 Rebellion – did just that, as Pearse and the other executed leaders inveterately showed by quoting its best-known lines in their last words and final letters, as so many of them did, but chiefly the mesmerizing lines: 'They shall be remembered forever / They shall be alive for ever, / They shall be speaking for ever, / The people shall hear them for ever.'[23]

At the heart of 'The Statues' stands an anomalous and – indeed – a contra-dictory application of the idea of 'darkness' as it figures in the phrase 'our proper dark'. The Druids are not kindred to the Greek philosophers nor is their version of literary culture – each letter a pantheistic alloy of sound and symbol identified with a type of tree in Ireland – identical with the Pythagorean cult of universal numbers. Image and number are classically opposed, yet Yeats sees the two orders as complementary and incomplete without the other. Hence Phidias's statues, in the poem, are said to possess 'proportion' while chronically lacking 'character' – as boys and girls, 'pale from imagined love', well know. It is 'boys and girls' of this type who start revolutions in the knowledge that 'passion could bring character enough' (to quote the poem again); and it is they who vivify a purely geometric idea of the kind associated with the name of Pythagoras by pressing their 'live lips' against the statues themselves – much as Pygmalion did with *his* statue in the Greek myth. For Yeats the Irish revolution participated in the nature of a wider process of millennial destruction and renewal which he envisaged famously in 'The Second Coming' as some 'rough beast' *slouching* 'towards Bethlehem to be born'. (*CP*, p. 210) Yeats's Pearse is no rational exponent of republican democracy tipped by strategy or accident into revolutionary violence but – as Terence Brown has recently reminded us – 'a magus who summoned a ghost out of the racial dark'.[24]

In poem after poem Yeats elaborated upon this idea with increasing relish. For him Pearse became the harbinger of a return of mythological forces under the form of modern violence; a Celtic avatar no less than a Fenian revolutionary.

> And yet who knows what's yet to come?
> For Patrick Pearse had said
> That in every generation
> Must Ireland's blood be shed.
> *From mountain to mountain the fierce horsemen ride.*
> ('Three Songs to One Burden, III'; *CP*, p. 374)

What Yeats sees spreading out from the imaginative drama of the Easter Rising is something like the overthrow of the Roman empire, plunging the world – as he remarks elsewhere – into 'a fabulous formless darkness'.[25] In that benighted state, he tells us, 'we are lost amid alien intellects, near but incomprehensible, more incomprehensible than the most distant stars.'[26] Here, indeed, he might be talking of the Anglo-Irish – men such as Henry Middleton in the first 'song' of this cycle – surrounded in their social twilight by the atavistic passions in nationalist Ireland.[27] Of course, the 'we' in that last sentence is much more like the empirical subject of contemporary British life than the national community denoted by 'We Irish' in 'The Statues'. In that poem – by contrast with this metropolitan man of letters who writes much of the prose – Yeats adopts the persona of a latter-day Irish druid-philosopher-bard in touch with supernatural sources of poetry and possessed of a revolutionary ardour for national independence while keeping the 'cold, logical intellect' of Bishop Berkeley – as he called it in *King of the Great Clock Tower* (1934) – strictly at bay.[28]

There is room here to consider a minute antithesis: for, since 'formless spawning fury' in 'The Statues' rhymes so well with the 'formless dark' of *Wheels and Butterflies*, then the 'proper dark' attributed to the Irish must be of a different sort from that which is merely formless. Hence we recognize in the two versions of the term a distinction between that kind of 'darkness' which is purely moribund and destructive and another – nearer to the Irish kind – which consists in passionate and instinctive knowledge. To be generative in the sense intended by Yeats, 'our proper dark' certainly must contain some forms within itself – forms such as the emblematic person of Cuchulain. And so it does. In his 'General Introduction', Yeats tells us that 'behind all Irish history hangs a great tapestry' and that 'nobody looking at its dim folds can say where Christianity begins and Druidism ends.'[29] It is against this background of merging pagan and Christian, ancient and modern, that he places Pearse: 'in the imagination of Pearse and his fellow soldiers the Sacrifice of the Mass had found the Red Branch in the tapestry.'[30] They found, in other words, their heroic inspiration in figures such as Diarmuid, Conchobar and Cuchulain. Another writer might say that the discovery was essentially fictive but Yeats has it that the spirits of the ancient heroes were *actually* present: Cuchulain 'stalked through the Post Office' when Patrick Pearse summoned him – to which his antithetical self, modern being at the opposite pole from such 'vague immensities', makes its *reply*. In all of this, 'The Statues' speaks of real presences, of true revenants and ghosts come from the past into our own time. (George Steiner's last work, *Real Presences*, illuminates this theme especially in the hermeneutic question that he poses, 'Is there anything real *in* what we say?')

In prose writings of the period, Yeats repeatedly made use of 'dark' and 'darkness' as terms for a generative power or its opposite in an antithetical arrangement of natural forces. In annotations to the 1929 edition of *The Winding Stair*, he wrote of one poem, 'I have symbolised a woman's love as the struggle of the darkness to keep the sun from rising from its earthly bed.'[31] Comparably, in the closing remarks of his profoundly undiplomatic 'General Introduction', he looks upon the contemporary form of Irish statehood as it appeared to him on the main street of the capital (a scene of some humiliation from the aesthetic standpoint):

> When I stand on O'Connell Street … where modern heterogeneity has taken physical form, a vague hatred comes up out of *my own dark* and I am certain that wherever in Europe there are minds strong enough to lead others the same vague hatred will have issued in violence and imposed some kind of rule of kindred. I cannot know the nature of that rule, for its opposite fills the light; all I can do to bring it nearer is to intensify my hatred.[32] [My emphasis.]

'My own dark': here corresponds with some exactitude to the coinage 'our proper dark' in 'The Statues' and probably talks to it. By it, Yeats surely meant that the racial consciousness of the Irish, with its promise of a dark illumination at the polar extreme from the commercial illuminations of Western civilization has failed – as Toynbee's sentence bears witness – and that he must now turn to yet darker sources of irrationalism for the 'Unity of Being' that he seeks. Hence his opening assertion that he never had been an Irish nationalist except for 'passing reasons' as he gives himself increasingly to European Fascism.[33]

Yet Ireland had provided Yeats with a context in which he could experience the interfusion of the natural and the supernatural, and indeed – at one point in its political history – the domination of the social order by atavistic, supernatural forces, sustained by the 'passion' of the revolutionaries. To some extent everyone in Ireland has experienced the upsurge of the atavistic in modern times – not so much through the persistence of 'fairy faith' or the literary revival of ancient legends as through the presence and activity of Irish nationalism both in its benign and its malignant forms. The point can be illustrated conveniently with reference to a literary dialogue between Seamus Deane and Seamus Heaney in 1977 during the course of which the former took issue with Conor Cruise O'Brien, a virulent critic of the Provisional IRA and the tradition of physical force republicanism they stood for: 'But surely', argued Deane, 'this very clarity of O'Brien's position is just what is most objectionable. ... In other words, is not his humanism here being used as an excuse to rid Ireland of the atavisms which gave it life even though the life itself may be in some ways brutal?'[34] Perhaps so – but in any case it greatly amplifies our appreciation of the real impact of the Irish literary revival to find that its spiritualized version of Irish national history could connect so powerfully with the political turbulence of the living Irish world so near to our own time. ('Atavism, sheer bloody atavism', was what Gerry Fitt, leader of the SDLP, said spontaneously on television in response to the Omagh Bombing in August 1998.)

III

In considering Yeats's way of engaging with the distinct but intersecting questions of individual and national spirit, it is impossible to infer anything like a definite system – other, that is, than the geometric schema of personal and historical phases which he set out in the lunar diagrams of A Vision. His own attempts at cosmological theory are generally unprepossessing as when, in the revised edition of A Vision he wrote that he regards the 'circuits of sun and moon ... as stylistic arrangements of experience comparable to the cubes in the drawing of Wyndam Lewis and the ovoid's in the sculpture of Brancusi', adding with some éclat in the closing sentence: 'they have helped me to hold in a single thought reality and justice.'[35] The effect of this disclosure on Louis MacNeice was to make him abandon any hope of finding real philosophy in *any* part of Yeats and to cast doubt on the poet's motives and capacity for the intellectual task that he had undertaken – as distinct, that is, from the talent required for the poetry he created in relation to those ideas. Yeats, he further thought, 'lack[ed] intuitive knowledge of people', a point confirmed by Mrs Yeats. Reflecting on the 'classification of human types' which comprises the business of *A Vision*, MacNeice noted that the elder poet 'declined to accept explanations offered by professional psychologists' on the peculiar premise that '[i]f life is to be conditioned by accidents, the accidents must be supernatural.'[36]

F.R. Leavis was likewise unconvinced by the intellectual performance, writing that '[i]t is characteristic of Yeats to have no centre of unity, and to have been unable to find one', the lack being most 'apparent in his solemn propoundings about the Mask and the Anti-Self, and in the related schematic elaborations.'[37] And Monk Gibbon, a (perhaps warrantably) embittered contemporary in Ireland, argued that Yeats was not a mystic at all. 'The mystic believes that there is some complete pattern, some Whole into which all the parts fit ... Yeats's mind moved, rather, amid isolated phantasmagorias, or at least in the same way that the mind moves in sleep, with sudden intense perception emerging from a background of vague cloud. It was intentionally undisciplined.'[38] Denis Donoghue, a highly sympathetic critic (also Irish), makes the same point in a more courteous fashion: 'In fact, strictly speaking magic in Yeats's later work served only the same purpose as the faery-islands in the early poems – to fence off an area of private ground within which his Spirit might roam at will.'[39] It may be, therefore, that Seamus Heaney's 'set question to the ghost of W.B. Yeats' on the location of the spirit is addressed to the wrong authority after all. That said, it would be a great mistake to overlook the visionary power of a poem such as 'Meru' in the 'Philosophical Songs'.

Almost uniquely among Yeats's writings it offers a version of mystical insight which takes the reader beyond the antithetical into the *néant*. While recognizably a poem in the tradition of Shelley's 'Ozymandias', it incorporates the intuition that culture and thought are fundamentally groundless in a manner quite distinct from the epithet 'boundless and bare' in Shelley's vision of ruin. Yeats 'desolation of reality' is the antithesis of philosophy; it is the zero-point of cultural annihilation, setting all the postulates and theories about poetry and race, literature and nation that he so warmly entertained at naught:

XII. *Meru*
Civilisation is hooped together, brought
Under a rule, under the semblance of peace
By manifold illusion; but man's life is thought,
And he, despite his terror, cannot cease
Ravening through century after century,
Ravening, raging, and uprooting that he may come
Into the desolation of reality[.]

(*CP*, p. 333)

This poem, dated 1934, offers the view that all thought necessarily debouches into nothingness and, if it suspends the question whether that nothingness is Buddhistic, existential or simply nihilistic, it possesses the special authority of one who has contemplated through a lifetime the ruin of class, caste, country houses, race and family in the Ireland all around him. Terence Brown has offered a fine appraisal of the poem 'Meru' in the course of his remarks on 'late Yeatsian orientalism' in general: 'To western ways of thought such ascetic intensity is distinctly unappealing and can be difficult to distinguish from nihilistic life-denial. And in Yeats's late poetry the way of the East can indeed seem the way of terrifying negation that leads to the knowledge that reality has its basis in non-being.'[40] And here he aptly quotes from 'The Statues': 'In this mood the East for Yeats in his last years is the Buddha, whose "empty eye-balls knew / That knowledge increases unreality, that / Mirror on mirror mirrored all the show" ' before offering a paraphrase of 'Meru', drawing up a line from Yeats's great poem 'The Tower': 'Eastern thought intensified his growing fear, as death approached, that there was nothing behind the 'superhuman mirror / Resembling dream' that man had made to disguise from himself the truth of nihilism from 'the desolation of reality'.[41] The wonder is that Yeats's religious, magical and mystical concern with self, friends and nation map on to a dangerously antagonist apprehension of nothingness – strictly cancelling the other idea with such a degree of exactitude (simultaneous and coterminous) that only a profoundly self-contradictory conception of the mind's structure can adequately comprehend them. For such a structure his own terms were the 'antithetical self', or *principle*, and 'The Mask'.

It might be said that much of the power of Yeats's poetry and thought arose from his personal capacity to yoke contradictory ideas together, belief and unbelief subsisting in such a way that both the archaic and the modern, the fanciful and the philosophic, find expression in his poems. Where does the spirit live? It is not demeaning, in the light of this exploration of his convictions, to say that the 'monuments of unageing intellect' are less philosophical ideas than imaginative works – poems, in short; and if that seems a solipsistic formula it is no more so than the antithesis between the Happy Shepherd and the Sad Shepherd with whose songs the *Collected Poems* begins. Both make use of a 'twisted, echoing shell' – the symbol of lyric art – but where one receives comfort from the shell's 'melodious guile' the other hears only its 'inarticulate moan' (*CP*, pp. 8, 9). In this it reflects the conundrum of modernity, the *significant* and the *arbitrary* confronting each other with an air of mutual exclusion while lacking the capacity to separate from the Hegelian clinch in which we meet them – a world that is all plenitude and all vacuity whichever way we turn. In such a world, as 'The Second Coming' avers, the best 'lack all conviction' and the worst 'are full of passionate intensity' – an observation that has pertinence as much today, in the age of global terrorism, as during the rise of Fascism.[42] What we take from it, in a Yeatsian context, is that scepticism and conviction are antithetical states of mind which are necessary to each other and actually subsisted together in the poet's mind.

Yet 'Meru' is more predicative than that as regards the condition of the modern world in as much as it speaks of all social institutions as illusory and of the human intellect as a 'ravening' thing which has now torn down all comfortable illusions, with the effect of facing what he calls in a darkly ringing phrase 'the desolation of reality' in a *vis-à-vis* that leaves us no less naked than the Buddhist monk or the king in Shakespeare's play unhoused upon a blasted heath. The question is, if Yeats can offer such a view of how we stand at the end of history, how may he also regard the universe as a place in which courage and grace and visionary thought have any part to play? Surely his desolation in 'Meru' is no less bleak than in any other poet of the Modernist movement – in the place of honour as chief doom-monger, perhaps, the Anglo-American doyen of cultural doom and gloom (and later escapist into High Anglicanism), Thomas Stearns Eliot.

IV

Faced with the difference between Yeats and his Anglo-American contemporaries, Eliot wrote: 'The difference between his [Yeats's] world and ours is so complete as to seem almost a physiological variety, different nerves and sense. It is, therefore, allowable to imagine that the difference is not only personal but national.'[43] W.H. Auden had the same idea when he posed the question how the Irish poet could call himself one of 'the last romantics' when all the world besides was caught up in all the -isms of a materialist outlook (futurism, communism, nihilism):

> ... mad Ireland hurt you into poetry.
> Now Ireland has her madness and her weather still,
> For poetry makes nothing happen: it survives
> In the valley of its saying ... [44]

This account has the advantage that it is attestably Yeats's own in 'Remorse for Intemperate Speech' where he writes 'Out of Ireland have we come / Great hatred, little room / Maimed us at the start / I carry from my mother's womb / A fanatic heart.' (CP, p. 287) Yet even if Auden had occasion to berate Yeats's *Oxford Book of Modern Verse* in 1936 as the 'most deplorable [anthology] ever issued ... under the imprint of ... the Clarendon Press', he ultimately forgave him for his 'feudal mentality' and his 'belief in fairies' on the grounds that 'art is a product of history, not a cause.'[45] This act of absolution required some Marxist gymnastics as regards the nature of poetry: 'Unlike some products – technical inventions, for instance – it does not re-enter history as an effective agent, so that the question whether [it] should or should not be propaganda is unreal.'[46] Relatedly, in spite of Yeats's fascistic leanings, he argued that the Irish poet shows himself to be 'one of us' through his increasingly modern way of engaging in 'the field of language': 'However false or undemocratic [Yeats's] ideas, his diction shows a continuous evolution towards what one might call the true democratic style. The social virtues of a real democracy are brotherhood and intelligence, and the parallel linguistic virtues are strength and clarity.'[47]

Unfortunately, however, the record of Yeats's thinking on the language question is almost diametrically at odds with Auden's account of it: 'Because I need a passionate syntax for passionate subject-matter I compel myself to accept those traditional metres that have developed with the language. Ezra Pound, Turner, Lawrence wrote admirable free verse, I could not. I would lose myself, become joyless like those mad old women.'[48] Needless to say, the language mentioned here is Gaelic and the 'mad old women' those speakers whom he met with in the West of Ireland. In these terms, at any rate, Yeats was not going to be easily assimilated to modernity and nor, for that matter, were others of his nation – if only for the reason that their metaphysical assumptions were significantly at odds with those of the secularized culture which formed so much of their contemporary English language and almost all of their posthumous audience. Otherwise stated, Ireland in the twentieth century embraced romantic nationalism largely sustained by Roman Catholic metaphysics – though not in Yeats's case – and with it, made the plea that the island-nation was the repository and last bastion of spirituality in the western world. More than purely political arguments, this plea served in fact as the justification and alibi for independence and though the nation that it valorized by such means was always apt to speak about the 'hemiplegia of emigration' it never on the whole found it tempting to address the larger philosophical condition which Yeats denominated as 'the desolation of reality' in 1934.

For the Irish nationalists of the revolutionary generation Ireland was a numinous realm as well as an island-nation and the view that Ireland had preserved the spiritual outlook that industrial England had trampled under-foot was endemic to the men and women who set their mark on its modern culture. In various – and sometimes mutually exclusive ways – such figures as George ('Æ') Russell and Douglas Hyde, D.P. Moran, and Patrick Pearse were on their guard against the intellectual depredations of English civilization (or 'syphilistation', as the Citizen calls it in *Ulysses*). This belief found its most ardent – and comical – expression when Patrick Pearse professed:

> The Gael is not like other men ... a destiny more glorious than that of Rome, more glorious than that of Britain awaits him, to become the saviour of idealism in modern intellectual and social life, the regenerator and rejuve-nator of the literature of the world, the instructor of nations, the preacher of the gospel of nature-worship, God-worship – such, Mr Chairman, is the destiny of the Gael.[49]

Neither, though Pearse called Yeats 'a third-rate English poet' about this time, was the latter's view entirely different. Thus, in 1899, he wrote of Irish peas-ants: 'The children of the poor and simple learn from their unbroken religious faith, and from their traditional beliefs, and from the hardness of their lives that this world is nothing, and that a spiritual world, where all dreams come true, is everything; and therefore the poor and simple are that imperfection whose perfection is genius.'[50] At about the same time he affirmed: 'I believe that the renewal of belief which is the great movement of our time will more and more liberate the arts from "their age" and ... that all will ... be more and more convinced that it is a revelation of hidden life, and ... the only means of conversing with eternity left to man on earth.'[51]

That was *not* the stuff of the liberal humanism that dominated English letters at that date – nor pragmatic imperialism, and least of all the philosoph-ical nihilism which would emerge as the dominant temper of twentieth-century Europe after the devastation of two world wars. It is Yeats's anomalous distinc-tion that he belongs so largely to the Irish romantic movement while, at the same time, holding his place as a spokesman for the idea of a 'decentred' polit-ical world, spinning out of control: 'Things fall apart; the centre cannot hold; / Mere anarchy is loosed upon the world' (*CP*, p. 211). In 1936 he professed to believe that this was a genuine prefiguring of the rise of European Fascism, arrived at in excited reverie 'some sixteen or seventeen years ago'.[52] In that interpretation 'The Second Coming' is quite literally a record of a prophetic moment rather than the utterance of a political pundit availing of Ireland's marginal location to identify a great historical shift that those nearer to hand cannot see by reason of too-close proximity to the 'cruelty of governments' in their own and neighbouring lands.[53] According to Conor Cruise O'Brien this was actually an utterance of 'the true Yeats ... watch[ing] bitterly or sardonically, a game he had no chance of playing'[54] – as if to say that he relished the spectacle of political violence that was no longer available in contemporary Ireland of the early 1930s. O'Brien tellingly notes that '[Yeats's] greatest poetry was written near the end of his life when his ideas were at their most sinister', and that this tendency connects with the rise of Fascism elsewhere than in Ireland, while his support for General O'Duffy's Blueshirts in the same period suggests that his 'horror' at the growing violence is more ambiguous than an indulgent reading of the poem in long retrospect might suggest.

What 'The Second Coming' conveys, above all, is the impression that Yeats's mind was focused on epochal shifts in the history of thought far beyond the scope of Irish romantic nationalism in the received sense. Here we face the ultimate irony of Yeats's belief-system: mysticism brings him to a position identical with nihilism; his metaphysics leads him to predicate the deepest apprehensions of agnosticism; his Kabbalah turns into a *néant* worthy of the most godless existentialist. In summary, it might be said that Yeats's romanticism is modernism by other means.

NOTES

1. *Collected Poems of W.B. Yeats* (London 1950), p. 398. Henceforth CP.
2. T.S. Eliot, 'Tradition and the Individual Talent', in *Collected Essays* (New York 1964), p. 9.
3. *Autobiographies* (London 1955), pp. 115–6.
4. 'General Introduction' [1937], rep. in *Essay & Introductions* (London 1961), p. 518. Yeats's fullest statement on 'Unity of Being' is to be found in *Autobiographies* (London 1955), p. 190.
5. A.N. Jeffares has called the third section of 'The Tower' – from which these lines come – Yeats's profession of faith. See *W.B. Yeats: A New Biography* (London 1988), p. 279.
6. *W.B. Yeats: Short Fiction*, ed. George J. Watson (Harmondsworth 1995), pp. 201–11; here p. 206.
7. Letter of 14 June 1915; quoted in Richard Ellmann, *Yeats: The Man and the Masks* [1948] (Oxford 1979), p. 213.
8. See 'Magic' [1901], in *Essays and Introductions* (London 1961), p. 28.
9. *Essays & Introductions* (1961), p. 526.

10. *The Works of William Blake* [...] *Poetic, Symbolic, and Critical Edition* [...] by Edwin John Ellis [...] and William Butler Yeats, 3 vols. (London 1893), Vol. 1, p. 240.

11. *Ibid.* pp. 240–1.

12. 'Four Years – 1887–1891', in *Autobiographies* (London 1955), p. 191.

13. 'Hodos Chameliontos', in *ibid.* p. 263.

14. 'Browning', in *Boston Pilot* (22 Feb. 1890), rep. in Yeats, *Letters to the New Island* (New York 1934), p. 104.

15. 'General Introduction to My Work' [1937], in *Essays and Introductions* (1961), p. 518. The 'amber' simile was the property of John Eglinton.

16. Berkeley wrote in his *Philosophical Commentaries* (ed. A.A. Luce, 1944): 'We Irish cannot attain to these truths' [Entry 392]. Yeats harped on this in his Preface to Mario Rossi and Joseph Hone's *George Berkeley* (1931), making much of the distance Berkeley felt from the philosophers of the 'neighbouring nation'. Professor Luce did not think that anything should be made of Berkeley's apparent nationalism à la Yeats, but Denis Donoghue considers that Berkeley, like Yeats, 'believed in something called the Irish intellect'. (See Yeats, 'Bishop Berkeley', in *Essays and Introductions*, 1961, p. 396, and his prefatory notes to *King of the Great Clock Tower* (1934), Sect. II; also Donoghue, *We Irish: Essays in Irish Literature and Society* (Brighton 1986), p. 6.

17. Viz., 'That we in coming days may be / Still the indomitable Irishry' ('Under Ben Bulben'), *CP*, p. 400. Yeats correspondingly argues that certain characteristics of the 'Irishry' may 'grow in importance in the future' in his 'General Introduction to My Works' (*Essays and Introductions*, 1961), p. 517.

18. *Idem.*

19. Seán O'Faoláin, *The Irish* (Harmondsworth 1947), p. 21.

20. 'General Introduction' (1961), p. 519.

21. See Hubert Butler, 'The Eggman and the Fairies' in *Escape from the Anthill* (Dublin 1985) and Geneviève Brennan, 'Yeats, Clodd, *Scatalogic Rites* and the Clonmel Witch Burning', in *Yeats Annual* No. 4 (1986). A full-length study of the Bridget Cleary affair and a fiction-treatment have been written by Angela Bourke and Carlo Gébler respectively.

22. *Essays and Introductions* (1961), p. 527. Yeats quotes further from Toynbee: 'Jewry and Irishry will each fit into its own tiny niche' (*idem*).

23. *Collected Plays* (London 1960), p. 86.

24. 'Celticism and the Occult', in *Celticism*, ed. Terence Brown (Amsterdam 1996), p. 221.

25. *Wheels and Butterflies* (London 1934), pp. 77–8. Yeats purports to quote an anonymous philosopher living at the time.

26. *Idem.*

27. See 'Three Songs to One Burden, II', in *Collected Poems* (1950), pp. 372–3.

28. *King of the Great Clock Tower* (1934), Sect. II; cited in A.N. Jeffares, *A New Commentary on the Poems of W.B. Yeats* [1968] (London 1984), p. 333.

29. 'General Introduction to My Work', 1937; rep. in *Essays and Introductions* (1961), p. 513–4.

30. *Ibid.* p. 515.

31. See Jeffares, *op. cit.* (1984), p. 326.

32. 'General Introduction', in *Essays and Introductions* (1961), p. 526.

33. *Idem.*

34. Seamus Deane, 'Interview with Heaney', in *The Crane Bag*, 1, 1 (1977), pp. 61–72.

35. *A Vision* [corrected edn] [1928] (London 1962), p. 25.

36. Louis MacNeice, *The Poetry of W.B. Yeats* (London 1941), p. 115.

37. Seamus Deane, 'The Problem and the Challenge', in *Revaluation: Tradition and Development in English Poetry* [1936] (London 1972), p. 75.

38. Monk Gibbon, *The Masterpiece and the Man, Yeats As I Knew Him* (1959), p. 128.

39. Denis Donoghue, 'Yeats and Modern Poetry: An Introduction', *The Integrity of Yeats* (Cork 1964), pp. 12–13.

40. Terence Brown, *The Life of W.B. Yeats: A Critical Biography* (Dublin 1999), pp. 353–4.

41. *Idem.*

42. *Ibid.* p. 211.

43. T.S. Eliot, Reviewing Yeats in *The Athenaeum* (4 July 1919), p. 552; quoted in Seamus Deane, *Heroic Styles: The Tradition of an Idea* [Field Day Pamphlets, No. 4] (Derry 1984), p. 17.

44. W.H. Auden, 'In Memory of W.B. Yeats', in *Collected Poems of W.H. Auden* [1976] (London 1994), p. 47.

45. Auden, 'The Public Versus the Late Mr. William Butler Yeats', in *Partisan Review*, 6, 3, Spring 1939, p. 47; rep. in *The English Auden*, ed. Edward Mendelson (London 1977); cited in Lucy McDiarmid, *Saving Civilisation*, 1984, p. xiii.

46. Auden, *ibid.* p. 51; McDiarmid, *op. cit.* pp. xiii-iv.

47. Auden, *idem*; McDiarmid, *op. cit.* p. 95.

48. 'General Introduction to My Work' (1937), Pt III; rep. in *Essays and Introductions* (1961), pp. 521–3.

49. Patrick Pearse, Address L. & H. [UCD], in *Collected Works, Political Writings and Speeches*, ed. Desmond Ryan (Dublin 1924), p. 221.

50. 'The Literary Movement in Ireland', in *North American Review* (Dec. 1899); revised in Lady Gregory's *Ideals in Ireland*, 1901 and reprinted from the original in John Frayne (ed.), *Uncollected Prose*, Vol. 2 (London 1975), pp. 184–96; p. 191.

51. Yeats's contribution to *Literary Ideals in Ireland*, ed. John Eglinton (1899); quoted in Louis MacNeice, *W.B. Yeats* (Oxford 1944), p. 84.

52. Letter to Ethel Mannin of 7 April 1936; quoted in Ellmann, *The Identity of Yeats* (London 1948), p. 282.

53. Letter to Mannin, in Ellmann, *op. cit.* p. 211.

54. *Passion and Cunning and Other Essays* (New York 1988), 'Some Stray Personal thoughts on Yeats and Music', p. 44.

W.B. Yeats's Poetry of Violence

CAROLYN MASEL

One aspect of Yeats's poetry that continues to impress us is its depiction of the heroic. Courage and passion are highly valued, and those who possess them – including the singing self – are celebrated at the centre of his universe. Yeats's contribution to modern poetry seems distinctive in this respect: we do not think of Wallace Stevens or T.S. Eliot in terms of heroic self-representation, and Pound's version of the heroic is a form of pastiche. However, as soon as we begin to reflect on the nature of the heroic in Yeats's poetry, we are compelled to confront the violence that appears to be an intrinsic part of it. This aspect of his work can seem quite foreign to readers encountering Yeats for the first time. Given current trends in pedagogy in Australia, the likelihood of encountering Yeats's most accessible poems and then proceeding to a more intensive study seems much reduced for the present generation, and this raises the prospect of Yeats, with his special meanings, including the various meanings of violence, being consigned to be read only by an informed coterie. In order to avoid this, it seems as well to confront his unfamiliarity directly. It has seemed pertinent, too, to revisit Yeats's treatment of violence at the present time, when it seems more than ever desirable to be level-headed in one's responses to violent events ostensibly precipitated by differences in ideology.

Yeats himself was, of course, surrounded – spatially and temporally – by large-scale military conflicts and was intensely aware of his non-combatant status (*The Collected Works of W.B.Yeats, Vol 1: The Poems,* ed. Richard J.

Finneran, 2nd edn [New York 1997], pp. 208, 242 [hereafter CW]). He might have felt distant from the allegiances of World War I (CW, p. 156), but the smaller-scale event that precipitated his most memorable poetry, the Easter Rising, at first shocked and overwhelmed him (Marjorie G. Perloff, '"Easter, 1916": Yeats's First World War Poem', The Oxford Handbook of British War Poetry, ed. Tim Kendall [Oxford 2007], pp. 227–41 [hereafter Perloff]). As a member of the Irish Republican Brotherhood, and later, as a Senator for the Irish Free State, he was actively involved in political negotiations while surrounded by turmoil and violence, and even in the last year of his life he discussed 'intensively' with his son the international situation that would result in the outbreak of World War II (R.F. Foster, W.B. Yeats: A Life, Vol. II, The Arch-Poet 1915–1939 [Oxford 2003], p. 623). Since that time, we have had further opportunity to reflect on supermen, political causes and heroes, as well as new manifestations of the horrors of which the human imagination is capable. We have had cause to lose faith in the words 'never again', perceiving patterns of violence in history that astonish and appal us. We have been enlisted, in our homes, as witnesses of armed conflict and its bloody results, and we bear the marks of having done so. Our intervening violent history has made it more difficult for a contemporary readership to arrive at an understanding of what Yeats meant by his imagery of violence, beyond noting that violence was something he valorized but was also horrified by.

Rather than trace Yeats's conception of violence chronologically, I want to begin by thinking about it thematically. I have chosen this strategy as one likely to engage students who might be impatient with the detail of Yeats's personal history as it intersects with wider historical conditions. There are three parts to this study of Yeats's treatment of violence. I begin with a brief consideration of the sheer physicality of violence; then I consider violence as occupying a spectrum between two poles, unmeaning and super-saturated meaningfulness, after which I examine the connection of violence to the Great House in Yeats's conception of it. I will conclude with some brief contextual remarks about Yeats's quest for eternity, so as to transcend the chaotic violence he has witnessed, and his setting aside of the eternal in order to celebrate a liberated heroic stance, in full knowledge of its transience.

It seems worth beginning with the simple observation that Yeats's conception of violence is grounded in the physical; it is overwhelmingly a thing of the body rather than the mind. This means that, for Yeats, violence is gendered; that is, violence is manifested differently by differently gendered characters. Female characters convey a bodily memory of violence, whether experiencing or inflicting it. So that when Crazy Jane tells the bishop that 'nothing can be sole or whole / That has not been rent' (CW, p. 264), her wisdom is grounded in her own experience of being torn asunder; her stiffness and pride in the pursuit of love are invariably compromised by the chaos of sexuality. Since her wisdom is of the body, she pledges herself to physical experience rather than to the Bishop's recommendation to attend to her soul. In her world, passion, whether love or hatred, is so intense that it can bring about violent death; sexual ecstasy is tantamount to being strangled or stabbed: the experience of 'Love is like the lion's tooth' (CW, pp. 264–5). Similarly, the experience of the young man who breaks his heart in two through the force of his pledge of undying love knows that 'Out of a desolate source / Love leaps upon its course' (CW, p. 267). His knowledge is as paradoxical in its expression as any declaration by Crazy Jane, but it lacks the extremes of affect that characterize her; he tends rather to be ruled by 'noble rage' (CW, p. 265).

The violence associated with sexual passion gets its most extended treatment in 'Her Vision in the Wood'. The speaker of that poem, furious at being 'Too old for a man's love', tears her body with her fingernails, 'that its wine might cover / Whatever could recall the lip of lover' (CW, p. 279). This action brings on a vision of a man, fatally wounded by a beast, attended by singing, grief-stricken young women, a scene reminiscent in some respects of the death of Adonis. Smitten with the contrast between the young people and herself, which they will never have to think about, being creatures in a transient vision, the elderly speaker curses the dying man. Then it seems 'that beast-torn wreck' turns and recognizes her – and, as she falls, shrieking, she recognizes the man as 'my heart's victim and its torturer', the lover of her dreams mortally wounded by the beast who is her own self. Eros and lethal violence are conjoined in this vision.

In its context in The Tower, 'Leda and the Swan' is another poem about the genealogy of violence, yet perhaps it gains something from being included in a discussion of poems about gendered physical violence. The final question of whether Leda was invested with the prophetic knowledge of the consequences of her rape is the focus of virtually every reading – hardly surprisingly, since it launches Yeats's conception of the gyres of history. This question is, as William Johnsen notes, present in every version of the poem, as if Yeats was hopeful of an answer (William Johnsen, 'Textual/Sexual politics in Yeats's "Leda and the Swan"', Yeats and Postmodernism, ed. Leonard Orr [Syracuse 1991], p. 83 [hereafter Johnsen]). However, it cannot be answered in the terms in which Yeats has asked it, for he is no more interested in Leda's having a separate history before her rape by the god than Zeus is. The poem's final question reifies divine power rather than questioning what Leda might know in any conception of her as a genuine 'other' (Johnsen, pp. 87–8). Johnsen's comments go some way toward accounting for the queasiness with which one responds to this poem. It is not only a matter of gender, in the end, but more of a subaltern issue: it is the fact of Leda's and the swan's being co-created in a colonial (orientalist) binary, for which the final question is proffered as a possibly adequate compensation: *if we could only answer that …* To read the poem is to endure a double brutality: once as a 'verbal witness' of the rape, with its attendant visceral detail, and once as someone cold enough to ask whether, had Leda been given a seer's knowledge of the genealogy of violence in which she was an instrument, that could have gone some way to offset her misfortune.

Violence may be physical and grounded in the body, but that does not ensure that it is meaningful. Indeed, one of Yeats's enduring fears is the meaninglessness of violence, as in the 'mere anarchy' of 'The Second Coming' (*CW*, p. 189). However, highly significant violence – such as the Easter Rising – presents its own challenges for representation. Yeats's Easter Rising poems show clearly that the significance of a violent event is not intrinsic to the event, for they envision the same event in radically different ways.

'Easter 1916' (*CW*, pp. 182–4) perfectly illustrates our Janus-faced relationship to time: unable to predict how events will turn out, we can look on them with hindsight as fated or destined. The poem is an anthem celebrating a heroic destiny, but with the contrary elements woven into it of doubt and perplexed wonder. The combination remains intriguing. The leaders of the Rising are transfigured through their sacrifice; Yeats describes each one and brings each into the pattern heard in his famous refrain of blood and beauty, with its heavy trimeter. Even that 'drunken, vainglorious lout', whose misdeeds Yeats adumbrates darkly (lines 33–5), proves capable of transformation; he, too, is taken up into the larger pattern, where his individual account is set at nought, and he is eventually able to be named. By contrast, Yeats reluctantly includes that leader of the insurgency who was a friend since childhood and who he would rather had remained young, beautiful and ignorant (lines 17–23). Constance Markiewicz may be numbered in the song, but, presumably because she did not make the blood sacrifice that would accord her the full status of hero, she is not named. (Thus, arguably, Yeats repeats the English humiliation of a capable military leader.) The effect of his continuous revision is that the narrative of the poem seems at once willed, as an important but difficult story requiring a vigilant response is willed, and driven, since the poet seems impelled to sing on the emerging nation's behalf. He dares to question the necessity for both the insurgency and the executions (lines 67–8), but, both having happened, he sets about his task as poet to mark the 'terrible beauty' they have brought to birth (lines 16, 39, 80). Notwithstanding, he keeps before him, as all great poets do, an awareness of the temptation of metaphor to distance, aestheticize and lie in the face of the absoluteness of death (lines 60–6).

'The Rose Tree' seems as complete a contrast as it is possible to derive from the same series of events (*CW*, p. 185). As if in answer to the question of 'Easter 1916' whether the deaths were necessary, the premise of 'The Rose Tree' is that they were indeed crucial to the cause of Irish nationalism. All but two of the insurgents have disappeared from the poem, and their mysterious disembodied dialogue structures it. The sacrifice of their 'own red blood' for the cause of the Rose Tree's health is a quasi-medieval image of martyrdom; the cause of Irish nationalism has become inseparable from religious fervour. With its violence, death and mystery, the poem achieves so authentically the qualities of the folk ballad that it is only the additional two lines in each stanza that point to its being a poem composed by a knowing individual rather than a ballad proper. The three rhyming lines in each stanza correspond with the three stanzas that compose the poem, which are also the three movements in the argument; it is simple, yet hugely meaningful. Indeed, it is arguably among the best lyric poems in the language.

The dangers of such beauty and simplicity should be apparent in January 2015, but there is abundant evidence to suggest they are not. 'The Rose Tree' is a poem of moral certitude; its rhetoric of dialogue is not even a playing out of dialectical positions, and it is as traditionally framed and coded as any political badge or emblem. As a verbal construct, it is perfect; as a political lyric, it is potentially deadly. It is not just an emblematic commemoration of events, but an emblem of sacrifice; while Pearse and Connolly are only offering their own blood, the poem could very easily be co-opted as a model by others for future pious acts of sacrifice involving the spilling of blood. In 'Easter 1916' Yeats explores the meaning of the Rising from a personal perspective, assuming the right to do so. At the same time he shields himself from the pressure of public scrutiny, or the prospect of it, by printing only twenty-five copies of the poem, in 1917, to be circulated and discussed privately (Perloff, p. 141). 'The Rose Tree' seems, by contrast, a thoroughly public poem, since it imitates a popular form and dramatizes courage, pride and honour. Yet Yeats was also circum-spect about its publication, waiting three years and embedding it in the context of his other, more doubt-ridden, political poems in 1920. Ultimately, however, it seems clear that, despite the evident differences in the two poems, both mani-fest a similar conception of violence. At worst it is chaotic, but at best violence is capable of giving a culture its profoundest meaning, a significance sealed in sacrifice. Bloodshed does not of itself sanctify (or else Constance Markiewicz had surely been named among the revolutionary heroes of modern Ireland's violent birth). One has to achieve the absolute: be killed by enemy forces, suffer a form of secular martyrdom. Such deaths alone are sanctified and themselves sanctify 'the Holy Land of Ireland' (*CW*, p. 271).

We can detect traces of that same ambivalence toward violence in Yeats's conception of the Great House. A vision originating in his research into Irish folklore with Lady Gregory (Michael Cade-Stewart, 'Mask and Robe: Yeats's *Oxford Book of Modern Verse* (1936) and *New Poems* (1938)', *Yeats's Masks YA No. 19*, p. 231), the Great House served for many years as a kind of bastion of the imagination. His conception of it dates from the time of Cromwell, but it also has ties with eighteenth-century poets' visions (*aislings*) of similar structures (Cade-Stewart, p. 232). The Great House is everlasting in the realm of the faery, for despite the worst depredations under Cromwell, the Sidhe can restore it 'in a minute' (Cade-Stewart, p. 231). Some kinds of colonial violence are thus excluded by the Great House, or healed by the fact of its persistence, yet an older colonial violence is also intrinsic to it, since the hierarchical society that inhabits it ultimately rests on force. It might be argued (not by me) that force and violence are not the same thing – that the one is defensive and even defensible, like a nation's boundaries or the class system, while the other is aggressive and worthy of repudiation – but in the case of the Great House, we are not talking about mere force: the propensity of the upper classes to perpetrate violence upon the lower classes is so entrenched that it becomes the subject of jokes. Furthermore, worryingly, they are jokes to which we, as readers, are party.

Thus, in the second section of 'The Tower', the serving-man who could guess Mrs French's wish 'ran and with the garden shears / Clipped an insolent farmer's ears / And brought them in a little covered dish' (*CW*, p. 199, lines 30–2). One responds with amazed horror at the serving-man's literal and wrong response, which is in essence a misprision of an idiom. More exactly, one registers all at once a recognition of the pun, an understanding that the serving-man's social position is connected with his inability to rise beyond literalism, and an understanding that Mrs French has more power than she can wield safely – that she is not, after all, one of the 'lords and ladies gay / That were beaten into the clay' (*CW*, p. 335). Horror and custom come together in that 'little covered dish', with the serving-man playing Salomé or Medea.

An almost symmetrical piece of violence occurs with the man who 'was drowned in the great bog of Cloone' (*CW*, p. 199, line 48), which has to do with the banality of the rhyme with 'moon'; it is as if the drowning of the man fulfilled a kind of banal inevitability. (Man driven astray by music and alcohol tries to glimpse fabulously beautiful woman and drowns.) As we read, the social strata unfold like a click clack (Jacob's ladder), so that we can see the full social hierarchy that Yeats is exploring, as he weaves the local history of his own chosen habitation with his conception of the ethereal, indestructible Great House. In the end, the allegiance he opts for is with the class to which he already belongs: 'The people of Burke and Grattan' (CW, p. 202, line 132), which he casts, a little evasively, as somewhere between 'slaves that were spat on' and 'the tyrants that spat' (lines 130–1). Yet there is perhaps also an honesty in this nomination, and a sense of having earned, through careful and prolonged exploration, a knowledge of the culture of the place of his stewardship that for someone of his privileged position would have been entirely optional. This declaration of allegiance certainly elicits some extremely lyrical celebratory poetry, where it is difficult to distinguish the singing voice from the imagery of plenty, and where one might be tempted to forgive the naturalization of privilege encoded there, so close are the rhythms of the verse to the unfolding of the vision of the tended landscape:

> The people of Burke and of Grattan
> That gave, though free to refuse –
> Pride, like that of the morn,
> When the headlong light is loose,
> Or that of the fabulous horn,
> Or that of the sudden shower
> When all streams are dry,
> Or that of the hour
> When the swan must fix his eye
> Upon a fading gleam,
> Float out upon a long
> Last reach of glittering stream
> And there sing his last song.
>
> (lines 132–44)

The undoing of uncritical acceptance of privilege marks the Tennysonian opening of 'Meditations in Time of Civil War', which, although an earlier poem, Yeats arranged to follow 'The Tower' – as though to recapitulate, and as quickly critique, that poem's last stance. Degeneration of the inheritors is the fear of those who bequeath their wealth, a 'marvellous' yet 'empty' sea-shell replacing Homer's 'abounding glittering jet' in a Nietzschean conception of the inadequacy of degenerate man to match his divine potential (CW, p. 204, lines 12–3), to the point where 'the great-grandson of that house … 's but a mouse' (lines 23–4).

It is clear that, at this point of the poem, violence is inextricable from creativity. This is a personal ethos rather than mere feeling. Importantly, it acknowledges the origins of land ownership in violence. Artistic making is also violent. The architect and the artist who realize in stone, bronze and marble the dream of the original owner are as violent and bitter men as he (lines 17–9). Yet all reach for 'sweetness', for 'The gentleness that none there had ever known' (line 21). In Yeats, this yearning toward an opposite state is cast as antithetical dreaming; but his apparently idiosyncratic system is not as different as it might at first appear from the formulations of other poets. One thinks especially of Wallace Stevens's later articulations of a theory of desire, whereby 'The dry eucalyptus seeks god in the rainy cloud' (Stevens 405) or, even more clearly, 'It was difficult to sing in the face / Of the object. The singers had to avert themselves / Or else avert the object' (Wallace Stevens, *Collected Poetry and Prose*, ed. Frank Kermode and Joan Richardson [New York 1997], p. 325). For Yeats, quite as dialectical a thinker as Stevens, the question is whether the ease and luxury of the realized dream of sweetness will corrupt – will 'But take our greatness with our bitterness' (CW, p. 205, line 40).

The answer, since Yeats is a poet, must be couched in terms of art. From the very beginning of the poem, Yeats positions himself in the chain of inheritance as a descendant as well as a legator. Section II consists of a nested set of analogies between man of violence and artistic maker that show a line of descent: just as the man-of-arms founded and defended his home, Thoor Ballylee, so Yeats creates his 'emblems of adversity'. And just as John Milton imagined being 'seen in some high lonely Tower' (*Il Penseroso*, line 86), while depicting 'how the daemonic rage / Imagined everything', so Yeats toils on 'in some like chamber' (CW, p. 205, line 15), imagining Milton. His 'emblems of adversity' pay homage both to Milton's poems and his suffering; thus inheritance enriches, even as it is seen that a rich tradition is also a burden of responsibility.

Like Sato's sword, Yeats's conception of poetry is of something wrought and tempered (which accords entirely with his practice of revision). Considering what a sword's work is – even when it is more prized as object than instrument – and considering its placement to spur him to action with pen and paper, Yeats seems manifestly uninterested in the performative (temporal) aspect of language in comparison with its monumental capacity. The present model of language has evidently descended far from Homer's 'abounding glittering jet' (CW, p. 204, line 12). The turmoil of the Civil War, the evident violence without, provides the impulse toward monumentalism. One sets out one's genealogy and bequests as though one had control over one's destiny as one might in a civilized place. Sato's sword provides a model of inheritance – of passing on the skills of sword-making – in which degeneration of the maker is not at all evident or necessary, but since 'only an aching heart / Conceives a changeless work of art', successful sword-making down the generations eventually produces such contained and passionate yearning that a whole civilized society seems to depend on it (Brian Arkins, *Builders of My Soul: Greek and Roman Themes in Yeats* [Gerrards Cross 1990], p. 91). Huge emotional power is banked up, just as powerful forces go into the perfect forging and tempering of a ceremonial sword; however, this highly controlled power is not to be confused with violence. It is, in fact, its very antithesis.

Yeats returns once more to the consideration of his own descendants, but this move is unhelpful. He is constrained to retreat to the simple bases of his choice of the tower for his home – love and friendship. He can only build a monument to these tried sources and to himself; he cannot make any predictions about the worth, or otherwise, of his descendants. His very young children are comparable to the moor-hen's featureless 'feathered balls of soot' (*CW*, p. 208, line 11), their mettle untested. Not so the 'Falstaffian man', whom fate (in the person of Yeats via Shakespeare) has marked out for non-inheritance, and whose jokey bravura elicits a certain admiration (*CW*, p. 208, lines 1–5). The case of the 'brown Lieutenant' with his half-dressed men is more equivocal. The broken pear-tree might turn out to be an appropriate symbol, as might the unpaired moor-hen guiding her chicks on the stream. A Senator for the Irish Free State in his late fifties might still yearn for the exhilaration of committed physical action, but he knows that a complex understanding, which includes an acknowledgment of what cannot be known with any certainty, militates against it as much as physical frailty.

It is at this point (section VI) that the poem comes into contact, one senses, with an even deeper emotional source. Random violence is the real threat, to sanity as much as to life, when 'A man is killed, or a house burned' (*CW*, p. 208, line 8). In one line 'The mother birds bring grubs and flies' (line 3), but two lines later they are gone, as though Thoor Ballylee were no longer a suitable home for a family. The honey-bees, that through their orderly industry produce sweetness, are summoned to redeem the birds' absence, perhaps because they stand for a whole social order that otherwise seems unattainable, or perhaps because they once filled another strong structure that had been overwhelmed – a lion's carcase – with sweetness (Judges 14:8–9). Locked in with their uncertainties, the poet and his family find the lack of clarity maddening. The terrible fact of the 'dead young soldier in his blood' (*CW*, p. 209, line 14) breaks down the dialectic that has operated up until this point as the whole poem's predominant method. The man's violent death is not the product of its contrary, nurturing love, but instead shows the inadequacy of that thought process. While the 'fantasies' that fed the heart are contrasted with its consequent 'brutality' (lines 16–7), both are linked in their failure to connect sufficiently with the actual world. Enmities kill; fantasies that feed enmities can be dispersed, and people can become agents in that process. Again, one cannot help pausing to note how pertinent Yeats's wisdom seems to the violent consequences of ideology in the present time.

One would want to add that Yeats is not under any illusion about the difficulty of effecting this dispersal: in an extended fantasy sequence (section VII), even he all but cries 'For vengeance on the murderers of Jacques Molay' (*CW*, p. 209, line 16). In 'How Jacques Molay Got Up the Tower: Yeats and the Irish Civil War', *ELH* 50:4 (1983), pp. 763–89, http://wwwjstor.org//stable/2872926, Elizabeth Cullingford explains that Molay belonged to the Knights Templar – that is, he was a Freemason – who was accused of heresy and burned to death at the stake in 1314 (Cullingford, p. 763). She helpfully traces Yeats's familiarity with Freemasonry through his uncle George Pollexfen and points out the similarities between its practices and the practices of the Golden Dawn (Cullingford, pp. 766–7). She also links the work of masons to Yeats's project of restoring Thoor Ballylee (Cullingford, p. 772). In Yeats's fantasy of 'Monstrous familiar images', ethereal visions of class-driven strife ('In cloud-pale rags, or in lace' [line 10]) transform into civil war, where 'Trooper belabour[s] trooper, biting at arm or at face' (line 12). Images of elegant Babylonian ladies alternate with 'grip of claw' and 'innumerable clanging wings' (*CW*, p. 210, lines 31–2). Violence itself is degenerate – and so, Yeats realizes, degeneracy has nothing to do with breeding; in the end it owes much more to a communal failure of imagination. The final, most important genealogical relation one has is with oneself, and so, in a markedly Wordsworthian conclusion, Yeats makes a connection between his present self and his boyhood self that is so strong as to resemble a typology.

'Meditations in Time of Civil War' shows a distinctive veering back and forth of thought and even action. At the end of the poem, Yeats 'turn[s] away and shut[s] the door, and on the stair / Wonder[s] how many times [he] could have proved [his] worth / In something that all others understand or share' (*CW*, p. 210, lines 33–5), just as, at the end of section V, he counts the moor-hen's chicks 'To silence the envy in [his] thought; / And turn[s] toward [his] chamber, caught / In the cold snows of a dream' (*CW*, p. 208, lines 13–5). Even when he finds particular trains of thought to be unproductive, such as the questioning of the worth of his descendants, he returns to them and continues to seek possibilities, using the dialectical method I have outlined. That method will never leave him entirely – it is the organizing principle, for example, in 'The Man and the Echo' – but it is never given such full thematic treatment again. 'Meditations' also gives us an example, in Sato's sword, of that search for eternal standards that is most obviously characterized by Byzantium, by the incorruptibility of gold and the inhuman mechanical quality of timelessness that sends the poet back to the natural world again. Eventually, he will recognize the incommensurability of the eternal and the human, and will liberate himself from the search for 'Monuments of unageing intellect' (CW, p. 197). The effect of that will be immense. In the last great turn of his career, beginning with *The Winding Stair and Other Poems* and culminating in his *Last Poems*, he will embark on the series of great late poems that are characterized by a heightened consciousness of mortality. That awareness will seem to liberate him further, to the point where he can ask the rider passing by his grave to 'cast a cold eye' equally on life and death. Heroes act bravely in the awareness of their approaching doom. Yeats shows himself in his last great poems to be among the very bravest.

Some Stray Personal Thoughts on Yeats and Music, Touching on McIntyre, Burns, MacLean and the Oral Tradition

JOHN PURSER

I am going to read my poems with great emphasis upon the rhythm, and that may seem strange if you are not used to it. I remember the great English poet, William Morris, coming in a rage out of some lecture hall, where somebody had recited a passage out of his *Sigurd the Volsung.*

'It gave me a devil of a lot of trouble', said Morris, 'to get that thing into verse'.

It gave me [says Yeats] the devil of a lot of trouble to get into verse the poems that I am going to read. That is why I will not read them as if they were prose.[1]

By the nineteeth century, poets and writers were performing in large theatres, which called for greater projection and a slower pace if there were to be any chance of being followed beyond the front stalls. In those days, before the microphone, something akin to a formal bardic delivery was often a practical necessity. With respect to the delivery of a political speech or a sermon, it was ever thus. The essentials in such styles of delivery are the essentials of music – pace, rhythm, pitch, emphasis, colour and tone, repetition: all qualities without any semantic necessities.

One of the most impressive survivals of a truly bardic delivery was that of Sorley MacLean. Sorley's voice was much imitated, and the measured pace of his speech, whether in conversation or performance, Gaelic or English, was mimicked and even satirized. Norman MacCaig pointedly looked at his watch when Sorley was reading or reciting.[2] MacCaig, himself deeply imbued with Gaelic culture, but without the language, was, perhaps, a little jealous of MacLean. Seamus Heaney wrote:

> Everyone imitated Sorley's accent, everything highly pitched and atremble; so, when you met him, you were meeting with the real performance – and he was no disappointment. Country people, when I was growing up, stood up when they were going to recite, and they formally recited. I took it to be that Sorley was a product of an oral culture; and, if you are going to recite, you make a job of it![3]

MacLean and Heaney knew what it was to experience an oral culture, albeit a literate one. Yeats, however, distanced as he was from Irish Gaelic oral tradition, experienced it primarily at second hand, in translation. His brother Jack made an effort to learn Irish Gaelic, but it came to nothing, and W.B. relied largely on Standish O'Grady and Lady Gregory's efforts in tackling the language. Yeats also read Carmichael's *Carmina Gadelica* as soon as it came out, which gave him access to aspects of Scottish Gaelic tradition, particularly those of incantation and seasonal rituals.[4] But for Yeats Gaelic was 'my national language, but it is not my mother tongue', and for that reason, even if he had learnt it, he maintained he could not have written in it with music and vigour.[5] O'Faoláin and O'Connor did not credit him with much vigour in English,[6] and MacLean held a dim view of Yeats's early poetry: 'now utterly discredited as being completely un-Irish and un-Celtic, and this being amply proved even to non-Gaelic speakers by the remarkable verse translations of Irish poetry being produced by men like Frank O'Connor.'[7] The later poetry MacLean was not only to admire; he was, by his own admission, strongly influenced by it.[8]

Authentic or not, the musicality of Yeats's verse is widely admired and sometimes related to the oral tradition in Ireland. By contrast, in 'The Rhetoric of Yeats', T.R. Henn asserts the importance of classical rhetorical devices, addressing aspects of Yeats's handling of tempo and rhythm in particular, and drawing attention to some of his favourite quotations in that context.[9] One might also draw attention to the extraordinarily beautiful philosophic prose of MacKenna's translation of Plotinus, which had prompted Yeats to declare it a 'masterpiece of English prose' – a statement one might qualify by describing MacKenna's work as a masterpiece of Anglo-Irish prose which, in its beauty and care for the rhythm and assonance as well as the meaning of words, has been matched in the last century only by Samuel Beckett.

Three useful essays on related topics appeared in *Yeats Annual No. 11*, with Helen Vendler writing perceptively on the poet's use of *ottava rima* and

Steve Ellis on 'Chaucer, Yeats and the Living Voice'. Vendler's essay makes many fine observations about Yeats's growing virtuosity with the form, manipulating pace and rhythm, moving the rhyming couplet from its usual concluding position, all with relevance to the semantic content. But in this thorough analysis there is no need to call upon any influences beyond the literary. Yeats could read these rhythms, sense these cadences, appreciate these formal devices, simply off the page.

That ability, however, can be too easily taken for granted. We know that W.B. often spoke his poetry aloud to himself, and his ability to read with a highly developed sensitivity to sound values may well have had some nurturing in a society in which eloquence, poetry and music had always been highly valued. That reputation for eloquence was an old one. Writing in opposition to Johannes Scotus Eriugena's *De divina praedestinatione* of 850–1, Prudentius comments on Eriugena's *celtica eloquentia* or Celtic eloquence.[10] In the context of parallel criticisms of Gaelic scholars of the time as *vaniliquus et garrulus* (vain and garrulous), the uncharitable critic might suggest that *plus ça change, plus c'est la même chose*. More kindly, one might say that a love of talk and a readiness to use pitch, rhythm and variety of cadence to assist it, is a characteristic of Irish speech. The Blarney Stone may represent a touristic stereotype, but such stereotypes can have a basis in realities that may also be assets.

Michael Sidnell, in an essay on Yeats's 'Written Speech', concluded provocatively that in Yeats 'there is another level of loss and aspiration, which has to do not with cultural antinomies but with the fact that writing is never speech and that poetry nevertheless attempts to cross *that* uncrossable linguistic gulf.'[11] This supposedly uncrossable gulf is, in my view, bridged so frequently that one might better claim 'an highway shall be there and a way'. It is in particular the way of the theatre and the cinema. It was also, as Yeats himself pointed out in *Explorations*, Chaucer's way, in which he concluded: ' ... all the old writers, the masculine writers of the world, wrote to be spoken or sung ... '[12]

With respect to poetry and oral tradition (which are at the heart of Sidnell's argument), one might cite the illiterate Duncan Ban McIntyre's great poem *Moladh Beinn Dorain*. It was printed and published in his own lifetime in the mid-eighteenth century, but is still said and sung within the Gaelic tradition by those who know it, in part through oral tradition but substantially through print. Being highly literate, but imbued with the oral tradition, such performers have no more difficulty in bridging the gap than did McIntyre's original poem when rendered into a print that he himself could not read in either language.

A similar misunderstanding between the written and the oral arises with respect to traditional and classical music. There are still many traditional musicians – singers in particular – who actively turn their backs on musical literacy. It is, of course, obvious that if one is either illiterate, or at best stumbling over one's letters or notes, one is likely to resent their presence when there is the chance of learning orally, with all the additional subtleties of transmission that that can offer. The oral tradition, equally obviously, transmits severe limitations in terms of the specific performance practice of one's models. Thus, in the world of Highland piping, some pipers are now having recourse to the written version of *piobaireachd* as in the Campbell *canntaireachd* manuscript of the late eighteenth century, because it offers alternatives to performing orthodoxies which have been developed and fostered, in some cases almost regimentally, within the oral tradition of piping. Nowadays, the use of recordings as models often substitutes for direct oral transmission. But is a recording a form of writing? It is a nice question.

What is true is that for anyone who is highly literate either musically or with words, the transition from sound to notation, notation to sound, speech to writing, writing to speech, is no longer a learned activity but as natural and instinctive as walking, though that too was at one time learned. However, while throughout Yeats's work there are many references to great writers and artists, where are the composers? In *Under Ben Bulben*, he travels through centuries of artists – if only to conclude that 'after that / confusion fell upon our thought'.

Many's the poet and philosopher that commands his attention, from Plotinus to Berkeley, Homer to Chaucer to Shelley. But the composers do not even gather abuse, though Elgar's imperial-style funeral march for Yeats's *Diarmuid and Grania* produced at the Gaiety Theatre in Dublin in 1901 earned his warm praise. If only by omission, Yeats does not appear to have been at home with anything resembling classical music or musical literacy.

But musical literacy does not guarantee sensitivity, it merely enables it, and W.B. appears to have been happier to align himself, as did his brother Jack, with a musical world closer to Irish tradition; hence, *Words for Music Perhaps*. But to write true lyrics, as opposed to 'perhaps' lyrics, is an art in itself, and it requires true musicianship if not at least some degree of musical literacy.

Yeats claimed with evident pride that in Ireland there 'lives almost undisturbed the last folk tradition of Western Europe.'[13] His meeting with MacDiarmid might have told him that the same could as truly have been said of Scotland. He was, perhaps, more aware of it than he was prepared openly to acknowledge. 'He " ... wanted to create once more an art, where the artist's handiwork would hide ... as we find it in some old Scots ballads ... " '[14] and he speculated that: 'if Shelley had nailed his Prometheus or some equal symbol upon some Welsh or Scottish rock, ... [his] art had entered more intimately, more microscopically, as it were, into our thought, and had given to modern poetry a breadth and stability like that of ancient poetry.'[15]

He frequently refers to Burns's work as to some kind of touchstone, and he surely must have recognized the inheritance of Burns in MacDiarmid when he not only anthologized, but quoted in his Introduction:

> O wha's been here afore me, lass,
> And hoo did he get in?

to explain a weariness with the Mona Lisa prompted by Walter Pater, and which he promises, and fails, to elucidate further on.[16] It is not easy to be more lucid than Burns or, in this quasi-ballad mode, MacDiarmid, with his focused yet conversational tone and his second, wonderfully pointed question in the shorter line. MacDiarmid was as highly critical as MacLean of the 'Irish literary Renaissance people' who 'only tinkered with the fringes; the whole Celtic Twilight business was a dodging of the issue.' If Yeats and other Irish poets had attempted subsequently 'to recover the master-key', MacDiarmid claimed he had the advantage of being able to do it through Scots which 'has enabled me to get far nearer to the goal'.[17]

Burns was, of course, fluent in two languages – Scots and English – and he was an amateur musician, able at least to read the treble clef, play the fiddle, sing (albeit with a rough voice) and, of course, he was a consummate lyricist. He was also educated and well-read. Whether Yeats classed him as a 'peasant' I cannot say – 'peasant' was a word which he used freely; but in preferring Burns's *Elegy on Capt. Matthew Henderson*, to Shelley's *Adonais* he was preferring a mode of address derived equally from the 'vernacular' and the more 'elevated' tone of a Shelley (for want of better words):

> Go to your sculptured tombs, ye Great,
> *In a' the tinsel trash o' state!*

is as poetically and socially sharp as anything Yeats was to write: 'I remember when I was twenty years old, arguing ... that Ireland ... could never create a democratic poet of the type of Burns, although it had tried to do so more than once, but that its genius would in the long run be aristocratic and lonely'. Was Yeats thinking of himself as that potential genius? He continues: 'Whenever I had known some old countryman, I had heard stories and sayings that arose out of an imagination, that would have understood Homer better than "The Cotter's Saturday Night" or "Highland Mary", because it was an ancient imagination ... '[18] This is not a convincing proposition when presented to anyone brought up in the literary tradition of Gavin Douglas's translation of the *Eneados* into Scots, but it does reveal a need to claim a piece of high literary ground for Ireland at a popular level.

In many respects, Burns had confronted the rhetorical problems that Yeats was to encounter in his search for 'a common speech'. It was not a wish to deny the rights of one or another mode of address so much as a desire for the freedom and ability to make use of variety, and this applied, in Scotland at least, to traditional music and song. Perhaps more significant than the fact that Burns was a master in the use of Scots was his skill as musician and lyricist in re-working traditional material which had, not infrequently, been modified by a variety of aesthetic approaches. I have discussed this in ' "The Wee Appollo": Burns and Oswald', but would add that something similar took place in Ireland in the Italianization of Irish melody by O'Carolan, and in the consummate marriage of lyrics and traditional melody in the works of Thomas Moore, albeit in more middle class and less varied veins.[19] Yeats himself was not a lyricist in the strict meaning of the word: nor was he a musician in any sense that might have enabled him to sing or set his verses to music in the way that Burns and Moore were able to do. But he was not only deeply sensitive to musical values in speech, but aware of aspects of the tradition that reach deeply into performance practice. This was equally true of MacLean who came from a family rich in music and song but who was not himself a singer or musician.[20] He went so far as to write that: 'I suppose the poet is the musician *manqué*, but just as surely the musician is the poet *manqué*, because, "this intellectual being, the thoughts that wander through eternity", are at most only implicit in the musician's art.'[21]

Writing as a musician, I would regard MacLean's corollary as a poor one, notwithstanding his having brought in Milton to his aid. All art, after all, 'constantly aspires towards the condition of music', does it not?[22]

Going beyond the lyric into poetry that bears some kind of extended theme and / or narrative thread, there is also an important memory of the pacing and rhythm of traditional performance. Yeats imagines Burns reading Thomson and Cowper and finding them 'too long', perhaps sharing with Yeats 'an Irish preference for a swift current'. He thinks such a preference 'might be mere indolence' and he mistakenly aligns the Scottish Thomson with the 'meditative, rich, deliberate' English mind: but by contrast, the pointed narrative thrust of the Scottish ballad and of Burns's narrative poetry make use of 'a timeless pattern' which Yeats recalls in the Scottish ballad of 'The Four Maries': 'The maid of honour whose tragedy they sing must be lifted out of history with timeless pattern, she is one of the four Maries, the rhythm is old and familiar, imagination must dance, must be carried beyond feeling into the aboriginal ice.'

This is an extraordinary piece of writing with its own beautifully balanced rhythm leading to that last arresting image of the aboriginal ice. And then Yeats asks 'Is ice the correct word?'[23] Perhaps not, but in seeking some kind of impersonal and universal expression that goes beyond the expression of individual emotion, Yeats was accessing that reality of traditional singing in which the 'performer' may use many oratorical techniques, but never intrudes his or her own emotion, though feeling it deeply inwardly, not in themselves, but in the characters whose story they transmit. It was in the context of drama that the ballad came to Yeats's mind.

Elizabeth Stewart is a traditional Scottish ballad singer, born into a centuries-old traveller tradition. I asked her whether, as she sang, she saw the story in her mind? This is how she replied:

> I ... Act it. When I sing it – any which song – any which ballad – I'm actually part of that ballad. If it's 'The Cruel Mother', I'm the cruel mother: if it's 'I Aince Had a Lass, I Likeit Her Weel', I'm the man that was hurt, nae, nae the woman, cos she went away wi somebody else, but I happen to be the man that was hurt. I take on his feelings. How would I feel if it was me that was seeing my love married to somebody else? I'm – I'm actually acting that part.[24]

But Elizabeth Stewart herself would never display her feelings personally. As Yeats writes: ' ... no actress has ever sobbed when she played Cleopatra, even the shallow brain of a producer has never thought of such a thing.'[25]

That understanding of the traditions of performance in the oral tradition – not forgetting the theatre and opera as surviving exemplars of oral tradition – is a vital element in W.B.'s work. At the same time, it is worth pointing out that Elizabeth Stewart (as was her mother) is a fully literate musician as ready to play a Beethoven sonata as sing a song. That was not a skill acquired by W.B., whose musical interests appear essentially to have been confined to the world of song and ballad. Jack certainly thought of his brother's poems in that context: 'The last few years ... he would talk about everything that was interesting to him or tell me some new ballad he had made ... '[26] Indeed, W.B. co-edited a series of Broadsides in the 1930s which, for the first time in the Cuala Press's publications of Broadsides, included music notation. Mind you, when Yeats concludes the second stanza of *The Soldier Takes Pride* with:

> March, march – how does it run? –
> O any old words to a tune.

one might be forgiven for being unsurprised that only the first four lines of each stanza of his lyrics seem to fit the tune provided by Arthur Duff.[27] James Stephens went to the trouble in a later *Broadside*, of pointing the rhythm of

The Main-Deep with accents, to ensure we know how it fits its tune. Duff is no longer credited as music editor, but with or without him, these Broadsides, which frequently ape the ballad tradition, fail to make use of the normal technique of underlaying the music with at least one stanza of the words.[28]

In *The Ballads and Songs of W.B.Yeats*, Colin Meirs pursued the Anglo-Irish ballad influence on Yeats's early work, and drew attention to W.B.'s homage to Davis, Mangan and Ferguson, as well as to Douglas Hyde.[29] While it is hard to accept that Davis's famous *A Nation Once Again* takes its form 'from the English [*sic*] literary ballads of Scott and Macaulay', Meirs brings to the fore many useful relationships and developments from the traditions of the Irish literary ballad. But what is most obvious throughout virtually all the literary criticism, be it by Yeats himself or his commentators, is the absence of any reference to the music. Lyrics are examined without acknowledgment that they were either designed to be sung, or taken up as song, and this despite the fact that they were commonly published with the music and, in the case of the 1911 edition of *The Spirit of the Nation*, with an Introduction by Grattan Flood, assessing the history of the published melodies in previous editions. One may huff and puff about the quality of lyric verse: the Germans are harsh about Müller's qualities as a lyric poet – harsh, that is, until they hear him sung in Schubert's settings, of which Müller (alas) had no knowledge. The point is that the true lyricist and, of course, balladeer, writes within a particular genre which seeks music even if it does not yet have it, and any critical appraisal should take that into account. The literary critic may shrink a little at Burns's 'warring sighs and groans I'll wage thee', but the words sing well and *Ae Fond Kiss* is a great song no matter which of the two favourite tunes to which it is sung is used.

Here we come to the fundamental problem faced by the musically illiterate who are bursting with musical notions: they have to rely on musicians:

> Yeats' distrust of the professional actor was as nothing when compared to his dislike of the professional musician … Forcibly as his ideas about music were expressed, he had no ear for music as it is understood in Western Europe. He could not hum a tune and his notion of pitch was wildly inaccurate, qualities which made his demands upon professional instrumentalists who took part very exacting.[30]

Thus George Barnes, recalling W.B.'s experiments with the presentation of poetry on radio in 1936 and 1937. A similar Radio Eireann broadcast from Athlone was, however 'a fiasco'. Yeats had asked one of the singers: ' … to clap his hands in time to the music after every verse, and it was very stirring – on the wireless it was a schoolboy knocking with the end of a penknife or spoon.'[31]

Yeats wondered, in the same letter, whether his 'old bundle of poet's tricks' was useless, but after the BBC broadcasts, Barnes stated he had used them 'with great effect', including having de la Mare's *Three Jolly Farmers* delivered as patter, and using the bones to accompany F.R. Higgins's *Song for the Clatter Bones*. It is still a decidedly raw poem, especially when accompanied in the *Broadside* by Jack Yeats's patently licentious singer purporting to accompany his song with the very bones of 'that Jewy woman' who 'peeled the clothes from her shoulder-bones / down to her spent teats'. Barnes states that 'Queen Jezzebel the witch' (which is as in the *Broadside*) had been substituted (with Yeats's permission) for 'Queen Jezzebel the bitch', 'in the interests of British morals'.[32] British morals were still in crisis mode in 1969 when I was invited by Scottish Television to find a substitute for 'bitches' in the libretto of my opera *The Undertaker*. I turned the ladies in question into 'vixens' and everybody's honour was thereby satisfied!

These quasi-musical experiments with the delivery of verse were not uncommon in the 1920s–30s. Most famous was, of course, Walton and Sitwell's *Façade*. The technical difficulties of its performance in Glasgow in 1930 led to Walton losing his way when conducting the work and handing over the baton gratefully to Erik Chisholm, who had also put on performances of Debussy's *La boîte à joujoux* and other works for reciter and instruments ranging from Schumann to Sibelius and Strauss.[33] The reason for Walton's embarrassment was that the reciter 'got hopelessly out in the rhythms'. He was also largely incomprehensible if not inaudible.[34] Perhaps knowledge of such difficulties with the genre is what prompted Yeats to insist that any music was to be interspersed rather than accompany the actual delivery of the verse.[35] But perhaps also there was a certain mystery attached to music which he simply could not penetrate, however Rosicrucian his inclinations: a spiritual hunger which he expresses with profound beauty:

> No matter what disaster occurred
> She stood in desperate music wound,
> Wound, wound, and she made in her triumph
> Where the bales and the baskets lay
> No common intelligible sound
> But sang, 'O sea-starved, hungry sea.'

It is *A Crazed Girl* who provokes those magnificent lines, but in the more general tenor of W.B.'s ways, there were always the voices of his own people. The richness of Yeats's diction arose not only from a wide and intensive reading at which he was clearly immensely fluent; and from the residual influences of

Kiltartanese, and the more authentic echoes of the Gaelic influence on Irish English to be found in the translations of Hyde; but also from the habits of speech of his own Anglo-Irish society, his garrulous father and Lionel Johnson not least amongst them:

> Lionel Johnson ... spoke with so much music that what had been in another monotony, became nobility of style ... even poor verses were beautiful upon his lips.[36]

That community from the generation of W.B. and Jack spoke with a soft musicality and easy but always lively flow of conversation, often touched with humour, and occasionally wonderfully pointed. Thus we find W.B. praising Jack's first novel, which might be described by some as in the garrulous vein of their father, in the following terms: 'It is a most amusing, animated book ... It is the best of talk and the best of writing.'[37]

Many of the community of those days wrote as they spoke, not only in their frequent letters, but in their more formal writing, including in their translations from Irish Gaelic. There was a stimulating range of such work from which to choose. Callanan, Lady Gregory, Hyde, O'Grady and many others. Yeats was equivocal about O'Grady's style, identifying an unwelcome influence of Macaulay, but he wrote to O'Grady in 1914 that 'every Irish imaginative writer' owed him 'a portion of his soul.'[38] The leading philologist, Whitley Stokes, who was a stern and demanding scholar of Celtic languages and who tore O'Grady's editions of Old Irish to pieces, was also an admirer of O'Grady's sensitive translations. Yeats recalled the music of O'Grady's voice, even though O'Grady was very drunk at the time:

> I had never heard him speak, and at first he reminded me of Cardinal Manning. There was the same simplicity, the same gentleness. He stood between two tables, touching one or the other for support, and said in a low penetrating voice: 'We have now a literary movement, it is not very important; it will be followed by a political movement, that will not be very important; then must come a military movement, that will be important indeed'.[39]

For myself, I recollect with nostalgia the voices of Whitley Stokes's nephews, and of many others – old people in my young days. Theirs was an entirely natural rhetoric, unaffected by the demands of public performance and radio transmission, or, indeed, by the need to impress their public with the depth of their thought; but the music of their discourse was part of a tradition of their society, and in that sense, one can fairly claim that the musicality of many of W.B.'s instincts, and even specific skills, was derived from tradition.

Besides the influence of classical rhetoric, Henn has drawn attention to the importance to Yeats of the power, resonance and strong cadences of some of the finest passages of 'traditional Anglo-Irish rhetoric.' One example he gives is that of George Fox's translation, *Sailing, Sailing Swiftly*, from the seventeenth-century Irish of Thomas Lavelle.[40] It gave its title to Jack's novel, *Sailing Sailing Swiftly* and it looks back to 'The Flight of the Earls'. The novel is a sad but curiously affirmative reminiscence reflecting on the failure of the attempted marriage of Ireland and England. Throughout it, there are echoes of the ballad and throughout Jack's own writings and paintings there are echoes of many more. The rhymes, rhythms, images and political realities embodied in that Anglo-Irish tradition had long been overtly promoted by Jack Yeats in the *Broadsides* of the early 1900s, published by the Cuala Press. Even if W.B. had not been brought up on and engaged with that repertoire, his attention was being drawn to it in issue after issue by Jack.

The *Broadsides* offer fascinating parallels with W.B.'s preoccupations, rhetorical, symbolic and political. After all, the two brothers were so alike, yet so different, creative and rich in their syntax and vocabulary. W.B. knew what his brother was worth as a writer even though he may well have suppressed Jack's plays at the Abbey:

> And now comes my brother's extreme book, 'The Charmed Life'. He does not care that few will read it, still fewer recognise its genius; it is his book, his 'Faust', his pursuit of all that through its unpredictable, unarrangeable reality, least resembles knowledge. His style fits his purpose for every sentence has its own taste, tint and smell.

Interesting that W.B. refers to only three of the five senses, omitting touch and hearing. I have written of this masterpiece, *The Charmed Life*, elsewhere, but W.B.'s acknowledgment of his brother's genius as a writer was not, I am sure, easily won and most certainly never solicited, and anyone who reads Jack's writings will soon realize that he had a mastery of the visual (as a great artist, naturally enough) but also a mastery of rhythm and tone.[41] They were brothers, they were brought up with the same family rhetoric and repartee, and if one of them had more access than the other to the inheritance of Irish Gaelic influences, it was surely Jack, who was immensely widely read, but who spent far more time in the West of Ireland (not least in the company of Synge) than did W.B. The musicality of W.B. Yeats is far from unique and, I would suggest, finds expression and inspiration in the works not only of those cited above, but in the voice and writings of his own brother, along with many another less celebrated member of that vibrant artistic community.

NOTES

1. BBC broadcast 1932.

2. Personal communication from Stewart Conn.

3. Seamus Heaney in interview with Dennis O'Driscoll in *The Dark Horse*, Winter / Spring 2011, p. 12.

4. W.B. Yeats, 'Magic' in A.N. Jeffares (ed.), *W.B.Yeats Selected Criticism* (London 1976), p. 89.

5. W.B. Yeats, 'A General Introduction for My Work' in A.N. Jeffares (ed.), *W.B.Yeats Selected Criticism* (London 1976), pp. 264–5.

6. See D. Torchiana, '"Among School Children" and the education of the Irish Spirit' in Jeffares and Cross (eds), *In Excited Reverie* (New York 1965), pp. 149–50.

7. S. MacLean, 'Realism in Gaelic Poetry' in W. Gillies (ed.), *Ris a' Bhruthaich* (Stornoway 1985), p. 19.

8. S. MacLean, 'Some Gaelic and Non-Gaelic Influences on Myself' in R. O'Driscoll (ed.), *The Celtic Consciousness* (Portlaoise and Edinburgh 1981), pp. 500–1.

9. T.R. Henn, 'The Rhetoric of Yeats' in Jeffares and Cross (eds), *In Excited Reverie*, (New York 1965), pp. 102–22.

10. Prudentis, *De praedestinatione contra Joannem Scotum*, in Patrologia Latina CXV.1194a, quoted in D. Moran, *The Philosophy of John Scotus Eriugena* (Cambridge 1989), p. 33.

11. M. Sidnell, 'Yeats's "Written Speech" ', *Yeats Annual* No. 11, p. 23.

12. Mrs W.B. Yeats (sel.), *Explorations* (London 1962), p. 221.

13. W.B. Yeats, 'Introduction' *Oxford Book of Modern Verse* (Oxford 1936), p. xiii.

14. W.B. Yeats, *Four Years* (Dundrum 1921), p. 41.

15. W.B. Yeats, *Four Years* (Dundrum 1921), pp. 40–1.

16. W.B. Yeats, 'Introduction' *Oxford Book of Modern Verse* (Oxford 1936), p. viii.

17. Letter from Chris Grieve to Kenneth Buthlay, 4.3.53 in A. Bold (ed.), *The Letters of Hugh MacDiarmid* (London 1984), pp. 863–4.

18. W.B. Yeats, *Poetry and Ireland: Essays by W.B. Yeats and Lionel Johnson* (Dundrum 1908), p. 6.

19. J. Purser, '"The Wee Apollo": Burns and Oswald' in K. Simpson (ed.), *Love & Liberty – Robert Burns A Bicentenary Celebration* (East Linton 1997), pp. 326–33.

20. 'Sorley and the Music of the Bards' *Ainmeal Thar Cheadan* Conference, Sabhal Mòr Ostaig, 16 June 2011, forthcoming in Scottish Gaelic Studies as *Guth Shomhairle*.

21. S. MacLean, 'Old songs and new poetry' in W. Gillies (ed.), *Ris a' Bhruthaich* (Stornoway 1985), p. 111.

22. W. Pater, *The Renaissance*, 'Giorgione'.

23. W.B. Yeats, 'A General Introduction for My Work' in A.N. Jeffares (ed.), *W.B. Yeats Selected Criticism* (London 1976), p. 267.

24. Recorded on *Bonnie Rideout – Harlaw, Scotland 1411*, Tulloch Music tm505, 2011, CD2.

25. W.B. Yeats, 'A General Introduction for my Work' in A.N. Jeffares (ed.), *W.B. Yeats Selected Criticism* (London 1976), p. 266.

26. Jack Yeats to Joseph Hone, 2.2.1939, Kenneth Spenser Research Library, University of Kansas, MS. 25.
27. Yeats, Higgins and Duff (eds) *A Broadside*, No. 12 (New Series), Dublin 1935.
28. Yeats and Higgins (eds) *A Broadside*, No. 4 (New Series), Dublin, April 1937.
29. C. Meir, *The Ballads and Songs of W.B. Yeats – The Anglo-Irish heritage in Subject and Style* (London 1974), p. 2.
30. G.R. Barnes, quoted in J. Hone, *W.B. Yeats 1865–1939* (London 1962), p. 457.
31. Letter from W.B. to George Barnes, 2.2.1937, quoted in J. Hone, *W.B. Yeats 1865–1939* (London 1962), p. 454. The broadcast was on the previous day.
32. G.R. Barnes, quoted in J. Hone, *W.B. Yeats 1865–1939* (London 1962), p. 456.
33. J. Purser, *Erik Chisholm, Scottish Modernist 1904–1965* (Woodbridge 2009), pp. 66 and 221.
34. J. Purser, *Erik Chisholm, Scottish Modernist 1904–1965* (Woodbridge 2009), p. 24.
35. J. Hone, *W.B. Yeats 1865–1939* (London 1962), p. 454.
36. W.B. Yeats, introduction to Lionel Johnson's essay in *Poetry and Ireland: Essays by W.B.Yeats and Lionel Johnson*, Dundrum 1908, p. 19.
37. W.B. Yeats to Jack B. Yeats, 18 July 1930, the artist's papers – now in the National Gallery of Ireland.
38. W.B. Yeats, *The Autobiography of William Butler Yeats* (New York 1938), pp. 189–90.
39. W.B. Yeats, *Dramatis Personae*, Dublin 1935, p. 47.
40. T.R. Henn, 'The Rhetoric of Yeats', in: Jeffares and Cross (eds) *In Excited Reverie* (New York 1965), pp. 106–7.
41. J. Purser, *The Literary Works of Jack B. Yeats* (Gerrards Cross, London: Savage, Maryland 1991), Chapter 11.

The Plays

Less to spoil: Dance in the Plays of W.B. Yeats

RICHARD LONDRAVILLE

PERFORMANCE EXPERIMENTS

In my years of interaction with the Yeatsian Noh, a primary concern has been the place of the dance in his plays. It seems to me one of the most important and at the same time most difficult elements to address properly. I attempted two productions of the Cuchulain cycle, one in 1971 at SUNY Potsdam, and the other in 1983 at the National Taiwan Normal University in Taiwan.[1] The first was a collaborative effort using faculty and students from literature, art and music. The result, although successful enough (it was selected for broadcast by PBS), reflected the disparate interests of these people. Yeats's words passed through the alembic of modern musicians, stage designers and dancers. The final production, arresting as it was, seemed to lack a necessary unity.

When I was a visiting professor at NTNU University in 1983, I was afforded access to the facilities of the national Chinese opera of Taiwan, including staging, costuming and makeup. This meant that I was able to use the structure of the Chinese opera as framework for the Cuchulain cycle;[2] I found Yeats's *Noh* remarkably adaptable to the Chinese opera, with its traditional elements fitting neatly into his idea of subjective theatre. I was able to incorporate Chinese opera dances at climactic points to emphasize Yeats's idea of the dance as focus of the emotion generated by the action. The Chinese audience had the advantage of recognizing costume, staging, and dance inherent in their opera. When Emer and Eithne Inguba were both onstage, for example, their dress, decorum, and makeup identified them respectively as queen and courtesan. In Yeats's productions in the West his audience had no such reference.

The production played to overflow audiences and caused a strong positive reaction in Taipei. Reviewers who were initially concerned about the corruption of the form of Chinese opera praised our efforts. On 31 May 1983, for instance, the (Taiwan) *Central Daily News* critic wrote, 'What a marvelous play! Foreign audiences were greatly amused, and Chinese audiences were enthralled. The script itself has been the weakest point of Chinese drama. The form of presentation has been perfectly refined after a long history of development. Yet the scenario itself is lagging behind. If this innovative experiment is well accepted, we may also try to stage other world plays in the style of Chinese drama.'

One of the most interesting suggestions was that the cycle be performed in a Taoist temple with only the gods as audience. Not incidentally, the Taiwanese also identified with Cuchulain fighting the waves as a symbol of their struggle against the overwhelming power of Mainland China.

Certainly the most gratifying reaction to this production occurred during the 1990 Yeats-Pound conference at the University of Maine in Orono. While Michael and Anne Yeats were watching a tape of the Taiwan production with me, Anne turned to her brother Michael and said, 'Oh, our father would have loved this!'

THE FUNCTION OF THE DANCE

Clearly one of the most striking elements in the Yeatsian *Noh* is the dance. Its climactic function in the plays focuses the audience's attention upon it as the highest moment in the drama. It is the summation and the quintessence of all the arts; since dance involves the whole being, it is more than the words that describe it. It represents for Yeats the unification of intellect with emotion, demonstrated by the similarly unified action of the dance. Who, indeed, can tell the dancer from the dance, or the artist from his art?

Yeats's prose and his poems included dances, dancers and dancing even in the nineteenth century, suggesting that his interest in the dance and the dancer is considerable. There is, however, no dance at all in Yeats's earlier plays; but once he had read of the *Noh* dance and its place in the drama, he was captivated by the idea: 'Instead of the players working themselves into a violence of passion indecorous in our sitting-room, the music, the beauty of the form and voice all come to climax in pantomimic dance.' The dance was the final touch that was to 'make credible strange events, elaborate words' (*Certain Noble Plays*, p. 221).[3]

The dance that enthralled Yeats, however, had little in common with most ideas of Western dance. He wrote further that:

> I have lately studied certain of these dances, with Japanese players, and I notice that their idea of beauty, unlike that of Greece, and like that of pictures from Japan and China, makes them pause at moments of muscular tension. The interest is not in the human form but in the rhythm to which it moves, and the triumph of their art is to express the rhythm in its intensity. There are few swaying movements of the arms or body such as make the beauty of our dancing. They move from the hip, keeping constantly the upper part of the body still, and seem to associate with every gesture or pose some definite thought. They cross the stage with a sliding movement, and one gets the impression not of undulation but of continuous straight lines (*Certain Noble Plays*, pp. 230–31).

The person most influential in Yeats's early views on the Japanese dance was Michio Ito, who became Yeats's Guardian of the Well in *At the Hawk's Well*. Ito had no formal training in the Japanese *Noh*, but from the above description of his dancing it appears that he came close to reproducing the *Noh* dance. Compare Yeats's account above to Faubion Bowers's comments in *The Japanese Theatre*:[4]

> In all Japanese dancing, movements are highly attenuated and suggestive (as opposed to literal). At times the dance seems so ethereal and remote from normal, day-to-day muscular activity that the dancers appear almost immobile ... The spectator is dazzled by the controlled tension and interiorized concentration of the human body. The dance may be completely understated, undermoved, and yet fully expressive and provocative of profound emotion (p. 174).

It is reasonable that Ito would have some ideas of the postures of the *Noh* dance without having been a *Noh* dancer, just as a dancer in the West would be almost certain to know something of ballet without having been a member of the *corps de ballet*. In any event, it was Ito who stirred Yeats's imagination:

> My play is made possible by a Japanese dancer whom I have seen dance in a studio and in a drawing-room and on a very small stage lit by a stage-light. In the studio and in the drawing-room alone, where the lighting was the light we are most accustomed to, did I see him as the tragic image that stirred my imagination (*Certain Noble Plays*, p. 224).

Once Yeats's imagination had been stirred by the tragic image of the dancer, his choice of the dance as a fitting climax for his plays never substantially changed.

Yeats had been trying to adapt his particular dramatic vision to the theatre of Ireland without much success, at least in his own terms. What success he had was in areas not close to his main interest, poetry. He wrote to Lady Gregory in 1919: 'We set out to make a "People's Theatre", and in that we have succeeded. But I did not know until very lately that there are certain things, dear to both our hearts, which no "People's Theatre" can accomplish'. (*A People's Theatre*, p. 224)

Indeed, he continues, the very success of that theatre has in some ways been 'a discouragement and a defeat' (p. 250), for a people's theatre meant concentration upon a realistic prose drama. Yeats had said as early as 1902, 'The only kind of drama that amuses me to write and amuses me to see is poetical drama, whether in prose or verse. I have therefore a desire to make a stage where prose would be as difficult as possible'.[5] But this desire for a poetical drama was subordinated to the main thrust of the Abbey theatre – dramatic realism – at least for Yeats the theatre director. Yeats the playwright continued to search for 'a mode of drama Shelley and Keats could have used without ceasing to be themselves, and for which even Blake in the mood of *The Book of Thel* might not have been too obscure.' (*A People's Theatre*, p. 225)

Yeats recognized in the *Noh* a different impetus from that of the Irish dramatic movement. The *Noh* appeared to be very close to Yeats's idea of perfect theatre, one removed from propagandistic purposes, concerned with 'the perfecting of the dramatic art' and little else. The *Noh* also has a particular appeal to a poet. Professor Makoto Ueda explains that the *Noh:* 'is primarily poetry rather than drama; it is poetry acted upon the stage. It imitates human actions, but it does so in such a way as to reveal the hidden essence of man and things, the "true intent" that only the sensitivity of an artist can feel' (*Zeami, Bashō*, et. al, p. 33).[6]

Here is a form suited to accommodate Yeats's dramatic ideas, one that appears to unify the arts. To quote Ueda again:

> The relation of an ordinary drama to painting and sculpture is not a particularly close one, because the drama, restricted by time and movement, tries to make the most of its dialogue and action; consequently the beauty of an ordinary drama is that of one continuous whole, not of one movement or of one moment that is part of the whole. But the *Nō*, because of its emphasis on intuition, minimizes the elements of time and movement; one little movement in a lengthy duration of time is made to suggest a great deal. In other words, the *Nō* drama, primarily a time art, is made to approach the space arts (*Zeami, Basho* p. 28).

The place of the dance in such an art form is obvious. Since the dance involves the whole body, since it is both pictorial and sculptural, it is the ideal medium to bridge the gap between the time and space arts. Dancing becomes not alone the quintessence of the arts, but the culmination of them all, a spontaneous manifestation of an inward emotion. As Ueda explained,

> Poetry is the expression of a personal emotion, and when the emotion becomes more intense, it takes the form of dancing. The origin of dancing is a spontaneous expression of emotion, a subconscious act, in contrast to our daily behaviour, which is in the main the result of our conscious thinking or will. It is significant that a dance in the *nō* drama is always performed by the protagonist – that is, a ghost, a deity, a mentally deranged person. What the protagonist wished to express reaches the level beyond the conscious; it cannot be stated in logical terms; consequently there is a need for symbolism in writing it out, for dancing in acting it out. As the language of poetry is highly stylized and evocative, so the movement of dancing is highly restrained and suggestive. Every action of the dancer has a symbolic meaning, because it is always an expression of some inner feeling. A *Nō* play reaches its climax with a dance, as dancing signifies the most intense form of man's psychical energy (*Zeami, Basho*, pp. 29–30).

Although the passage refers to the Japanese *Noh*, it would be difficult to find a more apt description of the function of the dance and the dancer in Yeats's work. This fusion of the artist with his art was a major concern of Yeats's until his death. In a letter written to Lady Elizabeth Pelham on 4 January 1939, he says: 'It seems to me that I have found what I wanted. When I try to put it all into a phrase I say, "Man can embody truth but he cannot know it." I must embody it in the completion of my life.' (*The Letters*, p. 922)[7]

The dance is one of the most easily verifiable of Yeats's debts to the Japanese *Noh*. There had been music in his plays for a long time before his reading of the Pound-Fenollosa plays, but he had never included a dance until this reading prompted him to write *At the Hawk's Well*. None of the existing forms of Western dance satisfied him. In *Four Plays for Dancers* he wrote: 'the dancing will give me the most trouble, for I know but vaguely what I want. I do not want any existing form of stage dancing, but something with a smaller gamut of expression, something more reserved, more self-controlled, as befits performers within arm's reach of the audience' (pp. 333–4).[8]

There appear to be opportunities for dance in some of the earlier plays; in *On Baile's Strand*, for example, Cuchulain's fight with the waves seems to call for a tragic dance. But Yeats chooses to have this particular action occur offstage – except in a 1926 production at Cambridge when the witches danced but Cuchulain did not (*The Letters*, p. 721: letter to Olivia Shakespear, 6 December 1926). It would be difficult to imagine that Yeats, after his exposure to the Japanese *Noh*, would miss the opportunity to stage Cuchulain's fight with the waves as a dance. His handling of the scene illustrates better than anything else what the dance came to mean in his plays:

> Fool. There, he is down! He is up again. He is going out in the deep water. There is a big wave. It has gone over him. I cannot see him now. He has killed kings and giants, but the waves have mastered him (*Variorium Edition of the Plays of W.B. Yeats, hereafter VPl*, p. 524).[9]

For whatever reasons Yeats chose to have the Fool describe Cuchulain's tragic fight with the sea, and there are sound reasons relative to staging difficulties and the difference in sensitivity between the Fool and Cuchulain, such a description cannot approach the intensity of dance at a climactic point. It is probable that other elements in the play make a dance unlikely at the climax of *On Baile's Strand*, but one can easily see that the general mood of Yeats's drama is greatly amenable to the dance.

And in fact, in my 1983 Taipei production, I staged this dance using a kneeling chorus moving undulating cloths of navy blue and aqua to represent the waves, while the fool narrated the action and Cuchulain fell to the inexorable sea (Londraville, in *YAA* No. 2, 1984). It was an idea that seemed to work.

It was fortunate for Yeats's drama that he had as his first dancer an artist with some sense of the Japanese aesthetic, and the dance which Ito performed in *At the Hawk's Well* pleased the playwright very much; he reported that Ito's 'minute intensity of movement in the dance of the hawk so well suited our small room and private art' (*VPl*, p. 417).

Yeats recognized the dramatic power implicit in the slow, disciplined, symbolic movements of the dance. Such a dance could be translated easily from its Japanese setting to the heroic age of Ireland, for the philosophy behind the Japanese *Noh* matched Yeats's aesthetic almost exactly. As Professor Ueda explained:

> The *nō* drama may be considered as an art which attempts to illuminate internal and external reality reflected in the deepest depth of the mind's eye, a level of reality which cannot be known through the ordinary senses. The world of the *nō* is primarily that of the subconscious. Two things which would be contrary to one another in the realm of the conscious are made to co-exist in the *nō* drama, like the sun shining at midnight (*Zeami, Bashō*, et al. pp. 24–5).

When a playwright is attempting to 'illuminate internal and external reality reflected in the deepest depth of the mind's eye', he must realize that the ordinary means of communication must be supplemented. Words illuminated by action may be the best means of communication in a realistic play, but these means fall short when attempting to communicate what is beyond words. It is at this point that the whole body must be used to convey emotions, and the words of the play are superseded by the dance.

The Japanese *Noh* explains the dance of the protagonist by means of the chorus, but Yeats most often chooses some other character to explain the dance, as for example, the Young Man in *The Dreaming of the Bones* who describes the climactic dance of Diarmuid and Dervorgilla. Yeats follows his Japanese model more closely in the relationship between the final song of the chorus and the dance. In *The Japanese Tradition in British and American Literature*, Earl Miner said that in Yeats's plays (as in the *Noh*), 'the climax often resolves the contrary forces of the play in a dance to music while the chorus chants its final song' (p. 2480).[10]

The dance thus fulfils its function of communication of the sense of climax. For without this communication even the sensitive audience that Yeats demanded might well be confused. Yeats's dance is always directly related to the action and is a logical outgrowth of the play rather than a superfluous addition. When a character in a Yeats play begins to dance, there is a sense of fitness, almost of inevitability; it is as if no other action could as well express the emotion felt by the dancer.

In *At the Hawk's Well*, Yeats is intoxicated with the new form he has invented. In choosing as his dancer the Guardian of the Well, he makes a variation from the Japanese *Noh*, which always has the main character or characters dance at the climax. Michio Ito, who first danced the part of the Guardian, was male, but the Guardian in the play is referred to as female. It may be that Yeats was making some concession to the practice of the Japanese *Noh* that has all of the parts played by male actors, or, what is more probable, he wanted to use Ito's skill in a central role and that role happened to call for a female.

The dancer in *At the Hawk's Well* is present from the beginning of the play, but she is covered with a black cloak that she does not throw off until the spirit of the hawk possesses her and she dances in a dress that 'suggests a hawk'. Her possession by the hawk-spirit is contagious; it catches up Cuchulain also. The First Musician tells us, 'the madness has laid hold upon him now'. Cuchulain leaves the well to chase the hawk-woman so that she may be 'perched upon my wrist', but retires from his fruitless chase to find that the water of the well of immortality has flowed while he was gone, and he has neither the hawk-woman nor eternal life.

The actions of both the hawk-woman and Cuchulain suggest a *pas de deux* more than a solo dance. Cuchulain seems as possessed by the same sort of madness as is the Guardian; as her dance goes on he rises to become part of that dance. There is a unity established when male and female, active and passive, join in the dance. It is admittedly a dance in which they do not order the steps, a dance of the seduction of the will, but it is nonetheless heroic, as least for Cuchulain.

In a play that has as its climax a dance, it would seem that that dance should be allegorical. This is not the case in *At the Hawk's Well*. The forces of the universe have demonstrated their power, not only over the passive Guardian, but also over the stubborn Cuchulain. And even after this power has been so convincingly demonstrated, when Cuchulain has lost both the woman and immortality, he is unbowed. He eschews the advice of the Old Man who warns him of the Sidhe, then shoulders his spear and shouts, 'He comes! Cuchulain, son of Sulatim, comes.'

Through the dance we have no specific clues concerning the nature of Cuchulain's experience, no acting-out of particularized emotions. We have instead the dance itself, in which emotions have become too grand to be contained within the normal media of expression, and must resolve themselves in sculptured action.

The non-representational quality of the dance seems to me a significant detail, for Yeats would have us know that it is the dance itself that is important, not the dance as representative of anything else. In a letter to his father written while in rehearsal for *At the Hawk's Well*, Yeats says:

> In the last letter but one, you spoke of all art as imitation, meaning, I conclude, imitation of something in the outer world. To me it seems that it often uses the outer world as a symbolism to express subjective moods. The greater the subjectivity, the less the imitation. You say that music suggests now the roar of the sea, now the song of the bird yet it seems to me that the song of the bird itself is perhaps subjective, an expression of feeling alone. The element of pattern in every art is, I think, the part that is not imitative, for in the last analysis there will always be somewhere an intensity of pattern that we have never seen with our eyes. In fact, imitation seems to me to create a language in which we say things which are not imitation (*The Letters*, p. 607).

It is in this departure from the realistic that Yeats's dance differs slightly from the Japanese *Noh*. In 'Yeats's Drama and the Nō', Yasuko Stucki suggests that dance in the *Noh*: 'is not presented in isolation from its content; the *Nō* dance either simply accompanies the spoken words by which the meaning of the movement is immediately self-evident, or creates the mood by purely abstract movements *after* the significance of the play has been fully revealed to the audience' (p. 118)[11].

The dance in Yeats's drama is (as Peter Ure says in his essay 'The Plays') often 'amplification of the gesture and appearance of a character and his recondite meaning' (p. 156), rather than the acting-out of the climax of the play. But

Yeats's idea of the dancer in his plays seems to me to be very close to Zeami Motokiyo's, who says that one 'should know the way in which singing and dancing in the *nō* are derived from a single spirit. When the spirit remains in the mind, it is called emotion; uttered in words, it is called poetry. When one cannot stop with poetry alone, he goes on to sing it out, waving his hands and stamping his feet in ecstasy' (*Zeami, Basho, et al.* p. 29).

As I have demonstrated earlier in this chapter, the dance in the Yeatsian *Noh* clearly does emerge from the logic of the play as the point at which words will not suffice to express the emotion aroused. It is true, as Stucki maintains, that the dance in the Japanese *Noh* tends to be more representational than Yeats's dance. But what seems to me more important is that Yeats's dance catches the essence of Zeami's idea of the art that goes beyond what can be expressed in words.

It is not strange that Yeats most often chooses the non-representation dance, for he does believe that 'there will always be somewhere an intensity of pattern that we have not seen with our eyes' and that the 'element of pattern in every art is ... the part that is not imitative.' Yeats is attempting to be indirect, symbolic in his dance. This does not mean that he chooses obscurity for its own sake out of some diabolical need to mystify his audience. He is attempting to express by symbolism what is inexpressible by other means. Speaking of Zeami, Professor Ueda says:

> His ideal is the union of the subjective and the objective, the observer and the observed ... An artist ought to catch this invisible spirit and present it through the things visible.
> This being the ultimate aim of art, the artist must rely on symbolization rather than description in attaining it. A symbol may lead one to an instantaneous perception of what cannot be analysed or described (*Zeami, Basho et al.* p. 27).

This passage could be as easily applied to Yeats's drama as to Zeami's. Yeats's alteration of the representational dance of the Japanese *Noh* to his own abstract symbolization of the emotion aroused is a modification of the Japanese model. Neither Yeats nor anyone else has maintained that he was attempting to follow the Japanese *Noh* exactly. But his modifications do not preclude the essential similarities between the two forms. Both treat the dance as a type of unified experience and the dancer as a type of unified creature. Yasuko Stucki maintains that 'the Dancer, for Yeats, is the central image of his idea of art; she is the embodiment of living beauty, devoid of a tormenting division between body and spirit, a perfect work of art in which artifice and imagination are coalesced' (*Yeats's Drama*, p. 118).

In *The Only Jealousy of Emer*, Yeats's next play after *At the Hawk's Well*, the figure of the dancer is perhaps the most striking to be found in all of his plays. Fand, the woman of the Sidhe, represents the fifteenth phase of Yeats's system in *A Vision*, the beauty and perfection that is beyond any human form. Fand dances before the figure of Cuchulain so that she may entice him from the earth and into perfection with her. But Cuchulain is kept from Fand by Emer's bargain with Bricriu, a god of discord. Emer agrees to renounce any chance of future happiness with Cuchulain in return for his release from Fand's power. Fand is enraged at her loss of Cuchulain, but it is questionable whether or not he could have merged with her perfection. Although he has great spiritual qualities, he has too much humanity to enter the fifteenth phase, where nothing human can exist. The glittering perfection which Fand represents is finally illusory for the human being. Entering the fifteenth phase would mean final assimilation into the universe, loss of personality, loss of human qualities.

Fighting the Waves, the prose version of *The Only Jealousy of Emer* that Yeats wrote for a more general audience, is notable for its slightly different treatment of the dance of Fand. Yeats did not consider *Fighting the Waves* in the same category with *The Only Jealousy of Emer*. In a 1934 introduction to the play he wrote that he didn't feel it was :

> always necessary when one writes for a general audience to make the words of the dialogue so simple and matter-of-fact; but is it necessary when the appeal is mainly to the eye and to the ear through songs and music. *Fighting the Waves* is in itself nothing, a mere occasion for the sculptor and dancer, for the exciting dramatic music of George Antheil (*VPl*, p. 567).

This later judgment of the play is considerably less enthusiastic than it was when he wrote to Olivia Shakespear on 13 September 1929: 'My *Fighting the Waves* has been my greatest success on the stage since *Kathleen-ni-Houlihan*, and its production was a great event [in Dublin] ... Everyone is as convinced as I am that I have discovered a new form by this combination of dance, speech and music' (*The Letters*, p. 767–8). It may be that the excitement of the Dublin production caused Yeats to value *Fighting the Waves* more highly than he would when considering it in a less exalted moment. In any event, the play does seem much more a spectacle, an occasion for Antheil's music, de Valois' dancing, and Van Krop's masks than an exposition of a 'deep of the mind'.

In the play many consider to be most like the Japanese *Noh*, *The Dreaming of the Bones*, Yeats for the first time chooses to make some description of the dance in the text of the play.

There are three characters in the play, excluding the chorus, and dress and masks indicate the supernatural quality of Diarmuid and Dervorgilla. A

Young Man in the play is mortal, an Aran fisherman caught up in the trouble of 1916. He serves as a representative of the here and now; his comments upon Diarmuid and Dervorgilla's sin are the comments of his nation and his age. He will not forgive them their ancient sin, and without this forgiveness they feel doomed to 'drift from rock to rock'.

The Young Man believes that the whole history of Ireland would have been changed for the better if Diarmuid and Dervorgilla had not betrayed their country to the invader.

> That town had lain,
> But for the pair you would have me pardon,
> Amid its gables and its battlements,
> Like any old admired Italian town;
> For though we have neither coal, nor iron ore,
> To make us wealthy and corrupt the air,
> Our country, if that crime were uncommitted,
> Had been most beautiful. Why do you dance?
> Why do you gaze, and with so passionate eyes,
> One on the other; and then turn away,
> Covering your eyes, and weave it into a dance?
>
> *(VPl,* p. 774).

Two purposes are served by this speech. First we are given the mortal judgment of the young man on Diarmuid and Dervorgilla, and second we have a description of the dance, which is for the first time integrated into the poetic text. This is the closest Yeats comes to following the rules of the Japanese *Noh* dance, in which the chorus speaks the words of the protagonist as he dances, or explains the significance of his dance. Yeats's young man continues to describe the dance, but he does so without explicitly describing either the dancers' action or their motivation, which indeed he could not do. He is a mortal watching supernatural spirits, and he can only report what he sees. But in his report there is something of the quality of the dance itself.

> So strangely and so sweetly. All the ruin,
> All, all their handiwork is blown away
> As though the mountain air had blown it away
> Because their eyes have met. They cannot hear,
> Being folded up and hidden in their dance.
> The dance is changing now. They have dropped their eyes,
> They have covered up their eyes as though their hearts
> Had suddenly been broken – never, never

Shall Diarmuid and Dervorgilla be forgiven.
They have drifted into the dance from rock to rock,
They have raised their hands as though to snatch the sleep
Though they can never reach it. A cloud floats up
And covers all the mountain-head in a moment;
And now it lifts and they are swept away.

(VPl, pp. 774–5)

This technique of having a character comment upon the dance by the principals is in the main effective, for it allows the poet to exercise some control over the choreography of his play, and it gives the audience and the director an 'authorized' version of what the dance represents.

The description by the Young Man is not so explicit, however, that it fixes forever the meaning of the dance. It is instead an interpretation by a young fisherman who, like ourselves, is in possession of only part of the truth. It opens the possibility of many more interpretations. The Young Man does not say that he understands the dance, but qualifies his observations with 'as though'. Their handiwork is blown away as though it is a consequence of their eyes meeting; they have covered their eyes as though their hearts had suddenly been broken; they have raised their hands as though to snatch sleep from the sky. What the Young Man infers is possible, even probable, but it is not the final explanation of the dance. Yeats means us to be informed by the Young Man concerning the nature of the dance, but the final explanation must lie in the consciousness of each perceiver. The communication of the dance is one of multiple meanings. The dance must remain indirect; it must communicate as symbol.

Calvary represents a departure from the line of Irish history and mythology that Yeats had been following in the Cuchulain cycle. The Christ represented in *Calvary*, however, has much more in common with the Irish hero than he does with the Christ of the New Testament. The audience must realize that this skewed Christ is not having a literal experience but is 'dreaming back' his passion and crucifixion. Like Cuchulain, Christ wishes for some positive answer or action that will make the universe conform to law. Like Cuchulain, Christ is doomed to the irrelevant heroic action. As Cuchulain fights the waves, so Christ is crucified. As the Blind Man and the Fool use Cuchulain's madness as an opportunity to steal bread, so the Roman soldiers divide the belongings of the crucified Christ.

The Roman soldiers are the dancers in *Calvary*, and their dance is not for themselves, but for Christ.

Second Roman Soldier.
    In the dance
We quarrel for a while, but settle it
By throwing dice, and after that, being friends,
Join hand to hand and wheel about the cross.

(*They dance.*)

Christ.   My Father, why hast Thou forsaken me?
                    (*VPl*, p. 787)

There is a unity of the soldiers and Christ, hinted at and foreshadowed by Christ's encounters with Lazarus and Judas, and re-enforced by the bird symbolism of the unifying dramatic image (see Londraville, in *YAA* No. 10, 1992). The dancers are at once outside the salvation effected by Christ and at the same time a part of his terrible delusion that he could perform an action that could have meaning outside of his own reality. The essential solitude of a character meant to be a surrogate for all mankind is twice as telling when he realizes this solitude for the first time.

The Cat and the Moon is a comedy that closely adheres to the *Noh* pattern established with *At the Hawk's Well*. Yeats was thinking of the *Kyogen*, the comic interlude that often comes between two *Noh*. In his 1924 introduction to the play, Yeats wrote that he intended his play 'to be what the Japanese call a "Kiogen", and to come as a relaxation of attention between, let us say "The Hawk's Well" and "The Dreaming of the Bones", and as the Musicians would be already in their places, I have not written any verses to be sung at the unfolding and the folding of a cloth' (*VPl*, p. 805).

The point in *The Cat and the Moon* of particular relevance here is the dances performed by the principals. In *The Nō Plays of Japan*, Arthur Waley suggests that The Blind Beggar and the Lame Beggar are very close to the stock characters of the Japanese *Noh*, the *Daimyō* and the comic servant, and the first dance which Yeats's characters perform is very like the ritual beating which the *Daimyō* often gives the servant (89). Yeats's stage directions explain: '*Blind Beggar beats Lame Beggar. The beating takes the form of a dance and is accompanied on drum and flute*' (*VPl*, p. 802).

The second dance has more importance; even in the farcical context of the play, the dance is described as 'a miracle', and represents a moment of illumination for the Lame Beggar: '*The Lame Beggar begins to dance, at first clumsily, moving about with his stick, then he trows the stick to the ground and dances more and more quickly. Whenever he strikes the ground strongly with his lame foot the cymbals clash*' (*VPl*, p. 804).

This moment of illumination is not equal to the realizations of a Christ or a Cuchulain, but the Lame Beggar is not an heroic person. The quality of his vision is akin to his own quality. Through the agency of the chorus he learns that he is 'blessed', 'a miracle', and this is enough for him. He will never feel the need to question the universe or his place in it. In his own way he is much closer to the vision of the saint than either Yeats's Cuchulain or his Christ.

In *The Resurrection* there is no dance on the stage. But in the dialogue of the Hebrew and the Greek, a Dionysian dance is described which has its own meaning to its followers. The Hebrew speaks:

> The priests of Dionysus are on the other side of the house, but they have hidden the image of the dead man, and from that I judge that they have raised their lunatic cry 'God has arisen, God has arisen!' They will cry that through every street of the city, making their God live and die as they please. But why are they silent – is it because they are hoarse that they dance silently, or is it some part of the play to seem, speechless at last, poor effeminate crack-pated men, with their imaginary joy? They are coming nearer and nearer, dancing all the while some kind of elaborate step, like the steps of an old Syrian dance. Look how they roll their painted eyes, as the dance grows quicker and quicker. Did ever man show such abandon in the expression of a real emotion? (*VPl*, p. 926)

At this moment of history, according to Yeats, a millennium is approaching. The world is shifting from the subjective, polytheistic stance it has occupied for the previous two thousand years and is preparing itself for the objective, mono-theistic era which Christ will bring. A new civilization is about to be born from everything that the previous civilization had rejected. It is reasonable, then, that the worshippers of Dionysus dance their crazed, silent dance; and it is also reasonable that this dance be performed offstage, for they are, as Peter Ure suggested in *Yeats the Playwright*,[12] worshippers of the 'dismembered' god (p. 124). Dionysus is dying, and the Christian era is being ushered in. The descrip-tions of the dancers show that they are possessed by their god, but their god is losing power, is falling out of phase. The objective Christian cycle is beginning, and the power of the new god and the new myth is gaining strength.

Therefore the dance described by the Hebrew has little in common with the dances in Yeats's other *Noh* plays. The closest thing to Yeatsian dancing in *The Resurrection* is the entrance of Christ – who never speaks, and whose movements are very slight, yet come at the climax of the play because the words have built toward that speechless pantomime and mystery.

The revelation in *A Full Moon in March* is closely related to Yeats's own thoughts concerning life and art at this period of his career. He has come back to the 'foul rag-and-bone shop of the heart', and the dance that the Queen makes before the Swineherd celebrates this knowledge.

Second Attendant.

Why must those holy, haughty feet descend
From emblematic niches, and what hand
Ran that delicate raddle through their white?
My heart is broken, yet must understand.
What do they seek for? Why must they descend?

First Attendant.

For desecration and the lover's night
                    (*VPl*, p. 989).

The Queen has realized that she cannot be complete in her virginal coldness, that fair must match with foul, that all things must be reconciled and unified. Her dance, therefore, is one of the simplest and purest forms of the *Noh* dance of enlightenment.

In Yeats's last play, *The Death of Cuchulain*, the poet constructs what one needs to appreciate its special form. In a prologue delivered by another of his old men, Yeats explains, among other things, the significance of the dance. He promises a dance, and wants to use the form 'because where there are no words there is less to spoil. Emer must dance, there must be severed heads – I am old, I belong to mythology – severed heads for her to dance before. I had thought to have those heads carved, but no, if the dancer can dance properly no wood-carving can look as well as a parallelogram of painted wood' (*VPl*, p. 1052). In this same speech, the Old Man also refers to Milton's *Comus*, which suggests Yeats's awareness of the dance-play tradition in Western art, although he seems to have taken very little of his own dance from the West.

When the old man says that he wanted a dance because 'where there are no words there will be less to spoil', it would appear that he is a strange mouth-piece for a poet, who must deal in words. Yeats is thinking of the dance as the supreme form of art; here, as elsewhere in his work, the dancer is the symbol of the unified personality, one whose every movement is a poem and who does not need to rely upon words to communicate. There will be 'less to spoil' because the message of the dance will not have to be interpreted through the imprecise medium of language.

It appears strange that the dancer in *The Death of Cuchulain* is Emer. She has no action in the play until her dance, and no lines at all. It is not that there is no other possible dancer, for there are three other female parts, Eithne Inguba, Aoife and the Morrigu. We might dismiss Eithne Inguba as too far removed from the spiritual to participate in a dance of enlightenment, and the Morrigu is a near-abstraction. This leaves Aoife, who has borne Cuchulain's son and remained his lifelong enemy. Her sisters have danced before him before, at other climactic moments of his life. (There was the hawk-woman to the young Cuchulain, the glittering Fand in *The Only Jealousy of Emer*.) Why does Aoife not dance at the climax of Cuchulain's life? Instead we see the faithful Emer, who otherwise has no place in this play, enter to perform the final dance before the head of Cuchulain.

It is obvious in the earlier Cuchulain plays that the Sidhe represent some sort of spiritual union to Cuchulain. What does Emer represent at this last moment of Cuchulain's life? We learn from the Morrigu, the goddess of war, that she 'arranged the dance', so there is something of god-like, fated arrangement which imbues Emer's dance. The implication of the Morrigu's statement is that not only the dance, but Cuchulain's death itself was arranged, that the men who gave Cuchulain his mortal wounds were no more than her puppets.

Emer's dance, then, is as fated as anything else in this world. Everything is arranged, but the truly heroic man acts as if he could control his own fate. This refusal to admit to any power greater than his is what makes the tragic hero.

In other plays we have seen extensions of Cuchulain's personality in the dances of the women of the Sidhe; in this last play we see another side of him. Emer's dance requires that she make obeisance to the head of Cuchulain, and perhaps it is fitting that she does; for Emer, who has always been tied to temporal reality, worships that part of Cuchulain that is flesh, even when the flesh has lost its vitality. As much as she loves Cuchulain, she cannot truly know him, for even as she bows before his severed head, a 'few faint bird notes' announce that his soul is elsewhere.

But Emer's role is not that of the mistaken mortal juxtaposed against the certainty of spiritual creatures. Here we see Yeats's theory of opposites that contain one another. Without mortality and frailty, we can have no knowledge of the spiritual. Emer, rather than one of the Sidhe, must dance in this last play so that Yeats's final dramatic work (and he certainly knew it was his last) could demonstrate that synthesis of fair and foul, flesh and spirit, which had become for him the ultimate revelation.

The dance became vital to Yeats's conception of drama after 1916. He calls these first plays 'plays for dancers', and a perusal of his letters will show that he used the term 'dance-play' again and again in the 1930s. But, as with other elements of the Japanese *Noh*, Yeats had anticipated the movement that he wished for his dance. He wrote in *Samhain: 1904* that 'actors must move, for the most part, slowly and quietly and not very much, and there should be something in their movements decorative and rhythmical, as if they were paintings on a frieze' (pp. 176–7). But it was not until he read the Pound-Fenollosa *Noh* redactions and saw Ito's stately dance that he recognized what he wanted in his drama.

The dance in Yeats's plays may be a Dantesque portrayal of passion, as in *The Dreaming of the Bones*, or a seduction of the will, as in *At the Hawk's Well*, but it seems most often to be a kind of illumination, when the character comes to some great personal truth. This realization may be danced by the character himself, as in *A Full Moon in March*, or by a surrogate, as in *Calvary*.

It is difficult to assess the quality of a particular illumination in a particular play, but some general remarks may be made concerning them all. The heroic character in a Yeats play often acts as if he had complete control of his fate, when in fact he is the inhabitant of a deterministic universe. The moment that he realizes that he cannot control his destiny is the moment of tragic intensity. But in at least one play, *The Death of Cuchulain*, the character acknowledges these deterministic forces which control him and still continues to act as if he controlled his own fate. This acting 'as if' seems to define a new type of tragic hero, for it is by acting this way that the character defies a deterministic universe. He creates his own style, he is his own man, regardless of what is done to him.

The images of the dancer as unified personality and the dance as unified activity so permeate Yeats's work after 1916 that one finds it difficult to read very far in his drama, poetry, or prose without encountering them. The dance has become a major tool with which he may hammer his thoughts into a unity.

It is fruitless to speculate how Yeats's dance might have evolved had he been nurtured in a tradition rather than being forced to go 'to Asia for a stage convention'. He would have had access to an audience and a ritual as I did in Taiwan. How might have that have changed his work? Finally, I believe that great art is more often created by the opposition of ideas than by recapitulation and refinement of accepted forms. As Yeats says in 'Anima Hominis',[13] 'We make out of the quarrel with others, rhetoric, but of the quarrel with ourselves poetry.'

NOTES

1. 'W.B. Yeats's Anti-Theatre and Its Analogs in Chinese Drama: The Staging of the Cuchulain Cycle.' *Asian Culture Quarterly* Vol. XI, #3 (1983): pp. 23–31.
2. See Londraville, in *Yeats An Annual of Critical Studies* No. 2, 1984 (USA).

3. W.B. Yeats 'Certain Noble Plays of Japan', *Essays and Introductions* (New York 1961).
4. Faubion Bowers, *Japanese Theatre* (New York 1952).
5. See Londraville, *Yeats Annual No. 8*, p. 95.
6. Makoto Ueda, *Zeami, Basho, Yeats, Pound: A Study in Japanese and English Poetics* (London and The Hague 1965).
7. W.B. Yeats, *The Letters of W.B. Yeats*, ed. Alan Wade (New York 1961).
8. W.B. Yeats, *Four Plays for Dancers* (London 1921).
9. *The Variorium Edition of the Plays of W.B. Yeats*, eds Russell K. Alspach with Catharine C. Alspach (New York 1966).
10. Earl Miner, *The Japanese Tradition in British and American Literature* (Princeton 1958).
11. Yasuko Stucki, 'Yeats's Drama and the Nō: A comparative Study in Dramatic Theories.' Modern Drama. Vol X (September 1966): pp. 110–22.
12. Peter Ure, *Yeats the Playwright* (New York 1966).
13. W.B. Yeats 'Anima Hominus' in *Essays* (New York 1924).

Breaking the Code: the Drama Workshop at the Yeats International Summer School, Sligo

SAM McCREADY

The Drama Workshop has for many years been a vital part of the annual Yeats International Summer School. During the two-week school, students have lectures in the morning, with seminars each afternoon. Students whose focus is the drama meet each afternoon for a practical exploration of Yeats's plays. These students not only discuss Yeats, they also physically experience his wonderful language and drama.

In 1998, George Watson, the Director of the Summer School, invited me to conduct the Drama Workshop. It was not my first visit to the school; my wife Joan and I had been at the first two Yeats Summer Schools in the early 1960s, when we performed the Yeats plays in the Sligo Town Hall with the Lyric Theatre Company from Belfast, the only theatre in the world to specialize in the drama of Yeats. With that company, under the inspired guidance of the founder, Mary O'Malley, I had learned the fundamentals of Yeats's drama. From that time, directing Yeats became a quest for me; how could I be faithful to Yeats's ideas on the theatre and yet make the plays accessible and engaging for a modern audience. This was the challenge I set myself when I agreed to direct the Drama Workshop at the Yeats Summer School.

The play I had chosen to work on was *The King of the Great Clock Tower*. I was full of enthusiasm when I first arrived but soon realized the difficulties of realizing my objective. Most of the students in the Drama Workshop had little to no experience of acting and limited knowledge of Yeats's plays. The workshop met for only two hours each day and there were few resources that I could draw on for the public presentation of *The King of the Great Clock Tower* which would take place at the conclusion of the Summer School. In the limited time available, we had to study the text, explore movement and speech, work with masks, learn the lines and work on costumes, lighting and sound for the final presentation. But I had fifteen enthusiastic students who responded wonderfully to my process; they were prepared to work hard, and the more they connected with Yeats's amazing drama of the Swineherd who comes to woo the silent Queen and for his labours is beheaded by the jealous King, the more excited they became about every aspect of the presentation. The response from the capacity audience to the performance in the Hawk's Well Theatre justified our hard work.

The experience convinced me that what I was doing was worthwhile, not just for me but also for the students and the many Yeats aficionados in Sligo. Performances of the Yeats plays were rare but at the Yeats Summer School I had the chance to ensure they were still being performed and appreciated. I responded very quickly to George Watson's request that I return the following year and I've been there almost every year since. In subsequent years I have been joined by my wife, Joan, and the choreographer Maddy Tongue, each of whom takes responsibility for an aspect of the workshop. Joan, Maddy and I are a team, and nothing I have done in subsequent years could have been done without their creative help.

In the Drama Workshop, we have worked on a number of the later plays: *At the Hawk's Well, The Only Jealousy of Emer, The Death of Cuchulain, Purgatory, Calvary, The Resurrection, The Words upon the Window-Pane,* and *The Dreaming of the Bones.* We've worked on those later plays because, although Yeats wrote some important dramas in his early career, with his discovery of the *Noh* Theatre in 1916 he became a major innovative force in the history of modern drama. These later plays are also very suitable for the Drama Workshop; they are short, usually lasting thirty minutes in performance, they are suitable for any number of performers and they are not gender specific (in the Drama Workshop, Christ has been played by a woman, as has the Young Man in *The Dreaming of the Bones*). The plays make minimal demands on staging and yet they provide the students with a multi-disciplined experience; speech, characterization, movement, dance, singing and mask work. They make use of all the art forms; they excite my imagination and challenge me as a director.

Despite having the responsibility of putting on the production in the Hawk's Well Theatre on the final night of the school, the emphasis in all we do in the Drama Workshop is on the students. It is important for us that the students get involved with a Yeats play text, that they have some practical experience of the demands of Yeats's theatre and that they become engaged with Yeats the playwright. If the workshop process is a good one, the final performance will most likely also be good.

No two of my productions of the same play are ever the same, principally because they represent a collaboration of all involved, students and teachers. Each year I emphasize that this will be a unique production: at no other time will we have the opportunity to work on this play together and I want the production to reflect that uniqueness. As a director, I also want to continually explore Yeats, to examine the plays from different perspectives that I might better understand them; I am constantly trying to break the code.

Thus, every production I have done at the school has been unique but I remember with delight the first production of *The Resurrection*. I set the play in a classroom with senior pupils studying the play and becoming bored. When the teacher leaves them to read the play silently they begin acting it out, initially reading from the text and then throwing the texts away and playing out the drama. The interpretation brought the play stunningly to life. Also memorable was the production of *At the Hawk's Well* in which Christ was danced by a Japanese student familiar with the *Noh*. Another actor spoke Christ's lines, and the concentration and *Noh*-inspired movements of the dancer held the audience mesmerized. In no other production of the play have I felt we were witnessing to such a degree Christ's 'dreaming through' his crucifixion, which is what Yeats intended. The dancer also played a special role in Joan McCready's production of *Purgatory*. The Old Man and the Boy were both masked but the presence onstage of the ghostly apparition of the Mother, danced by Maddy Tongue, connected this late play more closely with the *Plays for Dancers* which preceded it. For the same reason, masks were introduced into the quasi-naturalistic *The Words Upon the Window-Pane*. Mrs Henderson, the medium, assumed a mask when she channelled the spirits of Jonathan Swift, Stella and Vanessa, and a chorus (not in the original play) echoed the spirits' lines. These and other innovations in the production of the plays added immeasurably to my understanding of them and also explored their remarkable versatility and theatricality.

As may be appreciated, to mount a fully staged production of a Yeats play is a demanding process, not only for Joan, Maddy and myself, but also for the students. They have been part of an enormous learning curve, at times physically and mentally exhausting, and yet the satisfaction and joy they get from the process is palpable, so much so that a number return year after year. It delights us also that so many are determined to continue to work on the Yeats plays, either in production or as a focus of study for higher degrees. That is why we keep returning to the Summer School when invited. We find that, despite the energy and time we put into the workshop, we gain immeasurably from it, not only in our deepening appreciation of Yeats's drama but also in the close friendships we make.

What have I learned from all the productions I have done at the Yeats Summer School? I have learned to respect Yeats, and to follow closely his three guiding principles for the presentation of his plays: clear speech, minimum gesture and movement, simple costumes and staging. It's possible to ignore these principles and exploit the plays for theatrical ends, with extravagant settings, sound and lighting effects, exotic costumes or nudity (yes, it's been done), effects which may titillate the eyes of the average theatregoer but are not consistent with what Yeats wanted or believed; for Yeats, as with other contemporary playwrights, like Samuel Beckett, less is more.

Yeats wished for a Theatre of the Mind, a theatre to touch the imagination, like a conjuror with a magic wand. To create the state of reverie or dream in which his later plays function, each actor must enter into the drama as though taking part in some religious ritual. That is what I observed when I was permitted to observe backstage the famous Umewaka Noh Company. Priest-like, the leading actor, the *Shite*, was dressed by his attendants; there was a distinct air of reverence, a solemnity, as the players prepared to perform a drama that had remained unchanged for hundreds of years. The players were enacting a ritual, both offstage and onstage, and it is this sense of ritual that I believe is central to the performance of Yeats.

Yeats introduced ritual into *At the Hawk's Well*, and his other *Plays for Dancers*, with the opening and closing of a black curtain manipulated by the Musicians as they spoke the choruses, but he advised against using the curtain if the plays were performed on a conventional stage. Since the Drama Workshop performs the play in the Hawk's Well Theatre, I have devised many ways, consistent with each play, of creating the ritual. We have manipulated huge cloths and sheets; we have carried on to the stage large stones to mark out the acting space, we have built the set with chairs in full view of the audience, and so on. With the most recent production of *The Dreaming of the Bones*, the cast, dressed in black, entered in darkness, carrying lighted lanterns. There was an air of mystery; the audience was being drawn to some special place where something would happen. When the stage lights came up, the chorus took their seats in chairs lined across the back of the stage. There they sat, upright, still, powerful commentators who would witness the meeting of the Young Man and the wandering lovers, Diarmuid and Dervorgilla on a hillside in County Clare.

When these leading characters entered they stood very still, like living sculptures, trapped in some inexorable dream. Without distractions, the audience could listen to the words and become immersed in the drama.

I had a very strong cast in *The Dreaming of the Bones*, but the key to the success of the production was the absolute simplicity of the staging, the use of repetitive ritualized movements, the focus on stillness, the exquisite dance of longing and regret, choreographed by Maddy Tongue, the clear speech, and the strong internal connection that the leading players made with their characters.

Joan, Maddy and I will return to Sligo this year and we will joyfully set ourselves the task of meeting a whole new group of students and introducing them to the esoteric world of Yeats. We will work on one of his later plays, delighting in the activities of the workshop, the warm-up games, the movement, the vocal work, the reading and study of the text, and the friendships we make, but above all we will enjoy the journey to explore and reveal, to a degree, the remarkable plays of W.B. Yeats. Once more, I will attempt to break the code.

The Dreaming of the Bones: *chorus.*
Yeats Summer School, Sligo 2004

At the Hawk's Well: *the Young Man (Cuchulain) and the*
Woman of the Sidhe. Yeats Summer School, Sligo 2007

'The Labyrinth of Conscience' –
Uses of Dramatic Space in W.B. Yeats's
The Dreaming of the Bones[1]

MELINDA SZŰTS

Yeats's plays are often considered too theoretical and predominantly textual and are thus usually analysed merely on the basis of their literary value and indubitable merits in dramatic verse. Although the text-centred approach that focuses primarily on the plot, character-relations and stylistic registers might provide us with a better understanding of the written material and Yeatsian thought in general, it disregards the fact that the playwright viewed his plays not as mere literary texts but material written for performance whose true essence is called to life through stage representation. Yeats's global, performance-based approach[2] that regards the living body of the spoken, spatially presented material as the base of his work of art requires analyses that attempt to place Yeats's plays into the stage space, and try to look at the written text from a perspective that investigates the possibilities of the staged performance, its semantic layers and manifold relations to the audience.

I believe that Yeats's innovation in the theatre practice and stage dramaturgy of his time lies in a completely new perspective of spatial relations, which is in strong correlation with his performance-based attitude. However, Yeats's understanding of dramatic space and his onstage spatial constructions are far from being homogeneous, and varied from time to time, depending on the theoretical influences and practical circumstances he was working under. The heterogeneity of his dramatic visions thus requires us to narrow down the focus of our attention to a particular stage in the development of Yeats's stage drama-turgy, which, being a unified, organic system of its own, might count as an ultimate point of reference within the Yeatsian dramatic oeuvre. The 'Yeatsian revolution'[3] in the use of theatre space can be most fully presented through his *Four Plays for Dancers*, which, thanks to their performance-based nature, primarily rely on, and are thus determined by, spatial relations.[4]

Yeats's changes in the uses of theatrical space in the dance plays – abandoning almost all visible stage scenery, employing an open, platform stage and relying primarily on the place-making power of words[5] – served the purpose of breaking up the 'traditional' binary division of on- and offstage space to give way to a more complex and transmutable reality-structure. He developed a threefold division of dramatic space that allowed him to show how the realms of parallel dimensions (our own time-bound world and the eternal domains of the supernatural) can be intertwined through the mediating context of the theatre performance. In each play, the often self-reflexive meta-layer of the opening scenes can be called layer 1 (L1), which functions as a mere base on which the second layer (L2) of the playing space is projected. The poetically evoked, to-be-imagined dramatic space of L2, however, is again not a stable one, as in a most important moment, through one character's subjective media-tion, it is transposed to a third dimension (L3), the timeless dream-space of the supernatural. To see how Yeats's threefold space-world is constructed in the dance plays, and, if staged, how it contributes to the overall dramatic effect evoked by the performance, we should focus more elaborately on one represen-tative play: *The Dreaming of the Bones*.

Yeats's third dance play[6] is a drama of mobility. As its title suggests, Yeats placed the dramatic focus directly on the innermost domains of the dance plays' space-relations, the dream itself, whose essence lies in its variable, rela-tive qualities. The act of dreaming that we have seen from the outside in *At the Hawk's Well*, and as a parallel space bodied forth as the projections of the mind in *The Only Jealousy of Emer*, is here opened up and shown from the inside, leaving space for multiple interpretations and placing its audience in a spatial and temporal confusion.

Movement is an organizing principle that not only serves to visualize the spatial turmoil of dreams, but also defines the audience's position within the whole of the dramaturgical structure. A strong sense of motion is already evoked in the opening song, where the Musicians describe the turbulent upward movement of dreams, spinning up from the still centre of 'the dry bones of the dead', filling the valley to 'overflow the hills' in their circular, spiral stream. The 'widening gyre' of dreams that flows up in the cup-shaped setting embodies an ever-recurring pattern of movement we are immediately drawn into: the Musician-commentators from the very beginning take up the position of the audience to generate a feeling of shared consciousness in the theatre space. The fact that we see how lonely birds 'wheel about *our* heads' from an internal point of view is of prime importance, and is in strong relation to the play's historical focus. *The Dreaming of the Bones* actually is a Yeatsian history play, composed right after the Easter Rising,[7] which touches upon the questions of individual and shared, communal and national responsibilities, but does it in a beautifully composed, reversed dramaturgy by giving drama-turgical agency to the audience, and at the same time focusing on the personal, inner realms of one character. It is this duality of the plural and the personal that gives the play its most complex dramaturgical structure, and whose inter-play is presented primarily in its spatial arrangements.

The dramatic space of L2 is called to life as specified for place and time; we are in 1916, just after the rising, in the typically Irish setting of County Clare. We 'should not be afraid' in the concrete, familiar location of the opening scene that is described aptly enough to give us enough points of reference for orienta-tion, yet there is a strong sense of spatial confusion in the dramatic space – the whole imagined setting being 'covered up' in the misty darkness of the late 'hour before dawn'. It is stressed in the opening song that despite its three-dimensional spatial extensions, the place of the action is a spatialized metaphor for loneliness, where even 'sunlight can be lonely.' The lone figure of the Young Man enters the obscure place with a lantern, which is soon blown out by the Young Girl, making him totally dependent on the two Ghosts that appeared right after his entrance. Being lost in the dark, he has no other choice than to put himself 'into the hands' of the two shadows, who soon gain dramaturgical superiority by having a more reliable knowledge of the dramatic space.

Following closely the *Noh* tradition of space-minded dramaturgy, Yeats gives his characters dramatic weight by supplying them with manifold space-relations and locational attributes, and describes them according to their assigned places. Power relations in the first part of the play are in favour of the otherworldly creatures, who 'now the pathways where the sheep tread out and all the hiding places of the hills', whereas the Young Man 'would break his neck' if he was left on his own. The place names which he and his past are iden-tified with, however, bear common historical and cultural connotations for an Irish audience, as the fact that he was 'in the Post Office' and that he is seeking a hiding place to sail the western seas the following day tells everything about his identity, his political views and personal background. The same stands for the ghosts in the second part of the play; their spatially induced characterization gives a full account of their position and relationships.

Character-relations that are set in the first sequence of the play draw a nicely shaped triangular form,[8] which serves as an ultimate compositional pattern in the whole of the play, alternating with the circular movement of the gyre-like motion of the dream-set. The relation-map of the triangle visualizes the dramaturgical stance between the Ghosts and the Young Man, but also expresses the dual nature of the supernatural characters' relationship to each other. The Ghosts are masked, which is a strong visual means of distancing them from the unmasked figure of the Young Man, whose point of view and plane of reality the audience can thus easily identify with. However, the Young Man and the Young Girl formulate another pair within the triangle, not only by their names but through their physical and verbal engagement in the second part of the play. The Ghosts' internal relations are also presented through the space-game within the triangle by consciously rendering one player on the active side and leaving the other in total passivity on the other. The first sequence of the play is wholly conducted by the Stranger, with the Young Girl silenced on his side [see plate 1]. In the play's dual structure of shared and personal relations, the Stranger represents the pluralized, historical aspect that is repeatedly brought to the fore by referring to specific Irish place names and figures in history. The ruined Abbey of Corcomroe, Aughanish or Bailevelehan, the grey Aughtmana together with Donough O'Brien and the King of Thomond are all parts of the Irish cultural heritage, presented here to make the audience feel the personal story of the accursed, dwelling souls firmly bound to the whole of the Irish national past.

After the first sequence led by the dialogue of the two men, the stage is again set to motion by returning to the gyre-like cycles of the dream. The nature of this dream sequence in *The Dreaming of the Bones* is interesting both regarding its evocation and spatial representation, as the transcendence from L2 to L3 does not happen as abruptly as in the previous plays, which would make it absolutely obvious that it has actually happened. Here the border-crossing takes place in slow motion, without any overt sign to mark the act of trespassing. We might even claim that in the very first scene, with the appearance of the Ghosts, we are already placed into L3, the two creatures being only the embodied projections of the Young Man's mind. The fact that the dreaming process is so emphasized in the title, directly evoked in the opening song, and further referred to by the Stranger – 'In a dream ... some live through their old lives again'[9] – strengthens the idea that we are in the Young Man's dream from the very beginning.

The true engagement with the dreaming process, however, is brought about by the 'interlude' of stage motion accompanied by music. The cyclical movement around the stage evokes the same substance of dramatic space as the opening song; its fluid, changeable material draws the same map by its spiral turns. We learn from the Musicians' song that the three characters are slowly ascending; the owl being a point of reference for their gyre-like upward movement: first it is still 'crying above their heads', then it is seen 'at the foots level' to finally leave it 'far below them'. As opposed to the dream sequences in the previous plays, here the dreamer himself is moving; the smaller dance-circles are magnified and opened up to the whole of the playing area. This intensified representation might serve the purpose of drawing the audience into the heart of the process and letting them feel that they too are part of the action. 'The impact is like the sealing of a magic spell', says Cave: 'For the first time in his career as a dramatist, Yeats has discovered how a process of stylisation can transform the entire stage-action into powerfully allusive metaphor. The process requires an audience to enter imaginatively the meanings and interpretation that they draw from the experience.'[10] As the audience 'enter' the stage-world, they not only become part of the dream but of the cycles of history as well, whose ever-recurring pattern can be very effective on stage even if the spectators are not familiar with Yeats's theory of the gyres.

After the two rounds, the relation-map of the triangle is drawn again in another, more vivid, variation: the active part is taken up by the Young Girl, who, in contrast to the Stranger's cultural-historical approach, presents their story in most personal terms, employing mostly references to physicality and sexuality. Spatiality here is expressed not by mere references to Irish place names but through the Ghosts' personal relation to these locations: their very selves are defined by not coming 'from the Abbey graveyard' and thus being shut off from physical encounters with other lingering souls, who, 'being but common sinners ... can *mix* in a brief dream battle above their bones, or make one *drove* or *drift* in amity, or in the *hurry* of the heavenly *round* forget their earthly names'.[11] The lone lovers can only '*wander* side by side ... *hovering* between a thorn tree and a stone', until each time when they try to connect, 'the memory of their crime *flows up between* and *drives them apart*'.[12]

The triangle is broken for another circle around the stage, which takes the characters to the summit, and breaks the gyre-motion. When reaching the mountain top, the Young Man steps out of the shared dream, and by rejecting to help the pleading Ghosts, dooms them to eternal dwelling in their never-ending double-dream. Slowly, 'the horizon to the east is growing bright' and the unknown space of the dream-world is breaking up to let the familiar places of the

Irish scenery be seen by the Young Man – and through his poetic evocation, by the audience. The two lonely figures cannot see 'The Aran Islands, Connemara hills, and Galway in the breaking light' as they remain in the shadowy dream-space of L3 [see plate 2]. Their dance is shown again from the Young Man's point of view, who is watching them as they are being 'swept away', having 'lost themselves in a … self-created winding of the labyrinth of conscience'.[13] The ending strengthens the ambiguities generated by the shared dream-space and the subjective focus of the play, as Yeats leaves the interpretation of the Ghosts being mere visions of the Young Man's mind open. The protagonist only 'half believed' what he had seen was true, lifting or at least easing the heavy burden of moral judgement that was put on the shoulders of the specta-tors through their engagement with the action. It is not necessarily their (i.e. our) task to draw conclusions from the 'terrible beauty' of the Ghosts' treachery or the Easter Rising, as, according to Yeats's dramatic interpretation, personal and plural motives and responsibilities are too tightly woven, highly relative and ambiguous to build clean-cut conclusions on them. The Young Man closes down the sequence played in L2 by referring back to the dark and uncanny dream-dimension of L3: 'Terrible the temptation and the place!', giving way for the Musicians to turn the dramatic space back to its base.

Having seen some of the manifold variations of Yeats's unique handling of dramatic space in *The Dreaming of the Bones*, we might conclude that it is an ultimate representative of Yeats's space-minded, subjective dream-plays, whose truest meaning can only be accessed and delivered through performance – with the three dimensional embodiment of the space-relations suggested by the texts themselves. Through his poetic spaces, Yeats's words on stage are able to create worlds; showing us the diverging ways within and without labyrinths of the mind.

NOTES

1. This essay is an edited version of a paper given at the Hungarian Students' Scholarly Circles Conference in April 2015, titled 'The Labyrinths of the Mind' – Uses of Dramatic Space in W.B. Yeats's *Four Plays for Dancers*.
2. 'This is the very opposite of the over-literary approach to drama which some of Yeats's critics in the past have attributed to him. His feeling for the visual side of theatre was, in fact, sensitive beyond anything found in the playwrights writing for the English theatre of his time. He was in this respect a European even before he encountered the experimental Continental theatre in action', Katharine Worth, *The Irish Drama of Europe from Yeats to Beckett* (London 1978), p. 27.
3. Chris Morash and Shaun Richards, *Mapping Irish Theatre: Theories of Space and Place* (Cambridge 2014), p. 63.

4. In the *Noh* stage practice, Yeats finally found the way to devote enough time and attention to *spatiality* in its most complex sense; he could bring stories to life where the dramatic action was induced by the very location they took place in, and with the verbal evocation of the stage-space could draw the audience's attention to their multi-layered, semi-transcendental qualities. Peter Ure claims these 'place-minded' plays the most successful manifestations of Yeats's dramatic visions: 'one method of distinguishing his more successful plays from the others is that in them the story is about the place, or, to put it another way, that the characters have to come to just this place, and no other anywhere in the world, so that this story might happen', Peter Ure, *Yeats the Playwright* (London 1963), p. 29.

5. In his seminal work on the ontology and the spatial composition of the poetic image (*The Poetics of Space*), Gaston Bachelard defines words as mediators that have the quality to create and open up spaces and thus whole worlds inside and outside us: 'all important words, all the words marked for grandeur by a poet, are keys to the universe, to the dual universe of the Cosmos and the depths of the human spirit'. It is this shared, yet individually accessible universe, that is given dramatic substance in Yeats's mythical stage space, which is called to life through poetry. Gaston Bachelard, *The Poetics of Space* (Boston 1994), p. 198.

6. According to the rendering of the 1921 edition of *Four Plays for Dancers*.

7. William Butler Yeats, *Selected Plays*, ed. Richard Allen Cave (London 1997), p. 322.

8. The triangle is a general compositional pattern in all of Yeats's dance plays, which is most overtly manifested in the cloth-folding ritual. The three Musicians form a triangle 'with the first Musician at the apex supporting the centre of the cloth' (Yeats, *Selected Plays*, p. 114).

9. *Ibid.* p. 128.

10. *Ibid.* p. 325.

11. *Ibid.* p. 130.

12. Italics mine. *Ibid.* p. 313.

13. William Butler Yeats, *Four Plays for Dancers* (London 1921), p. 129.

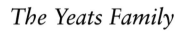

The Yeats Family

George Yeats – A Not So Reluctant Writer?

ANN SADDLEMYER

When W.B. Yeats was courting Georgie Hyde Lees in September 1917 he fled to Coole to gain the support of Lady Gregory. It was only weeks since Iseult Gonne had rejected him, a situation well-known by Georgie and of great concern to her mother. His daily letters[1] begin with a conscious need to prove his devotion to this new marital project, and we can observe him straining to set the right tone and clarify his hopes for their marriage: 'As the train passed through Wales I noticed a little house at the roadside & thought of Stone Cottage & myself walking home from the post to find you at the tea table.' 'You found me amid crowds but you will lead me to lonely places. Let us begin at once our life of study, of common interests & hopes.' 'Am I not Sinbad thrown upon the rocks & weary of the seas? I will live for my work & your happiness & when we are dead our names shall be rem[em]bered – perhaps we shall become a part of the strange legendary life of this country. My work shall become yours and yours mine & do not think that because your body and your strong bones fill me with desire that I do not seek also the secret things of the soul.' But despite his anxious pleas for a response, Georgie did not reply to Coole. 'No letter yet from you. <&> I keep wondering how you will begin the letter which seems full of mystery.' Still, Georgie remained silent.

I cannot believe she was shy – after all, they had known each other for at least six years, and marriage had first been spoken of two years before. Their introduction had been inevitable: in 1911, the year they were formally introduced, Georgie's widowed mother had married Olivia Shakespear's beloved brother Harry Tucker. Olivia's daughter Dorothy (who was to marry Ezra Pound) became Georgie's closest friend. By 1912 Yeats was staying with the Tuckers and Georgie in Margate, then later that year and again the next joined them in North Devon with Olivia and Dorothy; by now he was engrossed in a family friend's automatic script, and Georgie gained admission to the British Museum reading room to assist in the exciting occult adventure, sending him a businesslike report. Soon he was consulting her on horoscopes (she was meticulous), encountering her at séances (they were both frequent visitors), and then, apparently at his suggestion, he sponsored her membership in the Order of the Golden Dawn.

The well-worn story of Yeats's renewed courtship of Maud Gonne, then of her daughter Iseult, interrupted this friendship with Georgie. However, in March 1917 he finally claimed possession of Ballylee, the Norman tower across the fields from Coole, sketches of which he flourished among his women friends. When Iseult rejected him in August, he needed a wife more than ever. Fully aware of what she was taking on, Georgie was prepared – determined – to become that anchor. After a quiet marriage ceremony they retreated to Stone Cottage in the Ashdown Forest of Sussex. But the honeymoon was anything but traditional, Willy morosely suffering from stomach troubles and a guilty conscience – had he betrayed three people?

As is well-known, in an effort to retain her husband's interest and save her marriage George finally put pen to paper, trying her own hand at automatic script, and after some experiments producing 'a very profound, very exciting mystical philosophy', which her delighted husband began hammering into dialogue form. Now with him by her side, through the automatic script she was writing to him every day, and step by step they were creating a world vision and philosophy far more entrancing than mundane messages to Coole. She preserved most of the notebooks of the automatic script, and from them it is clear that from the beginning the project was a dialogue, not just between them, but drawing upon ghostly figures animated (and probably named) by George.[2] Work on the script continued intensely for three years, then sporadically until Willy had codified all he wanted for A Vision.

There will forever be debate as to whether the automatic writing was her hoax, a joint self-deception, or daimonic intervention. Did George believe in it? Towards the end of her life she would acknowledge that the system they developed through the automatic script and other methods came from 'their higher selves'. But the results are obvious. Clearly there were strong psychological advantages and equally strong emotional benefits to the role

Georgie consciously chose to play in selecting automatic writing as her creative medium. Her place in Willy's affections was assured and their marriage forged with a confidence and trust in each other's frank responses that would last until death. If their exploration proved nothing else, her generosity of spirit was obvious from the beginning, for in session after session she had to make room for the other women in her husband's life – his former mistress Mabel Dickinson and lighter loves were readily dismissed; surprisingly, Maud was easily disposed of, rapidly becoming the icon of his later poetry; Iseult, Olivia Shakespear, and Lady Gregory were more problematical, and would remain forces to be dealt with throughout her married life. More than that 'friendly, serviceable & very able' domestic partner he had hoped for, George was immediately established as the voice of truth, and for the rest of their lives together would continue to serve as unquestioned extension of his senses. She read aloud to him, served as his research assistant (where her linguistic skills and early study of philosophy were especially helpful), was typist and interpreter of his handwriting; WBY trusted her as critic both of his writing and the production of his plays, as editor and art adviser of his published works, as keeper of the hearth, guardian of the gate, and hence subtle discriminator of many personal influences.

In addition, the habit of discussion, of speaking of themselves and others at one or two removes, encouraged a process Yeats would develop more and more in his poetry – turning themselves and others into images. If poetry was the essence of his creative genius, then the automatic writing, whether consciously initiated or not, became the essence of hers. In helping provide those metaphors for poetry, might not the poet in turn have become her form of creation?

In addition to the almost daily chore at the writing table, George began to collect Willy's letters, and many of her own. But it is almost a year later that any reference is made to her side of the correspondence. By then they are living in County Galway supervising the restoration of Thoor Ballylee, and George is an active observer of Abbey Theatre affairs. When they are apart Willy needs to know details of 'how you got home & how all the beasts are'; he is relieved by her description of 'our household', and worries when he does not hear. The phrase will recur throughout their correspondence: 'Write often. I want to know every thing.' And as he works diligently away at transforming the details of George's automatic script into what would become *A Vision*, he also needs 'confirmation & a description' of various aspects of their new philosophical system.

In these early letters adventures with the Order of the Golden Dawn, experiences with mediums, and financial concerns over his sisters' Cuala industries (a lifelong battle), mingle with descriptions of household affairs, narratives about their many friends, unbuttoned descriptions of people and events and, always, Willy's work, creating the rich tapestry of their life together. In some cases they provide biographical and historical corrections to the popular narratives, suggesting subtle indications of intention and commitments without intermediary commentary.

His letters, sometimes as many as three a day, faithfully report on all his activities, whom he met, what he was reading and writing, even the clothes he bought. Hers relay all the news of Dublin and Ireland, the political situation at home and abroad, criticize the Abbey Theatre productions, remind him of appointments, comment on their friends' and her own activities and – very important – report on the development and activities of their two children. There are statements of belief, drafts of poetry, with comments by both. And they invariably include a description of the rooms in which they were written.

As the correspondence increased, so did its range: letters covered not just the Irish world of family, arts, letters, theatre, politics, society, but also the wider arena in which the many individuals mentioned in their gossipy, entrancing reports figured – actors, musicians, dancers, directors and designers; politicians, Senators and public servants; journalists, lawyers and priests; builders, doctors and country neighbours; mediums, occultists and philosophers; playwrights, poets and authors of detective stories – as well as intimate details of those whom we expect to encounter – members of the Yeats family, the Gonnes, Shakespears and Pounds, Gregory, and many of their Dublin circle. She and Willy years before had placed friends and strangers in their appropriate phases of the 'system' on the *Vision*'s wheel; this continued in their correspondence.

Always the letters flowed. George's letters, though not as frequent, were equally appreciated: 'Your letters are the best I have ever recieved [*sic*] they are so gay & vivid', he wrote; 'I thank you for your delightful letter – you are much the best letter writer I know, or have known – your letters have so much unstrained animation, so much natural joyousness.' She sympathized with Yeats's impatience over the desolation of Dublin during the years in which de Valera's conservative government controlled the arts and social life of Ireland. For George Yeats herself was easily bored and hated 'small talk'; she hungered, as she put it, 'for a mind that has "bite"' and which she appreciated in her husband's conversations. And always he trusted her judgment: 'I want your ideas on the subject – I am afraid of my own impulsiveness', he wrote concerning the selection of writers to be invited into his Irish Academy of Letters. Nor could he keep a secret from her; even if he thought he was enjoying an amorous secret intrigue, George knew all.

It was Maud Gonne who first observed to the Yeats sisters that George 'is most unselfish, never appears to assert herself at all, but from her face Maud thinks she *could* assert herself.'[3] And assert herself she did, from the moment she saved their marriage through the Automatic Script (an entry in 1919 reads, 'script depends on the love of medium for you – all intensity comes from that'). Despite references to an earlier correspondence, the first of George Yeats's letters that is preserved is from 1920, after their move to Oxford, the birth of their daughter Anne, their journey to the United States, and WBY's hasty mission to Ireland to rescue Iseult from an unhappy marriage to Francis Stuart. These early letters reveal much of the turmoil within the Gonne and Stuart households and the contrasting stability of the Yeatses': 'I feel it was right to come & I thank you for letting me do so', he wrote to Oxford from Ireland. ' – all that happens but shows me some new side of your goodness'. Her reply illustrates not only confidence, but sensible, studied wisdom: 'My thought is so much more for you than for her, because the spectator suffers more poignantly than the victim; his suffering being wholly subjective. As for my "goodness in letting you come" – that was really nothing but the foreseeing that you would have found it difficult to forgive me had I dissuaded you. If you cannot do much, at least you can do something.'

Why did they write so many letters? It is clear that the deliberate lacunae in Willy's reports on his activities did not escape his wife's antennae. Even during his later post-Steinach amorous adventures, he worked at sustaining a relationship, to continue a friendship with George. On her part, there was a clear determination to promote their partnership beyond her secretarial and administrative roles, to remind him of his family life, and most importantly to contribute to his creative work. Through their letters and the occasional telegram or telephone call, both maintained a presence during absence. Despite the gradual change in mode and manner from endearment to mere familiarity (such as the gradual more frequent use of 'Dobbs', one of George's childhood nicknames), there was an acknowledgment that they needed each other. Whenever they were apart, for whatever reason, the conversation kept going. And always, beyond the free give-and-take of ideas and questions, there was the added enjoyment of a good story to be well told and appreciated.

There is of course an element of posturing, as with all personal correspondence. When the collected edition of Willy's letters is complete, it will fill countless volumes, all bearing his inimitable voice and most of them clearly self-conscious. George frequently and cunningly subverted her own voice, leaving only questionable echoes to track. Unlike her husband who refined his voice at every opportunity, she destroyed papers and writings she thought unnecessary to the story of others, withheld personal knowledge if she could not weave it into the safety net of sanctuary, and frequently offered varying versions of what she *was* prepared to tell about herself. She even protected herself from those scholars she encouraged. When they got too close to her share of the story, she would dismiss them with the phrase 'That's private'.

Fortunately, many of George's letters to her most trusted friends do exist. She had few women friends, five or six at most – Dorothy Pound, Dolly Robinson, Sybil LeBrocquy (mother of the artists Louis and Melanie), several co-workers in the Dublin Drama League, and in later years the artists Elizabeth Rivers and Evie Hone (who fruitlessly tried to convert her to Catholicism). Although she had many acquaintances when Willy was in the Senate, two male friends especially were important to her – gentle Lennox Robinson ('Lynx' or 'Tinche' to his friends), and sensitive Thomas MacGreevy ('Tamsie' or – in moments of frustration – 'Painsy'). Tom MacGreevy was more like a younger brother – she could scold him, complain to him, talk about music and books. In turn, both men gave her their work to criticize, and confided their own problems. And all three wrote letters.

Lennox could be counted on in emergencies, even travelling out to France when the need arose, or house-hunting for her in Dublin; he was also discreet. They enjoyed going to the races (dog and horse) together, and were the strength behind the Dublin Drama League, when George's knowledge of modern languages and contemporary European literature was especially helpful. George held nothing back from Lynx, especially her trials, fears, and decisions about her husband and children:

> I seem to be inflicting a hell of a lot of letters on you & I hope I'll stop soon – but its your fault for being such a perfect oyster! I feel I can pour out all the vapourings & they wont go further or be supposed to be 'complaints' – ... I felt for years that life was quite unnecessary & if only a landslide would remove me they could have jointly a nurse a governess a secretary & a housekeeper & all get on so much better.[4]
>
> That ass-doctor came earlier than expected and filled W. with despair by telling him he need not expect ever to get back his original health etc. etc. So W. proceeded to have a complete breakdown, and 'of course he had never realised before how completely his interest in life had been in his work and if he isnt going to be able work and etc and etc' and 'You must tell Lennox. I know he has always thought I did not take my fair share of the burden of the Abbey .etc.etc.' So I made him dictate the beginning of a scenario for ballet, many letters and walked him into town today and he ate an enormous meal at the Majestic grill room and then wandered about looking at a seaplane which was taking people for short flights and landing near the Majestic on the sea, and only at 2–3 did he remember that he must be getting tired! I shall be thankful to get him to Rapallo and watch Ezra ginger him up!

Some day of course he will have to die but I do hope it will be in Dublin or at least London. ... More than ever I believe that no one should be dependent on anyone.

She disliked the boring and dull both in people and writing, and was intolerant of any pretension, dishonesty, or the second-rate, and all came out in her letters to Lennox:

... with you & Tom away Willy seems to have no one to hold his hand in the long evenings & he is a little 'off' Gogarty at present. Lately there have been swarms of hard-faced Americans there & none of them talk anything but sex & politics without even the saving grace of Quinn's lady who said after a lengthy conversation 'but I do like music too!' All nerveless & unwillable & rotten with age no matter how young they are.

Damn all the rich young men prancing round the world beautifully existing remote from a gross world by money & money & money. We'd a long afternoon of Stephen Tennant yesterday – so very tall, incredibly slim, with that pale delicate Ninetyish complection, large sad hazel eyes surrounded by the long dark up-turned eyelashes that so admirably match 'blond cendrée' hair with a deep wave in it from brow to nape of neck – long small boned hands ending in marvellously pollished [sic] pointed nails issue from 3 inches of beige silk cuffs (no turn-back; one large, individual, button) which in their turn emerge from brown suiting. But I didnt care for his taste in scent. He had just spent a week in Paris and had I am afraid been missled [sic] by one of these new Parisian Perfumes which disdain association with any flower – 'La Songe' 'Rêve d'amour' 'Pour troubler' and how it troubled the flat!... He'll spend the winters carrying his scent like a flag through all the most expensive hotels of Southern Italy – rich – rich ... He hadn't much conversation 'Fancy!' 'Really' 'How lovely!' and it was such a pity to just miss Gertrude Stein in Paris.

Did you ever read Morris? I have; aloud, for some three hours a day for some weeks. These over fertile writers ought, for the sake of younger generations, to undergo a Marie Stopes treatment. So treated Morris might have felt Chaucerian language incompatible with that vast efflorescence which covers everything he writes about, one cant read a description of a field and a tree without shivering to think how many leaves make the tree and how many blades of grass have gone to the greenness of the field. Horrid. Even when he describes bare places their lonely vastness is all pebbled, or still worse, sand. No. I do NOT like it. Then the clothes are encrusted with Embroideries ... Cuala ...

Where letters to Robinson were more confessional, George's correspondence with Tom MacGreevy tended to be philosophical, revealing more of her aesthetic tastes, more of her political views, and occasionally so personal that it was annotated 'burn this when read'.[5]

Chewing the cud over your expostulations on Anglo-Ireland that other day it occurred to me that truth was only to be discovered in an uncivilised country by the highly civilised and slightly mad foreigner. By foreigner I mean the object of your animosity, the Anglo-Irishman; probably the 'native' can achieve the high civilisation and slight madness necessary by a prolonged visit to some other country provided that he does not return to the motherland out of patriotism. Patriotism would destroy any country, its going to destroy England very soon. Up to about the middle of the war we wernt patriotic, everyone else was doing everything much better than we were, everyone elses goods were much better than ours. Then in spite of winning we began to come rather badly out of it, our unemployment is worse than anyone else's, we are very well hated by every other nation, we have a royalty who knits and collects postage stamps, breeds first rate bulls and fifth rate race horses, and so we have had to become patriotic to explain all these things to ourselves and hide them from the world.

The Divorce Speech has at any rate made people sit up – and whether they do so on a hard backed chair with their mouths in a horizontal line, or in arm-chairs with their mouths open, dont seem to much matter. But the Magical Sleep of hypocrisy & custom has had an abrupt waking! They are shocked at the mention of their immaculate O'Connell – but last night a good Catholic told W. the follow[ing] story – a man went to O'Connells house & found many pretty servant-girls waiting upon O'Connell. The man said 'What a lot of pretty maids you have. Where are they to be had?' And O'Connell's reply 'Upon the fur rug in the dining-room'.

Even more significantly, it is to Tom she admitted her further writing ambitions:

I drank four gins and its about two weeks ago and in the exhilaration produced thereby read Willy a play and he thought there was a play in it – in the first two scenes of it and damned the third fully comprehensively and thoroughly. I had a nervous breakdown for a week because when I had read one scene I realised what I was up to – he didnt know I ever did anything – but such small encouragement as I got has rather given me something to do, or to look forward to, not to production because I'm too critical to believe I'll ever do anything good enough, but at any rate to going on and not just getting through each day as it comes.

Although George finished the play, 'and it finished me', she rejected it as too 'impersonal' and 'really too punk for words.' However, 'rather proud of having done it, one got a sort of freedom', she moved on to a second play, 'more "ambitious" (I seem to hear that phrase as a commonplace of reviewers) with a theme more like to myself and what intrigues me.'

Unfortunately, no manuscript seems to have been preserved, nor is her playwriting mentioned again. We will never know what intrigued her, but clearly she needed a further outlet for her own creativity now that the days of automatic writing were over. She was serious enough about her writing to contemplate renting a studio outside of the house. When moving on to a novel, she remained secretive, scolding Willy for gossiping about it:

> How the devil am I to 'write a novel' if people ask how it progresses and I get involved therefore with biographical matter? I am doing it to amuse myself, and if I attempt to publish it shall do so under a pseudonym. Probably it will be burnt, but it is meant as an interest to myself, is not Irish or English, has no autobiographical or biographical associations. So leave me to stew in my solitary juice.

Again, the manuscript has disappeared.

A similar pattern can be traced in her other creative activities. Before her marriage she had studied painting at the Heatherley School in London (which her father-in-law had once attended). Her daughter Anne once noticed a portfolio stored in the house; but when she looked for it later, that too had disappeared.

Even from Willy, her closest friend, George Yeats concealed much. Perhaps her natural reserve was so strong she could not bear any public scrutiny; perhaps she was even more adept than her husband at creating a private mask. Or – I must reluctantly accept – George Yeats was just too clever for all of us.

NOTES

1. All letters here between the Yeatses are quoted from *W.B. Yeats and George Yeats The Letters*, ed. Ann Saddlemyer (Oxford 2011). All quotations are with the approval of Caitriona Yeats and the Yeats Estate.
2. See the *Yeats's Vision Papers*, vols 1–4, transcribed by George M. Harper, Margaret Mills Harper and colleagues (1992–2001).
3. See Ann Saddlemyer, *Becoming George: The Life of Mrs W.B. Yeats* (Oxford 2002) for details of George's early life.
4. George Yeats's letters to Lennox Robinson are in the Huntington Library, San Marino, California; many of them quoted in *Becoming George*.
5. George's letters to Thomas MacGreevy are in Trinity College, Dublin; many are quoted in *Becoming George*.

Anne Yeats (1919–2001)
A Twentieth-Century Artist

HILARY PYLE

Anne Yeats resembled the other artists of her family, her uncle Jack B. Yeats (1873–1957), and her grandfather, John Butler Yeats (1839–1922), in her urgent desire to be an artist true to her own time.

Her poet father took her birth seriously – he had an all-embracing wish for her, which he wrote down in the poem he composed for her, 'A Prayer for my Daughter'. One of his most important considerations was that she should not be so beautiful that she would be vain, and lose natural kindness and the ability to make friends: – he admitted that in this he was thinking of his former love, Maud Gonne.

> In courtesy I'd have her chiefly learned;
> Hearts are not had as a gift, but hearts are earned
> By those that are not entirely beautiful;
> Yet many, that have played the fool
> For beauty's very self, has made charm wise,
> And many a poor man that has roved,
> Loved and thought himself beloved,
> From a glad kindness cannot take his eyes.
>
> May she become a flourishing hidden tree
> That all her thoughts may like the linnet be,

> And have no business but dispensing round
> Their magnanimities of sound,
> Nor but in merriment begin a chase,
> Nor but in merriment quarrel.
> O may she live like some green laurel,
> Rooted in one dear perpetual place.

His prayer was well answered: Anne Yeats was courteous, and glad, and kind; and she was to live 'like some green laurel': generous, supportive to those who sought her out, and ultimately rooted in one dear perpetual place. Born in 1919 into what were troubled times in Ireland, she spent much of her youth abroad: but as an adult, whilst she travelled in Europe and Asia, she always returned to Dublin, dividing her living time between Merrion Square and Upper Mount Street, in the inner city, and the suburbs of Rathgar and Dalkey. In Dalkey she had a small but striking garden. On any visit to her Dalkey home the conversation in her sitting room adjoining a conservatory would be interspersed with bursts of exotic birdsong emanating from the unusual clock on her wall chiming the hours.

Though she wrote poetry as a girl, she used to say that by the age of twelve she had realized that she could never surpass her father, so she chose art as her profession. Not unnaturally her first influences, besides her mother who was artistic, were her aunts Lily (Susan Mary) and Lolly (Elizabeth Corbet) Yeats, leaders in the Irish Arts and Crafts movement since the beginning of the twentieth century, and still operating Cuala Industries as Anne grew to adulthood.

She received her first art lessons from her aunt Lolly, using watercolour. With her family she lived in Switzerland and Italy, retuning to Dublin when she was thirteen where she enrolled in the Royal Hibernian Academy School, then under the directorship of Maurice McGonigal, where she drew from the antique for five hours a day. Later, attending the National College of Art, presided over by Sean Keating, Anne reacted against the conservatism of both these artists.

However, before entering the College of Art, she took a position at the Abbey Theatre (all of the artistic Yeatses were involved with the Abbey Theatre at one time or another) as assistant to Tanya Moseiwitsch, which led to a period in Paris when she was eighteen studying at the Paul Colin's School of Theatre Design, returning to Dublin to become chief designer at the Abbey, doing sets and costumes for her uncle Jack's first performed play, *Harlequin's Positions*. Design was in her blood – her first tutor, her aunt Lolly, like her uncle, designed for the Cuala Industries. On leaving the Abbey, Anne worked freelance in other Dublin theatres as well as in Cork, and she was involved in other projects, such as the Unicorn and Red Bank restaurants in Dublin, as well as working on book illustration.

But, essentially, what she wanted to do was paint, and she started training at the College of Art. She approached Mainie Jellett, a pioneer of modernism in Irish art, for advice. She also consulted her uncle Jack, who had no time whatever for academic theories – he himself being largely self-taught – and he told her to paint life around her. This she took to naturally, working at first in watercolour, combining wax and ink in her technique: and experimentation like this became her lifelong practice.

Uncle Jack refused to give her art lessons, so she looked long and seriously at his paintings to understand what he was doing. She said that after twenty minutes of concentrated looking at one painting, everything thereafter that had seemed mysterious fell into place. Her work is quite unlike his. She would never lay so much importance on narrative or situation as he did, but now and again there are shared themes in their work.

She was not long in finding her own personal route. She was interested in international art, which at the time was mainly centred in Paris. Her first experience of School of Paris pictures had been in black-and-white reproduction in *The Studio* magazine: and in 1947 she went to Paris to see the canvases of Picasso and Braque as they were in reality, and these artists were her main influences about this period. Up to this she had worked totally in graphics – pencil or ink, warmed with a watercolour wash, sometimes varied with ink and wax – and she seems to have always enjoyed working in pen and ink. Now she prepared small studies for finished works that would be about twice the size; and she soon moved into oil. She held her first solo exhibition on her return to Dublin in 1948, and did not have another solo exhibition until September 1963. Instead she became involved in the Irish Exhibition of Living Art for twenty and more years, working closely with other *avant garde* Irish artists, principally women who excelled at this period.

From the beginning Anne had been fascinated by visual conundrums as they presented themselves. She had inherited the Pollexfen wit, and a fascination with visual ephemera, such as the traffic jam. In the 1970s she would do a series based on a piece of string.

A lasting pleasure was the abundance of song birds in Dublin's streets and gardens, which reappear constantly in her work of all periods. She was always contemporary and original in her style. Another concern was the lot of women, and their loneliness, explored in paintings such as *Bearing a Bundle, The Seat* and *Women and Washing,* this last now in the National Gallery of Ireland Yeats collection. She wasn't an active feminist, but, as an artist of her time, in the 1950s and 1960s anticipated the strong movement that would rise momentously in the 1970s.

During the 1970s she revived the Cuala Press (founded by Elizabeth Yeats, and later managed by her mother George) so as to reprint images of characters from *A Broadside*, such as *The Playboy, Theodore* and *Sarsfield*, as a celebration of the Jack B. Yeats centenary in 1971. In this she was assisted by Liam Miller of the Dolmen Press. At the same time she gave permission to the Irish Academic Press to reproduce the collections of *Broadsides* edited by her father in 1935 and 1937.

Throughout her life, she painted still life, particularly in her early French School influenced days. Her original linear manner in oil developed to become broad and painterly in the mid-nineteen sixties and then again her technique changed. She steeped butter muslin in thinned oil pigment, pressed it on canvas to make the image she wanted, aware that she could express movement, fluidity, and texture in a thoroughly contemporary way. In still life, the muslin patterning threw up chance images beside the central forms, and later formed a background to the entertaining and mysterious cats that stalked her imagination.

The most important and challenging event of her career was the commission in 1992 to paint a *Tribute* to her father for the Samuel Beckett Theatre in Trinity College, Dublin, on a canvas larger in size than she had ever attempted. Here she developed a symbolism deliberately for the purposes of conveying her own impression of the poet. She was inspired by W.B. Yeats's play *At the Hawk's Well* (1917) and his poem *The Hawk* – finding herself drawn to the sudden, unforeseen cry, and the bird's riveting eyes. The hawk, who was ever present but absent; invisible, inaccessible and everlasting. He tantalized the pilgrims who came to visit his well.

As always she approached her subject with preliminary drawings in pen and ink, making numerous sketches as she searched for the definitive image. She created the background of the painting by squeezing oil pigment straight on to the canvas and spreading it round. Over this she glazed the hawk with its mesmeric eye, a deliberately artificial form, the immortal shape hammered by craftsmen in her father's poem 'Sailing to Byzantium'.

In this new style and working on the same or a smaller scale, she turned to images that involved herself more personally – sunlit reeds, fish, the stalking cat, and of course birds. Technique had taken over and had become an integral part in the expressing of themes typical of the artist.

Latterly Anne Yeats painted little, but she continued to draw. She continued too to welcome scholars to look at her father's library, and to consult her uncle's archive, which she so generously presented to the National Gallery of Ireland in 1996. Sadly Anne died in early July 2001, some months before the official opening of the Archive Room built specially to accommodate the Jack B. Yeats Collection, and named the Yeats Museum. However, the collection is fortunate to include examples of her own work.*

Go ndéanaidh Dia trócaire ar a hanam.

---

* At the moment the Yeats collection has been suspended during ongoing alterations and extension to the National Gallery.

'Living in an elastic-sided world': John Butler Yeats and Lady Gregory

JAMES L. PETHICA

If obliged to characterize Augusta Gregory in less than a minute, one might begin with terms such as pragmatic, politically canny and decisive. The centrality of religious faith in her life would swiftly follow, along with the ways her career as a woman writer involved a constant negotiation between the demands of her own genius, and her instinct to help and collaborate with others. Her unflagging commitment to a moderate form of Irish nationalism would require emphasis, as would the element of Ascendancy self-interest and condescension lurking within it. Temperamentally a supporter of institutions – and most notably a founder of the Irish National Theatre – she always desired that her efforts as a literary and cultural nationalist, like all other aspects of her life, should help lead 'from things seen to things unseen'.[1] And one might close by highlighting her loyalty and generosity to those she cared for, and her capacity for ruthless dismissal of those she disdained.

Then, if obliged to repeat the task immediately for John Butler Yeats, one could for the most part simply invert these characterizations. He was indecisive, impractical and politically rather artless; was an atheist or skeptical positivist, who late in life termed God 'mainly a myth of the frightened imagination';[2] had a mighty capacity for self-involvement, and was quite content to depend on others for support as he indulged his own genius; happily shuffled off the bonds of his Irish life (albeit not his Irish identity) when settling permanently in the USA after 1907; and was a gadfly in his posture towards Nationalist politics since he cherished independence of thought above all. Suspicious of institutions, he was nonetheless the founding patriarch of a family of children far more successful than he was himself. And to close, one might stress that, unlike Lady Gregory, well-connected and socially astute but so often a loner psychologically, JBY was a wonderfully gregarious man.

As this thumbnail contrast might suggest, conventional friendship between two such different personalities and temperaments as JBY and the Dame of Coole was never likely. But these two powerful characters were repeatedly drawn together by their joint relationships with W.B. Yeats and with John Quinn. They were often rivals with one another for primacy with Yeats – with JBY trying to assert a continuing parental sway over a son who firmly resisted it, and Lady Gregory typically trying to avoid being perceived as merely an improved substitute for him as 'mother, friend, sister and brother' and 'more than kin' to the poet.[3] Each was sometimes a mediator or buffer for the other when their respective relationships with WBY or Quinn were strained or tested; and, occasionally, too, they were shared complainants and joint sympathizers in the face of high-handedness they perceived themselves as receiving from Quinn or WBY, or both. If the triangular elements of their relationship were often mutable, however, their direct dealings followed a largely predictable, and unequal, course, in which Lady Gregory adopted the role of manager and decisive figure of authority, and John Butler Yeats was content, most of the time, to be managed, or at least to offer a show of deference to her attempts to manage him.

The initial meetings between Gregory and Yeats *père* indeed in many ways established the core dynamics that would always exist between them. Lady Gregory, already firmly installed as W.B. Yeats's patron, advisor and collaborator after their first summer together at Coole, met other members of his family – his sisters Lily and Lolly, as well as John Butler Yeats, though not his brother Jack at this point – for the first time, in London, in late November 1897. A few days later she hosted them for a reception at the London Metropole Hotel following a speech W.B. Yeats gave to the Irish Literary Society on 4 December.[4] It was not quite as striking a debut introduction as Maud Gonne had managed in 1889 on first meeting the Yeatses, when she ostentatiously kept her cab waiting outside their Bedford Park house, and, as the Yeats sisters noted, wore both her slippers and 'a sort of a royal smile.'[5] But it was an arrival which nonetheless clearly signalled Lady Gregory's social position, her organizational centrality – and her ability to pay the bills.

Following the reception she observed in her diary merely that 'old Mr Yeats' was 'charming';[6] but when she finally saw him in artistic action for the first time two weeks later, sketching his son at Woburn Buildings, she was quick and astute in assessing him more fully: 'Found his father there sketching him, &not very successfully' she noted; 'probably knows his face too well – He has been at him for 3 days – [Yeats] writes that "it was very difficult to make him begin [sketching] & now it is still more difficult to make him leave off." '[7] And if this encounter, alone, was not enough to confirm JBY's impractical tendencies to her, the next day's news surely was:

> [He] was to set out for Dublin in the evening, to paint Standish O'Grady's portrait – but I heard next day he and with W[illie] started for the station, then found he had left his sketchbook & went back for that – & just as he had taken his ticket at Euston, the train steamed off – So then he decided to go by the next train & left his things at the cloak room & went back to Woburn Buildings – Then they set out the second time – & again he had left his sketch book – the other one, & had to return – but still they were in pretty good time at Euston, & they changed the ticket – but when he went to the cloak room, he had lost his luggage ticket and had to make a declaration – & while it was being made, the train went off! & then he was ashamed to go back to his family – & so went to the hotel for the night, & has been no more heard of – [8]

Her first written references to W.B. Yeats as 'Willie' notably coincide exactly with these first meetings with his father: prior to this she had initially termed him 'Mr Yeats' and then 'WBY.'[9] Since 'Willie' was the formulation JBY himself used in addressing his son, there's more than a hint that she co-opted an element of family position and power at the very moment of those first meetings with JBY, and that she did so quite deliberately. JBY would at first welcome both her forceful practical management of his son, and her loyal personal support, memorably dubbing her in 1899 the 'organizer of success';[10] but some degree of resentment at his sense that she had supplanted him in her influence would always linger in his response to her.

Despite her unpromising first impressions, Lady Gregory was determined, if not to bring JBY into her orbit, at least to make the most use of his talents she could. Well aware, via WBY, of the family's lack of money, she commissioned his father to make pencil sketches of Æ, Douglas Hyde, Horace Plunkett and other prominent Irish figures. As William Murphy observed, this commission had a decisive, transformative impact on JBY: 'at a stroke' it provided JBY 'with self-respect and an income' and it also significantly affected the course of his future artistic career by highlighting his abilities as a sketch artist, such that drawing, rather than oil paintings, made up the major share of his subsequent paid work.[11] It is important to note that her commission was not simply a pragmatic calculation on Lady Gregory's part, but the result of discriminating judgment. She was a capable amateur artist herself – she took regular lessons in sketching during the late 1890s, and her albums of sketches and watercolours from the 1880s and 1890s, now in the National Library of Ireland, show considerable talent. So she knew what she was advising. On the one occasion she sent a sketch of her own to JBY – a drawing of Thoor Ballylee, in a 1917 letter describing Yeats's plans for restoring the tower – he responded with surprise, having apparently, and rather characteristically, been quite oblivious to her artistic abilities: 'I had no idea you had so much talent in my line.'[12]

She would hold staunchly thereafter to her view that JBY should concentrate only on sketching as a career. As he prepared to sail for America in 1907, for instance, she emphatically and presciently warned John Quinn what to expect:

> Poor old Mr. Yeats, I did my best to discourage him from [this] visit and I don't think anyone has encouraged him, certainly his son hasn't. I hope he won't go, but if he does, let me give you this hint. Don't let him on any account touch paints or canvas. He is getting past his work in that direction, and there is no use encouraging him (Hugh Lane is very strong on this point). On the other hand, his pencil sketches are sometimes very charming, and he is content with very little for them, and if one doesn't turn out well, it means only a few hours to do another. He is as you know a charming talker, and if he only stayed for a short visit, and only worked with pencil, he might be sure his visit would be a success. But to start in oils would be fatal.[13]

Welcoming her commissions, and alert to the benefits her friendship brought to his oldest son, JBY eagerly encouraged her efforts to bring his younger son, Jack, likewise under her managerial ambit. He wrote flatteringly and appreciatively to Gregory after Jack stayed at Coole in 1899 that 'the liberating influence of your house and presence' had given his son 'ideas, ambitions, hopes that he never had before.'[14] Jack, however, would always remain studiedly resistant to her approaches, and JBY, for all his eagerness, was in turn never capable of benefitting from her would-be patronage. Her 1907 letter to Quinn shows readily enough what she might have done for JBY had he been the willing or disciplined client he failed to be.

On a personal level, the relationship quickly settled into a quite predictable pattern. Lady Gregory wasn't quite the millionaire rain-maker JBY always hoped would miraculously arrive to redeem his fortunes, but she was socially influential enough, so obviously powerful in her effect as patron to WBY, and so personally forceful, that JBY always regarded her with respect and approached her with some caution. His early letters to her typically adopt a tone that veers awkwardly between flattery – sometimes obsequious – and obvious admiration of her decisiveness and generosity. But he was never under any illusion about the fact that she had to a significant degree replaced him as a force in WBY's life. His jealousy and resentment would emerge most directly in a much-quoted angry letter he wrote to his son in June 1921, charging that Willie had wasted his genius: 'When is your poetry at its best? I challenge all the critics if it is not when its wild spirit of your imagination is wedded to concrete fact. Had you stayed with me and not left me for Lady Gregory and her friends and associations, you would have loved and adored concrete life for which as I know you have a real affection.'[15] It is a stunningly inapposite charge in one sense, given his own capacity for blithe indifference to 'concrete fact' and given Lady Gregory's notorious pragmatism, but – characteristically – it nonetheless encompasses a telling paternal insight into a, then, rarely acknowledged aspect of his son's imaginative tendencies. In more sober moments, however, his admiration for her would always predominate, even in the face of his distaste for her hauteur. 'On the whole I am very glad that Lady Gregory "got" Willie', he wrote in 1912: 'Arthur Symons never speaks of her except as the "Strega" which is the Italian for witch. I don't regret her witchcraft, though it is not easy personally to like her. ... I for one won't turn against Lady Gregory. She is perfectly disinterested. She shows this disinterestedness. That is one of the reasons why she is so infernally haughty to lesser mortals – or whom she thinks lesser mortals.'[16]

This clear-eyed mix of professional respect and personal coolness would be the predominant position adopted by Lily and Lolly Yeats, too. Their letters offer a catalogue of accounts of Lady Gregory cutting them ruthlessly in public, and of her unshakeable superiority and condescension. Here is Lolly for instance, in 1912 – 'I spoke to Lady Gregory one night at the play, but she was very cross and therefore rude, and dropped me or rather brushed by me without even replying to my salutation'[17] – and in 1910: 'she looked through me as if I came with a begging letter.'[18] Lily termed her 'the Juggernaut', telling John Quinn that she was lacking in tact 'but goes for what she wants straight over anything in her way.'[19] But at the same time the sisters were both consistently admiring of Gregory's determination and her loyalty to the causes and people she cared for (WBY of course being one of the latter). Writing to her father about Gregory's efforts to collect material for her memoir of Hugh Lane, Lily observed in 1919 that: 'Lady Gregory came out yesterday. What an old soldier she is. She walked out in the half dark from Dartry [station] in rain and a strong west wind. She wanted to get from us any little things we could remember about Hugh Lane. We had little to tell, but she said it would all help her.'[20] More simply, Lily would remark in 1926 that 'She is a wonder.'[21]

For her part, Lady Gregory quickly tagged JBY an 'enfant terrible',[22] and she used this phrase quite precisely to convey her sense that he was, in fact,

unable or unwilling to deal with the world in fully adult terms. On the few
early occasions they spent more than a few hours consecutively in one another's
company she would be exhausted by his need to be the centre of attention,
and annoyed by his lack of discretion and his controversial conversation. In
consequence, from early on, she was utterly businesslike in all her dealings with
him – laying out precise, circumscribing conditions on her commissions so as
to limit his capacity for procrastination and complication, and likewise sending
out reams of warnings to friends who planned to deal with him. A typical
example is her advice to Hugh Lane when he commissioned a series of portraits
from JBY in 1903. Lane should buy all the frames in advance, she urged, and
make them identical in size, so that JBY wouldn't end up giving offence to some
sitters by making their portraits smaller than others.[23] In her letters to JBY –
few of which survive, unfortunately – she generally wastes little time on flattery
or small pleasantries. In a rare moment of candour in 1914, JBY would thank
her for what he termed 'the first literary and expansive letter you ever wrote to
me, for generally you are abrupt and to the point.'[24]

But for all the constraints and temperamental differences between them,
there were occasions when the relationship did reach a significant level of inten-
sity – usually when their respective frustrations with W.B. Yeats or John Quinn
were involved, and home-truths of one sort or another had to be voiced about
the volatile emotional and creative triangles they were involved in with those
demanding and often imperious men. And there were occasions when they
became, rather involuntarily, provisional allies or at least mutual advisors in
the midst of larger controversies. One of these moments merits consideration
at length here, since in many ways it best characterizes the core tensions and
underlying mutual respect which held the relationship between JBY and Lady
Gregory together; and since it resulted in the most striking exchange of letters
between them that survives.

In October 1905 W.B. Yeats and Lady Gregory engineered the transfor-
mation of the Irish National Theatre Society from a democratic organization,
in which all members had one vote, into a Limited Company in which the
directorial triumvirate of Yeats, Synge and Gregory had, as she termed it 'abso-
lute power'.[25] When Abbey actress Mary Walker – also known as Máire Nic
Shiubhlaigh – resigned in response to Yeats's 'angry' pressuring of her into
signing a new contract in late December that year, WBY abruptly threatened
to sue her for breach of contract, in a heavy-handed salvo designed to demon-
strate his intention to use the directors' newly acquired power.[26] As he put it to
John Synge, he was 'dead certain that something must be done to show people
that we are not to be played with.'[27] But in a delicious and surely unexpected

turn of events, Mary Walker took refuge during the furore at Gurteen Dhas, the home of JBY, Lily and Lolly near Dundrum – she had worked for the Yeats sisters at the Dun Emer Press – thereby leaving JBY in effect in the middle between WBY and his unfortunate target, and thus unavoidably involved in the unfolding fight.

Privately, Lady Gregory deplored what WBY had done, having at once shrewdly recognized that Walker was a poor choice of test case for a display of toughness. As she told him in a letter:

> I could not bear taking sides as it were against you – & yet I feel it impossible, for your sake & that of the theatre which is bound up with you, that [the breach of contract suit] should come on – If it had been against her brother or any man, that would have been different, but the cry would have been that you were bullying a poor weak girl! I am not taking her part at all, I think her conduct has been extraordinarily irritating, & that the real insult lies in her having dared to take up so much so much of your time with her silly waverings – But I do think you made a mistake in the threat.[28]

It is a carefully phrased rebuke, which stresses her loyalty to Yeats, and which nominally upholds his imperious position by chiding Mary Walker for daring 'take up so much of [his] time'; but it also makes clear, amidst its insistence on his strategic folly, that he was indeed veering towards bullying. Publicly, she voiced no such doubts, and she promptly wrote to JBY characterizing anyone who wanted to hinder the new directors as the 'enemy', and charging that those who took up WBY's time, or her own time, and thus hindered them in their writing, were guilty of what she termed 'child-murder'.[29] Most remarkably of all, she lionized Yeats to his father in language of an extravagance she would never subsequently repeat – calling him a 'mythical bard … slaying all before him like the dragon of Wantley' and 'already started on the road to immortality.'[30] Overall, her letter to JBY constitutes a stern declaration of war against anyone who failed to side with the directors, and a resolute lecture about WBY's god-like genius. Ever the tactician, though, she combined iron fist and velvet glove by also sending a gift of a pheasant and urging JBY to look after Mary Walker's health.

JBY's reply, written on 8 January 1906, and surely one of his finest letters, is a masterpiece of subtle indirection in response to this absolute insistence. Careful flattery of Lady Gregory masks a sharp underlying critique of her arguments, while good general advice quietly encodes some unmistakable score-settling against his son. The letter opens by acknowledging the danger of his 'interposing' in someone else's quarrel, and by trusting that, once she has read the entire letter 'you will think that I am not merely impudent.' But then he fires a direct salvo at the 'mad poet' his son has become: 'Shut Willie up that he may do his work, or send him to America. At any rate act on your impulse and not on his.' If Lady Gregory were to come to Dublin to settle things, he counsels, 'on all sides would be frankness and discussion and the spirit of compromise. For everyone has the most entire trust in you – that is when <u>you are you</u>. They all feel that you have a man's mind, and the absolute disinterestedness out of which courage comes in inexhaustible resource.'[31] But the flattery here doesn't fully mask his insinuation that Lady Gregory indeed wasn't being herself when she publicly supported Yeats's line: 'everyone has the most entire trust in you – that is when <u>you are you</u>'. His letter shows he had skillfully detected her underlying reservations and knew that she was supporting Yeats out of loyalty, not from full conviction. Nor, in the end, does his wording disguise his under-lying investment in highlighting the differences between the poet and the Dame of Coole, and exacerbating them if possible, out of jealousy of his son. In his previous letter he had gone so far as to venture 'I am sometimes tempted to say that if a man has the gift of words he is thereby unfitted for every position in life except that of writing'[32] – a starkly hostile assessment of his son's practical abilities, and possibly of his reliability as a friend, too.

JBY knew he was on dangerous ground here, and the letter of 8 January begins and ends anxiously worrying about the likelihood of earning a 'bloody nose' for his interference. But – quite typically – he can't resist a parting shot, in the form of a postscript: 'A wise aristocracy in my mind should aim at being itself the best kind of democracy. Your autocracy would so desire, I further think. JBY.'[33] It's a brilliant touch, first appealing in class terms to Lady Gregory's judiciousness and superiority as a potential source of resolu-tion for the affair. At her aristocratic best – with her sense of noblesse oblige in full play – she might in fact be able to generate a compromise that would be acceptable to all, he suggests, by providing a 'wise aristocracy' to substi-tute for the actual democracy that the Abbey directors were now so intent on eliminating. And then that superb last touch: 'Your autocracy would so desire, I further think.' On the one hand it is the final flattery in a letter which flatters her, or appears to flatter her, throughout. But on the other hand it reminds her, by implication – 'Your' autocracy – that Yeats junior is a parvenu, who can't be trusted not to behave dangerously or foolishly. She knows how to handle power, and her autocracy, at its best, he implies, would indeed be a form of democracy; but that's not so for his son. He thereby perhaps aims to give her a last warning against her own worst impulses, and a last chiding for her will-ingness to support Yeats even against her better judgment. He's urging her to follow her best instincts – when 'you are you' you'll act fairly – and quietly

warning that if she supported his son out of loyalty, she would merely be abet-
ting an injustice. She must restrain him – 'Shut Willie up' – and she is the only
one in a position to do it.

Lady Gregory was well able to read between the lines, and his letter
certainly had some effect. Having also received a letter from Lolly, written
the same morning, that gave an account of WBY's 'sneering and offensive'
treatment of Mary Walker during two meetings at Gurteen Dhas, and which
also pointedly criticized Annie Horniman for speaking of WBY's 'bad temper
as if it was a feather in his cap',[34] she was far less inclined to try to defend
him. Replying, she now adopted a more conciliatory tone – no more talk of
the 'enemy' and 'child-murder' – though, typically enough, she didn't actually
concede any significant practical ground. The 'opposition' as she now termed
it must make proposals if there were to be a peace negotiation about the future
of the theatre – but, she quietly implies, there is, in fact, no one sufficiently
'responsible' to do this amongst the disgruntled theatre employees: they are too
immature, or too incompetent. JBY's critique of his son is left unanswered until
the very end of the letter, but here she retracts her lionizing language only to
suggest, instead, that she knows his failing full well, and that she requires no
lectures on the subject: 'you need not give me a list of Willie's crimes – he is not
so near sainted that the "devil's advocate" need thunder out the case against
him.'[35] The underlying implication is clear: she is willing to change the tone of
her rhetoric, willing to put herself in the role of mediator, and keen to find a
compromise position if possible that will save WBY from his folly in bringing
on an unnecessary and counterproductive fight; but her underlying loyalty to
Yeats should not be doubted, and JBY is powerless to disrupt their relationship
in any significant way.

The episode did not change the fundamentals of Lady Gregory's relation-
ship with JBY, but it epitomizes how, despite their very different value-systems,
there were times when they were of significant value to one another. JBY here
warns Lady Gregory against allowing her more ruthless side to dominate; she
in turn obliges him to temper his reactive hostility to his son, and to resist
any effort to undercut her relationship with the poet. Both benefit from the
exchange and exit with mutual respect for, if not admiration of, the other's
methods and skills.

After JBY's departure for the USA in 1907 Lady Gregory met him only a
very few more times – when briefly in New York during her American lecture
tours – but their correspondence if anything became more frequent. Although
she would become quite contemptuous of JBY's crafty resistance to coming
back to Ireland, and his breezy expectation of support from his son and from

John Quinn, she would at the same time find much to admire in his desire for freedom, and envied his escape from the partisan battles in what she called 'this unfortunate country.'[36] Her letters to John Quinn, who fulminated to her often about JBY's impracticality and egotism, nicely capture her mixture of dismissiveness and admiration of the old man's wily ways, and his capacity to escape responsibility and external discipline. In 1908, for instance, as it became ever clearer he would resist returning to Ireland, she told Quinn:

> As to old Yeats – it is irresistible to say 'I told you so'. Didn't I say he would be all right at pencil drawings, but once allowed to touch oils he gets hopelessly entangled and can no more get clear of his picture than a fly of a pot of cream. But no doubt he has been having a splendid time and I am glad that he has met with so much sunshine and affection, for Dublin is a hungry place and seldom offers a knife and fork to those who don't repay it in kind.[37]

And, again, in 1909:

> Poor old J.B.Y. It is wonderful how hopeful, how cheerful, how impossible he is. I admire him immensely at a distance, and I think him the most trying visitor possible in a house. Space and time mean nothing to him, he goes his own way, spoiling portraits as hopefully as he began them, and always on the verge of a great future! I should lock up his paints and only allow him a pencil and get occasional rapid sketches from him. I wonder if he is paying his hotel bill all this time, I hope so. He is certainly having the best time of his life. Dublin, never very hospitable, ignores him.[38]

Characteristically, she has her eye on the practical here: is he paying his hotel bill? In March 1915 she would take time out from her lecturing schedule to investigate the state of JBY's debts at the New York boarding house run by the Petitpas sisters, located on 29th Street between 8th and 9th Avenue, where he lived. She interviewed one of the Petitpas sisters at John Quinn's apartment, and, suspicious about the accuracy of the charges on JBY's statement of accounts from the sisters, pushed for a precise detailing of the alleged 'extras' above board and lodging he had received – 'wine, newspapers, Laundry' – and inquired carefully as to JBY's personal expenses on 'cigars, boots, linen, stamps – bus fare.'[39] (There is no evidence that she ever actually visited JBY at the Petitpas boarding house; John Quinn registered 'amazement and disgust' in 1911 when a New York newspaper erroneously reported that she was 'frequenting the place, dining there, etc,' and urged her to have her press agent publish a denial, since it was not, in his view, 'a place that you would go to' given the 'miscellaneous assortment of artists [and] pseudo poets' to be found there.)[40] The interview alarmed her, and knowing that JBY's outstanding bills would have to be paid off by his son, she reported to WBY that 'I have sent for Miss Pettipas [*sic*] again, to try if

she would reduce her terms, in consideration of your father's value as a "draw".'
But the tough Dame of Coole evidently for once met her match in this negotia-
tion, conducted on her 63rd birthday: 'Miss Petipas has been, but is as hard as
nails – says she cannot take less than the 9 dollars per week.'[41]

This experience did nothing to sweeten Lady Gregory's view of JBY in
his final years. She and John Quinn would latterly often take solace in sharing
their respective frustrations as patrons of both of the brilliant but difficult
Yeatses. 'Poor old Yeats, he does "tag" one', she wrote to Quinn, sympathizing
with his experience of being pigeonholed as merely a man of business by the
aging painter: but 'so does W.B.Y.' she added, 'And having tied on the tag,
they try to justify it. I have often told W.B.Y. this.'[42] Particularly after Yeats's
marriage in 1917, she became more openly resentful at being, as she saw it,
marginalized from both his daily life and from his affections, and in 1921 she
unloaded a powerful salvo to Quinn criticizing both father and son for their
failings, including an unpleasant cut at George Yeats, the woman she saw as
having replaced or eclipsed her:

> I do feel for you with old Mr Yeats. He as usual feels that he is living in an
> elastic-sided world, and that it will yield to his determination ... . I don't
> know what Yeats means by talking of want of money. His wife has money,
> though perhaps not so much as he was led to believe, and they live in extreme
> comfort, and ease – Of course but for your help and constant protection
> of him the old man would have had to come back long ago. He has always
> preached the domestic affections, and has as Yeats says spent his life in trying
> to escape from his family, and this time it seems as if he will succeed.

Only in her final sentences of this letter does her usual generous and Christian
viewpoint reassert itself and redeem what might otherwise have been unpleasant
score-settling: 'It is hard on you, because your kindness won't let you leave him
to his fate. Well "if a man does well and suffers for it and takes it patiently, that
is acceptable with God".'[43]

For some periods late in his life, JBY seems to have written almost as often
to Lady Gregory as he did to his son. He routinely sent his letters to Yeats to
Coole to be forwarded – on occasion inviting her to read them first[44] – and, as
he put it in 1916, sometimes wrote to her rather than Yeats both since it was,
as he acknowledged 'the easiest way of getting to him. And shall I confess it? I
look to you as my good friend (it is your own fault) as well as his.'[45] But when
he finally passed away in 1922, Lady Gregory was, typically, quite unwilling to
varnish over the awkward truths about either his career, or his uneasy relation-
ship with his son, in her letter to Yeats when hearing the news. One can hardly
call it a letter of condolence:

What a merciful death for your father, passing away in sleep! I think he would have resented the visible approach of death – How happy he was in believing to the last that his best work was still before him. I am glad he had not come back – I was afraid Dublin would have struck a chill – ... I am glad also he had won so much recognition while still in life, through his letters – You will miss them, tho' of course in other ways your mind will be more easy – he had always been an anxiety in one way or other![46]

On the one hand it is a rather cold, efficient and thoroughly pragmatic summation – one thinks of the closure of Robert Frost's poem 'Out, out – ': 'And they, since they / Were not the one dead, turned to their affairs.' But at the same time it is both honest, and, for its intended reader, an enabling, even generous, statement. It says clearly enough 'you don't have to pretend you are distraught, or that your feelings aren't mixed: I knew your father's limitations well; let's celebrate his virtues without having to misrepresent him or gloss over the truth.' It is a typical Lady Gregory letter to Yeats in many ways: business, the big picture, what is most honest, and what is best for creative achievement, come first, even if that runs roughshod over easier and more familiar conventions.

John Butler Yeats's 'elastic-sided world' was an expansive realm in which he flourished, but one the ever-pragmatic, orderly, ambitious Lady Gregory could never approve of. For him, she was admirably strong and goal-oriented, but in the end too self-repressing to be natural. For her, he was a swallow who most decisively refused to be kept to its first intent, and who quite happily flew past the nets which, in her hands, proved beneficial to so many others.

NOTES

1. Lady Gregory, 'The Felons of Our Land', *The Cornhill Magazine*, May 1900, p. 634.
2. William M. Murphy, *Prodigal Father: The Life of John Butler Yeats* (Ithaca and London 1978), p. 31.
3. W.B. Yeats, *Memoirs*, ed. Denis Donoghue (New York 1972), pp. 160–1.
4. The Metropole, located on Whitehall Place, between Trafalgar Square and the Embankment, close to the central administration buildings of the British Government, was one of the most luxurious and expensive London hotels of the period. WBY had given his lecture at the nearby Society of Arts building. Used by the Ministry of Defence for more than five decades from 1951, the Metropole building reopened in 2011 as the Corinthia Hotel.
5. Murphy, *Prodigal Father*, p. 160.
6. *Lady Gregory's Diaries 1892–1902*, ed. James Pethica (Gerrards Cross 1996), p. 157.
7. *Ibid.* p. 160.
8. *Ibid.*

9. See, for instance, *Lady Gregory's Diaries 1892–1902*, pp. 156–7, where AG first terms Yeats 'WBY' and 'W.' She evidently continued to address him as 'Mr Yeats' in her letters for some months after this – her first surviving letter to him, from April 1898 (Berg) is so phrased – but by later that year, and thereafter, she always began with 'My dear Willie'.

10. JBY to AG, 19 May 1899, Berg Collection.

11. Murphy, *Prodigal Father*, pp. 203–4.

12. JBY to AG, 11 June 1917, Berg Collection.

13. AG to Quinn, 22 December 1907, NYPL.

14. JBY to AG, 19 May 1899 and 27 May 1899, Berg Collection.

15. *J.B. Yeats: Letters to his son W.B. Yeats and Others 1869–1922*, ed. Joseph Hone (London 1944), pp. 280–1.

16. *Ibid.* pp. 151–2.

17. Lolly Yeats to JBY, 5 October 1912, NLI.

18. Lolly Yeats to JBY, 26 June 1910, NLI.

19. Lily Yeats to John Quinn, 5 April 1915, cited in Roy Foster, *W.B. Yeats: A Life. Vol. II The Arch-Poet* (Oxford 2003), p. 15.

20. Lily Yeats to JBY, 18 November 1919, NLI.

21. Lily Yeats to Ruth Pollexfen Lane-Poole, NLI.

22. *Lady Gregory's Diaries 1892–1902*, p. 217.

23. AG to Hugh Lane, 1 December 1903, Berg Collection.

24. JBY to AG, 10 November 1914, Berg Collection.

25. AG to Quinn, 1 November 1905, NYPL.

26. *The Collected Letters of W.B. Yeats, Volume IV, 1905–1907*, ed. John Kelly and Ronald Schuchard (Oxford 2005) p. 262 and *passim*. Born into an Irish-speaking and Nationalist family, Mary Walker (1883–1958) referred to herself as Máire Nic Shiubhlaigh after 1900 when she joined the Nationalists women's group Inghinidhe na hÉireann, but was usually still called 'Mary' or 'Máire' Walker by Yeats, Gregory, the Fay brothers and other key figures in the early years of the Abbey Theatre.

27. *Ibid.* p. 276.

28. AG to WBY, 3 January 1902, Berg Collection.

29. AG to JBY, 9 January 1906, Berg Collection.

30. *Ibid.*

31. JBY to AG, 8 January 1906, Berg Collection.

32. JBY to AG, 6 January 1906, Berg Collection.

33. JBY to AG, 8 January 1906, Berg Collection.

34. Lolly Yeats to AG, 8 January 1906, Berg Collection.

35. AG to JBY, 11 January 1906, Berg Collection.

36. AG to Hugh Lane, undated, Berg Collection.

37. AG to John Quinn, 6 June 1908, Berg Collection.

38. AG to John Quinn, 3 January 1909, Berg Collection.

39. AG to WBY, 15 March 1915, Berg Collection.

40. Quinn to AG, 13 November 1911, NYPL.

41. AG to WBY, 15 March 1915, Berg Collection.

42. AG to Quinn, 12 January 1919, NYPL. In his reply (5 February, NYPL) Quinn concurred about 'the "tagging" habit – I also have suffered from it. I often told Yeats he first forms a theory, & then tries to fit facts – & if they won't fit, he invents them.'

43. AG to Quinn, 2 January 1921, NYPL.

44. See, for example, JBY to AG, 20 June 1917 (NYPL); 'I want you to see it, because of my personal vanity, for I think it is a good letter' (Berg Collection).

45. JBY to AG, 4 December 1916, Berg Collection.

46. AG to WBY, 11 February 1922, Berg Collection.

The Art Which Is True Is as Lively as Life.
Jack B. Yeats's Modern Aspects of Irish Art Reconsidered*

ELISABETH ANSEL

In 1922 Jack B. Yeats wrote that painting is the 'greatest medium of all ... ; even greater ... than literature, because more simple'.[1] These lines belong to his only writing on art, *Modern Aspects of Irish Art,* and demonstrate that the artist was engaged with the paragone between painting and poetry. To the artist, painting was not only the first of all arts but also able to represent the country from which it emerges. Due to the national references the pamphlet has mostly been explored from a political angle. Nonetheless, not only the topos of the paragone,[2] but also other aspects in the artist's text, suggest an art historical reading. By examining the text in detail, this essay highlights the key ideas Yeats expressed in it. Further, I will analyse in which way the writing can be placed within the tradition of treatises on art, and moreover how Yeats can be regarded in the art world in his time. In this context, it will be necessary to also look at Yeats's education, including his family background and broader cultural influences.

Jack B. Yeats once explained the reason why he became a painter as follows: 'I'm the son of a painter, therefore, painting with me is easy for me'.[3] In turn his father, John Butler Yeats,[4] was aware of his influence as an artist

---

* This article is part of a larger research project on 'Der irische Künstler Jack B. Yeats (1871–1957). Die Suche nach nationaler Identität in der Moderne [The Irish Artist Jack B. Yeats. Modern Art and National Identity]' that I plan to submit as a dissertation thesis at Technische Universität Dresden in 2017.

and thought that neither Jack B. Yeats nor W.B. Yeats would have taken up an artistic profession if he himself had followed his career as a lawyer.[5] In an article on Jack B. Yeats's education he reported that his son began to draw at an early age and that he proved to be very talented at it.[6] He (and his friend York Powell) regarded him as 'best-educated' although he 'was never known to leave the lowest place in his class'.[7] According to JBY, this education was provided by Jack B. Yeats's grandparents in Sligo, the life in the west of Ireland and the fact that he 'kept to his own ideas, his own plans ... and diligently drew what he observed'.[8] Following his father's wish this keen interest in observation and drawing was later continued by a professional education at various art schools in London.[9] It is curious therefore that JBY, who advised Jack B. Yeats to attend art schools,[10] later showed little interest in this training by stating: 'What he did at the art school I could never find out. I fancy he was the wag and the wit and the storyteller, welcome with everybody ...'.[11] Here, it seems as if JBY undermines the impact the education might have had on him, in order to outline 'Jack's idea of self-education'.[12] This portrayal of a self-educated artist who draws from nature brings to mind classical art historical biographies as designed by Giorgio Vasari (1511–74) in his *Lives of the Artists*. In particular, conceptual parallels can be drawn to the vita of the ingenious shepherd boy Giotto di Bondone (*c.* 1266–1337): 'One day Cimabue ... came upon Giotto, who, while his sheep were grazing, was sketching one of them in a lifelike way with a slightly pointed rock upon a smooth and polished stone without having learned how to draw it from anyone other than Nature.'[13]

The biography of the 'daring naturalist',[14] who was regarded as 'the father of modern art',[15] was very well known at this time, especially since John Ruskin had published his monograph on the Italian artist in 1854. That JBY – who had moved to the artistic colony Bedford Park with his family in 1888 – was familiar with Giotto's life may be presumed because he was in contact with and influenced by the Pre-Raphaelites.[16] However, this recourse is not only convincing through the cultural exchange but also and more importantly for the reason that it underlines Jack B. Yeats's seemingly effortless mastership. By that reference, JBY places his son's artistic career in an art historical tradition and, by analogy with Giotto's life, assigns his son an initial and pioneering role in Irish art history. Then again, by concentrating on the self-education, JBY puts the academic influences of his son's training in the background. The passage rather implies that Jack B. Yeats's time at art school was nothing but a brief intermezzo. Actually, he studied for seven years at several art schools and it is hard to imagine that this education didn't have any effects on him at all.

He began his studies at the South Kensington School of Art in 1887 and moved to the Chiswick School of Art in 1888.[17] Between the years 1890 and 1893 he attended two schools in parallel, the West London School of Art and the Westminster School of Art, and finished his studies at the latter in 1894.[18] His tuition at South Kensington – where the education mainly focused on drawing and design – can be summed up as follows: Yeats got elementary instruction in art history and practised drawing from the antique and after that from the life. Alongside, he studied original art works in the collections belonging to the South Kensington School, in particular British Art. But he also got impulses from modern French art conveyed by the director of the South Kensington, Thomas Armstrong, who had worked in Paris beforehand.[19] At the Chiswick School of Art – which belonged to the Bedford Park colony – the training again focused on drawing (from models),[20] and at the Westminster art school pupils among other things worked from casts and later from the nude.[21] Altogether, the training provided Yeats with important technical skills, and introduced him to classical theoretical principles as well as to modern ideas.

Regarding the endurance and the consistency of Yeats's art training, it is not likely that he didn't approve of it. Instead, it has to be assumed that he was willing to receive a good training and to gather various artistic influences. Taking into consideration that Yeats had not only been trained at different art schools but had also been educated within the cultural context of his family home, he can truly be described as best-educated.

By the time Yeats wrote *Modern Aspects of Irish Art*, he had become a professional visual artist who not only had a clear understanding of what Irish art should be like, but also had certain political ideas. The contents of the booklet result from a lecture on Irish painting Yeats had given at the Irish Race Conference in Paris in 1922.[22] His 'vision of a politically free Ireland' and the close connection of art and politics become apparent in the lecture he held at the conference.[23] In it (and also in *Modern Aspects*) the artist stated that 'there is a country more ready than any other to lift painting into its rightful place, and that is Ireland, this land of ours'.[24]

Due to the historical background, both the lecture and the pamphlet *Modern Aspects of Irish Art,* clearly have to be considered within a political context. But despite this affiliation, it should not be forgotten that the main subject of the text is art itself, a fact that the literature has not yet discussed adequately.

Yeats begins his text with the statement that 'the majority of people like to think that the painter of pictures is a man who was born ambidextrous, and has been taught juggling'. According to him there have been only a few artists who haven't considered art as a 'trick of juggling' and instead have 'taken the side of nature'.[25]

He thus contrasts two different approaches, the true and the false painting, and takes these opposing aspects as the basis for his argument. At the same time Yeats discusses not only the artist and his art but also the reception of it, and criticizes that most people 'don't understand pictures [and] leave that sort of thing to the artists'.[26]

He then specifies that the false picture is not painted 'from nature, but from other pictures' in order to 'show ... cleverness'.[27] In turn true pictures are individual and demonstrate that the artist's 'eye [is] backed by his own memory and his own character'. Artists should not try to reach objective perfection: 'If the exact model is the highest aim of the artist, then the greatest artist in the world would be the man who painted a five-dollar bill on a sidewalk of New York so correctly, that the passers-by were actually trying to pick it up.'[28]

This example obviously relates to Yeats's visual experience he made during his stay in New York in 1904. Around this time trompe-l'oeil art was very popular in America where artists such as John Haberle (1856–1933) drew on the tradition of realistic still lives and connected it to modern life, for instance by depicting dollar notes in their paintings.[29]

Yeats rejects the tradition of trompe-l'oeil painting, which reaches back to Pliny's famous story of the competition between the ancient painters Zeuxis and Parrhasius. Zeuxis produced a picture of grapes so convincing that birds wanted to pick at them, whereas Parrhasius exceeded him in creating a lifelike curtain in front of a picture that Zeuxis asked to be drawn only to realize that the curtain was not real.[30] Yeats criticizes this technique of fooling the eye as 'it is the painter himself who makes the worth of the picture'.[31]

Further, for him, true pictures 'are not the outcome of science, they come from Life itself'.[32] Next to the opponents of true and false painting he thus introduces the contrasting terms of science and nature. For Yeats, the history of the scientific painting goes back to the invention of the perspective, when artists 'began torturing ... pictures with pavements and ceilings and walls covered with patterns so as to use the laws of perspective'.[33] As we have already seen from the trompe-l'oeil images, Yeats here again declines the illusionist character of art. Furthermore, this passage proves that he was well aware of Italian Renaissance art and of its theoretical principles constituted by artists, such as Leon Battista Alberti (1404–72). That Yeats was familiar with Alberti can be assumed as certain not only because of his art education but also because his library included a biography of Michelangelo (1475–1564) published by John Addington Symonds and which reports on Alberti too.[34]

Yeats continues that also modernist movements, such as Vorticism and Futurism, are attracted to science, and concludes that 'science is easier to follow than life. One can learn science from a handbook'.[35] According to him, the use of science does not lead to the right art; instead, the artist has to work from nature. In order to do so he has to use his skills of 'observation and memory', and follow his vision. Painting in this sense is the highest form of art and 'has not to be translated into words'.[36] In this Yeats refers to the paragone between painting and poetry, and gives his preference to the visual image as it is 'the greatest medium of all for the communication of the thoughts and feelings of mankind'.[37] This passage also brings to mind what his brother, W.B. Yeats, once wrote: 'When I look at my brother's picture, *Memory Harbour* ... I am full of disquiet and of excitement, and I am melancholy because I have not made more and better verses'.[38]

Furthermore, Yeats dissociates from the concept of imitation, and hereby also opposes the principles taught at his former art schools. He claims that the artist should refrain from copying other artists and from depicting nature in an idealistic manner. For Yeats, the aim of art is beauty but in contrast to the classical tradition it has not to be achieved through science or copying but only through truth to what the painter 'himself has seen'.[39]

Yeats goes on that the artist can communicate his visions best when he is 'part of the land and of the life he paints'. Hereby he ascribes Irish artists a central role in modern art as they 'have not too many false traditions about painting to get rid of' and can dedicate themselves to true art which 'is as lively as life'.[40] This idea of a new art exhibits strong analogies to Joshua Reynolds's (1723–92) *Discourses on Art* where the main advantage of English art is described as follows: 'One advantage ... we shall have in our Academy, which no other nation can boast. We shall have nothing to unlearn'.[41] The context of *Modern Aspects of Irish Art* suggests that Yeats refers to this idea in turn to distance Irish art from English just as Reynolds had distanced English art from Continental over a century before and to underline that Irish art is the real modern art.

Another reason that makes Irish art truly modern is the fact that 'life in Ireland is nearer to nature' and offers the painter the opportunity to see things 'with his own fresh eye'.[42] Yeats strongly recommends the orientation towards a vernacular art and advises against the focus on London or Paris as they are places 'of the very science of fashion'.[43] This programmatic refusal of European modern art surprises insofar as Yeats himself was influenced by French painters, such as Edgar Degas (1834–1917).[44] On the other hand, this negation serves the purpose to claim a new and genuine art that is free from 'false' traditions, and that emerges from a new country. Considering the Irish context, these lines can again be read as a statement against the English artistic tradition.

They remind one of William Rothenstein's characterization of English art: 'A general tendency among English painters has been ... to seek inspiration from pictures rather than from Nature.'[45] In his book on Francisco Goya (1746–1828) which Yeats kept in his library, he contrasted English painters and Goya who according to Rothenstein had made it his aim to 'preserve the freshness of nature',[46] an objective that Yeats, an admirer of the Spanish artist, likewise pursued. Thomas MacGreevy then also claimed Jack B. Yeats to be the 'first truly Irish painter' who didn't 'follow the English tradition' any longer.[47]

Subsequently, Yeats advances his idea of 'observation and memory' and brings up the thought, that not only 'every child in every corner of Ireland should be encouraged in this natural desire to draw what they see ... , but [also] every man and woman'.[48] He advises everyone to choose a scene, and to frame it by looking at it through a window. Subsequently one should 'make a square to represent the shape of the window frame, and then fill in as much as [the] memory holds of what [one] saw'.[49] Yeats here obviously draws on Alberti's idea of the picture frame as a 'finestra aperta', which is meant to create an objective vision of the world by using the scientific instrument of perspective,[50] and turns it into its opposite. More precisely, his concept of memory can be read as a riposte to the academic tradition as it is about the subjectivity of the artist.

This practice of drawing will enable everybody to become familiar with pictures of artists and enhance the pleasure of looking at images. Additionally, it will ensure that no longer only people who belong to the art world are in the position to judge pictures but also everybody else. To enforce the understanding between artists and the beholder it would be a great idea to organize 'loan exhibitions of pictures ... all over the country'. Finally, Yeats brings up the example of Russia where 'there was a very well arranged system by which a picture exhibition was brought to the far parts of that land'.[51] He hereby relates to the idea of the Peredvizhniki, the Society of Travelling Art Exhibits, which held their first exhibition in 1871 in St Petersburg. Thereafter the so called 'Wanderers' showed their art in a number of peripatetic exhibitions in many parts of the country, far beyond the capital.[52] They didn't consider it to be necessary to look at modern art abroad and in turn concentrated on rural Russia.[53] This focus on national issues and the aim to promote art to a wide audience explain why Yeats chose the example of the Peredvizhniki and moreover emphasized his demand that 'the roots of every art must be in the country of the artist'.[54]

In this essay, I have shown that Jack B. Yeats was a well-educated artist through his training at various art schools as well as through the influences of his artistic family. This education becomes apparent in his *Modern Aspects of Irish Art*, which can be read as a modern treatise on art, and which he wrote with an approach that is seemingly so casual that the various allusions are almost invisible at first sight. Close examination has demonstrated that Yeats was not only concerned with the classical theme of the paragone and the concept of imitation, but that he also discussed modern tendencies in art. In order to promote a modern Irish art Yeats dissociated from the academic tradition and instead pleaded for an authentic and individual process of painting. Finally, through this method of referencing he underlined the significance of Irish art, an art that he characterized as open-minded and in this sense modern and pioneering.

NOTES

1. Jack B. Yeats, *Modern Aspects of Irish Art* (Dublin 1922), p. 3.
2. The Topos (topic) of the paragone refers to the rivalry of the arts (painting, poetry, sculpture, etc.). It goes back to classical antiquity and was, in particular, taken up again by Italian Renaissance artists who debated the superiority of one art over the other. The topic remained popular throughout the following centuries. For further reading see, for instance, Heinrich F. Plett, *Rhetoric and Renaissance Culture* (Berlin and New York 2004), pp. 298–304.
3. Quoted in John Purser, 'Voices of the Past: Jack Yeats and Thomas MacGreevy in Conversation' in *Yeats Annual*, No. 11 (1995), 87–104 (p. 93).
4. In order to distinguish him from Jack B. Yeats he will hereafter be referred to by his signature 'JBY'.
5. John Butler Yeats, letter to Lily Yeats (11 June 1920) in *Letters of John Butler Yeats to his Son W.B. Yeats and others. 1869–1922*, ed. Joseph Hone (London 1999), p. 190.
6. John Butler Yeats, 'The Education of Jack B. Yeats' in *The Christian Science Monitor*, 2 November 1920.
7. *Ibid.*
8. *Ibid.*
9. Hilary Pyle, *Jack B. Yeats. A Biography* (London 1989), pp. 26 ff.
10. Pyle, *Yeats*, p. 25.
11. Yeats, 'Education'.
12. *Ibid.*
13. Giorgio Vasari, *The Lives of the Artists*, translated with an introduction and notes by Julia Conaway Bondanella and Peter Bondanella (Oxford 2008), p. 16.
14. John Ruskin, *Giotto and His Works in Padua*, reprint of the 1854 edition, London (Boston 1977), p. 23.
15. See Hugh Stokes, *The art treasures of London. Painting* (London 1908), p. 3.
16. W.B. Yeats, *Autobiographies. The Collected Works of W.B. Yeats*, vol. III, ed. Douglas N. Archibald (New York 1999), p. 67 and p. 114.
17. Pyle, *Yeats*, pp. 26 ff.

18. Bruce Arnold, *Jack Yeats* (London 1998), pp. 36 ff.

19. Pyle, *Yeats*, p. 26.

20. Margaret Jones Bolsterli, *The Early Community at Bedford Park. The Pursuit of 'Corporate Happiness' in the First Garden Suburb* (London 1977), pp. 69–70.

21. Anthony Anderson, *The Man who was H.M. Bateman* (Exeter 1982), p. 18.

22. Yeats Archive, Y1/JY/4/2/1. Yeats's vast collection of newspaper clippings also contains an article on the Irish Race Conference published by the Freeman's Journal in January 1922, demonstrating the artist's interest in the event. The article not only states that the two Yeats brothers will give a talk during the congress – W.B. on literature, Jack B. on painting – but also that the conference will be accompanied by an exhibition of Irish artworks, concerts, and plays.

23. Pyle, *Yeats*, p. 119.

24. Jack B. Yeats, 'Ireland and Painting' in *New Ireland*, 18 February 1922, p. 172.

25. Yeats, *Modern Aspects*, p. 1.

26. *Ibid.*

27. *Ibid.* p. 3.

28. *Ibid.* p. 2.

29. For further reading on American trompe l'oeil artists see Bruce W. Chambers, *Old Money. American Trompe L'Oeil Images of Currency* (New York 1988).

30. Pliny, *Natural History*, vol IX, libri XXXIII–XXXV, book XXXV (London 1984), 65–6, pp. 309–11.

31. Yeats, *Modern Aspects*, p. 2.

32. *Ibid.* p. 2.

33. *Ibid.* p. 3.

34. Yeats Archive, NGI/Y1/JY/24/3/4. John Addington Symonds, *The Life of Michelangelo Buonarroti. Based on Studies in the Archives of the Buonarroti Family at Florence*, 3rd edn (London 1901).

35. Yeats, *Modern Aspects*, p. 3.

36. *Ibid.*

37. *Ibid.* The fact that Yeats later also gained a reputation as a writer does not necessarily contradict his declared superiority of painting; it rather demonstrates the artist's constant engagement with the dialectic between word and image.

38. W.B. Yeats, *Autobiographies*, p. 72.

39. Yeats, *Modern Aspects,* p. 11.

40. *Ibid.* pp. 4–5.

41. Joshua Reynolds, *Discourses on Art*, ed. Robert R. Wark (New Haven and London 1988), Discourse I, p. 16.

42. Yeats, *Modern Aspects,* pp. 6–7.

43. *Ibid.* p. 5.

44. Pyle, *Yeats*, pp. 107–8.

45. Yeats Archive, NGI/Y1/JY/24/1/6/74. William Rothenstein, *Goya* (London, 1900), pp. 5–6.

46. *Ibid.* p. 14.

47. Thomas MacGreevy, 'Painting in Modern Ireland. The Rise of the National School' in *The Gael*, 27 February 1922, p. 19.

48. Yeats, *Modern Aspects*, p. 8.

49. *Ibid.* p. 9.

50. Leon Battista Alberti, *On Painting. A New Translation and Critical Edition*, ed. and transl. by Rocco Sinisgalli (Cambridge 2011).

51. Yeats, *Modern Aspects*, p. 11.

52. David Jackson, 'Sedition and tradition: the art of the Peredvizhniki', in *The Peredvizhniki. Pioneers of Russian Painting*, ed. David Jackson and Per Hedstrom (Stockholm 2011), pp. 16–37 (p. 22).

53. Per Hedstrom, 'The Peredvizhniki and Europe' in *The Peredvizhniki*. Jackson and Hedstrom (Stockholm 2011), pp. 40–53 (p. 43).

54. Yeats, *Modern Aspects*, p. 4.

Michael B. Yeats: A Committed Irish and European Legislator

MARTIN MANSERGH

W.B. Yeats, unintentionally perhaps, was one of the progenitors of national independence, not excluding the turbulent manner in which it came about, through the cultural revival in which he played a leading role. As the civil war came to an end, he referred in the Seanad on 19 April 1923 to 'when we began our imaginative movement which, for good or evil, had a little share in bringing about recent events'. If he had been living in the seventeenth century, his poem *Easter 1916* could have been viewed as the apotheosis of the executed leaders of the Rising. Yeats went on to serve in the Seanad of the Irish Free State for its first six years, and to chair a committee charged with designing Irish coins, using popular animal motifs.

Most of his Seanad contributions related to cultural concerns, with the notorious exception of his peroration on the insult that the disallowance of private divorce bills represented to the entire Anglo-Irish tradition (11 June 1925). There was never the slightest doubt that he remained a writer and poet first and foremost, and he did not seek a further term in 1928. At one point, he expressed the hope that the Government would not answer any questions in the Seanad on anything whatsoever, as otherwise, given that senators had national constituencies, the burden of post would become intolerable (19 March 1924). His postbag must already have been very large. He saw part of his role as senator as one of public education, and he defended the notion of a country-gentleman style leisured élite. He liked strong leaders such as Parnell and Kevin O'Higgins, and he identified with the Irish Free State. There is continuing academic debate as to how seriously he flirted with fascism in its early manifestations.

His son Michael B. Yeats (1921–2007) took up the parliamentary thread in his father's life, and made it his principal occupation in life. In retirement, he wrote a short but entertaining and instructive memoir, and its title *Cast a Cold Eye* was taken from the verse on his father's tombstone in their ancestral place, Drumcliffe, Co. Sligo. The sub-title reads *Memories of a poet's son and politician*. In effect, he could not escape, even if he had wanted to, from the many practical duties of being custodian of his father's legacy, especially after his mother George (Georgina) died in 1968.

Michael Yeats, who grew up with his sister Anne, was philosophical and even whimsical about their completely dysfunctional upbringing, especially where their father was concerned. Time was spent in Thor Ballylee, a tower house with few facilities but close to Lady Gregory's Coole Park, and then in Switzerland, where their father went for health reasons. At one point their mother had to embark 'on a long-term campaign to get us to know him better and to involve him in our lives', with only limited results. Michael regretted that it was only at Christmas 1938 on the French Riviera that he and his father began to have interesting and animated discussions about European politics, as war approached. A month later, his father was dead.

Michael had a Protestant schooling, and, not surprisingly given his own family background, he reacted against the continuing 'West British atmosphere' which he encountered. Like his uncle, Jack B. Yeats, the artist, though not cited as an influence, he sided with the de Valera republicanism of the Fianna Fáil political party. He became great friends at St Columba's, Rathfarnham with future Ulster Unionist leader and last Prime Minister of Northern Ireland, Brian Faulkner, though regrettably differences in politics later meant Faulkner kept his distance. Curiously, even at the height of the Troubles in the 1970s, Michael Yeats rarely spoke on the subject of Northern Ireland, either in the Seanad or the European Parliament, though his instincts were (constitutional) republican.

He was at Trinity College, Dublin for virtually the whole duration of the Second World War, entering in October 1939. Trinity at that time was a conservative and almost exclusively Protestant all-Ireland institution, very small compared to today, a marooned island in the capital. Like the ex-unionist *Irish Times*, its sympathies were almost entirely with the Allies. Unlike the newspaper, however, it kept its head down till victory was proclaimed, when, as in November 1918, its students in their triumphalist exuberance provoked a riot, drawn by Anne Yeats, his artist sister.

Michael's chapter on his years at Trinity makes no reference to his studies. However, Professor W.B. Stanford, Trinity Senator from 1948 to 1969, recalled that at a *viva voce* exam on Virgil's *Aeneid* he asked Michael Yeats to talk about poetry in general, 'and was flatly told that he had no interest in poetry'. This was no doubt a youthful reaction. Yeats did become active in debates in the College Historical Society, and rose to be its auditor. He achieved a great coup when he persuaded the Taoiseach Eamon de Valera to participate with Jan Masaryk, Foreign Minister of the Czechoslovak Government in exile in London and son of the State's founder, Tomáš Masaryk, in a debate on 'The Small Nations', a favourite topic of de Valera's. Yeats, also the son of a famous father, again found himself the conduit to de Valera for a dinner invitation from the Provost, which was politely declined. The photograph of the Auditor with Jan Masaryk appeared on the front page of the *Irish Times* the morning after.

Opening the debate on 1 November 1944, Yeats's contribution was idealistic, demanding equality between nations, whatever their size or military strength or natural resources. He argued that 'it was by the fate of small nations that one might judge the strength possessed by moral force in the conscience of nations'. He also thought that a primary objective of small States should be the development of closer political and economic relations between each other. Jan Masaryk was more naïvely optimistic about the future of small nations post-war than de Valera, who, while sympathizing with another small nation, Czechoslovakia, that had suffered so cruelly during the war and hoping that its agonies would soon be ended, was concerned about the creation of a new international organization in substitution for the League of Nations that would be subject to the dictatorship of the Great Powers (one of which, the Soviet Union, would veto neutral Ireland's UN membership till 1955). Masaryk fell to his death mysteriously in Prague in early 1948, as the Soviets completed the process of making Czechoslovakia a Soviet satellite. The debate was also notable for the impassioned contribution of Yeats's future Senate colleague, Owen Sheehy Skeffington, who denounced the Wilsonian declaration on self-determination, on the basis that the British response in Ireland to the sweeping victory of Sinn Féin in the 1918 General Election had been –'a régime of military repression and coercion unparalleled in history'. His mother Hanna, a noted public figure, was particularly proud of his speech.

Another Trinity society had an even bigger influence on Yeats's life. It was at a rowdy meeting of Cumann Gaelach (Irish Language Society) at which the Auditor Peter Kavanagh, brother of the poet Patrick Kavanagh, was being ejected down the stairs that Yeats first encountered his future wife Gráinne Ní hÉigeartaigh, whom he married in 1949. She was the daughter of P.S.

O'Hegarty and niece of Seán O'Hegarty, both of whom played a prominent role in the struggle for independence, her father writing a history of it, *The Victory of Sinn Féin,* while Secretary of the Department of Posts and Telegraphs. Her brother Seán was an Irish-language publisher. Their children were brought up Irish-speaking. She was to become one of the country's leading harpists and authority on Irish harp music. One of their daughters Caitríona is also a harpist, and another Síle was a broadcast journalist. A large car was needed to transport the harp, which meant that Yeats, who lived in Dalkey, could give southside colleagues a lift home after Seanad proceedings were over.

Michael Yeats had joined Fianna Fáil in 1943, with membership of a cumann (branch) in Rathmines. He fought two general elections as a Dáil candidate in 1948 and 1951, alongside the veteran Seán MacEntee. The Dublin South-East constituency was a three-seater, but, given that the three sitting TDs were all high profile, the other two being John A. Costello (1891–1976), Taoiseach from 1948 to 1951, and his famous Health Minister Dr Noel Browne (1915–97), Yeats had very little chance, but garnered around 3,000 votes on the first outing and 2,000 on the second. However, de Valera, recognizing Yeats's potential usefulness to the party, where he had been a member of the National Executive from 1948, nominated him to the Seanad, where he served till 1954.

His first term in the Seanad was fairly low profile. Always mindful of his family's Sligo roots, he spoke on rural development, turf production and the need for road maintenance, but was a strong advocate of the fiscal orthodoxy at that time; balanced budgets. In his memoir, he gave an interesting account of a Fianna Fáil Parliamentary Party meeting in 1953, discussing the difficulties the Government was still having with the Catholic Hierarchy over health legislation picking up the pieces after their veto on Noel Browne's Mother and Child scheme. According to Yeats, Dan Breen (a War of Independence veteran of note) stood up and said: 'It's a terrible pity that 30 years ago, when we had the chance, we didn't shoot a few Bishops'. Yeats added: 'de Valera looked glum'.

In the second half of the 1950s, whilst having no seat in the Oireachtas (Parliament), Yeats remained active in the organization and on the National Executive, and was a close observer of the political scene. In his memoir, he reflected on some of his contemporaries. He regretted that Dr Noel Browne, who had been welcomed into Fianna Fáil, was squeezed out of a party nomination in Dublin South-East in 1957, because he was a threat to MacEntee, but he concluded that in the long run Browne was probably too uncompromising to have stayed in the party. While Yeats respected de Valera, he clearly felt he hung on too long. He strongly identified with his Deputy Leader and successor as Taoiseach, Sean Lemass, and warmly welcomed his meetings with

Terence O'Neill, the Northern Ireland Prime Minister. His chapter on the first Lynch Administration (1966–73) is tellingly entitled *Without a Leader*. On the 1970 Arms Trial, he took the view that those trying to import arms 'genuinely thought that in this activity they were carrying out Government policy'. The court in acquitting the defendants seemed to have taken a similar view. He had retired from politics in 1979, so was not involved in the dramas of the 1980s under the leadership of Charles Haughey, about whom he had mixed feelings. He had been 'a brilliantly successful Minister', but following revelations in his retirement about the millions he had accepted when he was Taoiseach he had become 'a tragic and discredited figure'.

Yeats served continuously in the Seanad from 1961 to early 1980, being elected three times, on the Labour Panel in 1961, and on the Cultural and Educational Panel in 1969 and 1973, and twice being appointed as a Taoiseach's nominee in 1965 and 1977. His main contributions were on economic and social issues.

On 22 March 1962, speaking on the Central Fund Bill, he noted that 'things are better than they have been for a long time'. On 25 July, he remarked that ever increasing national income enabled the community to provide the better services that people wanted, and the next day accused the Labour Party of not being willing to raise taxes to increase public services. The previous month, on 24 June, he criticized a small rise in ministerial salaries from £2,000 to £2,200 as entirely inadequate, and he added: 'I regret the Government have not seen fit to give Ministers decent salaries'.

Yeats did also address other issues. Understandably, he was interested in copyright law, having no objection to the broadcast of reasonable extracts, but arguing that use of copyright material in advertising should require permission. Reflecting his background perhaps, Yeats did speak quite strongly against plans by a semi-State body to demolish Georgian houses to build its new headquarters along Dublin's Fitzwilliam Street interrupting a vista which was 'a magnificent architectural feature', but the Minister for Transport and Power Erskine Childers (from the same background) declined to intervene. The new HQ is now about to be demolished, having lasted no more than 50 years! More surprisingly, not just for a Fianna Fáil Senator but for the son of a poet who had famously lauded 'hard-riding country gentlemen', he was strongly critical of hunting and coursing. He argued in a debate on the Protection of Animals Bill (4 March 1964) with regard to one of the alleged justifications for hunting that 'no more inefficient or expensive system of ridding the country of vermin could be devised', and that he could not see why in a bill with that title 'it should be necessary to provide specifically for the infliction of suffering on animals'. Nor was he impressed with the economic justifications for such sports, which he likened to bull-fighting in Spain. Even the Bill's sponsor, Trinity Senator W.B. Stanford, described his position as 'brave'.

It was not just animals he cared about. On 2 March 1966, he also expressed hostility to corporal punishment in schools, highlighting the horrendous title of a 1946 Department Circular, *Instruction in regard to the Infliction of Corporal Punishment*, and arguing that there should be 'no question of giving leave to teachers to assault and batter children'. On 7 June 1967, he warmly welcomed Justice Minister Brian Lenihan's relaxation of literary censorship, commenting with regard to the banning of many books and authors of very great literary merit that 'many disgraceful things were done in the early years' because of 'bigoted cranks'. Senator W.B. Stanford noted in his memoirs that Yeats followed Senator Owen Sheehy Skeffington, who had concluded by saying that he was opposed to all censorship by the State, but that Yeats 'made a more constructive contribution'. On 13 December, Yeats complained of the small size of the Arts Council budget and that the National Library was grossly understaffed. He welcomed the proposed university merger between TCD and UCD, partly as a way round the episcopal ban on Catholics attending Trinity (24 January 1968). He warmly welcomed the exemption from tax conceded in then Finance Minister Haughey's 1969 Budget to writers, painters and sculptors, as representing the part of the Budget 'which will be remembered for generations long after the circumstances of the present day have been forgotten' (23 July 1969).

Yeats became a great expert on the electoral system. He was not a fan of the Single Transferable Vote system or Proportional Representation, with the alphabetical listing of candidates and the random distribution of later preferences. He strongly supported the referendum to substitute the British first-past-the-post system: 'The great advantage to us of the straight vote is that it tends to create a two-party system' (25 July 1968). Some years later, he conducted a very detailed forensic deconstruction of the then Minister for Local Government James Tully's redrawing of constituency boundaries. He argued that the bill was designed to copper-fasten the National Coalition's hold on the country for many years to come, but that the Minister had made a serious miscalculation. A very slight shift in opinion would be sufficient to turn the whole ship round the other way (10 April 1974), which proved an accurate prophesy when Fianna Fáil was swept back to power with a large majority in 1977.

Following the General Election of 1969, won by Fianna Fáil, Michael Yeats was put forward by his party for the position of Cathaoirleach (Chairperson) of the Seanad. The proposer Tomás Ó Maoláin called him 'a born parliamentarian', noted that he was the son of a father who had a worldwide reputation,

and praised his level-headedness, even temper and broadness of vision. His nomi-
nation was not an issue for the opposition parties, who spoke in favour of it.
M.J. O'Higgins of Fine Gael recalled that Yeats's father had been nominated to
the first Free State Senate by his party leader's father (W.T. Cosgrave). However,
despite Yeats's own Trinity background, he was opposed by two Trinity sena-
tors, Owen Sheehy Skeffington, seconded by the newly elected Mary Bourke
(President Mary Robinson, 1990–7). Having prefaced his remarks by saying that
he had known Michael Yeats for a quarter of a century (since 1944), Skeffington
expressed opposition on two grounds, one implausible, that Yeats had a muddled
grasp of procedure (something that he was in fact strong on), the other, only
partly true, that he was 'a deeply committed party politician', who did not think
his party was ever wrong, and who might find it difficult to be impartial and
who would be tempted to protect a minister. He added insult to injury by saying
he would have voted for his party colleague Eoin Ryan. What was fair comment
perhaps was his belief that Yeats in the body of the House would 'prove a far
more effective and useful Member than sitting in the Chair'. Some years later,
Yeats's reputation for understanding procedure was such that he was asked to
draw up new rules and procedures by the Bureau of the European Parliament, for
use after it became directly elected in 1979. As Cathaoirleach, Yeats led a number
of Senate delegations abroad, including to France and to Strasbourg, where he
decided that he would like to become a member of the European Parliament

     With Ireland's accession to the then EEC on 1 January 1973, Yeats was
appointed a member of the European Parliament, necessitating his resignation
as Chair of the Seanad. His colleagues were warm in their praise, Labour's J.
Fitzgerald saying that he had been 'brilliant' in his position, and 'very, very
fair to everyone'. Mary Robinson in her memoir *Everyone Matters* acknowl-
edged that, despite her initial opposition, Michael Yeats was 'a fine chair and
a committed and articulate senator', and cited him along with other distin-
guished senators, including Conor Cruise O' Brien, as amongst her role models.

     In the final phase of his parliamentary career, he exercised a dual mandate
in the Seanad and in the European Parliament between 1973 and 1979, making
a strong contribution to both. He would have preferred the Fianna Fáil MEPs
to have joined the Liberal Group in the Parliament, in which he was well before
his time, but the majority opted for the Gaullist alliance. It is obvious that
Yeats enjoyed the new stimulus, and that he was a strong believer in Ireland's
European vocation. He became the first Irish Vice-President of the Parliament.

     One of the issues he pursued most vigorously both in the Seanad and the
European Parliament was the under-representation of women in the higher
ranks of the public service and the workforce generally and the issue of equal

pay, which became the subject of an EEC directive. He highlighted in the
Seanad, for instance, that in 1972 0.6% of Principal Officers in the Irish Civil
Service were women, and that among 82 heads or deputy heads of depart-
ment there were none. In the EEC, the rule likewise seemed to be 'the higher
the position the fewer the women', based in part on the feeling men had that
women were intellectually inferior (25 July 1973). He did not let some Irish
trade unions off the hook either, especially the print unions. In the European
Parliament from 1973 on, he started hammering home the need for the EEC
Commission to ensure compliance with equal pay, and not to allow backsliding
by national governments. On 11 February 1976, he expressed vehement oppo-
sition to the Irish Government's application, under pressure from employer
organisations, for exemption from the requirements of the equal pay directive,
so that they could continue to have cheap labour. He called for 'outrageous
discrimination against women workers' to be eliminated. The Government's
application was unanimously rejected by the Commission. He also directed
fire against the Commission itself, where of 299 members of staff at the senior
A3 rank only 3 were women (17 June 1976), the inferior position being under-
pinned by a number of fallacious rationales. On International Women's Day (17
October 1976), he complained that, although the Directive had come into force
in February, in Ireland life had gone on as usual, and there was an unspoken
conspiracy, with the unions not that keen. Back home in the Seanad, in a debate
on the Employment Equality Bill in May 1977, he lambasted all-male interview
boards, with their assumption that the best qualified person for a job had to be
man, and ridiculed the banks for not having women cashiers, on the grounds
that the public would think that lodging money with them would be unsafe.
After the change of government in Ireland in mid-1977, while he moderated
his tone in the European Parliament a little, he still found the situation exceed-
ingly unsatisfactory, with private employers using the economic depression as
an excuse, and the government the budgetary situation to delay equal pay.
He deprecated the unions' promise to the employers not to use strike action
over equal pay. While he accepted there were enormous financial problems,
he said: 'We should be pushing for these things to be carried out: we should
not be giving a way out'. In parliamentary questions, he sought assurances
from the Commission that the introduction of work-sharing would not be used
to discriminate against women, and he also complained about a European
orchestra, in which at least 2/3 of the positions were reserved for men.

In his opening speech to the European Parliament on behalf of all the Irish
members on 16 January 1973, having evoked the historic cultural contribution
of Ireland to Europe, his main emphasis was on the need to reduce the great

economic and social disparities between different Western European regions. That and the handling of the recession arising from the first oil crisis at home and in Europe was another consistent theme of his contributions. At home, he was very critical of the initial expansionary budgetary policy of the National Coalition, leading to high deficits and high inflation. In Europe, he emphasized the importance of social policy. The EEC should not just be a rich man's club, nor simply a means by which could be exercised the full gamut of the activities of a self-seeking free enterprise society. In 1975 he drew up a report on the retention of the rights of employees in the case of mergers. He attacked the derisory amount of 1% for new actions in the 1976 Draft Budget as trying to run the Community on the cheap. He criticized the token sums allocated to the new Regional Fund, and the absence of any real increase in the 1978 Draft Budget. In a debate on enlargement in 1977, he argued that in the future vastly increased resources would be needed for the Regional and Social Funds, irrespective of enlargement. In the Seanad, on 5 December 1979, he spoke in favour of Greek accession, with membership looked on as a bulwark against any return to dictatorship. Indeed, he argued that 'all European democracies who can, economically speaking, withstand the pace of membership should be let in'. In 1978–9, he saw the agreement to create the European Monetary System as an opportunity to advance the agenda of progressively harmonizing living standards through greatly increased EU transfers. Again, he was ahead of his time, but it was not until 1988 under EU Commission President Jacques Delors that substantial Structural and (from 1993) Cohesion Funds were put in place, and they did greatly assist Ireland in catching up with average EU living standards.

As a parliamentarian who focused mainly on economic and social issues, Yeats was vocal in the European Parliament in favour of the establishment of the European Foundation for the Improvement of Living and Working Conditions. He also argued that there should be a Community presence, in terms of an institution, in each Member State. The European Foundation was established in June 1975, and by decision of the European Council was located in Loughlinstown, Co. Dublin. In 2015, it celebrates its fortieth year.

In the Seanad in 1975 Yeats strongly opposed the proposal of Dr Conor Cruise O'Brien, Minister for Posts and Telegraphs, to rebroadcast BBC 1 as a second channel, for the benefit of large parts of the country that did not have access at the time to multi-channel viewing. He was appalled by a proposal which seemed 'to disregard the entire concept of an Irish nation or Irish nationality'. The second channel should be left under Irish control. One of the reasons Ireland had joined the EEC was that 'we would be able to expose ourselves to a wider variety of cultures, and that we would escape from this dependence on

Great Britain'. It had been one of the reasons that the Abbey Theatre had been founded, to create an Irish company that could put on Irish plays. No *quid pro quo* was being offered. It was equivalent to having half our newspapers printed in Britain. It was a 'bloody insult to the Irish people'. 'No other country would dream of doing such a thing'. The O'Brien plan never went ahead.

In 1975, along with his party, he spoke out against the Criminal Law Jurisdiction Bill, which would have allowed terrorist suspects wanted in the North to be tried in the Republic, and claimed that the only people who wanted it were the Minister for Justice and the Northern Unionists. On 31 August 1976, he opposed a National Emergency Motion, which would have allowed the detention in custody of paramilitary suspects to be extended from two days to seven. He argued there was no comparison to the situation that obtained in World War II.

His last major speech in the Seanad was in support of Charles Haughey's Health (Family Planning) Bill (3 July 1979), where he confirmed his reputation as a liberal republican. The bill legalized artificial contraception for *bona fide* family planning purposes on prescription, in other words, understood to be confined to married couples only, but allowing doctors and chemists a conscience clause. Haughey (in)famously described it as 'an Irish solution to an Irish problem'. Yeats stated: 'My own view on the question of principle with regard to legislation of this kind is that the question of family planning or contraception is not a matter for the State'. If he were to write a bill from an ideal point of view, it would be a very different one. While it was easy to draft a bill, it was by no means easy to get majority support for it. The essential job of the bill was to get some kind of majority consensus, so that it had some prospect of becoming law. He noted that the Minister had engaged in endless consultation. Though fundamentally sharing the position of radicals such as Mary Robinson and Noel Browne, he did not share their scorn for the Minister's compromise and the need to proceed pragmatically.

In 1979 Yeats stood for election to the European Parliament in the Dublin constituency, the local and European elections went badly for Fianna Fáil, and he was not elected. He ceased to be active in the Seanad after December 1979, and resigned from it in April 1980 to take up a senior post of Director in the Council Secretariat. He was attached to the Energy and Research Directorate, which was very busy dealing with the effects of the second oil crisis after the fall of the Shah of Iran. He later had responsibility for relations between the Council and the European Parliament. As a former MEP, the contempt in which the Council then held the Parliament and the little store that it gave its opinions came as something of a revelation and shock to him. While supportive of the increased powers given subsequently to a much enlarged European Parliament, he was strongly of the view expressed in his memoir that 'in the years to come Ireland must make sure that we do not give up the right to defend our own national interests'. He saw the Council as essential to this, and unlike many other committed Irish Europeans he does not seem to have over-idealized the Commission as guarantor of the Community interest and the interest of the smaller States. This is even though on 10 February 1975, in line with Irish official thinking at the time, he expressed some suspicion about meetings of Heads of State and Government outside the formal institutional framework, and agreed with EU Commission President Ortoli 'that expediency might tempt us to take the low road of inter-governmental co-operation rather than the high road of integration'.

Yeats retired in 1986, having reached the age of 65. His memoir was completed in 1998, and he looked back in it with a good deal of satisfaction as the Celtic Tiger was reaching its height as to how far Ireland had come, especially in Europe. As guardian, with other family members, of the immense literary legacy of his father, he was exceptionally generous to academics and researchers, and to the State in donating the W.B. Yeats papers in his possession to the National Library of Ireland, where there is now the largest archived Yeats collection in the world. There are innumerable examples, worldwide, where the scions of famous statesmen and writers have gone down other roads, accepting large sums of money from the State to prevent a collection of papers from going abroad, or alternatively guarding copyright with the ferocity of Cerberus. There is a fine sculpture of Michael B. Yeats by John Coll at the top of the stairs down to the Yeats exhibition, which has been *in situ* since 2006 and is well visited every day. Warm tribute is paid to the help given by Michael and other members of his family in facilitating the exhibition. Michael died at the beginning of 2007.

Michael B. Yeats is certainly a model of the service that can be given by a committed parliamentarian in both Ireland and in Europe, whose focus was on the needs of the country and of the people, rather than solely or mainly on what populist catch-cries might help secure his re-election. For that reason perhaps, he had just moderate electoral success, and the length of his career and its continuity owed much to the support he received from three Taoisigh. As the title and sub-title of his book show, he had long reconciled himself to poetry and to being a poet's son. An explanatory tablet near the entrance of the National Library exhibition states: 'WBY and his brother and sisters went on to become the single most significant artistic family in twentieth-century Ireland'. While some of Michael's family were artistically gifted, his talents were in another direction, but he too in his own understated way brought honour not just to his family but to service to the State.

Tír na nÓg

Thomas Rice Henn (1901–74)
An Appreciation

GLEN CAVALIERO

Tom Henn was a polymath. Consider his credentials: scholar, soldier, teacher, sportsman, lecturer, administrator, poet. Yeats's tribute to Robert Gregory springs to mind – 'soldier, scholar, horseman, he.' Evidently this was a man who both by temperament and by experience was ideally suited to be a champion of a writer whom he considered to be 'our greatest poet since Shakespeare'. Henn was born in Sligo and spent his boyhood there: he had experienced from a child's perspective the landscape which Yeats mythologized; the local legends were in his bloodstream. He was twelve years old when in 1913 his parents moved south to County Clare, to occupy the family home so romantically called Paradise. Tom's later boyhood was therefore spent in a spacious landscape bordering the River Shannon as it neared the sea: the sense of a great current of water moving inexorably towards immersion in its destiny was to permeate his view of human history.

His autobiography *Five Arches*[1] contains a loving and evocative portrayal of the life he led there, written from the point of view of a sportsman who used a gun for purposes other than the random lawlessness of a period of social and political upheaval. Tom Henn knew the Irish peasantry at what was frequently a dangerous first-hand. 'In my own country, three known murderers lived within a short distance of my home; two policemen were put, alive, in a gas furnace in a certain town; a friend was buried alive.' The words are from *The Lonely*

Tower:[2] there can be few literary studies to refer to such atrocities with an equal particularity. Tom Henn's Ireland was very different from the world of dreamers conjured up in the two words 'Celtic Twilight'; it was the world that Yeats himself would come to encounter as he composed his greatest poems.

This adventurous boyhood was formative of Henn's work both as a scholar and a teacher. His wartime experiences and practical understanding of military affairs gave him a far wider outlook than the majority of academics could command – witness in *The Bible as Literature*[3] his account of the Israelites' wholesale slaughter of their enemies. He points out that whereas a mighty empire could afford to take captives, 'the Israelites had no great city and no adequate organisation to deal with prisoners. Therefore, as a purely practical measure, the army had to be put to the sword.' Such clear-sightedness makes uncomfortable reading, but Tom Henn was never a slave to contemporary social or moral attitudes.

In the post-war Cambridge world of the 1950s his lectures rivalled those of C.S. Lewis and F.R. Leavis in popularity, thanks in part to his deep resonant voice, his massive frame and sure sense of the appropriately histrionic gesture. His outlook was essentially one of demonstration, in this respect being out of line with the current emphasis on critical and political controversy. In *Five Arches* he was to write with prophetic insight of the limitations of ideology where a response to imaginative literature was concerned. With regard to the expansion of universities between 1957 and 1965 he commented that 'the supply of competent and experienced teachers was far behind the demand', resulting in a shift from academic to sociological credentials; while as to the current commercialization of literary studies he would surely have been wary of the emphasis laid on publication when making university appointments. What mattered to him was what a candidate had read and taken to heart. For it was his considered opinion that a recognition of the sovereign role played in literary studies by the imagination was essential to a proper understanding of an author's work. 'I do not think it is possible to make the teaching of literature a living thing without attention to the transcendental values.'

The Lonely Tower exemplifies this approach. The book is not only a tribute to Yeats's achievement as a poet: it reinforces that tribute by a close engagement with recurrent symbols and historical allusions. Imposing no theoretical interpretation upon its subject, it sets out to elucidate obscurities by testing their origins in non-academic life-experience, a method deployed also in the author's later study of Shakespearean metaphor, *The Living Image*.[4] These forays into explanatory interpretation are couched in phraseology that was courteous to their readers, phrases such as 'we may remember', 'I suggest' and so on – phrases that could be teasingly ironical when addressed to pupils at Cambridge. But he provided an example of scholarship that was in touch with his own experience, thus encouraging them to work towards a similar achievement of their own. And he could be frank: commenting on a passage from one of Yeats's letters to Sturge Moore, he readily admits, 'I do not know what this means.' As a literary scholar he was invariably companionable.

But for those of us who knew and loved him it was the man himself who stays longest in the mind. I am but one among very many who benefited from his humanity and willingness to take a risk. Thirty-seven years old at the time I met him, I had been acting as Chaplain to Anglican students in Edinburgh. My application to read for a degree in English had evidently proved daunting to more than one admissions tutor before I was advised to consult Tom Henn at St Catharine's. A meeting was arranged, and I entered for the first time that corner room which even today seems redolent of his presence. My first impression was of familiarity, for the large and slightly infirm figure that rose to greet me might have emerged from among the benevolent figures of my schooldays. It was an encouraging introduction.

There followed a year's wait before I could be admitted, and at my first supervision with him I was set an essay on one of Tom's principal areas of knowledge and concern – the seventeenth-century Metaphysical poets. This was clearly an acid test as to whether his gamble was to pay off. Rarely if ever have I worked so hard as I did in the ensuing week. As I settled down opposite Tom at its conclusion he remarked that since I was an Oxford man I could ignore the usual Cambridge practice by reading my essay aloud. He remained silent throughout but, I sensed, closely attentive until I wound up to the close. The silence went on – and, so it felt, on *and* on, interminably, only to he broken with a sigh. And then the verdict was pronounced: 'You depress me.' The silence resumed while I felt the bottom falling out of my entire enterprise. And then, 'There is nothing I can teach you.' And that was Tom Henn for you – the histrionic sense, the personal challenge with a compliment implicit in it, and the sheer mischief of playing such a game. Needless to say, there was a very great deal he was to teach me in the ensuing year, all of it communicated in a tone of scholarly urbanity. As often as not a glass of sherry would conclude the meeting.

Tom was to retire a few years after that and I realize more than ever how privileged I was to share in what I now realize to have been the very end of a particular approach to literary studies. The atmosphere of civility reflected a style of life such as Yeats had evoked in the relaxed formality of his elegies for Lady Gregory's Coole Park. His celebrated 'Monday Evenings' in his rooms in College realized something of this stylish atmosphere, being candle-lit for the reading by the assembled company of their unsigned poems, poems which Tom would gather up beforehand and distribute to those who seemed to him to be their appropriate readers. I was to experience this to my cost when he placed in my hands a poem of his own which he had read to me the week before: it had been written to mark the first anniversary of the death of his only son. Was this a case of a humility prepared to expose such a heartfelt piece of writing to the assessment of an audience of friends and pupils? As for myself, who not only had to read the poem aloud but also to open the following discussion, I decided to take the matter as being at once a challenge and an honour. Such latent ambiguity was yet another instance of Tom Henn's complicated temperament and of his sense of occasion. I did not respect him the less for it.

And it is possible for tables to be turned. One of his conversational strategies was to reply to a remark of one's own with some gnomic quotation uttered in a growling conspiratorial murmur. The words may have been those of Yeats or Kipling, or even his admired seventeenth-century poet, Nathaniel Wanley; but on one occasion some devil prompted me to challenge him. 'Tom, you made that up!' And he actually blushed and offered no reply. But that too was Tom Henn. How fortunate were those of us who knew him in having as a result so much to be grateful for and to remember.

NOTES

1. *Five Arches, with 'Philoctetes' and Other Poems* (Gerrards Cross 1980).
2. *The Lonely Tower: Studies in the Poetry of W.B. Yeats* (London 1950), second edition, revised, and enlarged, 1965.
3. *The Bible as Literature* (London 1970).
4. *The Living Image: Shakespearean Essays* (London 1972).

The Place of Shells

T.R. HENN
(1901–74)

I

I have taken the title of this lecture from the Irish form, *Sligeach,*[1] which means 'the Place of Shells'. Most of us, on holiday at some watering-place or wandering on the shingle of some lake-shore, are, instinctively, beachcombers; we look down to see what may be found, left by some ancient or modern tide. We may use them for decoration or just collect; and we have been familiar from childhood with the sea-roar which we can hear from the convoluted heart of certain larger shells, which is no more than the echo of our own restless blood. The heraldic emblem of Sligo is a shell, a scallop shell, which (as you will remember) is also the badge of the pilgrim to some great shrine, or to the Holy Land. May I remind you of Sir Walter Raleigh's poem?

The Passionate Man's Pilgrimage

Give me my scallop-shell of quiet,
My staff of faith to walk upon,
My scrip of joy, immortal diet,
My bottle of salvation,
My gown of glory, hope's true gage;
And thus I'll take my pilgrimage

> Blood must be my body's balmer;
> No other balm will there be given:
> Whilst my soul, like quiet palmer,
> Travelleth towards the land of heaven;
> Over the silver mountains,
> Where spring the nectar fountains;
> There will I kiss
> The bowl of bliss;
> And drink mine everlasting fill
> Upon every milken hill,
> My soul will be a-dry before;
> But after, it will thirst no more.

I would not press the thought that you and I are among the pilgrims to this place, though, indeed, we may well have needed our 'staff of faith' to journey here. My purpose this morning is to invite your attention to the historical energy and momentum that lie behind the centuries; to the turbulence of history that Yeats saw, and which he has dramatized in his characteristic way to inflame his imagination; and to offer some thoughts about the growth of a poet's mind – remembering Wordsworth's *Prelude* – in relation to the music of this countryside in his youth.

II

If we stand on the summit of Knocknarea – and you must carry a stone with you on your climb to put on the Cairn, else you will have no luck afterwards – we can watch the scene and the centuries mirrored as in some kind of glass. First and perhaps simplest, consider the geographical features which have made Sligo a centre of supreme military importance. For it is a point of passage; like Thermopylae, or Marathon, or the Plain of Esdraelon in Palestine. It stands across one of the great highways between Connaught and Ulster. There are at most only two strategic points where an army can cross; one, at low tide only, just below Hyde Bridge, and a second just above the upper bridge on John F. Kennedy Parade, and not far from the spot (so one account says) where the warrior Eoghan Bel has stood upright in his grave, holding his spear ready, throughout fourteen centuries. For a defending or invading force, the eastern flank is protected by Lough Gill, and, if you are a soldier, you will see the road around the lake is commanded by hills and wooded country eminently suitable for ambush. Westward, of course, you are protected by the Atlantic, moody and terrible; as the galleons of the Spanish Armada found when they were driven ashore on Streedagh Strand. The estuaries, bays, sandbanks make it quite impracticable to outflank your enemy by naval power, as in the Elizabethan and Cromwellian combined operations on the coast of Cork. Between Sligo and Drumcliffe lies the great plain – where Yeats saw Constance Gore-Booth ride. 'Under Ben Bulben to the meet' is a perfect arena for war-chariots and the set-piece battles of the heroic age. It was on the slopes of Ben Bulben that the Irish version of Venus and Adonis was enacted, the story of Diarmuid and Grania, and Diarmuid was slain by the enchanted ravaging boar. (That story and its symbols are as old as history.) You will see from Drumcliffe the cliffs that lie to the North-West of the Mountain, over which a troop of cavalry were driven to their death. And at least one whom I have spoken with has heard, on a foggy day on the plateau on the summit (you can reach it from the Waterfall at Glencar), the thunder of phantom hoofs, and seen the mountain grass spring up again, a few yards away, after the horsemen had passed. This, I think, stuck in Yeats's mind, for he mentions it twice:

> What marches through the mountain pass?
> No, no, my son, not yet;
> This is an airy spot,
> And no man knows what treads the grass. [2]

It was in a cavern in the side of Ben Bulben that the giant Dhoya, marooned by the Fomorian galleys in the bay of the Red Cataract (you can visit the great waterfall that plunges into the head of Ballisodare Bay, and remember that Kingsley's Tom the Water-Baby came down the Yorkshire hillside 'like a salmon over the Fall at Ballisodare') sought refuge in a cave beside Glencar, and for a time lived in great happiness with a mysterious daughter of the underworld. [3] And I fancy that it was on the Drumcliffe plain, on the edge of Lissadell, that the tiny, exquisite and difficult poem 'The Death of the Hare' came to being.

> I have pointed out the yelling pack,
> The hare leap to the wood,
> And when I pass a compliment
> Rejoice as lover should
> At the dropping of an eye,
> At the mantling of the blood.
> Then suddenly my heart is wrung
> By her distracted air
> And I remember wildness lost

> And after, swept from there,
> Am set down standing in the wood
> At the death of the hare.

You remember, too, Yeats's tribute to Constance Gore-Booth:

> What voice more sweet than hers
> When, young and beautiful
> She rode to harriers?[4]

III

It is a wild history on which you can look for the great cairn – which will never, I think, be excavated, and we shall never know if Queen Maeve really lies there or, as some think, at Croghan in County Roscommon – or perhaps from the tower of one of the churches. Let us glance at it for a moment. Sligo was invaded in AD 1235, and granted to Fitzgerald, an ancestor of the Earl of Kildare. He built a castle here in 1245, to serve as a base for his intended conquest of Tír Chonaill [Donegal]; and founded the Dominican Priory, whose splendid ruins you can visit. Within half a century that castle was destroyed *four* times by either O'Connor (Sligo) or O'Donnell (Donegal). In 1310 a new castle was built, and a new town laid out, by Richard de Burgh, the Red Earl of Ulster. Five years later the castle in its turn was destroyed by O'Donnell. In 1414 town and friary were destroyed by accidental fire, but were rebuilt about 1416 by Friar Brian MacDonagh. In 1470 Red Hugh O'Donnell took the castle once again from O'Connor: in 1595 the English, Leicester's forces, besieged the castle and destroyed the friary. In 1641 both town and friary were sacked by Cromwellian general Sir Frederick Hamilton. In 1645 the town, having presumably recovered from the sacking, was captured by Sir Charles Coote. In 1689 it was seized by the Williamites under Lord Kingstown, but was retaken by Patrick Sarsfield for King James. Then there seems to have been a period of the Pax Britannica, and of loyalty to the Hanoverian cause. At least we know that Sligo raised three whole regiments of militia – all with carefully designed and differentiated uniforms, for your soldier is a vain sort of animal – to repel the French invasion of 1798. I mention these odd fragments from the past only to suggest to you what a long and turbulent history this peaceful market town has had; that there are many buried dead about us; and that any place that has been much fought over seems to acquire (as we should expect) the character of being saturated with witnesses from the unseen world. It was Jack Yeats, the painter, who told me of an ancient piece of myth: that where a great mass of fresh water meets the sea by way of a short river as it does beside us here, a kind of magic is generated and spread upon the whole neighbourhood.

IV

These may be some of the influences of place on a poet's mind, and on the kind of poetry he writes. Of this general effect, one accepts it, I think, unconsciously. That the Lake District should have fired so greatly Wordsworth's imagination, that Cowper's poetry and his hymns should be related to the placid and comfortable waters of the Ouse, that Crabbe's grim realism should spring from that 'bold surly savage race' that you still find round Aldeburgh – we take these for granted; just as we see the praise of rivers in the song of poet after poet: Spenser, Marvell, Joyce. We accept (but cannot prove) how much of Warwickshire moulded Shakespeare; or how generations of writers have found themselves and their art in Greece and Italy:

> ... Whence turbulent Italy should draw
> Delight in art whose end is peace,
> In logic and in natural law
> By sucking at the dugs of Greece.[5]

But there is a world of difference between reading of the genius of place and meeting that genius face to face with the words moving in our minds. When I first saw the Cave of the Cumaean Sybil, on the south of the little sandy bay where Aeneas landed from Troy, its many mouths were filled with German machine-guns sited to fire on the beach; and it took on a strange metaphysical dimension from them. To see the long-extinct volcano of Solfatera where the ground rings hollow like a drum, with its pools of boiling mud, and to realize that you are walking on one of the classic entrances to Hell, is to understand, suddenly, something of Dante. So in the bible, above all books. One does not, I think, begin to realize the complexity and energy of its poetry until one has studied a little geography of the Holy Land; and begun to understand how the great images of its poetry spring naturally from the clash of the desert with the valleys that stand so thick with corn; of the importance of the springing well and the waters of comfort; of whirlwind and thunder; of sudden storms upon Galilee; of the imagery of the threshing-floor and of the scattering of nations like chaff before the wind; of Israel's fear of the sea and of its great beasts that take their pastime in it. These, and a thousand other images, even to the bulwarks that defend or break the nations, spring naturally out of the very inscape of place.

Perhaps, also, to understand fully these poems one needs to have been born and bred in one of the western Irish towns; to remember how it was the centre of your world, how the mountains and the rivers and the woods became a portion of your life forever; to have loved with a sense of possession even the roadside bushes where the cotters hung their clothes to dry. That a sense of possession was the very centre of the matter. Elsewhere you are only a passer-by, for everything is owned by no one.[6]

But there is another strange feature of the Sligo setting which has not, I think, been mentioned before.

All poetry is built on rhythm. Rhythm is in its turn built on stress, tone, pitch. All poets savour the juice of living words upon the tongue, 'bursting joy's grapes against his palate fine' in Keats's phrase. All poets have a stock of words which they taste and relish to a special degree. If we were to take three or four of the many poets here this morning, and analyse their vocabularies, we should find that they were in fact differentiated by a small individual vocabulary, perhaps a hundred or so, of words peculiar to themselves; of which they had, as it were, taken personal possession. We recall immediately some that Yeats was fond of: *wild* (in the Anglo-Irish songs); *arrogant; fanatic; ungovernable; murmuring* and *murmur; withered; ignorant; mummy* (and *mummy-dead*); *gear; magnanimity.* We should note the polysyllabic proper names that he tastes, rolls upon the tongue: 'the Great Smaragdine Tablet', 'the Mareotic Lake', 'Guidobaldo', 'Michelozzo', 'Rhadamanthus'; as well as the place-names round about Coole recorded in the poems of *The Seven Woods.* The list could be much extended. So, too, the nonce-words, those that are used only once in the poet's vocabulary of 10,666 words. But it is of the place-names of Sligo that I want to speak now.

I suggest that he found here a great reservoir of words that sing, as it were, of themselves. When we start to write Greek and Latin verse we are taught to keep notebooks of phrases, proper names, synonyms, embellishments of expansions, even clichés that have once been part of some ancient fabric of poetry, whether hexameters or elegiacs or sapphics; and which may legitimately be used again in our 'imitations'. To use these broken fragments of masonry with wit and precision, and to take advantage of allusions and references in depth, was once the mark of the scholar and of the poet who had served his apprenticeship among the classics. But if, as I believe happens here, the 'names' contain in themselves special rhythmical and musical qualities, if their complex musical values include this tone, pitch, stress so that they sing of their own accord, not only can the poetic craftsman weave them into his verse, but they may even suggest a sort of running tune, strongly remembered from childhood, out of which, or on which, the rhythm of a poem may grow.

Let us glance at some examples:

> Saddle and ride, I heard a man say,
> Out of Ben Bulben and Knocknarea.
> *What says the Clock in the Great Clock Tower?*[7]

Now *Knócknaréa* is, technically, the foot know as a cretic, common in Irish place names because the unstressed syllable –na (of) (as in Lugnagall) is a frequent link between two heavier stresses. *Bén Búlbén* on the other hand is the foot that prosodists call a bacchius, a kind of rhythmic foil to the *cretic,* sliding off on to a lighter stress after its two explosive but level initial stresses: *Ben Bulben.* But to my ear the strong *n*-sounds that follow the stresses give a kind of sinister weight, as of the very mountain itself: and these *n*-sounds are echoed (but with a different cadence, or resolution of the chord) in *Knocknarea.* In the same way,

> The light of evening, Lissadell,
> Great windows open to the south ...

Lissâdéll is again a *cretic,* but softened and the initial stress lightened, smoothed down by the liquid l's and resolved in the chord by the sibilants

Liss/a/dâll

– where the drama (as it were) of the rhythm is held up for a moment so that the final stress shall be heavier.

But in 'The Ballad of Father O'Hart' we may examine the last four stanzas:

> And these were the words of John,
> When, weeping score by score,
> People came into Coloney;
> For he'd died at ninety-four.

(a bad line, even with precedents from the *Lyrical Ballads*)

> There was no human keening;
> The birds from Knocknarea
> And the world round Knocknashee
> Came keening in that day.
>
> The young birds and the old birds
> Came flying, heavy and sad;
> Keening in from Tiraragh,
> Keening from Ballinafad.

Keening from Inishmurray,
Nor stayed for bite or sup;
This way were all reproved
Who dig all customs up.

Now I hold no brief for this poem, even if we are charitable to it as a ballad by a very young poet, whose words and rhymes do not yet 'obey his call'; but listen to the amazing variety of the place names:

Côloónêy, technically an *amphibrach* (x/x, two short 'arms' on either side of the central stress): wholly different in sound as well as position from *Coolaney.*

Knocknarea, again,

Knôcknâshée ('the hill of the faery folk') where we have lost I think something as contrasted with the sharper e-sound of *Knocknarea,* followed by

Tirárâgh (an amphibrach like Coloney)

mated with the complex and lovely *Bállînâfád* which is almost a metrical phrase in itself, and which slides over the two light syllables in the middle, to the strong beat at the end. Or we have the more famous lines from 'The Fiddler of Dooney' where the rhythm of the names seems to prepare us for the dance-setting:

When I play of my fiddle in Dooney,
Folk dance like a wave of the sea;
My cousin is priest in Kilvarnet,
My brother in Mocharabuiee.

We may note several things: that Yeats has cribbed – quite justifiably – a famous line from Shakespeare's *A Winter's Tale,* where Florizel praises Perdita (note here too those singing names of lovers)

When you do dance I wish you
A wave o' the sea ...

Again, hear the 'names' (I am thinking of 'Longinus') lengthen downwards as it were to the end of the verse.

Doónêy – the ordinary reversed iambic foot, the trochee

Kîlvárnêt – which is a strongly marked amphibrach again.

Móchârâbúiee –so that we end up with a four syllable beat:[8] and we remember that this, the rhyming of the monosyllable with a poly-syllable, is a most effective technical device in Donne and Marvell.

You will read and, better, hear many other examples:

Drómâháire is a cretic, like *Knocknarea,* but the heavier stress on the last syllable gives it a different pitch – 'He stood among the crowd at *Dromahaire*'.

Inîsfrée, the 'isle of heather', is of this form, but with a light accent on the first syllable which again gives a different effect: while in the line

> Castle Dargan's ruin all lit.
> Lovely ladies dancing in it.

the peculiar harshness of the open a's give yet another effect to what is techni-cally two trochaic feet of the order of / x | / x.

V

Now I do not think this is idle speculation. I believe that Yeats learnt, as so many poets have done, something of his word-music from Spenser. His essay on that poet, and the *Selection* he made from him, have received too little attention. Look where you will, you will find these singing names in *The Faerie Queene*: Phaedra, Acrasia, Scudamore, Britomart, Florimell, Cymoducé; and those of all the renaissance ghosts that jostle each other out of Ovid's *Metamorphoses*. We remember too Milton's great catalogue of the battles that saved Western civilization, as Satan reviews those superb troops of Hell:

> And what resounds
> In fable or romance of Uther's son
> Begirt with British and Armoric knights;
> And all who since, baptised or infidel.
> Jousted in Aspramont, or Montalban,
> Damasco, or Morocco, or Trebisond,
> Or whom Biserta sent from Afric shore
> When Charelmain with all his peerage fell
> By Fontarabbia.

You will remember, too, Wordsworth's

> To lie, and listen to the mountain flood
> Murmuring from Glaramara's inmost caves ...

And I remember from my own boyhood days in County Clare other mysterious and exciting names: Glenvarra, a long dark pool on a trout stream; Clondagad, with a ruined church and graveyard near it: Lough Lomáun, Thrummeragh, Clonderlaw, Gort Glas ... . Later in life Yeats fancied himself more in the Greek world, ready to 'Choose Plato and Plotinus for a friend ... '

We have 'the great Smaragdine Tablet': one can almost taste the name like a pistachio-nut; 'the many-headed foam of Salamis', the Mareotic Lake; all the names of poets, sculptors, painters that flit through the works: Guidobaldo, Michelozzo, Veronese, Mantegna. So Michael Angelo, out of which he extracts two wholly different rhythms (the second a kind of resolution of the chord)

> Michael Angelo left a proof
> On the Sistine Chapel roof ...

as against

> There on that scaffolding reclines
> Michael Angelo.

I do not think this fanciful, and your ears will note these subtle discriminations of sound: as they will have been trained to do by Shakespeare and Donne and Keats and Bridges. I suggest one caution only.

In Prosody, that ancient science, we can go just so far only. We may gesture towards stresses and accents, vowel and consonantal combinations, and can sometimes profit by such exercises. Only by these devices can we explore, for instance, Milton's exquisite counterpointing, by a kind of secondary rhythm, the primary wavemotion of the iambic line. But in the last resort we have no valid language for the critical discussion of rhythm, either in verse or in the movements of a play, though we commonly speak of rhythm as an aspect of dramatic structure, of the advance and retreat of sympathy, or participation, or alienation. In poetry there is one test only: your own ear, and what it tells you of the energy, momentum, the finality of the line. And that is why part of our study should concern (as Jon Stallworthy has shown)[9] the fragments from Yeats's workshop, the perpetual testing of the music by the ear, so that we may, if we are lucky, know for ourselves that perfection and finality that we call great poetry.

VI

And here I want to attempt to lay one heresy by the heel. Sometimes my young men come and say to me: 'O we aren't interested now in what a poem *sounds* like, we're only interested in how it *looks* on the page'. Granted that interesting and perhaps valuable effect can be achieved by typography, that the angels' wings of the seventeenth century or the experiments of, say, E.E. Cummings, have their place, the poet has always traditionally been the singer as well as the maker, the seer, the visionary, the unacknowledged legislator of the world. And for all those the voice seems to me essential.

It is for this reason (which Yeats would have approved) that the Sligo Yeats Summer School has insisted that poetry is, among much else, music; and that it should be read aloud, interpreted, discussed, in terms of the human voice. Here of course we are in a mysterious country, and a numinous one; the word or the Word, and its power, on Sinai or beside the Lake. And it may well be that we are in danger of losing our sense of the capacity of the voice to transmit meaning, and the subtle qualities of emotion that go with this kind of meaning; as well as the modulations of which a most delicate instrument is, after due training capable. We know that Yeats's own experiments with 'Speaking to the Psaltery' were not successful. Whenever I have heard attempts to read poetry against some kind of musical background I have nearly always been disappointed, even frustrated. I would even say that, with a few superb exceptions which we all know, poetry and music do not form too happy a union. A strong music allows you to get away with murder as regards poetry itself, and this the Elizabethan song-writers knew and often exploited in those often vapid and embroidered verses for madrigals. To interpret by reading aloud has from the beginning been a feature of Sligo, not only in the public readings of Yeats, and by poets of distinction, but by the students themselves. It is the first path to understanding. And one who has helped us so greatly is Mary Watson, the best reader of poetry whom I have heard.

You see, many people come to Sligo with, as it were, empty hands, saying in effect: 'I don't know much about Ireland, or Yeats, or indeed poetry. But I want to learn about these things.' And Sligo has always held such people to be immensely important. We have not yet had to impose any entrance test for registration. We have instead provided seminars, centres of discussion, where we can learn. It would have been only too easy to have pitched the standard at a level where we had only professors, university teachers, advanced students; and many Summer Schools and conferences do just that. It seems to me entirely fitting that a proportion here are not, and do not want to become, professional students of literature or 'to cough in ink'; but have come to get to know Ireland, and Sligo, and poetry. How many is, I believe, irrelevant. No teacher ever knows where the seed falls, or what grain may chance from it. No one can ever tell when the ripples from the stones thrown into the pool will end on some farther shore.

So we have lectures at a high level (probably from the most distinguished scholars in two continents), seminars at all levels, and discussions – wherever you will. Nothing is more admirable than the way in which students, in this sort of setting, begin to *teach one another;* and themselves learn as they do. And if the time is short, a mere thirteen days, it provides at least some of the tools (such as those in our bibliographies and other papers) for those who want to use them in the future. No university course, in whatever subject, can be more than a springboard for the future; unless indeed we were to return to the happy days of the Druid Bards, and prescribe a fourteen years' course for the final examination.

VII

This is, perhaps, a time at which we might reflect not only on the Place of Shells, and on music, and poetry, and history; but upon the fact of this International School. If it had been pre-planned instead of growing up spontaneously because of the character of Sligo Town and of the Sligo Yeats Society, it might have been more logical to have held it in one of the great Irish universities; where accommodation, administration, transport and the like would have lain to hand. It is not, I think, a secret that several American universities would have gladly caught it up into the resources of their wealth and scholarship. But this bad world seems to me (at times) to be over-planned. One of you said to me last year: 'This is the only place left where a poet can read his poetry without feeling self-conscious and over-organised.' I suspect that that was – is – only partly true: yet I know that many of the poetry competitions, festivals and such-like have not been altogether happy places. I like to think that here we are still casual, carefree, with no papers to write for credits, no prizes to compete for; and that we use to the full this unique and magical and very ancient place. Yeats's father boasted to his son of his family 'We have given a tongue to the sea-cliffs'. But the son gave more than that to sea, mountain and lake.

VIII

Yet I would not have it thought that one of our functions is less than that of providing a meeting-place for the most advanced and famous scholars. We are indebted to the very many who have taught here over the past decade, and to those who are not with us whose inheritance we use. Among those last are my own friends. Among them, Joseph Hone, the first of the Yeats biographers; Una Ellis Fermor, whose account of the Irish Dramatic Movement remains a classic; my friend and pupil Peter Allt.

IX

Yet there is so much more to be done: in scholarship, and in teaching. One day there must be a definitive edition, properly edited and cross-referenced to the plays and poems, of the Collected Prose. Remember two things; that Yeats's work, like Shakespeare's, or Milton's, or Arnold's, must be seen as a unity: and also that the volumes of essays, papers and prefaces that you know and use differ in some respects from their originals. When all the manuscript materials of A Vision are made available it will be possible to make a calm assessment of two important books, round whose walls so many scholars of note have marched blowing on a variety of ram's horns. When Warner's long-promised edition of Cornelius Agrippa is completed some new light will be thrown on Yeats's so-called 'magical' preoccupations being the end of the long road that led back from Blake through Swedenborg and Boehme; though I myself would question Yeats's contention that there was a time when Agrippa was familiar to every Irish farmer.

Such scholarship is vital; yet there is always the danger that Sligo might be tempted to keep its eyes fixed too closely on the sea-shore, on the smaller shells (however delicate) at its feet. We dare not view a great poet in a lesser setting than that of his time, his friends, and his age, his predecessors and contemporaries; and, ultimately, against the tradition of Western Europe. It would be only too easy, here, to fall into some kind of bardolatry, to let the appetite sicken, surfeit, die. Some form of dilettantism is an ever-present danger. So far we have tried (and it is my hope that we shall continue) to set beside him some of his great contemporaries: 'Æ', Synge, George Moore, James Stephens, Lady Gregory. Nor would it be wrong to predict that, as well as hearing them read their own work, some of the living here may join that tradition. Among the host of excellent books there is as yet no 'great' one to lead us through the whole labyrinth of the Irish Literary Revival. I use the word labyrinth with deliberation; for surely there is no literary movement or history so pronounced with the veering of its intrinsic history and politics, the friendships and hatreds so intense. Out of that comes, of course, the energy of the time; for – again –

> Out of Ireland have we come.
> Great hatred, little room.

X

The mystery of Sligo remains, and I would have it remain a mystery: as something which has grown organically, and (as some would say) by chance; out of a map of the 'Yeats Country' placed in the window by Tony Toher in the entrance to his chemist's shop on O'Connell Street, a request for a single lecture at the height of the tourist season. It has grown as the ancient universities have done. Some years ago the Yeats Society consulted me about the possibility of a University here. As I remember, my estimate of the cost of such a foundation today closed the discussion. But indeed with all the money and plant, the power of buying professors, you cannot make a University. This some have lately found; to their cost. Here at Sligo I would like to think that men and women will continue to come, as they have come from the time of Plato's academy onwards, to sit at the feet of famous scholars and poets. That, and not a degree or a diploma, is the essence of education. Granted that the time is all too short (though this may be one aspect of its strength); granted that many things are lacking in materials and accommodation (though there may be one day a worthy building[10] for us and the Museum); there is yet this fact that, year after year, men and women of the greatest eminence have come here to make this School. And I can find no reason other than the charity of great minds, the certainty of unjealous friendship and a passion for poetry, and the genius of the Place of Shells, of its people, and of the Society who have made a reality of what was once no more than a 'surmised shape', a living memorial.

NOTES

1. Sligo: the opening lecture, 1968. First published in *T.R. Henn's Last Essays* (Gerrards Cross & New York 1976).
2. 'Three Marching Songs', II. Yeats notes that airy 'may be an old pronunciation of eerie'. But we also use it of 'high places, and of their numen'.
3. See *John Sherman and Dhoya*, ed. R.S.J. Finneran (New York 1969).
4. 'Easter 1916'.
5. 'To a Wealthy Man ... '

6. From an essay by Yeats on William Allingham: quoted by Finneran. Preface to *John Sherman & Doya* (v. *supra*). For Palestine, see T.R. Henn, 'The Bible as Literature' (London 1971).

7. The king of the Great Clock Tower. See also the Variorum Edition of the Poems of W.B. Yeats (London 1957), p. 733.

8. The pronunciation that Yeats gives in a footnote is not (in my experience) quite accurate.

9. *Between the Lines* (Oxford 1963); *Yeats's Last Poems* (London 1968).

10. This came to pass, by generosity of the Allied Irish Bank Group when they presented 'The Citizens of Sligo' with the beautiful building of the former Royal Bank of Ireland on the banks of the Garavogue River, beside Hyde Bridge, in 1973.

Yeats: The Great Comedian

VINCENT BUCKLEY
(1925–88)

'Eliminate character from comedy and you get farce'; so Yeats said himself. To which we may add for ourselves, 'eliminate comedy from character and you get self-justification'. Everyone is familiar with the Yeats of legend, a poet humourless, self-elevating but for that reason seldom *bien élevé*, weaving plots for new aristocratic heroes, mythic (oh, yes, mythic), concerned centrally only with one character, his own, and concerned with that in a way that so thoroughly avoided comedy that it became a long and splendid exercise in self-justification. Yet, 'Comedy is joyous because all assumption of a part, of a personal mask, whether of the individualised face of comedy or of the grotesque face of farce, is a display, of energy, and all energy is joyous'. I for one believe this perception to be a valuable and integral element in Yeats's own work, both in poetry and prose; but I also think that it comes clear in the prose mainly in those parts of *Autobiographies* that were written after about 1920. So in looking at that work I shall leave aside all other considerations, however pressing and relevant, to take up some aspects of his humour.

It seems to me that he was a great prose writer, and that *Autobiographies* is one of the prose masterpieces of the century; it is creative in a way few biographies, or manifestoes, or cultural essays, or reminiscences, get within calling distance of being, and its creative power comes partly from its humour, a humour rooted in an immense variousness of energy and perception which, *because* it is so alive and purposeful, is the opposite of mere moodiness. I shall urge, then, that that variousness leads him to create himself in many shifting lights including humorous ones, and to create his contemporaries not in the way a reporter estimates his acquaintances but in the way a great artist controls the figures of his imagination. In power he seems to me far to exceed the Samuel Butler of *The Way of All Flesh* and to be at least the equal of Turgenev of *Fathers and Sons;* and in approach, though not of course in scope, he comes close to Proust.

The variety gained in his accounts of himself is a subject in itself, and for someone else; so, though I shall more than once refer to it in passing, my chief interest will be in his creation of figures whose comedy does not exhaust their interest but who, however dismal their fates, are given something of a comic cast. This applies, strangely enough, to Lionel Johnson and Henley, to Wilde and Dowson, indeed to almost all the self-destroyed of 'The Tragic Generation'; it does not apply to John Synge, a man whose bitter and reserved integrity as Yeats records it allows no entrance for the comic spirit: he was not self-destroyed, he merely accepted his death. It applies to John Taylor and Gavan Duffy, even to the revered O'Leary and the adored Maud Gonne; it does not apply to Parnell. Above all, it applies to George Moore, who is Yeats's one totally comic and totally sustained creation. In Yeats's account of him, personal bitterness (and we must believe there was some) is distanced to become a comic enjoyment of the great man as unwitting buffoon; and in the process the Archpoet himself becomes the Great Comedian.

Of the chief entries in *Autobiographies*, 'Estrangement' and 'The Death of Synge' date from 1908 and 1909 respectively; 'The Trembling of the Veil', with its five component sections, was written in the early 1920s; and 'Dramatis Personae', in which George Moore makes his stunningly successful appearance, comes from about 1934. Yeats was then not quite seventy, and a most sardonic verbal prankster. Looking at the prose works written forty years before, at those small collections with the revealing titles, 'The Celtic Twilight', 'The Secret Rose', 'Stories of Red Hanrahan', 'Rosa Alchemica', we could hardly believe the later vivacity to be possible. The little stories in 'The Celtic Twilight' are weak not so much because they are whimsical or incredible (born out of an endearing yet exasperating credulity) but perhaps for the opposite reason, that they are so lacking in conviction and in emotional pressure that they seem, quite simply, made up to adorn an ideological fancy that has not quite reached the stature even of a hope. They assert personality; yet it is personality that they lack. In the mishmash of country wonders, each recounted in a way that is flat and routine, we miss even the sense that the writer himself is drawn to wonder. Of course,

as we have them in the collection *Mythologies,* they have been rewritten with
the help of Lady Gregory to give them greater 'simplicity'. He would have done
better to save his naiveté with his breath; for, whatever masks were available to
him, that of a gaelicized Lady Gregory was not among them.

The slightly later stories from 'The Secret Rose' fare worse, if anything;
even the restraint that Lady Gregory had taught is now gone. There is no
sensible characterization, and the prose is perennially at the mercy both of the
glamour of names and of that seductive word, 'and': devices so transparently
diversionary that it is hard to see how any really intelligent Romantic could
have brought himself to adopt them. The almost inevitable result of Yeats's
mismanagement of event and dialogue in, for example, 'The Crucifixion of
the Outcast' is a kind of comic displacement of reality in the interests of an
undeclared solemnity:

> 'You may sleep', said Cumhal. 'I will sing a bard's curse on the abbot.' And
> he set the tub upside-down under the window, and stood upon it, and began
> to sing in a very loud voice. The singing awoke the abbot, so that he sat up in
> bed and blew a silver whistle until the lay brother came to him. 'I cannot get
> a wink of sleep with that noise', said the abbot. 'What is happening?

In some circumstances, unintentional comedy is worse than none at all.
Here, it is not that Yeats is unaware of the comic dimension; it is simply that he
keeps shading it off into a portentousness that he seems unable to distinguish
from it.

As for Red Hanrahan, Yeats later showed a surprising pride in his manage-
ment of that boyo:

> And I myself created Hanrahan
> And drove him drunk or sober through the dawn ...

The explanation of the pride is no doubt that Yeats saw the stories as a contri-
bution to folklore in depth. But that 'myself' gives the game away; and 'created'
is hardly the right word for what actually happens. Folklore certainly does
not benefit; and the stories are like nothing so much as scenery for an amateur
production of 'The Student Prince'. Hanrahan's doings are 'magical', and
uninteresting because elaborated solely for the *frisson;* and his personality
is uninteresting because so merely a matter of his doings. He seems to exist
in a between-stairs of the imagination; those fairy raths and peasant barns
have much more substantial inhabitants. He is not a creation, but a projec-
tion. In fact, Yeats seems to use Hanrahan's activities as a fantasy-completion
of his own activity as a poet; for example, in 'Hanrahan and Cathleen', the
story has no other point than to cajole Hanrahan into writing one of Yeats's

poems for him. Hanrahan does oblige, by writing 'Red Hanrahan's Song about Ireland'; which did not stop Yeats from later publishing it under his own name. There is more genuine invention even in 'Rosa Alchemica'; but this and its two companion pieces are, in the end, no more than standard Nineties writing; and the tendencies in them which show some promise of power are fulfilled thirty years later in *A Vision*, a book which, for all its fancifulness, is significantly systematic, and not impressionistic, in structure.

II

One may pause on the road to *Autobiographies* from such misguided gallantries and notice in *Explorations* signs of the qualities for which I am valuing Yeats. We are indebted to Mrs Yeats for this collection, and it is a much finer and more moving one than the better-known *Mythologies*. Generally, the documents it consists of are public ones, and chiefly it is concerned with the aspiration and dangers of an heroic theatre. So its tone is generally elevated, with a touch of the polemical here, and the admonitory there. The cadences move often like supernatural troops in battle; the trumpet rides through argument, and proofs sound like eulogies of the heroic slain. Anyone who loves Yeats for this power (tonal, stylistic, certainly, yet ethical as well) will read with joy his essay 'Samhain 1904: First Principles'. Yet even that magnificently resounding manifesto is less valuable to me than his wonderfully wise essay, 'If I were Four-and-Twenty', that comes fifteen years later. One would not have expected so elevated a journalism to leave room for any ironic self-awareness. Yet it does:

> When Dr. Hyde delivered in 1894 his lecture on the necessity of 'the de-anglicisation of Ireland', to a society that was a youthful indiscretion of my own I heard an enthusiastic hearer say: 'This lecture begins a new epoch in Ireland.' It did that, and if I were not four and-fifty, with no settled habit but the writing of verse, rheumatic, indolent, discouraged, and about to move to the Far East, I would begin another epoch by recommending to the Nation a new doctrine, that of unity of being.

It would be priggish to analyse in detail the movement of irony in this passage; but it is an irony obviously comic in emphasis, and the comedy surrounds both Yeats's audience and the image they have of *him*. I am thinking not of the 'youthful indiscretion', though that is charming certainly, but of the way in which the seeming self-pity of 'rheumatic, indolent, discouraged ... ' is resolved in 'and about to move to the Far East'. This is deadpan comedy; and though its ironies go deep, its surface is delightful, and delightfully revealing of the cultural situation in which it is written. So deadpan is it that one often cannot distinguish the intended from the unintended *coups* of comedy; yet one is quite certain that the distinction is there, as in the most amusing 'A Letter to Michael's Schoolmaster':

> As he grows older he will read to me the great lyric poets and I will talk to him about Plato. Do not teach him one word of Latin. The Roman people were the classic decadence, their literature form without matter. They destroyed Milton, the French seventeenth and our own eighteenth century, and our schoolmasters even today read Greek with Latin eyes. Greece, could we but approach it with eyes as young as its own, might renew our youth. Teach him mathematics as thoroughly as his capacity permits. I know that Bertrand Russell must, seeing that he is such a featherhead, be wrong about everything, but as I have no mathematics I cannot prove it. I do not want my son to be as helpless.

So direct, *so* pompous, *so* dogmatic, *so* helplessly indignant: it is all very serious, and all very comic, a serious joke, of which the most comic part is that very tone. Yet it is evident that Yeats means every word, even as he means his comedy. The view of life that can, without belittling an affirmation or mocking an eloquence, turn the tone of affirmation around to show how comic are the pretensions of speaker and audience alike is also one that leads to epigrams that sound like quips ('Logic is loose again ... ') and to straight-faced little anecdotes whose subject is evaluated in the very manner of their telling: 'Some thousands of examination papers were distributed to schoolchildren in a Northern industrial district with the question, "Who was the best man who ever lived?" The vast majority answered, "King George the Fifth." Christ was runner-up.' If this is great journalism, it is so because it is so revealing of competing dimensions in experience. As soon as you have been suitably surprised by one felicity – of phrasing, or characterization, or heroic suggestion – Yeats surprises you with another of such a different sort that you are led (somewhat uneasily if you are not Irish) to wonder if the whole method of exposition is founded on a joke. It is certainly not mere 'romantic' rambling, even when he calls it 'Reveries ... '. It is very persistent in his work, though generally not pervasive, and it is plainly a principle of economy and concentration. As often as not, it works by bringing the great and marvellous near to hand in one moment, then distancing it in another.

It is brought to its head in the best sections of *Autobiographies*. I always remember with pleasure that passage from 'Reveries over Childhood and Youth' in which he mentions his family's preconceptions about 'the English':

My mother had shown them to me kissing at railway stations, and taught me to feel disgust at their lack of reserve, and my father told how my grandfather, William Yeats, who had died before I was born, when he came home to his Rectory in County Down from an English visit, spoke of some man he had met on a coach road who 'English man-like' told him all his affairs. My father explained that an Englishman generally believed that his private affairs did him credit, while an Irishman, being poor and probably in debt, had no such confidence. I, however, did not believe in this explanation.

'My mother had shown them to me ... and taught me ... '; 'my father told ... '; 'my grandfather ... spoke of ... '; 'my father explained ... '; 'I, however ... '. Plainly it is not only the English, with their excessive mateyness, who are met with irony here; and the irony becomes truly comic when Yeats the child, though rejecting the explanation given, forgets to say a single word more of what explanation he would then have held, or would now hold, more plausible.

The recurrent impression of comedy comes partly, of course, from the expository method, which is that of a highly individual talk: conversational anecdote linked, but not always explained, by a generalization equally conversational in manner. A section will begin 'I had very little money and one day the toll – taken at the metal bridge ["the ha'penny bridge"] over the Liffey ... ' Always there is the seemingly pointless particular ('*metal* bridge ... '), always the easy connective. To say that such a method has often a ritual quality is not to say that it is inflexible; it is to say that Yeats has in a sense adopted the *persona* of the talker, that his whole method declares that adoption, but that within its terms he is remarkably flexible and free. This freedom is partly a matter of the extent to which, in the prose of his middle and old age, the adoption of *personae* has become native to his personality, and partly a matter of an astonishing flair for catching the 'interesting' stance and cadence in himself and the revealing stance and movement in others. To call this flair 'journalistic' would be accurate yet perhaps misleading; for there is in it a considerable profit to go beyond reportage and to create an economy of the things reported. It is this that enables him to create the sense of John O'Leary, both in 'Reveries' and elsewhere: an O'Leary incredibly noble in thought and gesture yet noble in a somehow remote way, uttering heartfelt gallantries that sound in the utterance as though they came from a man as acquainted with the fells of death as with the fields of life. 'There are things that a man must not do to save a nation', he says. But Yeats comments, shrewdly yet without obloquy: 'He would speak a sentence like that in ignorance of its passionate value, and would forget it the moment after'. And when, a hundred or so pages later, the anecdote is told again, we have an interesting addition: ' ... and when I asked what things, had said, 'to cry in public ... ' The effect of the addition is to give greater nobility yet also greater irrelevance (the dead have now encroached on our living-space), and so to be both more moving and more comic.

I would not want to emphasize the 'comedy' in the superb pen portrait of O'Leary, for Yeats's sympathetic admiration joins with his subject's nobility to create the dominant impression. Yet there *is* some quality of distance, of reserve, of a sense of paradox which never becomes criticism but does not remain unqualified admiration; and that quality does have an edge that links it in my mind with episodes and portraits that are unabashedly comic. I find this also in his deservedly famous evocation of his first meeting with Maud Gonne:

> Her complexion was luminous, like that of apple-blossom through which the light falls, and I remember her standing that first day by a great heap of blossoms in the window. In the next few years I saw her always when she passed to and fro between Dublin and Paris, surrounded, no matter how rapid her journey and how brief her stay at either end of it, by cages full of birds, canaries, finches of all kinds, dogs, a parrot, and once a full-grown hawk from Donegal.

The two sentences perfectly complement each other: the first a very fine epiphany of a moment's stance, and not entirely without self-consciousness; the second a careful manoeuvring of nobility into absurdity. In short, a double vision of the one grandeur, and one in which the juxtaposition of competing modes of perception creates its own comedy. Thirty years after the event, which began his servitude to Maud Gonne, is it her cage-birds that he remembers with wry humour; and is there some faint self-identification with that full-grown hawk?

It might be argued that the great and lambent sympathy of his account of Wilde, which begins a few pages later, contains no such comic qualification, even though it does not contain, either, the ecstatic admiration that is so qualified. Yeats's Wilde is a triumph of creative reconstruction resulting from a movement of imaginative sympathy; yet its final effect is, most emphatically, not one of admiration. Wilde is shown as a man betrayed, possibly, by some failure of self-awareness or of nerve; an outrageous flatterer, who does not care whether or not his flattery is noticed: 'Though to be compared with Homer passed the time pleasantly ... ', Yeats says pleasantly. Yeats was not himself a man to be flattered and not tell others of the compliment; but he *was* a man who had come to know his own past motives, and who was alternately amused and uplifted by his knowledge. Wilde, if we may generalize from this account, had no such gift. The great gifts which he did have were surrogates for the destiny which his cultural circumstances (in ways not stated) denied him: the destiny of a man of action. For Yeats, the secret of Wilde's wit, and the key to his downfall, was that he *was* a man-of-action *manqué*:

I think her son lived with no self-mockery at all an imaginary life; perpetually performed a play which was in all things the opposite of all he had known in childhood and early youth; never put off completely his wonder at opening his eyes every morning on his own beautiful house, and in remembering that he had dined yesterday with a duchess, and that he delighted in Flaubert and Pater, read Homer in the original and not as a schoolmaster reads him for the grammar. I think, too, that because of all that half-civilised blood in his veins he could not endure the sedentary toil of creative art and so remained a man of action, exaggerating, for the sake of immediate effect, every trick learned from his masters, turning their easel painting into painted scenes. He was a parvenu, but a parvenu whose whole bearing proved that if he did dedicate every story in *A House of Pomegranates* to a lady of title, it was but to show that he was Jack and the social ladder his pantomime beanstalk ...

... Such men get their sincerity, if at all, from the contact of events; the dinner-table was Wilde's event and made him the greatest talker of his time, and his plays and dialogues have what merit they possess from being now an imitation, now a record, of his talk. Even in those days I would often defend him by saying that his very admiration for his predecessors in poetry, for Browning, for Swinburne and Rossetti, in their first vogue while he was a very young man, made any success seem impossible that could satisfy his immense ambition: never but once before had the artist seemed so great, never had the work of art seemed so difficult. I would then compare him with Benvenuto Cellini who, coming after Michael Angelo, found nothing left to do so satisfactory as to turn bravo and quarrel with the man who broke Michael Angelo's nose.

The tone of this cannot be identified as a formula; but that is not because it is subtle but because it is various. If the writing has a panache equal to that of its subject, it is never wilful or posturing; on the contrary, whether or not Yeats's estimate is right, it is extremely intelligent and carefully pondered. He does not treat Wilde's dilemma lightly, yet he seems in a profound way to find it *satisfying,* not because it enables him to condescend, but because it comes to him as an example of the variety and strangeness of human personality. There is nothing here that we would call 'comic' in any glib way, and yet the very enjoyment of the human spectacle, laden with concern though it is, has a penumbra which is comic rather than tragic. The section ends, after all, with the words 'turn bravo and quarrel with the man who broke Michael Angelo's nose.' Yeats has a way of breaking off which itself indicates the tone that a section requires.

What is clear, as we follow through the logic of 'The Trembling of the Veil', and see one portrait succeed another, character climb on character, and anecdote call forth more anecdote, is that a wondering comic tone is diffused throughout. Yeats in his aging is a connoisseur of eccentricity, including his own;

but his method is not simply to accumulate examples of palpable eccentricity, as the pub talker does, but to turn a personality, a movement, a belief, a happening around until its eccentricity emerges. The total effect is less a quaintness than a suspension of belief about the nature of personality; for the eccentricity as often as not is that of people whose terrors have become inverted or whose aspirations have grown oblique. Anyone who assumes that Yeats was foolishly open-eyed about spiritualism should note the undeniably comic nature of many of his accounts of the behaviour of 'adepts'; a few are quite hilarious. It would be useless to pretend that most of the time he writes about the wastage of personalities and causes with simple amusement, bland or otherwise; in fact, he writes with an undertow of passion. But that passion, when it issues in judgment or anecdote, is so often sardonic; the anecdotes are so often turned or managed to bring out not only some paradox of action but some bizarre lack of proportion or of self-knowledge in the actors. There cannot be many portraits in all biography like his portraits of Wilde and Moore, the one his fated friend, the other his clinging enemy. And it is in the case of the latter that the account becomes unremittingly comic, and the farce of personality is allowed to emerge through a deadpan recounting which claims to be no more than straight reportage:

> It was now that George Moore came into our affairs, brought by Edward Martyn, who invited him to find a cast for *The Heather Field*. They were cousins and inseparable friends, bound one to the other by mutual contempt. When I told Martyn that Moore had good points, he replied: 'I know Moore a great deal longer than you do. He has no good points.' And a week or two later Moore said: 'That man Martyn is the most selfish man alive. He thinks that I am damned and he doesn't care.'

We must remember that this was written almost fifteen years after the account of Wilde, and is therefore at a still greater remove from the events it describes. It may be as well to remember also *where* it comes in the narrative. It is introduced with exemplary, and comic, abruptness immediately after an account of spiritualism and of Yeats's relations with the Gregory family, so that after the suggestion of nobility we may get, without pause, the suggestion of baseness. Its tone establishes the tone of all that is to follow for nearly fifty pages. Moore is presented as a boor priding himself on his sensibility, a man of the grossest spirit, whose every insult and stratagem, whose very offerings of friendship, are unintentionally revealing, and whose aspect is therefore unfailingly comic. All Yeats's powers of observation and mimicry, all his reserves of resentment and distaste perhaps, go into the creation of a buffoon whose buffoonery consists precisely in the fact that he has no good points: a man who, trying to be poetical, 'made the dying Diarmuid say to Finn: "I will kick you down the stairway of the stars" '; a man whose very nastiness is comic because so transparent, and whose social incapacity goes to more than Dickensian extremes:

> Even to conversation and acted plays, he gave an inattentive ear, instincts incapable of clear expression deafened him and blinded him; he was Milton's lion rising up, pawing out of the earth, but, unlike that lion, stuck half-way. He reached to middle life ignorant even of small practical details. He said to a friend: 'How do you keep your pants from falling about your knees?' 'o,' said the friend, 'I put my braces through the little tapes that are sewn there for the purpose.' A few days later, he thanked the friend with emotion. Upon a long country bicycle ride with another friend, he had stopped because his pants were about his knees, had gone behind a hedge, had taken them off, and exchanged them at a cottage for a tumbler of milk.

All this is not, certainly, a case of the farcical man talking himself into self-deflation; it is hard to know where Esau stops and Jacob starts in this sort of writing. If Moore appears unfailingly preposterous, even in his few generous moments, it is because Yeats's expository habit has entered into his preposterousness of speech and action to reveal no quality than that. Indeed, one may be surprised in retrospect by one's willingness to accept Yeats's account as being so little subjective, and having so compelling an authority. The reason surely is that, whatever polemical realities lie behind it, this is a *created* character:

> Moore had but his blind ambition. *Esther Waters* should have been a greater novel, for the scene is more varied. Esther is tempted to steal a half-crown; Balzac might have made her steal it and keep our sympathy, but Moore must create a personification of motherly goodness, almost an abstraction. Five years later he begged a number of his friends to read it. 'I have just read it,' he said. 'It has done me good, it radiates goodness.' He had wanted to be good as the mass of men understand goodness. In later life he wrote a long preface to prove that he had a mistress in Mayfair.

Moore's speech alone, though it is preposterous enough, is not allowed to create the required perspective; if it had, there might be pathos underlying the comedy. No; he 'begged' his friends to read it. And those two final sentences, so clipped and undemonstrative, so *final,* give the quietus to his implicit claim to either pathos or goodness. As Yeats presents him, he is a man who could not conceivably have done otherwise than turn all his pretensions into farce; he dooms himself to preposterousness. Whatever will be the place of the real George Moore, God's George Moore, in the history of literature and literary politics, Yeats's George Moore is surely one of the finest *comic* creations in our literature. The wonder is that the deflation of pretensions should be so complete yet carry so little cruelty, a quality that was evidently not native to Yeats. It is the tone of the reportage that does it, a tone always deadpan and unpretentious, the tone of one enjoying a *bêtise* which might have merely disgusted or angered other men.

III

Yeats is well known to have said, 'We begin to live when we have conceived life as Tragedy'. The tragic Yeats we have with us always. But in those years from (say) 1920 to 1935 he seems to have discovered in his own comic capacities a new ground for the rooting of that tragic sense. When we reflect how natural it was for him to give expression to those capacities by overseeing once more, in a long retrospect, the people and events that had once animated him in a different and much more disturbing way, we may think it also natural that he should express them in prose as well as in poetry. Maud Gonne, of all his familiars, most played the tragedienne; yet Frank O'Connor, a man himself brimming with sardonic humour, has recently called her a lifelong comedienne, and has produced anecdotes to prove it. Clearly Yeats also grew to perceive her and others in this light; but, not being in any usual sense a comic writer, he deals with them, generally, in a prose rhythm which retains its ability to render the noble as well as the ignoble aspects, and to cast a noble tone about them all. If Maud Gonne *was* a comedienne, her comedy consisted in her encouraging, and in presenting as a noble play, her own preposterous tendencies; she was, after all, an actress as well as a revolutionary. Yeats did nothing so wilful; his comic perceptions come from a new relaxation in his whole sense of being and its possibilities, and his task, insofar as he undertook it, was to recognize and control his own preposterousness and to bring it into relation with that of others. He is the Comedian-raconteur, not the Comedian-simple. But George Moore defeated him, by so unremitting an excess of the farcical; he could not be merely reported and ironically commented on, he had to be created as a totally comic figure.

Very few critics advert to this element in Yeats. I have searched through one collection of critical essays after another, and have found not a single essay on his prose comedy. Most people go to his prose to help explain his poetry; *he* resorted to it to help re-cast his past. The only passing reference I can find at all is Frank Kermode's remark, 'he brings to Irish peasant drama, for the pleasure of it, the force of his own considerable involuted humour, always, I think, based on ironic re-appraisal.' As can be seen, I agree with this remark. Anyone who wants 'sincerity' from *Autobiographies* might look for it not only in the wise and eloquent shrewdness of so many passages, and the sympathetic human feeling of so many others, but also at the dead centre of his comedy; he will find it there, and it will be deceptively unsmiling, as its comedy is too.

Yeats: The Poet

ALEC KING
(1904–70)

The indictment against Yeats has been:

That as a young poet he was a dreamer in the silly sense and that he never lost the attraction to hocus-pocus.

That, even though he learned to communicate his states of mind with poetic verve, they are the states of mind of a queer man: fascinating to look at, but impossible to adopt.

That he was a life-long poseur.

That he was under the impression that he was doing the great work of a poet, defending the imagination against the contemporary scientific positivism; but that the defence is really a defence of the fancy, not the imagination.

That he was a 'superior man'; that is, a poet believing in himself as the ground of all values, without the humility of the Christian, who believes himself to be the mouthpiece, by grace, of a system of transcendental values.

That he delighted, ridiculously, in his unchristened heart, and was more than happy to be ignorant of Christianity.

That his ignorance of philosophy and science make him a playboy
poet in such an age as ours.

My case for him is, of course, personal, in W.H. Auden's sense: 'the test
of a poet is the frequency and diversity of the occasions on which one remem-
bers him'. I find myself remembering Yeats on more occasions and on a greater
number of diverse occasions than any poet except Shakespeare, Herbert and
Marvell.

I put this, first, because I am perfectly aware my liking for Yeats is highly
personal, and that, if Yeats is 'silly', then it is a silliness I am personally in
love with. In fact, my valuing Yeats is that he is a fool, in the fundamental
sense; not merely superficially foolish, quirky, but a man who knew that we are
committed, as human beings, to a 'foolish' existence, and that only those who
accept themselves as fools can hope to be wise. Moreover the essential 'folly' of
existence – the ridiculous fact that humankind has to be transmitted through
a creature with an animal body, and innumerable inferior lusts – is central in
Yeats's poetry. It's a folly I think all minds worth anything come to in the end:
the medieval Mr Facing-Both-Ways, wobbling along his tight-rope, looking at
his kinsman animals, looking at his friends the angels; the 'pastoral' foolish-
ness, where you can imagine yourself turning to live with the animals because
they are so placid and self-contained, precisely because the angelic-serenity is
there also. Shakespeare never loses sight of this central ridiculous fact of exis-
tence, nor of the pretensions of people who forget it, the disasters of having to
act as if one were really not a fool, and the tragic laughter of the onlooker. And
Freud, with his long way round to Nirvana, is full of the same 'vision'; the still
small voice of reason can be heard, but only if we realize that it exists within
a sea of ridiculousness. Much of the contemporary neurosis is not something
new, but only the result of the decay of that imagination which helped men to
accept the foolishness of their personal lives as an essential pattern of all life.
Christianity has never lost sight of this: the central image of the God crucified
is a supreme idiocy. How many neurotic people hang themselves stiffly up on a
cross, not able to bear the idea that they are also those mocking voices, ances-
tral voices, crowding round in derision.

I'm calling all this to mind, because Yeats to me is the opposite of being
an oddity. This central foolishness was his constant preoccupation – something
he put finally in the most extreme way, in 'Love has pitched his mansion in the
place of excrement'.

My whole defence of Yeats starts from this. He lives as a poet, right
plumb in the centre of the human situation. And I have a sort of practical

proof that he does; because of the frequency and diversity of occasions on which I remember him.

Even his early dream poetry is acceptable on this basis, admitting it is dreamy and languid and precious and remembering that Yeats mocked at it himself for these qualities as he grew up, and could even say that, when he wrote it, he felt another self beside him with its tongue in its cheek. Yet the myths he so dreamily conceived are only partly the self-expression of a lonely mind incapable of standing up to the violence and 'otherness' of life. They are, also, the expression of the violence and otherness, by indirect approach. They have, that is, much of the validity of pastoral – which acknowledges and expresses indirectly the perfect piggishness of existence, by imagining a life where every piggish quality is absent. Yeats's early myth-poetry has also something of the quality we find in pastoral. Pastoral acknowledges itself as an elegant imaginative game by the quality of its verse or prose – the deliberate lightness and formality of language. We do the early Yeats an injustice by over-estimating the languor and drug-heavy characteristics of his poetry. Even here he writes with a certain fastidious and conscious beauty of phrase and cadence.

But above all, Yeats, quite seriously at the time, thought of his verse as relevant to the practical piggish world. His poems are not so much images of heroism, as of the possessed man, the man in the service of a divine madness of some sort. And, though he was soon to discover how little it could mean to his fellow countrymen in actual fact, he thought of his poetry as pressing back against the squalor of action and motive he felt around him, with an image of life possessed and dedicated and purified (as one can feel in texture of the verse).

You may not like this solemn poetry of possession; nor the early poems which may be called 'allegories of the imagination' – the Rose poems particularly in which Yeats devotes himself, in the tones of a religious celebrant, to the contemplation of a divinely beautiful symbol. But they do acknowledge what the imagination must be loyal to. Though Yeats was to find this mood, this way of acknowledging his loyalty, precious and rather absurd, he never lost the loyalty. Later in life he came to see that these holy haughty feet cannot be kept sacrosanctly in their niches; they must descend, not so as to disappear as apparitions, but for desecration and the lovers' night. By whatever word you name the absolutes, the ideas, the forms, they must enter into the gross body of existence and give it meaning. Yeats kept centrally in his mind all his life the notion that has its finest poetic expression in 'Leda and the Swan' – the descent of the divine into the animal in order to become operative. Jupiter 'desecrates' his divine power and wisdom by shaping it into the body of the swan, in order that Leda may be possessed.

> A sudden blow: the great wings beating still
> Above the staggering girl, her thighs caressed
> By the dark webs, her nape caught in his bill,
> He holds her helpless breast upon his breast.
>
> How can those terrified vague fingers push
> The feathered glory from her loosening thighs?
> And how can body, laid in that white rush,
> But feel the strange heart beating where it lies?
> A shudder in the loins engenders there
> The broken wall, the burning roof and tower
> And Agamemnon dead.
>   Being so caught up,
> So mastered by the brute blood of the air,
> Did she put on his knowledge with his power
> Before the indifferent beak could let her drop?

You might say that, in early life, Yeats was made to realize the two things separately – the gross piggish body of existence within himself within Ireland, and, preserved within his poems as in a niche, the Roses of all the World. As a mature poet he brings the two together – not only, I mean, in poems that deal as subject matter with this foolish mating of incompatibles and inseparables; but in the very essence of his poetic speech. He finds a way, through technical accomplishment, to express in poetry that double loyalty we all have to practise – the joy and excitement of finding the rose blooming everywhere, the smack-in-the-eye pleasure of feeling the palpable bodies for the rose to bloom in. Whitman gloated that he knew no sweeter fat than stuck to his own bones – not because he loved only the warm greasy stuff of his own carcass, but because, my God, it was that angelic substance. Fat, part of the divine generosity made palpable. Falstaff enjoys his grossness because it is at once full of divine and carnal humours. Yeats's developed style is palpable, warm, abounding, elastic; its body is good to touch, to fondle; but it never ceases to be a kind of song of pleasure in all the forms of vitality that pulsate within the material objects. He learns to talk about life with irony and humour, acknowledging its contradictions and foolishness, but the whole effect is one of rejoicing. By comparison, T.S. Eliot is a prune.

I like Yeats, then, for being at the centre of the human situation, and for knowing this 'folly' to the bone; for accepting it as one of the things to be gay about; for being, like Herbert and Marvell, gay about it. And being where he is, I like him for not knowing how to make up his mind about it, because it is impossible anyhow:

> Bodily decrepitude is wisdom, young
> We loved each other and were ignorant.

Shall I become a miracle bird on the bough of the Absolute tree; or shall I mock Plotinus' thought, and cry in Plato's teeth; shall I leave in my will everything to young upstanding men? To the perfect, formal, dolls of the Platonic heaven, a real baby is a noisy and a filthy thing – my dear, oh dear it was an accident. But who can get on without the fury and the mire of human veins, the gong tormented sea? The masterful images grew in pure mind, but began out of a mound of refuse, or the sweepings of a street; I must lie down where all the ladders start in the foul rag and bone shop of the heart – where Crazy Jane debates with the Bishop.

This is why the argument that he was a superior man is nonsense, as far as I'm concerned. The argument is that he substituted for the long-tested wisdom of the Church a one-man faith, and that his opposition to the accepted faith was based on a cult evolved in the crazy mind of Willy Yeats; that he was that kind of 'superior man' who could dispense with tried systems, and orthodox theologies, in the name of a private esoteric wisdom of his own.

The answer to these questions is that Yeats's poetry comes before any theology or accepted system; not in place of it. I would ask anyone who wanted to understand the situation in which religion makes sense, to soak himself in Yeats. The fact is that Yeats knows what it is in human life that religions interpret – or to put it another way, a great mass of his poetry is interested in human situations that could be discussed theologically. Far from being superior, he is, I think, basically more humble than Eliot, who practices Christian humility with a most unbending disdain; Yeats accepts life, Eliot finds a great deal of it disgusting.

As for Yeats's arrogant belief in his ancestors and his personal guardians, I like it because he is fundamentally right. Don't all sensible people carry round with them such 'images of greatness' – though not necessarily family ones? We may smile at the 'We must be free or die who spake the tongue Milton spake' attitude. But in fact it is the saving attitude, because it is not a personal arrogance, but the recognition of the myth to which the one gives allegiance. Anglicans, Catholics, Puritans, all know they have these renowned generations as ancestors; politically, socially, we do the same. It is precisely the danger of amorphous and ignorant democracy that individual greatness is measured in terms of footling material advantage, not of an impersonal tradition through whom the individual is fulfilled. Every age has to defend Man against the idiocies of contemporary men. A certain kind of aristocracy of temper, of assertion of the race through the individual, is necessary, and never more than in an atomic society. I do not find Yeats regarding himself as a singular man (in his

poetry), but as the present embodiment of a singular tradition. Nor is it sense
to say that the kind of virtues this tradition upholds could only be practised
in the freedom of rich country houses, as if men were the mere playthings of
their material environment. It is exactly that supposition, in fact, which is so
dangerous. Men have to resist their age as much as work with it; and they will
find their essential loyalties, their images of the human nature they need wher-
ever they are most highly visible and dramatically presented.

That is to say that I enjoy Yeats, as I do Lawrence, because he is so much
of his age to know that it must be fought tooth and nail, for certain dangerous
assumptions it believes in. He is anything, then, but a playboy in an age like
ours. His religious and unorthodox temper of mind, his intelligence, irony,
imagination, caught up in a poetry that likes to ring its bells and gongs and
get itself going into some resonant and sumptuous musical procession – if
this is eccentric, then it is all the more an indictment of us all. I like Yeats
because he is antithetical to this age – not only to the sea of journalistic glue
through which we wade, but to the careful, cold-headed, parenthetical, judi-
cious modern intelligence.

And if you feel he dramatized himself in all this, my own answer has to
be: who doesn't? Most people think of a person as dramatizing himself when
the drama he undertakes is an obviously queer private one. Yeats had some of
this, as a man. But as a poet, the drama he lives is neither queer nor private; it
is the drama of the poet, the imaginative poet, who throws himself into atti-
tudes in order to discourse to us through dramatic masks. How else can he do
it, if he needs to explore 'meaning' for us? You must make 'life', by some means
or other, stand up visibly and dramatically and declare itself. You can always
throw life into dramatic forms as Shakespeare does, or Eliot; but if you choose
to write, as Yeats and Rilke do, in the form of passionate discourse, you must
dramatize yourself.

So finally I like Yeats for the drama of his poetic personality – for some-
thing vividly, warmly, passionately presented – an image of a way of living
which, for me, has an extraordinary attraction.

Scholars

The Musicality of W.B. Yeats

DOUG SAUM

William Butler Yeats (13 June 1865 – 28 January 1939) took his first breath in a Dublin suburb, and spent most of his seventy-three years producing a varied and extensive body of literary work. Perhaps most remembered for his numerous volumes of lyric and dramatic poetry, he also produced: essays, speeches, translations, short fiction, longer fiction, autobiographies, journals (both personal and magical), letters, criticism, collaborative pieces, folklore, a mystical-philosophical system and highly stylized, cryptic dramatic plays. From his adolescence until just a week before he died, he was actively writing and revising. In addition he founded the Irish Literary Society (1892), served as a director / writer for the Irish National Theatre, studied occult matters with Mme H.P. Blavatsky in London, rose to prominence in the Hermetic Society of the Golden Dawn and its splinter groups (with his wife Georgie Hyde-Lees Yeats he produced a vast record of their occult communications with alleged spirit entities), was affiliated with Psychical Research Society investigations and served as Senator in the Irish Free State 1923–8. In 1923 he was awarded the Nobel Prize for Literature. His education was at times unorthodox and he took no formal university degree until he was awarded honorary doctorates from Queen's College Belfast, Trinity College Dublin and Oxford University. He is still well-remembered and his work is often quoted to this day. W.B. or Willie, as he was known within his family, has been the focus of the annual Yeats International Summer School in Sligo, Ireland since 1959.

We might expect that such an accomplished and prolific literary career would invite great interest; when we further recognize that the work was done with a quality rarely achieved in the history of letters, we realize that we are encountering a literary phenomenon, a name that I suspect shall one day roll as comfortably off the tongue as Chaucer's, Dante's, or Shakespeare's. We are left wondering how he did it. Was he a natural? Was he reared to it? Was he a seed that fell into the right soil? Was he touched by the Muse? Perhaps the answer to all of these questions is the same.

Even before he wrote that 'Words alone are certain good' in the first poem, 'The Song of the Happy Shepherd', of his first volume of poems, *Crossways* (1889), W.B. held a faith in the power of poetry. In a well-known passage from *The Trembling of the Veil*, he writes ' ... I had made a new religion, almost an infallible church of poetic tradition ... ' (*Au*, p. 116). In the sunset of his career, in what was once placed as the last poem in his last poetic volume ('Under Ben Bulben', *Last Poems*) he still trumpets his early faith when he exhorts Ireland's artists to follow what their ' ... great forefathers did / Bring the soul of Man to God.' This underlying faith brought him the high expectation of catalyzing a spiritual renewal for Ireland and the world. 'I used to tell the few friends to whom I could speak these secret thoughts that I would make the attempt in Ireland but fail, [to reform Ireland through "the applied arts of literature ... music, speech, and dance"] ... I had the wildest hopes' (*Au*, pp. 194–5). He wondered at the source of genius and creativity in the world; ' ... is it not because some knowledge or power has come to his mind from beyond his mind?' (*W.B. Yeats and the Muses*, Joseph M. Hassett [New York 2010], p. 1). To fully function in his church of poetic tradition, he would need to encounter his Poetic Muse.

There is some textual evidence throughout W.B.'s poems, early to late, that he thought of the Muse as a real factor in the creation of his poetic work. In a faery poem from an early play (*The Land of Heart's Desire*, 1894) called 'The Gates of the Day', he lays out his case for a metaphysical connection between the Poet and Nature worthy of Ralph Emerson's essay on 'Nature', but with the added bonus of including faeries dancing in a ring. As they shake their feet and toss their arms aloft the good folk sing of a land apart where the 'old are fair' and 'even the wise are merry of tongue'. The dance brings them communion with their highest notions of perfection in the land of heart's desire. For the human poet, however, the focus is not the dance so much as the sound of the wind passing over a hollow reed on the outskirts of the beautiful West of Ireland village: Coolaney in County Sligo. This reed brings him an inspired message from Nature (just as an ancient reed did to Greek poet Hesiod some

2500 years previously); his lonely heart withers away at its soothing sound. In this case, the role of the Muse is played by the naturally occurring common reed playing away at a divine healing tune that for the poet conjures images of the faery dance.

The Gates of the Day

The wind blows out of the gates of the day,
The wind blows over the lonely of heart,
And the lonely of heart is withered away.
While the faeries dance in a place apart,
Shaking their milk-white feet in a ring,
Tossing their milk-white arms in the air;
For they hear the wind laugh and murmur and sing
Of a land where even the old are fair,
And even the wise are merry of tongue;
But I heard a reed of Coolaney say,
"When the wind has laughed and murmured and sung
The lonely heart is withered away!"

(*Collected Poems*, Finneran, ed.)

Many years later W.B. would return to this image. In the untitled last poem of his *Responsibilities* collection he again identifies the reed with the Muse. 'While I, from that reed-throated whisperer / Who comes at need, although not now as once / A clear articulation in the air ... ' Now in his late forties he admits that his reed-throated Muse approaches him with less superfluous zeal than she did in his youth. She now comes 'at need' and no longer clearly articulates her messages in the thin air. For the middle-aged poet, the creation of poems is no longer the picking of low-hanging fruit as it once was. Yet still she comes; the poems still flow forth. The rest of this poem reveals a dejected Yeats, his fame fading and his priceless writings underappreciated to the point of being ' ... but a post the passing dogs defile.' Yet, he claims he can find that most divine of moods – forgiveness, even for the greatest wrongs – say for example George Moore's satiric barbs in *Hail and Farewell*. The Muse still soothes apparently, especially when the Muse is now associated with Lady Gregory's loyal hospitality.

While I, from that reed-throated whisperer
Who comes at need, although not now as once
A clear articulation in the air,
But inwardly, surmise companions

Beyond the fling of the dull ass's hoof,
– Ben Jonson's phrase – and find when June is come
At Kyle-na-no under that ancient roof
A sterner conscience and a friendlier home,
I can forgive even that wrong of wrongs,
Those undreamt accidents that have made me
– Seeing that Fame has perished this long while,
Being but a part of ancient ceremony –
Notorious, **till all my priceless things
Are but a post the passing dogs defile.**
     [My emphasis]

To finish this preliminary triad of Muse references in W.B.'s poems, I offer a later poem from 1937, just two years before his death, 'The Curse of Cromwell'. Here the Lemuel Gulliver-like narrator bitterly laments the rift in Ireland created by ' ... Cromwell's house and Cromwell's murderous crew.'

You ask what I have found and far and wide I go,
Nothing but **Cromwell's house and Cromwell's murderous crew,**
The lovers and the dancers are beaten into the clay,
And the tall men and the swordsmen and the horsemen
where are they?
And there is an old beggar wandering in his pride
His fathers served their fathers before Christ was crucified.
               O what of that, o what of that,
               What is there left to say?
All neighbourly content and easy talk are gone,
But there's no good complaining, for money's rant is on,
He that's mounting up must on his neighbour mount
And **we and all the Muses are things of no account.**
They have schooling of their own but I pass their schooling by,
What can they know that we know that know the time to die?
               O what of that, O what of that,
               What is there left to say?
     [My emphasis]

The Irish lovers, dancers, and beggar deemed an underclass by 'Cromwell's house / crew' in the first stanza are simply identified as **'we'** in the second. But 'we' are not alone against the might of the militaristic Roundheads. Notice that the Muses are included in this persecuted number. Even though this supposed Irish underclass may continue to serve the forceful conqueror, the narrator implies they are in reality superior to the invaders in that they are in league with the Muses and know the 'time to die'. They have the knowledge that can only be brought by the Muse.

Because of these and other instances in his poems, the topic I choose to engage herein concerns the musicality of W.B. Yeats. Though not a musician in the popular sense himself, he did skilfully manage the sounds within his poems as befits a great lyric poet. He rhymes, employs pleasant manifestations of assonance, consonance and rhythm, he makes crucial choices in metre, meaning and intentional ambiguity. Many people have praised his writing for its 'music', its ability to 'articulate sweet sounds together'. Two recent notable books deal with these matters; Helen Vendler's masterful *Our Secret Discipline: Yeats and Lyric Form* (Oxford 2007) provides for the serious reader of Yeats a systematic analysis of his poetic path. She documents his evolution as a poet, commenting on his near-misses and, more commonly, his spectacular successes (the poems where inspiration and form come together in dynamic, synergistic balance). Joseph M. Hassett's *W.B. Yeats and the Muses* (New York 2010) examines W.B.'s relationships with the nine women who most affected his poetry. Both of these books are helpful in considering the topic of the Muse and go a long way to make clear W.B.'s particular dance with his particular Muse(s). Instead of attempting to recapitulate their work, I'll take a simple, though perhaps radical approach in hope of adding a further dimension to this discussion. That dimension is time, historical and even prehistorical; I will draw upon the long view of human interaction with the Muse as assessed by anthropology, ethnobotany, and comparative mythology, though briefly. The meaning of the word 'muse' varies over its history. According to Julia Forster in her charming book *Muses: Revealing the Nature of Inspiration* (Sparkford, UK 2007), Pausanias, a second century AD Greek geographer and historian, maintained there were three muses originally. Melete, whose name means study or practice, Mneme meaning memory, and Aoide or song were all associated with Greece's Mount Helicon (*Muses*, p. 19). More commonly, nine Muses are reported. The aforementioned Hesiod, a shepherd and poet *c.* 700 BC, lived near Mount Helicon. He had encountered the Muses on the mountain and they told him to write poetry. He begins his lengthy poem the *Theogony* with these words: 'From the Muses of Helicon, let us begin our singing, that haunt Helicon's great and holy mountain, and dance on their soft feet round the violet-dark spring of the altar of the mighty son of Kronos [i.e. Zeus]' (*Muses*, p. 20). These nine Muses were immortal daughters of Zeus and Mnemosyne (memory) and each inspired and provided knowledge to men in arts, sciences, and humanities. A typical representation of their particular fields is represented here.

MUSE	Realm of Influence:
Calliope	Epic Poetry
Clio	History
Erato	Erotic or Love Poetry
Euterpe	Music, Lyric Poetry
Melpomene	Tragedy
Polyhymnia	Sacred Lyrics; Rhetoric; Geometry
Terpsichore	Dance
Thalia	Comedy; Bucolic Poetry
Urania	Astronomy; Astrology

(Forster, p. 21)

The Muses were taken seriously in Greece. Perhaps we've all read in school Homer's invocation to the Muse in *The Odyssey*; Pythagoras founded the first philosophical school and dedicated it to the Muses; Plato explains that Socrates held that 'not by art does the poet sing, but by power divine' (Forster, p. 24).

Over time and space, the notion of the Muse would change. Forster goes on to examine eight more discrete categories of Muses. (1. Archetypal; 2. Beloved; 3. Married; 4. Exotic; 5. Mutual; 6. Fated; 7. Iconic; and 8. Infant.) Dante, Petrarch, the troubadours of the Courtly Love tradition, Keats, Plath, Hughes, Lennon, Dali, Nin, Gauguin, Wordsworth, Rossetti, Rilke, Joyce and Charles Dodgson are but some of the artists she examines. She puts W.B. and George Yeats neatly in the Married Muse category, though to be fair the Muse had W.B. firmly in hand by the time he married Georgie Hyde-Lees on 20 October 1917 in his fifty-second year (on the day he wed he had ten volumes of narrative and lyric poetry published and a firm literary reputation).

The universal constant in all of Forster's Muse-forms is that each brings inspiration to the artist. This must be the heart of the musical matter. 'Inspire' is a beautiful word. 'To breathe in' is its common meaning. What have these inspired artists breathed in? Literally, I suppose the answer has to be 'air'. If it stops there, then that still doesn't help distinguish the inspiration of the artist from the non-artist. To proceed figuratively – air is wind; wind is spirit. Both the wind and Spirit go where they will. Wind could then symbolically represent the spirit or creative force which acts upon the artist. This co-mingling of mind of the artist and Spirit may seem routine to practised artists, but not everyone is used to this notion, so I mention it. To sum up, when touched by a Muse the artist may be seen to have breathed in a creative spirit that informs the work done by that artist.

What is the message of the Muse? It must be different from field to field, person to person. An inspired painter must, it would seem, receive different information than an inspired poet or scientist or dancer or mathematician. Yet there may be a commonality of experience when one is touched by the Muse. In W.B.'s short poem 'A Meditation in Time of War' he reports a sudden epiphany.

> For **one** throb of the artery,
> While on that old grey stone I sat
> Under the old wind-broken tree,
> **I knew** that **One** is animate,
> Mankind inanimate phantasy.
>
> 1920

[My emphasis]

Is this sudden knowledge the work of the Muse? Let's examine. The experience was brief – 'one throb of the artery'. When the word 'one' reappears in the third line its significance is magnified into the proper noun 'One' which may suggest divinity, or at least W.B.'s notion of 'Unity of Being'. Perhaps most importantly in this regard is the appearance of the word 'knew'. The Poet claims knowledge, not a hunch, not an educated guess, but a sudden **knowledge**. From this example, we might learn that the Muse's touch, though brief, leaves the gift of a bit of profound knowledge. The Poet experiences a moment of 'spontaneous grace' and, fortunately for us, leaves a residue of this encounter in the form of this short impacting poem.

Joseph Campbell, the wise authority in matters of comparative mythology, refers to a Muse as ' ... the inspirer of the spiritual life.' In his final series of lectures, *Transformations of Myth through Time*, he finds evidence of the concept of a female Muse in Paleolithic times and traces her evolution through the various goddesses of the fertile-crescent and beyond. He reminds us 'That when we think now of mother cults, everybody talks about fertility. But that's not the main inspiration of the goddess. That's only on the physical level. This is woman as muse. On the spiritual level she's the mother of our spiritual life' (*Transformations*, p. 64). So the concept of the Muse was already old when Socrates acknowledged that 'the divine sign' would come to him from time to time (*The Dialogues of Plato*, 'Euthyphro', p. 460). On the day of his death, Socrates speaks to his supporters (who would have him flee Athens and save himself) of the fact that his 'internal oracle' refuses to interfere with this day's severe events. 'Hitherto the divine faculty of which the internal oracle is the source has constantly been in the habit of opposing me even about trifles, if I was going to slip or error [*sic*] in any matter; … ' Now, with his death sentence impending, his internal oracle makes no sign that he should alter the course he has chosen, that is to face his death calmly and courageously. 'What do I take to be the explanation of this silence? I will tell you. It is an intimation that what has happened to me is a good, and those that think death is an evil are in error. For the customary sign would surely have opposed me had I been going to evil and not to good' (*The Dialogues of Plato*, 'Apology', p. 24). Socrates relies on his customary divine sign even unto his death.

In W.B.'s poems he expresses similar attitudes toward death. In his poetic sequence 'Upon a Dying Lady' (written for his friend Mabel Beardsley as she was facing cancer), the narrator recounts that even though her assembled friends may have trouble facing her demise – 'We have not for death but toys.' – she, like Socrates, will join the company of 'Achilles, Timor, Babar, Barhaim, all / Who have lived in joy and laughed into the face of death.' In W.B.'s translation from *Oedipus at Colonus*, he puts these words into long-suffering Oedipus's mouth 'I celebrate the silent kiss that ends short life or long.' Yeats's *Antigone* has the poor, loyal, child of Oedipus who, again like Socrates could have avoided death in acquiescing to the powers that be, refuse this option as she courageously 'Descends into the loveless dust' to hang herself rather than starve in madness as her uncle Creon decrees she must. Where does such courage originate? What can sustain it? Perhaps Socrates's internal oracle may help make this understandable.

As far as poetry is concerned, Socrates distinguishes between poets who are merely the craftsmen of language and those who have been touched by the Muse. ' … if a man comes to the door of poetry untouched by the madness of the Muses, believing that technique alone will make him a good poet, he and his sane compositions never reach perfection, but are utterly eclipsed by the performance of the inspired madman' (Forster, p. 24). Sprinkled throughout Plato's Socratic Dialogues are references to the authority of poetic lines as a reverent person might quote from the Bible. He even refers to the author of the epic poems of the Trojan War as ' … the divine poet Homer' (*The Dialogues of Plato*, 'Phaedo', p. 108). As Forster puts it, 'This heaven-sent madness … [creates poetry that] should send shivers down the reader's spine, make his eyes water and his hairs stand on end' (pp. 23–4). Of course there is nothing to say that an inspired, Muse-mad poet cannot also be a master craftsman and mage.

We have seen that the Muse is the source of inspiration in many fields of human activity and leaves the human contactee a boon of knowledge or creative spark; that the Muse is envisioned variously throughout time: as goddess, human female or male, or in the form of a natural object like the sound of wind over a hollow reed. Further, the artist's heart is opened through this experience. As Meister Eckhart wrote, 'what is taken in by contemplation must be given out in love' (*LSD: My Problem Child*, Dr Albert Hofmann, p. 180, Multidisciplinary Assoc. for Pyschedelic Studies. N.C. 2009). We have seen, and will further see, that the one touched by the Muse will cross the threshold of normal scepticism into a field of grateful subjective credulity concerning the inspiration. We have seen that with W.B. Yeats and with many more, the inspiration is transformed into artifice, poetry for Yeats, and lovingly spread among us through that ever-fascinating quality, Beauty. Consider W.B.'s poem of 1913, 'Paudeen'.

> Indignant at the fumbling wits, the obscure spite
> Of our Paudeen in his shop, I stumbled blind
> Among the stones and thorn-trees, under morning light;
> Until a curlew cried and in the luminous wind
> A curlew answered; and suddenly thereupon I thought
> That on the lonely height where all are in God's eye,
> There cannot be, confusion of our sound forgot,
> A single soul that lacks a sweet crystalline cry.

Beginning one place and ending another is the movement of 'Paudeen'. The apparently Protestant narrator begins in a black mood for having to endure apparently Catholic Paudeen's dimwitted awkwardness and ends in a rare and beautiful mood of blessed appreciation and forgiveness for all, even himself. He begins in blind rage and ends in vision beatific. That's quite a transformation of mood. Initial Tragedy gives way to ultimate Comedy. Was the fellow touched by a Muse to change so suddenly? Is there a Muse, as we've defined it, in this poem? If we rule out Paudeen and the narrator as antagonist and protagonist of this spare story, that leaves, as muse suspects, only natural objects: stones, thorn-trees, light, a curlew's cry and curlew's answer, and, once again, there is the wind. The message of knowledge of forgiveness must have come through Nature here as it did before in 'The Gates of the Day' before the narrator is granted the 'God's eye' view. And in only eight lines W.B. gives the world a poetic shortcut to profound catharsis.

Though the contented mood achieved by 'Paudeen's' narrator is rarely expressed so pointedly in his poems, the last stanza of 'A Dialogue of Self and Soul' reprises and announces the Self's life-affirming pronouncement in the face of the Soul's silence.

> I am content to follow to its source
> Every event in action or in thought;
> Measure the lot; forgive myself the lot!
> When such as I cast out remorse
> So great a sweetness flows into the breast
> We must laugh and we must sing,
> We are blest by everything,
> Everything we look upon is blest.

Surely such moments are peak experience. W.B. was to find that the native duplicity of the universe, moved along in gyres large and small, brought the full gamut of experiences to his door, good and bad, happy and sad, confused and crystal clear. His poetic accounting of his honest commuting from one side of this dichotomous line to the other is a 1929 poem called 'Vacillation', a poem in eight parts which begins, 'Between extremities, / Man runs his course;' and contains a similar scene of blessed epiphany in part IV:

> My fiftieth year had come and gone,
> I sat, a solitary man,
> In a crowded London shop,
> An open book and an empty cup
> On the marble table-top.
> While on the shop and street I gazed
> My body of a sudden blazed;
> And twenty minutes more or less
> It seemed, so great my happiness,
> That I was blessed and could bless.

1932

What do we call this type of experience? Spiritual? Visionary? Unity of being? One with Nature? Unio Mystica? These three peak experiences bear the same qualities as the encounter with the Muse. They are practically indistinguishable. Going down the checklist, both contain: 1). a specific source of inspiration, 2). a human contactee, 3). a boon bestowed to the contactee which may inspire a career in the arts or sciences and 4). communion with the Muse in a field of subjective credulity or gnosis concerning the inspiration. In human history these perennially powerful experiences have helped determine the structuring of myth, religion, business, art and play. We have been at the work of producing and controlling these very types of experiences far into the distant past, perhaps, if modern logic may be trusted on primeval matters, even to the Serengeti over three million years ago.

Here I feel a bit like the unexpectedly candid boy in Andersen's 'The Emperor's New Clothes'. For just as W.B. sought visionary experience (Aldous Huxley's term) through the Muse, he also sought it practically. 'There are experiences that most of us are hesitant to speak about, because they do not conform to everyday reality and defy rational explanation' begins Dr Albert Hofmann's highly serious memoir, *LSD: My Problem Child* (p. 29). Dr Hofmann is referring to 'time out of time' moments, the sort we've been considering. Visionary experience in humans is brought about through various methods. People have visionary experience spontaneously; they may have it as a result of prayer and meditation; visionary experience can be induced through fatigue, dancing and starvation of food, air and water; and humans, apparently, throughout the whole of our history, have induced such moments most reliably through the ingestion of psychotropic plants, fungi and plant derivatives. This may be the greatest story never told, or, at least, seldom told. And this is no digression, for these matters come into play when considering W.B. Yeats's life and art.

Though I claim no expertise in ethno-biology or human history, I detect a long-standing, clear pattern of human involvement with vision-inducing flora from reading in this arena. Who could doubt that omnivorous hominids like Lucy (*Australopithecus afarensis*) would hesitate for a moment to eat the mushrooms growing from the dung of the many nearby grazing ungulates? Mushrooms found in such an environment today would be suspected of containing psilocybin, a vision-inducing alkaloid. This is ages before the arrival of *Homo sapiens*.

Closer to modern times we have evidence of use, trade and artistic and linguistic representations of these psychoactive plants in virtually every civilization centre in human history. It is a long fascinating story that touches upon goddesses and mystery cults, the soma of Northern India, the likely ergot-derived *kykeon* drink of the Eleusinian Mysteries, the flesh of the Gods (sacred mushrooms) of the new world, and too many more to mention here. As we learn more about the role of these substances in human history, it is apparent to some that the words 'hallucinogenic' and 'psychedelic' are inadequate to describe the intended use of these compounds. The Eleusinian Mysteries, centered in Eleusis near Athens, flourished for nearly two millennia and was the most successful of the Greek Mysteries. In the fascinating and well-documented examination of this ancient institution, *The Road to Eleusis: Unveiling the Secret of The Mysteries*, classicist Carl A.P. Ruck, Harvard mycologist Gordon Wasson and the aforementioned bio-chemist Albert Hofmann, suggest the term 'entheogen' be used in lieu of 'hallucinogen'. In this word is embodied the idea of the Muse we've been addressing – the root of the word 'Theos' meaning God and the prefix 'en' meaning 'in'. So an entheogen is a substance that gives the subject the feeling of a divine consciousness awakening **in** the mind. This would have made the final initiation night rather a profound autumnal experience for the initiates at Eleusis. We might expect them to be literally **enthusiastic**. The Eleusinian vows of silence were extreme and popularly enforced, so the scholar must be a bit of a detective to summon the full meaning of Eleusis – it was finally destroyed in 395 AD. The findings of Hofmann, Ruck and Wasson are clear enough. The initiations at Eleusis were intended to create for the initiate a personal, powerful experience. The initiate in identifying with the Homeric Hymn to Demeter over a period of time, experiencing the sequential rituals (including baptism), and participating in a great culminating rite of initiation under the influence of an entheogen akin to – if not actually – LSD, gained a sacred, ultimate boon intimately known, but NEVER to be discussed outside Eleusis.

In 1890 Arthur Symons introduced W.B. Yeats to hashish, a very potent and condensed form of *cannabis* or marijuana (Foster, Vol I, p. 109). W.B. was in his mid-twenties. Roy Foster further reports that in 1896 'WBY had learnt to take hashish with the shady followers of the mystic Louis Claude de Saint-Martin in Paris, and with Davray and Symons the previous December.' W.B.'s use of hashish 'pellets' would be ongoing.

On another related front, in a sort of chemical breakthrough, the entheogenic alkaloids in the buttons of the peyote cactus – today the sacrament of the Native American Church – had been isolated and synthesized in the year 1896. Foster again, 'In 1897 he [W.B.] experimented with mescal [*i.e.* mescaline, or peyote buttons], supplied by [Dr] Havelock Ellis ... ' (*Idem*, p. 178). Dr Ellis described W.B., though unnamed, this way: he is 'interested in mystical matters, an excellent subject for visions, and **very familiar** with **various** vision-producing drugs and processes' (*Contemporary Review*, January 1898). [My emphasis]

Keep in mind that all of these pursuits were perfectly legal, known and, to some extent, practised in his social circles. The poet is attempting to induce visionary experience chemically. How long and to what extent he continued this strategy, I cannot yet say. We are still waiting for full information from his private writings.

By 1922 he could look back over his life and report of his attempt to create The Castle of Heroes with Maud Gonne. It was to be a school of Irish Mysteries or, in his words, 'I planned a mystical Order which should buy or hire the castle, and keep it as a place where its members could retire for a while for contemplation, and where we might establish mysteries like those of Eleusis and Samothrace' (*Au*, p. 254). This Castle of Heroes proved to be a castle in the air. It was never actually realized, unless you allow that his efforts at creating a uniquely Irish mystery experience were subsequently channelled through his theatre work and, of course, his poetry.

In this dialogue poem from *The Wild Swans at Coole* collection, 'The Saint and the Hunchback', W.B. casts words between a Hunchback and a Saint, the emblems of the twenty-sixth and twenty-seventh phases of his moon-phase / human personality schema. It seems these two are at odds. The cagey hunchback, while paying careful obeisance to this tortured, masochistic, confiding saint, acknowledges that they both have strong feelings about Alcibiades; the saint finds him a rogue, while the Hunchback can imagine no one more blessed.

> *Hunchback.* Stand up and lift your hands and bless
> A man that finds great bitterness
> In thinking of his lost renown.
> A Roman Caesar is held down
> Under this hump.
>
> *Saint.* God tries each man
> According to a different plan.
> I shall not cease to bless because
> I lay about me with the taws
> That night and morning I may thrash
> Greek Alexander from my flesh,
> Augustus Caesar, and after these
> That great rogue Alcibiades
>
> *Hunchback.* To all that in your flesh have stood
> And blessed, I give my gratitude,
> Honoured by all in their degrees,
> But most to Alcibiades.

Who, then, is Alcibiades? An Athenian of the Golden Age. When his father fell in battle great Pericles raised him; Socrates loved him steadfastly, though refused him sexually; eventually Athens looked to him as one if its leading citizens in war and peace for a time. He appears a beautiful, love-struck, drunken young man in Plato's *Symposium*. Never claiming to be a saint himself, he eventually did something that would earn the condemnation of Yeats's saint and praise from his hunchback. In 415 BC, Alcibiades profaned the Eleusinian Mysteries by staging his unofficial – and clearly outlawed and entirely underappreciated – versions of the most secret and sacred of Greek Mysteries. Held in some of the most aristocratic houses in Athens, there was intoxication shared with his disorderly friends as the secrets were divulged and the rituals re-enacted without sanction. (Whether this intoxication was of the entheogen barley drink of Eleusis – the *Kykeon*– is apparently not known for certain.) More details are available to the curious. Was this 'outing' of the Mysteries the act of a devil or holy man? W.B. offers two crippled perspectives; one a soul's, and one a body's; one of a deformed saint and one a hunchback. This poem could be W.B.'s cryptic commentary on the secret ceremonies of Eleusis, the ones he may have wished to adopt in his Castle of Heroes.

When W.B. and his wife, George, were essentially done with the spiritual field work that led to *A Vision*, he wrote a little poem that seems *à propos* to an examination of his relationship with the Muse, 'Gratitude to the Unknown Instructors' (1932).

> Gratitude to the Unknown Instructors
> What they undertook to do
> They brought to pass;
> All things hang like a drop of dew
> Upon a blade of grass.

Famously, the numerous spirits they contacted in 1917 and after through automatic writings, séances, sleeps, etc. came to bring the poet 'metaphors for poetry' (Introduction to *A Vision* from 'A Packet for Ezra Pound', 1937). But they also brought his philosophical system of paired antithetical gyres, phases of the moon related to human personality, understanding of the Great Wheel, an assurance of reincarnation, etc. For all of this and more, the Poet announces his gratitude. In other words, here we find what we expect to find in an artist touched by the Muse. Specific source(s) of inspiration, the instructors, 2). a human contactee, W.B., 3). boons bestowed to the contactee, manifesting in his work, 4). communion with the Muse in a field of subjective credulity or gnosis concerning the inspiration, and 5). a gratuitous impulse to share / rejoice, bless, etc. As he wrote to T. Werner Laurie on 27 July 1924, 'I dare say I delude myself in thinking this book [*A Vision*] my book of books' (Neil Mann, www. yeatsvision.com/Sitemap).

His gratitude is immortalized in his great poem from 1928's *The Tower*, 'Among School Children', in its ultimate metaphor. 'O body swayed to music, O brightening glance, / How can we know the dancer from the dance?' Helen Vendler trenchantly answers

> ... we cannot know ... the dancer from the dance ... The question implies
> wonder and joy, rather than an unanswerable enigma. Yeats has found some-
> thing to say for life: it is a solitary but nonetheless endlessly satisfying set

of creative inventions. By locating joy and identity in the 'enterprise' of our devising an individual dance, Yeats can acknowledge the truth of universal heartbreak without letting it entirely destroy the energy, delight, inventiveness, and continuity of being (Vendler, p. 286).

The living of one's individual life can be a dance as each chooses the next step. Vendler again,

> Although we have been given ... an art form – the dance – as a 'solution,' Yeats has, in an act of spectacular generosity, made his closing art form available to all. ... 'Among School Children' offers as its example of an art work the self-choreographed articulation of a life over time – an enterprise that every conscious creature must in some way undertake. ... Yeats has written a philosophical poem for everyone. ... He has stepped into the life of Everyman, and the poem is the greater for it (*Idem*, pp. 287–8).

In remembering that the word 'philosophy' means love of wisdom, Vendler's praise for this open-hearted 'philosophical' poem's universality, links W.B. Yeats's life-as-dance metaphor to the Muse that Joseph Campbell calls 'the source of our spiritual life'.

Therefore we all are dancers, figuratively if not literally, and those who listen to the Muse may dance in an inspired manner. Can there be any doubt that W.B. and most of his family were dancers of this special sort? Permit me to close with a Yeatsish version of an Irish blessing.

Not forgetting life's tragic dimension, may your body be swayed to the music you hear; may your glance be ever-brightening; and may your dance know all the gratuitous joy to which it is entitled.

Chaos, Prophecy and the Celtic Hero: 'The Second Coming' by W.B. Yeats, an Alternative Interpretation

CRAIG KIRK

The Second Coming

Turning and turning in the widening gyre
The falcon cannot hear the falconer;
Things fall apart; the centre cannot hold;
Mere anarchy is loosed upon the world,
The blood-dimmed tide is loosed, and everywhere
The ceremony of innocence is drowned;
The best lack all conviction, while the worst
Are full of passionate intensity.

Surely some revelation is at hand;
Surely the Second Coming is at hand.
The Second Coming! Hardly are those words out
When a vast image out of *Spiritus Mundi*
Troubles my sight: somewhere in sands of the desert
A shape with lion body and the head of a man,
A gaze blank and pitiless as the sun,
Is moving its slow thighs, while all about it

> Reel shadows of the indignant desert birds.
> The darkness drops again; but now I know
> That twenty centuries of stony sleep
> Were vexed to nightmare by a rocking cradle,
> And what rough beast, its hour come round at last,
> Slouches towards Bethlehem to be born?

Yeats's 'The Second Coming' (1919) was arguably written in response to turmoil in Europe and Ireland in that era. Yeats was a man who created his own perspective on the events of life and the world. Consequently, his insights were abstract and intuitive, requiring some understanding by his readers of his theories in order to make sense of his works. Despite this, 'The Second Coming' is immediately recognizable as dark and apocalyptic, with a depth and ambiguity that encourages speculative interpretation. My interpretation of 'The Second Coming' differs from the norm, but is based upon Yeats's preoccupation with mythology, spirituality, the supernatural and the occult. I think that in light of the tumultuous world events of the time, and Yeats's own theologies, that it may offer an alternative view on the central preoccupation behind the poem.

The form of the poem doesn't appear to be anything but free verse on first examination, but is loosely based enough on iambic pentameter to almost pass as blank verse. Additionally, the second stanza contains 14 lines, which bestows it with a sonnet-like structure without the rhyming elements of a sonnet. Thorne explains that metrically, Yeats uses variations in the basic iambic pattern to underpin the poem's theme, one of disorder and loss of direction.[1] Using 'solid' iambic pentameter interspersed with disordered lines enhances the loss of control; 'solid' lines of iambic pentameter such as:

> The falcon cannot hear the falconer,

are juxtapositioned among four-stressed lines such as:

> Turning and turning in the widening gyre

There are half-rhymes present in 'gyre' and 'falconer', 'hold' and 'world', but this is seemingly abandoned as the poem progresses. Perhaps all these attributes are a conscious manifestation by Yeats, where the content of the poem causes its very structure to become disordered.

Yeats uses repetition of stresses, sounds and alliteration to add gravity, strength and emphasis to the verse;[2] 'Turning and turning ... ' immediately produces a dizzying effect, whilst reinforcing Yeats's idea of the conclusion of a historical cycle with the use of two dactylic feet. (i.e. 1 strong, 2 weak stresses). Three stressed syllables, an iamb followed by a spondee in 'Thĕ blóod

/ -dim´med tíde' reflects the dark gravity of the 'anarchy'[3] which is 'loosed', while the doubling of the term 'loosed' enhances the loss of control. Yeats repeats the effect with 'Hardly are thóse wórds óut' to add drama and premonition to the description of his vision of the 'vast image'.

The last four lines of the first stanza are a fatalistic summation of the totality of the destruction of peace, purity and order, and the ascension of the strongest, most virulent political extremes; a particular abhorrence of Yeats's.[4] Political extremism, aquatic metaphors, 'ceremony' and 'innocence' are themes repeated in 'Prayer for my Daughter' (1919).[5]

In 'The Second Coming', Yeats accuses the 'worst' exponents of political extremes as being full of 'passionate intensity', fired up by bloodlust and warmongering; and the 'best' as 'lacking conviction', aimless and impotent in the face of the horrors of conflict. In 'A Prayer for my Daughter' Yeats personalizes 'intellectual hatred' and the 'opinionated mind', condemning its evils. However he optimistically proposes that 'all hatred driven hence' can enable innocence to be recovered and maintained despite contemptuous criticisms.

Yeats enlists aquatic themes in both poems, but pointedly, the imagery portrayed by these themes is different. Whereas in 'The Second Coming' the tide is an engulfing force that floods and drowns the 'ceremony of innocence', in 'A Prayer for my Daughter' the 'future years' have risen optimistically from the sea, and innocence is born in 'custom and in ceremony'. The moods of the two poems are dramatically different; summarized by their titles: 'The Second Coming' immediately infers Armageddon whilst 'A Prayer for my Daughter' is an anticipatory prayer of hope for an innocent entity that is yet to mature, be corrupted or tarnished. Yet the timing of the poems' composition, in close parallel with World War I and virulent Irish Republicanism, suggests Yeats reflecting on the events in the context of his own philosophies. In comparing the two equal-aged poems with their similar elements, it is possible to see one is of trepidation and the aftermath of war, where the other is a declaration of hope and optimism in the face of pessimistic criticisms.

Certainly, world events of the time influenced Yeats's mood, and strengthened his philosophies regarding the historical cyclonic gyres between pinnacles of peace and art, and cataclysms of warfare and bloodshed. As an ardent subscriber to mythology, the occult, the supernatural and spiritualism, Yeats entwined these elements within his works, both superficially and covertly.[6]

A Coat

I MADE my song a coat
Covered with embroideries

> Out of old mythologies
> From heel to throat;
> But the fools caught it,
> Wore it in the world's eyes
> As though they'd wrought it.
> Song, let them take it,
> For there's more enterprise
> In walking naked.
>   (1912)

I read his poem, 'A Coat' (1912) with great interest, as I believe it was a cry of despair from Yeats about critics and academics misinterpreting his imagery in the context of more contemporary culture instead of the ancient mythologies that Yeats revered. It led me to consider the sources of inspiration for Yeats's imagery in poems like 'The Second Coming'.

The second stanza begins like an evangelist awakening a sleepy congregation with the repeated announcement of 'The Second Coming'. The declaration triggers a vision, where he sees a troubling image from 'somewhere in sands of the desert': *'A shape with lion body and the head of a man'*.

This 'vast image from *Spiritus Mundi*' has understandably been commonly interpreted to be an Egyptian sphinx: 'sands of the desert', 'lion body and the head of a man' are superficially identifiable. However, when attempting to understand the poem, I found that academics have struggled to compose a definite theory while ever a sphinx is seen to be the 'image'.[7]

Yeats used diction that seemed to fit the description of the 'vast image' as a sphinx equivocally, as either Greek or Egyptian mythology's definition of the role of a sphinx seems inconsistent with the mood and theme of the poem itself. It led me to consider if other mythological beings might fit the description and decipher some of the meaning. In Roman mythology, Hercules was a great strong man who wore a lion skin, or *'lion body'*, on his back. The Greek equivalent was Heracles, also wearing a lion skin. The Irish version was Ogma, closely associated with and / or re-interpreted as Ogmios, from Celtic mythology.[8]

Ogmios had other characteristics, as well as being seen as the 'Celtic Hercules'. He was known as the God of Eloquence, poetry, oration and the creator of the Ogham script (an ancient Celtic runic language).[9] Such a character would certainly strike a chord with Yeats.

Distinct from Hercules / Heracles, he is described as being an old, balding man whose skin is dry and tanned almost black by the sun, he was also known as Sun-Face, and that he guided men to the underworld / land of the dead.[10] Such was his power of oratory that he is depicted as having chains coming from his tongue that are attached to the ears of men, guiding them willingly to the nether-world. As such, Ogmios would fit Yeats's description as possessing: 'A gaze blank and pitiless as the sun'. Further, as representing an <u>old man's gait</u>, the 'shape':

> <u>Is moving its slow thighs</u>, while all about it,
> Reel shadows of the indignant desert birds.

The 'shadows of indignant desert birds' could refer to the Stymphalian Birds that were vanquished by Hercules in his sixth labour, rediscovered in the Black Sea by the Argonauts, and later to be described by the second-century AD writer Pausanias as *'Arabian desert birds'*.[11] Their shadows 'reel', roused by 'Hercules / Ogmios' into the sky and whirling about each other, representative of the maelstrom of repercussions from his intercedence, echoing the gyre spirals of the falcon in the first stanza. The definition of the term 'reel' is more commonly thought of as a description of staggering revulsion, however it can also describe twirling and whirling movement, as in the traditional Irish folk-dance of the same name; where the participants move about each other in intertwining circular movements. As a devotee of ancient and traditional Irish / Celtic folklore, Yeats may have used the term 'reel' to liken the movements of the 'shadows of the indignant desert birds' to the whirling patterns of an Irish folk-dance, whilst equivocally insinuating fear and revulsion by the birds of the 'vast image from *Spiritus Mundi*'.

The affirmation 'Twenty centuries' echoes Yeats's philosophy of 2000 year cycles, emphasised by the balance of the rhyme and rhythm of the two words. In the sixteenth century, the French physician, Nostradamus, wrote books of prophecies titled 'Centuries'; in which Ogmios marches to Byzantium to despatch the powers of the Antichrist.[12] I consider that Yeats would have studied such texts, seeing parallels between his own philosophies and those of texts prophesizing Armageddon, such as Nostradamus. 'The Second Coming' mirrors elements of the text of Nostradamus.[13]

In Byzantium (now Istanbul) there is a district called Besiktas, which has several interpretations as to the origins of its name; one of which is 'cradle-stone'. Local legend has it that this name originated from a church that was built on a relic, a stone that came from the stable in which Jesus Christ was born.[14] I think it arguable that this paraphrases the pseudonym with 'stony sleep' and 'rocking cradle', to symbolize Byzantium, the ancient holy city that he venerates in 'Sailing to Byzantium' (1928).

A parallel can also be made that the 'stony sleep', i.e. the peace of the world, was 'vexed to nightmare' by the 'cradle', the 'cradle of civilisation' (Mesopotamia) representing humanity, being 'rocked' by World War I.

Being an unmistakable iconic image, 'Bethlehem' refers to the second coming of Christ. Following the prophecy of Nostradamus, however, Christ's safe arrival has to first be ensured by the accomplishment of the task that has 'to be born' by Ogmios, who, as an old man, will 'slouch' with 'slow moving thighs' to his prophesized destiny.

That W.B. Yeats created an enigma of a poem is unquestionable. I interpreted 'The Second Coming' as masking a positive resolution of Armageddon behind a veneer of puzzling dramatic imagery, albeit painted with a master craftsman's brush. I found that when the 'vast image from *Spiritus Mundi*' was reinterpreted as a mythological hero instead of a 'sphinx', the passages of the poem began to reconstruct themselves into a message of a powerful *good* moving inevitably towards a cataclysmic destruction of *evil,* in order to facilitate the birth of a new age. Surely this is a characteristic of Yeats's gyre system at hand.

NOTES

1. Sara Thorne, *Mastering Poetry* (Hampshire, New York 2006), p. 268
2. *Ibid.*
3. *Ibid.*
4. Dr Jennifer McDonnell, *The Poetry of W.B. Yeats II* (Armidale 2009) (podcast) audio recordings.
5. W.B. Yeats, 'Prayer for my Daughter' (1919)
6. Dr Jennifer McDonnell, 'William Butler Yeats (1865–1939)', *English 102 Advisory Materials* (Armidale 2009), p. 68; W.B. Yeats, 'A Coat', 1921.
7. Neil Mann, *The Second Coming* see http://www.yeatsvision.com/SecondNotes .html. 2007; Nicholas Grene, *Yeats's Poetic Codes* (Oxford 2008) pp. 104–6.
8. Encarta Encyclopedia 2004, 'Ogmios', Microsoft Corporation 2003.
9. See http://www.celtnet.org.uk/gods_o/ogmios; Indra Kagis McEwen, *Vitruvius: writing the body of architecture* (Cambridge, Massachusetts 2003), pp. 103–4; Encarta 2003.
10. J.A. MacCulloch, The Religion of the Ancient Celts, pp. 75–6, 1911, see http:// www.kernunnos.com/deities/ogmios/ogmios.html
11. Encarta Encyclopedia, 'Stymphalian Birds: Greek Mythological Beasts', 2003; see http://www.monstropedia.org/index.php?title=Stymphalian_BirdPausanias, Description of Greece 8. 22. 4 (trans. Jones) (Greek travelogue *c.* 2nd A.D.) see http://www.theoi.com/Ther/OrnithesStymphalides.html .
12. Nostradamus, quatrain 80, *Century V.* (1555) see http://www.sacred-texts.com /nos/cen5eng.htm
13. Nostradamus, verse 47, *Epistle to Henry II* (1557) see http://www.sacred-texts .com/nos/epistle.htm
14. See http://turkeytravelresource.com/view/57/besiktas; Encarta encyclopaedia, 'Beşiktaş' 2004.

Reconstructing W.B.: Memoirs of Yeats as Indices in Literary Ireland

KATY PLOWRIGHT

W.B. Yeats's epitaph must be one of the most famous of modern times:

> 'Cast a cold eye
> On life, on death.
> Horseman, pass by!'

The lines of course come from his late poem, 'Under Ben Bulben'. Yeats was an inveterate maker of his own image throughout his life, and in anticipating his own death, things were no different. Apocryphal tales placing emphasis on the textual representation of Yeats have sprung up: for instance, a neon sign announcing the poet's death was erected on Dublin's O'Connell Street. The representation of Yeats after his death, then, gained as much of its meaning from its medium as its message.

This paper will examine two collections of article-length biographical sketches of Yeats, in order to suggest the relation between textual elements, and larger movements in the literary scene. The first of these was edited by Lennox Robinson for the Abbey Theatre's *The Arrow* (1939), and the second by Stephen Gwynn for Macmillan's *Scattering Branches* (1940). The third case explored in this paper – Monk Gibbon's *The Masterpiece and the Man* (1959) – will show that this retrospective account presents a very different view of Yeats's relation to Irish literary culture, through bibliographic and editorial means.

The aim, in discussing these texts in their bibliographical context, is to explore the important role played by the author as an editorial principle, enabling the editor to encode the values behind the respectful act of collecting tributes to Yeats. In the short period 1939–40, which saw the first assessments of Ireland's literary potential without Yeats, an extension of authorial into national issues is perhaps inevitable. Yeats's own attitude to such notions of generic unity in collections of sketches and other minor writings was in line with this: in 1906, he wrote somewhat pompously to Stephen Gwynn about the collection *The Shanachie*: 'I do not find in the editing of this magazine any one selective mind or any one principle of selection … I don't believe that it is possible to make a good magazine without making up your mind who it is for whom you are making it and keeping to that idea throughout.' Yeats's idea of editorial principle is singular: it will become clear that the principles of editing used in these collections are versions of this emphasis on readership. It is still more relevant that Yeats's conclusion to his letter to Gwynn suggests the editorial principle of the third piece discussed in this essay: 'What Dublin wants is some man who knows his own mind and has an intolerable tongue and a delight in enemies … ' After examining the appearance of cultural unity as a generic art propagated by the biographical volumes of 1939–1940, the possibility that Dublin literary culture was less unified than fractured in Yeats's final years will be suggested, in order to contextualize the fiction of cultural unity.

It is to be expected that Yeats's death would result in a huge number of obituaries and tributes, and Roy Foster has usefully explored some of these with reference to notions of 'Irishness', in an article in the *Yeats Annual No. 12*, 1996. The first significant collection of biographical sketches, however, did not come out until the summer of 1939, with a special issue of the Abbey Theatre's occasional magazine, *The Arrow*. An analysis of the issue in terms of its organizational and commercial principles reveals not only information about the abrupt editorial decisions forced by Yeats's death, but also about the state of the critical canon as it stood just months after the poet's demise, and further, about the promotion of Yeats, whose works are advertised on the basis of his authorial stamp, in lieu of his high-profile public life.

The issue was an important event, as there had only been five previous editions of *The Arrow*: two in 1906, and one each in 1907, 1908, and 1909, all edited by Yeats. According to Lennox Robinson, the editor of the 1939 *Arrow*, the aim of the magazine had always been 'to comment on the work of the Theatre, to announce new plans and to answer criticisms.' This seems a fair comment, as previous editions had dealt with the controversy over J.M. Synge's *The Playboy of the Western World* (1907), and George Bernard

Shaw's *The Shewing-up of Blanco Posnet* (1909), with both of which Yeats had been personally associated. Preparations for a volume along the same lines had been 'far advanced' when the editor heard of Yeats's death, and postponed 'that controversial number'. The editor stresses the suddenly re-prioritized plans, thus paying homage to the importance of one of the theatre's founder directors, while simultaneously advertising the sensational nature of the next issue. Editorial changes were brought on directly by Yeats's death, and then appropriated within the wider purpose of homage to the poet. This declared purpose, however, fits strangely with the bibliographic appearance of the issue.

The arrangement of the biographical sketches collected within the volume, too, yields much information about the state of 'Yeatsiana' as a developing critical canon, and to put it more cynically, as a viable commercial product, less than six months after the author's death. The contributors include the poets John Masefield, F.R. Higgins, Austin Clarke, Oliver St John Gogarty and W.J. Turner, theatre men Gordon Bottomley and Lennox Robinson, and artists Edmund Dulac and William Rothenstein. At this early stage in the development of the posthumous critical arena, Robinson, in his role as editor, has to give acknowledgments for Masefield and Clarke's pieces, which have been printed previously elsewhere. It is clear that within the market for biographical sketches of Yeats, certain authors have to be re-printed from other sources, and their appearance in this collection has then to be recognized as derivative. The volume is effectively already engaged in textual interchange with journals and newspapers, although not as yet with other collections of sketches. It did not take long for this state of affairs to come about, and it characterizes the industry from here onwards.

The paratextual features surrounding the biographical sketches themselves suggest that this commercial aspect of the industry was already a major factor in the organization of the text. Of *The Arrow's* twenty-five pages, eight are made up of advertisements. The inclusion of some nine advertisements for Yeats editions and related works such as the plays of Lady Gregory and Lennox Robinson, as well as, of course, for the Abbey Theatre itself, suggests that something more than an act of altruistic homage is taking place, although the first line of the first actual piece, John Masefield's 'William Butler Yeats', reads 'The writers of the world will mourn the death of William Butler Yeats.' To surround such elegiac biographical pieces with texts which present the author and his movement commercially brings another level of meaning to the issue. The normal commercial aspects of magazine production apply: costs must still be covered by advertising. It is the emphasis of this advertisement which is striking.

Paratextual features, then, change the balance of the magazine's otherwise panegyric (not necessarily entirely idealized) presentation of Yeats. On the page facing the Contents list and Editor's Foreword, appears an advertisement for the Macmillan 'Coole edition' of Yeats ('The collected and definitive edition of the works of WB YEATS', the by-line boasts, a claim that was debated by Warwick Gould, Richard Finneran, Denis Donoghue and others, in the pages of the *Times Literary Supplement* in 1984). This advertisement is interesting because of the textual presentation of the author's symbolic importance to the edition. In the centre of the full-page advert, Macmillan's selling-point is put to the reader: 'This edition will be limited to 350 copies for sale; each set will have the author's signature; there will be five or six photo-gravure portraits of the author.'

The significance, in the context of a volume dedicated to biographical sketches, of an advertisement focusing primarily on the poet's textual 'body' (his autograph and portrait), cannot be overemphasized. The question has to be asked, in the words of Stanley Unwin, the nephew of Yeats's early publisher Fisher Unwin, in *The Truth About Publishing* (1926): 'What is the advertisement designed to achieve? Is it expected to make someone want to buy the book who has never heard anything about it or its author before … ?' Macmillan's emphasis on the centrality of the author's signature and physical image suggests that this advertisement aims at the reader who sees the edition as the textual representative of the author.

It is possible to understand the commercial function of bibliography as an attempt to understand the author. This is Simon Nowell-Smith's argument in *International Copyright Law and the Publisher*: 'The commercial aspects of bibliography are as important as the enumerative and analytical because they aid what he conceives as "the ultimate justification of all bibliographic exercise, the understanding of writers and their texts" … ' The advert assumes that it shares the appeal of the biographical sketches for a particular kind of reader. The key position of Macmillan's advertisement in *The Arrow* is not, then, merely an act of commercially astute textual manipulation. It represents a very specific way of thinking about the relations of the textual body to the author himself. Of course, this position relies on the correlation of textual body with a belief in the text's importance as the product of an individual author, but it is clear that this is exactly what *The Arrow* is playing upon. The acceptance of such an advertisement for this specific text and in this position in the volume was the result of a judgement both about the kind of reader *The Arrow* would attract, and the ethics of product-placing the author in an issue dedicated to 'commemoration' with all the elevated associations that word carries.

In 1940, *Scattering Branches: Tributes to the Memory of WB Yeats* appeared, edited by Stephen Gwynn, the high-profile literary Dubliner. The collection was perceived by its publisher as one of two major 'authorised' texts (the other was Joseph Hone's W*B Yeats, 1865–1939* [Macmillan 1942]). Charles Morgan mentions only these two texts in *The House of Macmillan*, although of course the commercial interests of Macmillan make this a predictable bias: 'a commemorative volume, *Scattering Branches*, edited by [Yeats's] old friend Stephen Gwynn, and an authorised biography by Joseph Hone.' That Yeats had very little confidence in Gwynn's editorial skills in *The Shanachie* affair, as we have already seen, has no effect on the publisher's belief in the status of the volume.

Gwynn's collection is of interest firstly because of its editor's conceptualized reading of the author's role in his project. Yeats, as we shall see, is claimed for the nation, as a national figure, in the editor's prefatory material, so that the context in which these pieces appear is of a more ambitious scale to that of the 1939 *Arrow*. They are explained not just as individual outpourings, but as elements in an ordered, organized textual body, which has as its aims both a canonisation of the poet (as if it had not already been achieved) and also an almost sacred image of the Irishness of Yeats. The second point of interest follows on from this: the editor's notion of his collection's generic status and purpose, which, again, is related to the presentation of a 'united Ireland' in the face of the challenge posed by Yeats's death.

Looking at Gwynn's contribution to the collection, as editor, and as contributor of the introductory sketch, it is clear that *Scattering Branches* performs a number of roles. It acts as a measure of the changing attitudes potential biographical sketchers held towards the project. Published roughly a year and a half after Yeats's death, the volume is still close enough to the event itself to be affected both by the personal qualms of authors, who feel that the industry's burgeoning state is too much, too soon, and by the feeling that the demands of such a volume are too time-intensive. Gwynn's preface is an interesting editorial version of these concerns:

> Three names are missing from this assembly which I desired to include. But the Poet Laureate [John Masefield] had already spoken his brief emphatic tribute in *The Arrow* and did not, in this tragic time, feel able to do more. T S Eliot preferred to write at leisure and to his own limit. Oliver St John Gogarty was fully occupied in a lecture tour through the United States. But these three poets may be counted as fully with the rest of us in paying homage.

Here, Gwynn establishes several points: firstly, his project is incomplete (names are missing). Secondly, each approached author has personal, generic or practical reasons for declining to contribute (Masefield felt his own role had been fulfilled, T.S. Eliot felt the volume was inappropriate, or at least, not to his own tastes as to time constraints and word count, and Gogarty was already off doing other work). Finally, Gwynn asserts the editor's right to assume their consent to giving the volume their blessing nonetheless, creating a symbolic textual fullness which, through the absence of the editor's own choice of contributors, cannot reasonably be claimed even on its own terms.

It is in the introductory sketch, also called 'Scattering Branches', that Gwynn's larger plans for his volume, on the same unified basis, become clear. Where the other contributors write about Yeats, Gwynn assesses Yeats according to the aims of this collection, and attempts to explain the principles behind the book through Yeats's role in Ireland. As a result, a certain conceptual framework comes to dominate his discussion. We can identify the editorial emphasis from the following passage: 'When an Irish poet had lived valiantly, it was only right that some such tribute should be paid, above all by those of his own allegiance.' Gwynn is doing what Roy Foster claims that certain obituaries do: he conflates the poet and nationalist politics, uniting Yeats and the political values of 'Irishness' in order to elevate Yeats to the level of an exemplary Irishman, seen by his peers as 'the poet who was to give to Ireland what Ireland in their judgement most needed.'

The principles Gwynn appears to be arguing for as far as genre goes are still more symbolic. On the subject of the ordering of his anthology, Gwynn collapses together the act of homage with the structure of the volume. He writes that 'after all, the order does not matter; each man brings his branch; I throw down mine, and make way ... ' Gwynn imagines the act of collection as a memorial act, before one even reads the sketches: within the covers of the book, the variety and individual perspectives of each writer are preserved while also being subsumed by the editor's own visionary operative fiction.

It is surely disingenuous, though, for Gwynn to claim that he 'throws down' his own homage and 'makes way', since his own editorial framework has decided the inclusion, ordering and context of each piece. And even for Gwynn to claim that each piece is an act of homage in line with his own view of Irish culture is anachronistic, if not ahistorical: there is no sense in which the extract from Maud Gonne's autobiography *A Servant of the Queen*, which appeared in 1938, can be said to be produced in a spirit of homage to the dead poet.

The editor's inclusion of the extract might qualify for this label, but again, it is the use which has been made of the sketch in the context of Gwynn's volume, rather than the sketch itself, which imports the appearance of intentional unity here. The editor, even if working from noble principles, still puts the need for a culturally unified act of homage above the actual history of each piece individually. His editorial policy is an example of the developing editorial emphasis on Yeats specifically as an Irish biographical subject, which places the representation of the author in the context of a larger ideological movement.

If the representation of Yeats as a national author immediately after his death was an editorial operative fiction, it may follow that the cultural unity implicit in such a role was not a reality either. A literary controversy of the 1930s may give some suggestion of the dissonant and fragmented everyday tensions of Irish literary culture before Yeats's death. This may help to contextualize the biographical volumes of 1939 and 1940, by establishing Yeats as a figure who was deeply aware of the commercial-biographical relationship, and who even manipulated his reputation in the publishing world in order to fulfil what he saw as the correct editorial path for a specific edition. This controversy involved the posthumous edition of Æ's journalism, which was eventually published as *The Living Torch* (1937). The series of events is described in Monk Gibbon's retrospective account, *The Masterpiece and the Man: Yeats as I Knew Him* (1959). In this case, the biographical arena is used to argue specific positions in relation to Yeats as a textual saboteur. The volume suggests something of the problems faced, particularly by Dublin writers, in accepting Yeats as a hero of national culture.

When Æ died in 1935, his work on the *Irish Statesman* was due to have been edited and collected for Macmillan by the young poet, Monk Gibbon, whose claim to fame was once that he was one of only three people about whom Yeats had ever pronounced his hatred. Gibbon's account of Yeats describes the publishing history of *The Living Torch* in terms which suggest that Yeats was solely responsible for the problems this seminal edition of Æ's work faced in being completed, and which allow us to make a case for the often hostile situation Yeats was capable of stirring up in Dublin circles. Gibbon was not only to have edited Æ's journalism, but also wished to provide a biographical introduction (an eighty-page sketch, which *did* actually make it to the final version). The source of Æ's journalism, *The Irish Statesman*, is given suitably nationalist credentials by Gibbon in his description of its purpose: it was re-founded after the Treaty by Plunkett, he says, 'to give voice to the aspirations of the nation in politics, literature and art.' Gibbon is attempting to canvas the patriotic reader, here, by invoking the idea of *The Statesman* as the mouthpiece of the nation. By contrast, Yeats's cynical comments are used to establish him in opposition to this virtue, as he meanly concentrates his venom on Æ's habitual fostering of young writers in *The Statesman*. Gibbon cites the apocryphal tale that Yeats had years before criticized a plan by Lord Dunsany for Æ to edit a journal: 'I hear, Lord Dunsany, that you are going to supply groundsel for Æ's Canaries.'

The planned publication of Æ's journalism was thrown into jeopardy when Yeats found out about the project, which had been approved by Æ's son Diarmuid Russell. Yeats approached the son with a plan that Pamela Travers (who had attended Æ in his last weeks) should edit the material for the Yeats sisters' Cuala Press. Diarmuid Russell then wrote apologetically to Gibbon to ask to be released from their agreement. Gibbon terms this 'deliberate tyrannical interference'on Yeats's part. Gibbon wrote to Macmillan explaining that the manuscript Yeats had seen was an aborted project, started at Æ's request, which he would now be able to develop according to the dead poet's wishes. Despite Yeats's claim to Diarmuid Russell that he did not think the Cuala edition would 'interfere at all' with the Macmillan edition, Gibbon was (at the time at least) in no doubt as to the purpose behind Yeats's actions: ' ... just as he had refrained from speaking at Æ's graveside, so he was now going to come between Æ and his posthumous fame by side-tracking into a smaller hand-printed edition what should reach a far larger audience, and by taking all the heart out of my enterprise before I ever began it.'

Frank O'Connor recalls Yeats at Æ's funeral, first commending O'Connor for his speech, and then lowering his voice to ask, 'Have you copies for the Press?' Yeats obviously had a keen sense of the textual requirements for a successful publicity operation, although O'Connor apparently did not, for he had prepared no copies for the Press. To return, from textuality in Yeats's literary relations, to the specific textual arguments around *The Living Torch*, then, a Cuala edition being issued only weeks before any other would undercut the later arrival: the anticlimax would mean the later volume would be seen as 'a mere gathering of the leavings'. Where Travers's version would be perceived as the primary and thereby genuine act of collection, Gibbon would be side-lined into a supporting role as a minor compiler of any uncollected pieces. The first act of collection, which Cuala would appear to have carried out, would leave Gibbon's volume appearing as a generic poor relation, a second collection rather than itself the result of original ground-work.

In support of Gibbon's case, it is clear that the Cuala Press carried a high status as a publisher of Irish writers, and so Gibbon might be justifiably worried about the knock-on effect on his own volume. Robin Skelton has written that the Cuala Press 'gave a large proportion of the best living Irish writers a public, and a reputation.' In Ireland at this time, the Cuala Press's list of authors was, after all, as impressive as Macmillan's. Although it only published small editions (its largest recorded edition was five hundred copies), under Yeats's editorship it published important works by Synge, Æ, Douglas Hyde, Katharine Tynan, Lord Dunsany, Oliver St John Gogarty, F.R. Higgins, Robin Flower, Frank O'Connor, J.B. Yeats and of course, almost thirty works by W.B. himself. In comparison to Macmillan's list from 1912 to 1942, the larger firm had only five more names than Cuala in their 'brilliant

Irish succession', to use Charles Morgan's words in The House of Macmillan.

Typographical evidence suggests that Cuala was an illustrious house-style. In 1961, for instance, the Dolmen Press (the Cuala's descendant) used the distinctive features of Yeats's era in Mary Ballard Duryee's *Words Alone Are Certain Good*, using the red and black type (though in Pilgrim rather than the usual Caslon font), frontispiece wood-cut by T. Sturge Moore, and an end-note giving the place and date of publication. Although this particular edition is likely to have satisfied private rather than public demand for poems by this obscure poet, the correlation between the distinctive Cuala imprint and the high-profile reputation of the house is clear.

It is possible, then, that Gibbon's claim that Yeats aimed to use the Cuala Press to limit Æ's posthumous profile may have some basis in reality. However, two of Yeats's past positions in relation to publication issues cast an equal amount of doubt on his assertion. The first piece of evidence against Gibbon is that on 7 December 1904 Yeats had written to William Allingham's widow, Helen, about the proposed Dun Emer selection of some of his poems: 'It would be quite a small book, let us say 25 poems, and, could not in any case interfere with the sale of ordinary editions.'

The phrasing is close to Gibbon's own, when he paraphrases Diarmuid Russell: 'WB had read my manuscript notes, he did not approve of them, and ... he would like Pamela Travers to edit a short selection from the same mate-rial for the Cuala Press, which he did not think could interfere at all with mine.' This suggests that Yeats's approach to negotiation – stressing Cuala's position outside the competitive world of commercial publishing – had not materially changed since the early 1900s. Yeats may have approached the Æ edition in exactly the same way, in the belief that the Cuala really posed no threat to larger works, in which case the most that Yeats could be accused of was sticking to persuasive techniques, which had been successful in the past.

The second element, which goes against Gibbon's claim of Yeats's unscru-pulous approach, is also from Yeats's correspondence. On 17 October 1918 Yeats had written to advise John B. Yeats about his autobiography, then in the planning stage. W.B.'s advice combines a concern to exert personal control over JBY's publishing relations, and the commercial sense that dual publica-tion can work in the author's favour: 'I think it should be published here by Macmillan & Co ... I think Cuala should publish in the spring a new volume of letters and Macmillan issue both volumes of letters together.'

It would have been consistent, then, for Yeats to take such a view once more in this case almost twenty years on. It seems more probable that he had in mind an expansion of the commercial possibilities before him than a limitation of distribution and publicity through channelling the work into a small edition. However, both interpretations of Yeats's actions are certainly possible, since no correspondence by Gibbon, Yeats or Macmillan & Co seems to have survived.

Gibbon's book also filters these textual contentions in bibliographic and bibliophilic terms. Gibbon emphasises his own appreciation of Yeats's publishing and bibliographic history: the illustrated wall-cards of 'The Lake Isle of Innisfree' and 'Into the Twilight', produced by Cuala, sent to Gibbon by Lily Yeats, and described in great detail in the book, come to represent the innocent homage Gibbon has mistakenly made to Yeats since youth. 'When I was twelve,' he writes. 'Lily Yeats sent my father a wall-card of "Innisfree", with illuminated capitals and framed with narrow, black adhesive tape. It was for me.' Again, 'Soon I would possess a copy of the Poems bound in jet-black calf, with a bright red-and-gilt spine ... ' In contrast with this youthful adulation of all Yeats texts, Yeats's own later editorial actions come to seem the cynical acts of a literary tyrant. The bibliographic element in Gibbon's text is a key to the bibliographical character of Yeats. The fiction uses a bibliographic emphasis to prepare the ground for the account of editorial antagonism between the two men.

It is appropriate that Gibbon's revenge should be achieved on a textually encoded level. When Macmillan decide in Gibbon's favour and Yeats's projected edition is refused permission, Gibbon's editorial mission is to appear the gracious victor: 'I gathered all the many wise and generous things that Æ said about Yeats in *The Irish Statesman*. They are all there, to a total of more than twenty pages. It was proof at least that I did not allow personal feeling into my literary transactions.'

Yet the attempt to purge literary antagonism through the edited text is hardly successful, for in 1959 he writes that 'as it was, I remained dignified and – God forgive me – still angry after twenty years.' Gibbon enacts a double revenge, through his 'generously' edited 1937 text, in which the material included in the collection belies the intention that decided its presence, and his 1959 representation of his own bibliographical sensitivity in contrast with which Yeats's bibliographic habits seem designed to disrupt the writing community. In fact, it is Gibbon who is the one with ulterior motives for his representation of the bibliographic and publishing of his relations with Yeats: the biographical account is tuned to the anti-elegiac purposes of destroying the view that Yeats was an ally in the textual projects of his colleagues.

The volumes of collected tributes by Robinson and Gwynn, and Gibbon's longer biographical study, mediate Yeats's involvement in and effect upon the contemporary literary scene and the texts that were produced. They show the lack of cultural homogeneity in this period, despite the best efforts of the editors to create operative fictions that work on a national level. I have examined the bibliographic and stylistic positions of both the immediate and retrospective versions of biographical representation, the collective and the individual act of textually reconstructing Yeats.

The active controversy of 'all Ireland's bard' effectively prevented the perpetuation, in the next generation, of the textual apparatus of homage which was evident in 1939–40, and Gibbon's text takes a belated place among the critical perspectives of his contemporaries Seumas O'Sullivan and Patrick Kavanagh. As we have seen throughout the literature surrounding Yeats's death, eventually the textual elements of the critical industry emerge in imaginative forms. In 1949 Patrick Kavanagh looked back with a satirical perspective on the posthumous industry in general, and was especially critical of the published war of words between Irish writers, alongside their habitual and hypocritical renunciations when one of them passed on: 'We must bring out a *Collected Edition*. The money's a minor consideration – What most we want to bring success. Is an end to petty bitterness, No more slashing notices in the press But something broadly generous.'

The controversial status of author and text, both within the Irish lists of Macmillan and the social world of writers, was the key in mediating the kind of discontinuity we have since come to recognize as a feature of the period. This dissonance is effectively excised from the text and paratext of the edited collections of tributes, although as we have seen, the competing demands of commercialization and homage cannot be easily reconciled, and so disrupt the text's declared elegiac function. What has become clear, in examining these writings, is that the attitudes towards Yeats revealed though the bibliographic emphases of certain textual bodies, during the sensitive period following Yeats's death, aim for an uncompromised national identity, and are in this sense always politically active. Ultimately, though, the textual elements explored in this paper lead to the issue of how Yeats himself dealt with the choice between the path of homage or the path of contention in his position as a powerful author in the Ireland of his old age, how he prepared the ground for his own posthumous reception. As Frank O'Connor puts it, 'he was always engaged, sometimes wrongly, but always warmly.' Yeats's epitaph may well be seen as 'perverse' by O'Connor, as the chilled misanthropy of the lines belies the very real link between the author and the textual controversies in his last years. Yeats himself was a vital figure in controversial editorial wrangling over the literary representation of other writers, and so it is perhaps appropriate that, despite short-lived textual attempts to assert cultural unity through tribute volumes, the same disruptive tendency was present after he himself had 'passed by.'

'A Presence which is not to be put by'

KRISTÓF KISS

An analysis of W.B. Yeats's 'Among School Children' and comparison with William Wordsworth's 'Ode: Intimations of Immortality from Recollections of Early Childhood'

The main focus of my essay is on W.B. Yeats's poem entitled 'Among School Children'. I give a possible specification of its interrelated imagery and aim at capturing the dramatic movement and play of the interaction of past and present, which is, in my opinion, a central theme of the poem. After the analysis of Yeats's poem, I continue with tracking down the images of 'Presences', 'tree' and 'dance' in William Wordsworth's 'Immortality Ode', and give a possible reading of Yeats's poem in light of Wordsworth's similar ideas and images that may have influenced Yeats in the way he built up his poem.[1] Although it would be beneficial to discuss the two poems to a similar extent, I will only discuss just a few parts from Wordsworth's poem, the most relevant ones for my analysis. The goal of the essay is to highlight and depict the important role of children, memories related to childhood, and the act of recollection in Yeats's poem, with the short comparison of the two poems serving to emphasize this idea.

According to Cleanth Brooks, there is a clear inner logic in Yeats' poem. The seemingly aimless byways, the reflections which follow each other may seem, indeed, purposeless in themselves, but they all add up to the questions and images appearing at the end of the poem, making it eventually a poem of an 'organised' stream of consciousness.[2] It can be said that the poem's central concept or image to which other images get connected, what the whole poem gets animated by are the oblique 'Presences'. 'The questions with which the poem ends flow out of the "blossoming or dancing" described in the last line of stanza eight ("Labour is blossoming or dancing where ... "), and this process is itself connected syntactically (the same sentence) by an invocation of "Presences" in the second half of the preceding stanza.'[3]

What is remarkable in Yeats's poem (and also in Wordsworth's 'Immortality Ode') is the way these problems and ideas get dramatized.[4] Thus, it seems to be a good strategy to follow the poem's progression concerning the understanding of its imagery and dramatic evolution. The poem opens with depicting children (probably the most important 'Presences' of the poem) and creating an atmosphere that seems just as light and neat as the everyday life of the children:

> I walk through the long schoolroom questioning;
> A kind old nun in a white hood replies;
> The children learn to cipher and to sing,
> To study reading-books and histories,
> To cut and sew, be neat in everything[5]

Already in the first stanza there is a dramatic change. The everyday life of the children gets disturbed by the appearance of the poet: 'the children's eyes / In momentary wonder stare upon / A sixty-year-old smiling public man.'

After this change in the first stanza, there is already another one coming between the first and the second stanzas. The careless atmosphere of the first stanza is taken over by the philosophic nature of the second. The syntax of the stanza has also become more complex. But the two stanzas are connected: the Ledaean body has been evoked in the poet by a child in the schoolroom.[6] Furthermore, however abrupt the change may seem, Yeats balances the everyday, the childlike and the philosophic in this stanza also in another sense. The Ledaean body was evoked by the 'tale that she / Told of harsh reproof, or trivial event', and this has turned the childish atmosphere into tragedy. It is through this reflection and retrospection the poet realizes that 'our two natures blent / Into a sphere from youthful sympathy.' This stanza ends with the following lines: 'Or else, to alter Plato's parable, / Into the yolk and white of the one shell.' It is in the *Symposium* where Plato has Aristophanes account for the origin of love in the following myth: men were originally double; in punishment for their attack on the gods, Zeus split them in two 'as you might divide an egg with a hair'; and ever since, the half-men have tried to unite with each other.[7]

So it seems that 'the youthful sympathy', the childhood memory is what connects the present and the past up to this point for the poet in the dramatic situation of the poem. The idea that past and present are connected is explicated in the following, third stanza. One can get a look at the poet's mind while continuously lingering on this subject. It seems that the poet returns for a while to the classroom: 'I look upon one child or t'other there / And wonder if she stood so at that age.' Finally, at the end of the stanza, memory gets projected into the present, past conquers present: 'She stands before me as a living child.'

It is the poet's memory and imagination that takes over, maybe without exaggeration, overrules his present state of mind. The beginning of the following stanza seems to confirm this statement, as: 'Her present image floats into the mind'. The poet realizes that he has been overwhelmed by his memories and by his imagination. The constant floating of the images in the speaker's mind can be interestingly tracked down. After the realization of memory's conquering, the poet tries to consciously discipline himself (in a classroom setting, as if being a child again): 'enough of that, / Better to smile on all that smile, and show / There is a comfortable kind of old scarecrow.' There is again an act of balancing temporal layers. After the poet has been enraptured by the imaginative, philosophic sphere of memories, he struggles to focus his attention on the present, where he identifies himself as an 'old scarecrow', as opposed to the Ledaean body.

In spite of seemingly arriving back to the everyday situation, the focus of the fifth stanza is devoted to philosophical questions: 'what youthful mother would think her birthpangs compensated if she could see at that moment her son as he is to look sixty years later.'[8] The question is probably formulated to dramatize the already present and vexing theme in the poem: the struggle of present and past. Another layer is introduced in the stanza, and that is the uncertain future. In terms of temporal layers, the stanza is made quite complex in this way. We are talking about a mother's past dreams and expectations concerning the future that is connected to the 'scarecrow' in the present, who has sixty or more winters on its head. Every temporal layer seems to affect the speaker in the present, even though he has been depicted as one who constantly struggles not to let his memories and imaginings overrule him in the present: 'struggle to escape / As recollection or the drug decide'. In terms of the dramatic tension that is present in the poem, recollection can be easily considered as a drug, the narcotic effect of which constantly makes the poet's attention divert from the present, on the one hand, and makes him face haunting questions through a stream of consciousness, on the other.

In the following, sixth stanza, there is again a kind of balancing: the poet returns from recollection to the schoolroom situation and gives the compressed

lore of three famous philosophers, Plato, Aristotle, and Pythagoras in the some-
what similarly careless, childish mood of the first stanza. But after making the
generalizations, the following conclusion is drawn: 'Old clothes upon old sticks
to scare a bird.' It is not only the scarecrow that is scared by the philosophizing
ideas (that are devoted to the *remembrance*, again, but in this case specified to
the philosophers). By not specifying the last image to the scarecrow, the image
of the bird comprises, starting from the image of the egg-shell (the state of
unity), the different kind of images connected to 'birds': the swan, the Ledaean
body; and the scarecrow. Through such an association of the 'bird' imagery,
the connection between past and present gets dramatized in the stanza. The
seventh stanza opens thus:

> Both nuns and mothers worship images,
> But those the candles light are not as those
> That animate a mother's reveries,
> But keep a marble or a bronze repose.

After following the speaker's stream of consciousness, which was an
on-going struggle with memories from which different images and philosophic
speculations grew out that constantly reached up to the poet's present and
thus affected him, an arriving at a static point, a repose could easily imply an
arriving at a conclusion. 'And yet they too break hearts'. The last one and a
half stanzas of the poem concern what have been prepared for throughout the
dramatic representations of the poem, what Yeats calls the 'Presences' which
'keep a marble or bronze repose.' As I have claimed via Lensing at the begin-
ning of my essay, the 'Presences' are connected with the two famous images of
the poem that are the constitutive elements of its rhetorical closure:

> O chestnut-tree, great-rooted blossomer,
> Are you the leaf, the blossom or the bole?
> O body swayed to music, O brightening glance,
> How can we know the dancer from the dance?

'As I.A. Richards has suggested of Wordsworth's "Ode," so here, "Among
School Children" is finally a poem "about" the nature of the human imagina-
tion itself.'[9] Indeed, the two poems are similar in the sense that both poems
can be interpreted from the organic interrelations that build them up, mostly
in terms of symbolism and dramatic progression. Before turning to pointing
out similarities between Yeats's poem and Wordsworth's 'Immortality Ode',
the nature of the 'Presences', the nature of the images and symbols appearing
in Yeats's poem has to be clarified. As Kermode puts it, 'There is a tormenting

contrast between the images ... and the living beauty. And out of this contrast grows the need for a poetic image which will resemble the living beauty rather than the marble or bronze. No static image will now serve; there must be movement, the different sort of life that a dancer has by comparison with the most perfect object of art.'[10]

Being able to create such images is 'the gift of divine imagination ... Only the imagination can make it live as a symbol, and that is the true life.'[11] Structurally then, the images of the tree and dancing (in other words, the 'Presences') are the culminations of the evolution of the poem's imagery (and the dramatic representation of the moving or floating of past and present), thus, they constitute the most organic life of the poem's symbolism.[12]

What is interesting is that similarities between Wordsworth's 'Immortality Ode' and Yeats's 'Among School Children' can also be tracked down through the images of the tree, the dance, and the presence. In the fourth stanza of the 'Immortality Ode', out of the natural setting, it is the image of the tree that will first appear to make the poet face the inevitable problem of his:

> But there's a Tree, of many one,
> A single Field which I have looked upon,
> Both of them speak of something that is gone:
> The Pansy at my feet
> Doth the same tale repeat:
> Whither is fled the visionary gleam?
> Where is it now, the glory and the dream?[13]

The image of a festival, of dancing and (self-generated) amusement appears twice in the poem. First, before this formerly cited significant tree appears, at the beginning of the fourth stanza (the beginning of which is ecstatic, even to a certain point of unpleasantness. As Brooks argues, 'the poet seems to be straining to work up a gaiety that isn't there'[14] but he also remarks that in terms of the poem's dramatic movement, this attitude is structurally well applied in this stanza.) The second time it appears, it seems that it has lost its strained atmosphere and appears more natural towards the end of the poem, in the tenth stanza:

> Then, sing ye Birds, sing, sing a joyous song!
> And let the young Lambs bound
> As to the tabor's sound!
> We in thought will join your throng,
> Ye that pipe and ye that play,
> Ye that through your hearts today
> Feel the gladness of the May!

The presence also appears in the 'Immortality Ode' and it does so in connection with the child in the eighth stanza, when the child is described as the 'best Philosopher':

> Thou, over whom thy Immortality
> Broods like the Day, a Master o'er a Slave,
> A Presence which is not to be put by

In Wordsworth's poem, the 'best Philosopher', the child, is referred to as the 'Presence', and this presence is what gets articulated in a self-defining way, first, when the poet gives praise

> ... for those first affections,
> Those shadowy recollections,
> *Which, be they what they may,*
> Are yet the fountain-light of all our day,
> Are yet a master-light of all our seeing;

And later, when they are characterized in the tenth stanza in the following way:

> We will grieve not, rather find
> Strength in what remains behind,
> In the primal sympathy
> *Which having been must ever be*[15]

The stanza ends with the following lines:

> In the soothing thoughts that spring
> Out of human suffering,
> In the faith that looks through death,
> In years that bring the philosophic mind.

So then, in a nutshell, the recollection of the child (the 'best Philosopher') grants the speaker the ability of exercising 'primal sympathy', having a 'philosophic mind'. It is through remembering childhood that one can have a 'philosophic mind', and it is in this sense that the 'Child is Father of the Man' in Wordsworth's poem.

The claim I would like to make is that the act of recollection and the role of childhood and children in this act have, in Yeats's poem, a similar significance. Yeats addresses the 'Presences' as things 'that passion, piety or affection knows', that are, according to Lensing, 'images carved upon the minds and hearts of lovers, nuns and mothers, and, by extension, all of us.'[16] These may be equated with what Wordsworth calls 'primal sympathy'. All the three themes of lovers, nuns, and mothers, the seemingly aimless recollective detours were motivated by the sight of children. 'Such image-making is man's enterprise; passion, piety and affection are the inescapable actions of the human heart.'[17] It may be that, as a poet, this is Yeats's 'thanks to the human heart by which we live'.

'Presences' then, if they are the symbolic achievement of the organized elaboration of the poem's imagery, can be interpreted as memories that can be related to childhood experiences and to the images that have been evoked through recollection. The presence of children, memories related to childhood, and the constantly present theme of learning in Yeats's verse is what makes the speaker learn at the end of the poem that one cannot know himself from his or her childhood, or his or her memories, concerning his or her personality, that 'we cannot know the dancer from the dance' in the ecstasy of the brightening glance precisely because actor and action are caught up in a moment of a fully human and altogether earthly enterprise: human love and its expression in act. In terms of tracking down the dramatic representation of the 'floating' of past and present through the imagery of Yeats' poem, and especially with interpreting the poem in the light of similar parts and images from Wordsworth's poem, it can be argued that Yeats's poem can be interpreted as an act of giving a lyric expression of the nature of poetic imagination, of the workings and the nature of recollection, of 'Presences' that can give 'Thoughts that do often lie too deep for tears'.

NOTES

1. For the sake of saving space I refer to Wordsworth's poem as 'Immortality Ode'.
2. Cleanth Brooks, *The Well Wrought Urn: Studies in the Structure of Poetry* (London 1949), p. 165.
3. George S. Lensing, '"Among School Children": Questions and Conclusions', *College Literature* 13, no. 1 (1986): 2, accessed 3 December 2014, http://www .jstor.org/stable/25111680
4. Brooks, *The Well Wrought Urn*, p. 163.
5. W.B. Yeats, 'Among School Children', in *The Major Works*, ed. Edward Larrissy (Oxford 2008), pp. 113–5.
6. Brooks, *The Well Wrought Urn*, p. 166.
7. *Ibid.* p. 167.
8. *Ibid.* p. 168.
9. *Ibid.* p. 172.
10. Frank Kermode, *Romantic Image* (London–New York 2004), p. 102.
11. *Ibid.* p. 121.
12. *Ibid.* p. 123.

13. William Wordsworth, 'Ode: Intimations of Immortality from Recollections of Early Childhood' in *The Collected Poems of William Wordsworth* (Ware: Wordsworth Editions, 2006), pp. 701–4.
14. Brooks, *The Well Wrought Urn*, p. 124.
15. Both italics are added by me in order to highlight the self-definitive style of the subject, a feature that can be also found at the end of Yeats's poem, concerning the 'Presences', 'dance' and 'tree'.
16. Lensing, 'Among School Children', p. 4.
17. *Ibid.*

W.B. Yeats Poetry Prizes

There are currently three *W.B. Yeats Poetry Prizes* in the world. The longest running is the *New York Yeats Society* followed by the *W.B. Yeats Poetry Prize for Australia*, and the *iYeats Poetry Competition* organised by the Hawk's Well Theatre Sligo.

iYEATS POETRY COMPETITION

The iYeats Poetry competition is an online national and international poetry competition produced by the Hawk's Well Theatre in Sligo. The competition has garnered a prestigious reputation for the calibre of both entrants and judges in its short lifespan to date. There are two categories in the competition; general and emerging talent (for poets between the ages of 16 and 25).

Judges have included Katie Donovan; James Harpur; Theo Dorgan; Paula Meehan; Gerald Dawe; Enda Wyley; Vincent Woods; Rita Ann Higgins; Niall MacMonagle; Mary Branley. The winning poems are published on the Hawk's Well Theatre website. www.hawkswell.com

Tawnytallon
Tamhnaig an tSalainn

The grassed fort shrinks like an old muscle
tired of fighting rain

Dockings fill the haggard, a ring of sycamore
grows skin and lidded eyes.

Though the redcurrants are gone,
the old woman still tastes berries.

The house sleeps rough, its small rooms
and careful trunk open to rain and swallows.

Fields divided between brothers,
each gift a small parcel of herbs and whin.

The people hard as grit, farmed salt,
they gathered whelk, burned shells for lime.

Everything was for sale, except this;
their father making letters with a stick in ash,

so words might warm them,
and stories settle in their flint bones.

2010 FIRST PRIZE: JANE CLARKE

Lighthouse Keeper

It's twenty years now since they unmanned the lantern,
left it unwatched and sent me away,
yet I often dream of that broad beam of light
sweeping the white caps, combing the waves.

Some summer's day take the ferry to Clare Island,
see a black and white tower overlooking Clew Bay,
where I first heard my mother say the rosary for sailors,
watched her fry herring on the wood-burning stove.

Where myself and my father cleaned rain-battered windows.
Polished brass instruments till they gleamed like stars,
peered through the telescope at kittiwakes and guillemots,
searched for the Seven Sisters in dark, winter skies.

These landlocked days I'm washed up like wreckage
and all I could wish for is tussocks of sea pinks,
grey seals sleeping on rocks pummelled smooth,
echoes of footsteps on spiral stone stairs.

2011 FIRST PRIZE: JESSAMINE O'CONNOR

Hellsteeth

His house is sinking
The tin roof crumbling
He was springtime
Up on rotten ladders
Painting it red
A balancing act
Juggling brush, can and glass
I used to sit on cushions outside
Looking up squinting
Pouring the drinks, laughing
Cautioning him on the treachery of ladders

Now a hedge eats the front of the house
I try not to see it
Flying past on the road
Because I can't stop
He is belly-deep in rushes
Or chasing pigs
His dog doesn't hear my car coming
There's nothing out-of-date to drink
No one there
Since he's been gone
Every day of the last ten years

2012 FIRST PRIZE: RICHARD HALPERIN

Snow Falling, Lady Muraski Watching

At the window
of her simple home

She watches snow slowly falling
forming little hills in the garden.

Her husband whom she loved
dead a long while and still missed,

the Emperor's court its hypocrites and good souls
very far away.

A brown bird alights
shockingly alive in the snow.

Why am I still here? She thinks,
How will it all end?

Arthur Waley the translator stands
just outside of view

captures it
captures it.

* * *

I look up from my café table
at posters on which models

smiling insincerely endorse things
of which no one has the least need.

In the sky above a silver airplane
is on its way
where?

POETRY IRELAND SECONDARY SCHOOLS COMPETITION

JOANNE HERAGHTY

'Ireland 2013'

Yeats said romance was gone and dead.
Back in the day when most tears were shed,
Times when the IRA were up and strong,
Days when they could be *seen* doing wrong.
Not right now, when it's just biased times;
The next Love/Hate enlightening their 'newest' crimes.
Our time does differ from the old.
And if Yeats could talk right now, a different story would be told.

We're due a time when they all come home
Cross the shores and along they come.
Times when they are safe to stay,
Unlike, the war years when they were forced away.
The times when Yeats said our heroes did us good.
Now, no novelty; no heroes: villains. Although, there should.
President Higgins, the 9th to stand.
Who speaks of 'our own Aisling' in this shared land.
Our time does differ from the old.
And if Yeats could talk right now, a different story would be told.

A hundred years, we're still the same.
When the 'recession' is so easy to blame.
A choice that Sinn Fein never got to make.
Led by Kenny, the government's mistake.
Choices made, nor law but religion.
Medical misadventures under moral obligation.
A jury given a choice of two verdicts: one story.
Savita's death, goes down in history.
Our time does differ from the old.
And if Yeats could talk right now, a different story would be told.

Our time when networks send youths to their grave,
An earlier landing caused by how others behaved.
Still mothers shed tears upon the pit of their sons,
Ashes to ashes, a new war has begun.
But, a type that is different in a virtual way,
For the past is the past and today is today.
That's how our times differ to those of 1913
And if Yeats were here right now, what real difference would be seen?

ANNUAL W.B. YEATS POETRY PRIZE FOR AUSTRALIA

Established in 1996 the prize ran until 2004 and was resumed in 2011. The competition recognizes the important role of poets and gives encouragement to their work.

The Australian Yeats Poetry Prize promotes the legacy and ideals of William Butler Yeats, as well as encouraging the compostion and publishing of poetry. Since the inception of the Yeats Poetry Prize, the entries have come from the length and breadth of Australia, and cover a broad variety of themes.

Judges included: Assoc. Professor Elaine Barry; Professor Kevin Brophy; Dr Penelope Buckley John Flaus; Dr Earl Livings; Brian McInerney; Dr Carolyn Masel; Dr Robyn Rowland; Dr Heather Sebo.

First Prize is AU$500 and Second Prize is AU$100 with Certificates for winners and commended. On occasion Highly Commended Certificates have been awarded.

The Prize winning and Commended entries are also placed on the Prize Website www.wbyeatspoetryprize.com

2013 JOINT FIRST PRIZE: JOHN CAREY

Brett and Arthur

Whiteley in the Rimbaud museum at Charleville,
naked, with a photo of the poet covering his face,
something of a larrikin touch to the homage,
good-humoured worlds away from the shit-on-God graffito
that Arthur would daub on walls around the drab town
he had to boomerang back to when he ran out of cash.

Nothing surprising at first in the lure of Rimbaud:
the flammable property of poetry, Art as an all-up bet,
ambitions beyond the station of any art or craft,
the siren-song of transgression, absinthe and hashish
as a leg-up to climb out of yourself into something
that would see the big picture, be the big picture.

In his own portrait of Rimbaud, Whiteley doesn't stray far
from the only clear photograph of the young poet
and fills most of the canvas with a rendering
of emanations from the poet's brain. Partial inventory:
rounded hillocks and boulders, a white staircase
curving and tapering back into yellow sand, in the distance,

a rearing shark with the hint of a quivering buttock,
a mouth like a hammerhead vulva and something
that looks like the island of Doctor Moreau. Brett's
copied-out passages from Rimbaud might suggest only
a cursory reading but the details of the picture
point to a strong grasp of motifs and sources.

I have seldom found the surrealist mode disturbing
where the psyche seems to reach out to the ambient world.
There is often a lush efflorescence in the works,
more fluid and dynamic than the clinging shapes,
the stalled moves and furred textures of nightmare. Here,
there's a South-Sea sunniness that undoes Arthur's ferocity.
For the better, perhaps. And Whiteley's other representation
of Arthur? The sculpture of two huge matches, one live, one dead?

I must have blinked and missed the flare in between. Or I needed
warmth in my life, not a conflagration. A lost weekend
in Hell was season enough and illumination best dammed
and released in a steady trickle of lucidity.

Brett asked the question about Van Gogh: "is Art worth a life?"
The answer for me is "no" if it didn't need to be. So what
do you do when you're not delirious? Arthur:
"I set myself up as an exemplary burnt-out case
and mind a shop in a hell-hole in Africa." Brett:
"I roll down my sleeves and get on with the job."

The Man With Only One Eye

The man with only one eye
was a careful man. He was a man
who, like the Roman sculptor returning
a dusty chisel to its leather pouch,
would place his menacing pencil flat
upon the table before lifting his hand
to touch his temple.

The man with only one eye
was not one who would trust his fate
to another. He was not some pagan
who would worship a doubtful idol
or a barren stone talisman. He was as
particular as a high priest studying
a plea for clemency.

The man with only one eye
was a careful man. And since he
followed no religion, entered no shrine
of any kind, he passed his days like a
goat listening as the howl of the wolf
came ever closer. For he was a man
with only one life.

2012 FIRST PRIZE: ANGELA DAWSON,

Restitution

Like the slender masts of deserted ships, shrugged of their meagre rigging,
The gum trees shoulder the alpine wind, point accusingly at the bruising
    skies,
At the very air that gave passage to their baptism,
And lean their burnt bodies, like black exclamations against a floor of white.

The forest should be in a winter sleep, but the scourge of flame has left the
    trees bereft,
And where they would be slumbering they stand hollow, in haunting
    desecration.
Draped with the tattered scarves of peeling bark, their shed skin makes a
    loose curtain
That rattles a death knell in the birdless air, in the feverish chill of wind
That creeps between their lean-to frames and waves the sheaves of bark
Above a delicate seam of fallen snow, like a thrown quilt.

A snap of dry wood resonates like a cracked knuckle in the hushed landscape,
Wrung by the hands of a penitent wind that reaches a crescendo,
Rolls-in then exhales like a tide through naked branches, and loses its
    momentum.

These tendrils of peeled bark trail in long ribbons from the frail husks of
    lissom trees;
They flutter and caress like fingers reaching between their spectral figures,
In eerie supplication, as if beseeching for a last embrace.
Leeched of life, in ghostly stance, they seem to huddle in the rigorous cold,
Their forlorn remains petrified by the char and lick of flames,
Reduced to residue and amputated limbs, in attitudes of horror and
    indignation.
In the hush of the alpine doldrums, these ships' masts make no journey,
Their dun, unclad limbs stiff and parched in this barren arboreal grave.
Lonely stanchions mark the ruins of the forest now, cutting into a rim of sky,
Their pitch skeletons gaunt and harried, stark against the winter chill.

The forest is dead; yet, at the ravaged feet of trees there springs a stalwart
    foliage

On tender shoots of green, their leaves twining hopefully on slender wrists of
    Eucalypt,
In reverence at the grave of their guardians, peering from snowy burrows
At the lofty heights to which their being makes them aspire.

From the ashes, the saplings begin their restitution, to flourish and endure as
    the seasons pass,
To reach for the high canopy as the decades unfold, and to be crowned again.
Their journey has barely begun, but in veneration for their fallen kings,
From the shivering ground their clamour rises: the forest is dead, long live the
    forest.
(Lake Mountain)

2011 FIRST PRIZE: JANEEN SAMUEL

www.rainforest/leeches

Enter the forest
and you're blundering inside a giant
green, antiquated
computer from before the days of silicon:
cables risen out of main-frame earth
coil and loop about you;
wires snatch at skin
snagging with small shocks;
birds amid leaves flash off-and-on
lives in the underbrush fizz
like sparks down hidden pathways;
everything is interconnecting, blinking
with thought too green and alien
to comprehend

but your input is required:
black filaments come looping
over leaf mould, each raised end
questing towards you;
they scale boots, drop from trees,
plugging into flesh – you tug
one from its socket and it loops
back into you; meanwhile two more
are replacing it – four,
eight, sixteen, thirty-two – the forest
is a hydra downloading you
into itself

and uploading in return
a byte of forest-thought: "I
am one fragment of a World-Wide
once-upon-a-time, now rent-and-ravelled
green Web, and you
and your kind are an inconvenient
virus I have spawned."

Night Train Australia 1940s

The train lies stretched
within a sleeping town.
On the puddled platform
incandescent light yellows the mist;
blackness pools about
the dull gleam of dented milk cans.

The engine pants;
water slides around its seams
glistens on each rounded stud;
white steam
gusts from the piston cylinder,
slicks the boiler's underbelly.

A shovel bites through coal
clangs against the firebox door.
The stoker pushes back his cap;
his forehead banded white
above a grimed and sweat-streaked face,
as he swigs from a canvas water-bag.

The porter's trolley trundles past –
cardboard cases and hat boxes,
their hand-lettered labels tied with twine.

In the refreshment room –
travellers bang down
logoed teacups
rimmed with tannin;
wrap their trench coats closer,
rush with vapoured breath
to wrench down the single handle
of narrow compartment doors.

The station master readies
his whistle in clamped lips,

swings a low arc
of lantern light.

Wooden windows
clatter down through ratchets.
The engine gathers power,
tautens the couplings,
finds the first slow rhythm
of wheel on track and ballast.
The train moves into night.

2003 FIRST PRIZE: JOAN KERR

Natural History

1.
This disease
is like a novel present
we don't want to open.
We eye it, warily.

This disease
is so civil. It knows how not to shock.
It mentions, as an afterthought,
the remedy is poison.

This disease
shakes hands with us.
Turn your hands to life, to love,
the grip remains.

2.
I place my fingertips on your back.
Twice before I've felt cold sweat
slick under my hand.
Something working as you slept, using dark
to run the body's trenches unobserved.

Unwilling sentry
stepping out into galvanic air.
Something's ready,
humming through the earth.

This is not malice, this is only history.
Expert, indifferent, exact.
No less or more important death,
no different size of grief.

3.
Orange cat sleeps by firelight
nose to tail
a perfect circle. The house holds its arms

around us and we breathe together
you and I, the cat, the fire, the house

now winter creeps
from the silent river
draws his pelt across the grass

this is the last of the red-leaved autumn years
this year he will come in as one coming home
curl up in my empty house.

2001 FIRST PRIZE: FRANKIE SEYMOUR

Night Mission

Half the night long we trudged in mud
in the dark of the moon,
knowing the slick curl
of the whispering water's edge
only by the mirrored starlight
in its inky ripple.

Cattle hooves
stampeding around us
invisible,
stark, drowned trees,
lean dark bars, black
on black of the star-jagged sky.

Hoarse stage whispers,
distances deceiving,
no landmarks,
only the need, the unanswerable,
uncompromising needs be there
when night thinned.

2000 FIRST PRIZE: TIM METCALF

Stages of Dying

denial
In anatomy class
we cut textbook lines
into the dull clay of our body.
We shook dismembered hands,
and bragged of cricket with arms and balls
for a joke.
We washed the formalin from our hands
for the next two days.

shock
A pregnant girl collapsed.
The scalpel cut quick and deep.
Her grey belly peeled apart.
The monitors ticked:
a mechanical requiem.
White gloves pulled out the baby
cold and dead like the streets
I wandered half that night.

guilt
As an intern
I was anxious, and obedient.
To cure at all costs
was the boss' creed.
I had no time for the old woman
we made betray her faith.
Soon after the transfusion
she died of cancer.

anger
Some drunken bastard
hit this woman with his car.
Her young breasts quivered
each time we thumped her chest.

Over half an hour
her face, burned alive,
set cold, branding for life
the mind of her child.

sorrow
Was it happy, his final memory?
This poor bloke, purple faced
and next in line for death?
I was naïve, yesterday,
regarding his broken heart.
Today I wouldn't go anymore.
Tonight I was drunk.
There were tears, briefly.

acceptance
I went to see an elder on his beach up north.
He didn't say much.
There was this sky-blue dreaming;
the ocean its luscent mirror,
flawless like an egg.
I heard he died around sunset.
That night a warm breeze blew
the soothing tune of the sea.

1999 FIRST PRIZE: JUDY JOHNSON

Girl On A Paling Fence

It's a trick the seven year old has been practising all morning; space-
    walking around
the palings with the balance bar of her arms outstretched. Her sandles
    are blue, the blue

of her mother's plastic necklace the girl once broke, then hid, piling its
    kaleidoscope of
planets into a box under her bed. Now she threads herself along the
    string of the fence.

looking down to two striped feet with their strapped-in cargo of toes.
Her father lies in the house behind, his limbs aligned for visitors. His
    polished shoes

rest exactly on one horizontal line of the chenille bedspread. In her
    pockets are the two things
she has stolen from his bedside table. No one has noticed. All morning
    her mother's eyes

have been like brown stones sinking beneath the weight of water. The
    girl does not touch the
heaviness of the objects she has taken for fear of a similar drowning. Still
    she knows their

dimensions; the tin that becomes the words 'cool' and 'slick' when held
    in the palm of the
hand, the sailor's face riding the crest of a wave, and the name *Dr Pat*.
    Her father once taught her

how to open the lid without spilling the contents. He let her twist it back
    and forth
while pressing down until she felt the seal give up its aromatic splinters.

In her other pocket is a hard black stem with a chewed end. She keeps
    the two apart by the
warmth of a body-width. She measures their coldness this way, as she
    measures the fence

by the flat spaces where she can place her feet and not by the spikes that
    divide them.
For months her dreams will be filled with impaled things, landlocked
    sailors buried above ground,

bushfires, but for now she remains balanced – the pipe on one side,
    tobacco tin
on the other, and in the middle her unlit heart.

1998 FIRST PRIZE: AILEEN KELLY (1939–2011)

The Lads

When she says 'our lads'
it's the boys hoisted out of sleep
packed with breakfast
and bunted off to learn for their long good.
Not only. It's the boys
her sons father and cosset.

Not only. It's the vanished great-uncles
three stringy brothers that her grandmother
kissed to English work or war and prayed
by mass and manners they might still be Irish.
The how-many-greats grand-cousins
who sailed surly from Cork or Carrickfergus.

The shot, the hanged. The crop-haired crop-eared
scrappers, the brains turned curdle
that should have been scholar or priest.
The quick-eyed old-faced youths hauled out
from skin-shed hulks to pick the rock
and starve in Botany Bay.

And no, with a pause with a headshake
but yes, most lost of someone's sons
crunched out of shape by noise
how could they ever grow human?
those blunt young heads baptized in old black bile
that only knew the strength of bomb and kneecap,
bewildered by a new silence, stupid from it:
every friend gone soft, the doors shut hard,
cold in the street that leads to hell through Omagh.

When she says 'our lads'
it's a blade to cut through boggy fibre,
tangled layers of generation
heavy for stacking. To build or burn.
Galway '98

1997 JOINT FIRST PRIZE: JUDY JOHNSON

Water-Wheel Man

Every dawn he is there swimming freestyle behind the waves. Each
limb-measured stroke seems to lift the sun further up and over the
    horizon.

Yet despite this, and the red sea parting beneath the directive of his
    palms,
he is clearly not God's understudy. A fulcrum pivots between his shoulder

blades; his pendulum neck swings 'No' to mortal implication
of each breath. And those curved hands are fixed in repetitious

scooping, up and over ... bailing out one small rowboat
          in the day already sinking

1997 JOINT FIRST PRIZE: PAUL HUTCHINSON

Brendan's Monks

Sweet Jesu! the bone-crush of a seventh wave, and a swill-
song for Epona ("oh sister, ride over us"), a prayer to Christus
Forkbeard: "Remember us, should our guts break open
and we wash into your bothy ... "Long after we forget land,
before we reinvent it, Brendan's our crazy father, constant
star-point, wind-leathered, blue-fingered, cormorant eye
bulging against webs of salt. Does every mad hero clasp
a shield of useless visions in front but only hold
the knowledge of the next word needed"? Against
the rosary clack of oars, sheets and rudder-pin, I know
it takes more handspans now to set the horizon.

So what does he go by, but memories of seagull spit,
soft vulvas of shellfish, a finger stain on the parchment's
creases, a lodestone buried at birth in his head. And if
we eat him, he'll just be wrought our newest god: no good
having this one's breath boiling in our dreams. Let me
tell you my plenty of them: one night the rowlocks
turned into quail soon minced by taloned skies,
each wave-swell bore a pannikin of wept berries;
once we fell right round the cauldron's starry belly; waking
once to smell of pigs, beeswax and bookdust; and once,
the black once I saw him, waist-deep, giant-fisted, cursing
God's ocean for burying his denied new land until he stopped
down deep to drag it and us up out of its coldest pit.

1996 FIRST PRIZE: JOEL DANDO

Ubi Sunt

On the surface those times that we did fall
in love. And the long climbs back out again.
At the centre, more intimate than all
of the dids are the didn'ts; the call
undialed, or left ringing; words that were not made flesh,
or once only – even then, but a press

of fingers to a not unwilling cheek.
My hand, you wondered why, stopped, poised to curl.
Flesh never doubts desire: Spirit was weak
to claim an uncertain future, the pearl
oystered in that moment. Some watchful streak
of fear, or honour, checked my will. I knew
the cost of what you promised, and withdrew.

But first the blackness oceaned us. My skin,
bathed in your solvent gaze, merged with the night
that skimmed your sleeveless arms, that you breathed in
and out. The dark was deep enough to light
the penumbra of what never happened.
Years on, my thoughts curve round that unfilled moment yet,
retracing futures lost in silhouette.

ANNUAL W.B. YEATS POETRY PRIZE OF NEW YORK

Established in 1994, the competition recognizes and encourages good poetry as part of the society's mission to promote and publicize the legacy and ideals of William Butler Yeats. To use Yeats's words, the aim is to 'sing what is well made'.

Annually, more than 100 poems are submitted, largely from within the USA, although submissions in English may be entered from other countries. Entrants may send several poems, each of which is judged separately and anonymously. There is a small processing fee for each poem. Awards include a $500 first prize, $250 second prize, and honourable mentions.

Judges, most of whom served for two successive years, have included Jessica Greenbaum, Billy Collins, Eamon Grennan, Campbell McGrath, Samuel Menashe, Paul Muldoon, Marie Ponsot, Alice Quinn, Grace Schulman, Harvey Shapiro, and Bill Zavatsky.

The winning and honourable mentions are placed on the Society's website www.yeatssociety.org

2014 FIRST PRIZE: MICHAEL MILLER

The Different War

Lifting his son from the sandbox,
He remembers the roadside bomb roaring,
The shuddering air subsiding.
He rushed to Riggins,
Lying unconscious in the wreckage.
Lifting him under the shoulders,
Pulling him away from the flames,
His body came apart at the waist.

II

Like a white hole in the black sky
The full moon glares
Upon the naked field
Where he walks at midnight,
Sowing it with his grief
For dead comrades.

III

When his wife lies upon him
He thinks of body armour;
How naked, how vulnerable he feels
Without it. But he is not in combat,
He is making love with his wife,
This gentle woman whose unfolding hands
Have never held a rifle.

IV

He watched the Medevac helicopter
Lifting Garcia in a Skedco harness
And imagined a stork
Carrying him in a white cloth
Away from the firefight
Where each wound was different,
Each death the same.

V

He dreamt he was vomiting bullets,
Shrapnel, grenades, then wiped
His mouth, stroked the snake wrapped
Around the dagger on his forearm
And went back to war.

VI

Pocked with bullet holes,
The veined rock rose at the foot
Of the mountain painted with
The words: Kilroy was Here.
But this was not France, not Germany,
This was the different war;
In his time, this was his war.
In the blue solarium

VII

He visited Henderson at Walter Reed
And recognized his face but not
The curling snakes of scar,
Not the smile that five surgeries
Had changed, and he felt
Embedded in the company of the maimed.

VIII

In the Taliban's domain
He had fought for his life,
Not for his comrades or 9/11
But to return to his son
Shouting, "Daddy!"
And his wife offering love
Through the portals of
Her body.

2013 FIRST PRIZE: ALISHA KAPLAN

A-6876

It's Sunday afternoon and
we're sitting on my roof,
talking about tattoos.
Damian won't get one
because he wants to be

pure. Lulu would if she
wasn't afraid of needles.
Jane has three and I think
They're all stupid but
I would never tell her.

I say I want to get a Zen
Buddhist symbol but I wouldn't
because I'm not a poser and I
couldn't be buried in a Jewish
cemetery and it would probably

kill my grandmother.
Then, as the Holocaust
often sneaks its way into
my conversations, I
mention her number.

Damian asks if she ever
considered getting it
removed. Jane says that would
make a great story. Lulu
shoots her a dirty look.

I agree, it would be
a good story, but not
one I could write because
my grandma would never
remove her number.

I know then that I can't
ever get a tattoo
because her number
will always be there,
a permanent souvenir

of pain far worse than needles,
far deeper than ink in skin,
so anything I write on my
body would be trivial,
no, an insult.

The only tattoo
I could get would be
my grandma's number.

2009 FIRST PRIZE: STEVE LAUTERMILCH

Basho Solo

Thirty years in a monk's
hut, island hermitage of an artist's boat cottage;
wayfarer rain and wandering storm,
now and then a cloud, a gathering mist
for a hiking companion.
Visitors,
the haze and fog that sidle in,
sun at their back, burning them away, ghosts
in steaming rags and tatters.

Syllables, whispering silence,
dissolving phrases, watery dregs of tea.
Language that floats and fades,
shuffles down a path, hedges and back roads
out of mind. In the one door and out the window.

Home.

Creaky gate where walk
leads to raft, river to plunge. Well fed
moon, stooping under the horse chestnut tree,
mad to get out of the rain –
leaves dripping or falling, streams that puddle
under your feet –
robe, mantle, sleeves
wet as your cheeks – every bone and sinew
in your skin bag aching or preparing.
Cloak like a rice sack torn open,
knots and threads catching on branches and thorns.
Bird neck craning this way that, trying to escape.

Basho.

Porous cup, fire cracked clay, fingers and palms
of a child always grasping, begging for more.

Trying to read the map.
Eyes, bleary and going blind, do you know, did you ever know
what you saw. Where you stand. Porch step. Deck.
Wobbling bottom of a leaky boat.

Deer's cry, bleating, water's ripple, chanting,
moon down on all fours, searching rushes
and scouring reeds, ears snatching at scraps of song,
hints and traces of notes lost in the bamboo –

Her hand, brushing the hair out of her eyes,
your fingers along her lips, a strand of her hair
caught on your tongue, the sudden spill of her breath
touching your face, reminding you, forcing you
to remember to breathe –

Rhythms and tones of a woods that always keeps changing,
always keeps time – the rise and fall of limbs
beyond hearing, beyond time,
beyond words –

Basho.

Tree leaves. Water leaves. Leaves.

2008 FIRST PRIZE: STEVE LAUTERMILCH

Gaia's Song

When I was young
water taught me how to speak.

Once I spoke, reed and stone and canyon wall
taught me to pause and listen and hear.

But light and shade and hazel leaves
broke that dream and brought me to my feet.

In a round of standing stones on holy ground I watched
the sun dawn and magnify in seed.

Grasses and flowers heavy with dew, dancing
long-haired corn rose and burned like children loose in a field.

Bearded rain, darkening earth, mountains like bears
asleep with snow, each of these took turns to lay me down to sleep,

bedding me away like the dragonfly in amber
the needled forest floor and rainbowed desert plain, the seep

of sand and rising mist, slip of fog clasping my hands
until my closed palms opened and were free.

Walking fish and swimming, diving birds took me
to the shore where every breath I breathed

joined everything that breathes.
Now a face looks back in every shape I see.

I hear a voice
on the lips of bud and berry, salmon and scree.

In the storm that whispers and in tongues of fire
a name is calling on every wave and tide. Who are you, easy

and hard in your ways, who come to talk but like a breeze
turn and die away.

Many you are named, and savage.
And sweet.

2007 FIRST PRIZE: CHARLOTTE MUSE

Song for Rana

Epigraph: The frog (Rana; of the family Ranidae) is disappearing all
    over the world.

Come back to our dreams with your cold and warty skin
your sideways eyes
your splayed hands clothes pin-fingered,
the litheness of your open thighs
ballooning of your singing throat
alarming,
alarming

We knew before the forests came
and went that you were magic.
We'll look past your crude disguise,
we told you. Fetch the golden ball
and you shall sleep upon our pillows singing
buttercup
buttercup

We wove you in, we made you songs,
mm-hmm, mm-hmm,
We thought you were unpleasant but we did,
mm-hmm,
A prince of a fellow, all in all,
we listened for you spring and fall
mm-hmm, mm-hmm, mm-hmm

When it was midnight, I held my breath
and kissed him handsome.
He waltzed me to my room.
Kick your shoes off, do not fear,
bring that bottle over here,
he sang, and I did. Outside,
under a black and silver sky
the voices of a thousand frogs
rang like muffled bells.

But who needs the frog
when the prince is underneath?
we asked ourselves,
netting frogs from their dark ponds
by the thousands. We'd hand one,
pickled in formaldehyde,
limp as a potholder,
to any biology student
who'd mine for the giblet heart,
the intestines rolled neatly as socks in a suitcase.
Such uses they found
for your body, Rana!
We've seen what makes you tick.
We know what makes you croak.

And now you answer
with an awful silence.

Please. Don't go.
We want you back.
We see now what we've broken.
We didn't mean to break it
break it break it. We didn't
mean to break it.

2006 FIRST PRIZE: MARY LEGATO BROWNELL

I Thought Only And Finally of Sound

(after Joseph Cornell's Aviary Boxes, Chicago Art Institute)

Never was I afraid of the city. It was the sound
of flight being let go of, and whenever I turned to the coming
height of its stones, as sparrow and finch – and to the wind, the wind
    taking my face –
stars would draw me to their degrees, and I would night by night
be Auriga's whitened thoughts – the man holding
the goat and her two across my back. Never had I wanted to

be an instant of will, to
tender about the city as a grey wing sound
dividing and crossing, or a word of wood or stone holding
shape in my hands, believing in form compassionate coming
to make safety of us all – all night
as we walked, all day as we dreamed. I understood the face

of the city as they saw its shimmering haste, its attention, the face
of its common offerings arched to the stone that held all other stones to
their roots, rain falling to the streets, slipping the night
of its shadows. And it was neither the city nor what they loved of it – the
    sound
of will or of sudden steps – that brought me to the aviaries, but the idea
    that coming
flight was not the work of wing, feather, adjustment, height holding

stone, wood, weight, feel. And in my first dovecote, pigeon was holding
her tappened fingertips against a worn clip latched to a metal rod. I
saw her press her face
close to the lathe levelled edge of a frame, to a spun handle, to a nail.
And in that coming
moment, in her pause and in her aim to
court what staying was, I heard the sound
of clay pipes, glass rings, memories, of lead shavings fitted against a night

dowel. And before she left, I hoped that in a night

of stars untimed, she would turn to happiness, holding
in the changing age of city, motion, sound,
the near touch of golden owl's lift, his tempered will against mine, and in
    his face,
not that pull of flight or stay – tree bark; galls; lichen to
stiffen the oval perch of his claws; moss. So I held to his coming

as if it were the return of a name, a word of will coming
against it all, and I made a box so fine and full of watching night,
that even your absence was radiant. Even your rest, taken. And you
    would rise to
it – the city still; time held close, its holding
like the envelope of wind you knew, like light falling across your face.
I thought only and finally of sound.

Let the sound of their coming wings rise, go by. We lose nothing. Let their
faces be bird-thin and shining. Let night remain. And may God forgive
    us as they move past – we
who are holding, to our stiffened chests, everything they had to offer.

2005 FIRST PRIZE: MARGARET J. HOEHN

The Geography of Distance

Every night, little towns like the one in which I live
disappear. The leave only their absence
in the creosote and sage;
on stony hillsides, with grey-needled pines;
along plains that sway with centuries
of sedges and oats.

It starts when the clerk of the five-and-dime
sweeps the dust from the floors,
slips off her apron, flips the sign
in the window to closed, locks
the door behind her. Cars on the main street
fade away, the grocery store empties,
the lights of the houses go out, one-by-one–
Then, distance settles in like an unlit road
unspooling through the years.

How many pockets the night has,
how many satchels it must carry
because the space between the stars
is never small or simple,
and darkness is never just a lack of light.

And what is distance, but the world
expanding in the darkness so far beyond oneself–
or maybe it is the wilderness within:
those stretches of deserts, of flatlands
and slopes, that inhabit the heart–
the miles pulled forth by longing.

Each sleepless hour is an endless road,
a longing, a clock that turns
overhead like a far away moon,
like a sadness of muted light. Each hour
is the estrangement of names, of memories
and landscapes, and all their permutations.

All night, I turn with the hands of the clock
toward the half-light of dawn, toward
the moment when distance must release
its clutch on these towns, must scatter
them back, like pages torn from nostalgia,
to the places where they belong.
Then night will pack its bags,
fold into itself, travel on.

2004 FIRST PRIZE: BARBARA CROOKER

All That is Glorious Around Us

(Title of an exhibit on The Hudson River School)

is not, for me, these grand vistas, sublime peaks, mist-filled overlooks,
towering clouds, but doing errands on a day of driving rain, staying dry
inside the silver skin of the car, 160,000 miles, still running just fine.
Or later, sitting in a café warmed by the steam from white chicken chili,
    two cups
of dark coffee, watching the red and gold leaves race down the street,
    confetti
from autumn's bright parade. And I think of how my mother struggles to
    breathe,
how few good days she has now, how we never think about the glories of
    breath,
oxygen cascading down our throats to the lungs, simple as the journey of
    water
over rock. *It is the nature of stone / to be satisfied /* writes Mary Oliver,
    It is the nature
of water / to want to be somewhere else, rushing down a rocky tor or
    high escarpment,
the panoramic landscape boundless behind it. But everything glorious is
    around us already:
on the pavement, where the last car to park has left its mark on the glis-
    tening street,
this radiant world.

2003 FIRST PRIZE: J. MICHAEL PARISH

Moths; Night-Fishing

It's not their fault that their wings and mouths are selfish—
that they use them to make trouble all around this mountain lake
or that their lust for the warm places has them recorded
among the Johns of the world, seeking from lippy globes of lamp and
          moon
nourishment, clarity, warmth, in all of which their brief faces shine like
life's first breath.

How pleasurable to be sliding across this smooth surface in a boat,
a skin of fog forming,
the immediate sound insects preening and probing, and the splash of fish
freeze-framed by a bolt of moonlight. Motor off:
the purest relaxation is the predator in his element?
civilization means we don't even have to purr anymore.

The slender bass, horizon-eyed, suspend in their aqueous humor
between gravity and the parabola of escape, and the methods
they choose to distinguish between my lure slowly spinning and the
fluttering wings of survival are the business of the world made plain.

Sligeach: Sligo – 'The place of Shells'
Slí Dhá Átha – 'The way of the two Fords'

'Sligo in heaven murmured uncle William / when the mist finally settled down on Tigullio' (Ezra Pound Cantos 77/473)

A poignant memory came upon me the other day while I was passing the drinking-fountain near Holland Park, for there I and my sister had spoken of our longing for Sligo and our hatred of London. I know we were both very close to tears and remember with wonder, for I had never known anyone that cared for such mementoes, that I longed for a sod of earth from some field I knew, something of Sligo to hold in my hand. It was some old race instinct like that of a savage, for we had been brought up to laugh at all display of emotion. Yet it was our mother, who would have thought its display a vulgarity, who kept alive that love. She would spend hours listening or telling stories of the pilots and fishing-people of Rosses Point, or of her own Sligo girlhood, and it was always assumed between her and us that Sligo was more beautiful than other places. I can see now that she had great depth of feeling, that she was her father's daughter … .Yet ten years ago when I was in San Francisco, an old cripple came to see me who had left Sligo before her marriage; he came to tell me, he said, that my mother 'had been the most beautiful girl in Sligo'. W.B. Yeats, Au, p.31

To the memory of those Sligo citizens

Founders of the Sligo Yeats Society

Initiators of the First Summer School in Ireland

The Annual Yeats Summer School

On the evening of 20 May 1958 at Sligo County Library, Stephen Street, a group of men and women – all of great vision – convened to discuss a Memorial to William Butler Yeats 'The Sligo Poet' (as his friend Oliver St John Gogarty always greeted him). The initial membership fee of five shillings each, paid by the six attendees, contributed a total of £1. 10. 0 (approximately £85 in 2015 value), which was the initial working capital. They had responded to a meeting between the then County Librarian Nora Niland and a visitor from Cambridge T.R. Henn, on how to honour the poet W.B. Yeats, in his home town. Tom Henn's suggestion to Nora Niland, 'The obvious way to commemorate the poet is by a summer school devoted to the works of the poet and his contemporaries', had led to this meeting of like-minded local people. And so it was that Sheelah Kirby, Eileen Lambert, Tom McEvilly, Rev. Fr Tom Moran, Nora Niland and Frank Wynne founded the Yeats Society and the International Yeats Summer School, Sligo in the heart of 'The Yeats Country'.

C. 1950 Sligo pharmacist T.P. 'Tony' Toher placed in the window of the entrance foyer of his shop on O'Connell Street (principal street of the town) a collection of 38 photgraphs of places associated with W.B. Yeats in the County of Sligo. He headed the exhibit 'The Yeats Country', by which Sligo is now noted today throughout the world.

What those who peruse these pages must never overlook, is that the founders were volunteers, and all they did, including the legacy we have today, comes from their selfless devotion to the task they undertook.

A Glimpse of the Geology of 'The Yeats Country'

GERRY FOLEY

William Butler Yeats may have been unaware of the influence of Sligo's geological past on his creativity; nonetheless he interacted with the sculpting hand of nature in a highly imaginative and passionate way. It was nature's great sculptures, the mountains, glens, lakes and rivers, the geology, which fuelled the dynamic images embedded in his poetry.

The shaping of the landscape was imperceptibly honed, over innumerable millions of years, by great geological forces, which are still very much at play today. The countryside reveals its epic tale through its rocky outcrops and stony crags. Great ice sheets hewing and plucking rocks, gouging out valleys, carving rivers in response to ever changing climates. Over eons frost, aided by the actions of the sun, wind and water, painted the geological canvas of the Yeats County of Sligo. Nature's artist followed the dictates of the cosmos long before humans appeared on Earth. The artist does not rest.

W.B. may not have been mindful of geological facts when he penned 'The Stolen Child' but one of its lines reflects a geological truth. 'Where dips the rocky highland of Sleuth Wood in the lake … ' It is a prehistorical fact, that these rock formations are part of a great range of folded highlands that protrude into the high mountains of Scotland and Scandinavia. At Slish the rock layers, which once lay horizontal, are now twisted and folded and dip under Lough Gill only to reappear as the protruding hump of the Ben Bo ridge, 'Peak of the Cow', near the town of Manorhamilton. Once upon a time they were sediments carried into a primordial sea; to settle into level planes like the unrippled surface of a tranquil lake. But the evolutionary forces of the planet Earth squeezed and distorted these rock beds into wrinkled strata like the waves in the sea. 'When I play on my fiddle at Dooney / Folk dance like a wave of the sea'. To the observant eye the subtleties of nature stand glaring obvious.

Near the third strand at Rosses Point another crest of these old rocky waves tantalising protrude through a grassy meadow near the foreshore. 'The Point', as it is known locally, was a place frequently visited by the Yeats family and it is here that the Garavogue River meets the wild Atlantic Ocean. The waters of this gentle river transport recycled sediments from the remains of the ancient continent and more recent geological formations, to be reconstituted into a future landmass beneath the salient water of Sligo Bay. The landscape is not static but imperceptibly changing. Nothing is permanent!

In the massive limestone outcrop at Dooney Rock, on the shores of Lough Gill, there is strong evidence, in the embedded fossilised corals, that a clear blue tropical sea once covered this area. Maybe the 'Fiddler of Dooney' plucked from the cosmos the eternal vibrations of an ancient sea. Some miles away, on the upper levels of the Ben Bulbin table land, identical coral-rich rock outcrops which were once at the same level as Dooney now lie at the higher altitude of some 500 metres above sea level. An imperceptible turbulence beneath the surface of the earth pushed the Ben Bulbin plateau high above the surrounding lowlands. High up in the grey limestone crags is a massive cave called 'Diarmuid and Grainne's Bed', which may have been the subterranean passage of a long vanished underground river.

The epic tale of 'Diarmuid and Grainne's Bed' was part of the folklore environment in which Yeats's creativity flourished.

Not far from the cave, deep within the old mine tunnels the ghosts of Barytes miners toil. Their voices echoed by dripping water down abandoned shafts. Old miners would talk of the mountain groaning and slowly shifting as if resettling in an uncomfortable bed. The mountain is not an inert but a moving dynamic entity with an existence of its own. All nature was alive, animated, in the mind of the poet. Through his unfettered imagination he was, and we can be, tuned into the subtle tales of nature.

The Ben Bulbin plateau is intersected by four great glens, each shaped by massive ice sheets during the last ice age which put the present touch to their majestic shapes. The glaciers, over 500 metres high, hacked and hewed their way through weaknesses in the rocky outcrops, giving the beautiful vertical-walled glens of Glencar, Glendaley, Gleniff and Glenade.

Across the bay the outline of Knocknarea portrays the direction of the ice flow, with its south facing humpback slopes and north facing steep crags over-looking Strandhill. Evidence as to the height of the glacier ice is abundant at the mound on its summit. The stone mound, built by stone-age people, is a mixture of limestone and metamorphic rocks and is reputed to be the burial place of the mythical Queen Maeve. The metamorphic gneisses originated in the Ox Mountains across Ballisodare bay: plucked from the mountain outcrops, they were carried and rolled by the advancing ice and deposited on the hill top when the ice sheets retreated. At the base of the cairn, on its southernside, is a very large rock weighing many tonnes that was transported here by the glacier from the Ox Mountains. The top of the ice would have been higher than the cairn. Thousands of tonnes of boulders and rocks were carried out into Sligo bay and on the Strandhill shore their rounded remains are being continuously washed up by the sea today.

Nothing is static, for the landscape is imperceptibly changing under our feet. A fraction of a millimetre of geological alteration each year goes unno-ticed in terms of human existence. From time to time faint tremors pass along the Ox Mountains and the mine tunnels moan and groan. To the poet and primitive people such events could be attributed to a sleeping giant under the surface. To William Butler Yeats this subterranean world is where the spirits, fairies and goblins dwell.

Geology shaped the Yeats Country landscape, which in turn moulded the native people and their folklore and ultimately fashioned the creative talents of W.B. Yeats which allowed him to forge his immortal verse. We are but grains in the sands of time,

> *Cast a cold eye*
> *On life, on death.*
> *Horseman pass by!*

Train Home

JOHN KAVANAGH

Looking out west beyond the Shannon
a sudden elemental shift
blooms into softer loosened light
floats over splayed horizon

canters toward mountain and sea
in air charged differently,
the open windowed,
raw ocean freshness
tingles on face and scalp

Fields undulate and ramble
endless lines of dry wall skirt and skim
— stone stitched tapestries
threading boundary and ditch

Haw and whitethorn lean, wind-sighed
and bow backed, an odd curiosity of oak soars
while bramble and scrub cluster
into knotted inpenetrables

The ground's stubborn rebuttal
of harrow and plough, seed scatter,

the back break of ditch-hoke and stone-heft
ghosts in grey ruin of castle and church

the windowless broken cottages
and their slow, crumbled release
of shape and form back into clay and air

It is here freed from the noise and clutter
of the city's swelling entropies
its hemmed in, concreted dissonance
we see things more clearly

the Sun's arced walk across the sky
a lemon Moon's charcoaled amble
the primrosed pre-dawn glow
of Venus heralding re-birth.

Sligo Town in the Childhood Days of 'Willy and Lily and Lollie and Jack'

FIONA GALLAGHER

In 1865, Sligo town, the home of W.B. Yeats's maternal grandparents, was the third largest port on the western sea-board.[1] The Middletons and Pollexfens were intimately involved in the economic life and development of his spiritual and childhood home place.

By the dawn of the fourth decade of the nineteenth century, Sligo was described as the 'chief mart of the north-west of Ireland', and had the look of a place of some consequence. Sligo was the leading market and retail centre between Ballina, Co. Mayo and Enniskillen, Co. Fermanagh by 1839; the largest port after Limerick and Galway, blessed with an extensive retail trade and 'without a due consideration of its geographical situation one might feel surprise at the very extensive warehouses containing groceries, clothes, cottons and cutlery'.[2] The Great Famine of the 1840s, while decimating rural County Sligo, had a limited effect on the urban area; Sligo town became a major emigration port, which paradoxically stimulated the local economy. In the years between 1831 and 1851, as many as 60,000 people sailed to the new world directly from Sligo. It was not until the 1850s that prosperity returned to the town itself. Frazer wrote of Sligo just before the Famine that: 'the streets in the older parts of the town were narrow, dirty, ill-paved, and badly suited to the bustle of an export trade; it had nevertheless much more the appearance of

a business place than any other town in [the province of] Connaught, a circum-
stance wholly owing to the spirit and enterprise of its traders.'

In the first half of the nineteenth century the town depended primarily on
sea transport, with its eastward road connection to Dublin still poorly metalled.
By 1820, a traveller's impression of Sligo was of a compact core, nestled at the
foot of its surrounding hills, with the great bay opening out to the west. Four
decades later, by the time the Yeats children came to spend their summers in
Sligo, a great period of expansion and change was sweeping the town.

New, wider approach roads had been constructed to the heart of the
town; the forty-foot-wide Mail Coach Road, almost 2000 feet long had been
constructed by 1810, in conjunction with the arrival of the mail-coaches; later
a bypass road, Temple Street, joined this coach road to the quays, passing the
large warehouses owned by Middleton and Pollexfen in Union Street. By 1853
a new embankment along the Garavogue estuary had been built, along with
the new Victoria Bridge, later renamed Hyde Bridge, spanning the river along-
side the extensive flour mills of Middleton and Pollexfen.

In 1800 sixty-five vessels entered the port, but by 1880 that figure had
increased to 540, with tonnage nearing 90,000, a clear indication of the expan-
sion of the port over the course of the century. Middleton and Pollexfen, the
firm belonging to Yeats's grandparents, was the largest ship owners by far in
Sligo town, and would continue their business until about 1910. Their steam-
ship service, founded in 1833, had in 1841, a regular service running between
Sligo and Glasgow, with a further regular service to Liverpool added in 1856.[3]

The most significant transport development of the nineteenth century was
the coming of the railway to Sligo town. A line was first proposed in 1845, but
it was not until 1862, that the Midland Great Western Railway extended their
line from Longford, with a terminus at the western end of Sligo town, and a
later extension to the quays.[4] The total cost was £450,000.[5] Sligo was now able
to combine the twin assets of a good harbour with fast transportation of the
imported goods by rail. One consequence of the expansion of trade through the
port was the development of the quays themselves; between 1800 and 1850, the
existing quays were re-aligned and strengthened. By 1880 Sligo's quays were
the longest on the west coast, apart from Limerick, at just over one mile long.[6]
These bustling quays were to influence the paintings of Jack B. Yeats, and
the poetry of his brother W.B. when as small boys they visited to inspect the
discharge of cargo from the ships docked there.

C. 1840 local government was reformed with a new Corporation elected
on a wider franchise to govern the Borough of Sligo, admitting the town's many
shopkeepers, and small rate-payers to the electoral process. Representation

of Catholics also increased, which in turn led to the development of a new Catholic merchant middle-class. Sligo was distinctive in Connacht, in that it had a substantial number of Protestants, the majority of them middle-class merchants and shopkeepers, with a number of industrialists and wholesalers. In 1861, when the population of the town was approximately 10,500, about sixteen per cent were Irish Church, and it was this merchant-class, Protestant entrepreneurial background that influenced Yeats's younger days.

By the 1850s Sligo was the fifteenth largest town in Ireland, with a population of 14,318 living within its boundary (measured in a one-mile radius from the Market Square; the present-day site of the Lady Erin monument, unveiled in 1898). In 1841 Sligo town held just 8 percent of the county's population; by 1901 that share had increased to 13 percent.[7] Sligo town was the sole sizable urban centre on the west coast between Galway and Derry cities.

The last quarter of the nineteenth century witnessed the erection of many fine public buildings allied to an increase in services to the rate-paying public. In 1847 a new constabulary barracks was erected, followed in 1879 with a new courthouse in Teeling Street. After a prolonged financial struggle, a new Town Hall was constructed in 1865, in 1815 a new county jail was erected on a six-acre site to the east of the town. (The local wags referred to it in its latter years as 'The Cranmore Hotel'.) Other public buildings soon followed; a workhouse on the northern side of Ash Lane, a good distance from the town, was opened in the autumn of 1846, and the District Lunatic Asylum (now a hotel) was opened in Ballytivnan in 1852. A new Roman Catholic cathedral was constructed in 1875, Sligo becoming a diocesan see for the first time; and a second Church of Ireland was erected on The Mall to cater for an expanding population. Thankfully all of these fine architectural edifices are still to be seen today.

In the two decades before 1869, the Sligo Grand Jury spent £20,000 on widening of the streets of the town.[8] In 1824 the old military barracks were replaced with new buildings, dominating Fort Hill until 1922 when they were burned down in the civil war. This barracks faced the rear of the last residence of the Pollexfen grandparents, *Charlemont*.

A new County Infirmary was built on The Mall in 1816, with a Fever Hospital following soon after. Dispensaries were set up to provide basic health-care. The rapid expansion of the town brought problems associated with a population living close together in dilapidated housing. In the 1850s Sligo was considered to be dirty and unsanitary; the river was grossly polluted by sewage and effluent from industrial processes such as soap boiling and tanning. Pollution was also destroying the salmon in the river Garavogue.[9] By the 1890s a more affluent and cleaner town was emerging. A modern sewerage scheme had been laid out, and clean, piped water brought to the town from the Kinsellagh reservoir; the contaminated wells and street pumps that had supplied the town for much of its history had been closed or connected up to the new water mains.[10] Hand-operated pumps connected to the new system were set up on the corners of several streets, to supply fresh water to the growing population. The remnants of these pumps were in existence until the late 1950s.

Industrially, nineteenth-century Sligo was dominated by the port. As old industry declined new ones evolved to replace them. The linen industry had declined sharply by the 1840s, and trade began to change from the supply of agricultural and maritime goods to consumer-led materials.

For example the number of cabinet makers increased, as did saddlers, tailors, watchmakers, and boot and shoe makers. Industry was well represented by four breweries, a large flour mills, a corn mill, and dozens of small workshops, such as soap makers, candle makers, hat makers, rope makers, cable makers and blacksmiths.

Large shops along with woollen and furniture warehouses opened, as did hotels, especially after the arrival of the railway. The new hotels played an important role in accommodating visitors to the markets and fairs. Banks were an important part of this growing prosperity and savings banks were opened in the early years of the century, followed by the larger national banks some years later, – one of which, the beautiful Royal Bank of Ireland building, in 1970 became The Yeats Memorial Building. These new buildings were evidence of the growing self-confidence of Sligo as a prosperous town. The shipping business expanded; emigrant agents established business and steam ships improved the links with Scotland, Liverpool and America.

The core of the town however, still retained its medieval Norman street pattern. Castle Street and Radcliffe Street, lined with attractive merchants' shops, ran from the ancient Dominican Friary to Knox's Street, which in 1899, was renamed O'Connell Street. From the site of the old Market Cross, in the centre of the town, Market Street and High Street ran steeply uphill, lined with scores of small grocery shops, haberdashers, tailors, public houses, woollen and linen drapers, milliners, tobacconists, and ironmongers. It presented a busy scene on an average weekday. Markets were held weekly in the adjacent market yard, a large enclosed area to the west of High Street. Knox's Street (O'Connell Street), was by the 1880s the premier business street in Sligo, with large amalgamated 'department' stores such as W.T. & G. Johnston's, the Sligo Wood & Iron Co. which included a large saw mills to the rear; a multitude of small grocers, drapers, and merchants. Stephen Street and The Mall were home to the financial institutions, legal offices, and the town-houses of the wealthy land-holding class; gentlemen's clubs, and up-market lodging houses were located on this more recently developed north bank of the Garavogue.

However, surrounding this affluent merchant-class core were the homes of the poor, who lived in small cabins and thatched houses on the edge of Sligo town. There were also several squalid lanes and alleys: Ramsay's Row; Middleton's Row (owned by Susan Yeats's uncle); Smith's Row; Armstrong's Row; and the Waste Garden Lane, with its tenement building known as 'The Blood Pan' tucked away behind the tall merchant houses in the town centre. This was quite a common situation in most Irish towns of that period. The suburban villa of William Pollexfen, *Charlemont* on Barrack Street, stood cheek-to-jowl with the cabins of the poor, which straggled up the hill towards the military barracks. On the southern side of the town, a similar situation was to be found on the South Gallows Hill and Mail Coach Road, both lined with deteriorating, thatched houses, unsanitary, overcrowded. They were described in 1901 by the local government health inspector as 'unfit for human in habitation'. Nevertheless, the plight of the labouring class would be ignored by the middle class, – both Catholic and Protestant – until the massive government-financed housing schemes of the 1930s.

The first Nationalist Corporation in Sligo was elected in 1898; many of the long-standing street names were re-named after Irish patriots; there was an air of change about the borough towards the end of the Victorian age. This period of Irish nationalism, along with the Gaelic revival was heavily influenced by the poetry, prose and plays of W.B. Yeats, as Sligo had earlier influenced his works and those of his brother Jack B. Yeats, artist and author.

NOTES

1. T.W. Freeman, *Irish towns in the Eighteenth & Nineteenth Centuries* in R.A. Butlin (ed.), *'The Development of the Irish Town'* (1977), p. 129
2. Inglis quoted in W.G. Wood Martin, Sligo, Vol. iii, p. 128
3. John C. McTernan, 'Memory Harbour: *The Port of Sligo*' (1992), p. 36
4. W.G. Wood Martin, *History of Sligo*', iii, p. 212
5. *Sligo Chronicle*, 5-12-1862
6. John C. McTernan, 'Memory Harbour: *The Port of Sligo*' (1992), pp. 25–8
7. CSO Census statistics, 1841–1911
8. W.G. Wood Martin, *History of Sligo*, iii, p. 201
9. 1837 Coms. Of Inquiry on State of Irish Fishers second Report, Minutes of Evidence, p. 31
10. W.G. Wood Martin, *History of Sligo*, iii, p. 184

The Tug of the Mythic

EARL LIVINGS

Nor is there singing school but studying
Monuments of its own magnificence
W.B. Yeats, 'Sailing to Byzantium'

COME AWAY

Where else but in Sligo can you turn around two street corners, minutes apart, and be reminded of the ever-present mythic history of Ireland? After one corner you see Knocknarea, with the giant cairn of Queen Meadhbh on its summit:

> The Host is riding from Knocknarea
> And over the grave of Clooth-na-bare;
> Caoilte tossing his burning hair
> And Niamh calling Away, come away.

After the other corner you see Ben Bulben in the distance, which prompts thoughts of Diarmuid and Gráinne's resting place and of course the familial and poetic history associated with the nearby church and its famous grave:

> Under bare Ben Bulben's head
> In Drumcliff churchyard Yeats is laid.
> An ancestor was rector there

Long years ago, a church stands near,
By the road an ancient cross.

No matter where one stands in Sligo and in the surrounding countryside, the landscape and its associated poetries tug at you, at your 'deep heart's core', and call from you the recognition that land, history, mythology and language depend on one another and are vital ingredients for the enrichment and enchantment of the soul.

I SHALL ARISE AND GO NOW

I first encountered Yeats in the early 1990s, when undertaking a Graduate Diploma in English at La Trobe University, Melbourne. The lecturer, like Auden many years before, praised the work but decried the investigations into magic, folklore and myth. He reluctantly acknowledged these as the scaffolding for the great poems, but unnecessary for understanding them. However, through the work of Kathleen Raine and my own explorations of those non-academic areas, which started for me long before I met Yeats, and of course through the poems themselves, I have come to disagree with that lecturer's assessment.

In 2009 I was fortunate to receive a Pierce Loughran Scholarship for the Yeats International Summer School (YISS). This paid for my accommodation and for the tuition fee. All I had to do was find the airfare and living expenses. What made this opportunity even more special was that I would be attending an amazing milestone: the fiftieth anniversary of the world's oldest literary summer school. Through the lectures and seminars and the atmosphere and landscape surrounding the venues and the town of Sligo, the two weeks would be filled with poetry, folklore, philosophy, biography, history and myth. I would also be attending readings by some of Ireland's and the world's greatest poets: Seamus Heaney, Michael Longley, Dennis O'Driscoll and others. With such a wonderful chance to immerse myself in the 'Learning of the Imagination', as Raine puts it in one of her books on Yeats, I soon found the money and organized the time away from my teaching job.

FROM CHANGE TO CHANGE

Nothing beats car trips with an ex-pat Irishman driver who is passionate about Irish literature, especially Yeats, and is a native of Sligo:

See that village? That is where Yeats heard the song that became 'Down by the Sally Gardens' and there's 'the field by the river' mentioned in the poem.

And from here, at the right time of the afternoon, as the sun is approaching the horizon, you can see the 'purple glow' of hills and lakes and, in the distance, the island that Yeats had planned to use for his Castle of Heroes.

Over there is Lough Gill, and the island that was the inspiration for 'The Lake Isle of Innisfree'.

Take a photo now, of Ben Bulben and Knocknarea 'together', with the whole coastline opened up and, there, between them, Sligo, from the Irish *Sligeach*, meaning 'a shelly place'.

And in that field, archaeologists found the remains of a great battle. Some consider it the site of the Second Battle of Mag Tuired (Moytura), which was fought between the Tuatha Dé Danann and the Fomorians.

And here is the building William Pollexfen, Yeats's grandfather, built, with the tower at the top so he could watch out for his ships coming into Sligo.

TO THE WATERS AND THE WILD

After the opening of the Summer School, we pile into coaches for a brief tour to Glencar Waterfall. We stop several times for photo opportunities, especially of a 'stream against the height' – a distant waterfall that, because of the shape of the valley walls and the force and direction of the wind, becomes a plume of mist, water falling upwards. This happens once every twelve months or so. What an omen for the next two weeks.

Sometimes this 'stream against the height' also happens at Glencar Waterfall itself, though not this day. A slight drizzle accompanies us as we follow the coruscating stream to the base of the fifty-foot waterfall. Closing my eyes and shutting out the sounds of conversations and clicking cameras, I easily imagine a young Yeats watching water drip from the tips of ferns and leaning over the pools 'among the rushes' to catch a 'slumbering trout'. On the way back, some of us stop in silence before a whitethorn tree draped with strips of coloured rags, clooties – messages to the Sidhe for healing or as an act of honouring them – and add our blessings.

After Evensong at Drumcliffe Church, I stand before Yeats's grave, a silent prayer of thanks. Then I glance back to Ben Bulben. So much history and mythology in soil and rock and water. Seeing these places brings the poems and the man into sharper focus. Seeing the landscape, I feel the tug of the mythic.

SING WHATEVER IS WELL MADE

Lectures in the mornings, dealing with Yeats's contemporaries, influences and traditions, and seminars on folklore and poetic form in the afternoons:

- Yeats as seen by, in comparison to, or associated with, other poets – Auden, MacNeice, Eliot, Pound.

- Yeats and family: the enormous debt to his father for advice and encouragement; the valuable contributions made to the Irish arts and crafts movement by his sisters Lily and Lolly; the early social sketches and the later expressionist-style paintings of Jack Yeats.

- Yeats and folklore, and Irish literary traditions, and Symbolism, and Sligo.

- Yeats's poems praised, dissected, explicated, understood. Their forms, their music, their meaning, their resonances.

So much to absorb during the day; so many conversations over a Guinness in the evening and well into the night, to the accompaniment of traditional Irish music. Bleary eyes in the morning. Eager hand reaching for pen and notebook.

CARROWKEEL

After a bumpy car journey, we climb a gravel path to the summit of one of the Bricklieve Mountains. This name is Irish for 'the speckled mountains', possibly because the quartz rocks on the outside of the passage tombs scattered across the range sparkle in the sun. Emerging from one of the tombs, I see Knocknarea in the distance and Lough Arrow, site of the Second Battle of Mag Tuired. Our guide points out Carrowmore, one of the other major megalithic complexes in Ireland. There is never enough time to experience fully such sites, their subtle mythic and psychological energies, their reverberating silences. Then again, as our guide notes, that's a good reason to return.

As we walk back to the car, one of our party stops for a moment, turns to me with a look of surprise and joy, and says she can hear the landscape talking to her in Irish. She has been studying the language for several years and this is the first time it has happened: her language training and her native experiences of the homeland somehow hooking into the contours and colours and textures and sounds of the landscape around her. I envy her this connection, this revelation, something non-indigenous Australians might find difficult, if not impossible, to experience in our own country.

DOLMEN AND CIRCLE

Carrowmore Megalithic Cemetery, Co. Sligo, Ireland

when we came the gods themselves
scattered boulders across plains
and forests like falling stars
they glitter at dusk at dawn
some too heavy for one clan's
blessing we rolled them hauled them
layers of pebbles beneath
them as many as the stars
made of them shapes whispering
the world around within us
hollows and mountain bulges
cast and swept by the sun's rim
and the darkness under this
raised the biggest to observe
that place each thing passes through
five boulders as three walls one
tilted on top sometimes more
pointing the way to sunrise
sometimes all covered by earth
mother and lover of each
we place our bones in bags stitched
from the skins of those we hunt
bury them in still corners
sing for moon sun stars passing
under the river-bright earth
seasons of meat shellfish fruit
leave the silent swirling dark
like a child blinking first light
stride the path till last light
strikes our eyes and once again
we gift our burnt bones to claim
water earth sky flame as breath

It is fascinating that the area has largely remained undisturbed for thousands
of years – no major buildings like forts, castles, churches, etc. The successive
inhabitants seemed to have recognized the numinous quality of the cemetery,

though some tombs were ransacked for building local dwellings. A curse on the landowner who completely demolished one tomb for his pasturing.

PLUCK TILL TIME AND TIMES ARE DONE

With a fire in my own head, I visit the hazel wood, which isn't far from my accommodation at the Yeats Village. I take photos while strolling down a disused, narrow road, but once inside the wood itself I put the camera away. Wet, soggy earth. No wildlife, except for insects and spiders. No noise, except for the occasional child's cry from distant picnickers. No wind.

I find an old tree stump, sit down, watch leaves and branches not moving. Feel myself relaxing, slowing, becoming centred. Think about 'hollow lands and hilly lands', about 'perfection of the life or of the work', then nothing at all.

Later, a gentle rain falls.

MEETING QUEEN MEADHBH

Where else but in dream
a week before I planned
to climb Cnoc na Ri
and leave a small green stone
in her cairn, one of two
I bought for this tradition,
labradorite, Merlin's stone.

I know the stories, from books
and from a taxi driver who says
the Queen loved men so much
when she died their wives piled
a mountain of rocks upon her grave
to stop her getting out.

I know as well what archaeologists claim:
the cairn a Neolithic tomb far older
than the time of bronze age warriors,
though what would such dissectors
of things and time know of the eternal
return in tales of love and the dead?

So she appears – after I scramble up

the mountain and walk a path
widdershins around the cairn. After
I drop the less flawed
of my two flecked stones between
grey and heavy rocks. After
bowing and moving away,
only to have the wind thrust me
back, lie me down to a second dream
in which I fight a guardian
none other than my own misshapen self –

So she appears, out of a flickering
haze of red and gold, speaks
of secrets and visions enough
to convince me to embrace
that hidden self, struggle, resolve.
I awake to waves of goose bumps
keeping me awake, more words.

Days later, all happens as foretold:
the climb, the path, the flat rock
that becomes a bed while I listen
to Atlantic winds shift the clouds,
ruffle the grasses, and the crack
between granite rocks where I drop
my link stone, hear it knock once
as it falls, then absorb silence.

I walk the many paths around
that mountain and across its fields,
over stone walls, past tufts of thistle,
hollows of red-yellow moss-blooms.
Black-faced sheep crop the hillsides.
Insects dart from me. Mist seeps
out from clefts, glistens a wood clearing
in which a lone, unseen bird summons
a courage to itself, again, again.

Away from the cairn, a hawk
quivers its wings against wind
and gravity, twenty seconds or more,

glides to another vantage point, waits,
glides again, a half dozen times,
then drops. I wait without counting,
rub the second stone in my pocket
as I walk back towards the edge.

(Note: Meadhbh is pronounced Maeve and Cnoc na Ri is pronounced Knocknaree.)

SINGING SCHOOL

After I walk back from Knocknarea, I go for a late lunch at Hargadon's Pub. During the meal, I pull out my notebook and continue studying *The Sacred Mythological Centres of Ireland*, which I had bought a few days before from Keohane's Bookshop. When the waitress brings my coffee, she sees the open book and asks if I am an archaeologist. Only in Ireland (and maybe Wales and Cornwall) would I be, and am, comfortable in saying, 'No, I'm a poet'. She doesn't comment on this admission, doesn't change her expression. No wonder. This is the country in which, during my previous trip here, a tourist guide quoted poetry while narrating facts and stories of the various sights / sites. For the next few minutes the waitress and I talk about Knocknarea and the tradition of leaving a stone on the cairn, a tradition introduced some years before to counter the loss of stones taken as souvenirs by tourists. When she goes back to work, I pat the Merlin stone in my pocket, return to my book, write notes towards a new poem, my own 'learning of the imagination'.

THE GREAT BATTLE

Myself must I remake
Till I am Timon and Lear
Or that William Blake
Who beat upon the wall
Till Truth obeyed his call

'Sorry about that Mr Yeats!'

ITA McMORROW-LEYDEN

From early childhood W.B. Yeats was always a giant on my shoulder, but I never really knew it until much later in life. His influence is everywhere, his poetry flows through our countryside and through our hearts and minds. He is to us in Sligo as Shakespeare is to Stratford-upon-Avon. Even our Theatre bears the name 'The Hawk's Well'.

My parents ran a family hotel, the Sancta Maria, in the seaside village of Strandhill at the foot of Knocknarea mountain ... meaning the hill of the King ... Cnoc na Ri ... but in Sligo we regard that mountain as the hill of the Queen.

Driving northwards into Sligo via the main Dublin Road, majestic Ben Bulben, our tabletop limestone mountain some 1760 feet tall, rises majestically in front of you. To your left you will see the soft shape of Knocknarea, almost like a woman's breast, with the cairn of the ancient legendary Queen Maeve forming the nipple. All of our mountains have their own stories. Someday the secret of the cairn will reveal itself. They say that someone of great importance is definitely buried up there. Yeats, I am sure, would have loved the experience of seeing his play *Purgatory* performed on the top of the mountain by the Sligo-based Blue Raincoat Theatre Company in 2013.

As a young girl I would guide our hotel guests to the summit. The tradition was to bring a stone and throw it on top of Queen Maeve's Cairn, then make a wish. I remember bringing up a middle-aged lady; she turned out to be a member of Rudolf Hess's family. In Hitler's Cabinet, he had been the deputy

Fuhrer; he was then serving his life sentence in Spandau Prison, for his horrific war crimes. She may have been his sister Margarete who was born in 1908. She wished to climb the mountain, because she had studied Yeats. It can be very dangerous if approached from Strandhill. It is best and much more accessible from the Glen Road near the Cullenamore strand in Ballysadare Bay. Approaching from the village of Strandhill you will pass The Glen containing 'the cleft that's christened Alt' in the poem 'Man and the Echo'.

What an event in summer of 2014 when once again the Blue Raincoat Theatre Company continued their experiential theatre in the landscape, by presenting *On Baile's Strand* on Cummeen Strand. It was a most memorable staging of a Yeats play in its place of origin, the countryside that had influenced Yeats. People came in their hundreds by foot, bike, car and even on horseback! Causing traffic jams at the entrance to the Coney Island road. It was so worth it! It was Neil Henry's great idea to set the plays where they had come from. I was proud of these young actors who are so enthusiastic about Yeats's epic plays. It was the wonderful landscape that caused the awakening of the poet's inspiration. Cuchulain's voice in its madness echoed from the surrounding cliffs as he battled the waves, it was pure magic.

We even had some food left from our picnic to share with the cast. They were on the wet strand since early morning and were starving! Many were past pupils of my own little people's theatre workshop, when they were very young.

Whenever I visit the places he has made famous, Yeats always comes to mind. I have gone to the Hazelwood because my head has also been bothered. In the nineteen-eighties recession when my development of shops and workshops was dissolving, there was always hope rising from the ashes. 'It had become a glimmering girl.' He is everywhere; in the days of my real estate business I would advertise: SITUATED IN THE HEART OF THE YEATS COUNTRY – that could mean miles from all amenities, schools, churches and shops. Or indeed, promoting local agri-tourism business: WITH PANORAMIC VIEWS OF THE YEATS COUNTRY.

Is it any wonder that Yeats was so struck by the heroic deeds and epic wars of the Sligo countryside? We have the 'Battle of the Bulls' (Queen Maeve) and 'The Battle of the Books' (St Columba), legends of the mountainous caves and those who hid therein (Grainne and Diarmuid). The entire place is haunted by a great wealth of folklore and sagas that could give Hollywood a run for its money. Yeats was spoilt for choice. If we look at just one character for example; the wealthy, beautiful Queen Maeve, the Celtic goddess herself, how crazy was she? Ruling over these lands of Connacht, causing lots of havoc and mayhem. Imagine sending her beautiful maidens to ride into battle, bare breasted in the hope that the soldiers would not harm them! Needless to say, they were savagely slaughtered!

I worked in Ardmore Studios under Robert Altman on his film *Images* starring Susannah York. Leonard Cohen was all the rage then, having recorded music tracks for a number of Altman's films. It was fantastic to see him in person when he performed in concert at Lissadell almost forty years later. We were awe-stricken with his love of Yeats. He rejoiced in the poetry. With Ben Bulben as a backdrop, we watched and listened, as the evening sun turned the embroidered heavens into 'the gold and silver light'.

When my world collapsed around me in the eighties, 'I did not really know what to do with myself', as the song goes, so I thought of recording a tape. One side would be Yeats poetry, the other, some of my own, also a few old Irish favourites like 'The Trimmings on the Rosary' by John O'Brien and 'The Four Farrellys' by Percy French.

I set about seeking permissions. One of the most important was to secure permission to record Yeats. It was such a thrill to receive a reply from W.B.'s son, the very kind Senator Michael Yeats. Yes, he granted me consent to record his father's poems but with a warning, 'My experience with people who have made recordings of this kind is that sales tend to be rather small.' I loved it! I still have his letter.

Frank and Georgie Wynne and their children lived near our family home in Strandhill. Frank was a founder member of the Sligo Yeats Society: Georgie worked as secretary for many years. Frank would often drop by for a night-cap with my father. I remember one night Mr Wynne was drafting a letter in the hope of securing the beautiful old Royal Bank Building at Hyde Bridge as a home for the Sligo Yeats Society. The anticipation, followed by the great excitement when it did come to fruition – the Yeats Memorial Building – proving yet again the great 'might of the pen'.

My father Joe McMorrow, being a founder member of The Sligo Drama Circle encouraged me to recite Yeats from an early age. We had lots of Irish nights in the hotel. My father going out into the highways and byways to collect musicians from far and near. What great characters! Josie McDermott and Joe O'Dowd were just two of the many musicians who played in the Sancta Maria Hotel. Joe played the fiddle in the south Sligo Coleman style. He was to me the real Fiddler of Dooney, he played gently in the background while I recited 'Fiddler', then brought the music to a great mad gallop of a crescendo and everyone would 'dance like a wave of the sea'! We always received tremendous applause.

I never did win the Yeats Cup at any of the local Feiseanna. I tried hard. But it eluded me! An adjudicator having listened to perhaps thirty or forty children, including me, recite, one after the other 'The Stolen Child' in competition for the Yeats Cup heard me on the following day in a different hall, recite my 'The Fiddler of Dooney'.

On receiving my mark sheet it read, 'If only I had heard this fiddler during the Yeats Cup yesterday, what a joy it would have been!' – Yes for me and all! – For me and all!

That was the one that got away on me. Sorry about that Mr Yeats!

Burial at Drumcliffe

JOHN CARROLL

A grave had been dug, flowers and soft green moss lined the sides and bottom of the grave. Prayers had been said and a large coffin had been lowered into the grave. A large crowd of people were standing around in silence.

A young boy had come along with his father. Now he stood on his own at the grave side. No one seemed to mind, so he stayed there taking it all in. Sixty-five years later he would be invited to revisit the scene

SLIGO TOWN, 17 SEPTEMBER 1948

With schools and shops closed, crowds of Sligo people lined the streets in silence to watch the funeral cortege, headed by the Mayor of Sligo and the members of Sligo Corporation wend its way to the Town Hall where the long black hearse slid into position for 'a lying in State' at the foot of the steps leading to the main entrance.

Town dignitaries stood there as did a guard of honour by a detachment of the Local Defence Force, along with people from many parts of Ireland. Later that same afternoon at Drumcliffe Churchyard in falling rain, my father Alf Carroll and his fellow Sligo man Kevin Murray filmed the proceedings from the church tower, with movie and still shots from their respective cameras.

The story in our family – father's own story – was that in the late 1920s, a native of Dublin, he was driving along the road north of Sligo town as he crossed the brow of a hill, the majestic long pose of Ben Bulben unfolded before him and that, there and then, he made up his mind it was in this part of Ireland he wanted to live.

Over the course of the next fifty years the Sligo landscape was to repay a hundred-fold his, and indeed our families' affection for it – most of all through what became a cherished relationship with its people – mainly from his work as an engineer in the creameries of County Sligo (these same creameries evolved from the great work of Æ and Horace Plunkett).

Yeats's burial at Drumcliffe, Sligo. Left to right: *Jack B. Yeats (under umbrella), Michael Yeats, Chevalier Thomas MacGreevy, Anne Yeats (with cape) and Mrs George Yeats. Behind McGreevy, in profile: 'McLoughlin The Mall'.* Above right, shoulder to camera: *Detective Sergeant Denis Hayden.* Foreground: *William Monds (brother of Bertie) and (*right*) John Carroll. (Photograph by the late Frank Kerrin, courtesy of Helen Kerrin)*

Thus the delightful poem of Seumas O'Sullivan's (1879–1958) has long been one of my favourites:

'The Starling Lake'

My sorrow that I am not by the little dún
By the lake of the starlings at Rosses under the hill,
And the larks there, singing over the fields of dew
Or evening there and the sedges still.
For plain I see now the length of yellow sand,
And Lissadell far off and its leafy ways,
And the holy mountain whose mighty heart
Gathers into it all the coloured days.
My sorrow that I am not by the little dún
By the lake of the starlings at evening when all is still,
And still in whispering sedges the herons stand.
'Tis there I would nestle at rest till the quivering moon
Uprose in the golden quiet over the hill.

Ben Bulben, presiding over a landscape discovered, cleared, grazed, tilled, celebrated, lived in and buried in for five thousand years and more.

No visitor to our home from outside of Sligo was allowed to leave without being taken to view Ben Bulben, to visit Tobernalt with its ancient Holy Well via the nearby Green Road atop Cairns Hill with its majestic panoramic vista, to imbibe Lough Gill and its wooded shore – Slish Wood, which Yeats adapted to 'Sleuth Wood in the lake', and the hidden Dooney rock where his fiddler played fairy music – and those mountains that glow purple at noon, Slieve da Ean, and back again to Lough Gill with its many islands, including Innisfree.

Once we in the Carroll family learned to swim, we were permitted to 'go up the Lake' on our own (which in the 1950s meant in the company of many others, as this was the playground for innumerable Sligo people). Having rowed up the Garavogue River from the Riverside embankment you meet Rat Island at the entrance to the lake proper. This islet lies close to Hazelwood shore and the tall reeds between the island and the shore block one's view of the open water ahead.

Tourists and anyone new to Lough Gill would go the long way around the island; we however with the lore handed down from generation to generation of Sligo dwellers, knew the lake and the name of this hidden waterway 'The Narrows' and so it was we bravely set to with

Topgallants braced
We drove straight through

And set our course
For —

To head for

Where dips the rocky highland
Of Sleuth Wood in the lake,
There lies a leafy island
Where flapping herons wake
The drowsy water-rats ...

Why we wondered did Yeats call it 'Sleuth Wood' when we know it is
'Slish'? The rhythms of poetry were far from our young minds in those days of
wonder and awe as we gloried in the nature surrounding us.

But who could find fault with a man who, on the other hand, had named
in his poems places that were part and parcel of our world:

'The hills above Glencar', 'furthest Rosses', 'Knocknarea', 'Dooney Rock',
'Innisfree' and above all our very own Rat Island?

For a decade or so, from the mid-1930s we lived in the village of Strandhill
at the foot of Knocknarea, bounded by the Sligo River and the wild Atlantic
ocean. The residents of Strandhill making their way to Sligo town pass within
a half mile of Cummeen Strand.

The complex landscape of the heart was still distant from us then, but the
hills, the waterways, the islands, the woods, the stone walled fields, cromlechs
and dolmens, the very sea itself came daily to our front door.

The Sligo poems of W.B. Yeats impacted on my father's appreciation of the
landscape – something which I, together with other family members, increas-
ingly shared. First, with the landscapes as part of the poem, but in the end the
poem merged into one's personal landscape.

In his introduction to Rabindranath Tagore's *Gitanjali* (Song Offerings),
W.B. Yeats delights in recalling his conversations with compatriots of the great
poet, one of whom told him how:

Every morning at three – I know, for I have seen it – he sits immovable in
contemplation, and for two hours does not awake from his reverie upon the
nature of God. This man goes on to speak of Rabindranath's relative, the
Maha Rishie, and of how 'once, upon a river, he fell into contemplation, and
the rowers waited for eight hours before they could continue their journey'.

Yeats acknowledges that the lyrics of Tagore

display in their thought a world I have dreamed of all my life long. The work
of a supreme culture, they yet appear as much as the growth of the common

soil as the grass and the rushes. A tradition, where poetry and religion are the same thing, has passed through the centuries, gathering from learned and unlearned metaphor and emotion ...

LISSADELL AND ITS LEAFY WAYS ...

The death of Hugh Gore-Booth, killed in action late in World War II on the Greek island of Leros, prompted the great Gaelic poet, Máirtín Ó Direáin (1910–88), to pay tribute to him in an essay titled 'Hugh Gore-Booth Nach Maireann (The Late Hugh Gore-Booth)'.

In September 1937 Máirtín Ó Direáin, on board the ferry *Dun Aengus*, on his way home to Inishmore, the largest of the Aran Islands, met by chance with Hugh Gore-Booth, who was visiting the islands for the first time and he was hoping to improve there his knowledge of the Irish language. They spent some days walking around the island together, Hugh reading phrases from his *Irish Beginners* book, with Máirtín as his tutor and treating the local people they met with a courtesy and respect which made a deep impression on Máirtín.

There is no mistaking the poet's personal regard for the Sligoman – and his sorrow on hearing of his death:

Chuir sé brón orm cinnte. Tá sé sínte I mball éigin uaigneach I bhfad ó Lissadell agus ó Shligeach. Ní fheicfidh sé go deo arís: —

'The light of evening, Lissadell,
Great windows open to the south ...

Faoi mar atá I dtús an dáin a chum Yeats ar a bheirt aintín iomráiteach. Go ndésns Dia trócaire ar a anam uasal.

(It certainly grieved me. He lies in some lonely place, far from Lissadell and Sligo. He will never again see: —

'The light of evening, Lissadell,
Great windows open to the south ...

As you find in the beginning of the poem which Yeats wrote about his two famous aunts,
May God have mercy on his gentle soul.)

Bertie Monds was born in 1917 at Ballynagalliagh in the Parish of Drum-cliffe. He later lived with his wife, Mona, and their family at nearby Milltown, half a mile from St Columba's, their parish church, where, succeeding his father,

John Monds, Bertie served as Churchwarden. His responsibilities included the heating of the church, general maintenance and the digging of graves.

My last conversation with Bertie was in July 2014, following his admission to the Sligo Regional Hospital during which he celebrated his 97th birthday. He talked to me about a horse belonging to Deirdre Roddy. He recalled opening the grave for the remains of W.B. Yeats in 1948 and also recalled my father being there.

Bertie Monds died in his own home at Milltown on Friday 15 August 2014 in the midst of his loving family. His nephew Alec Hunter told me of their last drive together in Bertie's gig, and of the pony losing a shoe, and of Bertie expertly replacing it by the roadside near Glencar.

Jack B. Yeats's (Cuala Press) illustrations of horse races on Drumcliffe Strand are captivating; one day I took the opportunity to ask Bertie if he remembered them. 'Remember them? I rode in them!' was his immediate response.

Bertie Monds (1917–2014), farmer, horseman, storyteller, Churchwarden, family man, staunch friend and obliging neighbour, personified much of what Sligo people love about Sligo.

It was indeed fitting that life's final courtesies should be rendered to the 'Sligo poet' by such a Sligo man.

Notes on Contributors

Elizabeth Ansel, MA, works as an assistant lecturer in the art history department at Technical University Dresden, Germany. Her main research interests are early modern European print culture and twentieth-century Irish art. Currently, she is writing her doctoral thesis on the Irish artist Jack B. Yeats.

Mary Legato Brownell is a teacher and poet from Jenkintown, Pennsylvania; she enjoys poetry readings as well as teaching and poetry conversations. She won First Prize in the 2006 New York Yeats Poetry Prize.

Vincent Buckley (1925–1988) essayist, poet, critic and Professor of English, University of Melbourne. He lectured at the University of Cambridge 1955–7. He had fourteen books of poetry published between 1954–85 as well as two other books, *Cutting Green Hay: Friendships, Movements and Cultural Conflicts in Australia's Great Decades*, 1983, and *Memory Ireland: Insights into the contemporary Irish Condition*, 1985 MUP (The University of Melbourne Press). The Vincent Buckley Poetry Prize, a biennial award that is offered alternately to enable an Australian poet to visit Ireland and to facilitate the visit of an Irish poet to Melbourne, was established to commemorate his life and work. http://australian-centre.unimelb.edu.au/prizes/buckley

John Carey, Chatswood New South Wales is a former teacher of French and Latin and a former actor. The latest of his four collections is 'One Lip Smacking' (Picaro Press 2013). He was joint First Prize winner of the 2013 W.B. Yeats Poetry Prize for Australia.

John Carroll Rev. Fr, a native of Sligo, is Roman Catholic Chaplain to Sligo General Hospital and Cregg House.

Glen Cavaliero F.R.S.L., Poet and Critic, is a Fellow Commoner of St Catharine's College Cambridge where he is a member of the Faculty of English

Jane Clarke was awarded First Prize in the 2010 iYeats Poetry Competition. Jane hails from a farming background in the west of Ireland, resides in County Wicklow. Her work has been widely published in magazines and Irish national newspapers. Her poems have won a number of prizes including *Listowel Writers Week Poetry*

Collection (2013) and she was shortlisted for the 2013 Patrick Kavanagh Poetry Competition. Her work is included in various anthologies including the recent *Roscommon Anthology*. Jane's website is www.janeclarkepoetry.ie

Barbara Crooker was born in Cold Spring, New York, in 1945, currently resides in Fogelsville, Pennsylvania. She began writing poetry in the late 1970s and has won many awards. Over 700 of her poems have been published in anthologies and magazines, as well as compiled in several chapbooks and books. She continues to write, teach workshops, and speak about the venues available for publishing poetry. Her latest collection, 'Gold' (2013), was published in the Poeima Poetry Series by Cascade Books. She won First Prize in the 2004 New York Yeats Poetry Prize.

Joel Dando ph.D. is Visiting Assistant Professor of English at St Michael's College, Colchester, Vermont. He specializes in Romantic Poetry in general and the life, poetry, and letters of Lord Byron in particular, literature and the visual arts, fiction and film. He was the inaugural winner of First Prize in the W.B. Yeats Poetry Prize for Australia in 1996.

Ann Margaret Daniel teaches and writes in New York City. Her articles, essays, notes, and reviews, covering topics from Oscar Wilde's trials to Bob Dylan and High Modernism, have appeared in books, critical editions, magazines, and journals including *The New York Times; Isis; Hot Press; The Times Literary Supplement*. She is currently working on a book about F. Scott Fitzgerald. Anne has degrees in American history and English from Harvard University (A.B.), Georgetown University (MA), and Princeton University (Ph.D.). Since 2002, she has taught in the literary studies and Humanities divisions of The New School University in Manhattan. Her specialty has long been Irish and Irish-American literature and culture. She has twice served as associate director of the Yeats International Summer School in Sligo, to which she has been a regular visitor since her High School days.

Maneck H. Daruwala is Associate Professor of English at Florida International University (the State University of Florida at Miami) where she teaches a variety of courses, especially in nineteenth- and twentieth-century literature. Her critical works include papers on Keats, Blake and Indian mythology.

Angela Dawson, a physiotherapist born in Manchester, whose first love was Wordsworth, now resides in Australia. She has performed at Overload Poetry Festivals in Australia. Her work has been featured on Community Radio. In 2012 she won both the Elwood Poetry Prize and First Prize in the W.B. Yeats Poetry Prize for Australia.

Denis Donoghue Professor Emeritus of English, University Professor and Henry James Professor of English and American Letters; Department of English. BA (1949), MA (1952), Ph.D. (1957) and D.Litt. (honoris causa) 1989 (National University of Ireland), MA 1964 (University of Cambridge). Denis Donoghue's teaching and writing engage modern English, Irish and American literature, and the aesthetics and practices of reading. Recent books include *Words Alone: The Poet T.S. Eliot* (Yale 2000), *Adam's Curse: Reflections on Literature and Religion* (Notre Dame 2001), *Speaking of Beauty* (Yale 2004), *The American Classics* (Yale 2005) and *On Eloquence* (Yale 2008).

Declan J. Foley born in Sligo town in 1950, moved to Melbourne in 1987. A former undertaker, now a Yeats scholar, he founded Bloomsday in Melbourne when Secretary of the Yeats Society of Victoria, and initiated the W.B. Yeats Poetry Prize for Australia. His previous Lilliput publication is 'The Only Art of Jack B. Yeats: Letters & Essays' (ed. 2009). He has organized John Butler Yeats Seminars at Chestertown NY in 2001, 2004, 2007 and at TCD in 2010. He is currently working on another John Butler Yeats collection of essays.

Gerry Foley A native of Sligo who has spent many years discovering the mountains of County Sligo, and Europe. He is a founding member of the Sligo Mountaineering Club, and an artist in many facets of that practice.

Fiona Gallagher A native of Sligo, and a local historian, she published *The Streets of Sligo* in 2008.

Beverley George writes poetry and children's books and her short stories have been commercially published. She has been a Writing Fellow of the Fellowship of Australian Writers since 1997; was President (2006–10) of the Australian Haiku Society; has presented papers on the Japanese genres of haiku and tanka twice in Japan and in 2009 convened a four day conference for haiku, attended by 57 full-time delegates from six countries. Currently, she is editor of 'Eucalypt: a Tanka Journal' [www.eucalypt.info] and 'Windfall: Australian haiku.' She won First Prize in the 2004 W.B. Yeats Poetry Prize for Australia.

Warwick Gould Emeritus Professor (English), Professor Gould has been Director of the Institute of English Studies since its inception, and Director of the Research Centre (est. Nov. 1999) in the History of the Book, for which the Institute is host institution. He has been Professor of English Literature in the University of London since 1995, and is Deputy Dean of the School of Advanced Study (2000–). He holds these posts on full-time secondment from Royal Holloway, University of London. He is currently editor of *The Yeats Annual*.

Richard W. Halperin, an Irish / American dual national residing in Paris received First Prize in the 2012 iYeats Poetry Competition, and another First in The New Tricks with Matches competition of University College Dublin. His poems have been published in a number of literary magazines, and several have received Honours in poetry competitions in Europe. His collection *Anniversary* has been translated into Japanese by Sakiko Tagaki (Kundai Bungei-sha Press, Toyko, 2012).

T.R. Henn (1901–74) was born in Albert House, Sligo town and educated in Fermoy, Cork and at St Catharine's College, Cambridge, where he was elected Fellow in 1926. He was Senior Tutor, 1945–7, and President, 1951–61. He served in the British army in the Second World War, rising to the rank of Brigadier. *The Lonely Tower* (1950) was a study of W.B. Yeats; he edited J.M. Synge in 1963, and embarked on the Coole edition of Lady Gregory with Colin Smythe towards the end of his life. He was Director of the Yeats Summer School in Sligo from 1962–8.

Joanne Heraghty is a former pupil of Grange Post Primary School, Sligo. Under the guidance of her teacher Miss Orla McArt, she won school poetry contests judged by *Poetry Ireland* in 2013 and 2014. 'Ireland 2013' received the Yeats' Day Poetry Ireland Award. At present Joanne is continuing her education with a post-leaving certificate course.

Margaret J. Hoehn lives with her husband and two children in Sacramento, California, where she practised law for many years. Her poetry has appeared in journals including *Nimrod, New Millennium, Peregrine, Inkwell, The Paterson Literary Review*. Her chapbooks, *Vanishings*, won the 1998 Hibiscus award, and *Changing Shapes* won the 1999 Howard Quentin Award. In 2000 she received the Hart Crane Award, and the annual poetry awards from Andrew Mountain Press, ByLine, and Briar Cliff Review. In 2001 she received the Southwest Writers Poetry Prize, the Calvin Fletcher Memorial Prize for Poetry, the annual poetry awards from Briar Cliff Review and Virginia Adversiaria, and her chapbook, *Balancing on Light*, won the Riverstone Chapbook Prize. She was awarded the 2002 Robinson Jeffers Tor House Prize for Poetry and in 2005 First Prize in the New York Yeats Poetry Prize.

Paul Hutchinson is a poet who resides in Melba Australian Capital Territory. He was joint winner of First Prize in the 1997 W.B. Yeats Poetry Prize for Australia.

Tomoko Iwatsubo is a Professor of English at the Faculty of Law at Hosei University, Tokyo. She has published a number of articles on W.B. Yeats in Japanese university journals. The essay 'Coole and Ballylee, 1931'; Yeats's elegy for the poetic demesne' is based on part of her Ph.D. thesis at the University of York.

Judy Johnson has published more than 300 poems in literary magazines across Australia and the UK. Many of them have won major awards. Her first collection, *Wing Corrections*, was on the Schools List in WA; her second, *Nomadic*, won the Wesley Michel Wright Award. She won First Prize in the 1999 W.B. Yeats Poetry Prize for Australia, and her verse novel, *Jack*, published by Pandanus Books, won the 2007 Victorian Premier's C.J. Dennis Prize for Poetry. Judy lives in the Lake Macquarie region of New South Wales.

Alisha Kaplan, Brooklyn, New York, won First Prize in the 2013 New York Yeats Poetry Prize.

John Kavanagh, a poet and playwright, is a native of Sligo. He is a winner of the Listowel Poetry Prize and his audio biography of W.B. Yeats (*Naxos*) won the Spoken Word Award. His plays have been produced in Ireland and the USA. He has published three poetry collections with Salmon Books.

Patrick J. Keane is Professor Emeritus of Le Moyne College and a Contributing Editor at *Numéro Cinq*. Though he has written on a wide range of topics, his areas of special interest have been nineteenth- and twentieth-century poetry in the Romantic tradition; Irish literature and history; the interactions of literature with philosophic, religious, and political thinking; the impact of Nietzsche on certain twentieth-century writers; and, most recently, Transatlantic studies, exploring the influence of German Idealist philosophy and British Romanticism on American writers. His books include *William Butler Yeats: Contemporary Studies in Literature* (1973), *A Wild Civility: Interactions in the Poetry and Thought of Robert Graves* (1980), *Yeats's Interactions with Tradition* (1987), *Terrible Beauty: Yeats, Joyce, Ireland and the Myth of the Devouring Female* (1988), *Coleridge's Submerged Politics* (1994), *Emerson, Romanticism, and Intuitive Reason: The Transatlantic 'Light of All Our Day'* (2003), and *Emily Dickinson's Approving God: Divine Design and the Problem of Suffering* (2007).

Aileen Kelly (1939–2011) grew up near Winchester U.K, graduated from Cambridge, moving to Melbourne in 1962. By profession an adult educator, specializing in the writing and reading of poetry, she worked with many writing groups throughout the State of Victoria. *Coming up for Light* (1994) won the Mary Gilmore Award for best Australian first book of poetry, and First Prize in the 1998 W.B. Yeats Poetry Prize.

Joan Kerr, Geelong, Victoria is a widely published poet and also, with Gabrielle Daly, the comic novelist Gert Loveday ('Writing is Easy' and 'Crane Mansions'). Joan blogs on books and writing at Gert Loveday-Fun With Books. She won First Prize in the 2003 W.B. Yeats Poetry Prize for Australia.

Alec King (1904–70) was a lecturer and later reader in English at the University of Western Australia, 1930–64; Professor of English at Monash University in Melbourne until his death in 1970. Born in Sherborne, Dorset U.K., he attended New College, Oxford, and the London Day Training College. He read Classics at Oxford and taught that subject briefly at a school in Western Australia. He published *The Control of Language* with Martin Ketley in 1939, a book on the varying uses of language, widely used in schools; *Australian Holiday* a children's book, with his wife, Catherine King (1904–2000), in 1945; *Wordsworth and the Artist's Vision* in 1966, and a number of pamphlets, mainly on the subject of Australian poetry.

Craig Kirk lives near Albury in New South Wales, Australia. Craig studied Business via Distance Education at the University of Southern Queensland as a mature student for some time before undertaking an Arts degree, majoring in History and Literature with the University of New England (Armidale, New South Wales), also by correspondence. During this time, Craig demonstrated acumen for literature, receiving high praise from lecturers regarding his analysis of works by Shakespeare, Browning, Conrad, Tennyson and W.B. Yeats. A business opportunity in 2012 necessitated a delay in Craig's studies, however he is currently working on a novel set in Europe, 1938, involving Irish, Spanish, German and Austrian participants.

Kristóf Kissa, native of Hungary, began studying at the Faculty of Humanities, ELTE in Budapest in 2009. He graduated with an MA in English literature in 2014, his thesis was on William Wordsworth's *Ode: Intimations of Immortality*. The idea was to interpret it through Wordsworth's own creative theory of poetry as described in the 'Preface' in *Lyrical Ballads*. In 2014 he started his first year as a PhD student at ELTE, continuing his research on Wordsworth and on the possible influence his work had on poets such as Dylan Thomas, John Montague and W.B. Yeats.

Peter Kuch is the inaugural Eamon Cleary Professor of Irish Studies at the University of Otago, New Zealand. He holds an Honours degree from the University of Wales and an MLitt and DPhil from Oxford, where he studied with Richard Ellmann and John Kelly. He has held posts at the University of Newcastle, Australia; Université de Caen, France; and the University of New South Wales, Australia; and been a Visiting Fellow at the Humanities Research Centre at the Australian National University and at Trinity College, Dublin. He has published widely on Yeats, Joyce, Eliot, Irish theatre, Irish literature, Irish and Australian film, literary theory, Australian literature, and Australian history. He is a commissioning editor for *The Irish Studies Review* (Routledge) and is on the editorial board of several journals. He is currently engaged in writing a cultural history of the performance of Irish theatre in New Zealand and Australia and is the representative for those countries on the international organizing committee of the Irish Theatrical Diaspora Project. Published works include *Writings on Literature and Art: Volume IV of The Collected Works of George William Russell (Æ)* and *Yeats and Æ: 'the antagonism that unites dear friends'*, Gerrards Cross: Colin Smythe.

José Lanters is a Professor of English and Co-Director of the Center for Celtic Studies at the University of Wisconsin-Milwaukee. She has published widely on Irish fiction and drama; her books include *Unauthorized Versions: Irish Menippean Satire, 1919–1952* (Catholic University of America Press, 2000) and *The "Tinkers" in Irish Literature* (Irish Academic Press, 2008). Professor Lanters delivered this paper at the 2002 Oconomowoc Joyce / Yeats weekend organized by Declan Foley.

Steve Lautermilch is a poet residing in Kill Devil Hills North Carolina. He was awarded the 2013 Linda Flowers Literary Award for his collection of poems 'Where Waters Meet'. He won First Prize in the 2008 and 2009 New York Yeats Poetry Prize.

Earl Livings has published poetry and fiction in Australia and also Britain, Canada, the USA, and Germany. He has a ph.D. in Creative Writing and taught professional writing and editing for 17 years. Earl is currently working on a Dark Ages novel and his next poetry collection. His writing focuses on nature, mythology and the sacred.

Richard Londraville is Professor Emeritus of English, SUNY Potsdam. He is noted for his publications on W.B. Yeats and his circle. His work has appeared in many journals, including *Yeats Annual* (UK), *Yeats: An annual critical and Textual Studies*, *The Journal of Modern Literature*, *Eire Ireland*, *Paideuma* and *English Literature in Transition*. He is a published poet and joint biographer with his wife Janis of Jeanne Robert Foster, a friend of JBY.

Sam McCready is an internationally respected actor, theatre director, teacher, painter, adjudicator, published author. Born in Belfast, he was a leading actor and founding member of Belfast's Lyric Theatre, and later a Trustee and Artistic Director of the company. He emigrated to the USA in 1984, when he was appointed Professor of Theatre at the University of Maryland, Baltimore County (UMBC), a position he held until his recent retirement.

He has directed in New York City and appeared as an actor in regional theatres in the U.S.A and Europe. He has directed the Drama Workshop at the Yeats

International Summer School since 1998. His publications include: *Lucille Lortel: The Queen of Off-Broadway* (Greenwood Press, 1993), *A William Butler Yeats Encyclopedia* (Greenwood, 1997); *Coole Lady; The Extraordinary Story of Lady Gregory* (Lagan Press, 2005); the memoir *Baptism by Fire: My Life with Mary O'Malley and the Lyric Players* (Lagan Press, 2008); and *The Great Yeats!* (Lagan Press, 2010).

Katy McDevitt *see Katy Plowright*

Lucy McDiarmid's most recent books are *Poets and the Peacock Dinner: the literary history of a meal* and *The Irish Art of Controversy*. The recipient of fellowships from the Guggenheim Foundation and the Cullman Center for Scholars and Writers at the New York Public Library, she is a former president of the American Conference for Irish Studies and is now Marie Frazee-Baldassarre Professor of English at Montclair State University. In October 2015 the Royal Irish Academy will publish her next book, *At Home in the Revolution: what women said and did in 2016.*

Ita McMorrow-Leyden is a member of an old Sligo family. Ita is noted for her involvement in innumerable community art and cultural projects, down the years, throughout County Sligo. Ita lives in the ancient townland of Carbury in the midst of the historical plain of Maugherow.

Winifred McNulty has published poetry in a number of journals, she has won the Boyle Arts poetry prize, the iYeats international poetry competition and in 2014, was shortlisted for the Listowel Poetry collection prize. She has performed her work at festivals, collaborating with singer Miffy Hoad as part of 'Lyric and Lilt', and on RTE's Sunday Miscellany. In 2012 with photographer Heike Thiele her book 'High shelves and Long Counters' was published by the Irish History Press. Winifred is from Leitrim and Leicester, she lives with Larry and Patrick on Blissberry Farm in Mountcharles, Co Donegal.

Niall J. Mann is a freelance translator and editor, whose work on Yeats has concentrated on *A Vision*. As well as essays in the *Yeats Annual* and elsewhere, he is the creator of the web site www.yeatsvision.com and co-edited the collection *W.B. Yeats's "A Vision": Explications and Contexts* (Clemson 2012). He is currently working on an introduction to *A Vision*.

Martin Mansergh Former diplomat, political adviser, and politician. Deeply involved in back-channel contacts and later Good Friday Agreement negotiations. Appointed Fianna Fáil Senator 2002, TD for Tipperary South 2007–11. Minister of State for Finance, the Office of Public Works and the Arts

(2008–11). Member of President Mary McAleese's second Council of State 2004–11. Author of *The Legacy of History for making peace in Ireland* (2003). Vice-chair of the Expert Advisory Group on Centenary Commemorations.

Dr Carolyn Masel (MA Melb, ph.D. Essex) is a Lecturer at Australian Catholic University, Melbourne, where she teaches a wide range of literature. She studied in Melbourne, Toronto and Colchester, and taught for many years in American Studies and English and American Literature degree programmes at the University of Manchester. She has a longstanding interest in poetry, especially modern poetry. Carolyn was co-Judge in the 2014 Yeats Poetry Prize for Australia.

Tim Metcalf is an Australian poet and doctor and has been described as one of Australia's most published doctor-poets. He lives at Brogo, New South Wales. He has specialized in remote area medicine since 1984 and has worked in NSW, Victoria, NT and British Columbia. In 2007 he was awarded the ACT Writing and Publishing Awards poetry award for his anthology of poems Verbal Medicine.

Michael Miller is a Poet residing in Amherst, MA. He has published a number of books of poems and is a regular read in the Amherst area. He won First Prize in the 2014 New York Yeats Poetry

Charlotte Muse lives, teaches, and writes poetry in Menlo Park, California. She's published two chapbooks: 'A Story Also Grows' and 'The Comfort Teacher' (The Heyeck Press). She is also co-author of 'Trio', a collection of poems with Toni Mirosevich and Edward Smallfield (Specter Press) Awards include the Allen Ginsberg Poetry Award, the Elinor Benedict Prize, two International Publication Awards from the Atlanta Review. These days, she holds private workshops, tutors Hispanic children in reading, and tries to keep a hopeful heart. She won First Prize in the 2007 New York Yeats Poetry Prize.

Jessamine O'Connor left Dublin for Sligo in 1999, where she lives with her family in an old train station by Lough Gara. In 2011 she won First Prize in the iYeats Poetry Competition, and won the Francis Ledwidge award. and has been placed in various competitions, and published in a number of journals. She facilitates the weekly *Wrong Side of the Tracks Writers* and in 2014 founded the poetry, art and music performance group *The Hermit Collective*.

Michael J. Parish, born in Decatur, Illinois in 1943, AB Princeton 1965, LLB Yale Law School 1968. Practised financial law on Wall Street for 35 years to the day. He won First Prize in the 2003 New York Yeats Poetry Prize.

James Pethica teaches in the Theatre and English Departments at Williams College. He has published widely in Irish literature – particularly on W.B. Yeats, Lady Gregory, and the Abbey Theatre – as well as Modern drama and poetry, and contemporary poetry. A past director of the Yeats International Summer School, he is currently completing the authorized biography of Lady Gregory for Oxford University Press, as well as a volume on her collaborations with Yeats. His book on Gregory's early Irish writings is forthcoming in 2015.

Gregory Piko lives in Yass, New South Wales. His poetry has appeared in various journals and anthologies including 'Page Seventeen', 'Famous Reporter', 'The Best Australian Poems 2012' (Black Inc, 2012), the Australian Poetry Members' 'Anthology: Poems 2013' and 'Haiku in English: The First Hundred Years' (WW Norton, 2013). He won joint First Prize in the 2013 W.B. Yeats Poetry Prize for Australia.

Katy Plowright (Katy McDevitt) earned a Distinction for the essay 'Reconstructing W.B.' for her Master of Studies in Research Methods in English from Exeter College, 1994. Her research interests include the marketing and reception of Irish poetry within Yeats's lifetime (1865–1939); Yeats's relations with Irish literary culture; Irish poetry after Yeats; modernism, particularly as it related to and reacted against its Victorian predecessors. She currently manages a publishing consultancy, Katy McDevitt Editorial Services in South Australia

John Purser is now a crofter on the Isle of Skye. He was the first manager of the Scottish Music Information Centre 1985–7 and a trustee of The John Muir Trust 2001–4. He is the author of *The Literary Works of Jack B. Yeats* (1991) and regularly lectures on Jack B. Yeats's literary work.

Hilary Pyle is Yeats Curator Emeritus at the National Gallery of Ireland. She has lectured internationally on the work of Jack B. Yeats, his father John Butler Yeats, as well as having published a number of books on the art of the Yeatses, including a seminal biography *Jack B. Yeats* (Andre Deutsch, London 1970, 2nd edn 1989)

Ann Saddlemyer, Professor Emeritus University of Toronto, Master of Massey College 1988–95, is an internationally known expert in the field of Anglo-Irish literature. Her most recent works include *Becoming George: The Life of Mrs W.B. Yeats* (2002, rpt 2003), which was shortlisted for the James Tait Black award for biography, and *W.B. Yeats and George Yeats: The Letters* (2011), both published by Oxford University Press.

Janeen Samuel could be described as a vet with literary ambitions. Though she now lives in South-West Victoria, she spent many years in Queensland, which is where she became acquainted with rainforest (and leeches). She has had stories and poems published in various magazines and anthologies, including *Award Winning Australian Writing*, Andromeda Spaceways 'InflightMagazine', and most recently the speculative poetry anthology *The Stars Like Sand* (Interactive Press). She won First Prize in the 2011 W.B. Yeats Poetry Prize for Australia.

Doug Saum a resident of Reno, Nevada, received undergraduate and graduate degrees from The University of Nebraska at Kearney (1974, 1976). Now retired, he taught English to high school students for thirty-four years. Doug's first remembered contact with W.B. Yeats was in his senior year of high school. He was asked to read 'The Lake Isle of Innisfree' and 'The Wild Swans at Coole' and being fascinated by the syntax of the first line of 'Innisfree', repeating it over and over. His Masters thesis is entitled 'William Butler Yeats: A Dialectical Analysis'. After a visit by the muse (8 June 1994) in 1996 he began putting the poems of W.B. Yeats to his original music. In spring of 2015 he finished this music project having produced nine CDs covering approximately 275 poems. He has presented these songs at Yeats-related events in Oconmowoc, Reno, San Francisco, Chestertown, New York City, Sligo, etc.

Frankie Seymour A lifelong human and animal rights advocate, Frankie Seymour studied history, sociology and English literature, with post-graduate studies in environmental science. Now retired, she writes poetry, songs, plays, non-fiction and speculative fiction, and occasionally dabbles in the romance and mystery genres. In 1993, she published an autobiographical account of her voyages aboard the Sea Shepherd in 1981 (*All Hearts on Deck*). Her work has been commended in many Australian literary awards. Her poems, stories and articles have been widely published. She won First Prize in the 2001 W.B. Yeats Poetry Prize for Australia.

Colin Smythe graduated from Dublin University (TCD) in 1963 and started his publishing company a couple of years later on the proceeds of the sale of his W.B. Yeats / Dun Emer / Cuala Press collection to Dublin City Library. He has since published works by and about Yeats, Lady Gregory, George Moore, George W. Russell ('Æ'), Shaw, Wilde, Carleton, Boucicault, Denis Johnston and other Irish literary figures, about a hundred works of literary criticism in his Irish Literary Studies, Ulster Editions & Monographs, and Princess Grace Irish Library series, as well as collections of plays in the Irish Drama Selections Series, biographies, SF and fantasy novels, and works on folklore and 'spooks'. In 1987 he acquired the stock of the Dolmen Press on its demise, following Liam Miller's death. He published Terry Pratchett's (1948–2015) first book in 1971, and his next four novels before becoming Terry's literary agent, a role that has rather taken over from his publishing activities. His Bibliography of the Writings of W.B. Yeats remains unfinished although 400,000 words have been written. He received an Hon. LLD from Dublin University for services to Irish literature in 1998.

Melinda Szüts, a native of Budapest, Hungary, completed her BA degree in English and Film Studies at the Faculty of Humanities, Eötvös Loránd University in 2013. In 2012 she studied Irish Literature at the Faculty of Arts, Humanities & Social Sciences at the University of Limerick. In 2013 and 2014 as a scholarship student at the International Yeats Summer School, she participated in the drama workshop, playing Dervorgilla in the 2014 production of 'The Dreaming of the Bones'. She wrote her BA thesis on the dramaturgical uses of masks and dance in the plays of W.B. Yeats, and submitted a paper on the uses of dramatic space in Yeats's *Four Plays for Dancers* for the Hungarian Students' Scholarly Circles Conference in 2015. She is currently working on her MA degree in English Literature (Shakespeare Studies, Twentieth Century Irish Drama) at Eötvös Loránd University. Melinda is founding member and acting head of the Hungarian Yeats Society.

Deirdre Toomey is Research Editor for the *Yeats Annual;* editor of *Yeats and Women: Yeats Annual No. 9* (1991), revised and augmented as *Yeats and Women* (Macmillan, 1997). Co-editor of *The Collected Letters of W.B. Yeats Volume II 1896–1900* (OUP, 1997) and co-editor of *Mythologies* (Palgrave Macmillan, 2005).

Helen Vendler is the A. Kingsley Porter University Professor at Harvard, where she received her ph.D. in English and American literature, after completing an undergraduate degree in chemistry at Emmanuel College. She has written books on Yeats, Herbert, Keats, Stevens, Shakespeare, Seamus Heaney, and Emily Dickinson. Her most recent books are *Dickinson: Selected Poems and Commentaries*; *Last Looks, Last Books: Stevens, Plath, Lowell, Bishop, Merrill*; and *Our Secret Discipline: Yeats and Lyric Form*. She is a frequent reviewer of poetry in such journals as *The New York Review of Books, The New York Times Book Review,*and *The New Republic*. Her avocational interests include music, art, and medicine.

Subscribers

The following people and organizations generously supported the publication of *Yeats 150*

Sligo Chamber of Commerce and Industry
County Sligo Tourist Development Association
Sligo County Libraries / Leabharlann Chontae Shligigh
Councillor Declan Bree, Sligo
The Carroll Family formerly of Strandhill County Sligo
The Carroll Family, Pearse Road, Sligo
Ailbhe Cunningham, Queensland, Australia
Paul and Peggy Davis, Melbourne
Anne Daniel
Padraic Feehily, Sligo
Helen Folcy, Mclbourne
Aelred and Bernie Gannon, Oconomowoc, WI. USA
Nial O'D. Dublin
Andrew and Paula Palmer, Melbourne
Higgins Family, Rosses Point, County Sligo
Joe B. McDonagh, Sligo
Tom and Mary McDermott, Australia
Ronan and Doreen MacEvilly in memory of Tom and Rita MacEvilly, Sligo
Ita McMorrow-Leyden, Dunfore Farm House, Ballinfull, County Sligo
Morrison family, Rosses Point, County Sligo
Mullaney Brothers, Sligo
Vincent and Catherine Raftery, Sligo
Doug Saum, Reno, NV. USA
Bill and Martina Verre, Delafield, WI. USA
Marea Walshe, Sligo
Malcolm and Martina Hamilton in memory of Frank Wynne
Maneck H. Darawula, Florida, USA
The Fagan Family, New York
Dr Patrick J. Henry, Sligo and Dublin

> Think where man's glory most begins and ends
> And say my glory was I had such friends.
>
> W.B. Yeats, 1937

Bibliography

Arkins, Brian, *Builders of My Soul: Greek and Roman Themes in Yeats* (Gerrards Cross: Colin Smythe/Rowman & Littlefield, 1990).

Auden W.H., *The Public v. the Late Mr. William Butler Yeats* (Partisan Review 6, 3, Spring 1939).

Bachelard, Gaston, *The Poetics of Space* (Boston: Beacon, 1994).

Bennett, Chris, *et al. Green Gold the Tree of Life: Marijuana in Magic & Religion* (Frazier Park, CA: n.d.).

Brooks, Cleanth, *The Well Wrought Urn: Studies in the Structure of Poetry* (London: Dennis Dobson Ltd, 1949).

Bowers, Faubion, *Japanese Theater* (New York: Hermitage House, 1952).

Campbell, Joseph, *Transformations of Myth Through Time* (San Francisco: Perennial Library, 1990).

Denson, Alan (ed.), *Letters from Æ* (London: Abelard–Schuman, 1961).

Ellmann, Richard. *James Joyce*. Rev. edn (Oxford: Oxford University Press, 1982).

European Parliament, *Official Journal of the European Communities*, 1972–3, 1978–9.

Flint, F.S., *Papers* (Harry Ransom Center, The University of Texas at Austin).

Foley, Declan (ed.), *The Only Art of Jack B. Yeats: Letters & Essays* (Dublin: The Lilliput Press, 2009).

Forster, Julia, *Muses* (Sparkford, Great Britain: Pocket Essentials, 2007).

Foster, R.F., *W.B. Yeats: A Life I: The Apprentice Mage 1865–1914* (NY: Oxford University Press, 1997).

Foster R.F., *W.B. Yeats: A Life II: The Arch-Poet* (Oxford: Oxford University Press, 2003).

Kain, Richard M., and James H. O'Brien, *George Russell (Æ)* (Lewisburgh, PA: Bucknell Univ. Press, 1976).

Kavanagh, Peter, *Patrick Kavanagh: Sacred Keeper* (The Curragh: Goldsmith Press, 1979).

Kermode, Frank, *Romantic Image* (London–New York: Routledge, 2004).

Hassett, Joseph M, *W.B. Yeats and the Muses* (New York: Oxford University Press, 2010).

Hofmann, Albert Dr, *Insight Outlook* (Atlanta: Humanics New Age, 1989).

Hofmann, Albert, *LSD: My Problem Child* (NC: MAPS [Multidisciplinary Association for Psychedelic Studies], 2009.)

Huxley, Aldous, *Moksha: Writings on Psychedelics and the Visionary Experience 1931–63* (London: Flamingo, 1994).

Johnsen, William, *Textual / Sexual Politics in Yeats's* 'Leda and the Swan' in *Yeats and Postmodernism*, ed. Leonard Orr (Syracuse: Syracuse UP, 1991), pp. 80–9.

Johnson, David M. *Socrates and Alcibiades: Four Texts* (Newburyport, MA: Focus Philosophical Library, 2003).

Joyce, James, *Ulysses* (New York: Vintage, 1986).

Larrissey, Edward (ed.), *The Major Works* (Oxford: Oxford University Press, 2008).

Leonard, J. (ed.), *Seven Centuries of Poetry in English*, 5th edn (Oxford: Oxford University Press. 2003).

Londraville, Richard, *Four Lectures by W.B. Yeats, 1902–4.* YAA #8 (1991), pp. 8–122.

— *I Have Longed for Such a Country: The Cuchulain Cycle as Peking Opera.* YAA #2 (1984), pp.165–94.

—, *The Unifying Dramatic Image in the Plays of W.B. Yeats* YAA #10 (1992), pp.115–39.

—. W.B. *Yeats's Anti-Theatre and Its Analogs in Chinese Drama: The Staging of the Cuchulain Cycle.* Asian Culture Quarterly Volume XI, #3 (1983), pp. 23–31.

Longford, Elizabeth, *A Pilgrimage of Passion: The Life of Wilfrid Scawen Blunt* (New York: Knopf, 1980).

McDiarmid, Lucy, *Poets and the Peacock Dinner: The Literary History of a Meal* (Oxford: Oxford University Press, 2014).

McDonnell, Dr J., *William Butler Yeats (1865–1939)* (English 102 Advisory Materials, University of New England, Armidale, 2009).

McKenzie, J.A. & J.K. (eds), *The World's Contracted Thus: Major Poetry from Chaucer to Plath*, 2nd edn (Heinemann Educational, Richmond Victoria, 1976).

Maddox, Brenda, *Nora: A Biography of Nora Joyce* (London: Hamish Hamilton, 1988).

Miner, Earl, *The Japanese Tradition in British and American Literature* (Princeton: Princeton University Press, 1958).

Morash, Cris and Shaun Richards, *Mapping Irish Theatre: Theories of Space and Place* (Cambridge: Cambridge University Press, 2014).

Murphy, William M., *Family Secrets: William Butler Yeats and His Relatives* (NY: Syracuse University Press, 2000).

Murphy, William M., *Prodigal Father: The life of John Butler Yeats (1839–1922)* (NY: Syracuse University Press, 2001).

Murphy, William M., *The Yeats Family and the Pollexfens of Sligo* (Dublin: The Dolmen Press, 1971).

O'Riordan, Manus, *Emergency Czechmate or Wartime Dialogue? Dev the Irish Institute and the Masaryk Affair* (Dublin: Irish Foreign Affairs, June 2013).

Padilla, M.R., *Mythological Gods* (Edimat Books, London 2004).

Plato, *The Dialogues* (New York: Bantam Books, 1986).

Purser, John W., *The Literary Works of Jack B. Yeats* (Gerrards Cross: Colin Smythe, 1991).

Pyle, Hilary, *Jack B. Yeats: A Biography* Savage (MD: Barnes & Noble Books, 1989).

Robinson, Mary, *Everybody Matters. A Memoir* (London: Hodder and Stoughton, 2012).

Seanad Debates, 1951–4, 1961–79 (Dublin).

Schultes, Richard Evans and Albert Hofmann, *Plants of the Gods: Their Sacred, Healing, and Hallucinogenic Powers* (Rochester, VT: Healing Arts Press, 1992).

Skeffington, Andrée Sheehy, *Skeff. A Life of Owen Sheehy Skeffington, 1909–1970* (Dublin: The Lilliput Press, 1991).

Stallworthy, Jon, *Yeats as Anthologist. In Excited Reverie: A Centenary Tribute to William Butler Yeats, 1865–1939*, eds A. Norman Jeffares and K.G.W. Cross (New York: Macmillan, 1965), pp. 171–92.

Stanford, William Bedell, *Memoirs* (Dublin: Hines 2001).

Stevens, Wallace, *Collected Poetry and Prose*, eds Frank Kermode and Joan Richardson (New York: Library of America, 1997).

Stevenson, R.L., *Letters to His Family and Friends, Vol 1*, ed. Sidney Colvin (New York: Charles Scribner's Sons, 1899).

Stucki, Yasuko, *Yeats's Drama and the Nō: A Comparative Study in Dramatic Theories* (Modern Drama. Volume X, September 1966), pp. 101–22.

Summerfield, Henry, *That Myriad-Minded Man: A Biography of George William Russell 'Æ' 1867–1935* (Gerrards Cross: Colin Smythe, 1975).

Thorn, S., *Mastering Poetry* (Hampshire New York: Palgrave Macmillan, 2006).

Ueda, Makoto, *Zeami, Basho, Yeats, Pound: A Study in Japanese and English Poetics* (London; London and The Hague: Mouton, 1965).

Ure, Peter, *The Plays. An Honored Guest: New Essays on W.B. Yeats*, eds Denis Donoghue and J.R. Mulryne (New York: St Martins Press, 1966).

Ure, Peter, *Yeats the Playwright*, New York: Routledge Paperbacks, 1966.

Untermeyer, Louis (ed.), *Modern British & Modern American Poetry*. Revised, shorter edition (New York: Harcourt, 1955).

Vendler, Helen, *Our Secret Discipline: Yeats and Lyric Form* (Cambridge: Harvard University Press, 2007).

Wasson, Hofmann, and Ruck, *The Road to Eleusis: Unveiling the Secret of the Mysteries* (Berkeley: North Atlantic Books, 2008).

Weller, Shane (ed.), *The Trial and Death of Socrates: Four Dialogues* (New York: Dover Publications, Inc., 1992).

Wellesley, Dorothy (ed.), *Letters on Poetry from W.B. Yeats to Dorothy Wellesley* (Oxford: Oxford University Press, 1964).

Wordsworth, William, *The Collected Poems of William Wordsworth* (Ware: Wordsworth Editions, 2006).

Worth, Katharine, *The Irish Drama of Europe from Yeats to Beckett* (London: Athlone Press, 1978).

Yeats, Michael. B., *Cast a Cold Eye. Memories of a Poet's Son and Politician* (Dublin: Blackwater Press, 1998).

Yeats, W.B. *Anima Hominus. Essays* (New York: Macmillan, 1924).

—, *A People's Theatre: Explorations* (New York: Macmillan, 1962).

—, *A Vision* (New York: Collier Books, 1973).

—, *Certain Noble Plays of Japan. Essays and Introductions* (New York: Macmillan, 1961).

—, *Last Poems: Manuscript Materials*, ed. James Pethica (Ithaca and London: Cornell University Press, 1997).

—, *Samhain: 190: Explorations* (New York: Macmillan, 1962).

—, *The Autobiography of William Butler Yeats*, Collier edition (New York: Macmillan, 1965).

—, *The Collected Works of W.B. Yeats. Volume I: The Poems*, second edition, ed. Richard J. Finneran (New York: Scribner, 1997).

—, *The Letters of W.B. Yeats*, ed. Alan Wade (New York: Macmillan, 1955).

—, *Oxford Book of Modern Verse* (New York: Oxford University Press, 1936).

—, *The Variorum Edition of the Poems of W.B. Yeats*, eds Peter Allt and Russell K. Alspach. Seventh Printing (New York: Macmillan, 1977).

—, *Uncollected Prose. Vol 1: First Reviews and Articles, 1886–1896*, ed. John P. Frayne (New York: Columbia University Press, 1970).

—, *Four Plays for Dancers* (London: Macmillan, 1921).

—, *Selected Plays*, ed. Richard Allen Cave (London: Penguin, 1997).

—, *The Autobiography of W.B. Yeats: Consisting of 'Reveries over Childhood and Youth', 'The Trembling of the Veil' and 'Dramatis Personae'* (New York: Collier Books, 1965).

—, *Essays and Introductions* (New York: Collier Books, 1968).

—, *Mythologies* (NYC: Collier Books, 1969).

—. Daniel Albright (ed.), *The Poems* (London: Everyman, 1998).

—, Richard Finneran (ed.), *The Poems: Revised* (New York: Macmillan, 1990).

WEBSITES

Cade-Stewart, Michael, *Mask and Robe: Yeats's Oxford Book of Modern Verse (1936) and New Poems (1938), Yeats's Mask* Yeats Annual 19: A Special Issue, ed. Margaret Mills Harper and Warwick Gould. Cambridge, UK: Open Book Publishers, 2013, pp. 221–58. http://dx/doi/org/ 10/11647/OBP.0038

Cullingford, Elizabeth, *How Jacques Molay Got Up the Tower: Yeats and the Irish Civil War*, ELH 50:4 (1983). 763–89. http://www.jstor.org/stable/2872926

Encarta 2004 encyclopaedia © 1993–2003 Microsoft Corporation.

Grene N., Yeats's *Poetic Codes* Oxford University Press, Oxford New York, 2008. at http://books. google.com.au/books accessed 16 September 2014.

Harvard University Library, Online Archival Search Information System, Stenbock, Stanislaus Eric, Count, 1860–1895. Papers: A Finding Aid.

Lensing, George S, *Among School Children: Questions and Conclusions* College Literature 13, no. 1 (1986): 1–8, Accessed 3 December 2014. http://www.jstor.org/stable/25111680

MacCulloch, J.A., *The Religion of the Ancient Celts* T. & T. Clark, Edinburgh, 1911 (extract) at http://www.kernunnos.com/deities/ogmios/ogmios.html accessed 20 September 2009.

McDonnell, Dr Jennifer, *The Poetry of W.B. Yeats (I and II)*, University of New England, Armidale 2009 (podcast) audio recordings.

McEwen, Indra Kagis, *Vitruvius: writing the body of architecture*, Cambridge, Massachusetts: MIT, 2003 at http://books.google.com.au/books

Mann, Neil. *A Vision Website* www.yeatsvision.com.

http://www.celtnet.org.uk/gods_o/ogmios

http://www.monstropedia.org/index.php?title=Stymphalian_Bird accessed 22 September 2009.

Nostradamus, M. Epistle to Henry II (1557) *Salon-de-Crau in Provence* http://www.sacred-texts.com/nos/epistle.htm.

Nostradamus, M. Century V. (1555) *Salon-de-Crau in Provence* http://www.sacred-texts.com/nos/cen5eng.html

Pausanias, *Description of Greece* 8. 22. 4 (trans. Jones) (Greek travelogue C2nd A.D.), Aaron J. Atsma, Theoi Project Copyright © 2000 – 2008, New Zealand http://www.theoi.com/Ther/ OrnithesStymphalides.html.

http://turkeytravelresource.com/view/57/besiktas

Robert Alden Rubin, *Some Heroic Discipline: William Butler Yeats and the Oxford Book of Modern Verse,* Dissertation. University of North Caroline, Chapel Hill, 2011. https://cdr.lib.unc.edu/ indexablecontent/ uuid:0ba7ce27-e6ad-4d27-a698-c9551fdfaf68

R.B. Russell, *The Lost Club Journal. Count Stenbock: A Brief Biography.* http:// www.tartaruspress.com/ stenbock.htm

W.B. Yeats, *The Collected Letters of W.B. Yeats,* New York: Oxford UP (InteLex Electronic Edition) 2002. http://www.nlx.com/collections/130

(no author listed) *A Secret Kept. A Brief Life of Count Stenbock.* http://www.mmhistory.org.uk/cce/Jo/

Milton, John. *Poems 1645* Rauner Library at Dartmouth College (Hickmot 172). The John Milton Reading Room, Dartmouth College. https://www.dartmouth.edu/~milton/reading_room/penseroso/ text.shtml

Perloff, Marjorie G. *'Easter, 1916': Yeats's First World War Poem, The Oxford Handbook of British War Poetry,* ed. Tim Kendall. Chapter 12, 227–41. Oxford: Oxford University Press, 2007. http:// epc.buffalo.edu/authors/perloff/articles/Perloff_Yeats-Easter-1916.pdf

Index

W.B. Yeats's headstone
(photograph: Hugh John Mullan)

'Under Ben Bulben'

VI

Under bare Ben Bulben's head
In Drumcliffe Churchyard Yeats is laid,
An ancestor was rector there
Long years ago; a church stands near,
By the road an ancient Cross.
No marble, no conventional phrase,
On limestone quarried near the spot
By his command these words are cut:

> *Cast a cold eye*
> *On life, on death.*
> *Horseman, pass by!*

September 4, 1938

Robert Gregory's woodcut pressmark
'Charging Unicorn'
from *Discoveries: A Volume of Essays*
by William Butler Yeats
(Dun Emer Press, Dublin, 1907)